UNIX Made Easy, Second Edition

John Muster & Associates

Osborne **McGraw-Hill**

Berkeley   New York   St. Louis   San Francisco
Auckland   Bogotá   Hamburg   London   Madrid
Mexico City   Milan   Montreal   New Delhi
Panama City   Paris   São Paulo   Singapore
Sydney   Tokyo   Toronto

Osborne **McGraw-Hill**
2600 Tenth Street
Berkeley, California 94710
U.S.A.

For information on translations or book distributors outside the U.S.A., or to arrange bulk purchase discounts for sales promotions, premiums, or fundraisers, please contact Osborne **McGraw-Hill** at the above address.

UNIX Made Easy, Second Edition

10 11 12 13 14 15 DOC/DOC 0 9 8 7 6 5 4 3 2 1 0

ISBN 0-07-882173-8

Acquisitions Editor: Wendy Rinaldi
Proofreader: Linda Medoff
Computer Designer: Marcela Hancik
Illustrator: Loretta Lian Au
Series Designer: Marla Shelasky
Quality Control Specialist: Joe Scuderi
Indexer: Richard Shrout

To you. In the hopes that you enjoy teaching yourself UNIX.

John Muster
Berkeley, CA 1996

About the Author

John Muster is a founder of Lurnix, a UNIX
education company that focuses on teaching the
UNIX operating system to new users. He is
president of Muster Learning Architects, which
specializes in developing educational materials
and programs for adults.

Contents

PART II

Examining User Support Features of UNIX

PART III

Working with Power Utilities

PART IV

Communicating with Other Users and Systems

PART V

Shell Programming and Customizing the Environment

Acknowledgments

In many a book I have read that the author never could have completed it without the understanding, patience, and support of their family. I now believe them. Catherine and Cassy, thank you very much.

The chapters in this book are in a constant state of evolution. For more than 15 years I have thoroughly enjoyed writing these chapters, teaching UNIX, listening to students' questions and suggestions, revising the chapters, teaching, revising.... The evolution of these exercises was possible because I have had the good fortune to be engaged with committed students at the University of California, and at corporate education facilities. Thank you for your comments and ideas.

From my earliest days, I have enjoyed watching the lights go on as people make sense out of what they are studying. Through the years of physics and computer science education I have enjoyed interacting with committed colleagues who have shared that same joy—and have affected how this book works. Thank you Phil Barnhart, Marjorie Conrad, John Coulter, Lillian Frank, Peter Kindfield, John Laubach, Albert Levy, James Miller, Walter Mitchell, Catherine M. Muster, John T. Muster, Bob Place, Siggy Selquist, Lyle Strand, and David Waas.

In addition to the colleagues listed in the first edition, the following associates made this book possible: Brian Haney, Carol Henry, Adrian Lim, Bee Ching Oh, Norman Pancner, Leo Pereira, Richard Rice, Wendy Rinaldi, Sean Rouse, and Vicki Van Ausdall.

Teach Yourself with UNIX Made Easy

The title of this book is not the ultimate oxymoron—Learning UNIX can be reasonably easy—if you approach it like you did when you learned how to ride a bicycle. Remember how your parents set up the overhead projector in the living room and showed you three quarters of a zillion slides in rapid succession, explaining the intricacies of micro-human bicycle propulsion? No, and you did not learn how to ride your bike by reading the manual either.

You got on your bike. Someone steadied it and at the precise moment that it was needed, gave you the specific, appropriate information that supported your mastering the needed skills: turn the handlebars this way, to stop just start peddling backwards, lean into the curve, avoid that rock....

The same is true as you master UNIX skills using *UNIX Made Easy*.

Get on to a UNIX system. Start at the beginning of the first Chapter and start peddling. The key is to actually do each exercise on a live UNIX system so you can see how it responds and exactly what you must do to get results. As you work through the chapters of this book, you enter commands, read about what is happening, enter more commands. Instructions in the chapters guide you carefully from the most tentative, initial steps, to exploring the essential features, through mastery of the editor, employing utilities, flying around the filesystem, controlling permissions, manipulating data, issuing complex commands to the shell, customizing your account, managing jobs and processes, using the Internet... to writing complex shell scripts.

Each step is specified; the implications are discussed as you investigate each feature.

This book can be your UNIX tutor—your shirpa—as you climb and teach yourself UNIX.

After the basic skills are mastered, you explore more complex features built on the basics. You carefully construct your knowledge of UNIX, adding each piece as it is appropriate.

The following diagram is designed to show the order you should follow as you work through the chapters in the book. Start at the top with the Tour, Chapter 1. When you have finished it you can move to Chapter 2, the Visual Editor, or Chapter 11, Motif, if you have an X-Windows workstation. Either way, complete vi, then go on to Utilities, Chapter 3, etc.

Chapter Roadmap

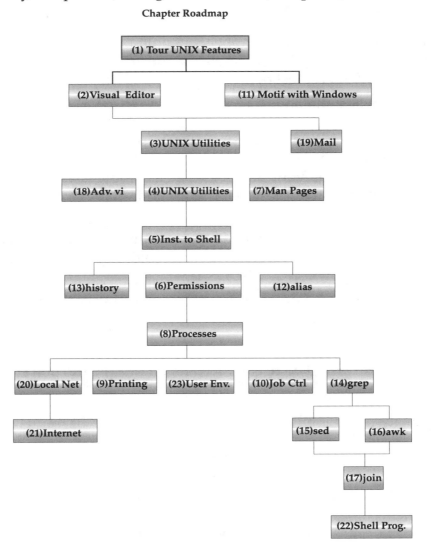

Experienced Users: Start at the beginning and quickly pass through a topic if you have done it several times before. Create all files as instructed because they are needed in later exercises. Wade in until you are in deep enough to swim, then carefully do each exercise. Most people, unless they are very experienced, find new skills even in the first chapter.

Conventions Used In This Book

In creating this book, we used the type faces available to help convey the meaning of the commands.

- If a part of a line to enter appears in **bold** text, it is a part of the name of a UNIX program or instruction and has precise meaning to the system. It must be entered exactly as is.

- Portions of commands that you enter are in *italics*. These are the portions of the instructions that are modifiable by users. For instance, we include suggested filenames in the commands we ask you to enter. You will later use the same command in conjunction with your own files. The italics indicate the portions of the command line you can change and still have it work.

- If a system file name or system variable is used in a command, it is in ***bold-italics*** indicating that it can be replaced with other system file names or system variables, but they must be spelled exactly as shown.

- A distinctive type of font is used for screen display output that is included in the book:

  ```
  This line is in monospace
  ```

- When you are asked to enter a command the instruction step is numbered.

Explanations generally *follow* the keyboard exercise. If results are puzzling, read on.

UNIX is a collection of powerful programs, is the foundation for modern operating systems, the ultimate user hostile interface, tinker-toys for adults, a fascinating and enjoyable programming environment....

Log on and let us guide you as you have fun and teach yourself UNIX.

PART I

Mastering Essential UNIX

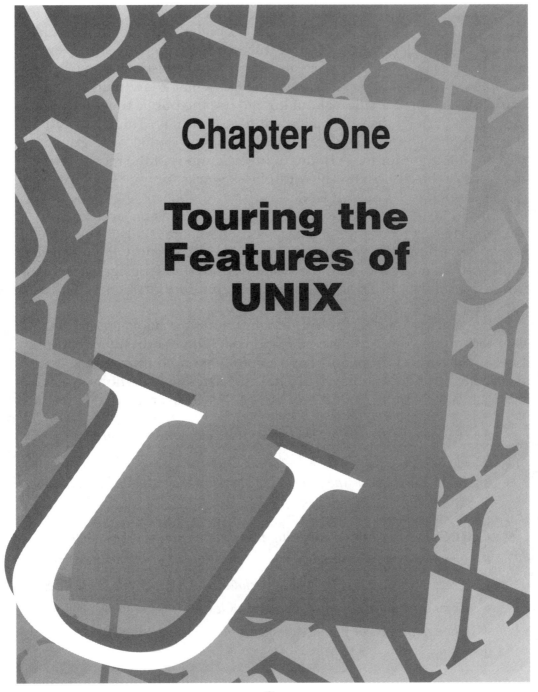

Chapter One

Touring the Features of UNIX

One way to visit a major city for the first time is to start at the top of one of its highest buildings. From that lofty perch, you can easily identify the major features and see the way streets and avenues are laid out. Your next step might be to consult a map or guidebook that provides basic facts about the city's major landmarks. You could then get information about how to use the public transportation system and briefly visit the major features of the city. This quick tour of the highlights would show you how the major systems work, giving you a foundation for more in-depth investigations of the most interesting parts of the city. That is how this book works for you. It's your guide as you teach yourself UNIX.

This initial chapter takes you on a guided, "hands-on" tour of the UNIX system. It focuses on mastery of fundamental skills that enable you to get around the system, use essential tools, identify the major features, and take advantage of the system's underlying design structures. You'll examine each aspect of UNIX through direct interaction with a functioning UNIX system.

After you've finished this introductory tour, the book's remaining chapters guide your further exploration of UNIX's individual features. Literally thousands of people have carefully worked through the exercises collected here and have read the associated explanations, teaching themselves to be proficient users of the UNIX system and its major features.

SKILLS CHECK: Before beginning this chapter, you should

- *Have access to a working UNIX system*
- *Be able to describe the formatting conventions presented in this book's introduction*

OBJECTIVES: After completing this chapter, you will be able to

- *Log on and off the system*
- *Create and manage files using various UNIX programs or utilities*
- *Copy, sort, move, remove, and print files*
- *Change the access permissions for a file*
- *Communicate with other users*

- *Collect data about users, the system, and its files using standard UNIX programs or utilities*
- *Properly communicate basic instructions to the UNIX command interpreter*
- *Connect the output from one program to the input of another*
- *Have the output of a utility saved in a file*
- *Move to specific standard directories and then return to your workspace*
- *Identify instances of running programs*
- *Create and execute a basic shell script*
- *Identify and make simple changes to a file's permissions*
- *Obtain information about UNIX from the on-line manual pages*
- *Change the password*

UNIX is a collection of user and system programs, called an operating system, that runs on equipment of essentially any size made by nearly all manufacturers. Although the UNIX operating system was initially developed at Bell Laboratories, the code was licensed to the University of California at Berkeley, where significant development took place. Additionally, several UNIX system manufacturers added on new features or modified the operating system to meet particular needs. The result is that UNIX is not a single operating system but rather is many slightly different flavors of the same general operating system. The various versions fall into two camps: those derived from AT&T's System V, and versions that have their origin in Berkeley's BSD code. To compound the complex issues arising from such divisions, the two camps often incorporated each other's code and ideas. In recent years, efforts to "unify" UNIX have been extensive, producing versions that have more consistency.

Today when manufacturers develop a UNIX computer, they must select and employ one of the several versions of the UNIX operating system. From the user's perspective, nearly all commands work the same in the most recent versions of UNIX. However, what differences do exist can be annoying. Because many older systems in operation are using AT&T or BSD operating systems, and because in the newest systems the merging of commands is not yet complete, many of this book's example commands are presented in both the AT&T and BSD forms. Unless your manufacturer has made proprietary changes in your machine or its operating system, at least one and possibly both versions of the commands presented here will work on your system.

1.1

Establishing Communication with UNIX

This initial section guides you through the steps needed to establish communication with UNIX: *logging on*. Because many installations have modified the login process to fit local environments, the steps listed here may not exactly match your situation. If an accomplished user is available to show you how to log on, get their assistance, and then examine the steps outlined here. Once you are logged on, the differences between systems largely melt away.

Obtaining What You Need to Log On

The UNIX computing environment is designed to serve many users at the same time. When the system's administrator adds a user to a system, an *account* or *login* name is created and assigned. Usually an initial *password* is also added. To gain access to the system, a user must specify the correct account name or login name and provide the appropriate password. When the login and password don't match, access is denied.

In addition to your login and password, there are a couple of other things you may need before starting to log on to the system. Here is a summary:

- If you are at an installation that lets you access several computers, you may need the name of the particular computer that you are assigned to use.

- The login name for your account.

- Probably a password for your login.

- Possibly the abbreviation for the type of terminal you are using.

This information will be supplied to you from one of two sources. If system administrators are in charge of maintaining accounts on your system, one of them will give you the needed information. If you are the first user on a new machine and have no mentor to assist you, check the user manual that is provided with your system. Look for a section entitled "Getting Started" or its equivalent. It will provide instructions on logging on as *tutor, user, guest,* or some other login name that implies the account is for exploring, not for system administration.

> *CAUTION: Your user manual will also include instructions for logging on as **root**, which is the account for the system administrator. Because this account carries substantial authority over system events and operations, it is unwise to log on as **root** until you have mastered the essential skills for using the system.*

The Login Process

Each step of the login process must be successfully completed. Figure 1-1 is a graphical depiction of the login steps described in the following paragraphs.

Selecting the System

If you're on a system that uses several computers linked together, you may be asked to identify the name of the specific computer you are to access, otherwise you are asked for your login name.

If you see a *login banner* instead of a request to identify a system, proceed to the next section, "Identifying the User Account."

1. If you are required to identify the system to access, the first prompt you see will be similar to one of the following:

   ```
   pad:
   request:
   system:
   ```

Type the identifying name of the computer to which you were assigned, and press (Return). When you type a name that the program recognizes, you are connected to that computer.

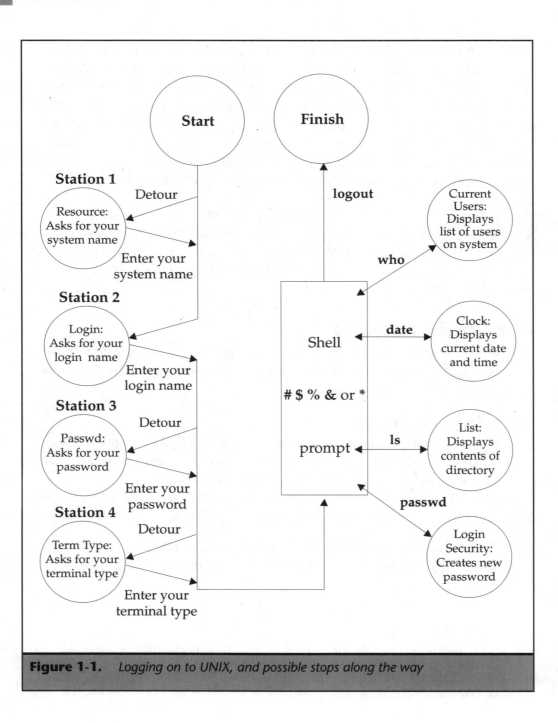

Figure 1-1. *Logging on to UNIX, and possible stops along the way*

Identifying the User Account

You are greeted with the login banner. It appears either in a graphical box in the center of the screen, or in plain type at the top-left of the screen.

```
login:
```

1. Identify yourself by specifying the name of your account, your *login*. On most systems, the login must be entered in lowercase letters.

2. After entering the exact account information, press the (Return) key.

Providing the Password

Whether or not you entered the login correctly, most installations require a password and the following prompt for password is displayed:

```
Password:
```

1. Enter your password exactly as it was provided to you. For security reasons, as you type your password it is not displayed on the screen.

2. When you have entered your password, press the (Return) key. If you provided a corresponding set of login and password entries, you are moved on to the next step.

    However, if either the login or password you supplied was incorrect, an error message appears, such as

```
Login incorrect
```

Following are some common mistakes when entering either the login or password that result in an incorrect login:

- You mistyped a numeral 1 for an "el" or a 0 (zero) for an "oh."
- You made a typing mistake.
- You used the (Backspace) to correct an error.
- You accidentally typed a segment in uppercase letters.

- The information you were given is wrong.

3. If you think you made an error in typing, reenter the login and password.

4. If your error was that you used uppercase to type something, the computer is now treating your terminal as a teletype terminal that will only work with uppercase letters. When this happens, most ordinary terminals display a backslash in front of the password prompt. Check to see if this has occurred.

5. To begin the login process again, hold down the [Ctrl] key and press the [d] key one time. This kills the login program. Another instance of the program immediately starts up, displaying a new login banner so you can start over.

Identifying the Terminal Type

Because UNIX can accept many different vendors' terminals that work in slightly different ways, the system must be informed of the type of terminal you are using. The information may be included in the startup files for your account, or you may be asked to enter a terminal type.

If the login program does not have the terminal information, the program will prompt you with the following:

```
Term:
```

1. The Terminal prompt often contains a default terminal setting in parentheses. If the default that is listed is correct, press [Return].

2. If you need to inform the system of a different terminal type, enter the abbreviation for your terminal. This abbreviation should be provided with your account information.

Manufacturers often construct new terminals that emulate the settings of standard terminals, particularly the vt100. Following are some common terminal abbreviations:

```
h19
hp
tvi925
```

vt100 (probably most prevalent)
wyse50
xterm

Meeting the Shell

Once you have successfully logged on, you may receive some informational messages, the screen may clear, one or more windows may be displayed, and a mouse may or may not be active.

If you are at a nongraphical terminal, or a graphical terminal that includes a terminal window, a prompt is displayed to inform you that you can start issuing commands. The prompt may be customized for your site, or it may be one of the default shell prompts, such as

```
$
```

or

```
%
```

The prompt is displayed on your screen by a program called the *shell* that reads your instructions and interprets them to the remainder of the system. On most systems, the shell is automatically started when you log on.

Starting a Terminal Window

If you are using a graphical workstation and there is no terminal window displayed with a shell prompt on the screen, you can probably start a terminal window.

1. Move the mouse cursor to an area on the screen not occupied by a window. Press and hold down the left mouse button. A window appears that probably includes the option

   ```
   New Window
   ```

   or

   ```
   Shell Window
   ```

2. Still holding down the mouse button, pull the pointer down until the New Window option is highlighted, and release the mouse button. A terminal window should start up. If not, ask an experienced user for assistance.

If you are using a Motif X Window interface, after you complete this chapter, you might consider completing the first few sections of Chapter 11, "Using the X Window System with Motif," before going on to **vi**.

Issuing a Command to the Shell

After you've successfully logged on, the prompt that is displayed on the screen is the shell command interpreter's way of asking what you want to do next.

1. With the cursor at the shell prompt, enter the following command:

   date

   and press (Return).

The **date** program runs. Its output, which includes the day, date, and time, is displayed on your screen.

Logging Off the System

You may not be ready to log off UNIX, but when you are, this exercise shows you how to do it. Unless your system is busy and logging back on is problematical, try logging off now and then log on again.

1. To log out, enter

   exit

   This usually logs you off the system.

2. If **exit** does not work, type one of these commands:

   logout

   or

$\boxed{\text{Ctrl}}$-$\boxed{\text{d}}$

(That is, hold the $\boxed{\text{Ctrl}}$ key down while you press the $\boxed{\text{d}}$ key one time.)

You have now logged off your system.

The steps you have just completed to log on are illustrated in Figure 1-1. Review the login procedure by examining the figure.

1.2

Instructing the Shell to Run Utilities to Obtain Information

The UNIX system includes a wealth of programs available to users. This section examines several standard programs that locate system data.

Determining Who Is on the System

In a multi-user environment, it is often useful to find out whether or not a colleague is logged on.

1. Log back on to UNIX if you logged out.

   The shell prompt is displayed. This means the shell is waiting for instructions from you, in the form of a command. Each command line you type now is sent to the shell, which interprets your instructions and executes whatever other programs you specify.

2. At the shell prompt, enter the following command:

   who

   and press $\boxed{\text{Return}}$.

A list of users currently logged on is displayed.

The command line you just entered instructs the shell to execute a program or utility named **who**. The **who** utility determines who is currently logged on and formats a display of information concerning those logged on users. In this instance, the *output* of **who** is sent to your monitor.

The output is of the following form. It will contain particular information associated with users currently on your system.

```
cassy     ttyh3     Jul 14 21:11
marty     ttyh3     Jul 14 21:11
kyle      ttyh5     Jul 14 11:11
anna      ttyi1     Jul 14 17:58
```

Fields in the Output of who

Each line of output represents a single user and consists of several *fields*. For instance, the components of the entry for *cassy* are as follows:

Element in who Output	Description
cassy	Login name of the user
ttyh3	User's terminal port
Jul 14 21:11	The month, day, and time of login

Each monitor is connected to the computer through a wire connected to a *port*—a connection on the back of the computer. Each port has a designation beginning with the letters *tty*. When you issue the **who** command, the **who** utility searches specific system files to determine the login name, port, and time each user logged on. The **who** utility then formats the information and outputs it (in this case, to the screen). After **who** has completed its work, it exits and the shell displays a new prompt, indicating that it is ready for your next instruction.

Interacting with UNIX

The procedure you just followed is the customary way you interact with UNIX:

- As soon as you log on, the shell displays a prompt indicating that it is ready to receive instructions from you.
- You enter a command, and press Return.

- The shell executes requested utilities.
- The utility retrieves information from the system. The utility's output is then displayed on your screen.
- The shell displays another prompt.

The interaction cycle is depicted in Figure 1-2.

Obtaining the Date and Time

Many programs on UNIX are time dependent. For example, you just used **who** to determine the date and time when current users logged on.

1. You directly access the current date and time information by requesting execution of the **date** program. Enter

   date

   and press Return. The output is displayed on your screen.

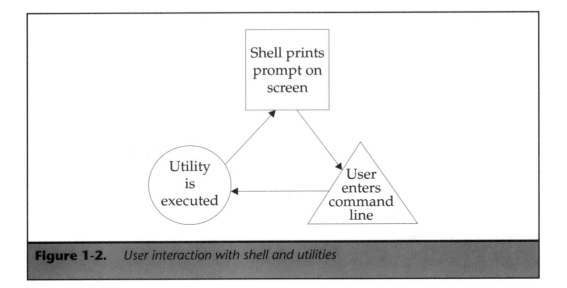

Figure 1-2. *User interaction with shell and utilities*

Making Corrections While Entering a Command Line

In this exercise you will enter the **date** command with an error in it and correct it.

1. Type the following four letters, but do *not* press (Return).

   dzte

2. Try using the (Backspace) key to back up the cursor and enter the command correctly. Press (Return).
   On many machines the (Backspace) does not do what you might expect.

3. Whether or not the (Backspace) key worked in step 2, again enter

   dzte

   Try backing up and retyping to correct the error, using each of the following:

   (Delete)
   (Ctrl)-(h)

   At least one of these keys works to move the cursor back and erase whatever you type.

NOTE: *You'll see how to customize the erase function and assign it to whatever key you want in the section on* **stty** *in Chapter 23, "Modifying the User Environment."*

Including an Argument in a Command

Included in UNIX is a program that provides a 12-month calendar for whatever year you choose. In this exercise you'll display a calendar and learn how to use *arguments* with shell commands.

1. Enter the following:

   cal *98*

Notice that the output displayed on your screen is not for the year 1998, but for the year 98 A.D.

In the commands previous to this one, you entered just the name of the utility you wanted run and the shell ran it. When you enter a command followed by other information, such as **cal** *98*, you are telling the shell (1) to run the **cal** utility, and (2) to pass to the utility the specific information that comes after the command—in this case, the number of the year you want displayed. Information passed to a utility is called an *argument* and has meaning to the utility. Arguments affect how utilities run.

2. Examine the calendar for 1752 by entering the following:

   cal *1752*

   This command instructs the shell to run the **cal** utility and to pass **cal** the argument *1752*, which **cal** interprets as the year to display.[1]

3. Display the calendar for the current year, using **cal**.

Reissuing Commands

If you use the C or Korn shell, you can tell the shell to repeat a command.

1. Type the command

   date

2. To reissue this command, enter

   !!

   If **date** runs again, you are in the C shell.

3. Enter

   date

   r

   If the **date** utility is executed twice you are in the Korn shell.

---

[1]September, 1752 is missing days that were dropped to compensate for inaccuracies of the previous (Julian) calendar, when the Gregorian calendar was started.

4. Enter

   cal *2000*

   The calendar for the year 2000 is displayed.

5. Repeat the calendar display by entering

   !!

   or

   r

The **!!** (C shell) and **r** (Korn shell) commands tell the shell to re-execute your last command line. You can also select command lines by number, and make changes in commands. This is called the *history feature*, and you'll examine C and Korn shell history in Chapter 13, "Accessing and Changing Previous Commands."

Examining the Components of a Shell Command

In the last few exercises you asked for and were given information. The shell puts a prompt on the screen. You say what you want done by entering the name of a program to run, possibly with an argument. Then you press the (Return) key. The results are displayed on the screen. Where does the information come from? Why is it displayed on the screen? Why isn't it placed in a file?

When people first use UNIX they sometimes get the impression that the shell "knows" who is logged on, the date, the ingredients of the calendar, and so on, and all we have to do is ask. Actually, the shell knows nothing. When you enter the command **date** and press the (Return) key, you are instructing the shell *to run the* **date** *program or utility*. This program is a separate program from the shell. What the shell *does* know is where utilities such as **cal**, **who**, and **date** are located on the system and how to get them executed.

After you press (Return) to indicate the end of the command line you want executed, the shell locates the code for whatever utility you placed as the first word on the command line. The shell passes the utility any arguments you included after the utility name on the command line, and executes the utility. In the case of the **date** utility, the program checks the system clock, and formats the display output. The utility sends the results out its output "door." By default, the output of a utility is connected to your display screen unless, as you will see, you request that the shell connect it to a file or even another utility.

Redirecting Output from a Utility to a File

When you issue a shell command to request a listing of current users, the **who** utility locates the needed information and formats the report. The default output destination for the results of the **who** utility is your screen.

1. You can instruct the shell to *redirect* the output of a utility away from your screen to a file. Type the following shell command line:

   who > *users_on*

   Nothing appears on the screen except the next shell prompt. There is no confirmation or acknowledgment that your command was successful. In UNIX, silence usually means success.
       In this command line, the **>** is the *shell redirection character.* Here the redirection character is instructing the shell to create a new file (named *users_on*) and to connect the output of **who** to the new file. The output is said to be *redirected* away from your screen to the new file. For a graphical description, see Figure 1-3.

3. Create a file in your account of the calendar of the year 1752. Enter

   cal *1752* > *lost-days*

       When a utility generates output it is displayed on the screen unless you tell the shell to redirect elsewhere. The previous command line uses the following general form: **utility** > *file*

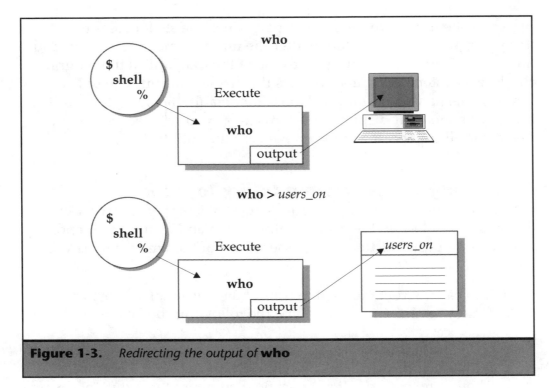

Figure 1-3. *Redirecting the output of* **who**

1.3

Using Utilities to Manage Files

In UNIX there are utilities for copying, renaming, moving, and removing files. This section examines how to use the file management utilities.

Listing Files in Your Home Directory

Because UNIX is a multi-user system, each user is given a separate
workspace or *home directory* to do their work. When you log on, you are
located in your home directory.

On UNIX systems, information is retained in files—system program
files, user-created files, as well as other types of files. In the preceding
exercises, you created two new files. You created the files; you own
them; you have access to them. The files are listed in your home directory.

1. You can request a utility to **list** the names of the files in your current (home) directory. Type the command

   ls

   and press (Return).

With this command line, you are asking the shell to locate and run the **ls** utility. When **ls** runs, it obtains the names of the files listed in your home directory and outputs a formatted display of those names. Because you did not ask the shell to redirect the output of **ls** anywhere else, it is displayed on the screen. After the **ls** utility completes its work, the program exits, the shell is notified, and the shell provides another prompt to see what you want to do next.

Viewing the Contents of Files

The UNIX system includes several utilities that display the contents of files on the terminal screen. Each utility handles the task differently.

One way to examine the contents of a file is to display it a screen at a time. This section examines two commands that work in similar ways:

- The **more** utility was developed for BSD and is included on all systems derived from BSD.

- The **pg** utility was developed at Bell Labs and is included in all System V versions of UNIX.

Many systems include both commands. Use whichever one works on your system. If you have both, try them both out in the exercises that follow to see which one you prefer. The following steps guide you through using each command.

Using more with a Long File

1. Try entering the following command:

   more *lost-days*

If **more** is available on your system, the first part of the file *lost-days* is displayed on the screen. If **more** is not available, you'll see something like this:

```
Command not found
```

2. If the first part of the contents of the file *lost-days* is now displayed on the screen, you can instruct **more** to display the next screenful of text or to exit. Press the [Spacebar] to see the next screen, or **q** to exit.

After **more** reaches the end of a file, it automatically quits and the shell again displays a prompt.

Examining a Long File with pg

1. To use the **pg** utility, enter

   pg *lost-days*

   If the first part of the file is displayed, **pg** is available on your system. If you see the "Command not found" error message, **pg** is not available.

2. When you are using **pg**, press [Return] to see the next screen of text. When **pg** reaches the end of the file, it displays a prompt:

   ```
   (EOF):
   ```

3. Press [q] or another [Return] to end the **pg** utility and return to the shell.

Displaying a Few Lines from a File

There are times when it is helpful to view the first few lines of a file to remind you of the contents or to confirm particular data.

1. On most systems, you can display the first few lines of a file by typing

   head *lost-days*

The **head** utility reads the first ten lines of file(s) named as arguments, in this case the file *lost-days*. You can pass a number argument to the **head** command to modify the number of lines that it reads and outputs.

2. Enter the following:

   head *-6 lost-days*

   The first six lines of the file are displayed. (Several are blank lines.)

3. Try using **head** to list the first eight lines of two of your files. To do this, you list the two filenames as arguments, as in the following example:

   head *-8 lost-days users_on*

4. On many systems you can also view the last lines from a file. Try this command and observe the results:

   tail *lost-days*

Displaying a File Without Interruption

The **pg** and **more** utilities display files one screenful at a time. Another utility displays files without interruption.

1. Enter the following command to see the contents of a file:

   cat *lost-days*

   Unless you have a screen that displays a large number of lines, the initial part of the file scrolls up off the screen.

2. Try the following:

   date > *today*
   cat *today*

   The first command instructs the shell to run the **date** utility. The > is instruction to create a new file named *today* and connect the output of **date** to the file. The second command tells the shell to run the **cat** utility and pass it one argument, *today*. The **cat** utility opens the file listed as an argument, reads the file, and writes each line to the utility's output, which is connected to your terminal. When a file is short, the **cat** utility is a quick way to display the file's contents.

3. Just like other utilities, the output of **cat** can be redirected. Enter the following variation on the last command:

cat *today* > *today2*

The following table examines what the last command instructed the shell to do.

Command Component	Instruction to the Shell
cat	Run the **cat** utility
today	Pass the argument *today* to **cat**
> *today2*	Redirect the output of **cat** to a new file, created by the shell, named *today2*.

Once **cat** is executed, it simply reads from the file *today* and writes to its output, which is connected to the new file *today2*.

4. Confirm the existence of the new file by listing the contents of your current directory:

ls

Because the **cat** utility reads each line from its input file and writes to output, the new file *today2* is a copy of the input file, *today*.

Copying Files

You have thus far created several files by instructing the shell to redirect the output of utilities such as **who**, **cat**, and **cal** to new files. The files you created are listed in your home directory, a workspace provided to you by the system. In later chapters, you will create additional new directories for storing files together that pertain to a given topic or task.

The files and directories you create are accessible from this, your home directory. The files are listed each time you type the **ls** command. You can also create new files by copying existing files.

1. To make a copy of *users_on* and give it the name *users_on_2*, type this command:

    cp *users_on users_on_2*

2. Obtain a listing of the files in your current directory.

    ls

    Notice that the new file is listed with your other files.

3. Examine the contents of *users_on_2* by typing one of the following commands

    pg *users_on_2*

    or

    more users_on_2

    The file *users_on_2* is an exact copy of *users_on*. Each file is a separate entity; either one can be modified or removed without affecting the other.

4. Create a copy of *lost-days* and name it *junk* by typing the following:

    cp *lost-days junk*

5. Create three other copies of files by entering

    cp *junk junk2*
    cp *lost-days lost-2*
    cp *lost-days lost-3*

6. Confirm that the new files were created, by entering

    ls

SUMMARY: *When you want to copy an existing file, use the* **cp** *command with two arguments, in this format:*

cp *oldfile newfile*

The **cp** *utility reads its first argument, oldfile, as the name of an existing file, and the second argument, newfile, as the name of a file to create as an exact copy of the first.*

Renaming Files from the Shell

When you create a file, you give it a name. Each file's name is used to identify and access the file. Filenames are not permanent but can be changed.

1. Examine the contents of your file named *lost-3*, using either **pg** or **more**.
2. Quit the **display** utility by entering

   q
3. Change the name of the file *lost-3* to *phon* by typing the following command:

   mv *lost-3 phon*
4. List your files with the **ls** command. Notice that the file named *lost-3* is absent; *phon* is there.
5. Display the contents of the new *phon* file using **pg** or **more**. It is the same file, with a new name.

When you use the **mv** utility to change the name of a file, you enter **mv** along with two additional pieces of information (the arguments) on the same line with the command. The first argument is the current name of the target file; the second argument is the new name you want to assign to the file. The command is in the format: **mv** *file newfile*.

It changes the name of *file* to *newfile*. Although the utility name implies that it **moves** the file, in this instance it just changes the name of the file. Later you will use the same **mv** utility to move files from one directory to another.

Removing Files

When a file is no longer needed, it is just taking up computer resources and should be deleted or **rem**oved from your account.

 1. Enter the following command to remove the *users_on_2* file:

  rm *users_on_2*

 2. Confirm that the file is removed.

  ls

 SUMMARY: *When you issue the* **rm** *command, you must provide the name of the file you want removed as the argument after* **rm** *on the command line. When you enter:* **rm** *filename, you are telling the shell to run the* **rm** *utility, and to pass* **rm** *one additional piece of information, the filename argument. The* **rm** *utility interprets the argument filename as the name of a file to be removed.*

Removing Files with Confirmation

There is a "silence" about the UNIX system that often disturbs people. For example, when you instruct **rm** to remove a file, all you get in response is the next shell prompt. The **rm** utility does not beep, buzz, or even send a message of acknowledgment. It silently does as requested and quits. The shell then prompts you for your next instruction.

 If you would like the opportunity to confirm your request to have a file removed before **rm** actually destroys it, you must tell **rm** to prompt you.

 1. A few steps back you created a file named *junk*. Request its removal now with the command

  rm **-i** *junk*

  and press ⟨Return⟩. The **rm** command displays a message asking if you really want *junk* removed.

 2. Press ⟨n⟩ and then press ⟨Return⟩ to abort the removal operation.

3. Confirm that you still have too much *junk* with

ls

When you enter the command **rm** **-i** *junk,* you instruct the shell to run the **rm** utility and to pass to **rm** two arguments: **-i** and *junk.* The **-i** is called an option and is interpreted by **rm** as instruction to ask for confirmation before removing any filenames listed as other arguments. Hence, **rm** asks you if you really want to remove the *junk* file.

4. Again request removal of the *junk* file with

rm **-i** *junk*

5. This time, instruct **rm** to go ahead and discard *junk,* by answering the inquiry with

y Return

6. Confirm that *junk* has been removed by entering

ls

Removing Several Files at Once
The **rm** command accepts multiple filenames as arguments.

1. Use **cp** to create a new file called *on2.*

cp *users_on on2*

2. Create two more files by entering the following commands:

date > *today3*
ls > *file-list*

3. Confirm that the files were created by checking the contents of your directory.

ls

4. Remove all three files at once with

rm *on2 today3 file-list*

This command line is instruction to the shell to run the **rm** utility and to pass it three arguments, the names of three files. The **rm** utility interprets all arguments as files to remove, so it removes all three files.

5. Confirm that the files were removed by entering

   ls

6. Attempt to remove a nonexistent file to see the error message.

   rm *xyz*

Creating a Combination File

In UNIX there are often several different ways to accomplish the same task, such as combining two files into a third. One way is to use the **cat** command.

1. Type the following command line:

   cat *junk2 today phon*

   When you enter this command, you are instructing the shell to run the **cat** utility and to pass it three arguments. To the **cat** utility, each argument is interpreted as the name of a file to be opened. Each line of the first file is read and written to output (the screen by default). After **cat** reads and writes all the lines from the first file, it opens the next file and reads and writes all lines, and so on until it reaches the end of the last file. The resulting output is a concatenation of the files.

2. In step 1, the output of the **cat** command was displayed on the screen. You can also tell the shell to redirect the output to a file. Enter

   cat *junk2 today phon* > *total*

3. Examine the *total* file by entering one of the following commands:

   more *total*

   or

pg *total*

The *total* file consists of the contents of the file *junk2* followed by the contents of the file *today* followed by the lines from *phon*. The > *total* portion of the command instructs the shell to create a new file *total* and to redirect the output of **cat** to the new file. All lines read by **cat** are written to the new file *total*.

When you look at the output, *total*, there is no way to tell where one file ends and the other begins.

SUMMARY: *You get work done in UNIX by interacting with the shell. The first word on a command line must be a utility you want the shell to execute. Utilities are used to change filenames, remove files, copy files, display the contents of files, and obtain information from the system. The output of a utility is displayed on the screen unless you instruct the shell to redirect it to a file. The behavior of a utility can be modified by including arguments after the utility on the command line. Thus far, options and filenames have been given as arguments to utilities.*

■ Review 1

Answers are listed at the end of the chapter.

1. When logging on, what does the error message

   ```
   Login incorrect
   ```

   mean?

2. What utility produces a list of currently logged on users?

3. When you enter the command **cal** *2001*, what are you asking the shell to do and what is the result?

4. What command tells the shell to repeat the last command?

5. What command results in the creation of a new file named *myfile* that contains a list of the names of the files in your current directory?

6. What does the following command line accomplish?

   who > *fileA*

7. What command makes a copy of *file1* called *file2*?

8. What do each of the following accomplish?

mv *file1 file2*
rm *file1 file2*
cat *file1 file2*

1.4

Employing the UNIX Toolbox of Utilities

The UNIX operating system user programs, or utilities, that you've examined thus far have located system information and output it to the display, and removed, renamed, and otherwise manipulated user files. Each utility program is a tool that performs a set of very specific tasks. This section examines utilities that read input from files; modify the data that they read; and send the output to your screen, to a file, the printer, or to another utility.

Printing a File

At this point in the chapter you have created several files and examined them on the screen. An essential feature of UNIX is printing files on paper.

Of the commands that you have tried so far, only **more** and **pg** are different depending on the UNIX system you are using. The UNIX commands to send a file to a printer for printing are also system dependent.

1. To print a file, try each of the following commands that send a file to a program that manages the printer, called a *spooler*.

   On System V:

   lp *lost-days*

   On BSD:

   lpr *lost-days*

   If the system responds to either of these commands with an error message about a lack of a destination printer, you will need to ask a colleague or your system administrator for the name of a printer available to you.

2. Once you have the printer name, type one of the following commands.

   The *dest* part of the argument refers to the name of the destination printer that you are selecting to print your file. Type in the printer name you obtained from your system administrator.

   On System V:

   lp -**d***dest lost-days*

   On BSD:

   lpr -**P***dest lost-days*

   If you have several printers available, the **-P** option in BSD, and the **-d** option in System V allow you to specify which printer to use. There is no space between the option and the destination printer name.

   NOTE: In these chapters, we will use the default form of the command, **lp** *or* **lpr**. *If you need to specify a printer, include the appropriate* **-P** *or* **-d** *option.*

3. Try printing several files from your account by entering one of the following commands, replacing *f1, f2,* and *f3* with names of three of your own files.

   lp *f1 f2 f3*

   or

   lpr *f1 f2 f3*

The print spooler utilities accept multiple filenames as command-line arguments and print all files named.

Sorting Lines in a File

Many files contain data concerning users or individuals. On UNIX, the file named */etc/passwd* (the *password file*) contains one line of information (a record) for each user. Every time a new user is added to the system, a new line is added (usually to the bottom of the file). As a result, the password file is not in sorted order. In the following exercise, you will sort the lines from the password file. To make visual examination easier, start by creating a file consisting of the first few lines of the file.

1. Create a file consisting of the first 20 lines of the password file on your machine, by entering

   head *-20 /etc/passwd > mypasswd*

2. Examine the file by entering

   cat *mypasswd*

 NOTE: *If the password file is quite small and the last line is **++**, it indicates that you are on a network and some other machine is responsible for maintaining most of the password entries. Without the **++**, a short list indicates there is a limited number of users on your machine. Either way, a small password file will work fine in these exercises.*

3. Sort the lines from the *mypasswd* file. Enter

   sort *mypasswd*

   The **sort** utility reads the file *mypasswd* and rearranges its lines. The output is displayed on the screen. The *mypasswd* file itself is not rearranged; rather, its data is read, sorted, and the output of **sort** is connected to your screen.

Sorting Multiple Files

1. Review the contents of two of your files by entering the following commands:

   cat *mypasswd*
   cat *total*

2. Use **sort** to sort the lines from the two files you just examined. Enter

   sort *mypasswd total*

   Examine the output. The **sort** utility reads both files (*total* and *mypasswd*) and sorts all the lines that it reads. The resulting output is the contents of both files, merged together and sorted, and output to the screen. The files are not sorted individually; instead the lines from both files are read and all the lines sorted into one output. Neither the original *total* nor *mypasswd* file is changed.

   In the **sort** order, lines beginning with numbers precede lines beginning with uppercase letters, which precede lines that begin with lowercase letters. Unless instructed otherwise, the **sort** utility sorts in ascii order (ascii is an acronym for the American Standard Code for Information Interchange). In ascii order, nonalphanumeric characters are first, then numbers, followed by uppercase characters, and then lowercase characters. Therefore, lines beginning with nonalphanumeric characters are first, then lines that begin with numbers, followed by uppercase lines, then lowercase.

3. On most systems you can examine the ascii order by entering this command:

   man *ascii*

Reversing the Sorted Order

To sort a file in reverse ascii order, you must specify an option to the utility on the command line, instructing it to work in a particular way.

1. Type the following command:

   sort -r *total mypasswd*

   Compare the output to that of the previous **sort**. In this case, you instructed the shell to run the **sort** utility and to pass it three arguments: the **-r** option and the two filename arguments. The **-r** is one of several options to the **sort** utility that instructs **sort** to change the way it functions.

NOTE: *More options to many of the utilities introduced here are examined in Chapter 3, "Using Basic UNIX Utilities."*

Listing Misspelled Words from a File

Many UNIX systems contain a spell-check program that examines files for misspelled words.

1. Examine *users_on* for misspelled words with the following command:

   spell *users_on*

   All strings in the file that **spell** does not find in the on-line dictionary are viewed as misspelled words in the file, and are displayed on the screen.

Deciphering Error Messages

When the shell or a utility is not prepared to interpret a portion of a command you enter, it sends you an error message.

1. Enter the following command that tells the shell to run a utility that is not available.

   copy

   The shell looks but cannot find it. It sends you the error message.

2. Enter

   cat *xyz*

   The **cat** utility tells you that the file does not exist.

3. Instruct the shell to run **cp** and pass it three arguments.

   cp *xxx yyy* zzz

   The **cp** utility informs you about its *usage*.

   The message says that to use **cp**, you can use the options listed in the brackets, and you must either give it two arguments or, if you want files copied into a directory, you can list several filenames providing the last argument is the directory in which you want the copies placed. This topic is explored in Chapter 4.

   The shell did not check to see if the files existed. The shell did not even interpret *xxx yyy* zzz as filenames. It just passed arguments. The **cp** utility did not get so far as to realize the *xxx* file does not exist. It just found three arguments, determined the last was not a directory, and so complained.

4. Try

   mv *abc def ghi*

   The **mv** utility functions in the same way.

Obtaining Information About Utilities

Throughout this book you try out new utilities. The exercises introduce how the utilities work, and later chapters explore them more completely. UNIX systems usually have an on-line manual that can be consulted.

1. To find out more about **sort**, enter

   man *sort*

   The display is a cryptic, programmer-to-programmer description of the utility.

2. Press the ⌷Spacebar⌷ to see the next page of the manual. If the ⌷Spacebar⌷ does not work, try ⌷Return⌷. In one of the first few pages, the various options are listed that **sort** understands. Find the **-r** option.

3. To quit the **man** display, enter

   q

Connecting Tools Together in Pipelines

In this chapter you have used each utility individually. An important UNIX feature is the capability it gives you to combine utilities in a command line. Each utility can be independently used to achieve a specific goal, or can also be connected to other utilities to accomplish more complex tasks.

Before UNIX, the way to use several utilities in a row was to employ temporary files. For example, to view a sorted list of who is logged on the system, you'd have to type the following series of commands. Try it.

1. Create a temporary file with the output of **who**.

   who > *temp*

2. Sort the temporary file and put the sorted output into a second temporary file, *temp2*.

   sort *temp* > *temp2*

3. Examine the contents of the output file, *temp2*, using **cat**, **more**, or **pg**.

4. List the directory's contents with **ls**.

5. Remove the temporary files *temp* and *temp2*.

UNIX provides an easier way to do this as the following exercises demonstrate.

Sorting the Output of who Using Redirection

The display that **who** provides is not in alphabetical order. You can have the shell send the output of **who** directly to **sort** for alphabetizing without using a temporary file.

1. Type the following commands and compare.

   who

   who | **sort**

   The pipe instructs the shell to connect the output of one utility to the input of another. The pipe symbol is usually found on the same key as the backslash.

The output of this command line consists of the lines from **who**, sorted in alphabetical order and displayed on the screen. No user temporary files are created or have to be removed.

2. You are not limited to one pipe redirection. To see the output of **sort** displayed one page at a time, enter

who | sort | more

or

who | sort | pg

3. Pipes and redirects can be combined. Create a new file for the sorted output, by typing this command:

who | sort > *sor_who*

4. Examine the file *sor_who*. The result of the previous **who** command line is that the shell connects the output of **who** to the input of **sort** and the output of **sort** to a new file, *sor_who*.

Counting Lines of a File

It is often useful to count the lines, words, or characters in a file. There is a UNIX utility that accomplishes that specific task.

1. Type the following command:

wc *total*

This command instructs the shell to run the **wc** utility and pass it one argument: *total*. The **wc** utility interprets arguments that don't have a - in front as files to read and examine. The output from the word count utility is similar to the following:

```
28     139     390  total
```

This output consists of the number of lines (28), words (139), and characters (390) read from the file, followed by the name of the file that was read.

2. Now have **wc** count the number of lines only, using the **-l** (lowercase "el") option:

wc -l *total*

The **-l** option instructs **wc** to output only the number of lines it reads from the input file. The minus sign tells **wc** that the l is an option, not a file to read as input.

Determining the Number of Current Users

You have seen that the output of **who** consists of one line of information for each user currently logged on. To determine the total number of people logged on, you can count the number of lines in the output of **who**.

1. Enter this command:

who | wc -l

The following describes how the shell interprets this command line.

Command	Interpretation
who	Instruction to the shell to run the **who** utility, which outputs one line of information about each user.
|	Instruction to the shell to connect **who**'s output to the input of **wc**.
wc	Instruction to run the **wc** utility, which counts elements in its input.
-l	An argument to pass to **wc**, which **wc** interprets as instruction to count only the lines.

As **who** completes its output of information about all users, the records are passed directly to **wc**, which counts the number of lines. The command line does not instruct the shell to redirect the output of **wc** anywhere, so it is displayed on the screen.

Locating Specific Lines in a File

It is often useful to locate the lines in a file that contain a word or string of characters.

1. The file *users_on* contains a record for each user who was logged on when you created the file. Type the following command, replacing *yourlogin* with your actual login name:

   grep *yourlogin users_on*

   The **grep** utility selects a line in the file *users_on* if it contains the string of characters that is *yourlogin,* and outputs it.

2. Now look for all lines in the file that contain the string *tty*. Enter

   grep *tty users_on*

This command line asks the shell to run the **grep** utility and pass it two arguments. Many utilities, including **sort** and **rm**, interpret all arguments as files to be acted on. They **sort** or remove them all. Not **grep**. To the **grep** utility, the first argument is the *target string*, and all *other* arguments are files to be opened and searched. In this case, **grep** looks through the file *users_on* for lines that contain the target string *tty*, and selects those lines. It outputs only those lines that have a match. The original file is not affected.

Determining How Many Times a User Is Logged On

The next exercise has utilities, pipes, and options working together to find out how many times a specific user is logged on.

1. Type the following command line, substituting your login name for *logname*:

   who | **grep** *logname*

   The output of **who** is connected to the input of **grep**. The **grep** utility searches its input for lines that include the string of characters it receives as the first argument—your login name. The output of **grep** consists of one line for each time you are logged on.

2. Pass the output of **grep** to the **wc** utility, to count the number of lines that include your login name. Type

who | **grep** *logname* | **wc -l**

The output is a number equal to the number of lines in the output of **grep**, which is the number of times the selected user is logged on. The schematic of the command line is

utility | **utility** *argument* | **utility** *argument*

1.5

Including Special Characters in Command Lines

When communicating with the shell, the only tool is the keyboard. The characters available on the keyboard and words created by combinations of those characters constitute the entire language used between you and the shell. To allow the use of complex commands, many characters have special meaning. You have used some already. The > symbol, for instance, is interpreted by the shell as instruction to connect the output of the previous utility to a file named right after the redirect. This section introduces others special characters used in shell commands.

Exploring Your Environment

The shell program that interprets your commands is started when you log on. Several pieces of information are given to your particular shell process, so that your computing environment is appropriate. You can examine how the environmental variables are set up.

1. From the shell, type the following.

In the Korn shell:

set

In the C shell:

printenv

or

env

The output is a listing of some of the variables that are currently set for your shell. Among the many lines displayed, you should find something like the following:

```
For C shell users:

USER      forbes
SHELL     /bin/csh
HOME      /users1/programmers/forbes
PATH      (/usr/ucb /bin /usr/bin /usr/local /lurnix/bin /usr/new .)

For Korn shell users:

HOME=/usr/home/brian
LOGNAME=brian
PATH=/usr/vue/bin:/usr/bin/X11:/bin:/usr/bin
SHELL=/bin/ksh
```

- The *user* or *USER* or *LOGNAME* variable is your account name that you entered when you logged on.

- The *shell* or *SHELL* line indicates which of several shell programs is started at login to interpret the commands that you enter: *csh* is the C shell, *sh* is the Bourne shell, and *ksh* is the Korn shell. They all handle basic commands in essentially the same way, and for now it makes little difference which is running.

- The *home* or *HOME* variable is the location of your workspace or home directory.

- The *path* or *PATH* variable lists the directories where the shell looks to find UNIX utilities you request.

The subject of local and environment variables is explored in some detail in Chapter 5, "Specifying Instructions to the Shell."

Evaluating Variables

The shell maintains a series of variables and their values. You can ask the shell to evaluate the specific variables.

1. The **echo** utility reads its arguments and writes them to output. For example, enter this command:

   echo *These words are arguments*

   The shell executes **echo** and passes it four arguments. To **echo**, arguments are just character strings to read and write as output. The output is therefore just the arguments from the command line.

2. Ask the shell to evaluate either the *USER* or *LOGNAME* variable and pass its value to **echo**, by entering

   echo $USER

   or

   echo $LOGNAME

   The **$** character has special meaning to the shell. It tells the shell to "locate the variable whose name follows, and replace this string with the variable's value." In the command you just entered, your login is the value of the variable, which the shell evaluates and passes as an argument to **echo**.

3. Having the shell evaluate *$LOGNAME* or *$USER*, and replacing the variable with its value, is very useful. Enter

   who | grep $USER

   or

   who | grep $LOGNAME

   The shell replaces the **$LOGNAME** with your login id and then passes that value to **grep** as its first argument. To **grep**, the first argument is its search string. The line from the output of **who** that contains your login id is selected by **grep** and output to your screen.

4. Have the shell evaluate some other variables. Enter

   echo $SHELL $HOME

   In this case, two variables are evaluated by the shell. The resulting values are passed to **echo** as arguments. The **echo** utility reads its arguments and writes them to output. By default, the output is connected to your monitor. The value of the first variable, *SHELL*, is the shell that is started up at login; the other variable, *HOME*, is where your home directory is located on the system. These variables were created when you logged on. Your shell and all other programs you run are given these variables and these values.

Selecting All Files as Arguments

Another special character you will use in UNIX command lines is the * (asterisk) or "splat."

1. If you list several filenames after the **wc** utility on a command line, as you did with **sort**, the **wc** utility will examine those files. Enter this command:

   wc *total lost-days*

   The number of elements in each file is counted and output.

2. To have **wc** examine all files whose names begin with the letter *l*, enter

   wc *l**

   The shell interprets the *l** as instruction to replace that string on the command line with the names of all files that start with the letter *l* and have zero or more of any additional characters following the *l* in their names (i.e., the * is a wildcard). The shell then runs the **wc** utility, passing it all arguments—the names of all files in the directory that were matched.

3. Confirm that the shell is expanding (replacing the string with) the * into filenames by entering

echo *l**

The shell replaces the string *l** with the filenames in the current directory that begin with the letter *l*. Those names are passed as arguments to **echo**, which writes the arguments to output.

4. You can also have the shell list *all* files in your current directory as arguments to **echo** by typing

echo *

The shell replaces the asterisk with the names of all the files in your directory and then executes **echo**. The **echo** utility reads its arguments (the filenames) and writes them to output, which in this case is your monitor.

5. Count all the elements of all the files in your directory by entering

wc *

The shell replaces the * with the names of all files in the current directory and passes all the names as arguments to **wc**. The **wc** utility examines all files listed as arguments, and displays output like this:

```
 8    39    190      junk
 9    29    175      on2
 8    39    190      phon
 1     5     22      today
12    59    310      total
14    80    220      users_on
52   251    899      total
```

The output from **wc** is a list of information pertaining to all input files, and then a total of these counts.

 NOTE: If you created a file named total, it will be listed in alphabetical order among the other files. The "total" at the end of the output is the sum of the statistics for all files examined by the utility.

6. You can also have the shell pass all filenames to the **grep** utility, so that **grep** searches through all the files in your directory. Type the following:

grep *Sep* *

This command line tells the shell to replace the asterisk with all the filenames listed in your current directory. The first argument passed to **grep** is *Sep*, which **grep** interprets as the target string. The remaining arguments are the names of all the files. The **grep** utility then searches each line in all files for the target string of characters, *Sep*.

Preventing Interpretation of a Special Character

You have seen how the characters * and $ have special meaning to the shell. Sometimes it is necessary to instruct the shell to not interpret special characters and to treat them as ordinary characters, instead.

1. Enter the following:

echo *

In response to this command, the shell does not expand the asterisk but passes it as an argument to **echo** uninterpreted. The **echo** utility reads it and outputs it to the screen. When a character is preceded by a backslash, the shell interprets it as just an ordinary character.

2. Enter the following:

echo \$*HOME*

The $ is *not* interpreted as instruction to evaluate the *HOME* variable. Because it is preceded by a backslash, it is just an ordinary dollar sign.

In the previous two commands, the arguments the shell gave to **echo** after it interpreted the * did not include the backslash. When the shell interprets * it reads the \ as a specific instruction—don't ascribe special meaning to the character that immediately follows. The only character that gets passed is the *. The \ is not passed to **echo**, it is instruction to the shell.

Not Interpreting the [Return]

When you press the [Return] key at the end of a command line, you are signaling the end of the command. The shell interprets the [Return] keypress as a special character, one that indicates the end of the command to be interpreted.

1. Enter the following command:

**who > **

and press the [Return] key.

The backslash instructs the shell to not interpret the character that immediately follows. Hence the [Return] keypress is not to be interpreted as the end of the command. At this point, the shell has not been told to process the command because no real [Return] has been received. It waits for more input. In fact, what you have entered so far is not a complete command. The shell needs to redirect the output of **who** to a file, but the filename is not included.

2. Enter the filename

users2

and press [Return] again. This time, the [Return] is not preceded by a backslash. The shell interprets it as a real [Return], so the command, which now spans two input lines, is processed.

3. Confirm that the new file was created by entering

ls
more *users2*

When you want a command line to span more than one input line, precede the [Return] with a backslash character to instruct the shell to not interpret the return's special meaning.

Not Interpreting Several Characters in a String

The backslash is interpreted by the shell as instruction to not interpret special meaning of the character that follows.

1. You can turn interpretation off for more than a single character. Enter

   echo '1*'
   echo '$HOME $LOGNAME'

   The output is the literal string of characters entered. The * and $ are interpreted as just characters, so the shell does not expand the * to match filenames. The **$HOME** is not evaluated for the variable value. The arguments passed to **echo** are just **1*** and **$HOME $LOGNAME**.

   The first single quote tells the shell to turn off interpretation of special characters. The second turns it on again. Because the special characters are inside the single quotes where interpretation is off, they are not interpreted.

Selecting Fields from a Database

One of the most useful functions of modern computers is database management. The UNIX operating system provides several utilities that are used with databases.

1. Type the following command:

   who | awk '{print $1}'

   The **awk** utility extracts the first field from each line of the output of **who**. The output of **awk** is displayed on the screen.

2. Change the command line to instruct **awk** to select the second field. Enter

   who | awk '{print $2}'

The following table describes the pieces of the command line.

Command	Interpretation
who	Instruction to the shell to run the **who** utility.
I	Instruction to the shell to connect the output of **who** to the input of the next utility, **awk**.
awk	Instruction to the shell to run the **awk** utility.
'　　'	Instruction to the shell to not interpret any special character between the single quotes, but to pass the enclosed characters as is, to **awk** as an argument.
{print $2}	The quoted string that is passed to awk. This instruction is interpreted by **awk** as "For every line of input, print out only the 2nd field."

The **awk** utility can be used to select and print specific fields, make calculations, and locate records by the value of specific fields. You will use it more extensively in Chapters 3, "Using Basic UNIX Utilities" and 16, "Data Manipulation with **awk**."

1.6
Redirecting Input to a Utility

Utilities receive input, do a task, and write output. Some utilities (**date**, **who**, **ls**) get their information or input from the system. Others read files. In this tour of the system, you have been using the > redirection symbol to specify where utilities are to write their output. For instance, when you enter **who** > *file1*, the output of **who** is connected to *file1*. If you do not redirect the output, the utility writes to your monitor.

When you issue a command like **who** I **sort**, you are instructing the shell to connect the output of **who** to the input of **sort**. You are specifying that the output of one utility become the input to another.

In this section you will examine how to specify a file as input to a utility.

Determining Where Utilities Read Input

If no input is specified for a utility, where does it get its input?

The Default Input Source

1. Enter the following command:

   sort

   and press ⌈Return⌉. The cursor moves to a new line. No shell prompt is displayed.

2. Enter the following lines:

   ```
   hello
   DDD
   2
   Hello
   110
   good-bye
   ```

3. Press ⌈Return⌉ to enter a blank line, and then press ⌈Return⌉ again. On a line by itself, enter ⌈Ctrl⌉-⌈d⌉. A sorted version of the lines you just entered is displayed on the screen.

   The ⌈Ctrl⌉-⌈d⌉ is the *end-of-file* (EOF) character. It indicates to the utility that there is no more input and that the utility can quit. The utility **sort** read the lines you entered, sorted them, and output the results to your display.

   The default input for a utility is the terminal keyboard. Because no input at all was specified in the preceding command, the **sort** utility read its input from the default input source, your keyboard. After receiving the ⌈Ctrl⌉-⌈d⌉, **sort** wrote the results as output.

4. For another example of the default input source, enter the following:

   sort > *sort-test*

5. Enter several lines of text as you did in step 2.

6. When you have finished, press [Return] to put the cursor on a line by itself, and press [Ctrl]-[d].

7. Examine the contents of the new file *sort-test* using **more** or **pg**.

In the command line in step 4, you instructed the shell to connect the output of **sort** to the new file *sort-test*, but you did not specify any input for **sort**. By default, input is connected to the keyboard if it is not redirected to another source. The **sort** utility read what you entered as input and wrote its output. Because you instructed the shell to connect the output of **sort** to the new file *sort-test* when **sort** wrote its output, it went to the new file.

Specifying a File as Input

When you want to designate a specific input source, there are two ways to get a file opened and read as input by a utility.

1. Enter the following command:

   sort *mypasswd*

   Here the shell is instructed to run the **sort** utility and pass it one argument, *mypasswd*. To the **sort** utility, the argument *mypasswd* is interpreted as a file to open and read as input. The file *mypasswd* is read, its contents sorted, and the output displayed by default on the workstation screen.

2. Enter the following:

   sort < *mypasswd*

   The results are the same as the command line you entered in step 1. A sorted version of the file *mypasswd* is displayed on the screen. In this command you are instructing the *shell* to open the file *mypasswd* and connect it to the *input* of **sort**. In the command line in step 1, the shell passes the filename as an argument to **sort**. In step 2, the < is instruction to the shell to open the file itself and connect the input to **sort**.

3. You can also connect files to the input of other utilities. For example, type

cat < *mypasswd*

In this case, you are instructing the shell to connect the file *mypasswd* to the *input* of **cat**. Because no output destination is specified, the output is by default connected to your monitor. Thus, the file *mypasswd* is read by **cat** and displayed on the workstation screen.

4. You have also been instructing utilities to open files, with commands such as

sort *mypasswd*

The same approach works with the **cat** utility. Type

cat *mypasswd*

The filename *mypasswd* is passed as an argument to **cat**, which opens it, reads it, and displays it on the screen.

Following is a summary of the redirection commands used thus far.

Command	Interpretation
utility > *filename*	Shell connects output of utility to *filename*.
utility < *filename*	Shell connects *filename* to input of utility.
utility1 | **utility2**	Shell connects output of **utility1** to input of **utility2**.

Redirecting to an Existing File

Thus far, you have used the > symbol to instruct the shell to connect the output of utilities to new files. What happens when you redirect output to an existing file depends on the shell you are using and the value of a variable *noclobber*?

1. To make sure that *noclobber* is off for the following demonstration, enter these commands:

In the C shell:

unset *noclobber*

In the Korn shell:

set +o *noclobber*

2. Create a new file and examine its contents by entering

ls > *test-list*
cat *test-list*

3. Instruct the shell to put the output of **date** into the same file and examine the file.

date > *test-list*
cat *test-list*

The original contents of the file are gone, *replaced* by the output of **date**.

When told to redirect to a file, the shell creates the file *if it does not exist*. If there is a file by that name, the current contents are *deleted* and the new output takes their place.

4. Instruct the shell to not clobber the files by entering the following:

In the C shell:

set *noclobber*

In the Korn shell:

set -o *noclobber*

5. Attempt to redirect output from another utility to the file.

ls > *test-list*

An error message is displayed in the Korn and C shells. The Bourne shell overwrites files with redirection and has no *noclobber* feature.

To turn off *noclobber*, you enter the commands you entered in step 1.

Creating a Text File with cat

You will usually create text files using an editor such as the UNIX visual editor, **vi**. However, you can quickly create small test files without first mastering an editor, by using one of several other shell commands. You will become familiar with the **vi** editor in Chapter 2.

1. Type the following:

   cat > *first_file*

   and press Return.
       The cursor returns to the beginning of the next line. Notice, however, that the shell does not display a new prompt. This command line instructs the shell to start the **cat** utility and connects its output to the new file *first_file*. There is no request to redirect the input, so input is still connected to the default—your keyboard. You are no longer in communication with the shell; what you now type is read by the **cat** utility.

2. Type the following lines:

   This is a line of text in the first-file.
   This is another.

   and press Return.
       The **cat** utility reads your input and writes it to a new file named *first_file*.

3. To inform the **cat** utility that you have finished adding text, press Return to advance to a new line and then press

   Ctrl-d

   This Ctrl-d (end-of-file or EOF character) tells **cat** there is no additional input. The **cat** utility dies, and the shell displays another prompt.

4. From the shell, obtain a listing of your files, using

   ls

The file *first_file* is listed.

5. Examine the contents of *first_file* by typing one of the following commands.

On System V:

pg *first_file*

On BSD:

more *first_file*

The *first_file* file consists only of the text you typed. No additional data about the file, such as the file's name or your name, is added to the file by the system. It is just the text you typed. The file's name is kept in the directory. The other information is in a system "file."

6. Create another text file with another **cat** command:

cat > *second_file*

Add some text, and return to the shell with Ctrl-d.

7. Obtain a listing of the files in your current directory with **ls**.

8. Examine the contents of *second_file* with **pg** or **more**. The file consists of the lines you entered as input to **cat**. For a graphical view of creating a file, see Figure 1-4.

The **cat** utility takes its name from the word con**cat**enate because if given several filenames as arguments, it reads all files and splices them together. The command **cat** > *filename* instructs the shell to connect the output from **cat** to the file *filename* and to execute the **cat** utility. By default, the workstation keyboard is connected to the input of **cat**. Whatever you type is read by **cat** from your workstation and written to the file. The **cat** utility is not very complicated; it simply reads input and writes output, making no modifications.

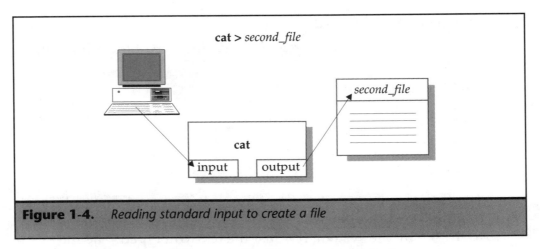

Figure 1-4. *Reading standard input to create a file*

Managing Input and Output with Redirection: A Summary

The role and effect of file input and output redirection symbols are summarized in the following table. The subject of redirection is examined more completely in Chapter 5.

Command	Input	Output	Effect
sort	Keyboard	Display screen	Whatever is entered at the keyboard is sorted and displayed onscreen.
sort > *file1*	Keyboard	*file1*	Keyboard input is sorted and placed in *file1*.
sort < *file2*	*file2*	Display screen	*file2* is opened by the shell and connected to the input of **sort**. The file *file2* is sorted and the output displayed on the screen.
sort *file1*	*file1*	Display screen	*file1* is passed as an argument to **sort**, which opens it for input. Contents of *file1* are sorted and written to output, connected to the screen.

Command	Input	Output	Effect
sort < *file1* > *file2*	*file1*	*file2*	Shell connects *file1* to input and *file2* to output of **sort**. The file *file1* is sorted and output placed in *file2*.
sort *file1* > *file2*	*file1*	*file2*	The shell passes *file1* as an argument to **sort** and connects output of sort to *file2*. The **sort** utility opens *file1* and sorts the lines, and the output goes to *file2*.

The two methods for opening files are needed because some utilities read all arguments as instructions and cannot open files.

SUMMARY: Utilities read existing files as input and act on the data. They can be used to accomplish many tasks including display, print, sort, search for a character string, and count the elements of a file or the output of another utility. Output from a utility can be redirected to another utility, a file, or, by default, is displayed on the screen.

■ Review 2

1. What is the effect of each of the following commands?

   a. **lp** *file1 file2*
   b. **sort** *file1 file2*
   c. **wc** *file1 file2*
   d. **grep** *file1 file2*
   e. **who** | **sort** > *abc*

2. What commands list the variables currently used by the shell?

3. What results from using the following commands?

   a. **grep** *$LOGNAME* */etc/passwd*
   b. **lpr** *chapter**
   c. **grep** *\$HOME fileA*

d. **sort** > *fileA*
e. **set** *noclobber*
 or
 set –**o** *noclobber*

f. **sort** < *fileA* > *fileB*

4. Redirection makes it possible to create complex command lines. Where a word is located on a command line is information to the shell. Consider the following command line. What is each piece: utility, input file, output file, argument?

 ------ ------ < ---- | ---- ---- > ----

1.7

Communicating with Other Users

Several UNIX utilities allow you to communicate with other users on your system or on the network. This section introduces you to two of them.

Writing a Message to Another User

Often, workstations attached to your system are located great distances apart. A utility provides a means of communication among the workstations. If you want to contact another user who is logged on, you can send messages to that workstation. This exercise is most useful if you and a colleague are using terminals that are adjacent so you can see what happens on each screen.

If that is not possible, use your own login and communicate to your own screen.

1. Start the message-sending process by typing the following command, using the login of your colleague for *other_login* or your own login if you are writing to your own screen.

 write *other_login*

2. If all goes well, the **write** utility sends a message to the screen that *other_login* is using, informing him or her that you are sending a message. Your keyboard is the input to **write**. Type a line or two of text. When you have finished, conclude the **write** session by returning to a new line and pressing

   [Ctrl]–[d]

3. When you want to use **write** to communicate with another user, use the **who** command to find a colleague who is logged on, and note his or her login. A user's login name is the first field in the **who** output.

4. When you are using **write** and you receive the message

   ```
   Permission Denied
   ```

   it means the user you want to **write** to has turned off permission for others to write to his or her terminal.

5. If you receive the message

   ```
   write:  other_login logged in more than once ...
   writing to terminal
   ```

   then *other_login* is logged on to at least two terminals or windows. You can verify this using the **who** utility:

   who

   In the output, note that for each instance that *other_login* is logged on, there is a unique terminal named in the second column.
      The **write** utility will connect to the first instance of *other_login* listed in **who**. You may override this default behavior by giving **write** a second argument:

   write *other_login* *other_terminal*

   where *other_terminal* is the specific terminal on which *other_login* is listed in **who**. This command line instructs **write** to connect to the terminal port where *other_login* is located.

6. You control whether people can write to your screen. To allow others to write to your display, enter the following:

mesg *y*

To deny access to others, enter

mesg *n*

Writing (Sending) a File to Another User's Screen

You can also use the **write** utility to send files rather than keyboard input to another user's screen.

1. Type the following command:

write *other_login* < *first_file*

The input to write is, by default, your keyboard. The < *first_file* portion of this command line instructs the shell to connect the file *first_file* to the input of **write** (to redirect the input for write away from your keyboard to the file). The **write** utility reads *first_file* instead of your keyboard and displays what it reads on the terminal that *other_login* is using The **write** utility cannot open files. It needs the shell's help.

Sending Mail to Another User

The **write** utility can be used only when the target user is currently logged on to the system. To send a message to a user whether or not they are not logged on, you can use the UNIX postal service.

1. For practice, send the file *first_file* as mail to yourself. Type the following command:

mail *your-login* < *first_file*

2. To receive your mail, wait a few minutes and enter

mail

Either a list of mail messages is displayed or the message scrolls across the screen.

3. If you see a list of messages and want to read the first message, enter its number

   1

4. To delete a message, enter

   d

5. To quit mail, enter

   q

To send mail to a user on another system, you need their mail address. The commands are in the following form.

mail *dimitri@machinename*

or

mail *cassy@muster.com*

Sending messages and files to users on other systems and using the full menu of **mail** features are explored in Chapter 19, "Sending and Receiving Mail Messages."

1.8

Modifying the User Environment

One of the strengths of the UNIX operating system is its flexibility. The system allows you to customize a variety of programs to your own liking.

Changing Your Password

One of the most important ways to customize your account is to choose a secure but memorable password. This is not only convenient, but necessary for maintaining security of everyone's data on the computer.

Before you begin the process of changing your password, decide on an appropriate new one. There are several words to avoid when choosing a password because they are easily guessed. Do *not* use

- Your login id
- Any first or last name
- Your address
- A word listed in a dictionary in any language
- Obscenities

Be sure to include both upper- and lowercase letters, and it is best to use a numeral or other character.

With all these considerations, you may find it difficult to create a secure password that can be remembered. One way to formulate a password is to use the first letters of every word in a memorable sentence. For example, if you enjoy the work of a particular author, your password might be

```
MfaiMT47
```

This looks difficult to remember. It *is* extremely difficult to crack— but it's easy to recall because it stands for

My **f**avorite **a**uthor **i**s **M**ark **T**wain,
and I am **47** years old

When you have decided on a new password and are ready to change your password, take the following steps:

1. Determine from a colleague or system administrator if your system is running NIS, the Network Information Service.
2. Once you have decided on a new password, type whichever of the following commands is appropriate. (If you are not sure whether you are on an NIS site, try the **yppasswd** command first. If you get an error message, try **passwd**.)
   If your system is running NIS, type

   yppasswd

Otherwise, enter

passwd

You are prompted for your *current* password. To protect you, the program will not continue unless you identify yourself by correctly providing the current password.

3. Type your *old* password and press (Return). You are now prompted for your *new* password.

4. Type your new password and press (Return). The program asks you to repeat the new password to make certain that you type it correctly.

5. Type your new password again and press (Return). When the shell prompt returns with no error messages, your password has been changed.

The **passwd** utility accomplishes tasks you cannot do. It actually changed a system file that you are permitted to alter. Because the **passwd** utility has that power, it grills you extensively to be sure you are legitimate and that you can remember the password.

Changing the Prompt

Throughout the chapter, we have talked about the shell prompt. There are three standard shell prompts, shown below. The prompt your shell displays, like much of your user environment, can be changed.

Prompt	Shell
$	Bourne and Korn shells
%	C shell
#	Any shell as *root*

1. You can find out which shell you are using by typing

   echo $SHELL

2. If you are using a C shell, type the following command:

set *prompt* = 'myname '

where *myname* is whatever you want the prompt to be.

3. If you are using the Bourne or Korn shell, type the following:

PS1 = 'myname '

Your prompt is now reset. This "personalized" prompt remains set until you log out. In Chapter 23 you will learn more about setting up your computer environment, and you will have the opportunity to permanently customize various asp'ects of your workspace, such as the shell prompts and how the shell behaves.

Renaming Commands for Personal Use

The C and Korn shells include an **alias** feature that permits you to rename commands—for ease of memory or to save keystrokes. You'll explore this feature more in Chapter 12. The Bourne shell, however, does not have an **alias** feature. If you are working in a C or Korn shell, try the following exercise.

If you have been using a system running the DOS operating system, you are used to getting a listing of your files by entering **dir**.

1. Try it on UNIX:

dir

Unless someone has already created an alias for your account, the shell tells you that

```
dir is not found.
```

2. Let the shell know that you are intending to use **dir** as a nickname for **ls** by entering the following.

In the C shell:

alias *dir* **ls**

In the Korn shell:

alias *dir*=**ls**

3. Try the **dir** command again. The output is that of the **ls** utility. You enter **dir**. The shell looks up **dir** in its alias list and finds out that you mean **ls** when you enter **dir**. The shell runs the **ls** utility.

4. Create an **alias** called **on** by typing one of the following commands.

   In the C shell:

   alias *on* **'who | sort'**

   In the Korn shell:

   alias *on=***'who | sort'**

5. Check to see if the **alias** worked. Type

   on

6. List your current aliases by entering

   alias | more

   What you see displayed is all aliases set at login, or by you in this session.

   In the setting of this alias, single quotes are used to tell the shell to *not* interpret the special characters *space* and | when it is interpreting the command line to create the alias. The shell interprets the quotes to mean "don't interpret the enclosed string." The shell sets the alias **on** equal to the *uninterpreted* string **who | sort**. Later when you enter **on** as a command, the shell checks its alias list, finds its meaning, and then runs **who | sort**.

7. Check the list of aliases. If your system does not have the command **rm** aliased to include the **i**nquire option, create the alias now. Enter one of the following commands.

   In the C shell:

   alias *rm* **'rm -i'**

   In the Korn shell:

   alias *rm=***'rm -i'**

8. Attempt to remove a file by typing

rm *filename*

and observe the result. The alias feature of the C and Korn shells allows you to customize the name you use for any command.

Aliases that you set at the command line last only until your current shell exits. In Chapter 23, "Modifying the User Environment," you will make aliases permanent.

Modifying the Permission on Files

As the owner of a file, you determine who has permission to read the contents of the file, or change the contents of the file. If it's a command file, you can specify who can execute it.

1. To view the permissions of the *users_on* file, type the following command:

ls -l *users_on*

The output resembles the following:

```
-rw-rw----  1  cassy       453 Jul 18 11:17 users_on
```

The **-l** option is interpreted by **ls** as instruction to provide a long listing of information about the file. The first field in the output, which consists of ten character places, shows the permissions currently set for that file. In Chapter 6 you'll explore setting file permissions in much more depth. For now, however, look at the second, third, fifth, and sixth characters of the permissions field. The first **r** and **w** indicate that *you* have permission to read and write to the file. The second **rw** indicates that other users who have been assigned to your group have read and write permissions for your file. The last three characters indicate the permission granted to all other uses who are not in your group.

For example, with the permissions field for a file shown in Figure 1-5, the following permissions are granted.

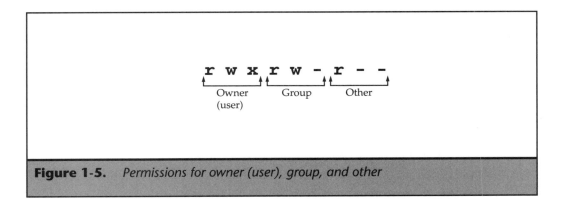

Figure 1-5. *Permissions for owner (user), group, and other*

Permissions Field	Permissions Granted
rwx	The file's owner can read, write, or execute the file.
rw-	Members of user's group can read or write to the file.
r--	Users who are not in the owner's group can only read the file.

Denying Read Permission on a File

You can change the permission on a file to make the file inaccessible by all users. (Since you own it, you can still change its permissions again at any time.) No user can read or copy your file if you don't grant read permission.

1. Type the following command to remove read permission from the file *users_on*:

   chmod -r *users_on*

2. Examine the permissions field for *users_on* by typing

   ls -l

   Notice that where the previous permissions were read and write permissions for you and group, the new permissions only include a **w**. You removed read.

3. Verify the state of the file's permissions by trying to display the file with the following command:

cat *users_on*

You immediately receive an error message saying that you do not have permission to read the file. Even though you own the file, if you deny yourself read, you can't read it. But you still own it. You can change the permissions again.

4. Return the read permission to the file with the following command:

chmod +r *users_on*

The **chmod** command is used to **ch**ange the **mode** of a file.

In Chapter 5, you will examine what each permission— **r, w,** and **x**— controls for files and directories, as well as how to specifically set the permissions for owner, group, and other users.

1.9

Programming with UNIX Tools

You can use UNIX to program in a variety of formats and languages. The UNIX operating system gives programmers a number of programming tools that either are packaged with the system or can be added.

Creating a Shell Script

One of the most basic and useful program tools is a *shell script.* You have been using the shell as an interactive command interpreter. It is also a powerful programming environment.

1. Type the following command to create a new file:

cat > *new_script*

2. Type the following lines.

> **echo** *Your files are*
> **ls**
> **echo** *today is*
> **date**

Press Return to move the cursor to a new line and enter Ctrl-d.

3. At this point, the file *new_script* contains a series of shell commands. Examine the file to be certain it is correct.

   cat *new_script*

   If there is a problem, remove the file *new-script* and return to step 1.

4. Display the permissions of the file by entering

   ls -l *new-script*

5. The permissions indicate that the file is not *executable*. To run the script, you must grant yourself execute permission. Type the following command to make *new_script* executable:

   chmod +x *new_script*

6. To see the new permissions, enter

   ls -l

   You now have execute permission, as well as read and write permissions for the file.

7. Execute the new script by typing its name:

   new_script

   All the commands that you typed into the file are executed, and their output is sent to the screen.

8. If you receive an error message such as

   `Command not found`

   type the following:

   ./new_script

This command line tells the shell exactly where to find the shell script *new_script*, in your current directory known as dot.

In summary, here are the steps to create and use a shell script:

- Create a file of shell commands.
- Make the file executable with **chmod**.
- Execute the file by entering the script name.

When you execute a script, the shell that is reading the script takes its input from the script, rather than your keyboard. It executes each line of the script as though it were a line you entered at the keyboard. All utilities in the script are executed. You will create many scripts in Chapter 3, "Using Basic UNIX Utilities" and in Chapter 22, "Programming with the Shell."

Determining Your Location in the File System

When you log on to the system, your shell is started and you are in your home directory.

1. To get a listing of where your home directory is located, type this command:

pwd

The **pwd** utility displays your **p**resent **w**orking **d**irectory. The output looks something like this:

```
/u1/staff/your_login
```

This is the *full path* of your present working directory. Your home directory on the right is listed in a parent directory, which in turn is in the one above it, and so on to the topmost directory, *root*.

2. Obtain a listing of the files in your current home directory with the usual command:

ls

The output is a listing of files that you have created. Their names are written in your home directory.

Viewing the File System from the Top

The top of the UNIX directory system is generally referred to as *root*, or sometimes "slash," because it is symbolized by the forward slash character.

1. Obtain a listing of the files and directories in the *root* directory with the following command:

   ls /

   The output is a listing of some of the system directories, including *dev*, *tmp*, *bin*, and *usr*. The listing also contains the first directory after *root* (/) that was in your path when you typed **pwd** from your home directory. This command told the shell to run the **ls** utility and pass it the / argument. The **ls** utility read the names of the files in the / directory and displayed that list on the screen.

2. Check to see what your present working directory is, by entering

   pwd

   Your current directory is not changed, even though you generated a listing of the contents of the **root** directory. The current directory is still your home directory. The **ls** utility allows you to obtain listings of other directories without actually changing directories.

Changing Directories

1. When you need to, you can change directories. To change from your present working directory to *root*, type the following command:

   cd /

   The command **cd** is instruction to change directory.

2. Confirm that your current directory is now the **root** directory by typing

pwd

The output is not terribly descriptive:

/

Your current directory is *root*, which is at the top of the UNIX file system.

3. Display a list of the files and directories in the *root* directory, with

ls

The listing is the same as was displayed when you entered the **ls /** command earlier. The directories *dev*, *tmp*, *bin*, and *usr* are system directories.

Returning Home

1. In Chapter 4, you will discover more about the directory system and how to move around within it. For now, return to your home directory with the following command:

cd

No matter where you are on the system, issuing the **cd** command with no argument will bring you to your home directory.

2. To verify that you are in your home directory, type

pwd

Creating a Directory

You are in your home directory. As a user you can create directories.

1. Create a subdirectory in your home directory by entering

mkdir *Private*

2. Confirm that the directory exist with

ls

Among your files now is a listing for the new directory *Private*. It is listed first, not because it is a directory, but because its name begins with a capital letter.

3. Change directories into *Private* by entering

cd *Private*

Because *Private* is a subdirectory of your home directory, you can change to *Private* from your home directory with the
cd *Private* command.

4. Confirm your location.

pwd

5. Ask for a listing of files.

ls

There are no files in your new *Private* directory. The files you created earlier are listed in your home directory, not the subdirectory.

6. Create a new file in *Private* by entering

cat > *secrets*

Enter a line or two of text and quit by going to a new line and entering Ctrl-d.

7. List the contents of the directory now.

ls

8. To return to your home directory, enter the usual

cd

Directories are used in UNIX like all in other computing systems—as places to store files that go together. For now, do all your work associated with this book in your home directory. In later chapters, you will create additional subdirectories.

Examining the Toolboxes That Contain the Utilities

Throughout this chapter, you have been issuing commands that call for the shell to execute a utility.

1. Enter the following misspelled command:

   datte

   The error message is

   ```
   Command Not Found
   ```

   Where is the shell looking? We ask our five-year-old to go upstairs and get a book that is on the desk or the nightstand. She leaves and returns with the book. It was on the desk or nightstand. Had it been on the bed with large red arrows pointing at it, she would have returned with the error message

   ```
   Book Not Found
   ```

   Just like the shell.

2. Enter

   echo $PATH

   The output is a series of directories:

   ```
   /bin:/usr/bin:/usr/local/bin:/usr/bin/x11:/usr/hosts
   ```

   This is the "desk" or "nightstand" list of places the shell checks for a utility when you ask for one to be executed. The shell looks first in the directory listed on the left, then the next, and so on.

   The */bin* directory contains some of the utilities available on the system in the form of binary files.

3. Obtain a listing of the utilities in */bin*. (Note: The */* is important; do not omit it.)

   ls */bin*

This command produces a list of the files in the directory */bin*. You may recognize some of these files—they are utilities you have already used, including **cat**, **rm**, **who**, and **ls**. These are the executable programs that are accessed when you type a command of the same name. As you saw when you examined your *PATH*, the */bin* directory is not the only directory that contains executable code. The path your shell examines can be modified to examine other directories. See Chapter 23, "Modifying the User Environment."

The Elements of the Password File

Many system files are consulted by utilities as they perform their jobs. When you log on, a program called *login* asks for your password and starts your shell. Your shell gets information like *USER* and *HOME* so it can access the needed information about your account.

An encrypted version of your password and other information about you reside in a file called */etc/passwd*. This file is read whenever you or any other user logs on.

1. Type one of the following commands.

   pg */etc/passwd*

   and press Return to page through the file, or type

   more */etc/passwd*

   and press the Spacebar to page through the file.

   If on a large network, try

   ypcat *passwd* | **more**

2. Locate the entry for your account.

3. Press q to stop and return to the shell.

4. Now examine your own personal entry in the */etc/passwd* file. Type one of the following commands:

   grep *$LOGNAME* */etc/passwd*
   grep *$USER* */etc/passwd*

```
ypcat passwd | grep $USER
ypcat passwd | grep $LOGNAME
```

In these versions, you are asking the shell to evaluate the variable *USER* or *LOGNAME* and pass its value to **grep** as the search target.

The records in the */etc/passwd* file consist of seven fields separated by colons. The general format is as follows.

```
login:password:uid:gid:misc-information:home:startup-program
```

The fields of the password file are described in the following table:

Field	Information
login	The login or name for your account. (May be a *.)
password	Your encrypted password. (May be a *.)
uid	Your user id; the unique number that is assigned to your account.
gid	Your group id. Each user must be a member of at least one group. Every user who has the same number in this field as you is in your group. You can share files with group members using permissions.
misc	The Miscellaneous field need not be filled. It contains information about the user.
home	Your home directory. This is your current directory when you first log on.
startup-program	The program that is started when you log on—usually either the C shell (*/bin/csh*) or the Korn shell (*/bin/ksh*).

Identifying Devices

When a terminal is connected to the computer, it is connected at a *port*. Each port is assigned a *tty* number. The *tty* is actually a special file that the system recognizes.

1. Enter

   who

   Every user logged on is logged on to a *tty* port.

2. Obtain a listing of the system devices with the following command:

   ls */dev* | **more**

   The output is a list of files in the */dev* directory. This directory contains information and files that the system uses to communicate with the disk drives, terminals, and other hardware devices. The group of files that begin with *tty*, such as *tty01* or *ttyp2*, are the terminal ports.

3. Find out which port your terminal is connected to. Type the following:

   tty

   The output is the number and path of your port, such as

   ```
   /dev/tty03
   ```

   This is the port through which the computer talks to you. It matches the number associated with your login in the output of **who**.

In UNIX, you create files, utilities are in files, and the terminal is a file.

1.10

How UNIX Does Its Work

Because UNIX is a multitasking system, it runs many programs at once. Each time you execute a utility, the system allocates memory, locates the needed code, and gives the request cpu attention—a *process* is underway. Any time you ask for a utility, you are asking for a process to run the code of the utility. Your shell is underway—it is a process.

Listing Processes

1. Obtain a listing of your current processes by entering one of the following commands:

   On System V:

   ps

   On BSD:

   ps -g

The output is a list of the processes currently associated with your login, along with some information about each process. For instance, the TT or TTY field is the *tty* number or port the processes are attached to. The PID is the id number of the process, and so forth. You will probably have at least two processes running—the shell and the **ps** command—and maybe several others. Each process is a program you have running on the system.

Listing Systemwide Processes

The **ps** command you entered in the preceding exercise gave you the status of *your* processes. You can also look at the processes running on the entire system, including those of all the users currently logged on.

1. Type one of the following commands.

   On System V:

   ps -ef

   On BSD:

   ps -aux

This output of **ps** includes more information than most users really want to know. It's a list of the process status of every process currently running on the system, along with a plethora of information on each process. For troubleshooting problems on the system, this information is very useful to system administrators and other people supervising the UNIX environment.

Backgrounding a Process

Many of the processes running on the system are not associated with a particular user but are important elements of the operating system. These processes are running *in the background*, and are invisible to most users. You, too, can run a process in the background.

1. Type one of the following commands to create a new file.

   On System V:

   ps -ef > *new_ps* **&**

   On BSD:

   ps -aux > *new_ps* **&**

These command lines tell the shell to run the **ps** command and redirect the output into a file named *new_ps*. The ampersand (**&**) at the end tells the shell to execute the whole command line in the background, and to return a new shell prompt so that you can continue working. When you execute the command, a number is displayed. This is the process id number of the **ps** utility as it is executed. When the process is finished, a message is sent to the screen.

This feature allows you to run time-consuming programs in the background while you continue work in the foreground. Obviously, with a command process as short as **ps**, backgrounding isn't so crucial; but there are times when it will save you time and work.

Avoiding Accidental Logout

If you accidentally enter a Ctrl-d to your login shell, you are logged out. The end-of-file character says "no more input, exit," so the shell exits.

1. You can tell the C and Korn shells to ignore end-of-file character with the following command:

   In the C shell:

   set *ignoreeof*

   In the Korn shell:

set -o *ignoreeof*

2. Now press Ctrl-d. You receive a message telling you to use **exit** or **logout**, not Ctrl-d.

You will soon customize your account to have *ignoreeof* and *noclobber* set at all times. For now, enter each after you log on to protect yourself from accidental overwrite and accidental logout.

SUMMARY: UNIX provides tools to communicate with other users on the local host, local network, and across the Internet. Tools also support your customizing how the shell functions, and what names are acceptable for utilities. You can create shell scripts, customize your prompt, and determine what processes are running.

■ Review 3

1. What results from the following commands?

   a. **write** *georgia*
   b. **mail** *georgia*
   c. **passwd**
   d. **set** *prompt*="*What's Next?* "
   e. **PS1**="*What's Next?* "
   f. **alias** *l* **ls**
   g. **alias**
   h. **ls -l**

2. What are the steps to create a shell script called *now*, such that when you enter *now* in the shell, output is displayed that tells you how many logins are currently logged on?

3. What command changes your current directory to *root*?

4. What command creates a new directory in your current directory named *Plan9*?

5. What command returns you to your home directory, no matter where you are?

6. What file contains a single line record for each user that lists the user's login id, user id, group id, and home directory?

7. What command outputs a list of the processes you have currently running?

8. What command instructs the shell to not accept Ctrl-d as a signal to log off?

■ Conclusion

UNIX is a multi-user, multitasking operating system. It includes numerous utilities that can be linked together for efficiency. As you probably noticed from this whirlwind tour, UNIX is a complex, powerful, and occasionally unusual operating system. In this chapter, you have been introduced to many commands and concepts. The skills you mastered in this chapter are the basis for more extensive investigations of the same topics in later chapters.

■ Answers to Review 1

1. What you entered for either the *login* or *passwd* was not correct.

2. **who**

3. It is a request that the shell run the **cal** utility and pass an argument to *2001*. The **cal** utility interprets the argument as a year. A 12-month calendar for the year 2001 is formatted and output. The output is displayed on the screen.

4. In the C shell:

   !!

   In the Korn shell:

   r

5. **ls** > *myfile*

6. The output of **who** (list of current users) is connected to a new file named *fileA*.

7. **cp** *file1 file2*

or

cat *file1* > *file2*

8. Changes the name of *file1* to *file2*.
Removes *file1* and *file2*.
Displays the contents of *file1* followed by *file2* on the screen.

■ **Answers to Review 2**

1. a. Prints *file1* and *file2*

b. Creates a sorted output consisting of the lines from *file1* and *file2*, merged together in ascii order. The output is displayed on the screen.

c. The output of **wc** on the screen is the number of lines, words and characters in *file1*, and *file2*, and a total of the elements of both.

d. The output of **grep** displayed on the screen is every line in *file2* that contains the string of characters *file1*.

e. The output of **who** is passed to **sort**, which sorts the lines. The output of **sort** is redirected to a new file *abc*.

2. **set, env, printenv**

3. a. The shell interprets **$LOGNAME** as the user's login id and passes that string the first argument to **grep**. All lines in file */etc/passwd* that contain the user's login id are selected by **grep** and output.

b. All files with names beginning with *chapter* and having zero more additional characters in the name are printed.

c. The shell does not interpret the **$** so passes *$HOME* as the first argument to **grep**, which selects all lines in fileA that contain the literal string *$HOME*.

d. Whatever the user enters from the keyboard is sorted and entered into a new file, *fileA*, or replaces an existing *fileA*.

e. The shell will not overwrite existing files when you redirect the output from a utility.

f. The contents of *fileA* are read and sorted, and output is placed in *fileB*.

4. **utility** *argument* < *input-file* | **utility** *argument* > *output-file*

■ **Answers to Review 3**

1. a. What you type is displayed immediately in user georgia's screen. She must be logged on.

   b. What you type is sent as a letter to *georgia* to read when she wants.

   c. Change your password.

   d. C shell prompt is changed.

   e. Korn or Bourne shell prompt is changed.

   f. The command **ls** will be executed when you enter **l**.

   g. A list of current aliases is displayed.

   h. A long listing of files is displayed that includes permissions.

2. Create *now* file with line **who** | **wc -l** in it, make it executable by entering **chmod +x** *now*, and then enter *now*.

3. **cd /**

4. **mkdir** *Plan9*

5. **cd**

6. */etc/passwd*

7. System V: **ps**

   or

   BSD: **ps -g**

8. C shell: **set** *ignoreeof*

   or

   Korn shell: **set -o** *ignoreeof*

COMMAND SUMMARY

Logging On and Off

exit	Kills the current shell. (See also **logout**.)
logout	Informs the shell you want to end the login session.
passwd	Changes user's password.

Working with Directories

cd *Dir*	Changes the working directory to *Dir*.
cd	Changes directory to home directory.
ls	Lists the contents of the current directory.
ls -l	Outputs a long listing of the contents of the current directory with one file or directory per line.
mkdir *Dir*	Creates a directory *Dir*.
pwd	Displays the full pathname of the current directory.

File Displaying Utilities

cat *file1 file2*	Concatenates *file1* and *file2*.
grep *word filename*	Searches for lines containing a particular *word* (or pattern) in *filename*.
head *filename*	Displays first 10 lines of *filename*.
wc *filename*	Counts the lines, words, and characters in *filename*.

Database Utilities

awk '{print $x}' *file*	Prints the xth field of *file*.
paste *file1 file2*	Combines *file1* and *file2*, line by line.

File Management Utilities

cp *file1 file2*	Copies *file1* to *file2*.

mv *file1 file2*   Renames *file1* as *file2*.

rm *filename*   Deletes *filename*.

rm -i *filename*   Same as **rm** *filename*, but asks the user to confirm the deletion.

Data Producing and Examining Utilities

tty   Displays the path and filename for the current terminal.

grep *word file-name*   Searches for lines containing a particular *word* (or pattern) in *filename*.

wc *filename*   Counts the lines, words, and characters in *filename*.

awk '{print $x}' *file*   Prints the *x*th field of *file*.

sort *filename*   Displays the lines in *filename* in sorted order.

spell *filename*   Checks the spelling in *filename*.

who   Displays a list of users currently logged on.

Printing

lp *filename*   On System V, prints *filename* on the line printer.

lpr *filename*   On BSD, prints *filename* on the line printer.

Communication Utilities

write *otherlogin*   Writes a message to another user's workstation.

mail *login < file-name*   Sends *filename* by electronic **mail** to *login*.

Redirection of Input and Output

utility *< filename*   Makes *filename* the input for **utility**.

utility *> filename*   Sends the output of **utility** to *filename*.

utility1 | utility2	Makes the output of **utility1** the input of **utility2**.

File Permissions

chmod -r *filename*	Removes permission to read *filename*.
chmod +r *filename*	Gives permission to read *filename*.
chmod +x *filename*	Grants execute permission on the file.
chmod -x *filename*	Removes execute permission on the file.

Shell Programming

set	Lists the variables that are set for your shell, and their values. In C shell, lists local variables. In Korn shell, lists local and environment variables.
env	Lists environment variables.
printenv	Lists environment variables.
$var	Evaluates a variable, *var*.
*	Expand to match filenames.
****	Interprets next character as ordinary character without special meaning.
' '	Interprets all characters between the single quotes as ordinary characters.
scriptname	Executes the commands in the file *scriptname*.

History

!!	In the C shell, reexecutes the last shell command.
r	In the Korn shell, reexecutes the last shell command.

Working with Aliases

alias   Lists your aliases and their values.

alias *string* '*command*'   In the C shell, accepts *string* as equivalent of *command*.

alias *string*='*command*'   In the Korn shell, accepts *string* as equivalent of *command*.

Setting the User Environment

set *prompt* = "*string*"   In the C shell, makes *string* the new prompt.

PS1="*string*"   In the Bourne or Korn shell, makes *string* the new prompt.

Process Monitoring

ps   On System V, displays current processes for this login session.

ps -g   On BSD, displays current processes for this login session.

Chapter Two

Editing with the Visual Editor

When writing text or computer programs, you need to create files, insert new lines, modify the content, rearrange lines, and make other necessary changes. Computer text editors were developed to help you accomplish these tasks. The UNIX **vi**sual editor, **vi**, is a powerful, command-driven screen editor. You give all your instructions to the editor by entering combinations of keystrokes. The **vi** visual editor is available on nearly all UNIX systems and is an essential UNIX tool. By using the **vi** editor, you can make specific and global changes to text—precisely and, with practice, easily.

In this chapter you'll use the visual editor to access files; move to various locations in them; and make editing changes within the file, such as adding text, deleting lines, reading in other files, and moving portions of files to different locations. Copies of the document in varying stages of development can be saved and printed.

SKILLS CHECK: *Before beginning this chapter, you should be able to*

- *Access and leave the system*
- *Execute basic shell commands*
- *Use* > *for output redirection*
- *Create a file using the* **cat** *utility*

OBJECTIVES: *After completing this chapter, you will be able to use* **vi** *to*

- *Create and access files*
- *Quickly find a specific place in a document*
- *Add text to files*
- *Move the cursor to particular words or lines in a file*
- *Delete or change words, lines, and blocks of text*
- *Cut and paste lines and blocks of text*
- *Undo your mistakes*
- *Properly move among editor modes*
- *Use the visual editor startup control file*

2.1

About vi

In the 1970s, people edited files on UNIX with the line editor by issuing cumbersome commands. There was no way to move the cursor to a particular word and make a correction. Instead, to correct the spelling of a word in the 14th line, you had to issue a command such as *14/s/misteak/mistake/*. A graduate student, Bill Joy, wrote the **vi** visual editor to allow movement of the cursor to make editing changes. An old editing program, **vi** is not a word processor and lacks many of the features available in today's PC word processors. There is no mouse support, no pull-down menus, and no page formatting.

It's not easy to master **vi**'s two *modes*—*command* mode and *append* mode—nor to keep track of the many commands you enter from the keyboard. However, even with these drawbacks, **vi** is an essential tool in UNIX for three reasons:

- It is provided as part of all standard UNIX releases.

- Once you master the basics, **vi** is a fast and effective editor.

- Many advanced **vi** features are very powerful and not available on other editors. The visual editor is actually the editor of choice for most advanced users.

In this first section you create a *practice* file using the **cat** utility. Then you use **vi** to move around in the file and make deletions. In later sections you'll learn to make changes and additions to the file, save the file, manage the screen display, and tailor the way **vi** works.

2.2

Working in an Existing File with vi

Files are central to the UNIX computing environment, as in any other. Business letters, college theses, program code, program output, data, e-mail, and data records are all files. The visual editor is used to create new files, as well as edit existing files. Even though a file is created using one utility, it can still be identified by its name and accessed by another utility, such as **vi**.

The visual editor, however, is built opposite most other editing environments. When you start a letter with a typewriter or a PC word processor, the one thing you can do right away is to type in or add text to the file. Not so with **vi**. When you start editing a file with **vi**, the one thing you *can't* do is add text. You can move around in the file, and delete words, lines, and characters; but you cannot add text to the file without first issuing an "I want to add text" command.

For that reason, it is easiest to learn to use **vi** by starting with an existing file.

Creating a Practice File

Let's begin by creating a practice file that you'll work with throughout this chapter.

1. Log on to your UNIX account.

2. One of the many ways to create a file on UNIX is with the **cat** utility. Start the process of creating a new file by typing

   cat > *practice*

3. Press ⌈Return⌋.

4. Type in the following lines. Be sure to make some mistakes as you type. In later exercises, you will use **vi** to correct them.

   This practice file will be used
   several times in this course.
   Although I am creating this file with the cat command,
   Later I will be editing it with the visual editor.
   a b c d
   2 3 4 5
   2 3 4 5
   A B C D
   E F G H
   (This is not making too much sense.)

> *Hello, I will be sure to add several more*
> *lines of text before quitting:*

5. To tell the **cat** utility that you are through typing text, do the following:

   a. Get to a new line by pressing Return.

   b. Then to end the input, press Ctrl-d.

   A shell prompt reappears.

2.3

Moving the Cursor with Direction Keys

You have just used the command **cat** > *filename* to create a new file. The *filename* you assign to a file (such as *first_file* or *practice*) becomes the identification label used by UNIX to locate the file when you want to work on it.

1. To start editing your new *practice* file with the **vi**sual editor, enter the command

   vi *practice*

   and press Return.

The cursor appears on the first line of the file. You are no longer communicating with the shell, but are in the **vi** control center or *command* mode. At this point the keyboard is used to issue commands for moving the cursor through the file and deleting text. As you will see, you cannot add text from command mode.

Moving the Cursor One Character or One Line at a Time

When editing a file, sometimes you need to correct the spelling of a word, remove specific lines of text, or insert additional code at various locations. You must inform **vi** exactly where you want to add text, or which specific character, word, or line you want to change. As a means of communicating with **vi**, you move the screen cursor to the appropriate location before you start an editing operation.

A fundamental way to move the cursor through a file is with the *direction keys*.

1. With the *practice* file displayed on the screen and the cursor at the beginning of the first line, press the Ⓙ key one time. The cursor moves down one line. If the cursor does not move, press the (Esc) key and then try again.

2. Most workstations also include arrow keys that move the cursor on the screen. Press the ⬇ one time now. If the cursor moves down to the second line, that means the arrow keys work in **vi** on your system.

    In steps 1 and 2 you used the arrow keys, as shown in Figure 2-1, or the Ⓗ, Ⓙ, Ⓚ, and Ⓛ keys, as shown in Figure 2-2, to move the cursor through a file.

3. Practice with each of the four arrow keys and the Ⓗ, Ⓙ, Ⓚ, and Ⓛ direction keys. Move the cursor up, down, right, and left through the text.

4. Move your cursor to a blank space, whether between words or accidentally placed at the end of a line. Spaces are considered characters.

5. Try to move the cursor beyond the text—to the right and left, above the first line, and below the last line.

    When you attempt to go beyond the existing text, the cursor does not move and the workstation either flashes or beeps.

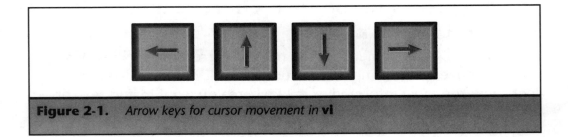

Figure 2-1.   *Arrow keys for cursor movement in vi*

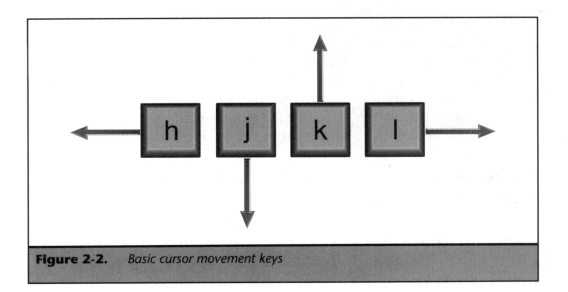

Figure 2-2. *Basic cursor movement keys*

Augmenting the Direction Keys

The number keys (1 through 9) located at the top of your keyboard can be used as part of the direction key commands. Try the following:

1. To have the cursor move four spaces down, type

   4

   and then press either ⬇ or ⓙ *without* pressing (Return). By preceding the direction key command with a 4, you have moved the cursor down four lines.

2. Move around the screen using augmented direction commands such as these:

   2 ⬆
   4 ➡
   3 ⬇
   4 ⬅
   3 ⓙ
   2 ⓗ
   3 ⓚ
   3 ⓛ

3. Many workstations will repeat an operation if you press the key and hold it down. Press and hold down a direction key now to see how it works on your workstation.

The arrow keys or the ⒣, ⒥, ⒦, and ⒧ direction keys—either alone or in conjunction with number keys—allow you to move the cursor to any character in the file. As you will see, there are more efficient ways to move the cursor long distances.

Conceptualizing the Visual Editor in Command Mode

As each series of **vi** commands is introduced in this chapter, a conceptual map is included to assist you in reviewing and conceptualizing the commands. Figure 2-3 is the conceptual map for accessing the command mode of **vi**.

1. In Figure 2-3, locate the box marked **Shell $ %**. Notice the arrow labeled **who** that leads from the shell to the circle describing what the **who** command does. The arrow is a two-headed arrow because when **who** completes its task, you are returned to the shell.

2. Find the arrow leading down from the shell, labeled **vi** *filename*. When you used the **vi** command earlier, you entered *practice* as the *filename*.

According to the conceptual map, when you are in the shell and type the command **vi** *filename*, you leave the shell and move into **vi**'s command mode. In command mode, you can move around, examine, and delete text from the file.

The command **vi** *filename* is a *one-way* command, in that it moves you from the shell to the **vi** command mode and leaves you there. Notice that the arrow labeled **vi** *filename* in the conceptual map has only one head, indicating that it is a one-way command.

At this point, you are "in" **vi**. The shell is no longer interpreting the commands you type; the visual editor is. It is only from **vi** command mode that you can begin editing a file.

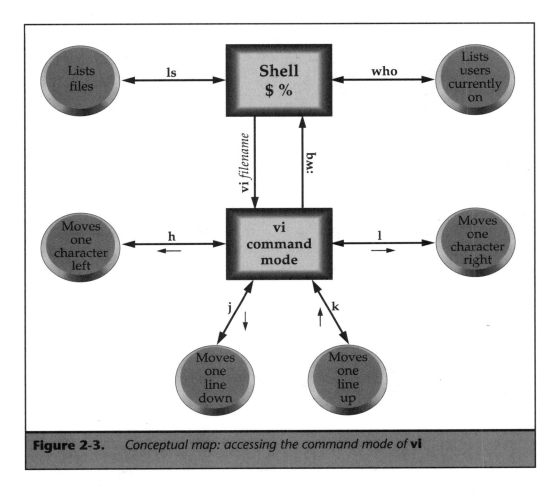

Figure 2-3. *Conceptual map: accessing the command mode of* **vi**

When you press the direction keys, the editor moves the cursor and then waits for your next command. You can type one cursor movement command after another without ever leaving command mode.

3. Find the arrows representing the direction key commands in Figure 2-3. These double-headed arrows indicate that the commands are *two-way* commands. These commands do not move you into another mode and do not require the use of the Return key. When you issue the commands, they take effect immediately, moving you around the file.

SUMMARY: *In command mode you can move the cursor around the screen. The* ⓗ*,* ⓙ*,* ⓚ*, and* ⓛ *keys on all workstations, and the arrow keys on most workstations, are used to move the cursor a space or line at a time within the contents of a file. These commands do not add letters to the file; they simply move the cursor. The action of each direction key can be augmented by pressing a number key before the direction key. The* **vi** *editor remains in command mode when cursor movement commands are used.*

Ending an Editing Session

You must inform the editor when you want to leave and return to the shell. On the conceptual map (Figure 2-3), locate the arrow, which moves you from **vi** command mode back to the shell.

When you begin editing a file, the editor creates a workspace, or *buffer*, for editing.

1. Leave the editor now and return to the shell by typing

   :wq

   When you have finished and you type **:wq**, you instruct the editor to **w**rite (that is, save) the buffer copy of the file you have been working on and **q**uit the editor.

Recovery from a Misspelled Filename

"Typos"—errors made while typing—are common mistakes when you are entering the name of an existing file. When this occurs, the editor will begin the process of starting a new file using the misspelled name. There is a way to access the correct file without leaving the editor, as follows:

1. Type the following command, misspelling the name of the file as shown:

   vi *praZtice*

   The editor searches for a file named *praZtice*. Unable to find a file with that name, **vi** starts an editing session for a new file, using the misspelled filename.

2. To tell the editor to access the correct file (*practice*) for **edit**ing and to throw away anything you have done in the misspelled file (*praZtice*), type

    :edit! *practice*

    and press Return.

    This command instructs the editor to abandon the empty file with the misspelled name and start editing the file named in the **:edit!** command.

2.4

Moving Efficiently to a Specific Target

Thus far you have been moving around the file character by character and line by line. There are several faster and more explicit ways to move the cursor.

Moving Forward to Specified Text

An easy way to move the cursor to a specific word in the text is with the forward search command, the slash. For instance, while editing your practice file you can quickly move the cursor forward to the word *be*.

1. From command mode, type

    /be

    and press Return.

    As you type the slash character / and each letter of the target word *be*, they appear in the lower-left corner of the screen. The characters are *not* entered into your file, however. The editor is displaying your forward search command on the workstation so you can see what you are typing.

2. After you press Return, the cursor moves forward to the specified word (*be*) in the text. If this doesn't happen, press Esc and try again.

3. Use the forward search command to locate another word, such as *text*.

After the target is located and the cursor moves to the new location, you are still in command mode. The search command is a two-way command.

Finding Other Instances of the Target

If a string of characters appears more than once in your file, the forward search command locates only the first appearance of the characters after the cursor. You can go on to others.

1. Search for the word *will* in your *practice* file.

2. Once you've located the first occurrence of the word, locate the next occurrence by entering

   n

3. Keep typing **n**ext. When the editor reaches the end of the file, it loops back to the beginning of the file and continues the search. The **n** command is a two-way command; you do not leave command mode.

SUMMARY: You must be in command mode to search for text characters. When you enter /targetword and press ⌈Return⌋, *the cursor moves forward through the text to the next occurrence of "targetword." When the editor reaches the end of the file, it goes back to the beginning and searches forward until it either locates the target or returns to your previous location. After the target is located and the cursor is moved to the new location, you are still in command mode. It is a two-way command. To go to the next occurrence, use the* **n** *command.*

Locating Characters, Not Words

You have seen how the forward search command finds the string of characters that you specify. This command is used to locate *character strings*, not words.

1. For instance, enter

   /it

The words *with*, ed*i*ting, *it*, ed*i*tor, and qu*i*tting are located.

You can also use the power of the forward search command to locate a string of several words. For instance:

1. Select and locate two words in your file. Try a command such as

   /several times

   Blank spaces can be included in a search string.

2. Move the cursor to some other locations in the file, using the forward search feature of the editor.

Searching Backward

You can also instruct the editor to search backward through the text to the next instance of the target word or character string.

1. Place your cursor in the middle of the file, using a command such as

   5 ⬇

   or

   5 ⓙ

2. Search for the next letter *e* by entering

   /e

3. Now reverse the direction of the search by entering

   ?e

   The cursor goes to the previous *e*.

4. Continue the reverse search by pressing ⓝ several times.

SUMMARY: *The / is used to instruct the editor to search forward for a target string; the ? is used to search backward. Regardless of which direction you are searching, you can move to the next occurrence of the word in the same direction using the* **n** *command.*

2.5

Moving the Cursor Word by Word

So far, you have used the ⒣, ⒥, ⒦, and ⒧ keys or the arrow keys to move the cursor one character or line at a time. And you've searched forward and backward to specified words.

You can also move the cursor through the text in word increments, either forward or backward.

Moving Forward in One-Word Increments

1. In the file *practice*, use the / command to position the cursor on any word in one of the first few lines of text.

2. Type the following lowercase command:

   w

   The cursor advances to the next word on the line. You do not use the / search command and you do not press ⸢Return⸣. You are in command mode, and the **w** simply instructs the editor to move ahead one **word**.

3. Type the **w** command several more times. Each time you do, the cursor advances forward to the *beginning* of the next word.

   The visual editor can also move the cursor to the **end** of a word and **backward** to previous words.

4. Enter each of the following commands and observe their actions:

   b
   e
   w

Moving Multiple Words

1. All of these word commands can be augmented to move through several words at a time. Try the following:

3b
2e
3w
4b

Figure 2-4 summarizes these commands.

SUMMARY: *The* **w** *command moves the cursor forward to the beginning of the next word. The* **e** *command moves the cursor forward to the next end of a word. The* **b** *command moves the cursor backward through your text one word at a time. All three commands can be prefaced with a number to move several words at a time.*

2.6
Deleting Text in Command Mode

So far, you have been moving around the file by issuing commands in the visual editor's command mode. Another important class of editing operations, available only from command mode, is removing text from a file. With **vi** you can remove one or more lines, words, or characters.

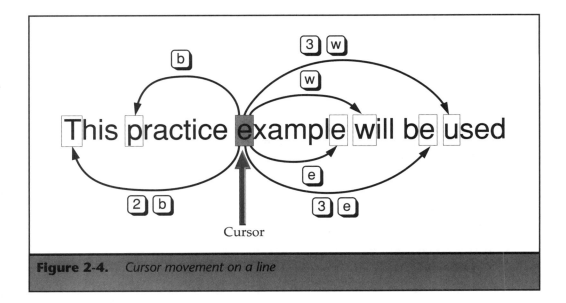

Figure 2-4. *Cursor movement on a line*

In the next several exercises you delete portions of your *practice* file. After using these procedures to explore the delete capabilities of the editor, you will then leave the editor *without* writing the changes, so the deletions you make will not be permanent.

Removing Whole Lines

One or more lines in a file can easily be deleted with the editor.

1. Move to the first line of text in your *practice* file. Place the cursor on any character in that line, and type the **drop-dead** command.

   dd

   You do not need to press (Return). As soon as you type the second **d**, **vi** does what you've requested and removes the line. Blank lines, as well as text lines, can be deleted with the **dd** command. The **dd** command is a two-way command; you type it from command mode, and after the editor deletes the current line, you are still in command mode.

2. To undo the deletion you just made, type the **u**ndo command:

   u

   The line returns to your file.

3. Like the direction keys, the **dd** command can be prefaced with a number to delete more than one line at the same time.

4. Issue this **vi** command:

   2dd

   The cursor line and the one following it are deleted. In the same fashion, typing **3dd** deletes three lines, beginning with the line where the cursor is located.

5. Use the ⊔ or ⏚ key to go to the last line in your file. Then type the command

   3dd

In this case, nothing is deleted, because you are requesting **vi** to remove more lines than are available to delete.

Deleting the Remainder of a Line

The visual editor does not limit you to deletion of whole lines.

1. Move the cursor to the middle of a long line in the *practice* file and type the following capital letter:

D

This capital **D** is instruction to Delete the remainder of the line, starting with the character under the cursor.

Deleting One or Several Words

In addition to deleting lines and parts of lines from a file, the editor lets you delete specific words.

1. Move the cursor to the first letter of a word, type the following **vi** commands, and observe the results:

dw
3dw

The **dw** command **d**eletes **w**ords and can be modified with a number, just like most **vi** commands.

2. Place the cursor in the middle of a long word and type

dw

This time the editor removes all characters from the cursor *to and including* the next space. To remove the whole word, place the cursor on the first letter as you did in step 1.

3. Place the cursor on the **(** character. Request deletion of two words with

2dw

Note that **vi** treats the **(** as a word and deletes it. The same is true for other characters that are not numbers or letters (*nonalphanumeric*).

4. Position the cursor on the beginning of one of the last two words near the end of any line of text. Type this **vi** command:

4dw

The last two words on the current line, as well as the first two words on the next line, are deleted. The editor accepts arguments that affect words on more than one line, unless there is a space at the end of the line.

Deleting Individual Characters

You can also delete specific single characters from a file.

1. Move your cursor to any character, such as the *H* in the word *Hello.*

2. Delete the character under the cursor with this lowercase command:

x

The **x** (x-out) command deletes only the single character under the cursor. It is the delete-one-character-at-a-time command.

3. The command **6x** does what you expect. Select a word with the forward search command and type

6x

Spaces between words on a line are characters just like letters or numbers. Thus, the **x** can be used to delete unwanted spaces anywhere in the file.

The following table summarizes the delete commands you have just used.

Object to Delete	Command
Character	x
Word	**dw**
Line	**dd**
Remainder of line	D

Summary of the Moving and Deleting Commands

The conceptual map of command mode, shown in Figure 2-5, illustrates the commands used thus far to move the cursor, delete text, and locate strings.

Quitting vi without Saving Changes

In this chapter so far, you have made quite a scramble of your *practice* file. Before continuing, you need to quit this editing session, return to the shell, and have the *practice* file remain as it was when you first called up the file at the beginning of this section.

1. From the command mode of the visual editor, type

   :q!

   Because you made changes to your file in this editing session, **vi** will not accept a plain **q** command. The editor does not know whether to save or discard the changes. The **!** says to the editor, "Yes, I know I made changes, but I really do want to quit." This command does not include a **w**rite (save), just a **q**uit. It says, "Quit the editor program, but don't write the changes I have been making."

   You are now back in the shell.

■ Review 1

Examine the conceptual map in Figure 2-5 and then answer the following questions. The answers are given at the end of the chapter.

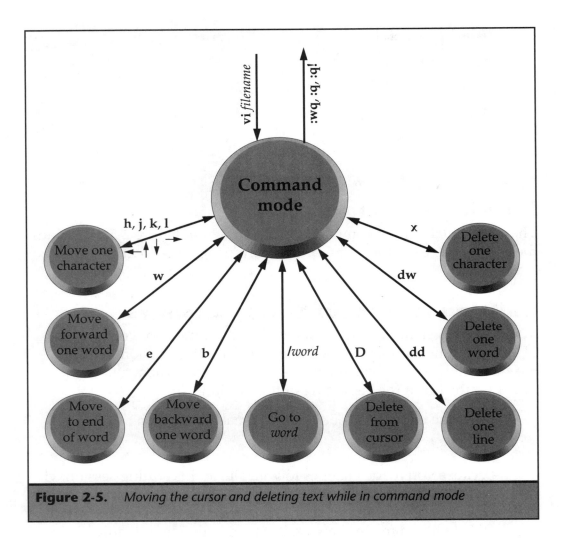

Figure 2-5. *Moving the cursor and deleting text while in command mode*

1. What command allows you to move the cursor one character to the left?
2. What command takes the cursor forward to the word "Administration"?
3. What command deletes the current line of text?
4. Where must the cursor be positioned to delete a line of text?
5. What command deletes eight lines of text?

6. What command deletes three words of text?

7. What command do you type to leave **vi** without saving the changes to the file?

8. What command moves the cursor to the end of the current word?

9. What command instructs **vi** to save changes and return to the shell?

10. What happens if you enter the following command in command mode: **2j3dw**?

11. What mode must you be in to move around a file?

12. What mode must you be in to issue the **dd** command?

2.7

Adding Text Relative to the Cursor

Thus far you have been moving around and deleting text from the file, but you have not yet added any text. There are several ways to add text, including adding new text to each side of the cursor, opening a line below the cursor, and opening a line above the cursor.

Appending Text to the Right of the Cursor

You have been instructing the editor to move the cursor around the file by issuing specific commands in command mode. To add text, you must leave command mode and be in *append* or *insert* mode. You need to issue specific command-mode instructions to inform the editor that you want to leave command mode and start adding text.

1. Call up the file *practice* with the visual editor. Type

   vi *practice*

   You are now in command mode, where the keys are used to issue position-change and delete commands, not to enter text.

2. Move the cursor to any character on the screen, and delete the letter by typing

   x

The **x** tells the editor to *delete one character* when you are in the **vi** command mode.

3. Move the cursor to the end of the first line in the file.

4. Type the following command one time:

   a

   Notice that the **a** is not displayed on the screen. Nothing appears to have happened. However, just as the **x** command instructs **vi** to delete one character, the **a** command tells **vi** to start **a**dding everything you type to the file, placing the new text in the file starting to the right of where the cursor is presently located.

5. Now type an **x** again. Because you're in append mode, the **x** appears on the screen and is added to the file; nothing gets deleted.

6. Now that you are in append mode, press Return and type the following text:

   I am now adding more text.
   Therefore I must be in append mode.
   The a command moves me into append·mode.
   Whatever I type is added to the right of the cursor.

   Examine the conceptual map in Figure 2-6. Note that the **a** command takes you out of command mode and puts you into *append* or *insert* mode. The **x** no longer means delete a character, it just means insert an *x*.

Leaving Append Mode and Returning to Command Mode

In the last exercise you opened a file with the visual editor. From command mode, you moved the cursor around with specific commands, and then typed the **a** command. The **a** told the editor to leave **vi**'s command mode and enter append mode. You then added text.

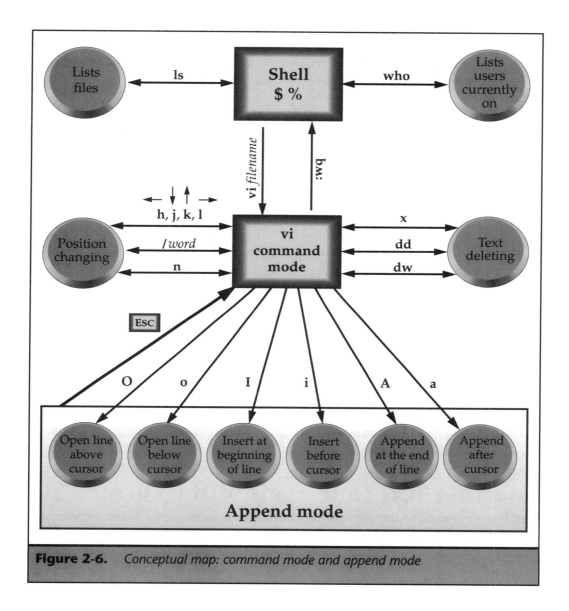

Figure 2-6. *Conceptual map: command mode and append mode*

As long as you are in append mode, every key you type will continue to be appended to the text; you do not return to command mode. When you have finished typing text, you need a way to instruct the **vi** editor to move you out of append mode and back into command mode.

1. Take a look at Figure 2-6. Find the command that appears on the arrow that moves you from append mode back to command mode. Press the "return to command mode" key:

   Esc

   Nothing appears to be different on the screen. Enter **x**. A character is deleted; **x** is now a command. You are again in command mode, where the keyboard is not for adding text but for issuing commands to move around in the file and to delete text. By pressing the Esc key, you move out of append mode and back to command mode.

2. To confirm that you are in command mode, press the Esc key a second time.

   If a beep sounds or the screen flashes, **vi** is telling you that it cannot move to command mode because you are already there.

SUMMARY: The Esc *key is an essential component of the visual editor. Whenever you are in doubt about where you are in* **vi**—*command or append mode—press the* Esc *key. In append mode,* Esc *moves you to command mode. In command mode,* Esc *produces a beep or flash indicating you are already in command mode. In either case, after you press* Esc *you are certain to be in command mode. From this point, you can decide what you want to do.*

Inserting Text to the Left of the Cursor

You have seen how the **a** command adds text *to the right of the cursor.* Another command is used to insert text *to the left of the cursor.*

1. In command mode, move the cursor to the beginning of a word on the screen. Type the **i**nsert command:

   i

2. Type the following text, and note how the existing text moves to the right as you type:

*The difference between the
i and a commands does not seem to be very
obvious.*

3. Return to command mode by pressing
[Esc]

NOTE: *You must always return to command mode to issue cursor movement commands.*

Comparing the a and i Commands

Both the **a** and **i** commands add text at the cursor. This next exercise demonstrates the difference between the two commands.

1. Place the cursor at the beginning of a line. Note where the cursor is located—this is its "original location."

2. Now type the *right of cursor* **a**ppend command.

   a

   and type the following text:

   XXX

   The first character in the line, the one the cursor was over when you entered the **a** command, remains at the beginning of the line. The added XXX was inserted to the right of the cursor location.

3. Press [Esc], and to return to command mode, then press [Return] to put the cursor at the beginning of the next line of the file.

4. Type the *left of cursor* insert command:

   i

   and type

   YYY

The text is added to the left of the cursor, the beginning of the line.

5. Try both the **a** and **i** commands with the cursor in various locations—at the beginning, middle, and end of a word; on both sides of a period; and at the end of a line.

SUMMARY: *The **a** and **i** commands move you from command mode to append mode. Every character you type after the **i** command is entered as text in your file, starting with the space to the left of the cursor. With the **a** command, text is entered to the right of the original cursor position.*

Opening a Line Below the Cursor

It is also possible to add text between two existing lines.

1. Make sure you are in command mode, then move the cursor to any location on a line in the middle of your screen. Type the **o**pen command (lowercase):

   o

2. Add text such as this:

   There certainly are a lot of ways to move from command mode to append!
   Each one starts adding text in a different place with respect to the cursor.

3. Return to command mode by pressing the [Esc] key.
   The **o** command opens space for a new line below the cursor line and before the next line in your file.

Opening a Line Above the Cursor

In addition to opening lines below the cursor, you can open new lines above the cursor.

1. Move the cursor to any location in any line.

2. Open a line above this line with the **O**pen command (uppercase):

   O

3. Now add some text, such as this:

   It is essential to be able to place
   text above the current line,
   especially when I want to enter text
   before the first line in a file.

4. Return to command mode by pressing the (Esc) key.

5. Move to the top of your file, and type text above the first line. As with the other append commands, you can continue typing as many lines as you wish; you are not limited to that one line.

6. Return to the **vi** command mode by pressing the (Esc) key.

7. Save the file as it is now written and return to the shell, by typing

   :wq

Summarizing the Append Commands

You have now added (appended) text on all four sides of the cursor. The commands used for these tasks are summarized in the following table and illustrated in Figure 2-7.

Append Mode Command	Action
i	inserts to the left
a	appends to the right
O	Opens a line above
o	opens a line below

Inserting Text at the Beginning of a Line

Often when you need to add text to the beginning or end of the line, the cursor may be located at a word in the middle of the line. Rather than overwork the arrow, you can issue specific text-adding commands.

1. Return to editing the file *practice* by entering

   vi *practice*

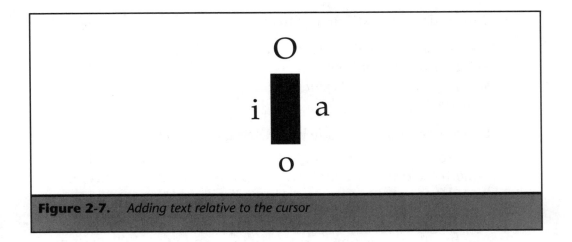

Figure 2-7.   *Adding text relative to the cursor*

2. Move the cursor to the middle of any line of text in your file and
   type the uppercase command:

   I

   The cursor moves to the beginning of the line. You are now in
   append mode, and anything you type is Inserted before the first
   character of the line.

3. Add some text, such as this:

   I was in the middle of a line,
   now I am adding text to the beginning.

4. Leave append mode and return to command mode by pressing

   [Esc]

   The **I** command is instruction to move the cursor to the beginning
   of the line, and change to append mode. Every character you
   type is Inserted as additional text until [Esc] is pressed.

Appending Text at the End of a Line

Adding text to the end of a line can be accomplished with the cursor
initially located anywhere on the line.

1. In command mode, move the cursor to the middle of a text line and type the uppercase command:

   A

   The cursor moves to the end of the line, and you are now in append mode.

2. Add some text such as the following:

   Adding text to the end of a line
   is easy with the A command.

   Return to command mode.

   All append commands move you into append mode until ⌜Esc⌟ is pressed. The various append commands differ only in where text is added to the file, relative to the cursor. Figure 2-8 illustrates where in the line the text is added in response to each command.

Moving Backward in Append Mode

Whenever you are in append mode, pressing essentially any key will place the appropriate character in your file and display it on your screen.

A few keys, however, don't produce text but instead cause an action to take place. The ⌜Esc⌟ key moves you from append to command mode,

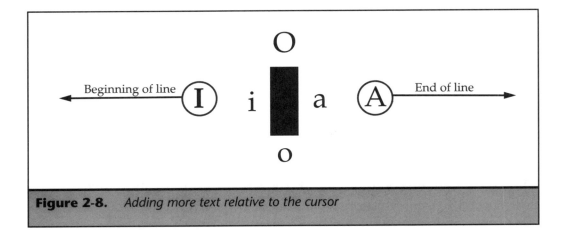

Figure 2-8. *Adding more text relative to the cursor*

as you have seen happen several times so far. The (Backspace) key moves the cursor back one space, removing the character you just typed without affecting your current mode.

If you are on a workstation that does not respond properly when you press the (Backspace) key, you can often use (Ctrl)-(h).

1. Make certain that you are in append mode.

2. Type in some text and then back up one space by pressing

(Ctrl)-(h)

When you are entering text in append mode, and you make an error, you can issue multiple backspaces. You can also press (Esc), and then go to the offending text and make changes. Easier, you can also move backward one whole word at a time through newly added text, without changing to command mode.

3. In append mode, add a few words and then press

(Ctrl)-(w)

Just as the (Ctrl)-(h) moves the cursor back one character and leaves you in append mode, (Ctrl)-(w) moves the cursor back through newly added text one word at a time. It stops abruptly when you reach text that was there before the current addition.

4. Add more text, which replaces, or overwrites, what was there.

5. Exit the editor by entering

(Esc)
:wq

2.8

Creating New Files with the Visual Editor

Thus far you have been moving the cursor around, deleting text, and adding text to an existing file. The visual editor is also used to create new files.

Invoking the Editor

Begin the process of creating a new file by typing

vi *journal*

The screen clears, a column of tildes lines up on the left of the screen, and you are placed in **vi**'s command mode. There is no text; a clean slate awaits your wisdom. But you cannot add text yet, because whenever you start the editor, you are in command mode.

1. Type the following command to go into append mode:

   a

2. Add a few lines of text.

3. Return to command mode.

Making Changes

1. Move around with your arrow keys, and delete a word or two. The editor acts the same whether you are creating a new file or editing an old one. The command to create a new file is exactly the same command you type to edit an existing file:

   vi *filename*

   In both cases, you supply the *filename*. One of two things happens when you type the **vi** *filename* command:

   - If the *filename* you enter already exists in your directory, **vi** accesses that file for you to edit.

   - If the *filename* you supply does not exist, the editor starts an editing session of the new *filename*.

2. Write the file, leave the editor, and return to the shell with the usual command:

   :wq

3. Obtain a listing of the files in your directory by entering

   ls

The new file is listed among the contents in your current directory.

Summarizing Mode Change Commands

Examine Figure 2-9. Editing a file begins in the shell with the shell prompt on your screen. You type **vi** *filename* and press (Return).

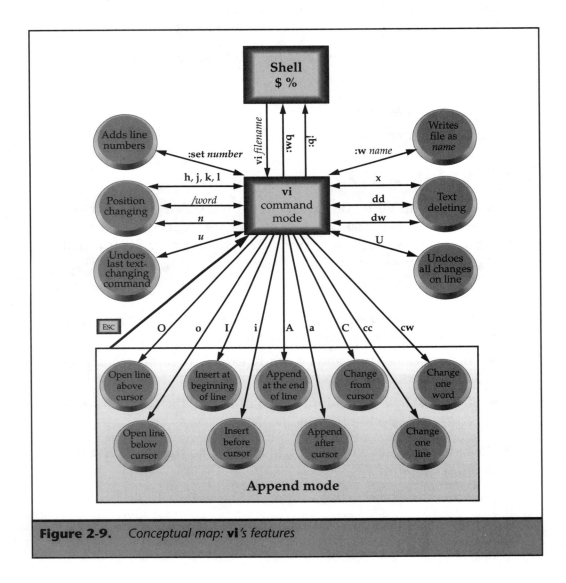

Figure 2-9. *Conceptual map:* **vi**'s *features*

This command instructs the shell to start the visual editor and pass to **vi** the *filename* argument. When **vi** starts up, you are placed in **vi**'s command mode, editing the file *filename*.

In command mode, you can move around the file using the direction keys or the search commands (*/word* and *?word*). You can also delete text.

To add text to the file, you must leave command mode and go into append mode. To make this transition, you use commands such as **a**, **i**, **o**, or **O**. Once you issue one of these commands, you are in append mode. Whatever you type is added to the file. When you press (Esc), you return to command mode. Issuing the command **:wq** is an instruction to write the file and quit the editor. The command **:q!** is a quit without saving.

2.9

Undoing and Repeating Editing Commands

Two powerful features of the visual editor are its *undo* and *repeat* functions. What they do is determined by what command was last typed.

Undoing the Last Command

Mistakez happen. Words are misspelled; lines are accidentally deleted; text is added that is no improvement. An essential tool for humans is the **u**ndo command, which undoes (rescinds) the most recent text-changing command.

1. Begin editing the file *practice* using **vi**.

2. Place your cursor on the first line in the file. Type

   2dd

   You are still in command mode; eight lines were removed.

3. Type the **u**ndo command:

   u

   The eight deleted lines return.

4. Type **u** again. Depending on your system's version of **vi**, either it undoes another text changing command, or typing **u** a second time rescinds the undo. Either the eight lines again disappear, or the two lines you deleted earlier appear again.

5. Open a new line and add some text.

6. Press [Esc] and then **u**. The added text is removed.

The **u**ndo command affects only the previous text changing command. You can only issue the **u**ndo command from command mode of the visual editor. However, you can move the cursor without affecting the **u** command.

Undoing All Editing Changes on a Line

There is a second **U**ndo command that undoes any number of changes that you've made to the line where the cursor is located, provided that you have not moved the cursor off the line.

1. Select a line of your text, and delete one word from the line.

2. Without leaving the line, move the cursor to another word and change its spelling. Return to command mode.

3. Without moving the cursor out of the line, type the lowercase command

   u

   Only the last change is undone.

4. Type **u** again. The word is again changed.

5. While still in the line, enter

   U

   The removed word reappears, and the altered word returns to its original state. Both changes are recorded.

6. Repeat steps 1 and 2, but this time, after you make the two changes, move the cursor to another line before typing the **U** command.

7. The **U** command fails. You left the line before entering **U**.

Following is a summary of the undo commands.

Undo Command	Action
u (lowercase)	**u**ndoes the effect of the last text change command given, even if you have moved from the line.
U (uppercase)	Undoes the effect of all changes made to the current line, provided that the cursor has not been moved from the line.

Repeating the Last Text-Changing Command

Frequently, you'll need to make an editing change to several locations in a file. For instance, suppose you need to add the text *This is an addition* to the end of several lines.

1. Select a line in the file, and move the cursor to any location in the line.

2. Type the command

   A

   The cursor moves to the end of the line; you are now in append mode.

3. Type this text:

   This is an addition

4. Without making any other text changes, press (Return) to move the cursor to the next line.

5. Return to command mode by pressing (Esc).

6. From command mode, type one single period to repeat your last **A** command. Yes, just a single period is the repeat command. The last text-changing command is repeated; the addition is made to this line.

7. Make the same change to another line using the period.

8. Delete a word, move the cursor to another word, and press period to delete the second word.

The period is the visual editor's "Play it again, Sam" command. It instructs the editor to repeat whatever text-changing command was just accomplished.

2.10

Saving Changes and the Original Version

When you begin editing a file, the editor creates a buffer, or workspace, for editing. When you finish and type the **:wq** command, you instruct the editor to write the buffer copy of the file and quit the editor.

Earlier in this chapter you quit the editor without saving the changes you made in the buffer copy of the file. To quit without writing changes, you entered the **:q!** command.

Saving the New Version

In some cases, you may decide that you want to save both the original file and its new, modified version. To save both, you must save the present buffer copy as a new file and then quit the editor without overwriting the original file.

1. Access the file *practice* and make a few changes to it.

2. To save a copy of the modified version of *practice*, type the following from the **vi** command mode:

   :w *newfilename*

   where *newfilename* is any name you want.

   A message similar to the following appears on your screen at the bottom of your file:

   ```
   "newfilename" [New file] 18 lines, 150 characters
   ```

You have instructed the editor to open a new file, *newfilename*, and write the buffer copy of the file you have been working on to that new file.

Protecting the Original Version

The next task is to protect the original version from being written over. The regular (**:wq**) command would write the new version over the old. You would then have two copies of the new version and none of the original. Your objective is to quit the **vi** editor *without* saving the changes to your file.

1. Enter

   :q!

2. Use the **ls** command to look at the latest listing of your files. Your directory now contains a copy of your original file *practice*, in addition to the modified copy listed under the new filename you chose.

◼ Review 2

1. What command do you type to add text to the right of the cursor?

2. How can you make sure that you are in **vi** command mode?

3. In what mode must you be to use the cursor movement direction keys?

4. What command must you type to add text at the beginning of the line where the cursor is resting?

5. Suppose you are editing the file *view* with the visual editor. You have made a series of changes but have not written the file. You decide that it would be best to keep the original version and save the modified version in another file called *room*. What commands should you type?

6. What command do you type to undo the effect of the last command that changed text?

7. What command repeats the last text-changing command?

8. How would you insert a new line right above the first line in the file?

9. If you are in append mode adding text, how do you move back two words without leaving append mode?

2.11

Making Text Changes

To effectively edit, you must be able to cut and paste lines and blocks of text, make word and line substitutions, break up lines, and join them together.

Cutting and Pasting Text

With the **vi** editor you can move and copy blocks of text.

1. Begin editing by entering **vi** *practice*.

2. Move the cursor to a line part way down the screen.

3. Type this lowercase command:

   yy

   Although it appears that nothing has happened, the **vi** editor has "**yy**anked" and made a copy of this line and is holding the copy in memory. The line that was copied is not deleted or otherwise affected by the **yy**ank command.

4. Move the cursor to a different place in your text. Type a lowercase

   p

   The line that was yanked is now **p**ut or **p**asted as a new line in the new location below the cursor.

5. The yank feature is most useful for copying blocks of text. For instance, to yank seven lines of text, beginning with the cursor line, type

   7yy

6. Move the cursor to a line where you want the yanked lines to be put, and type

   p

   A copy of the seven yanked lines of text now appears inserted as seven new lines below the cursor location.

Putting Lines in Several Places

When you yank lines of text, you are not limited to putting them in only one place.

1. Move to a new location and **p**ut the seven lines of text there.

2. Move the cursor to another location and **p**ut the lines of text there, too. The yanked lines of text have now been copied and pasted in three locations.

Determining Placement of Put Lines

Thus far, the lines have been put below the cursor line.

1. Yank the current single line by entering

   yy

2. Move to the first line in the file. Type the capital **P** and then lowercase **p**.
   With each command, notice where the line is placed. Uppercase **P** puts the copied text on the line *above* the cursor location, and lowercase **p** puts the copied text on the line *below* the cursor location.

Deleting and Putting Lines

The **yy**ank command makes a copy to be placed elsewhere. The delete commands can also be combined with **p**ut commands in a fashion similar to the **yy**ank command.

1. Select a line to move somewhere else in your file.

2. Position the cursor on any character on the line to be moved, and type

dd

3. Move the cursor to another location in the file where you want this text inserted, and then enter

p

Figure 2-10 illustrates deleting text, holding text in the buffer, and placing text.

 SUMMARY: To move a line of text from one location to a new location, you have to delete the line, move the cursor to a different location in your file, and then use the put command to reinsert the deleted text. When you use either the yank or delete command, you must put the yanked or deleted text in a new place before using any text-changing commands; otherwise, you will lose it. In between a yank/delete and a put command, you can use only cursor movement commands; you cannot save yanked or deleted text while you alter some other part of the text. For example, if you delete text, and then do another text-changing task before repositioning the deleted text, the deleted text is lost. You won't be able to reinsert it in your file with the regular put command. Instead, you must use buffers, the subject of a section in Chapter 18, "Using Advanced Visual Editor Features."

Replacing One Character with Another

You can remove one character and replace it with a single character, using the **r** command.

1. Move the cursor to any word you want, using the forward search command:

/word

2. Replace the first letter of this word by typing the command

   r

   and then following the **r** with any *replacement character*.

3. Try another example. Place the cursor at the first *o* in the word *too*. Type the **r** command, followed by the letter *w*. The first *o* in *too* is replaced by a *w*. The word *too* becomes *two*.

   The command **r r**eplaces the character located under the cursor with the very next character that you type. The **r** command is a two-way text-changing command. You are returned to command mode.

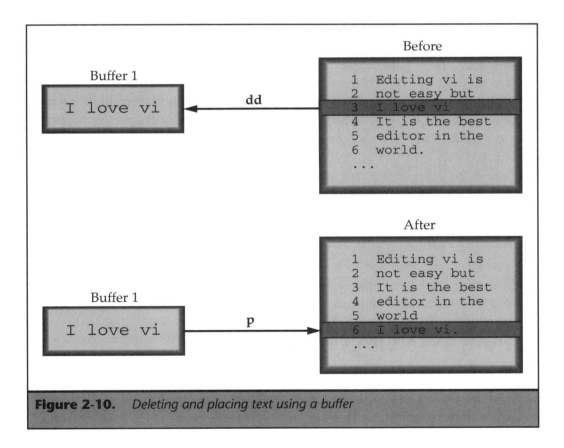

Figure 2-10. *Deleting and placing text using a buffer*

Breaking Up a Long Line

One important use of the replace command is to break one long line into two lines. When a line is too long, you need to place a [Return] in the middle, making it two lines.

1. Move the cursor to the space between two words in the middle of a long line.

2. Type the replace command (**r**), and then press [Return].
   You are replacing the space character between the two words with a [Return]. As a result, the second part of the long line moves to a new line. This works because when you press the [Return] key, it enters a special character that indicates a new line. You are left in command mode.

Typing Over Text Character by Character

The **r** command instructs the editor to replace the character under the cursor with whatever single character is typed next. At times it is convenient to replace a whole string of text character by character. Using the **r** command for this is cumbersome.

1. Make sure you are in command mode, and press the following uppercase command:

   R

2. Start typing. You are now in "typeover mode." Each letter you type replaces the single letter under the cursor.

3. After you have replaced some text with the typeover command, **R**, return to command mode with [Esc].

Joining Two Lines of Text

At times you'll want to join two lines together.

1. Select two short lines in your file, and position the cursor anywhere on the first line.

2. Type this uppercase command:

J

The two lines are now one.

Replacing a Single Letter with Other Text

You have learned how the **r** command replaces a single character with one other character. Often an author or programmer needs to remove one character and then substitute several characters or even pages for the deleted character.

1. With the cursor positioned over any character in the file, type this lowercase command:

   s

   The dollar sign ($) appears on the character. This dollar sign is placed over the last character that is being replaced.

2. Add text such as this:

   Is it true that I am now in append mode?
   I must be, text that I am entering
   is going onto the screen,
   and I expect into the file.

3. Press (Esc) to signal that you have finished typing text.

4. Select another character in the text and replace it with another, using the **r** command.

5. Choose another letter and substitute an entire sentence for it using the **s** command.

   Both the **r** and **s** commands add text in place of a single character in your file. However, the **s** command must be followed by (Esc) when you have finished typing text. This is not the case with the **r** command, because the extent of the replacement is always predetermined—one character.

The **r** command replaces one character with a single new character and then returns you automatically to command mode. Because **r** is a two-way command, you are not left in append mode and you do not use the (Esc) key.

In contrast, the **s** command substitutes the character under the cursor with whatever text you type until you press the (Esc) key. The **s** command allows you to substitute as many characters as you wish for the one removed character. You move from command mode to append mode and stay there until you use the (Esc) key to return to command mode. The **s** is a one-way command.

Likewise, after the **R** command is entered, the editor replaces each character the cursor passes over with only one character, but you must signal with (Esc) when you are ready to quit.

Substituting Several Words for One Word

It is also possible to change one word in your text into a multitude of other words.

1. Using the /*word* command, place your cursor on any word in the middle of the file.

2. Type the change word command:

   cw

   The dollar sign ($) appears at the end of the word, indicating the end of the text that is being replaced.

3. Add text such as this:

   XXX This is text entered
   after a cw command XXX

4. When you have finished, leave append mode by pressing (Esc).

Typing the **cw** command removes one word and moves you into append mode. Everything you type is entered into the file until you press (Esc).

Substituting Lines

The **s** and **cw** commands allow you to substitute text for a single character and for specific words, respectively. You can also substitute entire lines in your file.

1. Place the cursor anywhere on a line.

2. To substitute new text for the line, type the following lowercase command:

   cc

3. Add text such as this:

   And this is a new line of text!
   Well, actually two, taking the place of one.

   With the change line **cc** command, whatever you type is entered into the file in place of one line. Your replacement for the one line is not limited to only one line, however; you can append any number of lines at this point. The **cc** command deletes the line of text and moves you from command mode to append mode.

4. You remain in append mode, adding text. Return to command mode by entering Esc.

Changing the Remainder of a Line

You can change the remainder of a line, replacing it with new text.

1. Move the cursor to the middle of a line of text.

2. Type the following uppercase command:

   C

   The dollar sign appears at the end of the line, indicating the last character that is removed to make way for new text.

3. Add a couple of lines of text.
   The **C** command puts you in append mode and lets you **C**hange the part of the line from the cursor position to the end of the line. The characters from the left margin up to, but not

including, the cursor remain unchanged. Whatever text you type until you press (Esc) is substituted for the remainder of the line.

4. Write the changes and quit the editor by entering

(Esc)

:wq

The delete and substitute commands are summarized in this table.

Action	Character	Word	Line	Remainder of Line
Delete	x	dw	**dd**	**D**
Substitute	**s**	cw	**cc**	**C**

2.12
Avoiding Confusion Between the Shell and the vi Editor

So far, you have issued commands to the shell and to the visual editor, in both command mode and append mode. Each command interpreter acts on your commands in a different way.

Instructing the Shell

1. From the shell, type

who

A listing of users currently logged on appears on your screen. To the shell, the three characters **w h o** are interpreted to mean "Locate and Execute the utility named **who**." The **who** utility determines who is logged on and formats a report that is output, in this case, to your screen.

2. Leave the shell, and call up the editor to work on the file *practice* that you have been using in this chapter by entering

vi *practice*

You are now in command mode of the visual editor, editing a file.

Instructing the Command Mode

1. Place the cursor at the beginning of a word in the text and type the following three characters:

w

h

o

As you can see, the characters **w h o** have a very different meaning to the visual editor command mode:

- The **w** says move to the right one word.
- The **h** says move the cursor back one space.
- The **o** says open a line below the current line.

You are now in the append mode of the editor.

2. To complete the comparison, type the same three characters again. This time, in append mode, the effect of typing **w h o** is that three letters are added to the file.

3. Press [Esc] to return to command mode.

Comparing the Command Interpreters

The distinction between the two modes within the **vi** editor is a critical one. Whenever you leave the shell and enter the **vi** editor, you always enter command mode. A set of specific commands are understood and acted upon by **vi** in this mode. Keystrokes result in movement of the cursor, deletion of text, shifting into append mode, or leaving **vi** to return to the shell.

When you give an append command (such as **a** or **cw**), the editor starts treating every character you type as input to the file. You are moved out of command mode and into append mode. Once in append mode, virtually every character you type is put in the file as text and displayed on the screen. You remain in append mode until you press the Esc key.

Pressing Esc is necessary to return to command mode, regardless of which command you used to enter append mode. The Esc key is always the way back to command mode.

CAUTION: A common error on many systems is to try to move the cursor while you are in append mode instead of command mode. If you do this, on most systems a series of weird characters (^K^H) appears on the screen. The ^K or ^[A type characters are the control characters *associated with the arrow keys. Because you are in append mode,* **vi** *is happily adding the characters you type to your file. In this case, the added characters are the control characters. Should this happen, you need to press* Esc *and use the* **x** *command to delete the unwanted characters. On several recent releases of* **vi**, *you can use the arrow keys to move the cursor around while in append mode.*

2.13

Customizing the Visual Editor

Although Chapter 18, "Using Advanced Visual Editor Features," examines how to customize **vi** in detail, this section introduces the possibilities.

Adding Line Numbers to Your Display When Editing

It is often useful to know the line number for each line when you are editing a file.

1. Make sure you are in command mode by pressing Esc.

2. If you don't see line numbers on the screen when you're editing in **vi**, type the following command, which instructs the editor to provide numbers for the current editing session:

:set *number*

The editor displays line numbers on the left side of the screen. These numbers are part of the display only—they are not part of your file.

Requesting Showmode

One difficult aspect of working in **vi** is determining the mode you are in at any given time. On many versions of **vi** you can request that the editor keep you informed of the current mode.

1. From command mode of the editor, enter

   :set *showmode*

   Nothing appears to happen, but the attribute to **show** the **mode** has been set.

2. Start adding text by entering

   i

   If your version of **vi** includes *showmode*, the words *INSERT MODE* will appear in the bottom-right corner of the screen.

3. Press Esc.

4. Open a new line below the cursor. The *append* or *insert* mode is labeled.

5. Save the file and quit the editor.

Customizing vi with the Initialization File

Many programs in UNIX can be customized by recording instructions in a file about how you want the programs to perform. When you call up the visual editor, you can request line numbers on the screen by issuing the **:set** *number* command. You can also put similar instructions in a file that **vi** reads every time it is started up.

The initialization file for the **vi** editor is the file named *.exrc* (for **ex** **r**un **c**ontrol). As soon as you start editing with **vi,** it reads its *.exrc* file. Commands placed in the *.exrc* file determine how **vi** functions.

1. To edit the *.exrc* file, in your home directory type:

   vi *.exrc*

2. Add the following line as text in the file:

set *number*

Do not enter a colon at the beginning of the line; just type the words. If you like having the mode displayed, you can add the same command to your *.exrc*:

set *showmode*

Remember that instructions are added as text in the *.exrc* file, and do not include the colon.

3. Press [Esc] to leave append mode.

4. Examine the file. If there are any blank lines, remove them.

5. Write the file and quit the editor with **:wq**. You have created a file named *.exrc*.

6. Call up another file with **vi**.

vi *practice*

Without your having to ask for them, line numbers appear.

All of the commands within **vi** can be placed in the *.exrc* file in your home directory. They will be read in at the beginning of every editing session.

2.14

Changing the Display and Moving the Cursor

The commands in this section of the chapter examine two kinds of functions:

- *Cursor-positioning commands* move the cursor to a particular designated position in your file.

- *Display-adjusting commands* move the screen display forward or backward in the file relative to the cursor's current position and display a new section of text. The cursor has to follow along.

Moving the Cursor to Specific Targets

Examine Figure 2-11. The white square in the center (over the letter *m* in *move*) is the cursor. To move the cursor to the top-left (to the *T* in *This*), you type the uppercase command **H**. In this figure, the arrow connecting the cursor to this destination has the Ⓗ key printed next to it. Three other cursor movement commands are depicted: **w, 4b,** and **L.**

Returning to the Last Cursor Position

Often while editing, you'll need to move to a distant location in the file to check on some specific concern or perform an editing task. Once the task is completed, you'll want to return to your previous location and continue editing there.

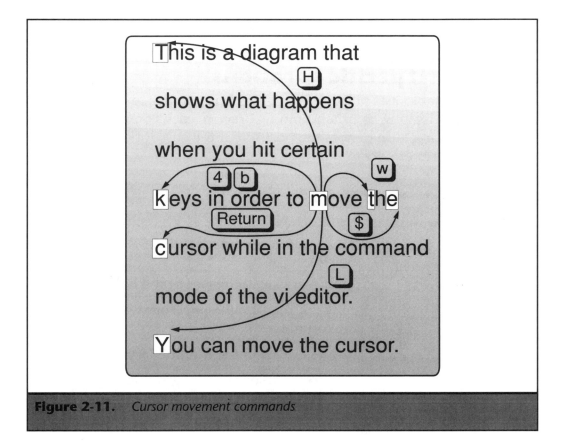

Figure 2-11. *Cursor movement commands*

1. First, before you move the cursor, mentally note the line number where the cursor is currently located.

2. Then use the **G** command to reposition the cursor to the distant line that you need to see. For example, move the cursor to line 11 by typing the command

   11G

3. At this location, add a line of text. Then return to command mode.

4. In command mode, type two single quotation marks (*not* double quotation marks):

   ' '

   You have just entered the secret passage back to your original location. The two single quotation marks return you to your previous location in a file, no matter where it is, and even though you have made a change to the file.

Moving to Specific Locations

The following table lists helpful commands you can use to move the cursor without leaving command mode. Practice each command several times, making sure to note the position of the cursor before and after you perform each command.

Cursor Positioning Command	Function
0 (zero)	Moves cursor to the beginning of the line it is on.
$	Moves cursor to the end of the line it is on.
*nn*G	Moves cursor to line *nn*, where *nn* is the line number.
G	Moves cursor to the last line in your file.
-	Positions cursor at the beginning of prior line.
+	Positions cursor at the beginning of next line.

Cursor Positioning Command	Function
nn l	Positions cursor at column *nn* of current line, where *nn* is the column number.
L	Positions cursor at lowest line displayed on the screen.
M	Positions cursor at line near midpoint of the screen.
H	Positions cursor at highest line on the screen.
f*x*	Moves cursor forward on the line to next *x*, where *x* is a specified character.
n	Moves to the next pattern identified in a previously issued /*word* or ?*word*.
' '	Returns cursor to the last line cursor was located on.

The commands you have just examined instruct the editor to move the cursor to a new location. If that new location is on the current screen, the cursor just hops to the new location and the screen display is not altered. However, if the new location is not in the text currently displayed, the cursor moves to that text and the screen display must follow along.

For instance, if you are at the beginning of a large file and you issue the **G** command, the cursor moves to the end of the file. Since that new location in this large file is probably not currently displayed, the display adjusts and shows the end of the file—the requested location.

Several of these commands are demonstrated in Figure 2-12.

Adjusting the Screen's Visual Display of Text

The cursor movement commands you used in the foregoing section relocate the cursor to a new character, word, or line, and the screen display follows along. These commands are line and text oriented, not display

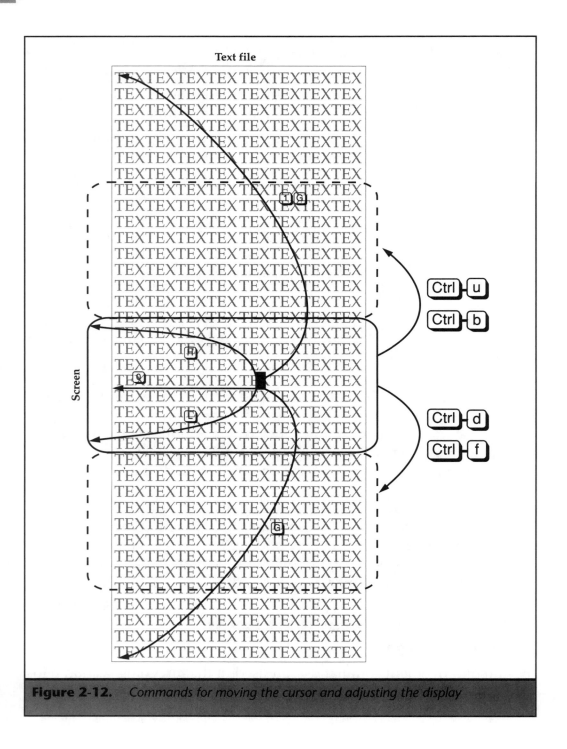

Figure 2-12. *Commands for moving the cursor and adjusting the display*

oriented. The screen display is determined by the cursor location. You can also move the display, forcing the cursor to follow along.

1. From command mode, press

   Ctrl - d

   This time the screen moves forward through the text, and the cursor comes along for the ride.

   The commands described in the following table are used to adjust the workstation's visual display and move forward or backward to a different block or section of text, regardless of its context.

2. Read through these display-adjusting commands.

3. Try each of them several times.

Display Adjustment Command	Function
Ctrl - d	Scrolls the cursor down one block of text in the file.
Ctrl - u	Scrolls the cursor up one block of text in the file.
Ctrl - f	Displays the next block of text in a file.
Ctrl - b	Displays the previous block of text in a file.
z*n***.**	Displays on the screen n lines of text, where n is the number of lines from 1 to 23. Remember the . (dot) is part of the command.
z.	Redraws the screen. This is similar to the previous command, except that it doesn't change the number of lines displayed. It is used to clear screen of unwanted information such as a **write** message.

Augmenting Display Commands

1. By placing a number before the commands Ctrl-d and Ctrl-u, you can modify the amount of text displayed on the screen. For example, scroll down through ten lines of text, and type

   10 Ctrl-d

   From now on, Ctrl-d or Ctrl-u will scroll ten lines, until you change the number to a different value. The command **z*n*.** is the instruction to display a specified number of lines when the screen is drawn. For instance, three lines will appear on the screen after you enter

   z 3.

   The dot after the number is essential.

 TIP: *You may want to use the* **z*n*.** *command to save time when editing, because the workstation will then display a smaller screenful of text more quickly. You might find that reducing the amount of information on the screen helps the eye to focus more easily, and is particularly helpful when locating certain words with the forward search command.*

■ Review 3

1. What command replaces a single character and returns you automatically to command mode?
2. What command instructs the editor to remove an entire line and put you in append mode?
3. What command removes all text from the cursor to the end of the line and puts you in append mode?
4. What command puts the line numbers on each line of the display?
5. What command moves the cursor back to the beginning of a word?
6. What command tells the editor to move the cursor to line 23?
7. What command tells **vi** to display only six lines of text?
8. What file is read by **vi** as it starts up?

9. What command puts the editor into typeover mode?

10. What command instructs the editor to combine the current and next lines?

11. What command moves the cursor to the top of the display?

12. How do you tell **vi** to scroll down a screenful of text?

13. How do you tell **vi** to refresh the screen?

2.15

Editing Blocks of Text

The visual editor offers several commands for copying a single line or many lines of text from one place to another in a file. These block-editing commands perform many of the same functions you learned previously with the two-way text-changing commands, but are easier to use when you are working with more than a few lines.

Copying Blocks of Text

Blocks of text, identified by line numbers, can be moved as a unit.

1. Display line numbers on your screen, if they are not already there, by entering

   :set *number*

2. From **vi** command mode, in the *practice* file, type the following command, including the colon:

   :2 **copy** *4*

   Press Return. A copy of line 2 is placed after line 4 in your file.
      With the **copy** command, the first number following the colon is the line number of the text that is copied. The copied text is placed *after* the second line number.

3. Now reverse the change made by the last command (copying a line) by entering the undo command:

   u

4. You are not limited to copying one line of text at a time. Several lines can be copied to a specific location in a single operation. Type the command

   :1,4 **copy** *7*

   A copy of lines 1 through 4 is placed after line 7. The original lines remain in place, but a copy is added to your text after line 7.

5. Examine Figure 2-13. It shows the effect of the following copy command:

   :1,8 **copy** *17*

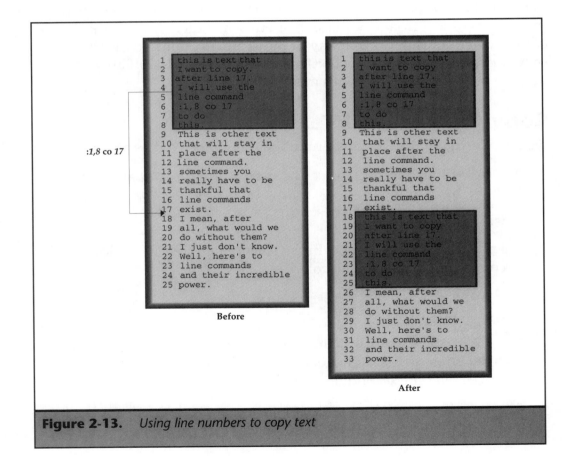

Figure 2-13. *Using line numbers to copy text*

Using Line Addresses

Editing commands that begin with a colon (such as *:1,4* **copy** *9*) operate on a block of text that is identified by its beginning and ending line numbers, which are separated by a comma. Hence, *1,4* represents lines 1, 2, 3, and 4.

Likewise, *57,62* represents the lines beginning with 57, up to and including 62. You saw two other examples of this format in the previous section.

> *CAUTION:* *Always be sure to type the lower number first; the editor does not understand line addresses such as* **62,57** *or* **9,2**.

1. The **copy** command can be abbreviated to **co**. For instance, type this command:

   :10 **co** *4*

   The editor makes a copy of line 10 and places it after line 4.

2. Special characters can be used with line commands. Try copying text to the very beginning of the file with this command:

   :10,14 **co** *0*

   Here, the lines 10 through 14 are copied and placed after line 0 (just before line 1).

3. To copy lines to the end of the file, type

   :10,14 **co** *$*

   The dollar sign ($) represents the last line, so lines 10 through 14 are copied after the last line of the file.

4. Suppose the cursor is on line 55, and you want to copy lines 55 through 65 to a position immediately after line 80. Type this command:

   :.,65 **co** *80*

   The dot after the colon represents the *current line*, that is, the line where the cursor is currently positioned.

Moving Blocks of Text

You have seen how the **copy** command lets you copy text to different locations in your file. You can also **move** the text from one location to another.

1. Type this command:

   :1,8 **move** *17*

   Examine Figure 2-14 to see the effect. The lines 1 through 8 have been moved to the new location, not copied. (Notice also that, in the figure, the **move** command is abbreviated to **m**.) The same conventions used for selecting a multiple-line block of text for the **copy** command are also used for the **move** command.

3. Before continuing, move another block of text in your file.

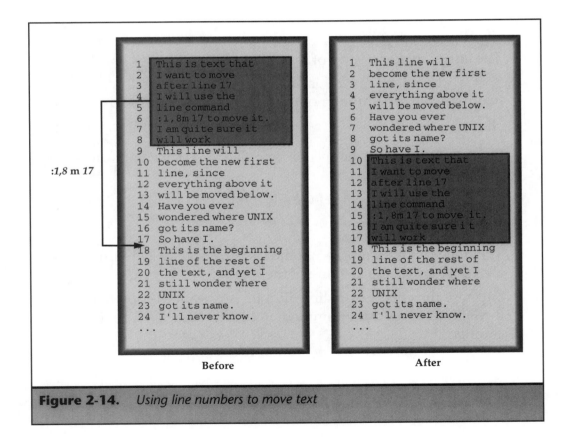

Figure 2-14. *Using line numbers to move text*

Deleting Blocks of Text

There are numerous ways to delete blocks of text in your file.

- To delete the first eight lines from a file, you can move the cursor to the first line and type

  8dd

- Or, *regardless of the location of the cursor*, you can type

  :1,8 d

This command instructs the editor to find lines 1 through 8 and delete them.

Figure 2-15 illustrates the previous delete command.

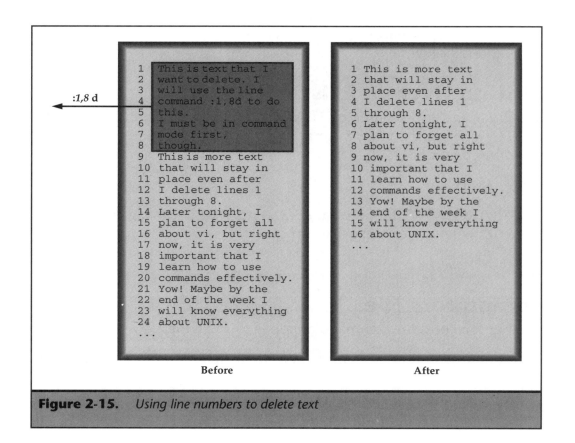

Figure 2-15. *Using line numbers to delete text*

Writing Out Blocks of Text

It is often useful to take portions of the file you are editing and create new files with them. To **write** a block of text from your current file out to a new file, you need two pieces of information:

- The line numbers for the first and last lines of the text you want to write out
- A new filename for the material to be written

1. From **vi** command mode, type this command:

   :1,7 write *newfilename*

   where *newfilename* is the name you choose for the new text.
   The lines specified by the line address (*1,7*) are copied and written into *newfilename*. The text from lines 1 through 7 now exists in two places—in the file you are currently editing (*practice*) and in *newfilename*.

Writing Over an Existing File

Sometimes the write command is used to overwrite, or replace, an existing file. Depending on how your account is set up, the shell may not allow the command

   :1,7 w *report.2*

to overwrite *report.2* if that file already exists. The following command will work whether *report.2* exists or not:

   :1,7 w! *report.2*

Adding to a File

Another type of write command appends text to a file.

1. Enter the following command to write lines 5 through 8 to the end of the file *report.2*.

   :5,8 w >> *report.2*

Reading In Files of Text

When editing a file, a writer or programmer often needs to *read in* the contents of a different file. Pieces of text or programs that are used frequently can be kept in specified files and read into another file when needed. Only a copy is made of the file that is read, leaving the original unchanged.

To read text into the current file, you need to know two things:

- The *name* of the file containing the material you want to copy into your current file

- The *location* (line number) in your current file where you want the new material to appear

1. From **vi** command mode, type this command:

    :3 **read** *report.2*

    This command instructs the editor to read the file *report.2* and place the text of that file after line 3 in the current file.

    If you enter the **read** command without specifying a line number, the file will be read in and placed following your current cursor location. The **read** command can be abbreviated as **r**.

    Because the **read** command is a text-changing command, you can undo it. If, after reading in a file, you decide you don't want to insert it after all, simply type **u**, and the lines you just read in will be deleted from your current file.

2. At the end of this chapter are command summaries of the colon, or line, commands you have learned so far. Practice these commands until you feel comfortable using them.

Review 4

1. What **vi** command places lines 1 to 33 of your current file in a new file named *report.10*?

2. What **vi** command overwrites the contents of an existing file named *report* with lines 29 through 200 of the file you are editing.

3. What **vi** command appends lines 36 through 74 of your current file onto the end of the file named *report.1*?

4. What mode must you be in to use the colon commands?

5. What command do you type to move lines 17 through 93 of your file to the end of the file?

6. What colon command deletes everything in a file following line 117?

7. How can you move a paragraph beginning on line 32 and ending on line 57, to the beginning of your file?

2.16

Integrating Features of the Visual Editor

Throughout this chapter you have used the fundamental visual editor commands to accomplish specific tasks. This final section steps you through a series of modifications in a document to demonstrate how the pieces fit together in an ordinary editing session.

Creating Test Files

Part of this exercise will involve reading in other files.

1. Because the number of users on your network may be large and the */etc/passwd* file extensive, the **head** command will be used to take only the first 20 lines from each in the following.

2. Create three test files in your home directory by entering these commands:

who | head -20 > *who-test*
head -20 /etc/passwd > *passwd-test*
ls > *ls-test*

Confirm the existence of these files by entering

ls

Complex Editing with the Visual Editor

The following exercise asks you to make a change and then provides the instruction to accomplish it. Try first to recall the needed command, then check out the written solution. Be sure to complete each step.

1. Use the editor to call up the file *passwd-test*.

   vi *passwd-test*

2. Go to the last line in the file by typing the following:

   G

3. Add two blank lines of text to the end of the file, followed by your name.

   o
   [Return]
   [Return]
   your name

4. Return to command mode.

   [Esc]

5. Read in the file *ls-test*.

   :r *ls-test*

6. Turn on the line numbers in the display if they are not already there.

   :set *number*

7. Add a line of text after the fourth line in the file and return to command mode.

   4G
   o
   some text
   [Esc]

8. Find the word *practice*, change it to *practicing*, and return to command mode.

/practice
e
s
ing
`Esc`

9. Read in the file *who-test* at the top of the existing file.

   :0 read *who-test*

10. Copy the whole file, and place the copy at the end of the file.

    :1,$ copy $

11. Go to the first line of the file and yank a copy of the first six lines. Then put copies after line 6 and at the end of the file.

    1G
    6yy
    6G
    p
    G
    p

12. Go to the word *root* and replace (substitute) the line with the phrase *root is gone*, then return to command mode.

    /root
    cc
    root is gone
    `Esc`

13. Go to line 7 and add the word *ADDITION* to the end of the line.

    7G
    A
    ADDITION

    `Esc`

14. Delete everything from line 10 to the end of the file.

    :10,$ d

15. Undo the deletion and bring the text back.

    u

16. Move downward one screenful of text.

    Ctrl - d

17. Go to the seventh line, and replace (substitute) the first four words with the one word *HELLO*.

    7G
    4cw
    HELLO
    Esc

18. Write the current file with the name *garbage*, and then quit the editor without saving the file.

    :w *garbage*
    :q!

■ Conclusion

The visual editor is a complex, command-driven, screen editor available on essentially all UNIX systems. When you call up an existing or a new file for editing, you are placed in command mode. From this interpreter you can issue commands to move around the file, commands to delete text, and commands to enter the append (text-addition) mode. There are usually several ways to accomplish every editing objective. You should select a set of commands that meet your needs. More will be added to your repertoire as you work through this book.

At the end of this chapter are command summaries of all commands examined in this chapter.

■ Answers to Review 1

1. h or ←
2. */Admin*
3. **dd**

4. Anywhere on the line

5. **8dd**

6. **3dw**

7. Type **:q!** to exit without writing the changes.

8. **e**

9. **:wq**

10. The cursor moves down two lines; then the editor removes three words.

11. Command mode.

12. Command mode.

■ Answers to Review 2

1. **a**

2. Esc

3. Command mode.

4. Enter **I** from command mode; then enter text from append mode.

5. **:w** *room* and then **:q!**

6. **u**

7. **.**

8. Go to the first line and enter **O**.

9. Ctrl-w Ctrl-w

■ Answers to Review 3

1. **r**

2. **cc** or **S**

3. **C**

4. **:set** *number*

5. **b**

6. **23G**

7. **z6.**

8. *.exrc*

9. **R**

10. **J**

11. **H**

12. `Ctrl`-`d`

13. **z.**

■ Answers to Review 4

1. *:1,33* **w** *report.10*

2. *:29,200* **w!** *report*

3. *:36,74* **w >>** *report.1*

4. **vi** *command mode*

5. *:17,93* **move $**

6. *:118,$* **d**

7. *:32,57* **move 0**

COMMAND SUMMARY

Cursor Movement Commands

ⓗⓙⓚⓛ⬅️⬆️➡️⬇️	Moves cursor one line up/down or one space left/right.
0 (zero)	Moves cursor to the beginning of the line it is currently on.
$	Moves cursor to the end of the line it is currently on.
*nn***G**	Moves cursor to the line specified by *nn*; for instance, **42G**.
G	Moves cursor to the last line in your file.
w	Moves cursor forward to the first letter of the next word.
' '	Moves the cursor to its previous location in the file.
e	Moves cursor forward to the end of the next word.
b	Moves cursor backward to the beginning of the current word, or, if at that location, to the beginning of the preceding word.
-	Positions cursor at the beginning of prior line.
+	Positions cursor at the beginning of next line.
nn|	Positions cursor at the column specified by *nn* in the current line; for instance, **42 |**.
L	Positions cursor at beginning of the lowest line displayed on the screen.
M	Positions cursor at line near the midpoint of the screen.
H	Positions cursor at the highest line on the screen.

Cursor Positioning Commands (Contextual)

fx Moves cursor forward on the line to next character specified by x.

Fx Moves cursor backward on the line to previous character specified by x.

/$word$ Moves cursor forward through text to next instance of *word*.

?$word$ Moves cursor backward through text to prior instance of *word*.

n   Moves to the next instance of the pattern identified in a previously issued */word* or *?word*.

Display Adjusting Commands

Ctrl-d   Scrolls the cursor down one block of text in the file.

Ctrl-u   Scrolls the cursor up one block of text in the file.

Ctrl-f   Displays the next block of text in a file.

Ctrl-b   Displays the previous block of text in a file.

zn.   Displays on the screen only n lines of text, where n is a number from 1 to 23. (For instance, **z4.** displays only four lines at a time.) Always type lowercase z, and don't leave out the **.** (dot).

z.   Redraws the screen. Similar to the **z**n. command, except that **z.** doesn't change the number of lines displayed.

:set *showmode*   Instructs the editor to display an indicator of the current mode.

:set *number*   Instructs the editor to include line numbers as part of the screen display, not as part of the file itself.

Text Deleting Commands

dd Deletes cursor line of text.

*n***dd** Deletes *n* number of lines of text; for example, **3dd**.

dw Deletes one word from text.

*n***dw** Deletes *n* number of words from text.

x Deletes the one character under the cursor.

*n***x** Deletes *n* number of characters from text.

:*nn*,*nn*d Deletes all specified lines from *nn* through *nn*, inclusive; for example, **7,23d**.

Undo Commands

u Reverses last text-change action. Works no matter where cursor is located.

U Reverses all text changes made to current line. Cursor cannot leave line between the changes and the **U** command.

Text-Adding Commands

a (lowercase) Inserts text starting with the position to the right of the cursor.

A (uppercase) Starts adding text at the end of the line.

i (lowercase) Starts adding text to the left of the cursor.

I (uppercase) Inserts text at the beginning of the line.

o (lowercase) Opens (or inserts) a line below the cursor line.

O (uppercase) Opens a line above the cursor line.

cw Changes only the one word under the cursor.

s (lowercase) Substitutes for a single character.

S (uppercase) Substitutes for an entire line.

:nn,nn **copy** *nn* Makes copy of lines *nn* through *nn* and places them after the line *nn*; for example, **7,23 copy 52**.

cc Substitutes for (replaces) an entire line (same as **S**).

C (uppercase) Changes the rest of the line (from the cursor position forward).

R Types over existing text.

r Replaces the one character under the cursor with the next character typed.

Text-Moving Commands

J Joins next line with current line.

:nn,nn **move** *nn* Moves lines *nn* through *nn* to after line *nn*; for example, **4,15 move 27**.

yy Copies line to buffer.

p Copies text from buffer and adds to file beginning with a next line.

Quit, Save, and Write Commands

:q Quits work on a file if no changes or additions have been made.

:wq Writes changes made to a file during that editing session, quits work on the file, and returns to the shell.

:q! Quits work on a file and returns to the shell, but does not write changes made during the editing session.

:w *filename* Writes file to new *filename*.

Chapter Three

Using Basic UNIX Utilities

One of the prominent features on the UNIX system landscape is its wide variety of powerful utility programs. Utilities are available to help you locate system information, sort lines, select specific fields, join data files, modify information, and manage files. Although the fundamental utilities are designed to accomplish a simple task, they can be easily combined to produce results that no single utility could produce by itself. This toolbox of utilities, along with the UNIX features that facilitate using several utilities at once, together provide you with a set of powerful solutions to computing problems.

In this chapter you use several utilities individually and in combination. You examine file manipulation utilities and use the basic forms of robust utilities that constitute the core user tools.

SKILLS CHECK: *Before beginning this chapter, you should be able to*

- *Log on to a UNIX system and issue basic commands*
- *Use an editor to create and modify files*
- *Move, copy, and remove files*
- *Place shell commands in a file and make the file executable*

OBJECTIVES: *Upon completion of this chapter, you will be able to*

- *Count the words, lines, and characters in a file*
- *Sort the contents of a file*
- *Identify and/or remove duplicate lines in a file*
- *Compare two files by identifying lines common to each*
- *Translate or remove characters in a file*
- *Search through files for a string of characters*
- *Select a portion of each line in a file*
- *Concatenate files*
- *Splice lines together*
- *Paginate long files*
- *Join together, from two or more files, lines that have a common value in the first field*

- *Make editing changes in a file, using a stream editor*
- *Select and modify the contents of a database file*

In this chapter you will use many different utilities. If you are comfortably familiar with a utility, you can just skim the text that describes it and enter the commands for review. Be certain, though, to read and complete the exercises for any unfamiliar utilities. Always create any requested files, because they are often used in later exercises. If the utility is unknown or only somewhat familiar to you, do all the activities. You'll need to read each summary, answer the review questions, and examine the command summary at the end of the chapter.

3.1

Making a Test File

You will be using the following file as input for several exercises in this chapter.

1. Use an editor to create a file named *test-file* with these contents:

```
File: test-file
This is a file
you will use with several utilities
to demonstrate how they work.
chocolate
chocolate
And he said,
"Use a utility with agility to avoid futility"
++++
13100
13101
11223
12133
11223
++++++
```

```
(and increase ability)
++++
```

3.2

Counting the Elements of a File

You can use a UNIX utility to count the number of lines, words, and characters in a file.

1. Enter the command

   wc *test-file*

   The output from the **wc** (that's **w**ord **c**ount, not water closet) utility consists of four fields:

   ```
   18      43      254      test-file
   ```

   The meaning of each field is described in Table 3-1.

2. In addition to counting the elements of files, **wc** can be used to count the words, lines, and characters in the output of previous utilities in a command line. Enter this command:

   who | wc

   The **who** utility outputs one line of information for each current user. The | is instruction to connect the output from **who** to the input of **wc**, which counts the elements. The **wc** utility then tosses the information that comes from **who** and just outputs its count totals.

Number of lines	18
Number of words	43
Total number of characters	254
Name of the file	*test-file*

Table 3-1. *Output Fields from* **wc**

Counting Only Lines

Like most UNIX utilities, the **wc** utility offers you options that instruct **wc** to run in different ways. You can tell **wc** to limit the count to lines, words, or characters, or any combination thereof.

1. For example, to request a count of just lines in the file, enter the **wc** command with the option **-l** (minus el).

   wc -l *test-file*

   The **wc** utility with its **-l** option produces a count of the lines in *test-file*. The counts of total characters and words in the file are not produced.
   Most command options or flags begin with a minus sign and are listed after the command name. You specify which optional form of the command you want by entering a *-flag*, such as the **-l** you just used.

2. Try each of the other options to **wc**, listed here:

Lines only	**wc -l** *test-file*
Words only	**wc -w** *test-file*
Characters only	**wc -c** *test-file*

Combining the wc Utility Options

More than one option can be used at the same time.

1. For example, enter the following command:

   wc -lc *test-file*

   Both the line count and the character count options are selected and the results displayed.

   SUMMARY: *The* **wc** *utility reads from its input or a file; counts the number of characters, words, and lines; and then outputs each of the three totals. Options are as follows:*

-l	Output the number of lines in the input
-w	Output the number of words in the input
-c	Output the number of characters in the input

3.3

Ordering the Lines of a File with sort

Another utility **sort**s the lines of its input and then outputs the ordered results.

1. Enter the following command to sort the lines from the file and have the output displayed on the terminal:

sort *test-file*

The resulting material is sorted as follows:

```
"Use a utility with agility to avoid futility"
(and increase ability)
++++
++++
++++++
11223
11223
12133
13100
13101
And he said,
File: test-file
This is a file
chocolate
chocolate
to demonstrate how they work.
you will use with several utilities
```

In its basic form, **sort** arranges the lines of a file in a sorted order by comparing the first and then subsequent characters of each line. The order that **sort** follows is the order in which characters are listed in the ascii character set.

2. Examine the ascii character set by entering this command:

man *ascii*

Table 3-2 shows the *ascii* chart from **man.** The numbers are the base 8 numbers associated with each character.

The beginning of the ascii character set comprises special characters such as *newline*, then some punctuation characters, followed by numbers, uppercase letters, lowercase letters, and so on. This is the order **sort** uses to sort the lines of a file, unless you provide specific command options to do otherwise, as you will soon see.

Sorting in Dictionary Order

The **sort** utility also has options. You can have **sort** ignore punctuation and other special characters, using only letters, digits, and blanks in its **sort**.

1. Enter

sort **-d** *test-file*

The **d**ictionary sorted output is as follows:

```
++++
++++
++++++
11223
11223
12133
13100
13101
And he said,
File: test-file
This is a file
"Use a utility with agility to avoid futility"
(and increase ability)
```

000 nul	001 soh	002 stx	003 etx	004 eot	005 enq	006 ack	007 bel
010 bs	011 ht	012 lf	013 vt	014 ff	015 cr	016 so	017 si
020 dle	021 dcl	022 dc2	023 dc3	024 dc4	025 nak	026 syn	027 etb
030 can	031 em	032 sub	033 esc	034 fs	035 gs	036 rs	037 us
040 sp	041 !	042 "	043 #	044 $	045 %	046 &	047 '
050 (	051)	052 *	053 +	054 ,	055 -	056 .	057 /
060 0	061 1	062 2	063 3	064 4	065 5	066 6	067 7
070 8	071 9	072 :	073 ;	074 <	075 =	076 >	077 ?
100 @	101 A	102 B	103 C	104 D	105 E	106 F	107 G
110 H	111 I	112 J	113 K	114 L	115 M	116 N	117 O
120 P	121 Q	122 R	123 S	124 T	125 U	126 V	127 W
130 X	131 Y	132 Z	133 [	134 \	135]	136 ^	137
140 '	141 a	142 b	143 c	144 d	145 e	146 f	147 g
150 h	151 I	152 j	153 k	154 l	155 m	156 n	157 o
160 p	161 q	162 r	163 s	164 t	165 u	166 v	167 w
170 x	171 y	172 z	173 {	174		175 }	176 ~	177 del

Table 3-2. *The **ascii** chart from the **man** Utility*

```
chocolate
chocolate
to demonstrate how they work.
you will use with several utilities
```

The line *"Use a utility with..."* is no longer the first line of sorted output. It is sorted according to where the *U* fits into the scheme, not the quotation marks. If a line begins with characters other than letters, numbers, or blanks, all those characters are ignored when you use the **-d** option. The sort takes into account only letters, numbers, or blank characters.

Sorting Regardless of Capitalization

The **sort** program can be told to ignore the case (upper or lower) of the letters in its input when sorting—that is, to fold the cases together.

1. For example, try this command:

    sort -f *test-file*

    The output displays the lines in ascii order, but with upper- and lowercase of the same letter together.

Reversing the Sort

The order of sorting can be reversed, too.

1. Enter this command:

    sort -r *test-file*

    The display is in reversed ascii order.

Sorting by Fields

The **sort** utility generally sorts lines based on the *first character* in each line, then if the first match, the second is examined, then the third, and so on. There is an alternative: you can sort by *field*. Many files consist of lines of data that are composed of separate fields. For example, examine the following text:

```
0. Dyllis B. Harvey nurturer
1. C. Lyle Strand inventor
2. Mitchy C. Klein explorer
3. Marjorie M. Conrad teacher
4. Orin C. Braucher farmer
5. David A. Waas professor
6. Peter M. Kindfield friend
7. Marge M. Boercker teacher
```

Each line in the file provides information about a particular person. Every line, called a record, is divided into five information fields that pertain to the person. The following relates the data from the first record to the associated field names.

Record Number	First Name	Middle Name	Last Name	Description
0	Dyllis	B.	Harvey	nurturer

A field is defined as a group of characters (a word, a number, a series of letters) where each group is separated from the next by some specified or default character. This character is often called the *field delimiter* or a *field separator*. The default field delimiter for **sort** is the space character.

Creating a Data File

To practice sorting lines by specific fields, you must use a data file that contains lines (records), with each line containing fields identified by a field separator.

1. Create a file named *respected* containing the text displayed above. Each line for each individual contains five fields of information about that individual.

2. Add one or two other people to the list, using the same five-field format.

Sorting a Data File by Fields

1. Sort the *respected* file according to last name (the fourth field) with the following command:

   sort +3 *respected*

   The **+3** tells **sort** to skip the first three fields and base the sort on the *fourth* and *following fields*.

2. An alternative way to achieve the same result on recent UNIX versions is to use the **-k** option. Enter

   sort -k 4 *respected*

The output is sorted beginning with the fourth field.

Sorting Starting with One Field

In the previous example, records are sorted based on the fourth field, which is the last names of the individuals. Because no two records contain the same last name, the sorting is without complication. However, because several individuals have the same middle initial, sorting on that field presents some questions.

1. To see how **sort** sorts by field when several records have the same value in the sort field, enter

   sort +2 *respected*

   The output is

   ```
   5. David A. Waas professor
   0. Dyllis B. Harvey nurturer
   4. Orin C. Braucher farmer
   2. Mitchy C. Klein explorer
   1. C. Lyle Strand inventor
   7. Marge M. Boercker teacher
   3. Marjorie M. Conrad teacher
   6. Peter M. Kindfield friend
   ```

   Notice there are two records with middle initial C. The **sort** utility found both Cs and decided the sort order by proceeding on down the lines to the next field. *Braucher* comes before *Klein*, so record 4 is output before record 2. Likewise, the three records for people with middle initials of *M* are arranged based on the contents of the next field, last name.

Limiting Sort

It is possible to instruct **sort** to sort only on a given field or range of fields.

1. Tell **sort** to only sort on field 3 by entering

   sort +2 -3 *respected*

The following display has characters in boldface type that are essential in making the sort decisions.

```
5. David A. Waas professor
0. Dyllis B. Harvey nurturer
2. Mitchy C. Klein explorer
4. Orin C. Braucher farmer
1. C. Lyle Strand inventor
3. Marjorie M. Conrad teacher
6. Peter M. Kindfield friend
7. Marge M. Boercker teacher
```

This instruction is to skip two fields (**+2**), and then stop with field three (**-3**). The records that have the same middle initial are now listed in the order they were read from the input file, which happens to be the same order as the numbers in field 1. *Klein* now comes before *Braucher* because it is first in the input file. Likewise, the *M*s are determined by the input order.

Including a Secondary Sort Field

Rather than defaulting to the order that the lines are read from the input file, you can specify another field as the secondary sort, to be examined only in cases of ties in the primary field.

1. Request the third field to be the primary sort field, and the second field to be the secondary sort field by entering

   sort +2 -3 +1 -2 *respected*

   The output is

   ```
   5. David Waas professor
   0. Dyllis B. Harvey nurturer
   2. Mitchy C. Klein explorer
   4. Orin C. Braucher farmer
   1. C. Lyle Strand inventor
   7. Marge M. Boercker teacher
   ```

```
3. Marjorie M. Conrad teacher
6. Peter M. Kindfield friend
```

In this version, the records with the same primary field value (middle initial) are sorted by the values in the secondary field, first names. For the two records with *C* in the primary, *Mitchy* is output before *Orin* because *M* precedes *O*. Three records have a middle initial of *M*, so the first names (field 2) are consulted: *Marge* precedes *Marjorie*, which precedes *Peter*. See Figure 3-1.

Reversing a Secondary Field

On most systems, each sort field can be handled differently.

1. Reverse the sense of the secondary sort field, while leaving the primary as is, by entering

   sort +2 -3 +1 -2 -r *respected*

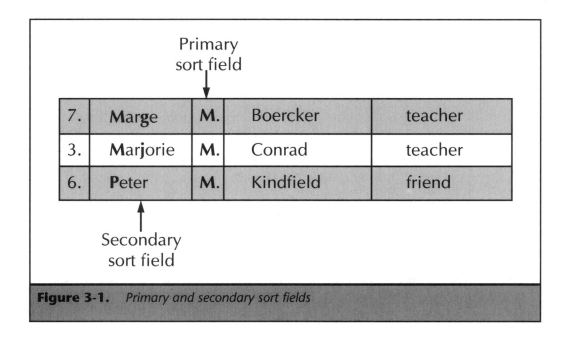

Figure 3-1.　*Primary and secondary sort fields*

The output is as follows. Because the secondary sort is reversed, *Peter* is displayed first among the records with middle initial of *M*.

```
5. David A. Waas professor
0. Dyllis B. Harvey nurturer
4. Orin C. Braucher farmer
2. Mitchy C. Klein explorer
1. C. Lyle Strand inventor
6. Peter M. Kindfield friend
3. Marjorie M. Conrad teacher
7. Marge M. Boercker teacher
```

With the **sort** utility you can specify complex sorts based on lines or fields, and you can instruct **sort** to use another field as a secondary sort criteria.

Using sort with a Different Field Delimiter

The file */etc/passwd* on your system contains information about users.

1. Examine the file by entering the following:

   head */etc/passwd*

   Each line looks like this:

   ```
   cassy:RstAk9?sMZ4pQb:1991:423:president:/usr/home:/bin/ksh
   ```

2. Have **sort** sort the lines in this file by entering

   sort */etc/passwd*

   In the *respected* file that you used a few steps back, the fields were separated by white space. In the */etc/passwd* file, the separator character is the colon.

3. The third field is the user's unique identification number. To see how **sort** handles the request to sort by specific field when the file does not use white space as a field separator, enter

   sort +2 */etc/passwd*

The results are not sorted by the third field, because **sort** expects spaces to tell it where the fields are located, and there are no spaces between the fields.

4. To request sorting by the third field with fields separated by the colon character, enter

   sort -t: **+2** */etc/passwd*

   Here the **-t** option instructs **sort** to use a different character for the **ta**b character or field separator. The new character, the colon, follows the **-t** option without a space between them. The records are sorted based on the third field, group id. The sorting is in ascii, not numerical value. In an ascii sort, the number 110 comes before 20 because 1 precedes 2 in the ascii character set. To sort in numerical order, include the **-n** option.

Redirecting the Output of sort to a File

In the examples entered thus far, the output of **sort** is sent to your work-station screen. As is usually the case in UNIX, you can have the output from a utility sent to a file, instead.

1. Enter

   sort *test-file* **>** *sor-test-file*

   The **sort** utility sorts the lines from the file named *test-file*, and the output of **sort** is placed in a file named *sor-test-file*. This new file can be edited, manipulated, or examined by other utilities.

2. Examine the *sor-test-file* using **more**, **pg**, or **cat**.
   Although **sort** is a powerful and flexible utility, it sorts only lines. Once it reads in the lines and sorts them, it outputs the whole lines, not just selected portions. Later in this chapter you will use **cut** and **awk**, utilities that overcome this limitation. Another constraint of **sort** is that, without the aid of other utilities, it cannot easily sort records consisting of multiple lines.

SUMMARY: The **sort** *utility takes all lines it receives as input and rearranges them into a variety of orders, including the following:*

sort without option	Alphabetical sort following the ascii order.
-r	Reverse ascii order.
-d	Output more like a dictionary; only letters, numbers, and spaces are evaluated in the sorting.
-f	Folded regardless of case. Sorted with upper- and lowercase of the same letter output together; if a tie, uppercase is first.
+n	Sort by specific field, where n is the number of fields **sort** is to pass over, beginning the sort with the n+1 field.
-n	Stop sorting at a specific field, where n is a number.
-k n	Sort by nth field.
-n	Sort by numerical value rather than ascii order with this option.
-tx	Change the field delimiter from tab or space to x, which can be any character.

3. Now that you have examined the **sort** utility and several of its options, examine the manual pages for other **sort** options on your system. Enter

   man *sort*

4. When you have explored enough, quit **man** by entering

   q

3.4

Identifying and Removing Duplicate Lines

Often when you sort a file such as information for an index or word list, the resulting output includes duplicate lines. The **uniq** program reads the input and compares each line with the line that precedes it. If they are identical, action is taken.

1. Look back at the *test-file* you created earlier and visually identify the identical lines in this file by entering

   cat *test-file*

2. To produce an output that includes *single* copies of the adjacent duplicate lines in *test-file* (which means additional copies are deleted), enter the following command line:

   uniq *test-file*

3. Examine the output:

   ```
   File: test-file
   This is a file
   you will use with several utilities
   to demonstrate how they work.
   chocolate            ← duplicate removed
   And he said,
   "Use a utility with agility to avoid futility"
   ++++                 ← duplicate remains
   13100
   ```

```
13101
11223                    ←duplicate remains
12133
11223                    ← duplicate remains
++++++
(and increase ability)
++++                     ← duplicate remains
```

This output consists of one copy of all unique lines and one copy of all duplicated lines that were adjacent to one another. Duplicates that were adjacent have been discarded, leaving one copy. All duplicate lines that are *not* adjacent still remain.

Removing All Duplicate Lines

In examining the output from the previous command, you see that the *chocolate* is, alas, gone, but there are two ++++ lines and two *11223* lines remaining. Because the **uniq** utility compares only *adjacent* lines, duplicate lines must be next to each other in the input to be **uniq**ed. One way to be certain all duplicates are adjacent is to first **sort** the file. Earlier, you sorted *test-file* and called the sorted version *sor-test-file*.

1. Examine *sor-test-file*, and then have **uniq** work on the sorted version by entering

   cat *sor-test-file*
   uniq *sor-test-file*

2. The sorted file has all duplicate lines grouped together. The **uniq** utility removes all but one of each set of duplicates.

3. Sorting and using **uniq** can be accomplished in one step. Enter the following:

   sort *test-file* | **uniq**

   In this case, after the contents of *test-file* are sorted, the output is sent to the input of **uniq**, which removes all but one copy of lines that have duplicates.

Identifying the Lines That Have No Duplicates

In *sor-test-file* there are some unique lines and some lines with duplicates. The unique lines alone can be selected, ignoring *all* copies of lines that have duplicates.

1. Enter the command

   uniq -u *sor-test-file*

   With the **-u** option, **uniq** examines the contents of the file and outputs only the lines that appear once in the file. All copies of lines that have duplicates are discarded. The truly **u**nique lines are the only ones selected.

Identifying the Duplicated Lines

The reverse of the **-u** option is also possible.

1. To ignore the unique lines and output one copy of the lines that have **d**uplicates, enter the command

   uniq -d *sor-test-file*

   With the **-d** option, **uniq** examines *sor-test-file* and outputs only those lines that are *repeated*.

   The **uniq** command with the **-d** option outputs a single copy of each duplicate line, no matter how often it is repeated in the file. Output consists of zero copies of all unique lines and one copy of all duplicated lines.

2. Now instruct **uniq** to inform you of the number of times each line is in its input.

   uniq -c *sor-test-file*

   Each line is output with a number at its left, indicating how many times that line is in the file. (Again, the input must be sorted.)

SUMMARY: *Unless an option is specified, the* **uniq** *utility compares adjacent lines in its input, discarding a line if it is a duplicate. If the input is sorted, the resulting output consists of one copy of all unique lines and one copy of all duplicate lines. Options are as follows:*

-u	Output only the unique lines.
-d	Output only a single copy of the lines that are duplicated; discard all unique lines.
-c	Output a single copy of each line with a number to its left indicating the number of times that line is in the input.

3.5

Comparing the Contents of Two Files with comm

The **comm** utility compares two files, line by line, and identifies three categories: lines found only in the first file, lines only in the second file, and lines that are in both files.

Creating an Example File

To examine how the **comm** utility compares data, you need two files of specific content. Some states in the U.S. are on the coast of an ocean; others are not. Some states are in the western U.S., and some are not. Some states are *both* in the west *and* on the coast.

1. Use the **vi**sual editor to create a file called *west* with the following contents:

```
California
Washington
Oregon
Nevada
Utah
```

2. While still editing the file *west*, tell **vi** to display special characters such as the ends of lines by entering the following command from the command mode:

   :set *list*

   A dollar sign is placed at the end of each line.

3. If any spaces exist at the end of lines or if any state is not spelled correctly, correct it.

4. Write the file and quit the editor.

5. Create a second file named *coast,* with the following contents:

   ```
   Florida
   Washington
   Maine
   Oregon
   California
   Georgia
   ```

6. Check to be sure the data is correct, with

   :set *list*

7. Write and quit the editor.

8. For **comm** to work properly, the files need to be sorted. Enter these commands:

   sort *west* > *sor-west*
   sort *coast* > *sor-coast*

Grouping Unique and Common Lines

Consider the diagram in Figure 3-2, which represents the lines in the two sorted files. Notice that some lines are unique to each file, and some lines are the same in both files.

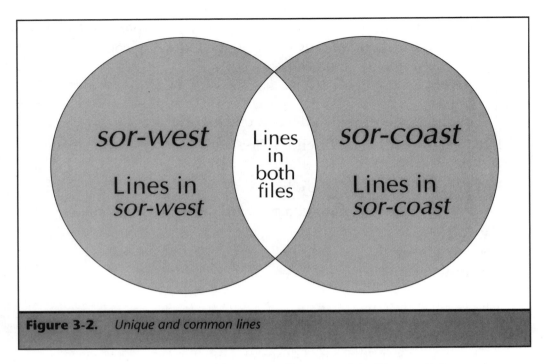

Figure 3-2. *Unique and common lines*

There are three groups of lines, as illustrated in Figure 3-3:

- Lines found in *sor-west* but not in *sor-coast* (western states not on the coast)

- Lines found in *sor-coast* but not in *sor-west* (coastal states not in the west)

- Lines found in both files (western states and on the coast)

Identifying Unique and Common Lines

1. To locate the common lines in the two sorted files, enter this command:

   comm *sor-west sor-coast* **>** *west-coast*

   This command instructs **comm** to perform the comparison and then write its output into a new file, *west-coast*.

2. Call up the file *west-coast* with the **vi**sual editor.

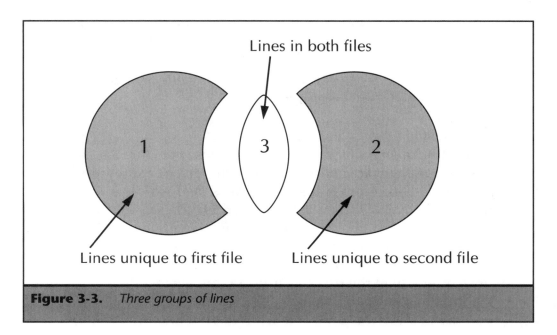

Lines in both files

1   3   2

Lines unique to first file   Lines unique to second file

Figure 3-3.   *Three groups of lines*

vi *west-coast*

The output of **comm** is three *columns* of data:

```
1               2                       3
                                        California
                Florida
                Georgia
                Maine
Nevada
                                        Oregon
Utah
                                        Washington
```

The three columns are as follows:

- The first column contains those lines that are only in the *first* file: *Nevada* and *Utah*.

- The second column contains those lines that are only in the *second* file: *Florida, Georgia,* and *Maine*.

- The third column contains those lines that are in *both* files: *California*, *Oregon*, and *Washington*.

3. While editing this output file, again ask the editor to display special characters by entering

   :set *list*

   You get a display, with lines shown like those in Figure 3-4.

   The special character **^I** is the tab character, representing the Tab key. When **comm** reads *California* as the first line in the first file and then also finds it in the second file, **comm** outputs two tabs and then the line *California*. The line *Florida* is found in the second file only, so **comm** precedes it with only one tab. *Nevada* is only in the first file, so **comm** outputs no tabs before the line. All lines uniquely in the first file, group 1, are against the left margin. All lines in the second file only, group 2, are in the middle, because one tab was output in front of each line. All lines in common, group 3, are on the right, because two tabs are output in front of each line.

4. Quit the editor and return to the shell.

5. To see how **comm** works, have **comm** compare the original unsorted files, *west* and *coast*.

   comm *west coast*

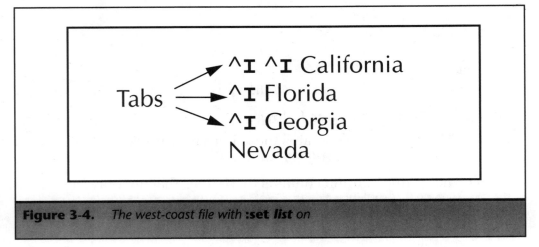

Figure 3-4. *The west-coast file with* **:set list** *on*

The output is not correct. Several states that are in common are listed as unique to each file. The **comm** utility compares the files line by line. When **comm** reads the line *California* in the first unsorted input file, then finds *Florida* as the first line in the second file, **comm** concludes that there is no *California* in the second file because there is no line starting with a letter earlier than *F*, for *Florida* in the second file. The input must be sorted because the program assumes it is and operates accordingly.

Selecting Unique or Common Lines

1. To *suppress* the printing of lines found in *sor-west* but not in *sor-coast* (group 1, as explained just above) enter the number 1 as a flag in the command line, as shown here:

   comm *-1 sor-west sor-coast*

   This command instructs **comm** to discard group 1, the lines unique to the first file. The output is group 2, the lines unique to the second file, and group 3, the lines in common to both files. The output consists of the lines found in *sor-coast* only and the lines found in both files (groups 2 and 3, above). Those lines found only in *sor-west* (group 1) are suppressed.

2. To list only those lines common to both files—that is, select group 3 and leave out groups 1 and 2—enter this command:

   comm *-12 sor-west sor-coast*

   With the *-12* flag, **comm** suppresses printing of groups 1 and 2, the lines unique to each file. Only those states in the west that are also on a coast are listed—the lines are in both files.

3. Likewise, a listing of western states not on the coast can be attained by entering

   comm *-23 sor-west sor-coast*

   This flag is an instruction to suppress groups 2, lines unique to the second file, and 3, lines in common. It outputs only group 1, lines unique to the first file.

SUMMARY: *The* **comm** *utility compares the contents of two files, line by line. It reports a table indicating the lines unique to each file, and the lines common to both. Because* **comm** *works only with one line at a time, input must be sorted. Options are as follows:*

-1	Suppress output of lines unique to the first file.
-2	Suppress output of lines unique to the second file.
-3	Suppress output of lines in common to both files.
-12	Options can be combined, like this. This combination is instruction to suppress lines unique to both files, so that only lines common to both are output.

3.6

Examining Differences Between Files

The **diff** utility indicates how two files are **different**. It reports the lines that are not the same; the location of these lines in their respective files; and what lines you need to add, change, or delete to convert the first file to the second.

1. Create a file called *alpha1* containing the following lines:

```
A  A
B  B
C  C
D  D
E  E
```

2. Create a second file, *alpha2*, containing these lines:

```
B  B
C  C
D  D
E  E
F  F
```

3. Find the differences between *alpha1* and *alpha2* by entering

diff *alpha1 alpha2*

The following output is displayed:

```
1d0
<AA
5a5
>FF
```

This output contains two kinds of lines. Lines such as *<AA* indicate that the line *AA* is in the first file, but not the second. Likewise, *>FF* is in the second file, not the first. The lines that include numbers and letters (*1d0* and *5a5*) indicate the location of the differing lines in their respective files and what needs to be done to convert the first file into the second, as outlined in the following table:

1d0	Line 1 needs to be **d**eleted from the first file to make the first line in the first file like the zeroth line in the second file.
5a5	Line 5 from the second file must be **a**dded as line 5 in the first file to make the first file the same as the second file.

4. In contrast, the **comm** utility just lists the lines unique to each and in common. Try this command and observe the results:

comm *alpha1 alpha2*

For more information concerning **diff**, consult the output of **man**.

 SUMMARY: *The* **diff** *utility compares two files and indicates what must be done to the first file to make it match the second. Lines unique to each file are marked.*

3.7

Translating Characters into Other Characters with tr

The **tr** utility reads input, and either deletes target characters or translates each target character into a specified replacement character. The output is a **tr**anslated version of the input.

Translating Specified Characters

The **tr** utility searches through every character in the input looking for the specified target character(s) and then acts on those characters.

1. To have a translation made of *test-file*, enter the following command:

   tr *1* X < *test-file*

   Here the **tr** utility is given two arguments, the number *1* and the letter X Each instance of the number *1* is located by **tr** and changed into an X. The output is displayed on your screen. The original file is not altered. This command line includes the < redirection symbol to tell the shell to open the file *test-file* for input to **tr**. The utility **tr** is not programmed to open files.

2. You can also make translations of several characters at the same time. Try this command:

   tr *"13S"* *"G&n"* < *test-file*

   The two arguments are in quotation marks to instruct the shell to pass both arguments to **tr** uninterpreted. As a result of **tr** 's efforts, the file is read, translations are made, and the translated version is output. All instances of the number *1* become a *G*. Every *3* becomes an *&*, and each *S* character becomes a small *n*.

1	$\rightarrow$	G
3	$\rightarrow$	&
S	$\rightarrow$	n

Translating a Range of Characters

With the **tr** utility you can also translate ranges of characters.

1. For example, enter the command

   tr "[*a-z*]" "[*A-Z*]" < *test-file*

   The output, sent to the terminal screen by default, is similar to the following:

   ```
   FILE: TEST-FILE
   THIS IS A FILE
   YOU WILL USE WITH SEVERAL UTILITIES
   TO DEMONSTRATE HOW THEY WORK.
   CHOCOLATE
   CHOCOLATE
   AND HE SAID,
   "USE A UTILITY WITH AGILITY TO AVOID FUTILITY"
   ++++
   13100
   13101
   11223
   12133
   11223
   ++++++
   (AND INCREASE ABILITY)
   ++++
   ```

   This command instructs the **tr** utility to read from *test-file* and translate all lowercase alphabetical characters [*a-z*] into uppercase [*A-Z*].

Deleting Specified Characters

The **tr** utility not only makes translations, but also simply deletes identified characters.

1. To delete listed characters from *test-file*, enter this command:

   tr   -d "*lc*+" < *test-file*

   All *l*'s, *c*'s, and +'s are removed from the output.

Passing Output from a Utility to tr

In addition to working on files, output from another utility can be passed to the **tr** utility to make translations.

1. Enter the following:

   ls | tr "[*a-z*]" "[*A-Z*]"

   The output of **tr** displayed on your screen is an all-uppercase listing of the output of **ls.**

SUMMARY: The **tr** *utility translates specific characters into other specific characters, and translates ranges of characters into other ranges. It also deletes listed characters. If two arguments are given, the characters in the first argument are translated into the characters listed in the second argument, with one-to-one mapping. One option of* **tr** *is discussed:*

   -d *argument*   *Instructs* **tr** *to delete all instances of each specified character in the argument that follows*

3.8

Merging Files with cat

One way to display files, especially if they are short, is with the **cat** utility.

1. Enter the following request to read a file and display it on the screen:

cat *test-file*

One argument, a filename, is given to **cat**. The **cat** utility opens the file, reads it, and writes each line to its output. In the above command, there is no instruction to redirect the output away from the default (the workstation screen), so the output is displayed there.

2. In an earlier step you created the files *coast* and *west*. To combine them into a new file called *states*, enter the following:

cat *west coast* > *states*

3. You now have three files: *west, coast*, and *states*. Examine the contents of *states*.

cat *states*

This new file consists of the contents of the first file followed by the second.

The general form for using the **cat** command to combine files is

cat *file1 file2* > *file3*

In the command above, the shell is instructed to redirect the output of **cat** to *file3*. The **cat** utility is instructed to open two files, read each one, and write to its output (which the shell has connected to *file3*). Both files are read and written sequentially. The two input files have been con**cat**enated into the output file.

 *CAUTION: The **cat** utility obtains input from the keyboard (the default) or from files. Its output is directed to the screen (the default) or to files. You must be careful to not use the construction **cat** file1 file2 > file1. This is instruction to the shell to erase file1 and connect it to the output of **cat**, and then to pass file1 as an argument to **cat**. By the time **cat** opens the file for input, it is empty.*

Numbering Lines of Output

Often programmers or data managers need to have line numbers included in the printout or screen display of a file, but do not want to actually modify the file by adding the numbers.

1. Enter the following request for **cat** to read a file:

cat -n *states*

Each line of output is numbered in the display; the file is not affected. If your version of **cat** does not include the **-n** option, you can number output lines using **pr**, which is examined later in this chapter.

 SUMMARY: *The* **cat** *utility reads the lines in all filenames given as arguments and writes all lines to output. Files can be concatenated, and displayed with numbers.*

cat without option	Reads input files and writes to output, which is the workstation display by default, and a file or utility if redirected.
-n	Numbers the lines in the output display

Review 1

1. What command results in a listing of the number of words and the number of lines in the files *practice* and *users_on*?

2. What command results in a sorting of the file *people*, ignoring case and ignoring punctuation at the beginning of the line?

3. What command sorts the file */etc/passwd* using the fourth field, group id, as the primary sort and the third field, user id, as the secondary sort?

4. Consider two files. The first file, *students*, is a sorted list of all students enrolled in the school. The second file, *paid*, is a sorted list of names of students who have paid their tuition. What command lists those students from the first file who have *not* paid their tuition?

5. What command displays the output of **who** in all capital letters?

6. What command creates a new file *chapter* consisting of the contents of the files *section1*, *section2*, *section3*, and *section4* with all lines numbered?

7. What command would produce a listing of what changes would have to be made in *names* to make it exactly like file *newnames*?

3.9

Searching Files with grep

Almost all text editors provide ways to locate words or any group of characters (called a *string* or *pattern*) within a file. On UNIX you can locate patterns in one or more files directly from the shell, without using an editor, by using the **grep** utility. Common uses for **grep** include quickly locating a pattern in a file, and identifying which of many files contains a specific pattern.

Searching Files and Printing Lines

1. The following is a basic **grep** command line. Enter it from the shell:

grep *he test-file*

All lines containing the pattern *he* in the file *test-file* are located and displayed on the screen. The line containing the word *they* is displayed along with the line containing the word *he* because **grep** searches for regular expressions. When a person sees the regular expression *he*, the person thinks of the word *he*. When **grep** sees this expression, it reads it as the letter *h* followed by the letter *e*. You see words, but **grep** sees two characters and they may be part of the words *the*, *they*, *mother*, and so forth.

2. The **grep** utility can be used to locate lines in a file that do *not* contain a particular string:

grep -v *he test-file*

In the output, **grep** has selected all the lines from *test-file* that do not contain the string *he*.

The **-v** option tells **grep** to reverse the sense of the search and to output all lines that do not include the target string.

Searching Through Multiple Files

The power of **grep** to search multiple files for a pattern is especially useful when you believe that you created a file with some known contents, but you cannot remember which of several files contains the target contents.

1. Choose a word that you believe you entered in one or more of your files. Then enter the following command line, substituting your chosen word for *pattern*, and your chosen filenames for *file1* and *file2*:

   grep *pattern file1 file2*

2. Search all files in the current directory for the word *the* by entering

   grep *the* *

   The shell replaces the * in this command line with the names of all the files in the current directory. The first argument passed to **grep** is the string *the*, and the remaining arguments are the names of all files in the current directory. Hence **grep** looks for the string *the* in all the files.

Command	Target to Search for	File to Search	File to Search	File to Search
grep	*the*	*file1*	*file2*	*file3*

Searching for Multiple-Word Targets

Often the goal is to locate a person's name or another string that contains multiple words (a string with spaces in it). In an earlier exercise, you created a file with the string *Lyle Strand* as text in the file.

1. To locate the file, enter this command:

grep "*Lyle Strand*" *

The quotation marks instruct the shell to not interpret the space between *Lyle* and *Strand* as delimiting two separate arguments, but instead to pass the string *Lyle*(space)*Strand* as one argument to **grep**.

2. Try the command without the quotation marks.

grep *Lyle Strand* *

Without the quotation marks, **grep** receives *Lyle* and *Strand* as *separate* arguments. It then searches for *Lyle* in a file named *Strand*, as well as all the other files in the current directory. Unable to locate the *Strand* file, an error message is displayed.

To pass a multiple-word target to **grep**, include it in quotation marks so the shell passes it as one argument.

Examining the grep Command-Line Syntax

The basic command line for **grep** is

grep *pattern filename*(s)

where *pattern* is a string of characters called a regular expression and *filename* is the name of one or more files to be examined by **grep**. The **grep** utility gets its name from "**g**lobal search for **r**egular **e**xpressions and **p**rint."

Ignoring Case in a Search

The **grep** utility is case sensitive when you specify the target string to use in a search.

You can instruct **grep** to **i**gnore case and match the target string, regardless of the case of the letters.

1. Enter the following command line:

grep **-i** *HE test-file*

The lines in *test-file* that contain *he* and *He* are selected because the **-i** option is interpreted by **grep** as instruction to ignore case.

Listing Filenames Without the Selected Lines in a Search

In the example **grep** commands shown thus far in this chapter, the output is the actual lines in the files that contain the target string, or that don't contain the string if **-v** is used. You can instruct **grep** to just list the filenames without displaying the lines if there is a match.

1. Enter the following optional form of **grep**, with the **-l** (minus el):

   grep -l *the* *

   The **-l** option for **grep** is interpreted by **grep** to mean list the file names, not the matching lines.

SUMMARY: The **grep** *utility is used to search through one or more files for lines containing a target string of characters. For a single file, it outputs the selected lines. For multiple files, it outputs the filenames and located lines. Options are as follows:*

grep without an option	Find *pattern* and output each line that contains it.
-i	Make matches ignoring upper- and lowercase.
-l	Output only a list of the names of the files that contain *pattern*.
-v	Output all lines where *pattern* is *not* found.

For additional information, see Chapter 14, "Locating Information with **grep** and Regular Expressions."

3.10

Selecting Portions of a File with cut

Data is often arranged in columns in a file. Columns of information, rather than lines, can also be extracted from a file, by using the **cut** utility.

Creating Example Database Files

1. With an editor, create a new file called *names.tmp*. Because **cut**'s default field delimiter is the tab character, enter the following text with the fields separated by tabs rather than by spaces:

   101 Tab *Bill* Tab *Z.*
   102 Tab *John* Tab *M.*
   104 Tab *Cassy* Tab *T.*
   106 Tab *Mary* Tab *L.*
   107 Tab *Santa* Tab *C.*

2. Create a second file called *numbers.tmp* as follows, with fields separated by tab characters:

   101 Tab *555-9136*
   104 Tab *591-1191*
   105 Tab *511-1972*
   106 Tab *317-6512*

Selecting a Field from a File

The simplest use of the **cut** utility is to extract one field from a file.

1. From the shell, enter the following command line:

   cut -f2 *names.tmp*

   The **cut** utility outputs the second field of the file *names.tmp*:

```
Bill
John
Cassy
Mary
Santa
```

2. To select the first field from the *numbers.tmp* file, enter

   cut -f1 *numbers.tmp*

   The elements of this command are as follows:

Command	Interpretation
cut	Instruction to the shell to execute the **cut** utility.
-f	The **cut** option to specify the extraction of field(s).
1	A number that follows the **-f** option indicates which field(s) to extract. In the previous step , a *1* requested the first field.
numbers.tmp	An argument that tells **cut** which file(s) to use as input.

Using Options with cut

The **cut** utility provides several useful options for manipulating data.

Changing the Field Separator

1. Instruct **cut** to use a colon as the field delimiter by entering the following:

   cut -d: -f4 */etc/passwd* | **more**

   The fourth field from the */etc/passwd* file is displayed because fields are separated by colons in the */etc/passwd* file. The **-d:** is instruction to use the colon as the field delimiter in the input.

Selecting Multiple Fields

Exact fields and ranges can be specified.

1. To select specific fields, enter the following:

   cut -d: **-f1,4** */etc/passwd*

   Fields 1 and 4 are extracted.

2. Enter the following to select a range:

   cut -d: **-f1-5** */etc/passwd*

   Fields 1, 2, 3, 4, and 5 are selected.

Selecting Character Ranges

1. The **cut** utility can be used to select by text character position instead of fields. Enter

   cut -c2-50 */etc/passwd* **|** **more**
   cut -c1-3 *numbers.tmp*

   Specific characters as determined by position from the left edge of the line are selected as output.

   SUMMARY: *The* **cut** *utility is used to read a file and extract fields, ranges of fields, characters, and ranges of characters. To extract by fields, each field must be separated by a field delimiter and, if other than a tab character, it must be specified. Selection may be made on the basis of a list of fields or characters or a range of those elements. Options include the following:*

-f*list*	Displays fields denoted by *list*. A *list* consisting of *1, 4* tells **cut** to display the first and fourth fields of a record. (*1-4* requests all four fields.)
-d*char*	Specifies a field-delimiting character other than the tab character. Use only when requesting fields with option **-f**.
-c*list*	Displays characters in the positions, denoted by *list*, in a record (for example, the character in position *3*, or characters in positions *5-10*).

3.11

Paginating Long Files

If you have been printing files, you have been using either the **lp** or the **lpr** utilities to spool files for printing. The **lp** and **lpr** printing utilities queue jobs and pass files to the printer. If the file is larger than a page, the file is separated into pages only by the separate sheets of paper. There are no margins separating the text from the top or bottom of whatever the printer defines as a page, nor are any of the pages numbered. Even the task of *paginating* a file involves formatting text.

When you want to determine how text is formatted, you must invoke one of several formatting utilities to act on the file. Manipulating layout with one utility and printing with another is typical of UNIX utilities. Each utility has a focus, doing its job well and carrying no extra baggage. In this section, you use the **pr** utility that outputs a file in pages to the screen or printer.

Creating a Long File

To complete the exercises in this section, you need to have a text file that is at least 200 short lines long.

1. Create a new file *prtest* containing a list of the filenames in your current directory. Enter this command:

   ls > *prtest*

2. Add the contents of your *practice* file to *prtest* by entering the following, which uses double-redirects to *add* to the file:

   cat *practice* **>>** *prtest*

3. Now add a listing of the files in */bin* to *prtest* by entering the following:

   ls */bin* **>>** *prtest*

4. Examine the file, determine the number of lines, and keep adding the contents of */bin* until the file is at least 200 lines long.

  more *prtest*
  wc -l *prtest*
  ls */bin* **>>** *prtest*
  wc -l *prtest*

Printing and Paginating a File

The **pr** utility's basic function is to read a file and output paginated text.

1. Observe the output of **pr** by paginating the file *prtest*. Enter

   pr *prtest*

   The output whizzes by on your screen. Like the **cat** utility, the **pr** utility just sends its output to the standard output without pausing.

2. So that you can see the text one screenful at a time, redirect the output of **pr** to **pg** or **more**. Enter either of the following commands:

   pr *prtest* | **more**

   or

   pr *prtest* | **pg**

   This time you are able to examine the output of **pr**. The pages are 66 lines long. Each page has a header at the top and blank lines at the bottom. The header contains the date and time the file was last modified, the filename, and the page number.

3. In addition to redirecting the output of **pr** to utilities like **pg** and **more**, you can also send the output of **pr** to the printer spooler utility by entering one of the following commands:

   pr *prtest* | **lpr**

   or

   pr *prtest* | **lp**

   The file *prtest* is now printed on your default printer. Because most printers use 66-line pages, each page contains 66 lines; this includes the page header, 2 blank lines at the top of the page, and 5 blank lines at the bottom of the page.

4. You can change the page length used by the **pr** utility. Enter the following with a **-l** (minus el) option:

   pr -l22 *prtest* | **more**

   or

   pr -l22 *prtest* | **pg**

   The option **-l** followed by the number 22 is instruction to **pr** to output pages with a length of 22 lines.

Printing and Paginating Multiple Files

You can also have **pr** paginate several files at the same time.

1. Enter one of the following commands to print two files without any formatting:

   lpr *practice users_on*

   or

   lp *practice users_on*

   Each file is printed on separate pages, but without page numbers; **pr** is not included in the command line.

2. Paginate each file with **pr** and send the output to the printer. Type either

   pr *practice users_on* | *lpr*

   or

   pr *practice users_on* | *lp*

   Each file is paginated by **pr** and then sent to the printer to be printed separately.

3. You can also use **cat** to combine the two files, **pr** to paginate the results, and then have the data printed as one output. Type either

   cat *practice users_on* | **pr** | **lpr**

   or

> **cat** *practice users_on* | **pr** | **lp**

The two files are concatenated, paginated, and printed as one file.

Modifying Page Layout

So far you have seen the basic use of the **pr** utility. You can use options to change the output of the **pr** utility, just as you can with other utilities.

Changing Page Headers

By default, **pr** puts a header on each page. You can change the content of the header.

1. Change the header for *prtest* by entering one of these commands:

   pr -h *MyFile prtest* | **more**

   or

   pr -h *MyFile prtest* | **pg**

   Instead of the name of the file, *prtest*, the header title for each page is now *MyFile*. Using the **-h** option, you can change the header title so that it briefly describes the contents of the file.

2. A one-word header title is not always useful. By enclosing a header title inside double quotes, you can include several words. Try one of the following commands to make a more descriptive header:

   pr -h *"My test file for pr"* *prtest* | **more**

   or

   pr -h *"My test file for pr"* *prtest* | **pg**

   The title argument following the **-h** option can include spaces or other shell special characters providing the argument is quoted.

Creating Numbered Listings

In an earlier section of this chapter, you used **cat** **-n** to produce output that had numbers included to the left of each line. In many earlier versions of UNIX, the **-n** option was not available.

1. Another way to obtain line numbered output is with **pr**. Enter the following:

   pr -n *prtest* | **pg**

   Every line, including any blank lines, is numbered on the printout.

Depending on the version of UNIX you are using, either **pr -n** or **cat -n** outputs numbers. In recent versions, both utilities work.

Skipping Pages from the Beginning

When examining very long listings, you might want to pass over the first several pages and paginate the remainder.

1. To skip the first two pages of *prtest*, enter the following command. Do not include a space between the + and the page number. It is one argument.

   pr +3 *prtest* | **more**

   The resulting output starts on the third page, as specified by the +3 in the command line.

Printing with Multiple Columns

The **pr** utility allows you to print several different files in separate columns on the same page, or to print one file in several columns on the page.

Printing Multiple Files Side by Side

With **pr** you can compare two or more files by printing them side by side on the same page.

1. Enter this command:

   pr -m *coast west prtest* | **more**

   The three files are displayed side by side in three columns. If you are using System V UNIX, the columns are 23 characters wide and separated by a space. If you are using BSD UNIX, the columns are not separated, the first two columns are 24 characters wide, and the third column is as wide as the third file's longest line.

In the output, long lines are not split up. Any line that does not completely fit within a column is cut off at the end of the column. For example, if there is a line in the first file that is 40 characters long, only the first 23 characters are printed.

NOTE: By using **pr** *with the* **-m** *option, you can check two or more files for differences, or similarities. This is useful for comparing lists that contain short lines. On the other hand, if the files contain long lines, your comparison using the* **-m** *option cannot be thorough, because most of the lines are truncated.*

Printing One File with Multiple Columns

You just instructed **pr** to output several files together with each file occupying a column on the display. You can also instruct **pr** to output one file in two or more columns, as in newspaper stories.

1. Have **pr** output the file *prtest* in three columns on the screen. Enter

   pr *-3 prtest* | **more**

   In the three columns just displayed, any lines longer than the column width are truncated, as occurs with multiple files above.

2. Print the file *prtest* in three columns, this time on the printer. Enter either of these commands:

   pr *-3 prtest* | **lp**

   or

   pr *-3 prtest* | **lpr**

   By using **pr** with the **-***number* option, you tell **pr** to print the output with that number of columns instead of one column.

SUMMARY: The **pr** *utility is used to read one or more files and format (paginate) output with headings into one or more columns. Options are as follows:*

pr without option	Provides a header that displays the filename, page number, as well as date and time of last modification of the file.
-h *title*	Allows you to replace filename in header with a *title* of your choosing.
-m *file1 file2*	Outputs files side by side. Lines may be truncated.
-n (n is any number)	Outputs the file in *n* columns. Lines may be truncated.

3.12

Putting Lines Together with paste

You've seen how the **cut** utility cuts out selected data from a file. The **paste** utility, as its name implies, lets you put data together. It's very useful when you want to combine lines from various files.

1. Instruct **paste** to operate on the lines of two different files. Enter

   paste *names.tmp numbers.tmp* **>** *combined*

2. Call up the file *combined* with the visual editor.

   vi *combined*

   The file contents are as follows:

   ```
   101 Bill Z.   101 555-9136
   102 John M.   104 591-1191
   104 Cassy T.  105 511-1972
   106 Mary L.   106 317-6512
   107 Santa C.
   ```

   The first line output by the **paste** utility consists of the first line of the first file combined with the first line of the second file. Then the second line of the first file is combined with the second line of the second file, and so on, until **paste** reaches the end of both files.

3. Instruct the visual editor to display special characters.

    :set *list*

    Between the pasted lines, the display includes a **^I**, which is the symbol for the tab character. The **paste** utility reads in a line from the first file, adds a tab, then adds a line from the second file. The default output separator is the tab character. As examined in the next exercise, it can be changed.

4. Quit the editor and return to the shell.

Recall that **cat** places one file *after* the other. The **paste** command, on the other hand, places them *side by side with a separator character included*. To see the difference, consider the following commands and their output:

cat *alpha1*

```
AA
BB
CC
DD
EE
```

cat *alpha2*

```
BB
CC
DD
EE
FF
```

cat *alpha1 alpha2*

```
AA
BB
CC
```

```
DD
EE
BB
CC
DD
EE
FF
```

paste *alpha1 alpha2*

AA	BB
BB	CC
CC	DD
DD	EE
EE	FF

Changing the Field Separator

With **paste** you can specify a character for the delimiter that is used in the output.

1. Have **paste** include a + as the output separator, by entering

   paste -d+ *alpha1 alpha2*

   The output consists of the lines from the two files pasted together with a + between them.

   Essentially any character can be used as the delimiter. If the character has special meaning to the shell—such as the characters * $ ~ & ; " '—the character must be surrounded by quotation marks.

2. Enter

   paste -d'$' *alpha1 alpha2*

   A dollar sign is placed between the pasted lines.

   In addition, \t is understood by **paste** to be the tab character;

\n is the newline; \\ is the backslash; and \0 is interpreted to be empty (no separator character).

3. Try the following:

paste -d'\t' *alpha1 alpha2*

paste -d'\n' *alpha1 alpha2*

paste -d'\\' *alpha1 alpha2*

paste -d'\0' *alpha1 alpha2*

Pasting the Lines of One File Together

The **paste** utility combines lines from two or more files when it is given multiple filename arguments. You can also instruct **paste** to combine the lines of a single file.

1. Enter the following one-file-argument command:

paste -s *alpha1*

The output consists of the lines from *alpha1* spliced together as one line using the tab character as a separator.

2. Instruct **paste** to use a space as the separator in the output, by entering

paste -s -d' ' *alpha1*

In this command line, the space must be in quotation marks to tell the shell to pass the space to **paste** uninterpreted.

SUMMARY: The **paste** *utility connects lines from 2 to 12 files. Lines are connected in numerical order. The* **paste** *utility can also be used with options:*

-d*char*	Change separator to *char*
-s	Paste lines together from a single file

3.13

Combining Selected Lines with join

Corresponding lines or records from two files can also be joined together based on the numerical value of a common field. This function of joining records based on field value is the core of relational database operations.

Joining Records Based on Join Field

1. Examine the contents of the *names.tmp* and *numbers.tmp* files once again. Enter

   cat *names.tmp numbers.tmp*

   The first column of each file contains a column of room numbers (101, 102, and so on). Looking at the displayed data, you can determine the phone number for Mary L. She is in room 106, and room 106 has a phone number of 317-6512. By joining those two pieces of information, Mary's phone must be 317-6512.

   If your objective were to create a joined file that has names matched with their respective phone numbers, you would need to **join** all the appropriate records from the two files. Clearly, the field that can be used to connect the corresponding lines or records of the two files in this example is the room number, called the *join field*.

2. To join the two files, enter

   join *names.tmp numbers.tmp*

   The output is useful information, showing both name and phone number for each room number that has a record in both files:

   ```
   101 Bill Z. 555-9136
   104 Cassy T.591-1191
   106 Mary L. 317-6512
   ```

The default field for joining records is the first field. When **join** reads the first line from the first file, it finds a 101 in the first field. Reading the first line from the second file, **join** also finds a 101. The join field from both records has the same value, so **join** outputs all fields from both records as a single line. See Figure 3-5 for a graphical view.

Examining the Need for Sorted Input

Because **join** compares lines from each file a line at a time, the files to be joined must be in sorted order.

1. Modify the *numbers.tmp* file to have the record for room 104 placed at the top of the file.

   104 Tab *591-1191*
   101 Tab *555-9136*
   105 Tab *511-1972*
   106 Tab *317-6512*

2. Have **join** read the two files and join the appropriate lines.

   join *names.tmp numbers.tmp*

   The output is quite different. Lines that you know share the same value in the join field are not joined. The **join** utility does not read a line from the first file and compare its join field value to all the lines in the other file, but instead only compares it to the first or next line. In this case the files are not in ascii order. The **join** utility finds a 104 in the join field of the first line in the second file, and concludes that there can be no record with a 101; it is already at 104. Files must be sorted for **join** to work properly. Chapter 17 examines more features of **join.**

   SUMMARY: The **join** *utility puts together—joins—lines from separate files if and only if the lines are related to one another through the presence of an identical value in a specified field, and both files are sorted (in ascii order) on the specified join fields.*

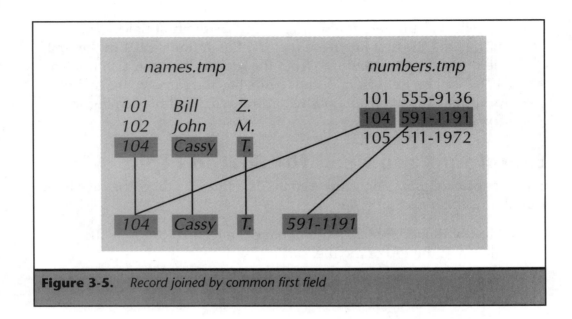

Figure 3-5. *Record joined by common first field*

3.14
Editing from the Command Line with sed

When you begin editing a file using the visual editor, the file is read into an editing or buffer space in memory. The whole file is there; you make changes anywhere in the file you want to work. Available memory prescribes a limit to the size of the file that can be edited. Another way to edit a file would be to read in just one line, make changes, write the line, and read in another. With such an approach, very large files can be edited. An editor that works on the lines of a file one at a time is a **stream** editor, **sed**.

Creating a Sample File

To examine stream editing, you need a file of specific content.

1. Use the visual editor to create a file called *caffeine* with the following contents:

```
coffee coffee coffee
coffee
1996   coffee   coffee
1996   decaf   coffee
1997   coffee   coffee
```

Changing Target Words

Suppose your caffeine addiction has changed flavors, and you want to replace the word *coffee* with the word *chocolate* at every instance where *coffee* occurs in the file *caffeine*. Without calling up a text editor, you can create a version with substitutions.

1. Enter the following command:

   sed '**s**/*coffee*/*chocolate*/' *caffeine*

   The output has only the first instance of *coffee* changed to *chocolate* on each line. This **sed** command contains the following instructions:

Command	Interpretation
s	Instructs **sed** to make a **s**ubstitution.
/*coffee*	The string *coffee* is the target to be searched for on each line. It is the target string to be replaced.
/*chocolate*/	The replacement string. In cases where there is more than one instance of the target word on a line, only the first is substituted.

   The file *caffeine* is not altered. Only the version that is output by **sed** is edited. Not every instance of *coffee* is changed in the output.

Changing All Instances of the Target

The previous **sed** command located the first instance of the target word on each line it read as input. You can instruct **sed** to change multiple instances occurring on each line.

1. Enter the following **sed** command including the **g**lobal request.

   sed '**s**/*coffee*/*chocolate*/**g**' *caffeine*

   Each line of the file *caffeine* is read and each instance of the target string is changed to the replacement. The resulting lines are displayed on the screen. The **g** after the replacement string instructs **sed** to **g**lobally affect each line; making substitutions for *all* instances of the target encountered, not just the first.

Selecting Lines and Then Making Replacements

The previous **sed** commands instructed **sed** to examine all lines of the input. You can request that **sed** act only on lines that meet a specified criteria.

1. Enter the following:

   sed '/*1996*/**s**/*coffee*/*chocolate*/**g**' *caffeine*

   The /*1996*/ in front of the substitution specification instructs **sed** to select a line only if it has the string *1996* in it. If a line is selected, then, if the string *coffee* is located on that line, **sed** substitutes *chocolate* for *coffee*. Lines are selected for further processing if the target string matches; a substitution takes place on the line if the substitution target is matched. The line with *1997* did not match *1996*, so, it retains its *coffee*. See Figure 3-6.

Making a Substitution for the Line Search Target

In the previous example, a target was specified for locating lines, and then a different target for a text substitution was provided. The line target can be used as the substitution target, as well.

1. Enter the following, which does not specify a substitution target:

   sed '/*1996*/**s**//*2003*/**g**' *caffeine*

   Lines are selected if they have the line target string present: *1996*. The *1996* is replaced with the string *2003*. In this command, no substitution target is specified; the two slashes after the **s** have no target between them. When no substitution target is specified, the line selection target is used for substitution. Lines are selected if they contain the line search target string, and then that string is replaced. Chapter 15 explores additional features of **sed**.

> **SUMMARY:** *The* **sed** *utility takes an input line, makes whatever editing changes are requested, and then outputs that line. It is a stream editor that uses the editing commands of the* **ex** *line editor.*

3.15
Manipulating Data with awk

The output of **who** consists of one line for each user who is logged on to the system. Each line, called a *record*, consists of several fields of particular information about the user. UNIX data is often stored in files with individual lines (records) containing multiple fields. The **awk** utility is designed to locate particular records and fields in a database, modify them, perform computations, and then output selected portions of the data. Thus **awk** is particularly useful for information retrieval, data manipulation, and report writing.

The name of the **awk** utility is derived from the names of the programmers who wrote it, **Aho**, **Weinberger**, and **Kernighan**.

1. For this section of the chapter, create a file called *food* and enter the following text:

   milk dairy 2.00
   hamburger meat 2.75
   cheese dairy 1.50

   The *food* file consists of three records. Each record contains three fields: name of product, kind of product, and the price. The fields are separated with spaces. A space is the default field delimiter for **awk**.

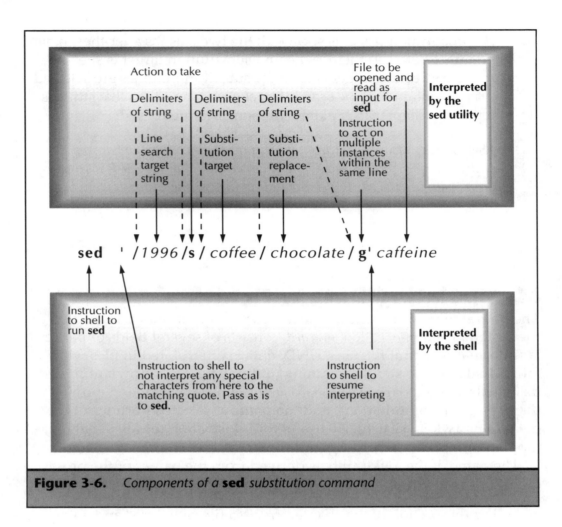

Figure 3-6. *Components of a* **sed** *substitution command*

Selecting Lines and Printing Fields

The **awk** utility does its work by selecting records based on the presence of a specified pattern, and then performing a prescribed action on the selected record.

1. Enter the command

   awk *'/dairy/* **{print $3}***' food*

This command line instructs **awk** to select each record in the *food* file that contains the character string *dairy*, and then to perform the action of printing the third field (*price*) from each of the selected records. In this example, the pattern used to select the lines was not in the field (3) that was output. You can use one field for selection and then output an entirely different field(s).

The components of the command line are as follows:

Command	Interpretation
awk	Instruction to the shell to execute the **awk** utility.
' '	Instruction to the shell to not interpret special characters inside the quoted string, but rather to pass the enclosed characters *as is* to the **awk** utility.
/dairy/	Instruction to **awk** to select lines that have the string *dairy* in any field. Lines that contain this pattern are selected for whatever action is specified.
{print $3}	Instruction to **awk** to output, **print**, the third field, **$3**, of the selected lines. The action, identified by curly braces, is performed on all the lines that have *dairy* in them. The **print** statement is one of **awk**'s many possible actions.
food	This argument tells **awk** which file to read for input.

Changing the Field Delimiter

In the previous examples, the fields in the records are delimited by spaces. Often data files use other characters as field separators. Login information is kept in the */etc/passwd* file, where fields are delimited with colons.

1. Have the system display your password record by entering the following, where you replace your actual login id for the string *yourlogin*.

   grep *yourlogin* */etc/passwd*

2. If you are on a stand-alone system, the password file is on your system; otherwise, it is on a network server. If you do not get an output line consisting of several fields separated by colons, you are probably on a network server. Request a display from the network server by entering

   ypcat *passwd* **| grep** *yourlogin*

3. You can instruct **awk** to use the colon as field separator. Enter the following:

   awk -F*:* **'{print $1, $3, $4}'** */etc/passwd* **| more**

   or

   ypcat passwd | awk -F*:* **'{print $1, $3, $4}' | more**

4. After you have examined a screenful of data, quit **more** by entering

   q

   The output consists of just the first, third, and fourth fields of all records in the password file.

   The fields are separated by colons in the input; **awk** is instructed to use the colon as the field delimiter because the command line included the argument **-F** followed by a colon. However, because of the commas in the **print** statement, **awk** displays its *output* using a single space between fields. For additional information about **awk**, see Chapter 16.

   SUMMARY: The **awk** *utility locates records that are stored in rows and columns (records and fields) in files (databases). It modifies records, performs computations, and outputs selected fields. One option is examined:*

   -F*char*   *Changes field delimiter to char.*

3.16

Sending Output to a File and to Another Utility

When you construct a command line, the output of a utility can be sent to only one place, either a file *or* another utility. Using redirection, it cannot be sent to both another utility *and* a file. There may be times when you want to have the output of a utility sent to a file for later examination, and at the same time have the output redirected to another utility. Because splitting of output cannot be done by the shell, another UNIX utility was created to accomplish this goal.

1. Enter the following command:

    ls | **tee** *current-files* | **wc -w**

    The output of **wc**, the number of files in the current directory, is displayed on the screen.

2. Examine the contents of your new file, *current-files*, by entering

    more *current-files*

    The file *current-files* contains the output of the **ls** utility. As you saw, the output of **ls** is also passed to **wc**, which counts the number of words. The output of **wc** is displayed on the screen.

    The **tee** utility reads from input (the output of **ls**) and then writes each line to output, which is connected to **wc**. In addition, **tee** reads its first argument, *current files*, and creates a file of that name. A copy of all the lines it read from input is also written to the file *current-files*.

SUMMARY: *Like a plumber's tee that sends cold water in two directions, the* **tee** *utility sends what it reads from its input in two directions: to a file named as an argument and to standard output.*
Standard output is connected by defaut to the workstation screen, or can be redirected to another utility, or even to another file. The **tee** *utility does not modify the data in any way.*

Review 2

1. What command tells a utility to search through every file in the current directory for the name *Catherine Thamzin*?

2. How would you output only the first two fields of */etc/passwd*?

3. How can you print the */etc/passwd* file with page numbers, line numbers, and a header entitled *Passwd File*?

4. Your company has acquired a skateboard manufacturing division, and you want to send out a mailing. You have a form letter in the file *form_letter*. You are told that the letter's salutation of "Dear Sir" should be changed to "Hey, dude." How can you accomplish this change?

5. What command could you enter to have the output of **who** placed in a file named *on-11pm* and a sorted version of the same data placed in a file *sorted-11pm*?

3.17

Creating Scripts Using Utilities

In the previous exercises you issued UNIX commands that called utilities, which in turn obtained or transformed data. Often it is more convenient to put complex commands in *script files* and execute the script rather than issue long commands at the command line. Corrections can be easily made to a script file without having to reenter the whole command, possibly introducing new errors. This section guides you through making several scripts that employ the utilities examined earlier in this chapter.

Listing Only Directories

The output of **ls** includes the names of the files and directories in the current directory. Sometimes, a listing of just the directories is useful.

1. Create a new script file named *mydirs* and type in the following command line as the only text in the file.

   ls -F | grep /

2. Make the file executable by entering

   chmod +x *mydirs*

3. Run the script by entering

   mydirs

   or

   ./mydirs

   The output consists of the names of the directories listed in the current directory. Filenames are ignored. The command line in the script calls for the **ls** utility to be run with the **-F** option. The following describes the components of the command line in the script.

ls -F	Instruction to the shell to run **ls** and give it **-F** as an argument. To the **ls** utility, the **-F** is a flag, or option. It is instruction to place a slash at the end of each directory name listed in its output. The default output of **ls** is to output every filename on a separate line. (On BSD and the most recent versions of UNIX, **ls** outputs filenames in columns if it is sending output to a terminal.) However, when sending output to another utility, **ls** lists one name per line.
|	Instruction to the shell to redirect the output of **ls** to the input of **grep**.

grep /	The **grep** utility is executed and given one argument, the slash character. To **grep**, the first argument is always interpreted as the search string. Hence, **grep** looks for a slash in each line of input. Lines with a slash character anywhere in the line are output and, in this case, displayed on the screen. Only the directory names in the output of **ls** have a / and, therefore, only directories are selected by **grep**.

Determining Whether Friends Are Logged On

On a large system there may be hundreds of users. It is often important to determine whether one of several colleagues is logged on.

1. Create a file named *friends* that contains, in alphabetical order, your login id, as well as the login ids of some of your friends and colleagues who have accounts on your system.

2. Use the editor to create a script named *friends-on* and type in the following contents:

who | **sort** | **cut -d" " -f1** > *logins-on*
join *logins-on* *friends*
rm *logins-on*

NOTE: If you are on a network you might want to use **rwho** *instead of* **who** *to obtain a listing of all users on the local network.*

3. Make the script *friends-on* executable.

4. Run *friends-on*. The output is a list of your friends who are currently logged on.

In this script **join** is used. You could also use **comm**. The following describes the contents of the script.

First Line of Script	
who	Instruction to the shell to execute who, which creates a list of current users.
|	The output of **who** is redirected to **sort**.
sort	Instruction to the shell to execute **sort**, which sorts the lines that it gets from **who**.
|	Instruction to connect the output of **sort** to the input of **cut**.
cut	Execute **cut**, a utility that can select fields from all lines of input.
-d" "	An argument passed to **cut**, which **cut** interprets as instruction to identify fields as groups of characters separated by a space. The delimiting space character is quoted in this command line to instruct the shell to pass the space to **cut** as a part of an argument, rather than interpret the space itself, in the usual way, as a separator of command-line tokens.
-f1	An argument passed to **cut**, instructing **cut** to output only the first field from all lines.
> *logins-on*	Instruction to the shell to connect the output of **cut** to the file *logins-on*.

Second Line of Script	
join	An instruction to the shell to run the join utility.

Second Line of Script

logins-on friends	Two arguments to be passed to **join**. The **join** utility interprets the two arguments as names of files to be opened and read. A relational join is computed using the contents of the two files, producing a list of users who are in the *friends* file and in the output of **who**.

Third Line of Script

rm *logins-on*	Instruction to execute the **rm** utility, giving it one argument, *logins-on*. The temporary file *logins-on* is removed.

Identifying the Number of Times You Are Logged On

A user may be logged on to UNIX on multiple ports. If so, **who** generates multiple lines of output for that user. If you log on in different locations, it is wise to make sure you do not leave a terminal unattended. This script assists by determining the number of times you are logged on.

1. Create a script named *num-on* containing one of the following lines:

   who | grep $LOGNAME | wc -l

   or

   who | grep $USER | wc -l

   (Use **$USER** if your system does not recognize **$LOGNAME**.)

2. If convenient, log on at a second workstation or start another terminal window at your workstation.

3. Make the script *num-on* executable and run it. The number of times you are logged on to the system is displayed.

The following describes the components of the *num-on* script.

who	Instruction to the shell to run the **who** utility, which produces a line of output for each instance that each user is logged in.
|	Instruction to the shell to redirect the output of **who** to the input of **grep**.
grep *$LOGNAME*	The *$USER* (or *$LOGNAME*) is a variable that the shell evaluates as it parses, or makes sense out of the command line. The shell removes the string of characters **$USER** from the command line and substitutes the value of the variable, the user's login id. When the shell executes **grep** it passes **grep** one argument, the value of the **$USER** variable, the user's login id. The **grep** utility searches each input line (the output from **who**) for instances of the target string, the user's login id. Only lines that include the target string are output by **grep**.
|	Instruction to connect the output of **grep** to the input of **wc**.
wc -l	Instruction to execute **wc** and pass **wc** one argument, **-l**, which **wc** interprets as instruction to output only the number of lines it receives from **grep**. This number is the number of lines in the output of **who** that contains the user's login id, hence the number of times the user is currently logged on.

3.18

Determining the Number of Unique Words in a File

In the previous exercises you had the shell redirect the output from one utility to the input of another using pipes. By employing several utilities at once, you can accomplish tasks much more complex than any single utility can accomplish.

This pipeline feature of UNIX is very useful, and central to effectively manipulating data with UNIX utilities. As Peter said while running the PickPepper utility, primitive programs prove positively powerful when properly piped.

It is sometimes instructive when examining your writing to know how many different words you are employing. This exercise guides you through the creation of a complex script that reads a file and outputs both the number and a list of unique words that are in the file.

The **uniq** utility is used to output unique lines from a file or other input. To prepare the data from a file so that **uniq** can work properly, punctuation and blank lines must be removed; differences in case for the same word must be rationalized; and the words must be in a sorted order, one word to a line.

Removing Punctuation

In any file of text, usually some punctuation is attached to words that must be removed for **uniq** to work.

1. Create a file named *wordsUsed*. Enter the following line, substituting the name of one of your files for *filename*:

   tr -d *'",;?.'* < *filename*

2. Make the script executable and run the script. The output is the contents of the file, with punctuation characters removed.

   In this command line, the components are as follows:

tr	Execute the **tr** utility.
-d ' '	Pass **tr** two arguments: **-d**, and the characters inside the single quotes. The **-d** is interpreted by **tr** to be its delete option.
" , ; ? .	Hence **tr** searches for literal " , ; ? or . characters in the input, and deletes those characters.
< *filename*	Instruction to the shell to open your *filename* and make it the input to **tr**.

Making All Characters Lowercase

Once punctuation marks are removed, there is still the matter of capital letters: some words are capitalized and others are not. To properly remove duplicates, each duplicate must match case, as well as characters. A simple solution is to just make the whole file lower- or uppercase.

1. Add a backslash to the end of the first line, and add a second line to the script, so the contents become

    tr -d '",;?.' < *filename* \
    | **tr** '[A-Z]' '[a-z]'

2. Run the script and examine its output. It's completely lowercase. The components of the added text are as follows:

\	Instruction to the shell to ignore special meaning of the next character, which is a (Return). Hence multiple lines in the script are seen by the shell as one line of input.
| **tr**	Instruction to connect the output of the previous utility, which was **tr**, to the following utility, another **tr**, and to execute the second **tr** utility.

' '	Instruction to the shell to not interpret the enclosed characters as having significance to the shell. The text between the quotes is passed, as is, to **tr**.
[A-Z]	The first quoted argument passed to **tr**, which **tr** interprets to be instruction to search for all uppercase letters as targets for replacement.
[a-z]	The second quoted argument passed to **tr**, which is interpreted as the replacement characters. All uppercase letters are replaced with their matching lowercase letters.

Putting Each Word on a Line

The output of the script has many words on each line. To remove duplicate words with **uniq**, they must be one to a line. To accomplish this task, the code for a character in the *ascii character set* is used.

1. Examine the ascii characters and their associated codes by entering

   man *ascii*

   The character with a number **012** beside it is the *newline* character. Lines in a file are separated by this character so that terminals and printers are able to display individual lines.

2. Modify the script file to include the following lines:

   ```
   tr -d '",;?.' < filename \
   | tr '[A-Z]' '[a-z]' \
   | tr ' ' '\012'
   ```

3. After completing the changes, run the script. Each word is on a line by itself.

   The additions to the script are as follows:

Command	Interpretation
l tr	Run the **tr** utility, which locates specified characters and replaces them with other specified characters. Connect the output of the previous utility, **tr** to this **tr**'s input.
' '	Pass to **tr** a first argument consisting of a space. The **tr** utility interprets its first argument to be the character(s) to be located and ultimately replaced by the character(s) listed in the second argument.
'\012'	Pass to **tr** a second argument, \012. The backslash instructs **tr** to use the **ascii** character associated with this number, 012, the newline, as a replacement character. The target character, space, is replaced with the newline character everywhere in the file. The resulting output of **tr** consists of every word from the input file on a new line.

Removing Blank Lines

The output includes whatever blank lines were in the input file. They can be removed.

1. Include the **sed** utility in the script by modifying the script to read

   tr -d ' ",;?.' < *filename* \
   l **tr** '[A-Z]' '[a-z]' \
   l **tr** ' ' '\012' \
   l **sed** '/^$/ d'

2. Run the script again. Blank lines are removed.
   The new script line consists of the following:

sed	Connect the output of **tr** to **sed** and execute the **sed** utility.
' '	Instruction to the shell to pass the enclosed string to **sed** as an argument without interpreting any characters.
/^$/ d	The argument passed to **sed**, which **sed** interprets to mean "locate lines that consist of a beginning ^ and ending $ with no text in between (blank lines), then delete (**d**) those lines."

Sorting the Lines

For **uniq** to remove duplicates, they must be adjacent.

1. Modify the script as follows:

```
tr -d '",;?.' < filename \
| tr '[A-Z]' '[a-z]' \
| tr ' ' '\012' \
| sed '/^$/ d' \
| sort
```

2. Re-run the script to confirm the effect of the sorting.
   The added commands are as follows:

		Connect the output of **sed** to the input of the next utility, **sort**.
sort		Run the **sort** utility, which sorts all lines it receives from **sed**. Because every word is on a line by itself, the output is a sorted list of words from the file, one word to a line. If the file contains ten instances of the word *the*, they are listed on sequential lines.

Removing Duplicates

At last, the data is ready for **uniq**.

1. Modify the script:

```
tr -d '",;?.' < filename \
  | tr '[A-Z]' '[a-z]' \
  | tr ' ' '\012' \
  | sed '/^$/ d' \
  | sort | uniq
```

2. Run the script. All duplicate lines are removed.
   The addition to the script is

|	Connect the output of **sort** to the input of **uniq**.
uniq	Run the **uniq** utility, which ignores adjacent identical lines. Multiple lines containing the same word are reduced to just one line containing that word. The output consists of a sorted list of unique words from the file, each word to a line.

Writing to Both a File and the Next Utility

The resulting unique lines (words) are displayed on the screen. The last addition has the output placed in a file and has the lines counted.

1. Complete the script so it looks like this:

```
tr -d '",;?.' < filename \
  | tr '[A-Z]' '[a-z]' \
  | tr ' ' '\012' \
  | sed '/^$/ d' \
  | sort | uniq \
  | tee words.out | wc -l
```

2. Run the script and examine the contents of the new file, *words.out,* which is in your current directory.

The new pieces of this script are as follows:

|	Connect the output of **uniq** to the input of the next utility, **tee**.
tee	Run the **tee** utility, which reads from its input and then writes both to output and to a file named as an argument.
words.out	The name of the file **tee** creates. A copy of every line **tee** reads from input is written to the file.
|	Connect the output of the previous utility, **tee**, to the next utility, **wc**.
wc	Run the **wc** utility.
-l	Instruction to **wc** to only count and display the number of lines, ignoring the number of words and characters. Because each word in the input is on a line by itself, the output from **wc** is the number of words.

There is no utility in UNIX that tells you the number of unique words included in a file. By piping several utilities together you can determine it.

In summary, the program accomplishes the following:

tr -d ' ' ",;?.' < *filename* \	←	Removes punctuation
| **tr** '[A-Z]' '[a-z]' \	←	Makes all words lowercase
| **tr** ' ' '\012' \	←	Replaces spaces with newlines
| **sed** '/^$/ d' \	←	Removes blank lines
| **sort** | **uniq** \	←	Sorts and removes duplicate lines

| **tee** *words.out* | **wc -l**   ← | Makes file of unique words and passes to **wc**, which counts lines

The diagram in Figure 3-7 identifies how the data is passed and transformed by the script's utilities. The arguments passed to each utility are labeled ARGS.

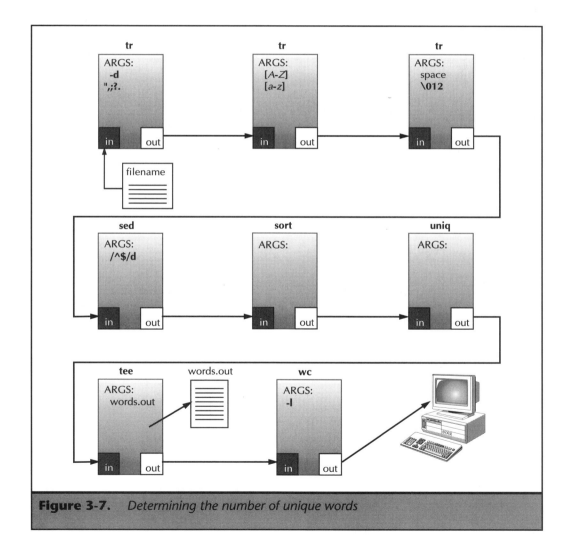

Figure 3-7. *Determining the number of unique words*

■ Conclusion

In this module you used a variety of UNIX utilities and employed basic versions of some utilities that are examined in detail in later chapters. The utilities took input, made transformations (such as selecting, modifying, or combining data), and then output results.

Each of these utilities completes its basic task well. To have a utility work in specific ways, you must employ options for the utility, called by *-flag*. More complex tasks are accomplished by passing the output of one utility to another, refining the output data. Often it is efficient to put complex commands that involve multiple utilities in script files, to have them executed by entering the script's name rather than the complex command.

■ Answers to Review 1

1. **wc -wl** *practice users_on*

2. **sort -fd** *people*

3. **sort -t**: *+3 -4 +2 -3 /etc/passwd*
   or
   sort -t: **k** *4, 4* **-k** *3, 3 /etc/passwd*

4. **comm -23** *students paid*
   or
   comm -13 *paid students*

5. **who** | **tr** "[*a-z*] "[*A-Z*]"

6. **cat -n** *section[1-4]* **>** *chapter*

7. **diff** *names newnames*

■ Answers to Review 2

1. **grep** "_Catherine Thamzin_" *
2. **cut -d**: **-f1,2** _/etc/passwd_
   or
   awk -F: '{print $1, $2}' _/etc/passwd_
3. **pr -h** "_Passwd File_" **-n** _/etc/passwd_ | **lpr**
4. **sed** '_s/Dear Sir/Hey dude_/**g**' _form_letter_ > _skateboard_letter_
5. **who** | **tee** _on-11pm_ | **sort** > _sorted-11pm_

COMMAND SUMMARY

awk *pattern {action} filename* — Performs the action on all records in *filename* that contain *pattern*.

cat *file1 file2 > file3* — Creates new *file3* with copies of the contents of *file1* and *file2*.

comm *file1 file2* — Shows the common and unique lines in two files. Compares *file1* to *file2*.

cut *option filename* — Outputs selected fields from *filename*.

diff *file1 file2* — Shows lines that are different in each file and how to modify first file to match second.

grep *expression filename* — Outputs all lines in *filename* that contain the regular expression.

join *file1 file2* — Combines lines from *file1* and *file2* that contain common fields.

paste *file1 file2* — Combines line 1 from *file1* with line 1 from *file2*, etc.

pr *filename* — Paginates named file (*filename*).

sed *command filename* — Executes specified **sed** editing command(s) on *filename*.

sort *filename* — Sorts the contents of the file *filename*.

tee *filename* — Reads from input and then writes both to output and to a file *filename*.

tr *'string1'* *"string2"* < *filename*	Reads input and translates *string1* characters into *string2* characters.
uniq *filename*	Removes duplicate adjacent lines from *filename*.
wc *filename*	Counts words, lines, and characters in *filename*.

Chapter Four

Creating and Changing UNIX Directories

On UNIX , files are collections of information stored on the system that can be accessed, modified, copied, and removed. In the same sense, a library contains books of information that can be accessed, copied, removed, and even modified. In a library the cards in the card catalog or records in the on-line catalog provide users with information about the books, as well as how to locate the books in the stacks. In a similar way, directories contain filenames and an index number that is used to locate information about the files, as well as the actual files on disk.

In this chapter, you create and use new directories, called *subdirectories*, within your home directory, and access the files within these subdirectories.

The UNIX *file system* or *directory structure* allows you to create files and directories accessed through a hierarchy of directories. For example, a letter to a client named Forbes on July 2, 1996, can be a file named *Forbes7.2.96* listed in a directory named *Correspondence*. The *Correspondence* directory can be listed in another directory, and so on. Such an arrangement is essential to locating information quickly on the system. If you are an experienced DOS user, the directory structure examined in this chapter will be familiar because the DOS file system is similar to the UNIX file system. The workstation screen is a small porthole through which you look into your collection of files. When a carefully designed hierarchical file system is in place, you can access the needed information with minimal effort.

SKILLS CHECK: Before beginning this chapter, you should be able to

- *Access and leave the system*
- *Create, display, and print files*
- *Execute basic shell commands*
- *Redirect output of a utility to another utility or to a file*
- *Name, copy, and remove files*
- *Access and modify files using the* **vi** *editor*

OBJECTIVES: *After completing this chapter, you will be able to*

- *Create a directory*
- *Change to a directory*
- *Use the complete pathname for a file*
- *Specify the path to a file relative to a user's home directory*
- *Use parent and current directories in path specifications*
- *List a file in more than one directory*
- *Move directories and their contents*
- *Remove directories*
- *Find files on the system*

4.1

Employing Directories to Create Order

Using directories is a fundamental UNIX skill, because nearly everything on the system is a file and all files are listed in directories. A directory does not actually contain files; rather it is a list of the names of files it references, as well as information concerning how to locate each file.

Until now, you have not needed to concern yourself with directories, because everything you have created has been listed in the one directory you access when you log on.

1. When you log on to a UNIX system, you are placed in your *home directory*. Log on now to your account.

   As you have experienced before, you are automatically in your home directory.

2. Files you create are accessed from your home directory. Enter

   who > *f_name*

   The new file *f_name* contains the login names and other information concerning users currently logged on to the system. You did not specify where the new file is to be located. As a default, the file is created in your current directory, which at the moment is your home directory.

All filenames you include in a command refer to files listed in your current directory, unless you specify otherwise.

3. Ask for a listing of the filenames in your current directory. Type

ls

The names of the files you have created appear on the screen. If you have only a few files, this listing is brief. However, if you have many files, this listing fills up the screen and is difficult to read. By using directories, you can store similar files together and have shorter listings in each directory.

4. Figure 4-1 illustrates the relationship between your home directory and some of the files probably listed in your home directory.

If your home directory does not have files named *practice*, *journal*, and *f_name*, create them now using an editor, as they are needed in exercises in this chapter. Append a few lines of any content to each file.

In the figures of this chapter, one graphic representing a directory has a boldface outline, indicating that it is your *current directory*—your present location in the file structure. In Figure 4-1, the home directory is the current directory.

People often think of UNIX directories as holding files much as physical file cabinets contain files. Although this metaphor is commonly used, it is not strictly accurate and is misleading. A directory does not actually "contain" files. Rather, for each of its files, the directory contains only the name of that file and an index number that leads to information about that file and the file itself.

The **ls** command reads the names of the files listed in your current directory and then outputs those names. The file's index number or *inode number* can also be shown.

5. Enter this command:

ls -i

to list the filenames and index numbers for the current directory.

```
21128  first_file
21327  food
21106  names.tmp
21107  number.tmp
21189  ordered_1
21133  phon
21083  practice
21325  prtest
21333  test_file
21084  users_on
```

The index number, or inode number, leads to a small data structure called an inode on the hard disk. The inode stores information about the file (such as its owner, permissions, and so on) and the disk addresses where the file is actually located. A directory contains only a file name and an index number for each of its files and directories.

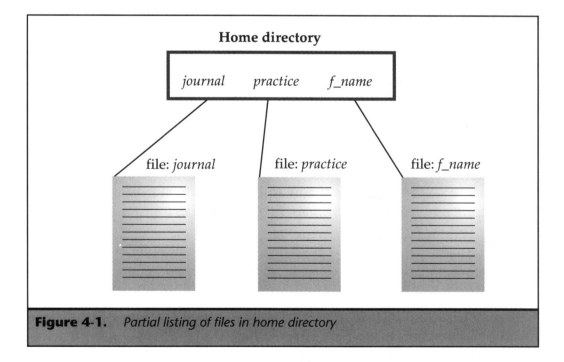

Figure 4-1.   *Partial listing of files in home directory*

Your home directory, then, is just a file containing the name and inode number of each file you have created that is listed in your home directory. The inode contains the remainder of the information about the file and the addresses needed to locate the data.

Creating Directories

You can create additional directories. New directories are usually created and listed in your current directory.

1. Create a new directory to be listed in your current, home directory, by typing the command

   mkdir *Projects*

   Use the name *Projects* for the new directory because that is the name used in the following instructions and figures.

   The command **mkdir** is used to **make** a **dir**ectory. The new directory is generally listed in whatever directory you are in when you create it and is often called a subdirectory. Each new directory you create can contain a list of additional files and other directories.

2. Obtain a listing of the contents of the current directory, by entering

   ls

The new directory, *Projects,* is probably listed first unless you have filenames with uppercase letters. By giving directories names that begin with uppercase letters and naming files in lowercase, you can have the directories listed first when **ls** is run. So, to keep directories at the top of the **ls** output, use names like *Programs, Mail,* and *Memos* for future directories.

 NOTE: In this book, user-created directories are given names with initial letter capitalized. UNIX, however, does not require capital letters in directory names.

Figure 4-2 is a depiction of your home directory. The graphic for your home directory is in bold. The one for the new *Projects* subdirectory is not, to indicate that although you created a new directory, your

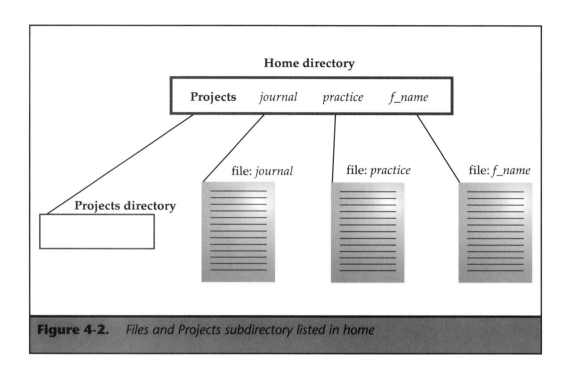

Figure 4-2. *Files and Projects subdirectory listed in home*

home directory is still your current directory, the one in which you are working.

Changing Directories

You can inform the shell that you want to change to a different directory, making it your current directory.

1. Change your current directory to the newly created *Projects* directory by typing

   cd *Projects*

   The command **cd** is the **c**hange **d**irectory command. Figure 4-3 indicates that your current directory is no longer your home directory; the subdirectory *Projects* is now your current directory. It is shown outlined in bold.

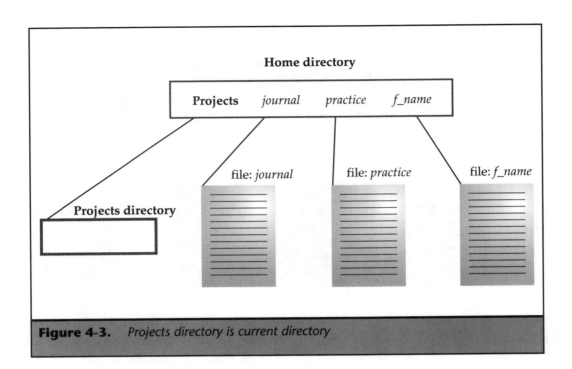

Figure 4-3. *Projects directory is current directory*

Examining the Path to Your Current Directory

Regardless of your present location in the file system, you can identify your current directory.

1. Examine the path to your current directory, *Projects*, by typing

   pwd

   The *path* is a list of directory names separated by the / (slash) character. In this example, the last directory listed is *Projects*. The one before it is the parent directory of *Projects*. The *Projects* directory is listed in its parent directory, which in this case is your home directory. Your home directory is listed in its parent directory, and so on.

   The **pwd** command prints the **pathname** of your current or working directory. The topmost directory, called *root*, is symbolized by the first forward slash (/) in the pathname. All other directories from *root* to the current directory are separated by slashes.

Listing the Contents of the Current Directory

On several occasions, you have obtained displays of the names of files listed in whatever directory was your current directory at the time.

1. List the contents of the directory that is now your current directory (*Projects*), with the usual command

   ls

   This time, nothing is listed. You have no ordinary files in the new *Projects* directory. The files that appeared when you last entered **ls** still exist, but not in this directory. The **ls** command displays only the names of the files listed in your current directory. You changed your current directory to be *Projects*, rather than the home directory, by typing the **cd** *Projects* command.

Creating Files Within a Subdirectory

1. With *Projects* as your current directory, create a new file named *testing*. Enter

   vi *testing*

2. Add a few lines of text to the new file.
3. Create another new file with the name *practice*, and add a line or two of text indicating that you are in a file in the *Projects* directory.
4. After you have created the two new files, list the filenames in the *Projects* directory by entering

   ls

   The files *practice* and *testing* are listed

Figure 4-4 illustrates the relationship between your home directory and its files. The files you just created in the *Projects* subdirectory are included.

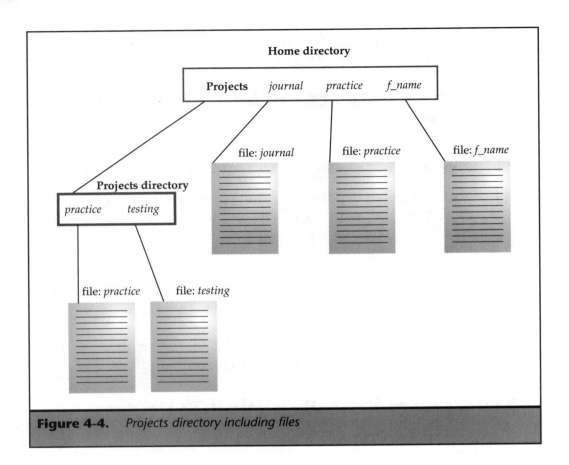

Figure 4-4. *Projects directory including files*

Returning to Your Home Directory

You used the command **cd** *subdirectory* (in this case **cd** *Projects*) to change the current directory from your home directory to the *Projects* directory.

1. To again make your home directory your current directory, type

   cd

2. Confirm that your current directory is now your home directory by typing

   pwd

The output of **pwd** is the same as when *Projects* was the current directory, except that your home directory is now the last directory listed and *Projects* is not listed.

No matter where in the file system you are currently working, the **cd** command, without any directory name as an argument, returns you home, making your home directory the current directory.

3. Change to the *root* directory by entering

   cd /

4. Confirm that you are at *root* by entering

   pwd

5. Return to your home directory by entering

   cd

6. Confirm you are home with

   pwd

7. Get a listing of the names of the files in your current directory by entering

   ls

   Projects appears, along with your other files, including a file named *practice*. Your home directory is again your current directory.

8. Examine the contents of the file *practice* with

   cat *practice*

   This file *practice* is *not* the one you just created in the *Projects* directory.

NOTE: Files can have identical names only if the files are listed in different directories.

Listing the Contents of a Subdirectory

When you run **ls** to determine the contents of your current (home) directory, the new subdirectory *Projects* is listed. However, **ls** does not output the names of the files listed in *Projects*, a subdirectory of the current directory.

1. You can list the contents of *Projects* without **cd**ing into it. Enter

   ls *Projects*

The way to get a listing of the contents of a subdirectory without leaving the parent directory is to use the **ls** command with the name of the subdirectory as an argument.

When **ls** is given *directory_name* as an argument, it displays the contents of the directory called *directory_name* provided *directory_name* is listed in the current directory. The **ls** command does not return a listing of information about the directory itself, but rather its contents.

Distinguishing Between Files and Directories

In this book, directory names have an uppercase first letter, to distinguish them from ordinary file names. The **ls** utility provides another way to identify directories.

1. From the shell, type the command

   ls -F

2. Examine the **-F** list. Directory names are displayed with a **/** appended to the end. The slash character is not a filename extension, but just a character added to the display by **ls** to indicate the nature of the object.

Filenames displayed with an asterisk (*) at the end are *executable* files, such as the scripts you created in Chapter 1 and Chapter 3.

The **ls** command interprets the **-F** option to mean "display a list of all files and directory names listed in the current directory, identifying directories with a slash, and so on."

Moving a File into a Subdirectory

To impose order on the chaos of an untamed home directory, you can move the listings of files from your home directory to a subdirectory.

1. Move the listing of *f_name* from the current directory to the *Projects* directory by typing this command:

   mv *f_name Projects/*

2. List the files in your home directory to see if *f_name* is still there. Type

   ls -F

   The file is not listed; it has been moved.

3. List the files in the *Projects* directory by typing

   ls -F *Projects*

   Your files *practice*, *testing*, and *f_name* are listed. The listing for the file *f_name* has been moved to your *Projects* directory.

4. Create a new file in your current home directory named *home-file*, then copy it into the *Projects* directory.

   cal *1996* **>** *home-file*
   ls
   cp *home-file Projects/*
   ls *Projects*
   cat *Projects/home-file*

   The syntax of the commands you just used to **m**ove or **c**opy files from the current directory to a subdirectory is as follows:

   mv *filename subdirectoryname*
   cp *filename subdirectoryname*

■ Summary

When the last argument in a **cp** or an **mv** command is a directory, the file is moved or copied into the directory, with the file retaining its original name.

Avoiding Mistakes When Moving Files into Directories

When you are moving a file into a subdirectory, what happens if you misspell the directory name?

1. Create a new file *trouble*. Then attempt to move it into the *Projects* directory; but when you type *Projects,* misspell it.

   date > *trouble*
   more *trouble*
   ls
   mv *trouble ProjectZ*

2. Get a listing of the files in the *Projects* directory.

   ls *Projects*

3. The file *trouble* is not there, so try the current directory.

   ls

   The file *trouble* is missing from here, too; but there is a new listing named *ProjectZ.*

4. Examine the file *ProjectZ*

   more *ProjectZ*

   The file *trouble* was renamed to *ProjectZ* when you issued the command

   mv *trouble ProjectZ*

   If the **mv** utility is given two arguments, it changes the names of the file listed as argument one to the name listed as argument two, unless the second argument is a directory. If the second argument is a directory, the file is moved into the directory. Because there was no directory named *ProjectZ*, the **mv** utility changed the name of *trouble* to a new filename, *ProjectZ.*

5. Change the name of the file back to *trouble*.

   mv *ProjectZ trouble*

6. This time, when entering the **move** command, place a slash after the directory name.

mv *trouble ProjectZ/*

This slash signals that you want the file *trouble* to be moved into a *directory* named *ProjectZ*. Because the shell cannot find *ProjectZ*, on most systems you receive an error message. Without the / at the end of the directory name, **mv** interprets your misspelled directory name as simply the new name for the file in a rename request.

When you issue the command **mv** *file directory* the system does not move the electronic file into the subdirectory. Directories do not contain files. Instead, the name and inode number, which provide information about the file, are erased from the current directory and written in the subdirectory. The new directory now lists the file's name and location information. This process of changing the location where a file is listed from one directory to another is commonly called *moving* the file.

Changing Filenames When Moving Files

In the commands you've used so far in this chapter, the files kept their original names in the new directory listings. You can also change the name of a file as you move it.

1. Create a file and move it into a subdirectory, with a new filename, by entering the following:

touch *junkness*
ls
mv *junkness Projects/treasure*
ls *Projects*

The file *junkness* is now in the *Projects* directory under a new name, *treasure*.

The syntax for the command to move a file listing from the current directory to a new directory and also change its *filename* is as follows:

mv *filename subdirectoryname/newfilename*

Removing Files from Subdirectories

You have just used the **mv** command to move a file from the current directory into a subdirectory, while remaining in the parent directory. You can remove (delete) files from a subdirectory in much the same way. Try this series of commands to remove the files *treasure* and *home-file*:

ls *Projects*
rm *Projects/treasure Projects/home-file*
cd *Projects*
ls

The files *treasure* and *home-file* are removed.

Creating Subdirectories Within Subdirectories

Earlier in this chapter you created the *Projects* directory as a subdirectory of your home directory. You can also create a subdirectory to be listed in the *Projects* directory.

1. Check to see that the *Projects* directory is still your current directory by typing

   pwd

2. Create a new subdirectory called *Code*.

   mkdir *Code*

3. Leave the *Projects* directory, and change to your new *Code* directory.

   cd *Code*

4. Make sure the *Code* directory is your current directory, with

   pwd

   This time the output of **pwd** consists of the path to your home directory, followed by */Projects/Code*. The new subdirectory, *Code*, is listed in the *Projects* directory. The *Projects* directory is listed in your home directory, and your home directory is listed in some other directory, and so on to the topmost directory, / (*root*).

5. Use an editor to create a file named *report3* in your *Code* directory that contains the following:

```
This is report 3 created in the Code directory.
```

6. List the files in the current directory by typing

ls -F

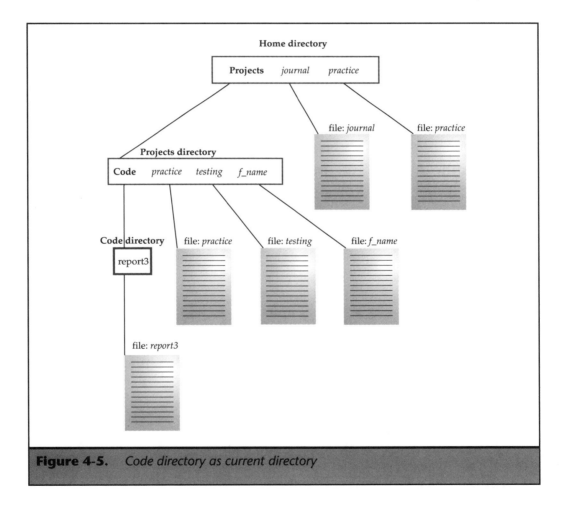

Figure 4-5. *Code directory as current directory*

You now have the file named *report3* listed in the *Code* directory, which is listed in the *Projects* directory, listed in your home directory. At this point your directory structure should look like the one in Figure 4-5.

Moving Through the File System

1. Change your current directory back to your home directory with

   cd

2. List the files and directories in your home directory with

   ls -F

   A complete listing of all the files and directories located in your main or home directory is displayed. The *Code* subdirectory and the file *report3* are not included because they are not listed in your home directory. Instead, they are listed in directories that are one or more levels beneath the home directory.

3. Enter the following commands, to move through the path to the *Code* directory and view the *report3* file:

   pwd
   cd *Projects*
   ls
   pwd
   cd *Code*
   pwd
   ls
   cat *report3*

   Your current directory is now your *Code* directory.

■ Review 1

1. What is the command to make a directory named *Proposals*?

2. What command changes your current directory to the *Proposals* directory?

3. What command changes your current directory back to the home directory?

4. What shell command can you enter to identify your current directory?

5. What **ls** command option tells **ls** to distinguish files from directories in its output?

6. Your home directory is your current directory, and you enter the command line **cd** *Projects.* You then create a file named *confused.* What directory will list the *confused* file?

7. How is it possible to have two files with the same filename in your account?

8. Assume your home directory is your current directory. What command will move a file named *florence* to a directory named *Proposals,* which is a subdirectory of the home directory?

9. Assume you want to move the file *ideas* from the current directory to a subdirectory named *Work,* and you enter the following command:

mv *ideas work*

When you examine the *Work* directory, the file is not listed there. Where is it?

4.2

Specifying Pathnames

In this section you use pathnames to identify files listed in subdirectories.

Using Pathnames to Change Directories

In the previous section, you moved through the directory system by entering a series of **cd** commands, such as **cd** *Projects* and **cd** *Code.* You typed a **cd** command for each directory change. There is an explicit way to reach distant directories in one **cd** command.

1. Make your home directory your current directory by typing the command

   cd

2. Examine Figure 4-5 again. Change your current directory from home to the *Code* directory in a single step by typing the following command. (Be careful to leave no spaces between the directory names and the / character.)

   cd *Projects/Code*

3. Check the path to your current directory by typing

   pwd

   Your current directory is now *Code*.

The command **cd** *Projects/Code* is the efficient way to change your current directory to a subdirectory (*Projects*) and then on to its subdirectory (*Code*).

The *Projects/Code* argument is a list of directories that describes where a directory or file is listed. *Projects/Code* is a pathname. In this case, *Code* is listed in *Projects*, which is listed in your current directory. This path instruction tells the shell to look in the current directory for a listing of *Projects*, then to look in *Projects* for a listing for *Code*, and then to make *Code* the current directory.

The shell keeps track of your current directory. A file name or directory name in a command line refers to a file or directory listed in the current directory. Pathnames are the mechanism used to inform the shell what path to follow to access a file or directory that is *not* listed in the current directory.

Using Pathnames with Utilities

Pathnames can also be used to make shell commands function on files not listed in your current directory. After the previous exercise, your *Code* directory is now your current directory. A few steps back, you created a file in the *Code* directory called *report3*.

1. Change directories to your home directory by typing

cd

2. Type the command

vi *report3*

This command results in one of two events. The editor begins the process of creating a new file called *report3* in your home directory. Or, if you already have a *report3* in the home directory, the editor will access that file. In either case, however, you do not access the *report3* file that is listed in the *Code* directory.

Leave the unwanted file and return to the shell by entering

:q!

3. To get to the desired *report3* file, you could change directories to your *Code* directory and then edit the file. Or, you can use the more efficient pathname. Use **vi** now to edit the *report3* file listed in your *Code* directory without changing your current directory from your home directory. Enter

vi *Projects/Code/report3*

NOTE: A pathname of a file combines both a directory path to the directory where the file is listed and the file's name, all separated by slashes. You can work with any UNIX utility on a file not listed in your current directory, by using the file's pathname.

4. Now make some changes or additions to *report3*, leave the file, and return to the shell.

Your current directory is still your home directory. Even though you worked on the file listed in a different directory, you did not change your current directory from your home directory. When you wrote the file with the **:wq** command, it was written to its directory, not to your current directory.

Copying Files into Other Directories Using Paths

Pathnames are particularly useful with the **cp** and **mv** commands. You can copy or move files from one directory to another.

Examine Figure 4-5. In this exercise, you'll copy the file *journal* to the *Code* directory and give it a new name.

1. Make sure your home directory is your current directory.

   cd

2. Type the following command (leave no spaces between the names and the / characters):

   cp *journal Projects/Code/journal2*

   With this command, you are giving **cp** two arguments, which tell the **cp** utility to

   - Make a copy of the *journal* file listed in your current directory.
   - Open the *Projects* directory to obtain information on the location of the *Code* directory.
   - Open the *Code* directory.
   - List the copy of *journal* in the *Code* directory.
   - Give the new copy the name *journal2*.

3. Confirm that *journal* was properly copied and listed in its new directory. Change from your home directory to the *Code* directory and list the files, by typing

   ls -i
   cd *Projects/Code*
   ls -i

   Because *journal2* was created as a copy, a duplicate electronic copy of the file is made. The new directory listing includes a new inode number that contains information needed to locate this new copy. Both the original and the copy can be edited independently.

4. Type this command:

cat *journal2*

and examine the contents of *journal2*.

SUMMARY: *The general form of the* **cp** *command is as follows:*

cp *filename Directory1/Directory2/newfilename*

where filename is a file in the current directory; Directory1 is listed in the current directory; Directory2 is listed in Directory1; and newfilename is the new name given to the copy of filename when it is listed in its new home, Directory2. You don't need to include the newfilename in the command. Omitting the newfilename results in the copy of the file having the same name as the original file. The same name is acceptable because the second file is in a different directory.

Listing the Contents of Subdirectories

1. Return to your home directory by typing

cd

2. From your home directory, use the explicit pathname to examine the contents of the *Code* directory. Type

ls *Projects/Code*

Any command that takes a *filename* or *directory name* as an argument will work using explicit pathnames like this one.

4.3

Specifying Paths with Directory Special Characters

UNIX has several characters that have special meanings in pathnames. Each character stands for a specific directory. Before exploring these special characters, you need to create two new directories.

1. Make certain you are in your home directory by typing

   cd

2. Create a directory named *Docum*.

   mkdir *Docum*

3. Now type the command

   ls -F

   Your new directory *Docum* is among the files and directories listed.

4. Change to the *Docum* directory.

   cd *Docum*

5. Create a file named *readme* in the *Docum* directory. Type

   vi *readme*

6. Enter a few lines of text and write this new file; then return to the shell.
   The file *readme* is now listed in the *Docum* directory, which is listed in your home directory.

Creating a Subdirectory Using a Pathname

Thus far you have only created subdirectories for whatever directory you were in (the current directory). You can also create subdirectories for remote directories.

1. Move back to your home directory. Enter

   cd

2. Make one more directory in the *Projects* directory, named *Corresp*. From your home directory, enter

   mkdir *Projects/Corresp*

3. Change to the *Projects* directory.

cd *Projects*

4. Find the names of the files and directories listed in the current directory, *Projects*, by entering

   ls -F

5. The new directory *Corresp* that you created while in your home directory is now listed in the *Projects* directory. Change to that new directory by typing

   cd *Corresp*

6. Create a file named *replies* in the *Corresp* directory, and add a few lines of text to it. Save the file and return to the shell.

7. Leave the *Corresp* directory and return to your home directory, with

   cd

   Your directory hierarchy now matches the structure in Figure 4-6.
       Look at Figure 4-6 and consider the following statements: You can change directories to directories located below the current directory, and you can change from a subdirectory back to your home directory. You have not yet, however, changed from one subdirectory to another subdirectory located on a different branch of a directory tree (from *Code* to *Docum*, for instance). The special characters introduced in the next section allow for changes of this kind.

8. Make sure you are in your home directory by typing

   pwd

9. Change to the subdirectory *Code,* by entering

   cd *Projects/Code*

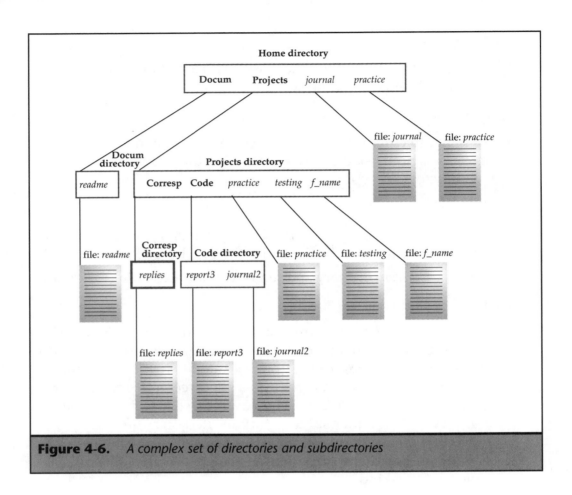

Figure 4-6. *A complex set of directories and subdirectories*

Explicitly Calling Your Home Directory

1. Your present working directory is *Code*. Without changing directories, obtain a listing of the files in your home directory by typing one of the following commands.

   For C and Korn shell users:

   ls ~

   For Bourne shell users:

   ls $HOME

2. Examine your current directory path.

pwd

Your current directory is still *Code*. The ~ and $*HOME* are interpreted by the shell to mean the user's home directory. Hence you are given a listing of the files in your home directory, while remaining in *Code*.

3. Access a file that is in your home directory without changing directories. Enter

more *~/practice*

This is the instruction to examine your home directory, look there for a file *practice*, and display it.

4. Change to the */tmp* directory by typing:

cd */tmp*
pwd

5 Return directly to *Code* by entering one of the following commands.

For C and Korn shell users:

cd *~/Projects/Code*
pwd

For Bourne shell users:

cd $*HOME/Projects/Code*
pwd

The previous **cd** command is instruction to examine your home directory for a directory named *Projects*, then look in *Projects* for the directory called *Code*, and make *Code* your current directory.

Using Parent Directory Names

There are other efficient ways to move around the file system. The techniques in this section are useful when you are unsure of where you are within the directory hierarchy, and when you want to enter more complicated commands.

1. Obtain a listing of all files in your current directory by including the **-a** option with the listing command, as follows:

   ls -a

   Your listing looks something like this:

   ```
   .       ..       journal2    report3
   ```

   You are in the *Code* directory and the files *journal2* and *report3* have appeared before. Dot and dot-dot are also listed.

2. Try the **more** or **pg** command to figure out what kind of file the dot is.

   pg .

   You receive a message indicating:

   ```
   pg:   . is a directory
   ```

3. Now examine the dot-dot (..) file by typing

   pg ..

   The output tells you the .. file, too, is a directory.

4. Confirm that your current directory is the *Code* directory.

   pwd

5. Change to the dot (.) directory by typing the command

   cd .

6. Determine the path to the dot directory by typing

   pwd

   The output of **pwd** says that your current directory is again *Code*. But *Code* was also your current directory before you typed the **cd .** command.

7. Obtain a listing of the contents of the dot directory.

ls .

The single dot is the name of your current directory. The dot is how your current directory accesses itself. All directories refer to themselves as . —it's the personal pronoun of Cyberville.

8. Change your current directory to the dot-dot directory by typing

cd ..

9. Determine your current directory by typing

pwd

You are now in the *Projects* directory. In Figure 4-6, *Projects* is the parent directory of the *Code* directory where you were located. The command **cd ..** has changed your current directory to the *Projects* directory, the parent.

The .. (dot-dot) is the listing for the parent directory. The parent directory is the directory located one level above your current directory.

10. Confirm your present location with

pwd

11. Now move up two directories with

cd ../..
pwd

12. Make *root* the current directory and try to go to its parent.

cd /
cd ..
pwd

At any directory level (except for the highest directory), you can type **cd ..** and you will change directories to the next higher (parent) directory.

13. Change back to the *Code* directory by typing the command

cd ~/Projects/Code

or

cd *$HOME*/*Projects*/*Code*

> **SUMMARY:** *It is possible to change directories in both directions within the file system. The command* **cd** *subdirectory changes from a directory to the subdirectory. The directory name must be specified because several directories may be listed in one parent directory. The* **cd** *.. command changes from a subdirectory to its one and only parent directory. The dot-dot symbol can be used because each directory has only one parent directory. The tilde ~ is used to specify the user's home directory as the starting point of a path. The dot specifies the current directory, and the / placed at the beginning of a path is instruction to start the path at* **root**.

Moving and Copying Multiple Files to Subdirectories

So far you have used the **cp** and **mv** utilities to change the names of files and to copy files within the same directory. You have also used these utilities to move or copy a single file into a subdirectory, as with the **mv** *practice Projects/* command. This section examines how to use **mv** and **cp** to move and copy multiple files into other directories.

Both commands have been used thus far with two arguments, such as **cp** *file1 newfile1*.

1. Make sure you are in your home directory, and try entering a **cp** command with these three filenames as arguments:

   cd
   cp *practice users_on journal*

   The **cp** utility displays an error message telling you only two arguments are acceptable, unless the last one is a directory.
       Commands with three filename arguments, such as **cp** *file1 file2 file3*, are ambiguous. Should the new *file3* contain both of the other files? Is *file1* copied and given two names? Because no clear meaning is attached, an error message is displayed.

2. Commands such as the following, however, *do* make sense. Enter

cp *practice users_on Docum/*
ls *Docum*

Again, three arguments are given to **cp**; but because the last argument is a directory, the meaning is clear. This command is instruction to copy both files (listed as the first two arguments) into the subdirectory (listed as the last argument.)

Both the **cp** and **mv** utilities accept more that two arguments, providing the last argument is a directory.

3. Create a new directory called *Archive*s by entering

mkdir *Archive*s

4. Copy several of your files into the *Archive* directory by entering

cp *users_on practice journal Archives/*
ls *Archives*

Just as you have done here with **cp**, you can use **mv** to move multiple files into a directory. Both **mv** and **cp** can affect many files as long as the last argument is a directory.

5. While you are in your home directory, create three files by entering

touch *cassy dimitri owen*
ls

6. Move all three files to your *Docum* directory by entering

mv *cassy dimitri owen Docum/*
ls

Because *Docum* is a directory name listed in the current directory, and it is the last argument in the command line, all three files are moved into that directory. They are no longer listed in the current directory.

7. Change directories to *Docum* and confirm that the listings have been moved. Enter

cd *Docum*
ls

Moving Files into a Parent Directory

1. Change directories to the *Code* directory, a subdirectory of *Projects*, which is in turn a subdirectory of your home directory, by entering

   cd
   cd *Projects/Code*

2. Confirm your current directory with **pwd**.

3. Move a file from the *Code* directory into its parent, the *Projects* directory. Type

   mv *report3* ..

   The last argument is a directory, namely the parent directory. So, **mv** moves the file into the .. directory. Because the *Projects* directory is the parent of *Code*, you have just moved the file *report3* from *Code* into *Projects*.

4. Return to the *Projects* directory.

   cd ..
   pwd

5. Confirm that the listing for *report3* was moved into *Projects*.

   ls -F

6. Now, move *report3* back to *Code*.

   mv *report3* *Code*

7. Create three files and then move them to your parent directory.

   touch *megan daniel betty*
   ls
   mv *megan daniel betty* ..
   ls

   The directory .. is a directory listed in the current directory. Since the last argument in the command line is .. all three files are moved into that directory.

8. Change to your parent directory and confirm that the listings have been moved, with

cd ..
ls

Examining the Full Path to Directories

The / (slash) character, which is used to separate directories and file names, is a path starting point. As examined before, the / by itself is also a directory.

1. Change to the / directory. Type

   cd /

2. Find the path to your current directory by typing

   pwd

   The output of **pwd** is a forward slash. The / is the name of the directory at the top of the directory tree.

3. Attempt to change directories to the parent of the / directory. Type

   cd ..

4. Find out what your current directory is by typing

   pwd

   Your current directory is still the / directory. Unlike any other directory, / is its own parent. Every file on the system is listed in the / directory or in one of its subdirectories. The / directory is called *root* because all other directories branch from it.

5. Change back to your home directory by typing

   cd

6. Examine the path to your current directory.

   pwd

The output of **pwd** is a list of directories starting with the /
character. If a pathname starts with a /, that first slash character
is the *root* directory. The remaining / characters in the list are
there to separate directory names. The output of **pwd** shows the
path from the / directory to your current directory, and is called
the *full pathname.*

Including Other Users' Logins
in Directory Paths

In earlier exercises you used the tilde (~) with the Korn and C shells as
a symbol representing your home directory. It can also be used to specify any user's home directory. On nearly all systems, the system
administrator can log on as the user *root*, after entering the appropriate
password. Once login is complete, a shell is started and the current directory is set to *root*'s home directory as specified in the */etc/passwd* file.

1. Examine the *root* entry in the password file by entering

   grep *root* */etc/passwd*

   You'll see a display much like the following:

   ```
   root:wAbLL/MiFOxBI:0:1:Operator:/:/bin/ksh
   ```

   The fields of this line are separated by colons. The sixth field is
   the home directory of *root*, usually /.

2. Request a listing of the contents of the home directory for *root* by
   entering the following command. Do not put any space between
   the ~ and the user id *root*.

   ls *~root*

   The files and directories listed in the *root*'s home directory are
   displayed.

3. Obtain a listing of the contents of the home directory of another
   user on the system by entering the following command, where
   otherlogin is the login id of a friend.

   ls *~otherlogin*

The contents of the home directory of the user whose name you specified are displayed if you have appropriate permission.

SUMMARY: *The tilde used alone is interpreted by the C and Korn shells to mean your home directory. The tilde attached to the login name of any actual user is interpreted to be that user's home directory. Paths to files may be specified starting with the tilde.*

For the tilde to work, the shell must determine where the home directory for your colleague, *otherlogin,* is located.

4. Request a display of the */etc/passwd* record for *otherlogin.* Enter

grep *otherlogin* */etc/passwd*

or

ypcat *passwd* **|** **grep** *otherlogin*

The next to last field in */etc/passwd* is where the home directory for *otherlogin* is recorded.

The shell consults the */etc/passwd* file when you use the tilde.

5. The shell interprets the tilde. Enter

echo ~

echo ~*root*

6. The tilde is interpreted to mean a home directory of a user; it cannot be used to specify any other kind of directory.

People often attempt to use the tilde to change directories to a directory that is an ordinary directory, not a user's home directory. For example, attempt to go to the */tmp* directory with the following command.

cd ~*tmp*

The error message indicates that there is no user on the system called *tmp.* Although there *is* a *tmp* directory, there is no user *tmp,* hence there is no *tmp* home directory.

4.4

Accessing Files in Remote Directories

Because the **cd** command allows you to move around a UNIX file system, at any moment your current directory could be any directory on the system. If you want to access a file that is not located in your current directory, you must specify a path to the file.

The following bulleted list shows summary commands for examination. Make sure you are in your home directory. In the previous sections you examined the following ways to specify a file's location:

- Specify the name of the file. For example:

wc *practice*

This is enough information if the file is listed in the current directory.

- Specify the path to a file starting with a directory that is listed in the current directory:

wc *Projects/Code/report3*

This is an instruction to first open the directory *Projects* listed in the current directory, then locate the requested subdirectory, open it, and so on. A path to a file beginning at the current directory is termed a *relative path*.

Specify a path to a new file named after one of your parents. You can start at *root*, regardless of your current directory:

touch */tmp/name*

ls */tmp/name*

This is an instruction to examine the *root* directory for the requested subdirectory, open it, and so on. A path starting at *root* is an *absolute path*.

In addition, the C and Korn shells allow you to

- Specify a path beginning at your home or any other user's home directory, regardless of your current directory. For instance,

wc *~/practice*
wc *~otherlogin/practice*

where *otherlogin* is a user. The second instruction is to look up the home directory for *otherlogin* in the */etc/passwd* file, and then use the path to that home directory in the command plus whatever additional path is specified.

Starting the Path Specification in the Current Directory

Perform the following exercises to explore examples of the various ways to provide a path to a file.

1. To access a file or directory that is listed in the current directory, you simply specify its name. Enter

wc -l *practice*
ls *Projects*

2. When you want to access a file or directory listed in a directory that is listed in your current directory, you specify the directory, then a slash, then the target file or directory.
Make sure you are in your home directory, and then create a new file in the *Projects* directory called *actions*.

cd
vi *Projects/actions*

3. Add text that is a brief description of how to access files at a distance, then write the file and quit the editor.

4. Obtain a listing of the files in the current directory, with

ls

The file *actions* is not listed in the current directory.

5. List the contents of the *Projects* directory.

ls *Projects*

The new file is listed.

SUMMARY: *A subdirectory is a directory listed in the current directory. In all instances where you want to access a subdirectory, you just specify its name. It is listed in the current directory, so the shell locates it.*

A common mistake is to use a slash in front of the requested directory—for instance, **cd** */Projects*. This is instruction to start at *root* and look there for the directory, *Projects*. The requested directory is not found and an error message is presented.

6. Change to the *Projects* directory, and obtain a word count of the *users_on* file, which is listed in your parent directory. Enter

cd *Projects*
wc *../users_on*

7. Because the .. directory is listed in the current Projects directory, it can be used as the starting point for the path to a file or one of its subdirectories. Enter

pwd

The output indicates that you remain in the *Projects* directory.

8. Access the *readme* file, which is located in *Docum*, which is located in your parent directory (see Figure 4-6).

more *../Docum/readme*

This command is instruction to look in the current directory for a dot-dot directory (your parent), then look in .. for the directory *Docum*, and then look in *Docum* for a file named *readme*.

9. Enter **cd** to return to your home directory.

The same procedure is available for specifying subdirectories of directories listed in the current directory, such as

ls *Projects/Code*
wc *Projects/Code/journal2*

Specifying the Absolute Path

Within any directory, all files and/or directories must have unique names. Except for *root*, all files and directories must be listed in another (parent) directory. The result of these two conditions is that every file on the system must have a unique pathname from *root*.

1. Identify the absolute path to your present directory.

pwd

The output of **pwd** is something like this:

```
/home/cassy
```

 *SUMMARY: The absolute path to every file in a directory consists of the path to the directory followed by a slash and the file's name. For example, the file passwd located in the **etc** directory has an absolute pathname of /etc/passwd.*

2. Ask for a display of the file *practice* located in the current directory by entering

wc *path-to-this-directory/practice*

Using the *cassy* example from above, you would enter

wc */home/cassy/practice*

Every file has an absolute pathname. It always starts at *root* (/) and includes the appropriate subdirectories. The file with an absolute path of

```
/home/cassy/Projects/code-phone
```

specifies that the file *code-phone* is located in the *Projects* directory. It must be a uniquely named file in that directory. *Projects* is listed in *cassy* and must be unique there, and so forth.

Specifying Paths Using Home Directories

The path specification can start at any user's home directory and proceed from there.

1. Change to the */tmp* directory by entering

   cd /tmp
   pwd

2. Without changing directories, get a listing of the files in your *Code* directory by entering

   ls ~/*Projects/Code*

   This command line is instruction to access the user's home directory, locate a listing for *Projects*, access *Projects*, locate a listing for *Code,* and then access *Code* to determine the names of all files listed there. The starting point is not the current directory, nor *root*, nor the parent; the starting point is simply the home directory of whichever user issued the command.

Accessing Directories Using All Methods

The activities in this section utilize the various methods of path specification you have studied in this chapter. It is suggested you read each instruction and try to accomplish the goal before reading the solution.

1. Make sure you are in your home directory, then obtain a display of the names of the files listed in the ***tmp*** directory, which is listed in *root*.

   cd
   ls /tmp

2. Confirm that you are still in your home directory by entering

   pwd

3. Copy your file *practice* to the */tmp* directory, and give the file a new name such as your login name.

   cp *practice* */tmp/yourloginid*

   (Instead of typing *yourloginid*, you could use the shell variable—either **$LOGNAME** or **$USER**, depending on your system.)

4. Without changing directories, obtain a listing of the files in */tmp*.

   ls */tmp*

5. Change directories to */tmp*, confirm your location, and obtain a listing of files.

   cd */tmp*
   pwd
   ls

6. Copy the file, *yourloginid* (which you just created here in */tmp*) back to the *Code* directory, which is in *Projects* in your home directory. Then obtain a listing of the files in *Code*.

   cp *yourloginid* *~/Projects/Code*
   ls *~/Projects/Code*

7. Change directories to *root* and confirm your location.

   cd */*
   pwd

8. Without changing directories, copy the file *report3*—which is located in *Code*, in *Projects*, in your home directory—to the *Docum* directory. (See Figure 4-6.)

   cp *~/Projects/Code/report3* *~/Docum*

9. Create a file named *friend-listing* in your *Projects* directory, containing the filenames listed in the home directory of a friend. Make *Projects* your current directory and confirm that the file was created.

> **ls** ~*login-of-friend* > ~*/Projects/friend-listing*
> **cd** ~*/Projects*
> **pwd**
> **ls**
> **more** *friend-listing*

10. While in the *Projects* directory, create a file named *greeting* in your parent directory containing the word *hello*.

> **echo** *hello* > *../greeting*
> **ls** *..*

11. Copy the file back to your current directory.

> **cp** *../greeting* .

12. Copy all files listed in your parent directory into the *Docum* directory.

> **cp** *../** ~*/Docum/*
> **ls** ~*/Docum/*

■ Review 2

1. Assume your current directory is not known. What command changes your current directory to a directory named *Education*, which is listed in a directory named *Proposals*, which is listed in your home directory?

2. From your home directory, what command do you enter to edit a file *kirby* that is listed in the *Proposals* directory?

3. From your home directory, how can you create a directory *Rejected*, listed in the *Proposals* directory?

4. How would you copy a file *selquist* from your home directory into *Education*, a subdirectory of the *Proposals* directory?

5. What command changes directories to the parent directory?

6. What command changes to the *Marilyn* directory listed in your home directory?

7. Assume that directories *Programs* and *Letters* have the same parent directory. How do you change your current directory from *Programs* to *Letters*?

8. How would you move the file *report7* in the current directory to the parent directory?

9. How can you copy all files from the current directory to the parent?

4.5

Managing Files from More Than One Directory

Whenever you create a file, it is listed in a directory, its parent. A listing for a file in a directory is called a *link*. You have accessed each file so far either from the parent directory, by specifying the file's name, or by including the parent directory in the pathname to the file. On UNIX, you can list or link a file to multiple directories.

1. Make sure you are in your home directory.

   Use the **vi**sual editor to create a file named *testing-links*.

   cd
   vi *testing-links*

2. Add the following text; then write and quit the editor.

   This file is listed in my home directory.

3. Confirm that it is listed in the current directory, your home directory, by entering

   pwd
   ls

4. Change directories to the *Archives* subdirectory and get a listing of its files.

cd *Archive*s
ls

Notice that the file *testing-links* is not listed in *Archive*s.

Listing a File in a Second Directory

1. Instruct the shell to also list the *testing-links* file using the name *testing2* in this directory.

ln *../testing-links testing2*

The file is being listed in or **linked** to a second directory. In this example, the file is given a different name in the second directory. It could be the same name, if you wish.

2. Obtain a display of the files now listed in your current directory.

ls

The file *testing2* is listed.

3. With **vi,** access the file *testing2* and add the following line:

And now listed in Archives, too

The *testing-links* file listed in the home directory is available in this directory with a new name, *testing2*.

4. After writing the file and quitting the editor with **:wq,** return to your home directory.

cd

5. Examine the *testing-links* file from your home directory.

more *testing-links*

The line you added when you accessed the file from the *Archive*s directory is in the file. It is the same file listed or linked to two directories. Figure 4-7 describes the linked file.

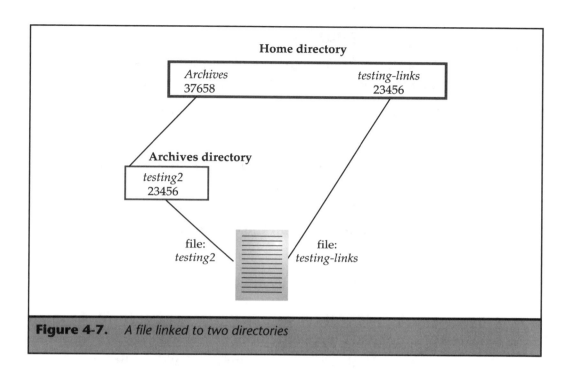

Figure 4-7. *A file linked to two directories*

6. Earlier, the index numbers, or inode numbers, for files were listed with filenames in a directory. Request a listing of the inode numbers for the current directory, by entering

   ls -i

7. Note the index number listed next to the *testing-links* file in the output of **ls**.

8. Likewise, examine the file index numbers for the *Archive* directory.

   ls -i *Archives*

   Both files, *testing-links* and *testing2*, are listed with the same inode number; they are the same file. There is only one file with one inode; however, it is listed or linked to two directories.

Removing Linked Files

Every file's index card, the inode, keeps track of the number of directories that list it. Each instance of a file listed in a directory is one link.

1. Obtain a long listing of the files in the current directory with

   ls -l

   In the listing, the field to the right of the permissions is the number of links or the link-count. The file *testing-links* has two links: the current directory and the *Archives* directory.

2. Remove the *testing-links* file from the current directory, by entering

   rm *testing-links*
   ls

   Although it was originally created in this directory, the file is now removed and not listed here any more.

3. Does that mean it is also removed from the *Archives* directory?

   ls -l *Archives*
   more *Archives/testing2*

   The file is still listed in *Archives* and is still the same file. When you remove a file, you remove its listing in the specified directory. If after the removal the number of links remaining is 1 or more, the file is kept. Only when it is no longer listed in any directory (i.e., when the link count goes to zero) is the file actually removed.

*SUMMARY: A file can be linked to multiple directories using the **ln** command. The first argument is the current filename; the second argument is the new directory, where the file is to be listed. A file is removed from any linked directory with the **rm** command. When it is removed from the last directory, it is actually removed.*

4.6

Moving Directories and Their Contents

You have used the **mv** command to move files into directories and to re-name files within a directory. Directories are just files that contain the names of other directories and files, with their associated index or inode numbers. Many file management operations are performed by modifying the contents of a directory. For instance, to change the name of a file is to change its entry in its parent directory. To create a new di-rectory is to create an entry in one directory that includes the new directory name and its inode, so that the shell can **cd** to or access the new directory.

Because directories are just files, it seems reasonable that you can change the name of a directory and move it in the same way you move and change names of other files. You can, as the next series of exercises demonstrate.

Changing a Directory's Name

Directories initially get named when you create them. The names can be changed by their owner.

1. Make sure you are in your home directory and that the *Projects* directory is listed.

   cd
   ls -F

2. Change the name of the *Projects* directory by entering

   mv *Projects Old-projects*

3. Obtain a listing of the contents of your current directory.

   ls -F

Notice that there is no *Projects* directory listed in your home directory anymore. However, *Old-projects* is listed.

4. Change directories into *Old-projects* and examine its contents.

cd *Old-projects*
ls -F

The contents are not changed; only the name of the directory is different. There is only one place the directory is named: the entry in your home directory that was modified to read *Old-projects* instead of *Projects*.

5. Return to your home directory and change the name of *Old-projects* back to *Projects*.

cd
mv *Old-projects Projects*

Moving a Directory

Whenever you create a directory, it is listed in your current directory. You can change where a directory is listed.

1. Obtain a listing of the files and directories in the current (your home) directory.

ls -F

The directories *Projects* and *Archives* are both listed.

2. Move the listing for the *Projects* directory from your current directory to the *Archives* directory.

mv *Projects Archives*
ls
ls *Archives*

Projects is now listed in *Archives*. Figure 4-8 depicts the directory structure before and after the move.

Your current directory, which is the parent directory of its subdirectories, contains the subdirectories' names and inode numbers. If you are owner of a directory, you can change the

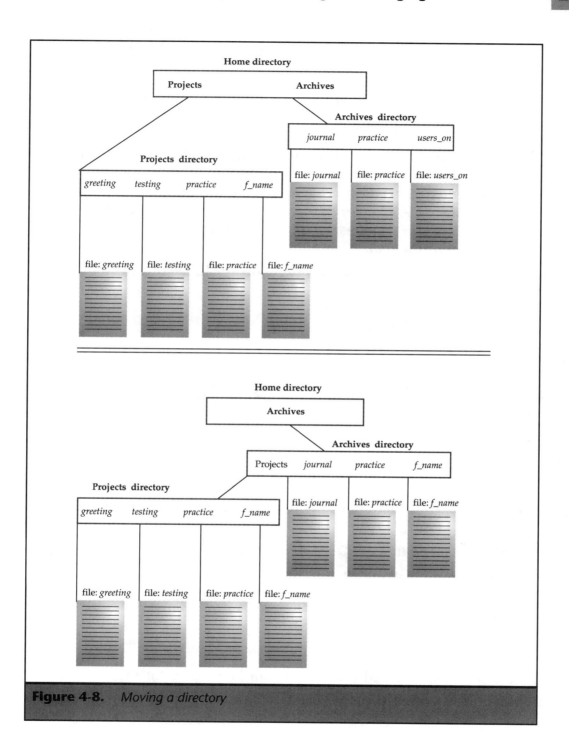

Figure 4-8. *Moving a directory*

directory where it is listed. If you change the listing, you "move" the directory.

3. Examine the contents of *Projects*, now listed in *Archives*.

   ls *Archives/Projects*

   When a directory is moved, its contents come along undisturbed. Moving a directory is just moving the listing for the directory from one parent directory to another. It does not affect the contents of the directory except that there is a new parent directory listed. It does not affect the moved directory's subdirectories at all.

4. Move the *Archives* directory back to your home directory by entering

   mv *Archives/Projects* .

4.7

Removing Directories and Files

UNIX provides commands to remove directories, just as there are commands to remove files.

CAUTION: Always use remove commands with great care, because often there is little chance of recovering lost items. Make sure you are in the appropriate directory for each of these activities.

Removing an Empty Directory

Two commands are available for removing a directory. The first command removes an empty directory—a directory with no files in it.

1. Move to your home directory with

   cd

2. List the files and directories in your home directory with

   ls -F

3. Change to the *Docum* directory by typing

   cd *Docum*

4. Check to see if there are any files in the *Docum* directory by typing

   ls

5. If there are any files in the *Docum* directory, remove or move them.

6. Return to your home directory with

   cd

7. Remove the directory *Docum* by typing the command

   rmdir *Docum*

8. Confirm that the *Docum* directory is gone by typing

   ls

9. Attempt to remove the *Archives* directory even though it contains files.

   rmdir *Archives*

   The error message indicates that the *Archives* directory is not empty, and **rmdir** does not remove the directory. Leave it as is.

Removing a Directory and Its Files

You have seen how the **rmdir** command removes empty directories. You can remove directories that are either empty or that contain files with an alternative command.

To remove a directory containing files, you must first locate the directory you want to remove. Use the **cd** command to change to the appropriate directory, or use pathnames to execute commands from your current directory.

1. To remove the directory *Code* from the *Projects* directory, first change to the *Projects* directory.

   For C and Korn shell users, type

cd *~/Projects*

For Bourne shell users, type

cd *$HOME/Projects*

2. Double-check that you are in the proper directory and that *Code* is listed.

pwd ; **ls**

3. Attempt to remove the *Code* directory. Type

rmdir *Code*

The directory cannot be removed with **rmdir** because it still contains files, so you receive an error message:

```
rmdir: Code: Directory not empty
```

4. To remove the directory *and* its files, type

rm -r *Code*

The **-r** option of the command instructs **rm** to recursively remove files. The utility starts by removing everything in the directory, including its subdirectories. Then it removes the directory itself.

5. Confirm that *Code* has been removed by typing

ls

Not only was the *Code* directory removed, but so were all the files in the directory, and any subdirectories you might have created in *Code*.

CAUTION: The **rm -r** *command has significant impact and should be used very carefully. Double-check that the directory you are removing doesn't contain any subdirectories that you may need. Move anything you want to keep to another directory before you use the* **rm -r** *command.*

4.8

Locating Files with find

As you create more and more complex directory structures, it becomes easier and easier to lose files. Fortunately, UNIX provides a utility that searches through directory trees to locate files.

Locating Files by Name

The file *practice* is located in several of your directories. They can all be located using **find**.

1. Make sure you are in your home directory.

   cd

2. Ask **find** to locate each file with the name *practice* and inform you of their pathnames by entering

   find .. -name *practice* **-print**

   The **find** utility often takes some time to complete its work. As **find** is working, it reports to your workstation both its output and any error information that is appropriate. You see the pathnames of files named *practice*, as well as information about which directories you cannot examine because of their assigned permissions.

   Following are explanations of each part of the command line in the above example.

Command	Interpretation
find	Instructs the shell to execute the **find** utility, which searches a directory and all of its subdirectories.

..	This argument specifies the starting point directory—in this case, the parent of your current directory. The result is a search of all directories listed in your parent directory, which includes your home directory and its siblings.
-name *practice*	Instructs **find** to locate all files with the specified name *practice*. In addition to locating files by name, **find** can also locate by age, owner, permissions, and so on.
-print	Specifies that the full pathname of each occurrence of the file(s) matching the selection criterion should be output. In addition to printing, **find** can be instructed to remove located files, change file permissions, or employ essentially any shell file manipulation command.

Locating Files by Owner

The **find** utility is used to locate files based on a variety of criteria.

1. Create a subdirectory in */tmp*, naming it with your last name.

   mkdir */tmp/your-last-name*

2. Copy three of your files to the new directory you just created in */tmp*.

   cp *practice names.tmp states* */tmp/your-last-name*

3. You now own three files located in one of */tmp*'s subdirectories. Instruct **find** to locate files owned by you by entering

   find */tmp* **-user** *yourlogin* **-print**

   The path to all six files is displayed.

   The result of this command is a display of all files belonging to the selected owner that are located in the directory tree that has */tmp* at the top.

Command	Interpretation
find	Instructs the shell to run the **find** utility.
/tmp	The first argument to **find**, instructing it to start its search in the */tmp* directory and search all directories below that.
-user	An option to **find**, instructing it to search for files by owner, not by name or any other criteria.
yourlogin	This argument directly follows the **user** argument and is interpreted by **find** to be the username whose files should be located. All files belonging to this user in the directory tree starting at */tmp* are located.
-print	Once files are located, this action takes place; in this case, the path to the selected files is output.

Putting find's Output in a File

In the previous exercise, the **find** utility completed a search of the directory tree below */tmp* and displayed the output on the screen.

1. Instruct the shell to redirect the output of **find** to a new file.

   find */tmp* **-user** *yourlogin* **-print** > *my-tmp-files*

2. After **find** completes its search, examine the output file *my-tmp-files*. In this file you see a listing of the pathnames for the files you own in */tmp*.

Locating and Removing Files by Owner

The **find** utility can be used to perform actions other than printing.

1. Enter

   find */tmp* **-user** *yourlogin* **-exec rm -r** {} \;

   The execution of this command results in the deletion of all files and directories belonging to the selected owner that are located in the directory tree with */tmp* at the top.

The command line just above, is interpreted as follows:

Command	Interpretation
find	Instructs the shell to run the **find** utility.
/tmp	The first argument to **find**, instructing it to start its search in the */tmp* directory and search all directories below that.
-user	An option to **find**, instructing it to search for files by owner, not by name or any other criteria.
yourlogin	This argument directly follows the **user** argument and is interpreted by **find** to be the username whose files should be located. All files belonging to this user in the directory tree starting at */tmp* are located.
-exec	Instruction to execute the command that follows it.
rm -r	Command to remove all files and directories recursively.
{ }	Symbol for the located filename(s). Whatever filename(s) **find** locates is substituted into the command following **exec** at the position of these curly braces. Hence, all located files become arguments to **rm**, and they are removed.
\;	Tells **find** where the **exec** command ends. A semicolon (*;*) is always required at the end of the command part of the **-exec** action. The backslash before the semicolon is required to tell the shell to not interpret it. If there's no backslash, the shell will interpret the *;* as a command separator.

The **find** utility, with the use of the **-exec** option, can be used to execute any command utilizing the filename(s) that has been selected.

The **find** utility is a powerful search tool. It allows you to search through specified directory trees, based on a variety of criteria, and then perform actions on the located file. The manual pages, as well, contain information about all the options, selection criteria, and actions that **find** interprets.

Review 3

1. What command would you enter to move the file *eakins*, which is in your current directory, so it's listed in your home directory?

2. What is the difference between the commands **rmdir** and **rm -r**?

3. Assume you are in the *Projects* directory, which has the subdirectories *Old-projects* and *New-projects*. What is the command to move the *Bookproject* directory from *New-projects* to *Old-projects*?

4. You are in your home directory where there is a file named *users_on*. What command will list the file in both your home directory and in the subdirectory *Projects*?

5. What command locates all files named *core* anywhere on the file system?

6. What command creates a new file named *myfiles* containing the names of all files owned by you on the system?

Conclusion

At this point you have moved around the file system and created and used directories. You have also accessed files using the special directory characters (., .., / and ~) and pathnames. You have removed directories and located files "misplaced" in the file system. By storing files in subdirectories, you can organize and manage your files, keep old copies of files, and remove groups of useless files. Files are accessed by specifying the pathname of the file. If no pathname is specified, the current directory is searched. The *root* directory, a home directory, the parent directory, and the current directory can all be used as starting points for the path to a file. The full pathname for a file is the list of directories, beginning with *root*, that must be traveled to access the file.

Directories, since they are a type of file, can be moved, removed, and renamed, the same way as files. Treating and maintaining a well-ing a well-defined and functional file structure is a necessary condition for the effective and efficient use of one's system.

◼ Answers to Review 1

1. **mkdir** *Proposals*

2. **cd** *Proposals*

3. **cd**

4. **pwd**

5. **ls -F**

6. *Projects*

7. The files exist in different directories.

8. **mv** *florence Proposals/*

9. The file is in your current directory, now named *work*.

◼ Answers to Review 2

1. **cd** *~/Proposals/Education*

2. **vi** *Proposals/kirby*

3. **mkdir** *Proposals/Rejected*

4. **cp** *~/selquist ~/Proposals/Education*

5. **cd** *..*

6. **cd** *~/Marilyn* or **cd $HOME/***Marilyn*

7. **cd** *../Letters*

8. **mv** *report7 ..*

9. **cp** * ..*

■ Answers to Review 3

1. **mv** *eakins* ~ or **mv** *eakins* *$HOME*

2. **rmdir** only removes empty directories, but **rm -r** removes a directory and all of the files and subdirectories.

3. **mv** *New-projects/Bookproject Old-projects*

4. **ln** *users_on Projects*

5. **find** **/** **-name** *core* **-print**

6. **find** **/** **-user** *$LOGNAME* **-print >** *myfiles* (or *$USER* on BSD systems)

COMMAND SUMMARY

cd *pathname*   Changes to the directory specified by *pathname*.

pwd   Displays the full pathname of your current directory.

mv *filename path/newfilename*   Moves the listing for the file named *filename* into the directory specified by *path*, and renames the file *newfilename* if it is specified.

mv *directoryname path/new_directory-name*   Moves the listing for the directory named *directoryname* into the directory specified by *path*, and renames the moved directory *new_directoryname* if it is specified.

cp *filename path/newfilename*   Puts a copy of *filename* into the directory specified by *path*, and names the copy *newfilename* if it is specified.

ls -a   Displays a list of files and subdirectories in your current directory, including files with names beginning with a period/dot.

ls -F   Displays the names of files in your current directory and places a / after directory names. Executable files are displayed with a *.

mkdir *directory*   Creates a new directory called *directory*.

rmdir *directory*   Removes *directory*, but only if it contains no files or subdirectories.

rm -r *directory*   Removes *directory*, as well as everything it contains.

Chapter Five

Specifying Instructions to the Shell

In UNIX, hundreds of utilities are available that accomplish many useful tasks. Among the many utilities are the command interpreters, or shells, that you use to communicate with the rest of UNIX. In the chapters of this book you have been examining the three most prevalent shells: Bourne, C, and Korn. You have learned how to enter shell command lines to instruct the shell to execute other utilities to accomplish tasks. When you enter a UNIX command line, the shell reads the command line and interprets each instruction, then sets up redirection of the utility's input and output, evaluates variables, passes arguments, and ultimately executes the specified utilities.

In this chapter you examine how the shell and other utilities interpret your command lines and accomplish the tasks you request. You have to "talk shell" when you issue commands. The shell interprets the grammar (*syntax*) of command lines in very specific ways. And of course, it does what you *say*, not what you mean. So it's important to employ correct shell grammar when you make requests and thus communicate your intentions exactly. The shell then does as you intend, and you get work done.

SKILLS CHECK: *Before beginning this chapter, you should be able to*

- *Create, edit, move, copy, view, and remove files*
- *Make directories and move around in the file system*
- *Use basic utilities to manage files and manipulate data*
- *Redirect output from utilities to files and to other utilities*
- *Issue basic shell commands including appropriate arguments*

OBJECTIVES: *Upon completion of this chapter, you will be able to*

- *Issue commands to the shell that establish where utilities read input, and write output and error information*
- *Use the command line to pass complex arguments to utilities*
- *Use the shell's special characters to communicate your intentions to the shell*
- *Identify the function of each element in a complex command line*

- *Construct command lines that include evaluation of local and environmental variables*
- *Use quotation marks and backslashes to control interpretation of special characters*
- *Instruct the shell to include the output of a command line as part of another*

The fundamental elements of the UNIX computing system are files, processes, and hardware. The hardware, which comprises the central processing unit (cpu), storage devices, working memory, connecting bus, and cables, could be used to run any one of several computing systems. When the hardware is running UNIX, the core program, called the *kernel,* manages the schedule of tasks undertaken by the cpu, allocates primary memory, and handles the input/output of terminals, disk drives, and other peripherals. The UNIX kernel program virtually defines UNIX. (This complex, extensive program has consumed an enormous number of programming hours. There is, however, no truth to the rumor that programmers who spend their time removing the kernel's rough edges are called Kernel Sanders.)

When you are logged on to UNIX, you do not communicate directly with the kernel. Rather, you tell the shell what you want and it translates your requests into the proper kernel *calls.* These calls instruct the kernel to do the work you request. When you ask the shell to run a utility, the shell must find the compiled program located in a file in the file system on the hard disk. Next, the shell asks the kernel to start a new process to run the code and to give the new process some computing time on the cpu.

In fact, even the shell is just another utility. It is started when you log on, to serve as the interface between you, other utilities, the file system, and the kernel. The shell's code is in a file in the directory */bin;* the shell gets cpu time; it sends messages, which the kernel places on your display; and generally behaves like any other utility.

One of the shell's primary functions is to read the command line you issue, examine the components of the command line, interpret the pieces according to its rules of grammar (syntax), and then do what you request. This chapter's exercises begin with a detailed look at how the shell interprets simple commands, and then proceeds through an investigation of how the shell works with complex command lines that call for programming, passing of information, and interpretation of special characters.

5.1

Interacting with the Shell to Execute a Utility

The basic way you communicate with the shell is to enter a command line that requests execution of utilities. When you examine the events carefully, even a simple command communicates a lot of information from your head to the shell. A continuous cycle takes place:

- The shell displays a prompt.
- You enter a command.
- The utility runs, or you get an error message.
- The shell displays a new prompt.

In fact, a lot happens between your entry of a command line and the execution of the utility—the second and third steps of this cycle. The shell must interpret each aspect of the command line.

Consider what happens when you enter the command **ls**:

- The shell interprets these two characters as a request to execute the **ls** utility. Why is it not interpreted as instruction to read the contents of a file named *ls*? Or to move the cursor to a lower section?

- Entering **ls** results in a utility being run. Where is the utility code located?

- The **ls** utility locates the names of the files in your current directory and then formats a listing as output. The output comes to your display. Why does it not get put in a file? Or on someone else's display?

- If you enter the command **ls -l**, the output is a long listing of the files in your directory. Is **ls -l** a different utility than **ls**, or is it the same code acting differently?

- If you enter the command **ls-l**, you get an error message indicating that the command **ls-l** is not found. But we know the **ls** command does exist. Why the complaint?

To answer these questions, let's take a closer look at the series of events that occur when you enter a command.

Parsing the Command Line

The commands you enter, such as **ls -l**, consist of words or *tokens*. The shell interprets some tokens as utilities, but how does the shell identify a string of characters as a token in the first place? For a command line that consists of one word or token, it is easy. The (Return) identifies the end of the command and therefore certainly the end of the single token. But how does the shell identify individual tokens in a long command line?

There is no music without the silence between the notes.

ThereisnoEnglishwithoutthespaces.

Likewise, the shell uses white space to identify the words or tokens of a command line.

1. Enter the following, including the several spaces between the tokens, and observe the results:

   ls   -l

2. Enter the following with three tabs and no spaces between **ls** and **-l**.

   ls (Tab) (Tab) (Tab) **-l**

   The shell runs the **ls** utility and passes it an argument **-l**, because the shell accepts white space—that is, (Tab) or (Spacebar) keypresses—in addition to the (Return) keypress, as *token delimiters* on the command line.

3. Enter the following:

ls -l | wc
ls -l|wc
ls -l|wc>*filesLS*

Without the spaces around the | and > redirection characters, the shell still identifies the **ls**, **-l**, **wc**, and *filesLS* strings as separate tokens on the command line.

The shell interprets white space, redirection characters, and other special characters as separating (delimiting) the command-line words or tokens.

Identifying Utilities to Execute

One of the steps the shell must accomplish in interpreting a command line is identifying the utility to run. In every shell command line you have ever entered in UNIX, a utility that the shell attempts to execute is listed as the first word or token on the command line.

Initial Word on a Command Line

1. Whatever string of characters you provide first on the line followed by a space, (Return), or other token delimiter is interpreted by the shell as a utility. Enter these characters at the prompt

abcdefg hij

The shell responds that the utility *abcdefg* is not found. The string *abcdefg* is the first token on the command line, so from the shell's perspective, it must be a utility. Unable to locate it in the directories the shell searches, the shell reports the error message.

Token Following Pipe Redirection Symbol

1. The initial token on a line is where the first utility is located. Its output can be redirected (piped) to another utility. Consider the following command:

   ls | wc

   When **wc** is placed after the pipe, the shell interprets **wc** as a utility to be executed, and connects the output from **ls** to the input of **wc**.

2. Now enter this command:

   ls | *abcde*

   This time the shell attempts to execute the utility *abcde* and pass it the output of **ls**. The shell again complains that the utility does not exist.

A word or token placed immediately after a pipe or at the beginning of a command line is interpreted by the shell as a utility to be executed.

Token Following In-Line Return

You can have the shell run one utility after another on a single command line without redirecting output.

1. Enter the following:

   ls; cd /*tmp***; ls; cd**

   The shell runs the **ls** utility and then, after the **ls** is completed, the change directory is accomplished. After you are in /*tmp*, **ls** is run again. After **ls** produces a list of files in the current directory, /*tmp*, a final **cd** brings you home. All is one command line.

   You do not need to press [Return] and execute the four commands on four individual command lines. Instead, you use semicolons (;) to separate commands on the line.

2. The shell interprets the semicolon as an in-line (Return). Enter the following and observe the results:

date; *abcd*

The first token after a semicolon must be a utility.

Following Conditional Execution Symbols

You can run a command based on the outcome (success or failure) of the preceding pipeline in the same command line.

1. Have the shell run the following:

cat > /etc/passwd && ls -l

You see an error message that you do not have write permission for the password file. The command **ls -l** is not executed. This is because the **&&** is interpreted by the shell as instruction to run the command that follows only if the preceding command line executed successfully.

2. Try this command line:

date && echo *hello*

This time, because the **date** command is successful, the **echo** is run.

3. Enter

cat > /etc/passwd | | ls -l
date | | echo *hello*

You again receive an error message that **cat** cannot write to the *password* file, but this time the **ls -l** command *is* executed. When the first command line runs, the command line after the | | does not execute. The shell interprets the | | as instruction to execute the command line to the right of the | | if the command to the left fails, and *not* execute the right if the left is successful. The **&&** is the other way: if the command line that preceded **&&** is successful, then execute the command line following **&&**. If the preceding command line is not successful, don't run the line that follows.

The first token after a | | or **&&** begins a new command line; it must be a utility.

After a Backquote That Includes Output of a Utility in a Command Line

Often it is useful to put the output of one utility in a command line that executes other utilities.

1. Enter the following commands and observe the results.

    echo *today is date*
    echo *today is* **`date`**

    The resulting output of the second command line includes the *output* of the **date** utility, not the word *date*. The shell had the **date** utility executed and replaced **`date`** on the command line with its output. The **echo** utility received as arguments *today is 23 April....* This is because the shell interprets the back quote character as instruction to have whatever is inside the back quotes executed and then to place the output on the current command line, replacing the back quotes and the command line they enclose.

2. Create a file named *some-files,* and include in it a line of text listing the names of four files in the current directory. For example, your *some-files* file might have this line:

    ```
    first-file   names   lost-days   west
    ```

3. Once *some-files* is created, enter this command line:

    ls -l **`cat** *some-files***`**

    The shell takes the output of the **cat** *some-files* command substitution and places it in the command line, creating an internal command line of

    ls -l *first-file names lost-days west*

    The four filename arguments and **-l** are passed to **ls**. A long listing of the four files is displayed.

4. Try the following two commands:

echo *My home directory is* `‛pwd‛`
echo *My home directory is* `‛abcd‛`

and observe the results.

In a command line, the first token after a back quote must be a utility. It starts the command that is substituted.

Placement of Utilities on the Command Line

Examine the following schematic of a command line. Each blank line represents a token.

_____ | _____ && _____ ; _____ ‛ _____ | _____ ‛ || _____

In this case, every token must be a utility.

utility | utility && utility ; utility ‛utility | utility‛ || utility

In summary, utilities are

- The first command or token in a command line
- The token that follows a pipe (the utility to receive input)
- The token that follows **&&** (the utility to run if the previous utility is successful)
- The token that follows a **;** (the utility to run after the command to the left of the semicolon is complete)
- The token that follows a **‛** (the utility to run for output to replace backquoted command line)
- The token that follows **||** (the utility to run if the previous utility is *not* successful)

■ Identifying Processes Associated with Execution of Utilities

When a utility is doing work—reading files, performing calculations, following instruction in its code—a *process* is underway. The shell's redirection of output and input is related to how processes are started.

Identifying Your Current Processes

1. You have used the **ps** utility in other exercises. This utility searches the kernel's table of running processes and outputs information concerning the processes that belong to you. Obtain a list of your current processes by entering one of the following commands:

   ps

   or

   ps -g

   Your shell process is listed, as is the process running the **ps** utility.

The output of the **ps** utility includes a *process identification number* (PID) for each process that you are running. Every process on your system has a unique PID so the kernel can manage each process individually.

Whenever you run a utility, a new process is started that executes the code, keeps track of variables, and generally accomplishes whatever the utility does.

Running a Command Line in the Background

When you enter a command line, the shell interprets it, executes needed utilities, and waits until the utilities complete their work. You can ask the shell to interpret, execute, and not wait but instead present a new prompt to you for continued interaction.

1. Enter the following command and observe the results:

   sleep 5

   When **sleep** has counted to 5, it dies. Your shell's wait is over, so it presents a new prompt.

2. Put sleep in the background by entering

   sleep 5 **&**

   When you enter the second **sleep** command line, the shell immediately presents a new prompt. You can then enter a new request. A command consisting of utilities, arguments, and redirection terminated by a [Return] is called a *job*. With the **&**, the whole *job* is placed in the *background*. The cpu still works on the job. The shell does not wait. Both get cpu attention.

Suspending a Job

The C and Korn shells allow you to *suspend* a job in midstream and return to it later.

1. Enter this command:

   vi *practice*

2. Add a line of text to the *practice* file.

3. Return to the command mode of **vi** and press

   [Ctrl]-[z]

   The job is suspended, not killed.

4. Enter

   ps

   The output shows that **vi** is still a process on your process list; however, it is not active. It is suspended.

5. Bring the job back into the *foreground* by entering

   fg

6. Put the file away and quit the editor.

   You can interrupt a foreground process and return momentarily to the shell using [Ctrl]-[z].

The topic of job control is explored thoroughly in Chapter 10, "Managing UNIX Jobs."

Identifying Multiple Processes from One Command Line

Processes are started after the shell completes its interpretation of a command line.

1. Enter this command:

   sort | **grep** *aaa* | **tee** *bb* | **wc**

   Because you have not specified an input source for **sort**, it is reading from your keyboard.

2. Suspend the job by entering

   [Ctrl]-[z]

3. Request a list of processes currently running, with

   ps

   All of the processes that you requested in the **sort, grep, tee, wc** job you entered above and then suspended are still running. Each utility included on a command line results in one process executing the code of that utility.

4. Bring the job back to the foreground by entering **fg** then [Ctrl]-[d].

Starting a Process to Run a Utility

The shell you are using is an active process, running in the foreground. The kernel has assigned a PID to your shell process. Environmental and local variables for it are kept in memory, shell code was located and is being executed. The input to the shell process is connected to your keyboard. Error messages and output from the shell are connected to your screen. The resources allocated to a running process are called a *process space* or a *process image*. Figure 5-1 depicts your shell process.

When you issue a command to run a utility, such as **ls**, the shell interprets the command line and then executes the utility **ls**—no simple task. Executing a utility involves the following steps:

- The first thing the shell does is request that the kernel make an *almost* exact copy of its own process space. The copy of the process space (Figure 5-2) includes the environmental variables, such as your user id, your search path, and your home directory. Environmental variables are passed to child processes. Because the new (child) process space is a copy of the shell, it has its input, output, and error connected to your screen and keyboard, as they are for your shell process.

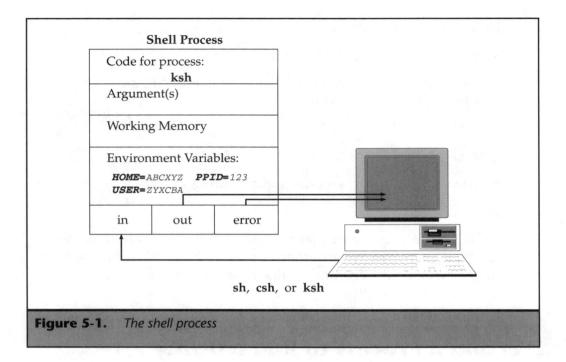

Figure 5-1. *The shell process*

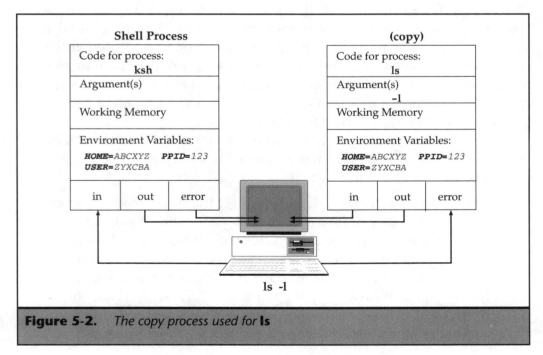

Figure 5-2. *The copy process used for* **ls**

- Next, the shell locates the code for the requested **ls** utility, has it loaded into the new process space, and has the process executed.

The result is that the **ls** utility code is being executed in a process that is quite similar to the shell's. When **ls** finishes creating a list of your files in the current directory, it writes to its output, which is connected to your screen because the shell's output was connected to your screen, and you did not redirect it.

Several users can be running the same utility at the same time because each is running a *different* process. Each process has access to the same utility instruction file, which was loaded when the utility was executed.

Running a Process Redirecting Input and Output

Consider what happens as you enter the command

> **ls** > *myfiles*

The shell again requests a copy of its own process space. Once the copy is created, the output is, by default, connected to your screen. Your instructions on the command line include the redirect symbol and a token that follows it, namely: > *myfiles*.

The shell interprets the > as instruction to redirect the output for the new process away from the workstation screen and attach it to the file *myfiles*. When the process runs the **ls** utility, its output goes directly to the file. (See Figure 5-3.)

You have also, in previous exercises, told the shell to redirect output of a utility to the input of another utility, and the output of a utility to a file. You've entered commands such as this:

> **who** | **grep** *yourlogin* | **wc -l** > *n-on*

The output from **wc** is placed in a new file and contains the number of times you are currently logged in. In this case, the command line tells the shell to run the **who** utility, which creates a list of logged-on users, and to connect the output of **who** to the input of **grep**. Then **grep** selects any line that includes your login. The output of **grep** is connected to the input of **wc**, which counts the number of lines in its input (which is the output of **grep**). The output of **wc** is then redirected to a new file.

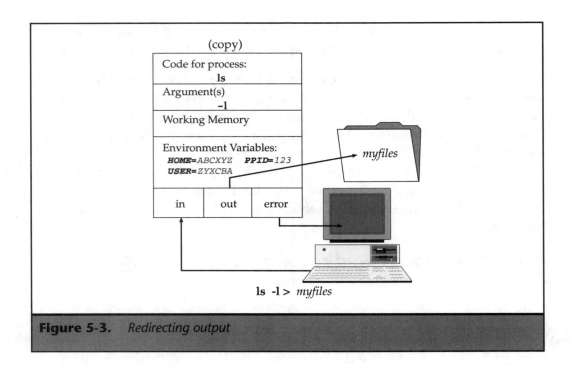

Figure 5-3.   *Redirecting output*

All of that is possible because the shell starts with copies of its own process space or resources, then does redirection of the default output and input.

Once the redirection of input, output, or error takes place and arguments are passed, the *processes* are started and the instructions in the utility file are read, or *loaded*, into memory.

Saying that a utility is "doing something" is another way of saying that the system is running a process that is following the instructions in the utility file.

 SUMMARY: *Redirecting input and output from the default (workstation) destination to files and other utilities is one of the functions of the shell. The shell's output, input, and error are connected to your workstation. Creating a new process begins with making a copy of your shell's process space. The input, output, and error are therefore initially, by default, each connected to your workstation, and remain there unless you instruct the shell to redirect one or more of them to another utility or to a file.*

Passing an Argument to a Process

Another task performed by the shell in interpreting your commands is to pass arguments to the utility being run. In an earlier exercise, you entered **ls-l** and received a message that the command was not found.

1. Examine the following command line:

ls -l *practice*

When you enter this command, including the space between the **ls** and the **-l**, the output is a long listing of the file *practice*. As you have learned, the shell uses white space as one of the ways to identify the pieces of a command line. The **ls** is the first token on the command line, so from the shell's view, it must be a utility. The **-l** is the second token. The filename *practice* is the third. These second and third tokens are the two *arguments*—strings of characters that have no special meaning to the shell. They are not the first token; they do not follow a redirection symbol and thus cannot be utilities. The shell is programmed to pass these strings to the preceding utility as arguments for the utility to interpret. To **ls**, the **-l** argument has special meaning; it is instruction to produce a long listing.

The **ls** utility interprets any arguments not preceded by a minus sign, such as *practice,* as the names of files. The result of this command, then, is production and output of a long listing of information about the file *practice*.

Any tokens left over on a command line when the shell has completed its interpretation are passed as arguments to the associated utility. Each utility interprets its arguments in its own way.

Using Options as Arguments

Command options, as well, are interpreted as arguments by the shell. You can specify more than one option to a utility on a single command line, each preceded by a minus sign.

1. Enter the following multiple-argument command line:

ls -a -l

The shell passes two arguments to the utility. These options tell the **ls** utility to output a long listing of **a**ll the files in the current directory.

2. For further flexibility, you can often specify two or more option flags on the command line as one argument. Enter these two commands and observe the results:

ls -al
sort -rd *practice*

Only one argument, **-al** or **-rd**, is passed to each utility; however, the utility interprets the one argument as instruction to follow the code of two options.

Comparing the Shell's View of Options with the Utility's View

Options have meaning to the utility; from the shell's view, however, the options are just arguments to be passed to the utility.

Examine the following utilities and their arguments, enter them if you wish:

ls -l
wc -l
pr -l *15 practice*

In all three instances, the shell passes the same argument, but it is interpreted very differently by the three utilities. To **ls**, the **-l** means produce a long listing. To **wc**, the **-l** is instruction to just output the count of lines in the input. To **pr**, the **-l** is instruction to make the page length equal to whatever argument follows.

Identifying the Function of Tokens on a Command Line

The shell is programmed to ascribe the role of each command-line token or word *based on its location* in the command line.

1. Enter the following:

   date > *wc*
   cat *wc*

   The first command instructs the shell to run the **date** utility and connect its output to a new *file* named *wc*. The second command instructs the shell to pass *wc* as an argument to **cat**, which in turn interprets *wc* as a file to open and read. The shell does not interpret *wc* as the utility to execute because the location on the command line says otherwise.

2. Enter another version:

   wc **-wc** *wc*

   In this case, the shell is told to execute the **wc** utility and then pass it two arguments: **-wc** and *wc*. To the **wc** utility, the two arguments are interpreted as instructions to output only the count of words and characters from the input file named *wc*.

3. Consider the following schematic of a command line containing a pipe character. Each blank line represents a token. What role must each token have?

   _____ _____ | _____ ; _____ _____ ` _____ _____ `

   The various tokens have specific roles.

   - The first token on a command line must be a utility to execute.
   - The token that follows a pipe, semicolon, or back quote must be another utility.
   - Any tokens left must be arguments to the foregoing utility.

   Thus the roles for each token in this example must be

   utility *argument* | **utility** ; **utility** *argument* `**utility** *argument*`

   This schematic represents a command line such as

   ls **-l** | **wc** **-l;** **grep** *alec* `**cat** *myfiles*`

4. Here is another example. What role must each token play in the following command line?

_____ _____ | _____ _____ > _____; _____ > _____

This command-line schematic is like the previous one, except here the output of two utilities is redirected to a file using the > redirection symbol. Whenever the > is used, the output from the previous utility is redirected not to a utility, but to a file. The token following the > must be a file.

5.2

Redirecting Output and Error

The preceding section examined how utilities and options are identified on the command line and how redirection takes place as processes are executed. This section explores output and error redirection in more detail.

The Output Redirection Symbols

Two symbols are used to tell the shell to redirect output: the > and the |. These two output redirection characters have distinct roles and cannot be interchanged.

1. Enter the following command, which asks the shell to redirect the output of **who**.

   who | sort

   The output from **sort** is displayed on the screen because you did not ask the shell to redirect it elsewhere.

2. Now enter

   who > *sort*

   When you enter this second command, you are greeted with a new shell prompt.

3. A new file named *sort* is in your current directory. Examine it with

   more *sort*

The command line **who** > *sort* instructs the shell to run the **who** utility and connect its output to a new file to be given the name of *sort*.

Both the | and > redirection symbols redirect the output from utilities. The pipe redirects output only to another utility. The > redirects only to a file.

Redirecting Output to an Existing File

When you redirect the output of a utility to a *filename,* the shell creates the new file. What happens when the file you specify already exists depends on the shell you are using and how the *noclobber* is set.

1. Make sure *noclobber* is off, so the shell will clobber (overwrite) existing files when redirecting output.

   In the C shell, enter

   unset *noclobber*

   In the Korn shell, enter

   set +o *noclobber*

When you redirect the output of a utility to an existing file, the Bourne shell interprets your command as instruction to overwrite the existing file. The Korn and C shells, as well, will overwrite the existing file if the shell variable *noclobber* is turned off.

Overwriting an Existing File

When you enter commands such as **sort** *file*, the **sort** utility reads the contents of *file* and outputs a sorted version. The original file itself is not sorted.

1. Often you will want to sort the file itself and may mistakenly enter commands like the following. Let's find out why these commands don't work. Make a copy of *practice* and then sort it using redirection, as follows:

   cp *practice pract-2*
   sort *pract-2* > *pract-2*

2. Now examine the contents of *pract-2*.

   cat *pract-2*

   What has happened? The shell first completes the interpretation of a command line, does all output redirection, and *then* executes the utility. In the **sort** command you just entered, the > *pract-2* is instruction to redirect the output of **sort** to an existing file. The shell empties the existing file before it attaches the output of **sort** to the file. The process running **sort** is then started and given the argument *pract-2*, which **sort** interprets as a file to read. When **sort** opens the file, it finds it is empty, making sorting quite easy! Many an important file has been lost by accidentally overwriting it with output.

Actually Sorting an Existing File

To sort a file, you can have **sort** read a file, sort the lines, and then have **sort** put the output back *in the original file.*

1. Create a file named *experts* and include the following lines:

   ```
   Georgia Holmes
   Marge Boercker
   Lillian Frank
   Mary Place
   Mary Lloyd
   Lelia Braucher
   ```

2. Instruct **sort** to sort the file and then replace its output back into the file, overwriting the unsorted version. Enter

   cat *experts*
   sort -o *experts experts*

3. Examine the *experts* file now.

   cat *experts*

   It is sorted.

The components of this command line are as follows:

Command	Interpretation
sort	Instruction to the shell to execute the **sort** utility.
-o	To the shell, this is an argument to be passed to **sort**. To **sort**, the **-o** is an option, interpreted as instruction to write the output to a file named as the next argument, rather than to standard output.
experts (first argument following **-o**)	This first occurrence of the argument *experts* follows the **-o**, so when **sort** is finished sorting its input, it writes to the file *experts*.
experts	This second occurrence of the argument *experts* is interpreted by **sort** as the name of a file to open, read, and sort.

The **sort** utility opens the file *experts*, reads it, sorts it, and then writes the output back to the file *experts*. Because the shell is not asked to redirect the output, it does not empty the file.

Protecting Existing Files

By turning the *noclobber* variable on, the C and Korn shells can be instructed to *not* overwrite files when you redirect the output from a utility.

1. Set the *noclobber* variable *on*, by entering one of the following commands.

    In the C shell:

    set *noclobber*

    In the Korn shell:

    set -o *noclobber*

Escaping noclobber in the Shell

There may be times when you actually do want the shell to overwrite a file while you have the *noclobber* variable set *on*. You can specifically instruct the shell to overwrite a file even though you set *noclobber*.

1. Make sure *noclobber* is on and then copy the file *experts* and use it in redirection. Enter the following commands:

   cp *experts experts-3*
   date > *experts-3*

2. Instruct the shell to overwrite using the output of a utility.

   C shell:

   date >! *experts-3*

   Korn shell:

   date >| *experts-3*

3. Confirm, with the **cat** utility, that the file was overwritten.

   cat *experts-3*

By placing the exclamation point (!) after the output redirect symbol (>) in the **date** command, you instructed the C shell to overwrite the file, if it exists. In the Korn shell, the >| is instruction to overwrite even if *noclobber* is set.

Avoiding Accidental Removal of Files with Other Utilities

Even when *noclobber* is turned on, you can still accidentally destroy files using utilities such as **cp** or **mv** if you copy or move an existing file and use the name of another existing file as the second argument. That's because the shell is not redirecting output, so *noclobber* has no effect. To protect yourself from accidental removal of files with the **cp** and **mv** utilities, employ the **-i**, inquire, option to the utilities.

See Chapter 23, "Modifying the User Environment," for information about making *noclobber* and **-i** options a part of all shells you execute.

Adding to an Existing File

With *noclobber* set, you cannot redirect the output of a utility to an existing file, but you can still *append* the output to the end of an existing file.

1. Enter

   ls >> *experts-3*
   cat *experts-3*

   The output of **ls** is at the end of the *experts3* file.

Redirecting Error Messages

When the shell or a utility is unable to perform a command, an error message is issued. Unless you redirect it, error output is displayed on your workstation screen. These error messages can be redirected from your screen into a file. The various shells work differently in this regard.

Korn and Bourne Shells

You can redirect standard error into a new file with Korn and Bourne shells.

1. Redirect standard errors into a file named *myerrors* by entering the following command. (Note: This command will not work as intended if your current directory has a file named *enlightenment*. If you have a file with this name, replace *enlightenment* with another name in the following command line.)

   ls *enlightenment* **2>** *myerrors*

   With the **2>** errors added to the command line, no error message is displayed, even though you do not have an *enlightenment* file and the shell generates an error.

2. Now examine the file named *myerrors*; enter

   more *myerrors*

   The error message is in this file.

   With the C shell, you cannot send only errors to a file.

C, Korn, and Bourne Shells

You can redirect both standard error and standard output together to the same file using any of the shells.

1. To redirect *both* standard error and standard output to the same file, enter one of the following commands.

   In the C shell:

   ls -l *enlightenment* **/etc/passwd >&** *err+out*

   In the Korn and Bourne shells:

   ls -l *enlightenment* **/etc/passwd 2>&1** *err+out*

2. Examine the result by entering

   more *err+out*

   The file contains both the long listing of the **/etc/passwd** file and the error message "enlightenment not found."

   In the C shell, the **&** after the redirection symbol tells the shell to route the standard error output, along with the standard output, to the named file. In the Korn and Bourne shells, the **>** *err+out* redirects standard output from the **ls** utility to the file. With **2>&1**, you are adding standard error.

C and Korn Shells

You can redirect all error output from jobs running in the background. You may not want to have your screen constantly bombarded with these background error messages as you are working in the foreground. If your system is lightly loaded try one of the following commands.

1. In the C shell, enter

   find .. -name *temp* **-print >&** *mytemp* **&**

   In the Korn shell, enter

   find .. -name *temp* **-print 2>** */dev/null* **>** *mytemp* **&**

The **find** utility looks for all files named *temp* in all directories starting with your parent directory. If a *temp* file is found, its full pathname is placed in the *mytemp* file. Then,

- In the C shell, when error messages occur—for instance, when a directory cannot be accessed—these error messages will also be placed in the file. Finally, the command is running in the background to allow you to perform other tasks.

- In the Korn shell, errors are sent to the "bin bucket in the sky," */dev/null*, the output to your *mytemp*.

■ Review 1

1. What is a token? How does the shell decide where one token ends and another begins?

2. What is the result of running the following?

   mail `` `cat `` *list* `` ` `` `<` *message*

3. Which tokens must be where on the following line?

   _____ | _____ _____ < _____ | | _____ `\_\_\_\_\_` _____

4. What is the result of running the following?

   cat *file1 file2* `>` *file1*

5. How can you overwrite a file if *noclobber* is set in the C shell? In the Korn shell?

5.3

■ Using Shell Characters to Specify Filenames

You can create filenames that contain common names with number or letter extensions. Then, by entering shell commands that contain special characters, you can match and select the filenames in groups. As the shell examines each command line you enter, it looks for the special characters. Some characters are interpreted as *wildcard* characters and used for matching unspecified characters of a filename. Other characters are used to select a range of characters for matching with filenames. This feature is often referred to as filename *expansion* or filename *matching*, because you can select many filenames while entering only one name with special characters embedded.

Matching Filenames Using Wildcard Characters

We often name files using a scheme that creates a relationship among the files. Using wildcard characters, you can list groups of filenames that have similar characteristics.

1. For instance, create empty files with the following commands that employ **touch**:

   touch *chap chapter2 chapter5 summaries*
   touch *chapter chapter3 chapter5A chapter57 chapter62*
   touch *chapter1 chapter4 index chapterA chapterR chapter2-5*

   The **touch** command changes the date associated with an existing file named as an argument. If the file does not exist, **touch** creates it as an empty file. It is a quick way to create files.

2. Obtain a long listing for a selection of these files. Enter

   ls -l *chap**

   This command contains the asterisk (*) wildcard character, which matches any character. The shell matches the string *chap** with names of files in the current directory. It replaces *chap** on the command line with all the filenames that begin with the characters *chap* followed by zero or more additional characters of any kind. Thus, the files named *chap*, *chap62*, and so on, are selected. The matched filenames are passed to **ls** as arguments. The **ls** utility then produces its long listing about those files.

3. The question mark (**?**) is another filename-matching character that is more limited. Enter the following command:

ls *chapter?*

This time, neither *chapter* nor *chapter5A* is selected, because the **?** character matches any *one* character—no more, no less.

The ***** and **?** are two of the special *metacharacters* interpreted by the shell.

As the shell interprets the command line, it does not open files. it just matches the filenames with the string of regular and metacharacters you enter, and then passes this list of matching filenames as arguments to whatever utility precedes the arguments on the command line.

Selecting Filenames Within a Range

You can have the shell match filenames that include letters or numbers that fall within a specified range.

1. Enter this command:

   ls *chapter[2-5]*

   In this case, the files *chapter2*, *chapter3*, *chapter4*, and *chapter5* are selected, but neither *chapter1* nor *chapter5A* are included in the output. The number *1* is not included in the specified range, and the filename *chapter5A* has a character after the number, which is not specified in the requested range. The file *chapter2-5* does not match because the [2-5] on the command line is interpreted by the shell as instruction to match one character, not the string *2-5*. Even the file *chapter2-5* is not selected. The square brackets tell the shell to match any filename that has *one and only one* number, in the range *2-5*, following the letters *chapter*.

2. To include *chapter5A,* in the selection, change the command to

   ls *chapter[2-5]**

   Adding the ***** tells the shell to expand the filename *chapter* to include one character from the list of numbers *2, 3, 4, 5,* and then zero or more of any other characters.

3. You can select filenames that contain more than one specified range of characters. Try this command:

ls *chapter*[1-9][1-9]

The selected filenames now include *chapter57* and *chapter62*, because they are the only filenames that start with *chapter* followed by one number and then followed by another number.

4. The characters listed in the brackets need not be a range. A list of acceptable values works, too. Enter

echo *chapter*[R3A1]

The output is *chapter1*, *chapter3*, *chapterA*, and *chapterR*.

Using the Curly Brace Expansion Characters to Specify Filenames

The curly brace characters { and } are also used for matching and creating multiple filenames from one pattern.

1. Enter the following:

echo *chapter*{1,3,5A}

2. Use the curly braces to attempt to select all files in a range.

echo *chapter*{1-7}

The curly braces match existing filenames but not ranges.

3. The curly braces can be used to expand a range for creating files or directories. Create five new files by entering

touch *ABC*{1,2,3,4,16}
ls *AB**

The shell creates new files with the name *ABC* and then adds each of the strings in the curly braces, hence *ABC1*, *ABC2*, *ABC3... ABC16*.

4. You may wish to make multiple directories that all begin with the same name. Enter this command:

mkdir ~/*this_is_a_long_directory_name_that_I_type-{one,two,three}*

5. Now examine the results:

ls

Notice that you have created three new directories:

In the command you just entered, the curly braces around the strings *one*, *two*, *three* tell the shell to use each portion to create a new file or directory name.

5.4

Storing and Retrieving Information Using Shell Variables

In the foregoing sections you learned the basics of how the shell interprets command lines, matches filenames, and executes processes to run the requested utilities. Next you will look in detail at the complex steps taken by the shell when it interprets a command line. First, you'll examine variables—creating them, evaluating them, and passing them to child processes.

Evaluating Existing Variables

When your shell was executed, it was given the names and values of many variables. You have been using them in commands such as these:

echo *$HOME*
echo *$USER*   (or *$LOGNAME*)
who | **grep** *$USER*

1. Ask for a listing of many of the current variables and their values by entering

set | **more**

The variables displayed are available to you because they are in your shell's memory.

Creating and Changing Variables

The shells each use their own syntax for creating a variable.

1. Enter one of the following commands:

   In the C shell:

   set *AA = 200*

   or

   set *AA=200*

   In the Korn and Bourne shells:

   AA=200

   All of these commands instruct the corresponding shell to place in memory the variable named *AA* with a current value of *200*.

2. Ask the shell to evaluate the variable in a command line by entering

   echo *$AA*

   The shell replaces *$AA* with *200* and passes *200* as an argument to **echo**.

   The shell interprets the **$** character as instruction to locate in the shell's memory the variable that has the name of whatever character string follows the **$**. Once the variable and value are located, the shell replaces the **$** and variable name with the variable's value on the command line. The result is the command line **echo** *200*. When executing **echo**, the shell passes one argument, the value of the evaluated variable, *200*, and **echo** writes its argument to standard output usually connected to your screen.

3. A variable's value is not etched in stone. Enter one of the following commands.

   In the C shell:

   set *AA = wonderful*

   In the Bourne and Korn shells:

AA=wonderful

4. Evaluate the *AA* variable now by entering

echo *$AA*

The new value assigned to the variable is reported.

Determining the Command-Line Role of a Variable

So far in these examples, the variables were placed on the command line as arguments to the **echo** utility. Using arguments with **echo** is a good way to have the shell evaluate variables and display the result. The location of a variable among the other tokens on the command line determines the ultimate role of that variable's value in the execution of the command.

1. Set the value of a new variable to the name of a utility. Enter one of the following commands.

   In the C shell:

   set *L=ls*

   In the Bourne and Korn shells:

   L=ls

2. Instruct the shell to evaluate the variable using it as an argument, by entering

   echo *$L*

3. Have the shell evaluate the variable when it is the first token on the command line. Enter

   $L

   The names of the files in the current directory are displayed. When you enter $L and press (Return), the shell is passed the command line $L for interpretation. It interprets the $ as a request to evaluate the variable L. The shell consults its memory and determines that *L* has a value of the character string *ls,* which is then placed on the command line, replacing the $L token. The $L was the first token on the command line. When the *ls* replaces the variable on the command line, it becomes the first token. Because the first token followed by a space *must* be a utility, *ls* is interpreted as the **ls** utility, so the shell executes **ls,** which lists the filenames in the current directory.

4. Change directories and repeat the command from step 3. Enter these commands:

   cd */tmp*
   $L

   The names of the files in the */tmp* directory are displayed. The variable is again evaluated to be *ls* and the **ls** utility is run, because of the location of **ls** on the command line. The shell keeps the variable names and values in its memory, not in a file. Therefore, regardless of your current directory, shell variables are available.

5. Change back to your original directory.

 *NOTE: The $L variable results in the **ls** utility being executed because the shell interprets variables before it determines which tokens are utilities to be executed. If the shell were to look for utilities before evaluating variables, the shell would complain about not finding the utility $L.*

Setting the Value of a Variable to Include Spaces

For programming purposes and user convenience, you will often need to set the value of a variable to include characters that are special to the shell.

1. At the shell prompt, set two variables, each consisting of a string of characters that includes a space.

   In the C shell, enter

> **set** *CC='-l -i'*
> **set** *DD='practice test-file'*

In the Korn or Bourne shell, enter

> *CC='-l -i'*
> *DD='practice test-file'*

2. Confirm the values by entering

> **echo** *$CC*
> **echo** *$DD*

Now each variable has a value that consists of two strings of characters separated by a space.

3. Employ the variables in the following command lines:

> **echo** *$CC*
> **ls** *$CC*

The variable *CC* has a value of *-l -i* when the shell evaluates it. Thus, after the variable's value is substituted, **ls -l -i** is the result. The shell executes **ls** and passes it the two arguments. The output is a long listing (**-l**) with inode numbers (**-i**) included for each file.

4. Extend the use of variables with the following commands:

> **echo** *$CC*
> **echo** *$DD*
> **ls** *$CC $DD*

A long listing, with inodes for the files *practice* and *test-file*, is output. The shell evaluates all variables, creating the command line **ls -l -i** *practice test-file*.

5. Variable interpretation can be carried to the limit with

> *$L $CC $DD > $L*

As a result of this command line, the shell interprets the $L variable (created several steps back) as **ls**, the $CC as *-l -i*, and $DD as *practice test-file*. The result is again the command line

> **ls -l -i** *practice test-file > ls*

6. Examine the history list for your C or Korn shell:

history

Notice that the list displays the command lines as you entered them, rather than after variable evaluation.

Avoiding Interpretation of a Space

When you created the *CC* and *DD* variables, you included quotation marks around the value for the variables.

1. Enter one of the previous commands, this time without the quotation marks.

In the C shell, enter

set *CC* = *-l* *-i*

In the Bourne and Korn shells, enter

CC=-l *-i*

An error message is displayed.

When you create variables for either shell, the value of the variable can be only one token or word on the command line. Often, however, you will need to include a space in a variable's value. To the shell, the space is a special character, interpreted as a token separator. When you entered the command without the quotes, the shell was allowed to interpret the space in the usual way. The shell thus interprets the *-l* as one token and the *-i* as another—too many arguments for variables creation, so a complaint is lodged.

To get the value *-l* *-i* passed as one token, you must put quotes around the argument to tell the shell to *not* interpret the space, as you did when you created *CC* and *DD* earlier.

Not Giving Local Variables to a Child Process

Thus far in this chapter, the variables you have created and evaluated have all been kept in the memory of your login shell. When child processes are started, many essential variables are passed to them, including *$PATH, $HOME, $USER*, or *$LOGNAME*, and so on. Such variables are called *environmental variables* and are given to child processes when they are started. The environmental variables are part of the parent process that is copied when a child is started.

But what about other variables? Are user-created variables such as *AA* given to child processes when they are executed?

1. Confirm that the following variables are set in your current shell:

   echo *$AA*
   echo *$DD*

2. Regardless of the shell you are using, start a child C shell and ask for evaluation of an environmental variable and of two of your local variables. Enter

   csh
   echo *$HOME*
   echo *$AA*
   echo *$DD*

   Only *$HOME* is an existing variable in the memory of the child process. The child shell was given the value for *HOME*, but not for the variables you created.

3. Exit the C shell, start a Korn shell, and again evaluate the variables.

   exit
   ksh
   echo *$HOME*
   echo *$AA*
   echo *$DD*

A child Korn shell works the same way: children do not automatically get local variables from the parent shell.

4. Exit the Korn shell and confirm that the variables are still available in your parent shell.

exit
echo $*AA*
echo $*DD*

Passing Environmental Variables to Child Processes

Variables such as *AA* were created in your current shell, are in its memory, and are available as long as that shell exists. They are *local variables*; they are not passed to child processes. The C, Bourne, and Korn shells allow you to pass user-created variables to child processes, but the mechanisms employed by the shells are rather different.

Creating a C Shell Environmental Variable

In the C shell, local and environmental variables are separate entities having lives of their own.

1. Make sure you are in a C shell. Instruct the C shell to create a new environmental variable, *AA*, by entering

setenv *AA 6060M*

The C shell syntax for setting environmental variables is

setenv *variable-name variable-value*

No equal sign is used.

2. Ask the C shell to list all of its environmental variables by entering

printenv

or

env

The variable *AA=6060M* is on the list.

3. Start a child C shell and evaluate the *AA* variable. Enter

   csh
   echo $*AA*
   printenv

   or

   env

   When the child process (and it could be *any* process) is created, the environmental variables and their values are given to the child shell. They are in the environmental variable list.

4. Start a "grandchild" process. Child shells do not have to be C shells to inherit environmental variables created in the C shell. This time try a Korn or Bourne shell. Once the new process is running, evaluate the variable.

   ksh
   echo $*AA*

   The environmental variable created with **setenv** in the C shell is a part of the child's child process.

5. Exit the Korn shell and the child C shell, returning to where you created *AA*.

   exit
   exit

Resolving Variable Conflicts in the C Shell

When you created the environmental variable *AA* you gave it the value of *6060M*.

1. Ask the shell to evaluate the *AA* variable with

   echo $*AA*

The value of *wonderful* is displayed. You have two variables called *AA*—one local to which you assigned a value of *wonderful*, and one environmental variable that you gave a value of *6060M*.

2. Tell the C shell to display its local variables:

set

3. Ask for the C shell's environmental variables by entering

printenv

or

env

Notice that the variable *AA* is on both lists but with different values. The local variable *AA* was created using **set** *AA wonderful* and is in the list displayed when you enter **set**. The environmental variable *AA* was created with **setenv** and is displayed when you enter **env** or **printenv**.

When you request evaluation of any variable, the C shell checks the list of local variables first. If the variable is located there, the local value (in this case, *200*) is used. Only if the variable is not found in the local list does the C shell examine the environmental variables list where the value (*6060M*) was found. The result is that in the C shell, a local variable takes precedence over an environmental variable of the same name.

When a child process is created, only the environmental variables are passed, so when you request evaluation of the variable by a child, the environmental value is the only one available.

Exporting a Variable from a Korn Shell to a Child Process

In the Korn shell, there is only one mechanism for creating a variable. Once created, though, any variable can be made *exportable* to child processes.

1. Create a new Korn shell variable, **LL** by entering:

LL = Fun
export *LL*

2. Create a child shell of any kind. Enter the appropriate command for a shell.

   csh

   or

   ksh

   or

   sh

3. Evaluate the *LL* variable.

   echo $LL

4. Start a "child of the child" process and evaluate the *LL* variable.
   Once you tell a Korn or Bourne shell to export a variable, it is given to all child processes and all their children, and their children's children, and so on. All children receive the variable.

5. Exit from the child shell, and return to the C shell where you created *AA*.

Listing Variables

In the C shell, local variables are listed when you enter the command **set**. Environmental variables are listed when you enter **env** on some systems and **printenv** on others.

With the Korn and Bourne shells, the **set** command gives you a listing of *all* variables—those that are exported and those that are local. To see just the exported variables, enter **env** or **printenv** in the Korn shell.

Removing Variables

Once a variable is set, you may need to remove it. The shells differ in this procedure, too.

Unsetting Variables in the C Shell

At this point you have a local variable and an environmental variable named *AA*.

1. Remove the local *AA* variable.

   echo $*AA*
   unset *AA*

2. List the current local variables.

   set

   AA is not there.

3. Request that the shell evaluate the variable *AA* and then list the current environmental variables:

   echo $*AA*
   printenv

   or

   env

   The display says that *AA* is still a variable and has a value of *6060M*, which is the value you gave *AA* when you created the environmental variable. Even though you removed the local C shell variable several steps back, the environmental variable *AA* still exists. Its value is used when the variable cannot be located in the local list. *AA* is listed with the environmental variables.

4. Instruct the shell to unset the *AA* environmental variable by entering

   unsetenv *AA*

5. Confirm the environmental variable is gone with

   echo $*AA*
   printenv

   or

env

To remove a local variable in the C shell, enter **unset** *local-variable.* To remove an environmental variable in the C shell, enter **unsetenv** *environment-variable.*

Removing Korn Shell Variables

The Korn shell removes variables using the same **unset** command:

1. To remove the *LL* variable in the Korn shell, enter

   unset *LL*

   Once *AA* is removed, it can not be exported. It is not available in local or any child shells.

2. Enter

   set
   env

   or

   printenv

   It is gone.

Removing Variables by Exiting the Shell

1. Create a child shell of any kind, for example a C shell. Set the value of a new variable.

   csh
   set *college='A great experience'*
   echo *$college*

   The value of the variable *college* is in the child shell's memory.

2. Exit the child shell and return to its parent, and then evaluate the variable *college* in the parent shell, with

   exit
   echo *$college*

When a child shell exits, it takes its memory of all variables with it. Parents are not informed of variables set in child processes.

TIP: *At the moment, you have several variables in your current shell. If you log out of the shell and return, these variables will not be in your new login shell. They die with the shell. If you want your shells to always create certain variables whenever you start them up—specific variables of interest—you can arrange this by putting the commands in control files that are read by new shell processes when they are created. See Chapter 23, "Modifying the User Environment."*

Mixing Shell Variables with Other Text on the Command Line

At times it is essential to append text to the end of shell variables—for example, when you wish to add a filename to the end of a variable that contains the value of the correct path to the file.

The next exercise assumes you have a directory named *Projects* in your home directory. If you don't have it, make one before continuing.

1. First, create a variable for the *location directory* by typing one of the following commands:

   C shell:

   set *locat* = *'~/Projects'*

   Korn shell:

   locat='~/Projects'

2. To tack a new directory name to the end of the variable, type

   echo $*{locat}/Internet-idea*

   Displayed on the screen is

   ```
   ~/Projects/Internet-idea
   ```

3. Create a new directory in *Projects*. Enter

> **mkdir** ${*locat*}/*Internet-idea*
> **ls** ~/*Projects*

(**or ls** $*locat*)

4. You can also place the curly braces around the text added to the end of the variable. Type

echo $*locat*{/*Internet-idea*}

The output is the same as from the command in step 2. The curly braces tell the shell where the characters for a variable stop and other characters begin.

5. Enter

echo {$*HOME*}/*abc*/*cde*/*fgh*

The output is the path to your home directory, followed by the characters /*abc*/*cde*/*fgh*. The pair of curly braces { } identify a string that must be kept together for variable evaluation.

6. The $ can be inside or outside the braces. Enter

echo {$*USER*}*ABCD*
echo ${*USER*}*ABCD*

SUMMARY: *Variables are labels attached to values that can change. Variables are kept in a process's memory, available to the user. Child processes are given copies of variables only if they are designated as environmental variables. You can delimit variables with respect to other characters with the { } special characters.*

5.5

Interpreting Special Characters

Many characters have special meaning to the shell. For instance, you used the $ to designate variables to be evaluated, in commands such as **echo $*PATH***. The shell located the variable *PATH* and passed its value as an argument to **echo**. In other commands you had the shell replace the * with the names of all files in the current directory. When the shell interprets a command line, it must make sense out of whatever special characters you include as instructions.

To Interpret or Not to Interpret...

That is the question. Whether 'tis nobler to evaluate a variable or leave it as a character string...

1. Enter the following commands and observe the results:

   echo $HOME
   echo \$HOME
   *

   The shell interprets special characters, except when you tell it not to. One way to turn off interpretation is with the backslash character; the backslash tells the shell to ignore any special meaning attached to the character that follows. In fact, there are three characters the shell interprets as instruction to turn off interpretation of other special characters.

2. Enter the following:

   echo *
   echo *
   echo "*"
   echo '*'

To the shell, the * is the filename-matching character. However, when the * follows a backslash or is inside single quotes or double quotes, the shell interprets the * as just an asterisk. For the **echo** commands above, if the * is interpreted, the shell replaces it with all filenames in the current directory. Hence, **echo** gets as arguments all file names. It then writes its arguments (filenames) to output, which is connected to your screen. If the * is not interpreted by the shell, the argument that is passed to **echo** is just the * character.

These three characters—backslash, a pair of single quotes, or a pair of double quotes—have special meaning to the shell; namely, to turn interpretation off or on when reading a character or string of characters.

In the following table, characters that are special to the shell are listed in the far-left column. Across the top, the column heads are the three characters that turn off interpretation. The table contains some information you've already learned about how the special characters are interpreted. In the remainder of this section you'll examine whether a special character is interpreted or not interpreted with respect to the backslash, single quotes, and double quotes and backslash. Fill in the table.

Special Character	When Inside " "	When Inside ' '	When Preceded by \
Space	_____	_____	_____
Newline	_____	_____	_____
?	_____	_____	_____
*	not interpreted	not interpreted	not interpreted
[	_____	_____	_____
{	_____	_____	_____
>	_____	_____	_____
<	_____	_____	_____
|	_____	_____	_____
$	_____	_____	not interpreted
`	_____	_____	_____
"	_____	_____	_____
`	_____	_____	_____
\	_____	_____	_____

Interpretation of Filename-Matching Characters

1. Make sure you have files named *chapter1* and *chapter2* in your current directory, by entering

touch *chapter1 chapter2*

2. Evaluate the other filename-matching characters. Enter these commands.

echo *chapter[0-9]*
echo *chapter\[0-9\]*
echo *"chapter[0-9]"*
echo *'chapter[0-9]'*
echo *chapter{1,2}*
echo *chapter\{1,2\}*
echo *"chapter{1,2}"*
echo *'chapter{1,2}'*
echo *chapter?*
echo *chapter\?*
echo *"chapter?"*
echo *'chapter?'*

The shell turns off all filename-matching special characters when protected by any of the three protection mechanisms.

Fill in the blanks in the previous table indicating that the [, {, and ? are not interpreted following \ or inside single or double quotes.

3. Enter

echo *'*

and press (Return).

If you are using a C shell, you receive an error message that there are unmatched quotes. This is because the shell interprets the first single quote as instruction to turn interpretation off. The shell is not told to turn interpretation back on with a matching single quote before you pressed (Return), so it complains.

In the Korn shell, you are now facing the secondary prompt—the Korn shell's way of telling you that you can't be finished with the command line. Like the C shell, the Korn shell, too, turns off interpretation when it encounters the first single quote. When you press a (Return), it is not interpreted as a (Return) because interpretation is off. The shell is still waiting for a (Return) to interpret as the end of the command.

4. Type an asterisk and another single quote, and press (Return).

The * is not interpreted; it's inside quotes and is passed as is to **echo** as an argument.

Interpretation of Quotes

1. Enter

echo "'"
echo '"'

2. The shell passed the enclosed quote in each case. The shell does not interpret single quotes if they are inside double quotes; nor does it interpret double quotes inside single quotes.

3. Now try

echo \'
echo \"

The shell interprets the quotation marks as just quotation marks without any special characteristics if they follow a backslash. Single quotes are not interpreted if they are inside double quotes. Double quotes are not interpreted if they're inside singles.

Variable Evaluation

Variables can be interpreted or not depending on how they are quoted.

1. Try placing a variable in the clutches of the "don't interpret" characters. Enter these commands:

echo $HOME
echo \$HOME
echo '$HOME'
echo "$HOME"

The backslash and single quotes both prevent evaluation of variables, but the shell evaluates variables even when they are inside double quotes.

2. Interpretation of double-quoted variables make several useful constructs possible. Enter

echo *I'm in $HOME*

An apostrophe to us is a single quote to the shell. Interpretation of the variable is turned off but not back on. With this command you get either a complaint (C shell) or a secondary prompt (Korn or Bourne shell).

3. If you have a secondary Korn shell prompt, enter a closing single quote and press Return.

4. Instruct the shell to not interpret the single quote, by entering

echo *"I'm in $HOME"*

The single quote is not interpreted, but the variable **$HOME** is—because the shell interprets **$** if it's inside double quotes.

Turning Interpretation On and Off

When trying to make sense out of quoted strings, the first look can be quite baffling. Consider the following:

"chapter[0-3]" chapter[0- 3]" chapter[0-3]"

Is the middle *chapter[0-3]* buried inside many quotes or not quoted at all?

1. Enter

echo *"chapter[0-3] " chapter[0-3] " chapter[0-3]"*
echo *'$USER ' $USER ' $USER'*

In both examples, the middle string is interpreted.

To make sense out of "shell quoting," imagine the shell maintains a series of on/off switches associated with the special characters. For each character, interpretation is either on or off.

Character	Interpretation
'	The shell starts at the left end of the command line and finds a single quote. The shell turns off interpretation of essentially all special characters. (Interpretation of the [and] characters is off.)
chapter[0-3]	All characters from the first quote are passed to **echo**, uninterpreted until the shell encounters a matching single quote. This string is passed to **echo**.
'	Shell finds the matching single quote and turns interpretation back on.
chapter[0-3]	Interpretation is on, so the filename matching takes place and a series of filenames are matched and given as arguments to **echo**.
'	Interpretation is turned off.
chapter[0-3]	This string is passed uninterpreted.
'	Interpretation is turned back on.

2. Enter the following:

    echo '*$USER*"*?' *$USER* '"$USER"'

Examine this command line from the left. The first single quote turns interpretation off, so the string *$USER*"*? is passed uninterpreted. The next single quote turns interpretation back on, and **$USER** is evaluated to be your login id. The third single quote turns interpretation back off, so "$USER" is passed literally. The last single quote turns interpretation back on, so the (Return) is evaluated. Figure 5-4 describes the interpretation.

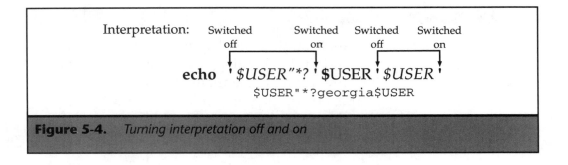

Figure 5-4. *Turning interpretation off and on*

Mixing Single and Double Quotes

By including both single and double quotes on a command line, we can examine their interactions.

1. Enter the following command (using **$LOGNAME** instead of **$USER**, if appropriate):

   echo ´"$USER"´

   The shell interprets the first single quote as instructions to turn off interpretation of the double quotes and **$** variable characters. Thus the argument *$USER* is passed as an uninterpreted string of characters.

2. Reverse the process by entering

   echo "´$USER´"

   In this case, the output is your user id surrounded by single quotes. The shell interprets the first double quote as instruction to turn off interpretation of the single quotes. Thus the **$** is still interpreted, and the variable evaluation takes place. The argument sent to **echo** is the value of the evaluated variable surrounded by the uninterpreted single quotes.

The key here is that, although **$USER** is surrounded by single quotes on the command line, those single quotes are inside double quotes, and therefore have no special meaning.

Using Back Quotes

1. Enter the following commands and observe the results:

echo *today is date*
echo *today is* `date`
echo *'today is* `date`*'*
echo *"today is* `date`*"*
echo *today is* \ `date\`

The shell interprets the backquote character as a request to perform command substitution. It says, "Replace the back quotes and their included command with the results of running the included command." If the back quotes are preceded by a backslash or inside a pair of single quotes, the back quotes are not interpreted. Inside a pair of double quotes, however, the back quotes *are* interpreted. Fill in the appropriate fields in the table.

The following table summarizes special-character quoting.

Special Character	When Inside " "	When Inside ' '	When Preceded by \
space	not interpreted	not interpreted	not interpreted
newline	not interpreted	not interpreted	not interpreted
?	not interpreted	not interpreted	not interpreted
*	not interpreted	not interpreted	not interpreted
[	not interpreted	not interpreted	not interpreted
{	not interpreted	not interpreted	not interpreted
>	not interpreted	not interpreted	not interpreted
<	not interpreted	not interpreted	not interpreted
|	not interpreted	not interpreted	not interpreted
$	interpreted	not interpreted	not interpreted
`	interpreted	not interpreted	not interpreted

Special Character	When Inside " "	When Inside ' '	When Preceded by \
"		not interpreted	not interpreted
'	not interpreted		not interpreted
\	interpreted	not interpreted	not interpreted

There are some differences between the shells.

2. Enter the following command in both the Korn and C shells:

echo *ABC[1-4]*

The C shell informs you there is no match with the files in the current directory. The Korn shell, upon finding no match, *passes the string uninterpreted* to **echo** as an argument.

5.6

Executing Commands in Scripts

In several exercises, you placed command lines in script files and had the shell execute them by entering the script names. Script execution is an important role for the shell.

Processing Processes

The currently running processes are listed when you request them.

1. Enter

ps

or

ps -g

Your current processes should include the **ps** and your shell. If you have more than one shell process currently running, count the total.

Identifying the Process Running a Script

When you ask to have a script executed, some process is doing the work. Which one?

1. Create a variable by entering

   In the C shell:

   set *a="Danny Colon"*

   In the Korn or Bourne shells:

   a="Danny Colon"

2. In your home directory, create a script called *programA* with the following contents (use **ps -g** if appropriate):

   echo *hello*
   echo *$HOME*
   ps
   echo *The value of a is $a*
   b="Gene Calhoun"
   echo *$b*

3. Make the script executable and run it.

   The results of the **ps** indicate that a new shell was running when the script was being executed. The new shell did not know the value of the local variable *a*, but did know the environmental variable's value.

   When you created a new variable in the child shell, the Korn/Bourne shell syntax was used.

   Whenever you ask a shell to execute a script by entering the script name, a child shell is executed to read the file and execute the commands. Your primary shell is protected from any disasters that may be in the script's code.

   - If your current shell is a Bourne shell, the child is a Bourne shell.

   - If your current shell is a C shell, the child is a Bourne shell. Because the Bourne shell is used by the C shell to execute scripts, the library of current scripts, written in the Bourne shell syntax, is available to C shell users.

- If your current shell is a Korn shell, a child Korn shell interprets scripts. Because the Korn shell syntax is a superset of the Bourne, all Bourne scripts still run in the Korn shell.

4. Add the following lines to the script *programA*.

echo *You are in* **`pwd`**
cd */tmp*
echo *you are now in* **`pwd`**
ls

5. Run the script and then determine your file system location.

programA
pwd

The script runs, it tells you that you are in your current directory, and then tells you that you are in */tmp*. After the script is complete, your current shell tells you that you are in your home directory.

The child shell evaluated the variable, ran **ps**, ran **echo**, made the trip to */tmp*, ran **pwd** while in */tmp*, and then the child shell exited.

Your current shell is informed and displays a prompt. You ask for a **pwd**. Your current shell is *still* in your home directory. The child took the trip and as usual did not inform the parent. It did not go to */tmp*.

Having the Current Shell Read a Script

When you enter a script's name, a child shell is executed to read the commands from the script and execute them.

1. Instruct your current shell to do the work.

In the C shell:

source *programA*

In the Korn or Bourne shells:

. *programA*

2. After the script runs, ask for your current location.

pwd

Your current shell is now actually in */tmp*. The output from **ps** does not include a child shell to run the script. The **source** and **.** commands instruct the respective shells to read the file. All commands are executed by the current shell. No child shell is executed for the task.

3. Return home by entering **cd**.

Passing Information to a Script

Some variables have particular meaning to the shell.

1. Create a script called *arguments* with the following contents.

> **echo** *hello*
> **echo** *$1*
> **echo** *$2*
> **echo** *$3*
> **echo** *$**

2. Make the file executable and run it.

> **chmod** *755 arguments*
> *arguments*

The variables have no values, so blank **echo** lines are displayed.

3. Run the script again by entering

> **arguments** *Butch Kaye Jason Amber Brandon*
> **arguments** *Helen Chellin Jerry Cathy Isaac*

The shell interprets **$1** as the value of the first arguments on the command line, **$2** is the second, ... **$*** is all arguments. User information can be given to a process by employing arguments.

4. Enter the following:

> **arguments** *"Bob Purdy" "Margot Smith"*

The result of the **echo $1** and **echo $2** lines in the script are displayed. The shell interprets the command line as containing only two arguments to be passed to **echo**—not four. Although there is a space between *Bob* and *Purdy*, the shell does not interpret the space as separating two arguments because the space is inside quotes. Interpretation of spaces is off. *Bob Purdy* is one argument, not two. *Margot Smith* is another.

5.7

Employing Shell Variables to Customize Interaction

Earlier in this chapter you instructed the shell to modify its behavior using the shell variable *noclobber*. Once a variable is set, the shell interacts differently. For instance, when ***noclobber*** is set on, the shell does *not* overwrite existing files when you redirect the output of a utility to a file.

In the C shell, variables are set by entering a command such as

set *noclobber*

and turned off with a command such as

unset *noclobber*

In the Korn shell, you turn a **set** variable on by entering a command such as

set -o *noclobber*

and turn it off with

set +o *noclobber*

NOTE: *To see a full list of* **set** *options available in the Korn shell, enter the command* **set -o**. *You'll get a list of options and the current status of each. See Chapter 23.*

Requesting the Shell to Complete Filenames

Because typing command lines with absolute accuracy is difficult to do, UNIX has a feature that allows you to give only part of a file or directory name and ask the shell to complete it. Operation of this feature differs among the shells.

Filename Completion in the C Shell

1. Make sure you are in a C shell.

2. Create two files by entering

   touch *zadigAAAA zadigBBB*

3. Request the shell to do filename-completion by entering

   set *filec*

4. With the filename-completion variable entered, type

   ls -l *za*

   but do not press [Return].

5. Press [Esc].
   The command line on the screen changes to

   ls -l *zadig*

   When you entered the *z* character at the end of the **ls -l** command and then pressed [Esc], the shell attempted to complete the word you started as the name of a file in the current directory. However, a complete filename was not produced, because the shell could not distinguish between two existing filenames. If no filename in the current directory matches the characters you enter, the shell will also beep. (In this situation, you need to enter additional characters until the shell can select a unique filename.)

6. Give the shell more information—enough to uniquely identify the filename. Enter

   A

   and press [Esc].
   The command line changes to

   ls -l *zadigAAAA*

7. Press (Return) to run the command.

8. You can also have the shell complete filenames in directories other than your current directory. Enter

    touch */tmp/AABBCC*
    ls -l */t*

    and press (Esc). The display is now

    ls -l */tmp/*

    Enter

    AA

    and press (Esc). The line **ls -l** */tmp/AABBCC* is probably displayed. When you have given the shell enough information to specify the file, press (Return).
       A long listing of the file in */tmp* directory is produced.

9. Remove it using file completion:

    rm */t* (Esc) *AA* (Esc)

The filename completion feature looks for matching file or directory names in directories specified on the command line—in this example, the */* directory. You can continue this process of entering characters and using (Esc) to produce a full pathname of a file or directory.

Filename Completion in the Korn Shell

The filename completion feature of the Korn shell functions in the same manner as in the C shell, except that instead of using the (Esc) key to request filename completion, you use the (Tab) key.

1. Exit the C shell and start a Korn shell.

2. Set the filename-completion variable in the Korn shell by entering

    VISUAL=vi
    set -o *vi-tabcomplete*

3. Try the same exercise in filename completion with the Korn shell as you did with the C shell, except you must use the (Tab) instead of (Esc).

Setting a Search Path for Directories

When you want a utility executed, you just enter its name. The shell searches through the directories listed in the *PATH* variable and finds the utility. When you want to change directories, however, you must explicitly state the path to the directory when you enter the **cd** command. There is also a way for you to designate directories in a *directory search path* that the shell can use to find directories, analogous to the utility search path.

1. Create the following directories and files. (Replace *LOGNAME* with *USER*, if appropriate.)

   mkdir */tmp/$LOGNAME*

2. If you are in the C shell, enter

   set *cdpath=/tmp*

   If you are in the Korn shell, enter

   CDPATH=/tmp
   export *CDPATH*

   The directory path variable now has just one directory that will be searched. You can add more.

3. Make sure you are in your home directory.

   Attempt to change directories to a directory with the name of your login, by entering

   cd $LOGNAME
   pwd

   You are in the directory */tmp/$LOGNAME* even though you did not just now explicitly indicate */tmp*. The shell examines the current directory and then the list of directories in the directory path variable for a directory with the name provided as an argument to **cd**. It found the directory named the same as your *LOGNAME* in */tmp*.

   When you enter a **cd** command, the shell searches the path listed in the C shell *cdpath* or the Korn shell *CDPATH* variable—just as it does when it attempts to find a particular utility file by searching the directories in the *path* or *PATH* variable. You can include multiple directories in your directory search path, as in the *path* and *PATH* variables, which list several directories. The format of both *cdpath* and *CDPATH* is the same, respectively, as that of *path* and *PATH*. The directories are searched in the order that they are listed.

4. Create a useful directory path by including some of the directories you commonly use.

Creating a Personalized Shell Prompt

If you don't like to see a % or $ as a shell prompt, you can create another. For example, you may want to have the full pathname of your current directory displayed as a prompt. Unfortunately, if you were to set the prompt to include your current directory, when you then change directories the prompt would indicate you were still in the previous directory. The next two sections describe how you can tailor your prompt in the C and Korn shells to include your current directory.

Including the Current Directory in the C Shell

1. Enter the following from the C shell command line:

alias *prom* **'set prompt="($***cwd***) "'**
alias cd 'cd \\!* ; *prom***'**

2. Change directories to */tmp*. The prompt changes.

In the C shell, these two **alias** command lines solve the problem mentioned just above, of displaying the current directory. Here you first created an alias named *prom* that sets the prompt to include the current directory (the value of *cwd*), followed by a space. The **cd** command is then aliased to be a regular **cd** followed by running the *prom* alias. Whenever you change directories, the prompt is reset to reflect the new location.

Including the Current Directory in the Korn Shell Prompt

The Korn shell evaluates the prompt automatically every time you change directories. Enter the following:

PS1='$PWD $ '

The variable *PWD* has a value equal to the path to the current directory. It is set every time you change directories, so evaluating it shows you your current directory.

Specifying the Code to Execute

After you enter a command that requests a utility to be run and the shell interprets the command line, the shell must locate the code for the program. The C shell variable ***path*** and the Korn/Bourne shell variable ***PATH*** contain a list of directories that are searched by the respective shells to locate the code for a utility.

NOTE: If you add a new directory of commands, or load a new application on your system, the path should be changed to include the directory where the new commands are located. Instructions on changing the path by modifying your housekeeping files is in Chapter 23, "Modifying the User Environment."

1. List the value of your *PATH* variable by entering

   echo $*path*
   echo $*PATH*

   The list of directories that is displayed tells you the places the shell checks for the utilities you include in any command line. Notice that one of the directories in your path is */bin*.

2. Obtain a long listing of the code file for the **ls** utility. This utility is located in the directory */bin*, so enter

   ls -l */bin/ls*

The output is similar to the following:

```
-rwxr-xr-x 1 root   65536 Jun 23 1995 /bin/ls
```

This file contains the executable program **ls**. It is the compiled version of the program, which includes a lot of control characters that will disrupt a workstation dramatically if you try to display the file using ordinary file-reading utilities.

3. Examine the character strings in the file by entering

   strings */bin/ls*

   A list of disjointed words and phrases is displayed. The **strings** utility ignores all machine code and outputs only the strings of ascii characters that it finds in its input. The displayed output from **strings** consists of the error messages and other character strings included in the binary file of **ls**.

4. To run a utility, you can provide the shell with the path to the utility code file, rather than have the shell check the path to find the code. Enter

   */bin/*ls **-l**

   When you provide a path to a utility, the shell does not have to use the search path to locate the utility.

The Elements of the Search Path in the C Shell

1. Make sure you are in the C shell.
2. To examine your current C shell path, enter

   echo $*path*

   The output is a series of directories, such as

```
(/usr/local /usr/ucb /bin /usr/bin  .)
```

   Each directory to be searched is separated by spaces. The **.** represents the current directory, which in this example is the last directory searched by the shell for commands.

   The *path* variable is a local variable. Normally, you assign its value in the *.cshrc* file so that its value is available to each C shell you create.

In addition to *path*, the C shell also maintains (but does not use for locating commands) the environmental variable *PATH*. This variable contains the same information as *path*, but in a format that is acceptable to other shells, such as the Bourne and Korn. *PATH* is then exported to them and used if you request a child Korn or Bourne shell. In the C shell, the two variables are intertwined, in that whenever you change the value of one, the other is automatically updated to reflect the change.

Changing the path Variable in the C Shell

The *path* variable can be changed to add new directories.

1. In your home directory, create a directory named */bin* if you do not already have one there.

   cd
   mkdir *bin*

2. Modify your path with the following command:

   set *path* = (*$path* ~/*bin*)

   This command sets the value of *path* to be the current *path* plus *bin* located in your home directory.

3. Confirm the new value for *path*.

   echo $path

4. Create a script named *2day* in your *bin* directory containing one line:

   date

5. Make the script executable and run it to confirm that it works.

6. Change directories and attempt to run the script by entering these commands:

   cd */tmp*
   2day

Even though the script is in your C shell path, the C shell does not find *2day.*

7. Enter

rehash

8. Now run the script.

2day

At login when you change the directories listed in the path variable, or when instructed with **rehash**, the C shell searches the complete path and creates a cheat-sheet (*hash table*) of utilities and the directories in which they are located. Once the table is created, the shell can locate a utility much faster because it only needs to consult the table rather than a dozen directories.

Once you modify the contents of a path directory, you must either log out and log back in, or enter the **rehash** command, to get the shell to re-create its table of utilities to reflect your changes.

Modifying the Path in the Korn/Bourne Shell

Unlike the C shell, the Bourne and Korn shells maintain only one path variable, *PATH*.

1. If you are not in a C shell, start one and enter

echo *$PATH*

2. Exit the C shell, and start a Korn shell.

3. Enter

echo *$PATH*

The format of the Korn shell *PATH* variable is the same as that of the C shell *PATH* variable. Notice, however, that the directory paths are separated by colons, not spaces. Also, because the path is one long string and not a list of directories, parentheses are not used.

4. Add a new directory to the existing Korn shell path list, by entering

PATH=$PATH:~/bin
export *PATH*

In this case, you are adding *~/bin* to the end of the string of directories in your path.

5. Create a new script in your */bin* directory and make it executable.

6. Change directories to */tmp* and run the script.

Because the Korn shell actually checks the directories listed in the *PATH* variable rather than referring to a hash table, you can modify the path and the shell can immediately locate the script.

In the Bourne and Korn shells, you can modify *PATH* with the following method:

Assign a string of directory names to *PATH,* as in

PATH=/bin:/usr/bin:/usr/local
export *PATH*

Including the Current Directory in the Path

A colon (:) at the beginning or end of a path string is interpreted by the Korn shell as instruction to search your current directory. You can also place an empty field using two colons :: or explicitly request the current directory, anywhere in the path, using a dot. If your current directory is to be included in your *PATH* variable, for security reasons it is best to have it listed last, as in

PATH=/bin:/usr/bin:/usr/local::

■ **Review 2**

1. How do you create a local variable named *tuesday* with the value *8-5* in the C shell? In the Korn shell?

2. How do you create an environmental variable called *OCT* with the value *NOT_PAID* in the C shell? In the Korn shell?

3. You have a global variable *LEVEL#* in the Korn shell with value *one*, and you start a child Korn shell. In the child shell, you enter the command *LEVEL#=two*. You now start another child (grandchild) shell. What is the value of *LEVEL#* now?

4. How do you enable filename completion in the Korn shell?

5. You want to find all records containing the string *happy* in some files. You know that their names begin with *monica*, followed by some character followed by one number between (*0, 1, 2, 3*) followed by one other number (*3, 4, 5, 6, 7,* or *8*) followed by more characters. What is the shortest command to find the records?

■ Conclusion

The UNIX shells are powerful command interpreters that read your command lines and take requested actions, including redirecting output, evaluating variables, performing command substitution, passing arguments, and executing utilities. Special characters are interpreted or not interpreted depending on whether or not, and how they are quoted. Words or tokens in command lines have meaning to the shell based on their location in the line, on the content of the tokens, and on their relationship to other tokens. The shell interprets a full programming language from the command line or by reading shell scripts.

You'll find an extensive examination of the shell's programming language in Chapter 22, "Programming with the Shell."

■ Answers to Review 1

1. A token is a string of characters (word) separated from other strings by white spaces, redirection symbols, or other special characters.

2. The file message is sent via **mail** to all users whose logins are in the file *list*. **cat** opens, reads, and outputs the logins from *list*. The shell passes the output list of logins to **mail** as arguments.

3. **utility** | **utility** *argument* < *file* | | **utility** `utility` *argument*

4. The shell issues error message warning you that the file you want to create already exists if *noclobber* is set.
   The shell empties *file1* to receive data and **cat** combines empty *file1* with data from *file2* and puts it in *file1* if *noclobber* is not set.

5. In the C shell, use >!
   In the Korn shell, use >|

■ **Answers to Review 2**

1. C: **set** *tuesday=8-5*
   Korn: *tuesday=8-5*

2. C: **setenv** *OCT NOT_PAID*
   Korn: *OCT=NOT_PAID*
   export *OCT*

3. *two*

4. **set -o** *vi-tabcomplete*

5. **grep** *happy monica***?***[0-3][3-8]**

COMMAND SUMMARY

Input, Output, and Error Redirection Characters

| Redirects output from prior utility to next utility

< Opens file on the right of symbol and connects it to the input of the utility on the left

> Redirects output of utility on the left into the file named to the right

>> Output from utility on the left is appended to the file on the right

>! Redirects output of utility on the left into file on the right; overrides *noclobber* feature (C shell)

>| Redirects output of utility on the left into file on the right; overrides *noclobber* feature (Korn shell)

>& Redirects the combination of standard output and standard error to the file on the right (C shell)

2> Redirects standard error to the file on the right (Korn shell)

2>&1 Redirects the combination of standard output and standard error to the file on its right (Korn shell)

Command-Line Control Characters

; Command separator. Executes each pipeline separated by ; as a separate command, although they are on the same command line

& Causes the command to be run in the background

&& Causes execution of pipeline on the right when pipeline on the left executes successfully

|| Causes execution of pipeline on the right when pipeline on the left does not execute successfully

` **and** ` Denotes beginning and end of command to be run and replaced by its result prior to the execution of other elements on the command line

Interpretation Controlling Characters

" " Turns off (and on) shell interpretation of some special symbols

\ Turns off interpretation for next single character

// Turns off and on interpretation of most special characters

Filename-Matching Characters

* Expands to match any number of any character (except . as first character in a filename) to be matched

? Expands to match any one character to be matched

[ ] Defines list of characters from which one is to be selected for matching

{ } Defines string to be included with adjacent string for matching or for generating new file or directory names

${ } Evaluate variable named in curly braces and merges with adjacent string

Shell Variable Commands

In the C Shell:

set *variable=value* Initializes or changes the value of local variable to *value*

setenv *variable* Initializes or changes the value of environmental variable to *value*

set Displays all local variables and their values

printenv *variable* Displays environmental variable and its value (BSD)

printenv Displays all environmental variables and their values (BSD)

env Displays all environmental variables and their values (System V)

unset *variable* Removes local variable

unsetenv *variable* Removes environmental variable

In the Bourne and Korn Shells:

variable=value Initializes or changes value of *variable*

export *variable* Makes *variable* environmental

set -o Special option of **set** command. Displays all options of **set -o**

set Displays all local variables and their values

printenv Displays all environmental variables and their values (BSD)

env Displays all environmental variables and their values (System V)

unset *variable* Removes *variable* (local and therefore environmental)

Initializing Shell Variables

set *filec* Turns on filename completion (C shell)

set -o *vi-tabcomplete*	Same as above (Korn shell)
set *noclobber*	Prevents overwriting files with redirection (C shell)
set -o *noclobber*	Prevents overwriting files with redirection (Korn shell)
set *cdpath=(/path)*	Sets path for user's **cd** command search (C shell)
CDPATH=*/path*	Sets path for user's **cd** command search (Korn shell)

Job-Control Commands

Ctrl-z	Suspends currently running foreground jobs
fg	Brings last suspended or backgrounded job to the foreground.
bg	Places suspended job in the background (will resume running there)
ps	Creates snapshot of process activity

Chapter Six

Setting File and Directory Permissions

ontemporary UNIX systems manage files that can vary greatly in their importance—from state secrets to casual notes. Hence, files on a UNIX system need different levels of protection. If a file contains, for instance, plans for a new product, then only a few users should have access to read the file. Its availability must be fairly restricted. In contrast, a memo intended for everyone must be accessible by all employees.

UNIX systems routinely store information in files and read program files. Even workstation terminal displays and other hardware are managed as files. Whether or not a user has access to each file is determined by a *set of permissions* attached to the file. By changing a file's permissions, you determine which users can read, modify, and/or execute the file. Fundamental UNIX security for users and for the system is based on carefully prescribing who has access to each file, through the permissions attached to files and directories. This chapter investigates how the UNIX file permissions work and how to modify them.

SKILLS CHECK: *Before beginning this chapter, you should be able to*

- *Access and leave the system*
- *Create and display files*
- *Name, copy, and remove files*
- *Execute basic shell commands*
- *Use several shell commands in combination*
- *Access and modify files using an editor*
- *Use the UNIX directory hierarchy system*

OBJECTIVES: *After completing this chapter, you will be able to*

- *Determine the permissions various kinds of users have for a specific file*
- *Change permissions for a file*
- *Change how the system assigns default permissions to new files*
- *Determine who is permitted access to a specific directory*
- *Change permissions for access to a directory*
- *Change the default permissions for new directories*

- *Modify permissions for whole directory trees*
- *Assign permissions appropriately*

6.1

Modifying Read and Write File Permissions

A person working on a UNIX system issues commands, enters data, writes programs, changes directories, and obtains information. All these activities are accomplished by accessing files that are utilized in three ways:

1. When you examine the contents of a file with utilities such as **pg**, **cat**, and **vi**, you *read* the file. The file is not changed, only read.

2. When you have completed editing a file and you type **:w**, you *write* the file, making changes.

3. When you issue a command, you *execute* a command file or a script located on the system.

If you own a file, you may either allow or deny permission for yourself and others to read, write, or execute the file. You can modify the permissions on a file for three classes of users: the owner or user (yourself), other members of your group, and all other users.

The first section of this chapter examines file permissions using letters and numbers to represent permissions. The second section investigates directory permissions. The last section examines how files and directories get their initial permissions.

Using Read and Write Permissions

To examine the contents of a file, you must have read permission for that file. To modify a file with an editor such as **vi**, you need both read and write permission for the file.

1. Call up an old file, such as *practice*, with the visual editor:

   vi *practice*

   You are able to read the file. Its contents are displayed on the screen.

2. Make a change in the file by adding some lines, such as

These are two new lines
I am adding to practice in this permissions chapter.

3. Write the file and quit the editor with the **:wq** command. You are able to make changes to the file because you have write permission.

Changing Permissions for a File to Read Only

You can restrict access to a file. For example, you might want a letter to be available to read but not to change in any way. To prohibit changes, you remove the *write* permissions for that file.

1. Examine the permissions of the *practice* file by entering

ls -l *practice*

The permissions displayed for this file are probably

```
rw-rw-rw-
```

The first **rw** tells you that the current permissions attached to the *practice* file allow you, as owner, to read and write the file.

3. Change the permissions, removing the write permission by typing this command:

chmod -w *practice*

The **chmod -w** *filename* command is instruction to **ch**ange the **mod**e, or permissions, for the file to remove write permission (minus **w**rite).

4. Obtain a listing of the permissions now, with

ls -l *practice*

Notice that you no longer have a **w** for **w**rite permission.

5. Use **vi** to call up the *practice* file again and make other changes to its contents.

6. Attempt to write the file with the usual **:wq** command. The resulting error message is something like

   ```
   File is read only
   ```

   You cannot write the changes. Because you do not have write permission, you are able to read the file, but you cannot alter the file's contents.

7. To return to the shell, you must quit the editor. Quit without attempting to write by typing the editor command:

   :q!

Changing Permissions for a File to Write Only

With one command, you can change the permissions for the *practice* file to add write permission and deny read.

1. Modify the permissions on *practice* by entering

   chmod -r+w *practice*

2. Examine the permissions on *practice*:

   ls -l *practice*

3. Attempt to read the file using

   cat *practice*

   The shell responds with an error message:

   ```
   practice:  Permission denied
   ```

   This error message indicates you do not have read permission on the file, hence you cannot read its contents. However, you still have write permission for the file. It is possible to write to a file, even if you cannot read it.

4. You can instruct the shell to connect the output of a utility to the end of an existing file. Type

date >> *practice*

This command specifies the output of **date** to be appended to the *practice* file. Because you have write permission for the file, you can add text.

5. Attempt to determine whether the addition was made to the file. Enter

pg *practice*

You are not allowed to examine the file because you do not have read permission for the file.

Adding Read and Write Permissions to a File

In the previous exercise, you limited the permission to only write for the file *practice*.

1. Reset the permissions for *practice* to allow reading, by typing

chmod **+r** *practice*

2. Use **pg** or **more** to confirm that you are able to read the file.

3. Notice that the date is the last line. It was added when you only had write permission for the file.

6.2

Using Execute Permissions

As you saw in earlier chapters, shell commands can be placed in a file and run all at once. This technique of creating command files, or *shell scripts*, can make your work more efficient and reduce errors.

Creating a File of Shell Commands

Shell scripts are created just like any other file, usually with an editor.

1. Ensure that you are in your home directory.

   cd

2. Create a new file named *inform*.

   vi *inform*

3. Place the following lines in the *inform* file:

   date
   pwd
   echo You have the following files
   ls

4. Write the file and return to the shell.

5. To run a shell script like any other UNIX command, you type its name and press ⌈Return⌋. From the shell, type

   inform

   If you get an error message that says

   ```
   command not found
   ```

   it means your path does not include searching for *inform* in the current directory.

6. Enter this command to specify looking in the current directory for the script *inform*:

   ./inform

   Instead of executing the *inform* command, you receive an error message:

   ```
   inform:   execute permission denied.
   ```

   Although the file contains a valid shell script, the shell does not execute it, because you do not have permission to execute the file even though you created it.

7. Examine the permissions of *inform* by entering

ls **-l** *inform*

Notice that you have read and write only; that is not enough. Once you have written a file of commands, you must set the file's permissions so that it will be an executable file.

Changing Permissions to Make a File Executable

The error message you received in the preceding exercise lets you know that the shell attempted to execute the file *inform*, but found that you did not have permission to execute it. This is only a plain, ordinary, non-executable file. You need to change the permissions for *inform* to be executable.

1. To make *inform* executable, type

chmod **+x** *inform*

The **+x** option grants execute permission for the file.

2. Examine the permissions now.

ls **-l** *inform*

Notice there is an **x** in the third field, indicating it is executable by you.

3. Execute the new **inform** shell script by typing

inform

You are treated to the display of the name of your current working directory, the path to your current directory, and a listing of all files in your current directory. The shell commands placed within your **inform** file are all run. The script is executable, and the shell executes it.

To make a file executable, the owner must change its permissions (or file mode) to include execute permission.

6.3

Examining the Long Listing for Files

Throughout the previous chapters, you determined the current permissions for your files using the **ls** command. In this section you examine the different parts of the long listing by **ls**.

1. Obtain a long listing of the files in your home directory by typing one of the following commands.

   On System V:

   ls -l

   On BSD:

   ls -lg

This command outputs a long listing on your screen similar to the following:

```
total 9
drwxrwxrwx 4 cassy staff    544  Nov 13 17:04 Projects
-rwxrwxrwx 1 cassy staff   1452 Sep 7   11:58 inform
-rw-rw-rw- 1 cassy staff   1452 Sep 7   11:58 journal
-rw------- 1 cassy staff   1064 Sep 2   21:14 practice
-rw-rw-rw- 1 cassy staff   6100 Oct 12  11:32 practiceA
```

The first piece of information seen here (*total 9*) indicates the total number of data blocks used by the current directory—in this case, 9. Each line that follows is the long listing of information for one file or directory in your current directory.

Identifying the Fields in a Long Listing Entry

In a long listing entry, or record, the information for each file or directory is divided into seven fields. In the example just discussed, the first record's fields are as follows:

Permissions Field	No. of Links	File's Owner	File's Group	Size in Bytes	Date of Last Modification	Directory or File Name
drwxrwxrwx	4	cassy	staff	544	Nov 13 17:04	Projects

Permissions Field

This first field is ten characters long and may have a **d** as the first character:

drwxrwxrwx

or

-rw-rw-rw-

When the first character is a **d**, the listing is for a directory. The remaining characters specify the permissions for the directory. The listing for the file *inform* has a minus sign in the first position of the first field because *inform* is not a directory, but a file.

Links

The second field in each record is a number, such as *1, 2, 3, 4,* and so on. This number indicates the number of directory entries that refer to that file. In a previous chapter, you created the *Projects* directory in your current directory. There are four directories that have entries that refer to the *Projects* directory: *Projects*'s parent directory lists *Projects*; the *Projects* directory lists itself as the **.** directory; and the two subdirectories of *Projects* each has a listing for its parent, *Projects*, the **..** directory.

Files generally have a *1* in this field, indicating that they are listed in their parent directory only. If a file is listed to two directories, it is said to be *linked* to both directories, and has a *2* in this field.

Owner

The third field of the long listing is the login name of the owner of the file (in some contexts, the owner is called the user). In this example, *cassy* is the name of the file owner.

Group

The fourth field is the name of the group associated with the file. In this example, the group is *staff*. Groups are used to gather together various users who need to share access to the same files. Groups in UNIX are like departments in a company—the group is a name for several users working on a similar project. Every user belongs to at least one group. Access to a file can be granted for all users in a group and denied to members of all other groups.

Size

The fifth field of the listing is the length of the file in bytes.

Modification Date

This sixth field tells you the date the file was last altered.

Filename

The last field is the name given to the file.

Determining Who Can Modify Permissions

Throughout these chapters you have changed the permissions of *practice* and other files. For system security reasons, there are limits to what files you can affect.

1. Determine who you are by entering one of the following commands:

   whoami

   or

   who am i

   The output you see is your login name.

NOTE: *If you are **root**, log out and then log back on as an ordinary user; then continue with step 2.*

2. Determine the current permissions of the file *date* in the */bin* directory by entering

   ls -l */bin/date*

   The output shows that although everyone can execute the date utility, you are not the owner of the */bin/date* file.

3. Attempt to make */bin/date* writable by everyone, by entering

   chmod +w */bin/date*

   The permissions are not changed, and an error message indicates that you are not the owner of the file. Only the owner can change file permissions.

Examining the Permissions Field

Reexamine the permissions for all the regular files in your home directory, by entering either **ls -l** or **ls -lg**. In the permissions field there are ten slots for each file. For example:

```
-rwxr-x--x
```

Every slot is occupied either by a minus sign or by a letter. A minus sign in a slot indicates that the particular permission is denied. If a letter appears in the slot, it indicates a permission is allowed. The letters you see will usually be **r**, **w**, **x**, or **d**, and for some files you might also see **b**, **c**, **l**, **p**, **s**, or **S**, **t**, or **T**.

Directory

The first slot indicates whether the listing is for a directory, a plain file, or a special UNIX file. A **d** indicates a directory; a minus sign specifies a file other than a directory. The first character in the permissions field for the file *inform* is a minus sign, indicating that *inform* is a regular file.

The file *Projects* is a directory, as indicated by the **d** in the first character location.

In addition to the **d**, this location may also hold a **b**, **c**, or **l** for some files. These characters indicate special permissions associated with the file, which are of interest to the system administrator.

File Permissions

The remainder of the permissions field is divided into three sets of three slots each. Depending on how your account is set up, the record for *practice* could look like this:

```
-rw-r--r--
```

Following the first dash or *d*, there are three sets of permissions. The first set, **rw-**, determines what you as owner (user) of the file can do with the file, as follows:

- The first of these three slots contains either an **r**, indicating the owner has read permission and can view the contents of the file, or a minus sign to indicate that read permission is denied.

- The second slot contains either a **w**, indicating the owner has write permission and can alter the contents of the file, or a minus sign to prevent the owner from altering the file.

- In similar fashion, the third slot indicates whether or not the file can be executed. An **x** means the owner has execute permission; a minus sign means the owner does not.

In summary, the presence of an **r**, **w**, or **x** in the first set of permission slots, or permission bits, indicates that the associated permission is allowed; a minus sign indicates that this permission is denied for the owner of the file.

File Permissions for Group and Other

When you create a file of any kind, you are the owner of that file. As owner, you are responsible for setting permissions for yourself (often referred to as *user* or owner), for others who are in the same *group* as yourself, and for any *other* person who might have access to the system.

Examine the permissions for the files in your current directory by entering one of the following commands:

ls -l

or

ls -lg

In the long listing output that appears, the name of the owner and group are the third and fourth fields. The three sets of characters that comprise the permissions field determine file access for three different types of users on the system: user, group, and other.

User	Group	Other
rwx	r-x	- -x

The same permissions field rules for the owner (user), examined earlier in this chapter, apply for group and other. The middle three positions determine the read, write, and execute permissions for users who are members of the same group as the owner. This is done so that people working on the same project can have access to the same files and resources and also place different restrictions on the rest of the system's users. The last three slots determine permissions for everyone who has an account on the system, but is not the owner nor in the owner's group.

For example, consider the following permissions field:

```
-rwxr-x-r--
```

The object is a file; the user has read, **write**, and execute permission for the file. Other members of the same group as the owner have read and execute permission, but not write permission. They can see and execute the file, but they cannot alter it. All others have permission to read, but not to write or execute the file. Every file has an associated permission field for user, group, and all others on the system.

In summary, the three permission fields have the following meaning:

- User permissions determine what you can do with the file if you own it.

- Group permissions on files determine what people in your group can do with your files, and what you can do with files owned by other members of your group.

- Other permissions determine what users who are not the owner nor in the owner's group (other) can do with the files you create, and what you can do with files owned by users not in your group.

6.4

Changing File Permissions Numerically

There are two ways to change the mode or permissions for files, using the **chmod** command. One method is to use **chmod** with letter arguments for the permissions, such as **-w**, **+x**, and **-r**, to add or remove permissions. You have already used this method several times. Another method allows you to specify permissions with numbers that represent the permissions.

1. Examine the permissions of the *inform* file by typing

   ls -l *inform*

2. Change its mode to be read and write only, using

   chmod -x *inform*

3. Examine the permissions with

   ls -l *inform*

   The permissions field probably looks like this:

   ```
   -rw-r--r--
   ```

   Until now you have changed a file's mode by explicitly telling the system what change you want, using **chmod**—for example, **chmod +x** *filename* to add execute permission. Numbers are also used to change permissions explicitly.

4. Type the following:

chmod *700* *inform*

5. Examine the permissions now granted by displaying a long listing for the file.

ls -l *inform*

The output is

```
-rwx------ cassy staff July 14 9:37 inform
```

which indicates the user has full **read**, **write**, and **execute** permission for the file. The group and other users have no access.

Using the numerical approach (as in **chmod 700**) to specify the permissions for a file allows you to specify the exact permissions you want to be granted, regardless of the current permissions. The number *700* grants **rwx** to owner. The following section examines how to specify other permissions.

Using Numerical Permissions for Read, Write, and Execute

1. Type the following:

chmod *400* *inform*
ls -l *inform*

2. The **ls** command outputs the long listing for the file. Only an **r** is present in the owner's permissions field.

3. The *400* grants read only to the owner. Change the permission again and examine the results by entering the following commands:

chmod *200* *inform*
ls -l

Only **write** permission is granted to the owner.

4. Now assign only execute permission, by entering

chmod *100* *inform*

5. Deny all permissions by entering

chmod *000 inform*
ls -l *inform*

The basic number permissions are as follows:

Number	Permission
4	read
2	write
1	execute
0	deny all

Assigning Combinations of Permissions

Users seldom grant only one of the three permissions to a file. Often a combination, such as read and write, is specified.

1. Change the permissions for *inform* to include both read and write for the owner, by entering

chmod *600 inform*

Combination permissions are specified using the sum of the values for the specific permissions, as follows:

Permission		Number
read	=	*4*
write	=	*2*
read and write	=	*6*, which is (*4* + *2*)

Identifying All Possible Combinations of Permissions

In the following list, the numbers *1*, *2*, and *4* are used in combinations that add up to produce *3*, *5*, *6*, and *7*. Each of the combinations of *1*, *2*, and *4* adds together to produce a number that no other combination yields. All possible numbers from *0* to *7* are specified.

Composite Number		Basic Permission Number
0	=	*0*
1	=	*1*
2	=	*2*
3	=	*2+1*
4	=	*4*
5	=	*4+1*
6	=	*4+2*
7	=	*4+2+1*

This set of unique numbers is used with **chmod** to establish the permissions for files. The numbers *1*, *2*, and *4* are assigned permission values as follows:

1	Allows execute permission
2	Allows **write** permission
4	Allows **read** permission

These primitives (*0, 1, 2*, and *4*) can be added together to grant any combination of permissions. The basic permissions for a file are as follows:

0	Grants no permissions
1	Grants execute permission only
2	Grants **write** permission only
3	Grants **write** and execute permissions (*1 + 2*)

The sum of *1 + 2 = 3* means that execute and write permissions are both granted, but read permission is denied. Additionally:

4	Grants read permission only
5	Grants read and execute (*1 + 4*)
6	Grants read and write (*2 + 4*)
7	Grants read and write and execute (*1 + 2 + 4*)

Thus the three numbers *1*, *2*, and *4* can be used to express the eight possible states involving combinations of execute, write, and read permissions.

Table 6-1 summarizes the uses of numbers for permissions assignment.

Numerals	Sum	Resulting Permissions
4 2 1		r w x
r w x		*4 2 1*
- - -	*0*	- - -
- - *1*	*1*	- - x
- *2* -	*2*	- w -
- *2 1*	*3*	- w x
4 - -	*4*	r - -
4 - *1*	*5*	r - x
4 2 -	*6*	r w -
4 2 1	*7*	r w x

Table 6-1. *Using Numbers for Permissions Assignment*

Granting Combinations of Permissions Numerically

In this exercise you change the permissions on the *inform* file to all possible combinations and examine the effect of the changed permissions.

1. Change the permissions of *inform* to **rwx** for you, the owner.

   chmod *700 inform*

2. Now attempt to execute the script, read the script, add a new line to the bottom of the script file, and get a listing of the file.

   inform
   more *inform*
   echo date >> *inform*
   ls *inform*

3. Have your current shell read and execute the commands in the script. Bourne and Korn shell users, use the dot command; C shell users, use **source**.

   . *inform*

   or

   source *inform*

   You were able to do all five actions in step 2, as indicated in Table 6-2.

4. Change the permissions on **inform** to *600*. Then issue commands from the previous steps to determine whether you can execute, display, modify, and list the file. Keep track of the results of the effect of permission on the appropriate commands in Table 6-2.

5. Proceed by changing the permissions on **inform** to each of the others, and complete the table.

chmod Parameter Issued Resulting Permission for User	700 rwx	600 rw-	500 r-x	400 r--	300 -wx	200 -w-	100 --x
inform	Yes						
more *inform*	Yes						
echo date >> *inform*	Yes						
ls *inform*	Yes						
. *inform* or **source** *inform*	Yes						

Table 6-2. *Tracking Permissions in the **inform** File*

What are essential permissions for executing a script? What permission is needed to have **ls** list the file? From the previous exercise, you can see that

- Read permission is needed to access the contents of the file.
- Write permission is needed for a user to make any change in a file.
- Both read and execute are required to execute a script, because the script must be read by the child shell created to execute the script.
- Regardless of the permissions on the file, **ls** is able to list it. The **ls** utility does not access the files or their inodes to produce a simple listing of the files in a directory. Instead, **ls** must read the filenames listed in the current directory itself. If you can read the directory, you can obtain an **ls**, no matter what permissions the files have.
- When you ask the shell to read a file and execute its contents—either with the C shell **source** command or Bourne/Korn's dot command—you only need read permission. The current shell is already active. It doesn't have to be executed. It just reads the file.

NOTE: If you are familiar with base 2 arithmetic and binary numbers, you have recognized that the three numbers 4, 2, and 1 are 2 squared, 2 to the first power, and 2 to the zeroth power. Permission numerals are simply the octal sum of the three bits.

Changing Permissions for Group and Other

The numeric values used to set file permissions can be used to specify permissions for any of the three sets (user, group, and other) in the permissions field.

1. Type the following command to add full permissions for your group:

   chmod *770 inform*

2. Check the permissions for *inform*. Type

   ls -l *inform*

   Both the user and the group have read, write, and execute permission for the file. Others are denied access.

3. Type the following command, which grants full permissions to everyone:

   chmod *777 inform*

4. Check how you have changed the permissions for ***inform*** with

   ls -l *inform*

   The permissions now show **read**, **write**, and execute for user, group, and all other users.

5. Try out the following permissions-changing commands. First enter the **chmod** command to change the *inform* file's permissions, and then examine the results with the **ls -l** *inform* command.

Put the resulting permissions in the following table:

Command	Resulting Permission
chmod *777 inform*	rwx rwx rwx
chmod *751 inform*	___ ___ ___
chmod *640 inform*	___ ___ ___
chmod *000 inform*	___ ___ ___

Determining Which Permissions Apply

Permissions are usually most restrictive for other, less so for group, and least restrictive for the owner of a file. If they are not—if group actually has more permissions granted than owner—it raises some interesting problems.

1. Change the permissions for *inform* to be **rwx** for other, **r-x** for group, and grant no permissions to yourself, the owner.

   chmod *057 inform*
   ls -l *inform*

   The permissions displayed are

   ```
   ---r-xrwx
   ```

   You, as owner, appear to have no granted permissions. But you are in your group. Are you granted your group's permissions?

2. Attempt to execute and read the script:

   inform
   cat *inform*

   You have no access to the file.

As the Figure 6-1 indicates, the process of determining your permissions for the object begins with establishing whether or not you are the

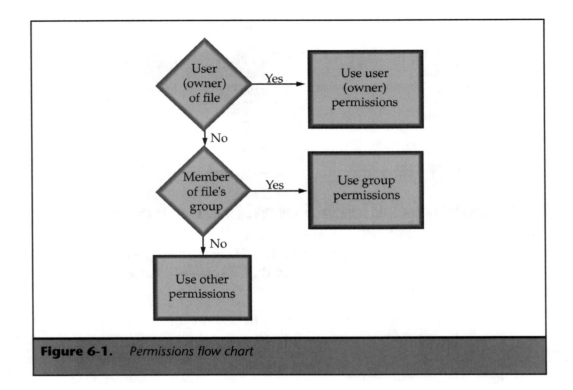

Figure 6-1. *Permissions flow chart*

owner. If the answer is yes, you are granted the owner's permissions as established in the first three permission bits. The question of what group you belong to—of what the group permissions are—is never raised; you pass the owner test and are given that permission set. The same thing happens with respect to members of your group. If other users attempt to access this file, they must fail to be the owner, fail to be in the group, and are then assigned "else," or other, permissions.

■ Review 1

1. What command gives you a long listing of your filenames in the current directory, including the permissions attached to each file?

2. What permissions are granted, to which classes of users, for a file with the following permissions field:

   -r-x------

3. What command would you use to change a file's permissions to include read, write, and execute permission for the owner of the file only?

4. What would a file's permissions field look like after you changed its mode to include read, write, and execute permission for the user only?

5. Fill in the blank spaces in the following table:

Permissions	Argument to Enter with chmod
-rwxrwxrwx	777
	751
-rwx- - - - - -	
-rw-r- -r- -	
	640
	400
	000

6. Read the following conditions, and then describe the permissions on a file with these conditions. You, the owner, can access the file with **vi** and write changes. The file contains a series of shell commands such as **ls** and **who**. When you enter the file's name at the command line, the commands listed in the file are run. Members of your group cannot make changes to the file, but when they issue the file's name to the shell, the internal commands do run. Other users can use **pg** and **more** on the file, but when they issue the filename to the shell, the internal commands do not run.

6.5

Changing Directory Permissions

When you type **ls -l**, the output reveals that directories have the same kind of permissions field as regular files, except for the **d** in the leftmost position. Directory permissions are much the same as for files. The owner of the directory changes the permissions, and the owner determines which users have access to the directory and its files. Assigning permissions to directories is done with the same letters and numbers that are used for assigning permissions to directories as are used with files.

Directories are special files containing names of files and other directories, each entry listed with its associated inode. Permissions for directories determine what you can and can't do to the directory itself. For instance, what permission would you expect is needed for a directory that would allow you to change the name of a file listed in it? What permission is needed to obtain a listing of the files in a directory? In this section you learn how to modify directory permissions and see the effects of your changes.

Using Permissions to Control Directory Access

The owner of a directory has the responsibility for setting its access permissions. Directory permissions, like file permissions, include read, write, and execute.

1. Create a new subdirectory, *Mybin,* in your home directory by typing

   mkdir *Mybin*

2. Examine the specific permissions attached to *Mybin.*

   ls -ld *Mybin*

   The **d** option to **ls** instructs **ls** to provide a long listing of the directory itself, not its files.

3. In an earlier chapter, you examined the actual contents of a directory. Display the contents of your current directory now, with

   ls -i

   The display is the directory's filenames and associated inodes.

NOTE: *In the following exercises you will work with the directory you just created, Mybin, from its parent directory. First, you need to create some files.*

4. Copy the *inform* file into the new *Mybin* subdirectory, by entering

   cp *inform* **Mybin**

5. Change to the *Mybin* directory and create eight test files, by entering the following commands:

   cd *Mybin*
   touch *old0 old1 old2 old3 old4 old5 old6 old7*

6. Run the ***inform*** file to make sure it is executable.

   inform

7. Return to the parent directory.

   cd ..

Listing the Files in a Directory

At the moment, your current working directory is the parent of *Mybin*.

1. Obtain a listing of the files in *Mybin* by entering

   ls *Mybin*

   The output on your screen is not the files in your current directory, but the files listed in *Mybin*. You can read the filenames.

2. Change the permissions of the *Mybin* directory to be only write and execute, with

   chmod *300* *Mybin*

3. Instruct **ls** to list *Mybin*'s permissions, rather than the permissions of its contents, by entering

   ls -ld *Mybin*

   The output indicates you do not have read permission for the directory, only write and execute *(d-wx------).*

4. Attempt to obtain a listing of the files in *Mybin*.

ls *Mybin*

Without read permission for the directory, you cannot read the directory's contents, hence you cannot get a listing of its files.

Denying Write Permission for a Directory

With a file, write permission must be granted before a user can modify the contents of the file. The same is true for directories.

1. Modify the permissions on *Mybin* to exclude write, and examine the results.

chmod *500 Mybin*
ls -ld *Mybin*

The directory has only read and execute for the owner. Write is denied.

2. Obtain a listing of the files in *Mybin*.

ls *Mybin*

You can list the directory's contents because you have read permission. You are reading the directory to determine its files.

3. Attempt to change the name of the file *old5* by entering

mv *old5 old5.bak*

Without write permission, you cannot modify the contents of the directory. You cannot change the name of a listed file, remove a file, or add a file. To make any of those changes requires modifying the content of the directory (i.e., writing).

Examining the Need for Execute Permissions

The directory permissions read and write are similar to the same permissions on regular files. The execute permission, however, works differently for directories.

1. Change the mode of *Mybin* to read and write only, by removing execute.

   chmod *600* *Mybin*
   ls -ld *Mybin*

   Execute is denied.

2. Attempt to change directories to *Mybin*.

   cd *Mybin*

   The shell returns an error message similar to the following:

   ```
   Mybin: Permission denied
   ```

   Execute permission for a directory determines whether or not you can make the directory your current directory.

3. Attempt to execute the script *info*, which is in *Mybin*.

   Mybin/*info*

   Without execute permission, you cannot **cd** into a directory, nor can you use the directory in a path to its contents. Here, you cannot execute *info* because you cannot access the directory to get to the file. You still have execute permission on the file itself; but because you cannot use its parent directory in a path, you cannot get to the file.

NOTE: *To* **cd** *to a directory, or to use the directory in a pathname, you must have execute permission for that directory.*

Examining the Effect of Directory Permission

In the following section you will examine the effect of assigning various permissions to the directory *Mybin*, keeping track of the results in Table 6-3.

Starting in your home directory, assign the first permission listed at the top of the table to *Mybin*. Then try each of the commands listed in the left-hand column of the table. Write down in the appropriate columns of the table whether or not the command was executed without error.

Complete the following exercise, first for permissions set to **700**, and then change the directory permissions to **600** and try the commands again. Continue until you have completed the table.

1. Change the mode to **700** by entering

   chmod 700 *Mybin*

2. Confirm the permissions in the directory by entering

   ls -ld *Mybin*

3. Obtain a listing of *Mybin*'s files by entering

   ls *Mybin*

4. Change directory to *Mybin* by entering

   cd *Mybin*

5. If the previous command was successful, return to the parent directory by entering

   cd ..

   (If you were not able to change directories to *Mybin*, you are still in the parent directory and can continue to the next step.)

6. From the parent directory, read the *info* file, which is in *Mybin*.

   cat *Mybin/info*

7. Request that the *info* script be run.

   Mybin/info

8. Create a new file in *Mybin* called *new7* by entering the following:

   who > *Mybin/new7*

9. Remove an old file by entering

   rm *Mybin/old7*

10. Get a long listing of *Mybin*'s contents.

    ls -l *Mybin*

    The results of entering the above commands when *Mybin* has permissions of **700** are entered in the first column of Table 6-3.

11. Change the permissions to **600**.

12. Repeat steps 1 through 11 above, using *newfile6* in step 8 and *old6* in step 9 when appropriate. Write the results in Table 6-3.

    Continue with each successive permission (and use the appropriate files, i.e., *newfile5* and *oldfile5* with parameter **500**) until the table is completed.

Step	Command Issued	700	600	500	400	300	200	100	000
1	**chmod 700** (or **600**)	Yes							
2	**ls -ld** *Mybin*	Yes							
3	**ls** *Mybin*	Yes							
4	**cat** *Mybin/inform*	Yes							
5	Mybin/*inform*	Yes							
6	**who >** *Mybin/new7*	Yes							
7	**rm** *Mybin/old7*	Yes							
8	**ls -l** *Mybin*	Yes							
9	**cd** *Mybin*	Yes							
10	**ls**	Yes							
11	**inform**	Yes							
12	**cd ..**	Yes							

Table 6-3. *Tracking the Results of Changing Directory Permissions*

13. Repeat steps 1 through 10 above, using *new6* in step 8 and *old6* in step 9. Write the results in Table 6-3. Continue with each successive permission until the table is completed.

These exercises reveal the following:

- Read permission is needed to list the contents of a directory with **ls**.

- Write permission is needed to create files in or remove them from a directory (write to the directory file).

- Execute permission is needed to make a directory your working directory with **cd**, or to pass through it as part of a search path.

- Both read and execute are needed to get a long **ls** listing. Although read permission is enough to run **ls**, it is not enough to run **ls -l**. The information needed for the long listing is not held in the directory itself. Only the filenames are in the directory. The permissions, owner, and so forth are listed in the inode. The only way to access the inode is through the directory, which requires execute permission.

Limiting Execute in a Path

Having execute permission for directories has important consequences.

1. For the *Mybin* directory, make the permissions **rwx** for the owner, and then add a new directory named *Testing*.

   chmod 700 *Mybin*
   ls -ld *Mybin*
   mkdir *Mybin/Testing*

2. Change directories to *Testing*, check your location, and return to the current directory.

   cd *Mybin/Testing*
   pwd
   cd ../..
   pwd

   You are able to change directories through *Mybin* to *Testing*.

3. Change the permissions of *Mybin* to deny execute.

   chmod *600 Mybin*
   ls -ld *Mybin*

4. Attempt to change to the *Testing* directory.

   cd *Mybin/Testing*

   Because you do not have execute on the *Mybin* directory, you cannot use it in a path to reach *Testing*.

Granting Execute Permission Only

You have seen that, without execute permission, you cannot change into or through a directory. Is execute enough?

1. Change the permissions for the directory *Mybin* to be only **x**.

   chmod *100 Mybin*
   ls -ld *Mybin*

2. Attempt to change directories to *Mybin*, get a listing of its files, and then change directories to *Testing*.

   cd *Mybin*
   pwd
   ls
   cd *Testing*
   pwd

   With only execute permission on a directory, you can **cd** into it, but you cannot get a listing of its files. You can change directories from it to a subdirectory.

A 13-year-old boy was in the kitchen. His mother asked him if she could get some things out of the closet in his room. He replied that it was the holiday season and presents were all over his room. He didn't want anyone looking around in there. Mom said she wanted into the closet, not the room. He agreed that she could go through his room *with her eyes closed* and, once in the closet, turn on the light, open her eyes, and get what she needed. He granted her execute but not read permission to his room.

Establishing Directory Permissions for Group and Other

The permissions on directories are specified for user, group, and other, in the same fields of the long listing that are associated with file permissions.

1. Restore full permissions to owner for *Mybin* by typing

   chmod *700 Mybin*
   ls **-ld** *Mybin*   .
   ls **-l** *Mybin*

   No one but you can obtain a listing of the files in *Mybin* using **ls**. All group and other permissions are denied. They cannot **cd** to *Mybin* or use that directory in a path to access any files in it or below it—regardless of the permissions granted for the individual files.

2. Allow all users in your group to have execute permission to your directory *Mybin*. Enter

   chmod *710 Mybin*
   ls **-ld** *Mybin*

   This command allows the owner total access to the directory. It does not allow group users to **ls** or write files in the directory. However, they can **cd** into it. Other users who are not in your group are denied all access.

3. Allow your group and others to change directories into *Mybin* and to obtain listings of files. Enter the following:

   chmod *755 Mybin*
   ls **-l** *Mybin*
   ls **-ld** *Mybin*

6.6

Changing Permissions for Files in All Subdirectories

Thus far, you have changed the permissions for individual files within their own directory. The **chmod** utility can also change the permissions for *all* files in a directory and all of its subdirectories.

1. Issue the following commands to change to your home directory, and to create a subdirectory that contains several files, another subdirectory, and additional files.

   cd
   mkdir *Dir-A*
   ls -ld *Dir-A*
   cd *Dir-A*
   touch *A AA AAA*
   ls -l *
   mkdir *Dir-B*
   ls -ld *Dir-B*
   cd *Dir-B*
   touch *B BB BBB*
   ls -l *
   cd

   The resulting files and directories are illustrated in Figure 6-2. The new directory, *Dir-B*, contains a series of files with limited permissions. *Dir-B* is listed in the *Dir-A* directory, which is listed in your home directory.

2. Change the permissions for *all* the files and *both* directories by issuing one command:

   chmod -R *777 Dir-A*

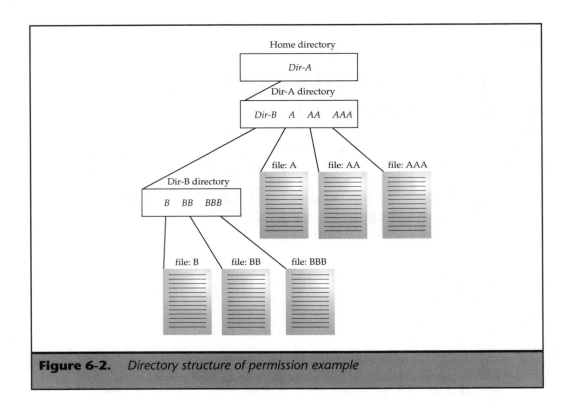

Figure 6-2. *Directory structure of permission example*

3. Check the permissions of the directories and files:

ls -ld *Dir-A*
ls -l *Dir-A*
ls -ld *Dir-A/Dir-B*
ls -l *Dir-A/Dir-B*

The **-R** option to the **chmod** utility is instruction to **R**ecursively descend down through the directory tree and change the permissions for all the files and directories.

6.7
Identifying Other Permissions

When cruising around the file system, you will sometimes see permissions **s** and **t** for files, rather than **r**, **w**, or **x**. The **s** and **t** permissions can only be set by the superuser, not by ordinary users. This section introduces these remaining two permissions. For a detailed account of these superuser permissions, consult the **man** section on **chmod** in Section 2 of the Reference Manual, or look in a system administration text.

Running Programs as Root

The */bin/passwd* file is a program that UNIX users run to change their passwords. Encrypted passwords are kept in the */etc/passwd*, or */etc/shadow*, or another system file, depending on your system. Ordinary users do not have write permission to the password file.

1. Enter the following commands:

   ls -l */etc/shadow*
   ls -l */etc/passwd*

2. Even though you lack write permission to the password files, you have probably run the *passwd* program to change your passwords, thus changing the file. For instance, enter

   ls -l */bin/passwd*

The output includes one or more unusual permissions:

```
-rwsr-xr-x   3    root   94208    Jun 29 1995   /bin/passwd
```

On a network system, examine the permissions for *yppasswd*. This output indicates that the file's owner is *root*. Only *root* can write the file. The owner also has an **s** instead of an **x** in the execute field. The **s** indicates that when anyone who has permission to execute this program does so, the program runs with the identity of *root*, not the identity of the person who actually runs the program. Because the *passwd* program runs as *root*, and because root has write permission for the password file, running *passwd* changes the user's password.

Setting Group Id

Often applications on systems need to be available to any member of a specified group. The programs are owned by a member of the group, and other group members have execute authority. If the execute permission slot for a program contains an **s**, anyone with execute permission for the file runs the file as though they were a member of the group, even if they are not.

Keeping Programs Resident

When a program is executed, the code for the program is read into memory. While no one is using the code, it is deleted from memory. To have the code remain in memory after the last user has completed running the program, the system administrator can *set the sticky bit* on the program. This improves system performance when very common programs are run, because the code does not have to be read in first. A **t** in the permissions field indicates that the sticky bit is set.

Directories, as well, can have the sticky bit set. In this case, the sticky bit prohibits a user who has write permission on the directory from removing or changing the name of files belonging to another user.

6.8

Setting Permissions When Files Are Created

In UNIX you create files in three ways: you can copy an existing file into a new one; you can use a utility such as an editor or **tee** to create a file; or you can specify that the output of a utility be sent to a new file, using redirection in a shell command. When you run **ls -l** after you create a new file, the new file has permissions set, without your intervention. You are not consulted first; the initial permissions are automatically assigned.

Examining the Default Permissions

Thus far in this chapter you have examined how to modify existing permissions on files and directories. This section investigates how the initial settings are established.

In an earlier chapter, you created the command file *inform*. The operating system initially set the permissions for you, the owner, as read and write. Initially, you were not allowed to execute the file. At creation, permission settings were included for other users who were members of your group and for all others. These default permission settings are determined by the **umask** value.

As you will see, the **umask** is so named because its value determines which permissions are *masked*, or *not set*.

1. To ensure that you can access the files used in the following exercises, check to make sure you are in your home directory.

2. Obtain the current setting of **umask** by entering

   umask

   A number such as *22* is displayed.

This **umask** setting determines the value of permissions for new files as they are created. Changing the **umask** has no effect on existing files. The **umask** setting is initially determined by default on the system and can be modified from the shell command line, or through entries in a user's startup files.

> *CAUTION:* *Be careful. For some reason, especially in late October, people often enter unmask, but it's* **umask***.*

Specifying Directories Permissions

To explore how directory permissions are affected by **umask**, the following exercises guide you through changing **umask** values and then creating new directories.

1. Create a new, empty directory for these next exercises.

   mkdir *DIRS*
   cd *DIRS*
   pwd
   ls

2. You are about to change the value of the **umask**. First, write down the present value so that you can change it back later.

Original **umask** value:_____

3. Reset the **umask** to *000* by entering

umask 000

4. To confirm that you have changed the **umask**, type

umask

The **umask** is now *000*, which may be displayed as *0*. (It doesn't make much difference whether a checking account has $0. or $000. in it.)

5. With the **umask** at *000*, create a new directory and determine its permissions:

mkdir *DIR000*
ls -ld *DIR* *

The output is

```
drwxrwxrwx
```

The permissions of the directory are wide open—readable, writable, and executable by everyone.

When the **umask** is set to *000*, nothing is masked out and all permissions are granted for new directories.

Creating a Directory with Write Masked

A directory created while **umask** is *000* has full permissions granted to user, group, and other.

1. Change **umask** to be *022* and request confirmation.

umask 022
umask

2. With the **umask** at *022*, create a new directory and examine its permissions:

mkdir *DIR022*
ls -ld *DIR* *

The new directory created while the **umask** is *022*, has permissions of

```
drwxr-xr-x
```

The owner has **rwx**, the group **r-x**, and others **r-x**. What permissions are missing or *mask*ed? Nothing is masked from the owner, *0*. Group is missing write permission, *2*, and other is missing *2*. The missing or masked permissions are *022*.

The following table summarizes how **mkdir** determines permissions for a new directory when the **umask** is *022*.

	Directory Permissions Granted			
umask	Owner	Group	Other	
000	rwx 421	rwx 421	rwx 421	Directory permissions granted if nothing were masked
022	0 - - -	2 -w-	2 -w-	Permissions masked by **unmask** at current setting
	rwx 421	r-x 4-1	r-x 4-1	Resulting directory permissions

Permissions masked when the **umask** is set to *022* are as follows:

- *0* Nothing is masked from the owner's permissions.
- *2* The permission **w**rite is masked from group.
- *2* Other is also missing **w**rite.

Masking Different Permissions for Group and Other

In the last exercise, when a new directory was created the write permission was masked for group and other, because there were **2**s in the second and third fields of **umask**.

1. Change the **umask** by entering

   umask *037*

2. Create another directory by typing

   mkdir *DIR037*

3. Check the directory's permissions by typing

   ls -ld *DIR* *

   This time the directory's permissions are

   ```
   drwxr-----
   ```

   The owner has full **rwx**, the group has just **r**ead, and others are granted no permissions. The directory's permissions are **740**: read, write, and execute by the owner, and read for the group. With the **umask** set at **037**, no permissions are masked from owner, **w**rite and execute (**3**) are denied to group, and all (**7**) permissions are denied group members.

   The following table summarizes how these permissions for a new directory are determined when the **umask** is **037**.

	Directory Permissions Granted			
umask	**Owner**	**Group**	**Other**	
000	rwx	rwx	rwx	Directory permissions granted
	421	*421*	*421*	when nothing is masked
037	0	21	421	Permissions masked
	- - -	-wx	rwx	by **umask** at current setting
	rwx	r- -	- - -	Resulting directory permissions

4. Change the **umask** to the following values. With **umask** at a value, create a directory, and then examine the permissions for that directory.

Setting of umask	Resulting Directory Permissions
023	d - - - - - - - - -
066	d - - - - - - - - -

SUMMARY: If the **umask** *is set to* **000**, *no permissions are masked and any directories created have full* **rwx** *for all users. A nonzero in any field of* **umask** *specifies the permissions that are denied to the owner, members of the group, and others depending on which field is not zero. The* **umask** *values and resulting permissions are as follows for each of the three fields:*

0	Denies no permissions hence, grants all three permissions, **rwx**
1	Restricts execute permission only, granting **r** and **w**
2	Restricts **write** permission only, granting **r** and x
3	Restricts **write** and execute, granting **r**
4	Restricts read permission only, granting **w** and x
5	Restricts read and execute (*1 + 4*), granting **w**
6	Restricts read and **write** (*2 + 4*), granting x
7	Restricts read, write, and execute (*1 + 2 + 4*), granting no permissions

Identifying File Permissions with Nothing Masked

A particular **umask** setting results in different permissions for files than it does for directories.

1. To examine the resulting file permissions when nothing is masked, change the **umask** value to *0* by typing

umask 000

2. Create a file named *file000*.

   ls > *file000*

3. Check the mode of *file000*.

   ls -l *file000*

At this point, the file is readable and writable by everyone. When the **umask** is *000*, the default permissions for a new file are *666* (readable and writable by owner, group, and others). As you can see from this example, even though the **umask** is set to *000*, when a file is created, it still does not have execute permission. No one, not even the owner, is granted execute permission until it is specifically added by the **chmod** command.

Denying Write for New Files

The **umask** is used to mask permissions for new files.

1. Set your **umask** to *022* by typing

   umask *022*

2. Create another file called *file022* and check its permissions.

   touch *file022*
   ls -l

The permissions are **read** and **write** for owner, and **read** alone for group and others (*644*).

When the **umask** is set to *000* and you create a file, the file's permissions are set to be as open as possible without granting execute (*666*). When you reset the **umask** to *022*, the new file has permissions of *644*. The write (*2*) is masked or denied for group and other.

The following table summarizes how initial permissions are granted to files when the **umask** is *022*.

umask	File Permissions Granted			
	Owner	**Group**	**Other**	
000	rw 42	rw 42	rw 42	File permission granted when nothing is masked
022	0 - - -	2 -w-	2 -w-	Permissions masked by **umask** at current setting
	42 rw-	4 r- -	4 r- -	Resulting file permissions

File Permissions When Execute Is Masked

At file creation, execute is never granted. If **umask** also *masks* execute, what is the result when files are created?

1. Set the **umask** to *023* by typing

   umask 023

2. Create another file named *file023* and check its permissions:

   touch *file023*
   ls -l

   The new file created while **umask** is *023* has permissions of

   ```
   -rw-r--r--
   ```

This result is exactly the same as when the **umask** was set to *022*. The only difference between the two is that *023* calls for masking the execute permission for other users. Because files are not granted execute at creation—at all—it makes no difference whether the **umask** grants or denies execute for files.

The following table summarizes how permissions are granted to a new *file* when the **umask** is masking execute. At file creation, execute is not granted; hence, there is none to be masked. Masking execute for files is irrelevant.

	File Permissions Granted			
umask	Owner	Group	Other	
000	rw 42	rw 42-	rw 42-	Directory permissions granted when nothing is masked
023	0 - - -	2 -w-	21 -wx	Permissions masked by **umask** at current setting
	42 rw	4 r- -	4 r- -	Resulting directory permissions

A graphical description of how **umask** works is presented in Figure 6-3.

Predicting Permissions for Files

In this exercise you change the **umask**, then calculate the permissions
for a file, then check the permissions.

1. Set the **umask** to *037*.

   umask *037*

2. Create another file named *file037*.

   touch *file037*

3. In the following table, write down the permissions you expect
   file037 to be granted at creation.

	File Permissions Granted			
umask	Owner	Group	Other	
000	rw- 42-	rw- 42-	rw- 42-	Directory permissions granted when nothing is masked
037	___ ___	___ ___	___ ___	Permissions masked by **umask** at current setting
	___ ___	___ ___	___ ___	Resulting file permissions

Directory

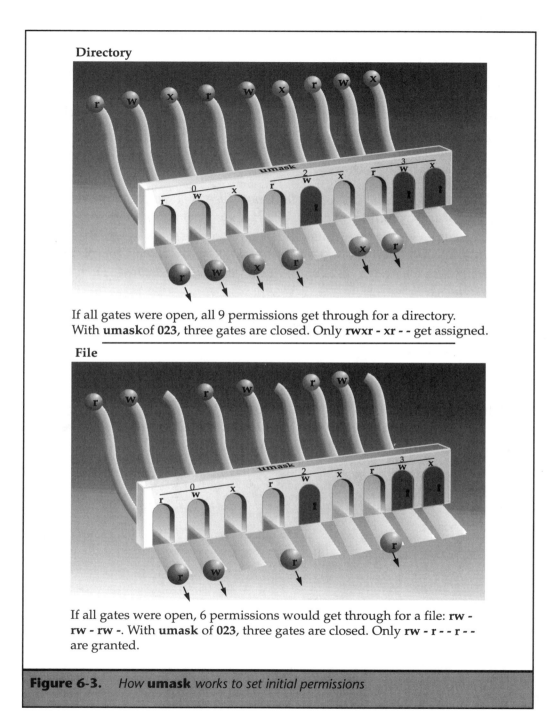

If all gates were open, all 9 permissions get through for a directory. With **umask** of **023**, three gates are closed. Only **rwxr - xr - -** get assigned.

File

If all gates were open, 6 permissions would get through for a file: **rw - rw - rw -**. With **umask** of **023**, three gates are closed. Only **rw - r - - r - -** are granted.

Figure 6-3.   *How **umask** works to set initial permissions*

4. Check the new file's permissions against what you wrote in the table. Type

ls -l *file037*

The file's permissions are read and write by owner, and read by group (**640**). The **umask** worked as expected: The file is not writable or executable by the group; nor is it readable, writable, or executable by others.

SUMMARY: *If the* **umask** *is* **000**, *new files are created with read and write for user, group, and other. The execute permission is not granted at file creation. When the* **umask** *is not zero, permissions are masked for new files. Although* **2** *masks* **write** *and* **4** *masks* **read**, *the* **1** *for execute has no effect because execute is not granted when files are created. There is nothing to mask.*

Predicting Permission for Files and Directories

Because file and directory permissions are affected differently for the same **umask**, it is useful to compare the results.

In this next exercise, you'll predict and compare permissions for files and directories. Change the **umask**, create some files and directories, and check resulting permissions to complete the following table.

Directory and File Permissions		
Resulting Directory Permissions	**umask**	**Resulting File Permissions**
drwxrwxrwx	*000*	rw-rw-rw
_____	*022*	_____
_____	*023*	_____
_____	*033*	_____
_____	*037*	_____
_____	*077*	_____
_____	*777*	_____

6.9

Inheriting Permissions When Files Are Copied

Clearly, the **umask** affects permission when new files are created, but does it affect all new files? Whether or not the **cp** command retains permissions when files are copied depends on the version of UNIX you are using.

1. Set your **umask** to **777**, return to your home directory, and create two files:

   umask 777
   cd
   touch *newfile777*
   who > *who-file777*
   ls -l * 777 *

   Notice that, at this point, new files are created with no permissions granted at all.

2. Earlier in this chapter you created a new file, *inform*, in your home directory that contained several shell commands. You made it executable, and then executed it. Examine the permissions for the *inform* file.

   cd
   ls -l *inform*

3. Make a new file, by copying the *inform* file.

   cp *inform inform1*

   Because you have read permission for *inform*, you can copy it into *inform1*.

4. Attempt to execute the new file. Type

   ./inform1

   If this new file is executable, proceed to the next steps; otherwise, use a **-p** option by entering

> **rm** *inform1*
>
> **cp -p** *inform inform1*

5. Check the permissions of both files. Type

> **ls -l** *inform inform1*

The file *inform1* inherited the same permissions as *inform* when it was copied.

   When you copy a file, the new copy of the file has the same permissions as the original. Depending on your system, the **umask** has no effect on files that are created by copying other files. If you do want to have **umask** take effect when making a duplicate file, you must use a utility other than **cp**.

6. For instance, copy the file *inform* to a new file named *infoX* using the **cat** utility. Enter

> **cat** *inform* > *infoX*

7. Attempt to execute the new file.

> *./infoX*

You cannot execute the file.

8. Check the permissions.

> **ls -l** *infoX*

The new file has the permissions determined by the **umask**. In this instance, you instructed the shell to redirect the output of **cat** to a new file. The shell follows **umask** instructions when creating files.

9. Before continuing with the upcoming Review section, go back to the earlier section "Identifying File Permissions with Nothing Masked" and find the original **umask** value that you recorded. Reset the **umask** back to that value. Or, just log off and log back on.

■ Review 2

1. What permissions are granted on a directory with the following permissions field?

   `drwxr-xr--`

2. What command sets the permission fields of all newly created files so that no one other than the owner can write to the file?

3. What command sets the permissions fields of all newly created directories to read, write, and execute for owner, and execute only for everyone else?

4. If **umask** is *022* and the permissions on a file named *scriptA* are **rwxr-xr-x**, what are the permissions for the resulting files when you enter the following commands?

   a. **touch** *abc*
   b. **mkdir** *def*
   c. **who** > *ghi*
   d. **cp** *scriptA scriptB*
   e. **wc** *scriptA* > *wcA*

■ Conclusion

The UNIX operating system includes a collection of files. Some are essential for system operation; others contain valuable information. Still others are powerful programs that should be employed only by certain users. Many files are simply useful to one or more users.

Each file and directory has an associated set of permissions that determines what users can do to the file or directory. The owner of a file or directory is responsible for managing its permissions.

Files and directories are granted initial permissions at creation determined by the **umask** setting at the time. When files are copied, permissions are copied as well.

For a file, read permission is needed to access the file's contents with a utility; write is needed to make changes to the file; and execute is needed to run the commands in the file. If the file is a script, execute is necessary, but not sufficient. The shell must read the file, so read is also required. The contents of a directory must be read to run **ls**, hence read permission is needed. To add a file, remove a file or change a file's name, the user must have write permission in the directory. To **cd** into a directory or include the directory in a path, the user must be granted execute permission.

Two methods are available for changing the permissions: letters (**chmod +x**) and numbers (**chmod 700**).

■ Answers to Review 1

1. **ls -l**

2. Read and execute permission for the user, but not write permission. None to group or other.

3. **chmod 700** *filename*

4. The permissions field should appear as follows:

   ```
   -rwx------
   ```

5. The table should be filled in as follows:

Permissions	Argument of chmod
rwxrwxrwx	777
rwxr-x--x	751
rwx------	700
rw-r--r--	644
rw-r-----	640
r--------	400
---------	000

6. The permissions field should appear as follows:

```
rwxr-xr--
```

■ Answers to Review 2

1. Owner may list the contents, add/remove files, and change directory into the directories and execute files. Group may list contents and change directory into the directories and execute files. Others may list contents only.

2. **umask *022***

3. **umask *066***

4. a. **rw-r- -r- -**
   b. **rwxr-xr-x**
   c. **rw-r- -r- -**
   d. **rwxr-xr-x**
   e. **rw-r- -r- -**

COMMAND SUMMARY

ls -l Produces a long listing, including permissions, of the files contained in the current directory.

chmod *mode filename* Changes the permissions on *filename* to those represented by *mode*.

umask *mode* Changes the default permissions on new files created to a permission value equal to *777* minus *mode* for directories, and a permission value equal to *666* minus *mode* for plain files.

Mode Summary

r Allows read permission for designated user

w Allows write permission for designated user

x Allows execute permission for designated user

4 Allows read permission for designated user

2 Allows write permission for designated user

1 Allows execute permission for designated user

PART II

Examining
User Support
Features of
UNIX

Chapter Seven

Obtaining Help from the On-Line Manual

Part of the UNIX system's power is its offering of an extensive variety of UNIX utility programs, application programs, and programming support libraries. These diverse UNIX facilities are too numerous for most of us to remember in detail. While working, you'll often need to recall the syntax of a particular option or command from this or that utility. The needed information is available from the *UNIX Programmer's Manual*, often called the *UNIX Reference Manual*, which is available both in hardcopy and on-line.

A hardcopy version of the Reference Manual is provided with most systems and can usually be found in terminal rooms or work areas. On many systems, the entire Reference Manual is available on-line.

This chapter examines how to access information in both versions of the manual.

SKILLS CHECK: Before beginning this chapter, you should be able to

- *Access and leave the system*
- *Execute basic shell commands*
- *Use several utilities in combination*

OBJECTIVES: After completing this chapter, you will be able to

- *Display the on-line manual pages that describe specific commands and files*
- *Search for specific on-line manual pages by keyword or regular expression*
- *Find related manual entries through cross-referencing*
- *Use the permuted index found in many hardcopy versions of the Reference Manual*

The UNIX Reference Manual is an indispensable part of the UNIX system. It contains readily available, detailed documentation on the uses and functions of all standard utility programs, many application programs and libraries, as well as information on UNIX system files and system programming libraries. The Reference Manual also contains supplementary information on related special files and commands for each entry. In addition, examples and error conditions are often provided.

7.1

■ Accessing the On-Line Manual

On-line Reference Manual pages can be displayed on your workstation screen just as they would appear in hardcopy form. If your system does not have the on-line manual, you may want to find a system that does, or skip to Section 7.2.

Displaying a Manual Entry

From the shell, you can request that individual manual entries be written on the workstation screen.

1. Examine the on-line manual entry for the **cat** utility by entering

   man *cat*

   Part of the first page of the output is shown here:

   ```
   CAT(1)              UNIX Programmer's Manual          CAT(1)

   NAME

        cat  -  concatenate and print files

   SYNOPSIS

   cat [ -u ] [ -s ] [  -v  [-e]  [-t]  ]  file  ...
   ```

2. On most systems, the **man** utility displays each manual entry one screenful at a time. If your system does not provide a screen-by-screen display of the manual, you can explicitly include the appropriate utility necessary for this function by piping the output of **man** to a paging utility, as follows:

   man *cat* | **pg**

   or

   man *cat* | **more**

Organization of Manual Entries

Every manual entry follows the same basic organization. The top line of the output includes the name of the utility, followed by a number in parentheses that refers to the section of the manual where the entry is located. Words at the left margin in all capital letters, such as NAME and SYNOPSIS, introduce the various sections of the entry.

1. Advance through the manual pages for the **cat** utility, examining the headings and text.

2. You may be familiar with the **copy** command from the DOS world. To see if UNIX has a similarly named command, type

   man *copy*

   The **man** utility responds with this message:

   ```
   No manual entry for copy
   ```

   This message does not necessarily mean there is no **copy** command. It does mean there is no entry in the manual for **copy**.

3. Examine the manual entries for a few of the commands you have used, such as **date**, **wc**, **more**, **pg**, **who**, **vi**, **cp**, and **sort**. Take special note of the options available for each utility.

Searching Through a Manual Entry

Often manual entries are very long, and it is difficult to access the portion that contains what you want. You can search for specific words.

1. Call up the manual entry for **ls**.

   man *ls*

2. With the first page displayed, ask for a search through the entry. Search for the word *column* by entering

   /column

   Press (Return), and the display advances to the first page that includes the word *column*.

3. Press ⓝ to advance to the next instance of the word *column*.

Entries in the manual tend to follow the structure of a newspaper story: usually the most critical information comes first. By reading just the first few sections, you can examine the most important features of the utility.

As you saw in the previous example, you can search for a particular entry in the manual by using

/entry

where *entry* is a word in the current manual entry that you want searched.

When you are using **man** in most environments, you can use all of the features offered by the **more** command.

4. To exit the **man** utility, enter **q**.

Organization of the Manual Sections

Manual entries are grouped into a number of categories called *sections*. There are eight standard sections in the manual, numbered 1 through 8. Some systems have a few optional sections, such as N for New, L for Local, and X for eXperimental. Descriptions of the most common sections are summarized in Table 7-1.

On Santa Cruz Operations' version, called SCO UNIX, the sections are named as follows:

- ADM (System Administration)
- C (Commands)
- M (Miscellaneous)
- F (File Formats)
- HW (Hardware Dependent)
- S (Subroutines and Libraries)
- CP (Programming Commands)
- DOS (DOS Subroutines and Libraries)
- LOCAL (Local Utilities)

Section	System V	BSD
1	Basic utilities invoked by users or programs at command-level interpretation	Basic utilities invoked by users or programs at command-level interpretation
1C	Commands for communication with other systems	Commands for communication with other systems
1G	Commands used primarily for computer graphics or computer aided design (CAD)	Commands used primarily for computer graphics or computer aided design (CAD)
1M	Basic administration utilities	Public Accessible Commands, General Utilities
2	System calls, the C language interface, error numbers, and signals	System calls, the C language interface, error numbers, and signals
3	The subroutine libraries available, usually in **/lib** and **/usr/lib**	C programming language library functions
3C	C programming language libraries	
3S	Standard I/O routines	Standard I/O routines
3M	Mathematical library routines	Mathematical library routines
3N	Networking support library	Internet library functions

Table 7-1. *UNIX Reference Manual Categories*

Section	System V	BSD
3X	Specialized libraries	Minor libraries and miscellaneous runtime facilities
3F	FORTRAN programming language libraries	FORTRAN programming language libraries

Table 7-1. *UNIX Reference Manual Categories (continued)*

Accessing Manual Entries from a Specific Section

Sometimes a command needs to be described in general terms in one section of the manual, and in detail in another. Commands are often listed in more than one section of the UNIX Reference Manual.

1. Examine the manual entry for **chmod** by typing

   man *chmod*

2. Browse through the manual entry to the end, or enter the search request command for the section entitled SEE ALSO. Among the entries listed under SEE ALSO is

   ```
   chmod(2)
   ```

   This refers to a listing for **chmod** in Section 2 of the Reference Manual. Section 2 contains the description of UNIX system calls.

3. To look at the Section 2 entry for **chmod**, enter

   man *2 chmod*

   The entry describing the system call **chmod** appears on your screen. If the manual page did *not* appear, the system you are using may not have a full set of manual pages installed.

In summary, the command to look up an entry in a specific manual section is

man *section command*

where *section* is the section number and *command* is the title of the entry.

Determining the Contents of a Manual Section

Most sections (and some subsections) of the manual include a special entry that describes the contents of the section.

1. To find out what Section 1 of the manual contains, type

   man *1 intro*

   The output of the command displayed is similar to

```
INTRO(1)            UNIX Programmer's Manual     INTRO(1)

NAME

     intro  -  introduction to commands

DESCRIPTION

     This section describes publicly accessible com-
mands, listed in alphabetical order. Certain distinc-
tions of purpose are made in the headings:

(1)        Commands of general utility

(1C)       Commands for communication with other systems

(1G)       Commands used primarily for graphics and
           computer-aided design
```

This entry is the introduction to Section 1 of the manual. The *intro* entries are written in the same format as other manual entries. They contain descriptions of the section and any of its subsections, along with references to other useful information.

Not all sections and subsections have an *intro* entry. The inclusion of an *intro* for an on-line manual section is most often determined by the space considerations on your machine.

7.2

Navigating the Elements of a Manual Page

In this section you will examine a manual entry in depth.

1. Display the manual entry for the **cat** utility again.

man *cat*

Here is the entire entry for **cat.** The headings (NAME, SYNOPSIS, and so on) are generally in the order shown here, but there may be some variations in your system.

```
CAT(1)            UNIX Programmer's Manual          CAT(1)

NAME

     cat  -  concatenate and print file

SYNOPSIS

cat [ -u ] [ -s ] [ -v [-t] [-e] ] files ...

DESCRIPTION

     Cat reads each file in sequence and writes it on
the standard output. Thus cat file displays the file
on the standard output, and cat file1 file2 >file3
concatenates the first two files and places the
result in the third.

     If no input file is given, or if the argument -
is encountered, cat reads from the standard input
file.
```

OPTIONS

-u   The output is not buffered. (The default is buffered output.)

-s   cat is silent about non-existent files.

-v   Displays non-printing characters so that they are visible. For example, Ctrl-X is printed as ^X; the delete character (octal 0177) is printed as ^?. Non-ASCII characters (with the high bit set) are printed as M-(for meta) followed by the character of the low 7 bits.

-e   Used with the -v option; displays a $ character at the end of each line.

-t   Used with the -v option; displays tab characters as ^I.

WARNING

Command formats such as

     cat file1 file2 >file1

will destroy the original data in file1 before it is read.

SEE ALSO

     cp(1), ex(1), more(1), pr(1), tail(1)

The Header

The first line of the manual entry is the header. Its exact format varies among UNIX installations, but it usually includes the name of the manual entry and a number enclosed in parentheses that indicates the manual section from which the entry was taken.

NAME Line

Look at the first heading following the header line:

```
NAME

    cat  -   concatenate and print file
```

This line consists of the primary name of the command, and then any alternative name of the command, followed by a brief description of the command's function. In the hardcopy version of the manual, this line is the table of contents entry.

SYNOPSIS/Syntax Section

The SYNOPSIS or Syntax section summarizes the *usage* of the command.

```
SYNOPSIS

cat  [  -u  ]  [  -s  ]  [  -v  [-t]  [-e]  ]  files ...
```

For a command such as **cat**, usage means the proper method of typing the command, including any valid arguments the command may take.

Throughout the manual, square brackets [ ] are used to denote optional arguments. If a command has many options, the word *options* appears in the brackets instead of a list of the actual options. Where brackets are nested, as with the

```
[  -v  [-t]  [-e]  ]
```

in the **cat** example, you cannot choose the **-t**, **-e**, or **-te** options without the **-v** option.

NOTE: Each UNIX system may have its own specific set of available options. In addition, each system may require or allow the use of certain options with or without other options.

Following the bracketed options is the word *file ...* or *files ...*, indicating that one or more filenames may follow the **cat** command at that position.

Some manual entries are for important system files. In these cases, the SYNOPSIS consists of the full pathname of the file.

1. Look at the entry for the ascii database in the manual, by typing

   man *ascii*

   The SYNOPSIS section for ascii consists of this line:

   ```
   cat  /usr/pub/ascii
   ```

   If the entry is a programming library function, the SYNOPSIS may include the file that contains the entry and any additional information you need to use the file.

2. Examine the UNIX C programming language library routine, **rmdir**, by typing

   man 2 *rmdir*

   The **rmdir** function is the C language subroutine equivalent of the UNIX **rmdir** shell utility. You see this manual entry:

   ```
   RMDIR(2)         UNIX Programmer's Manual         RMDIR(2)

   NAME

         rmdir  -  remove a directory file

   SYNOPSIS

         int  rmdir  (path)

         char  * path;

   . . .
   ```

Here the SYNOPSIS consists of the proper method of using the function from within a C program.

DESCRIPTION Section

Return to the manual entry for **cat** and examine the next heading: DE-SCRIPTION. This section of the manual entry is invariably the longest and discusses the entry in detail. In this case, DESCRIPTION outlines the correct methods of using the **cat** command, and the expected results.

OPTIONS Section

The OPTIONS section describes the function and use of each option or flag available with a given utility. Most people access the **man** pages to identify the exact option needed to accomplish a task. In this example, you can see that **cat** accepts the **-v** and **-t** options. These options are used together in the following command:

cat -vt */etc/termcap* **| more**

This command asks **cat** to display the */etc/termcap* file, with the non-printable characters displayed, and tabs displayed as **^I**.

On some systems, the list of command options will appear under DESCRIPTION.

WARNINGS Section

Some utilities must be used with care because of their far-reaching effects. In our **cat** example, the WARNINGS section of the manual cautions you about using **cat** with redirection.

```
WARNINGS

    Command formats such as

        cat file1 file2 >file1

    will destroy the original data in file1 before it is
    read.
```

The WARNINGS section contains information on common usage mistakes and tips for avoiding difficulties.

SEE ALSO Section

References are placed in this section to lead you to other related entries in the manual and, occasionally, to technical papers, journal articles, or

books. For the **cat** entry, there are cross-references to the entries for
cp(1) and **pr(1)**, among others. Remember, as you saw in the heading
for **cat**, the number in parentheses following each of these cross-refer-
enced entries indicates the manual section containing that entry.

FILES Section

The FILES section lists the names of files associated with the entry.
Sometimes you'll also find a short description of each file's use. For example, listed in the FILES section of the manual entry for the **at** utility
are the files **/usr/lib/atrun** and **/usr/spool/at**.

DIAGNOSTICS Section

This section describes the more unusual diagnostic messages a utility
may produce.

BUGS Section

The BUGS description includes information about the known bugs and
deficiencies of the utility, and occasionally a method for correcting the
problem. Because the material covered in the WARNINGS and BUGS
sections is topically similar, on many systems the two sections are combined under the BUGS heading. On systems that use both headings, the
information presented in each section is determined by intent. WARN-
INGS pertain to problems of improper usage (or sometimes improper
design) of a command. BUGS addresses program design deficiencies
and tells where a program can deviate from its expected behavior.

7.3

Searching with Keywords

The on-line manual consists of a number of files in the **/usr/man** directory (and in the case of System V, the **/usr/lib/help** directory). On many
systems you can have the **man** utility search the on-line manual database for all entries containing a specific keyword. As with any reference

book, it is easier to search the manual's table of contents than to search the entire book for a specific piece of information.

Searching for Utilities That Perform a Function

UNIX provides a utility for locating manual entries through *keyword pattern matching*. Descriptions of each entry in the manual's table of contents or in a special on-line help database are searched for occurrences of the keyword. All entry descriptions that contain a match for that keyword are returned. This process is similar to that of the **grep** utility.

The keyword searching capability is not available on all systems.

1. Suppose you have forgotten the command to send a file to the printer. Do a keyword search for the word *printer* to see which entries relate to printers.

   man -k *printer*

   If **man -k** does not work, try **apropos** *printer*. Among the entries listed, you will find either the **lp** command for System V, or the **lpr** command for BSD. Both commands send files to a line printer for printing.

2. Do similar searches using the keywords *move, edit, help,* and *file*.

3. Search the table of contents for the word *copy* by typing

   man -k *copy*

   The output is similar to the following:

   ```
   arff, flcopy (8)            - archiver and copier
                                for floppy

   bcopy, bcmp, bzero, ffs (3) - bit and byte string
                                operations

   cp (1)                      - copy

   dd (1)                      - convert and copy a
                                file
   ```

```
fork (3F)                    - create a copy of this
                               process

rcp (1C)                     - remote file copy

uucp, uulog (1C)             - UNIX to UNIX copy
```

Each of these table of contents entries contains the word *copy*, either in the title or in the brief description that follows. You will find the output from the search to be familiar; the lines are taken from the NAME section for each of the returned entries. The **man -k** command performs a pattern-matching search of the NAME section for each related entry in the on-line manual.

The keyword may be any combination of letters. Notice that the first two entries in the **man -k** output do not contain *copy* as a separate word; instead, *copy* is part of the title word. When doing a keyword search, **man -k** searches for all instances of the string *copy*, whether or not it is a word.

Titles separated by a comma indicate shared entries. If you examine the entry for **arff**, you also see the entry for **flcopy**, and vice versa. The two commands are identical in everything but name.

Using More Than One Keyword

You can use more than one keyword argument during a keyword search of the table of contents.

1. Search for a utility that identifies duplicated or repeated lines (that is, the two words are interchangeable). Type this command:

   man -k *duplicate repeat*

   You get a display similar to the ones shown here:

   ```
   dup, dup2 (2)        - duplicate a descriptor

   uniq (1)             - report repeated lines in a
                          file

   yes (1)              - output string repeatedly
   ```

All manual entries that have *any* of the keywords you specified appear in the output. The default is an *or* operation. If one keyword or another is found in the manual entry, the utility is selected for the output. This is particularly useful in a search for a keyword with common synonyms. In the above example, you can see that the **uniq** utility finds repeated lines in a file. If you had searched only for the keyword *duplicate*, you would not have found **uniq**.

To examine the *keyword* possibilities in UNIX, enter

   man -k *keyword*

All programs that include *keyword* in the title or summary are listed.

■ Review 1

1. What command displays the manual entry for **man**?

2. There are three entries titled *sleep* in Sections 1, 3, and 3F respectively. How would you examine the entry in Section 3?

3. What command would you type to search the **man** table of contents for all references to the word *file*?

7.4

■ Requiring Two Entries to Limit the Search

In the previous exercise, you searched for a single keyword. At times the goal is to search for one keyword *and* another. You can perform more complex keyword searches by combining a keyword search command with other utilities.

Searching for Combinations of Keywords

You have seen how to use **man -k** to search for lines containing one or several keywords, but how do you search for a specific line with several keywords in it? By sending the output of a search to the **grep** utility, you can retain only the lines that contain several keywords.

1. Find all lines in the table of contents that mention either the word *receive* or the word *send*, by entering

   man -k *send receive*

   The lines from the table of contents that contain the words *send* or *receive* appear on your screen.

2. You can distill the output further by sending the results of the multiple-keyword search to the **grep** utility to select only those lines containing *both* words. Try this command:

   man -k *receive* | **grep** *send*

   The **man -k** command produces all entries with descriptions containing the pattern *receive*. The output of the **man -k** command is then sent to the **grep** utility, which retains only those descriptions containing the pattern *send*. Therefore, only the lines that contain both the word *send* and the word *receive* are selected.

   In summary, to perform a keyword search for lines containing a combination of keywords, use this command:

   man -k *keyword1* | **grep** *keyword2* | **grep** *keyword3* . . .

Searching a Specific Manual Section

The **-k** option tells **man** to search for keywords through all sections of the manual. You can search a specific section of the manual by using **grep** and regular expressions.

1. Search the table of contents for lines containing the word *system*, piping the output to **pg** or **more**.

2. Restrict the output to lines from Section 1. Type this command:

   man -k *system* | **grep** *"(1"*

   The output is similar to the following:

```
hostid (1)       - set or print identifier of current
                   host system

hostname (1)     - set or print name of current host
                   system

msgs (1)         - system messages

sendbug (1)      - mail a system bug report to bugs@isi

sysline (1)      - display system status on status line
                   of a workstation

time (1)         - print a command's elapsed, system
                   and user times

tip, cu (1C)     - connect to a remote system

uptime (1)       - length of time system has been up

users (1)        - compact list of users who are on the
                   system

who (1)          - who is on the system
```

This output is considerably shorter than what would be produced by a keyword search through the entire table of contents for the word *system*.

7.5

Outputing Manual Pages to a File or Printer

The output of **man** is normally sent to the screen. You can also instruct the shell to redirect the output of **man** to a file or to the printer.

1. Redirect the manual entry for **man** by entering this command:

   man *man* > *man.manpage*

2. Now examine *man.manpage* with the editor by entering

   vi *man.manpage*

Included in the output on many systems are a number of control characters that make the output difficult to read. If you had printed the **man** output, the control characters would have been included in the printed output, as well.

3. One way to dispose of these characters is to redirect **man** output to an intermediary utility. Quit the editor, and from the shell enter one of the following commands.

For BSD:

man *who* | **colcrt** > *who.manpage*

For System V:

man *who* | **col -bx** > *who.manpage*

4. Examine the *who.manpage* by entering

vi *who.manpage*

The control characters are removed.

5. To print the output of **man**, enter one of the following commands.
For BSD:

man *who* | **colcrt** | **lpr**

For System V:

man *who* | **col -bx** | **lpr**

The **colcrt** and **col** utilites remove the terminal control characters.

7.6

Browsing Through the On-Line Manual

The **man** utility can be used for looking randomly through the Reference Manual. Investigating the manual in this way can uncover some interesting relationships between utilities. This is one of the best ways to increase your knowledge of the UNIX system.

To browse through the manual, first consult an entry for a familiar utility, and then look up the entries listed under the SEE ALSO header.

1. Look up the manual entry for the **grep** utility in Section 1. Type this command:

   man *1 grep*

2. Scan through the entry and look for the SEE ALSO header. One of the entries there is

   ```
   sed(1)
   ```

3. Examine the manual entry for **sed** in Section 1 by typing

   man *1 sed*

   The **sed** utility is a stream editor that reads from standard input, makes changes, and writes to standard output. Its most common use is pattern search and replacement.

4. Look for the SEE ALSO header again. One entry listed is

   ```
   awk(1)
   ```

5. Look up the entry for **awk** in Section 1. Type

   man *1 awk*

   You will find that **awk** is a pattern scanning and processing language.

6. Notice that each of the entries you have looked at has mentioned *process scanning*. Continue to browse, and you are referred to a utility called **lex** and then to a compiler generator called **yacc**.

7.7

Using the Hardcopy Manual and the Permuted Index

The original hardcopy version of the UNIX Reference Manual contained the eight numbered sections in one volume. Some recent versions have split the manual into three volumes:

- The *Users' Reference Manual* contains information about the standard UNIX commands, utilities, application packages, and games.

- The *Programmer's Reference Manual* contains information on the programming libraries, system calls, protocols, and special files.

- The *System Administrator's Manual* consists of procedures, files, application packages, and commands useful to system administrators.

The hardcopy manual contains the same manual pages as those displayed by the **man** utility, sorted alphabetically into the eight sections described earlier. This makes searching for entries somewhat tedious—because if you don't already know in which section to look, you must search several sections to find the entry you want.

Fortunately, the hardcopy manual comes with an index. On many systems, the index is a *permuted index*, also known as a *keyword-in-context index*. A permuted index allows you to do keyword searches similar to those done automatically by **man -k** or **apropos**.

Using a Permuted Index

Consider the following book titles:

> *The Golden Gate*
> *Interview with the Vampire*
> *One Hundred Years of Solitude*

The keywords for this list of titles are the words *Golden, Gate, Interview, Vampire, One, Hundred, Years,* and *Solitude.*

A permuted index of these titles is an alphabetized listing of certain rotated versions of the titles.

```
Gate, The Golden
Golden Gate, The
Hundred Years of Solitude, One
Interview with the Vampire
One Hundred Years of Solitude
Solitude, One Hundred Years of
```

```
Vampire, Interview with the
Years of Solitude, One Hundred
```

Specifically, in the preceding permuted index

- Each title appears exactly once for each keyword it contains.
- Each entry has had its words cyclically shifted until it begins with a keyword.
- Each keyword in a title appears at the beginning of some shifted version of that title.
- No duplicate entries appear.
- The shifted titles appear in alphabetical order.

In the hardcopy version of the manual, the permuted index of command names and titles appears in this equivalent but easier-to-read form:

```
          The Golden    Gate

                 The    Golden Gate

                 One    Hundred Years of Solitude

                        Interview with the Vampire

                        One Hundred Years of Solitude

One Hundred Years of    Solitude

   Interview with the    Vampire

        One Hundred    Years of Solitude
```

1. Suppose you want to find the title of a book that contains the keyword *Vampire*. If you scan along the words to the right of the wide center space in the preceding list (it is sorted alphabetically), you will find this entry:

```
Interview with the    Vampire
```

2. Now look at the permuted index for the hardcopy manual. Search for entries that contain the word *editor*. You will find something similar to the following:

```
screen-oriented      editor based on ex          vi(1)

(visual) display

ed(1) red(1) text    editor                      ed(1)

ex(1) text           editor                      ex(1)

sed(1) stream        editor                      sed(1)

edit(1) text         editor(variant of ex)       edit(1)
```

There are references to five editors: **vi**, **ed**, **ex**, **sed**, and **edit**. By looking at the permuted index, you can find the entry you are looking for.

■ Review 2

1. What command would you type to find all Section 1 entries containing the keyword *directory*?

2. What part of a manual entry refers to other manual entries?

3. While searching a permuted index for a particular word or phrase, which column do you look at?

■ Conclusion

In this chapter, you consulted the on-line or hardcopy manual for assistance with UNIX utilities. If your system allows, you can also search the table of contents to find an appropriate entry relating to your questions. If you cannot search the on-line table of contents, you can use the permuted index of the hardcopy manual to search for entries relating to a topic. By using the manual, you can get descriptions and instructions for commands, or find the right command to perform a task.

■ Answers to Review 1

1. **man** *man*
2. **man** *3 sleep*
3. **man -k** *file* **|** **more** or **man -k** *file* **|** **pg**

■ Answers to Review 2

1. **man -k** *directory* **|** **grep** *"(1"*
2. The part under the heading SEE ALSO
3. Search the column to the right of the blank center column.

COMMAND SUMMARY

man *section*   Displays the on-line manual entry named *command*
command   from Section *section*.

man -k *word(s)*   Displays all lines in the table of contents containing
any word listed in *word(s)*.

Chapter Eight

Controlling User Processes

UNIX is a multiuser, multitasking computer environment. At any given moment several users can be on a UNIX system, each having different operations under way. One user may be editing a file in the foreground and at the same time performing a database update in the background. Meanwhile, other users are running whatever programs they need. The system itself is also running tasks, handling central processor scheduling, reading and writing to the disk, sending mail, printing jobs, and completing other system functions.

When you enter a command line at the shell prompt and press (Return), the shell arranges for execution of the utilities specified in the command line. When a utility is executed, instructions located in a command file are loaded into memory and followed by the system, resulting in some action being performed for you. Most of the commands that you have used so far—**vi**, **cat**, and **who**, for instance—are utilities. The shell, too, is just another program or utility.

When a utility is being executed, a *process* is under way. Computer memory is addressed, the CPU performs calculations, information is written back to and from memory, output is written, and the process dies. When a utility such as **vi** is being executed by several users (or several times by the same user), each execution of the program is a separate process. When UNIX was designed, multitasking was a main objective. The goal was to allow several tasks to be accomplished at the same time. The problem was keeping all the activity straight. Processes were the solution.

As you are working on the system, you are interacting with processes. When a utility is not responding as you expect it to, you need to request a listing of current processes, and often will proceed to stop, kill, or restart the processes involved.

In this chapter, you will investigate how the hardware and software execute utilities via processes. Knowledge of the execution of a process will help you monitor and control your processes more effectively.

SKILLS CHECK: Before beginning this chapter, you should be able to

- *Move files and change directories within the UNIX file system*
- *Issue complex commands to the shell*

- *Employ permissions to specify access to files and directories by the owner, groups of users, and other users on a system*

OBJECTIVES: *After completing this chapter, you will be able to*
- *Display process information and identify problems with processes*
- *Describe the life cycle of a process*
- *Terminate problem processes*

8.1

Processing Processes

A *process* is the data, CPU activity, memory accesses, and other events associated with an instance of a program's execution. For instance, you request **date**; a process runs the date code. Some processes, such as **date**, run only a short time; others run continuously. All processes, however, go through a life cycle that begins with their creation (*spawning*) and ends with their death (*exiting*).

You log on to your system. A shell process begins. You enter commands to the shell. The shell interprets the commands you type in, executes the utilities requested, waits, then after the utilities are finished, asks you what you want to do next.

Identifying Your Processes

1. Display information about processes currently running, with one of the following commands:

On SYSTEM V:

ps

On BSD:

ps -g

The output shows at least two processes running, as shown in the following table. In your output, the numbers shown in the first three columns will be different. There may be other columns such as STAT.

PID	TTY	TIME	COMMAND
8464	2	1:20	ksh
9512	2	0:05	ps

2. Using the output displayed on your terminal from the **ps** command, fill out the following chart:

PID	TIME	COMMAND

In this example, two processes are listed, and you have recorded three pieces of information for each process:

- A PID (pronounced "pee-eye-dee")
- The time
- The command

PID   The numbers in the PID column are **P**rocess **ID**entifiers. As processes are created in UNIX, each is assigned a PID, somewhat like a customer receiving a number when entering a busy bakery. The numbering of PIDs begins with 0 at system startup. If 1,207 were the PID of your **ps** process, it might or might not be the 1,208th process started on your system since the last time the system was rebooted. PID numbers do not simply increase forever. Each system has a maximum process identification number and, when this number is reached, the numbering starts over again from the first *available* number greater than 1.

TIME   This is the CPU time used by the process so far. Because systems are quite fast, this is often zero.

COMMAND   The items listed in this column are the names of the utilities associated with each of the processes you have running. (In this example, a shell and **ps** are listed.)

Examining Processes as Temporary Entities

All processes have a definite beginning time and ending time.

1. When you run **ps**, one of the processes listed is **ps**. When the **ps** utility is running, it lists all the processes that are running at that time. Thus it lists itself.

2. Run the **ps** utility again. Type

   ps

   and fill out the following chart based on this new output.

PID	COMMAND

Compare the PIDs for the shell process in this and the previous table. It is the same PID, and, therefore, the same shell process as before.

Compare the PIDs for the **ps** process in the two tables. They are different. The second instance of executing the **ps** utility is a new one.

When a user enters a utility name at the shell prompt, a process is created to carry out the instructions contained within the utility. The process completes its task, writes its output, and dies. If the user then enters the same command name again (as you just did with the **ps** command), a new process is created, with a new PID.

Examining the Life Cycle of a Shell Process

Most processes live short, happy lives executing utilities. They perform their functions and then die.

1. Log out now and then log back on.
2. After you have logged on again, get a list of the processes you are running. Type

   ps

   or

   ps -g

   and compare the PID of your current shell with the PID of your previous shell, which you noted in the tables on the previous pages.

This is a new shell process. It has a new PID. When you logged out, you killed the old one. The shell process that you are now using was created when you logged on. It cycles through the following steps until you log out:

- Print a prompt
- Wait until the user enters a command line
- Interpret the command line
- Execute the utilities named in the command line
- Wait for the utilities to complete
- Print a prompt
- Wait

The third step, *interpret the command line*, was examined in detail in previous chapters dealing with other shell commands.

When you enter the command **exit** or Ctrl-d, the shell process finally does what all processes do when they reach the end of a file or receive an exit command—it dies. Shell processes go through the same life cycle as other processes. Because they are ordinary processes, they can interpret your commands and spawn other processes as requested.

Connecting to a Process Through a Port

A process is more than just the instructions in the utility being executed. A process maintains information about itself, about the user, and about how the system is executing the process. The first part of this information that you have already seen is the PID. Another column of information about the process revealed by the **ps** utility is the associated port or *tty*.

1. Enter the **ps** command again, to examine the processes you are currently running.

The value displayed under the TTY column heading is the same for all the processes you have just entered. It corresponds to the port on the computer where your terminal display is attached. Each *tty* can have a number of processes attached to it.

Most user processes need to read input from and write output to a terminal display. Thus, most user processes must be informed of the *tty* or port to which they are attached. These data are stored with each process and are displayed as part of the output of the **ps** command.

Transforming a Utility into a Process

Earlier, we defined a utility as a set of instructions stored in a file, and a process as an instance of the execution of these instructions. This does not explain where utilities and processes are located, nor why a process is called a process. The answers to these questions are based on the functions performed by three important pieces of hardware:

- The disk
- The main memory
- The CPU

Figure 8-1 and the following paragraphs describe each of these components and their relationships.

Disks   Disks are magnetic storage devices that are relatively slow to read and write, but are permanent. All files, including utilities, are stored on a disk.

Main Memory   Main memory is a collection of computer chips that temporarily store information. The instructions contained in a utility are transferred from the disk to main memory and are then executed by the CPU.

CPU   The central processing unit (CPU) is the computer logic chip that executes instructions. The CPU cannot execute instructions directly from the disk; rather, it deals exclusively with instructions stored in main memory. The CPU processes data at a much higher rate than any magnetic disk can provide it.

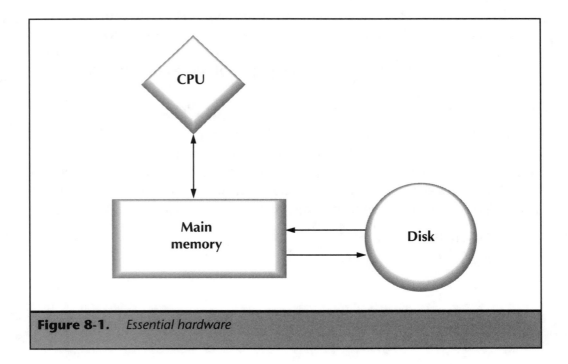

Figure 8-1.   *Essential hardware*

The Steps of a Process

The sequence of events in the life of a process is as follows:

- The shell process is running. It places a prompt on the screen.

- You type in the name of the utility that is to be run and press Return.

- The shell interprets the command line, instructing the kernel to execute the utility. The shell process sleeps until the newly requested process dies.

- The kernel's execution of the new process includes loading the utility's instructions from disk into main memory, for use by the created process.

- The system adds an entry referring the new process to a *ready queue,* which has entries for all of the processes in the system that are ready to run. The process then waits for attention from the CPU.

- Eventually the system, according to its scheduling parameters, gives a waiting process its share of CPU time.

- After the CPU reaches the end of the instructions, the process dies.

- The exit status of the child shell is passed back to the parent shell, which ends the parent's wait.

- The system then frees the locations in main memory occupied by the process, so that it may be used by other processes.

- After the shell wakes up, the CPU continues with the shell utility's instructions where it left off. The shell now displays the prompt and waits to receive new input from the user.

SUMMARY: A process is an instance of a running program, the instructions of which were loaded from the disk to main memory and executed by the CPU.

8.2

Using the ps Utility to Obtain Data About Processes

You can obtain a great deal of information about processes.

1. To generate a long listing of your processes, type this command:

   ps -l

2. More fields are included in the **-l** display than were displayed in the earlier outputs. Using the data displayed on your screen, locate the following four fields and fill in this chart:

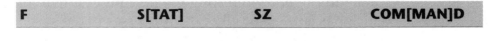

F	S[TAT]	SZ	COM[MAN]D

Following are descriptions of the fields in this display.

F This mysteriously named field contains a number indicating what Flags are set for the process. For this purpose the only meaningful number is the one that indicates the process is in memory. Which of your processes are in memory? Certainly **ps**—it must be in memory when it is running, and it must be running while it is performing its function. And probably the shell that is running, **csh** or **ksh**, is in memory. Most processes are in memory at any given moment.

S[TAT] The State field contains a capital letter indicating the state of the process. The most common states are sleeping (S), and running or runnable (R). Other states are idle (I) and traced (T).

- A process is sleeping (S) if it has been idle (I) for less than 20 seconds.

- If a process is runnable (BSD), the process is currently in the run queue and can be run whenever the CPU is free. A process that is actually being run by the CPU is said to be running (System V). If you have a multiprocessor System V, you might see several processes listed with state R, indicating that more than one CPU is busy running a process.

- A process is idle (I) if it has been inactive for longer than 20 seconds.

- If the process is stopped by a signal from the parent process, it is in the traced (T) state.

SZ The SiZe field contains a number that indicates the size of the process in memory. If you can read hexadecimal (base 16), you can use this field to determine the relative sizes of processes. Depending on which system you are using, the process size may be given in kilobytes, blocks, or pages. Details such as process size unit of measurement are best determined by checking the manual pages of your system.

1. To access the manual pages for **ps** on your system, enter the command

   man *ps*

2. Scroll through the pages to find the process size unit for your system.

COM[MAN]D This label refers to the actual command being run by the process.

Identifying the Parent Process

A process is much more than a series of instructions for the CPU to follow. Important data are associated with each process, including the workstation (*tty*) to which it is attached, a list of open files to which it can write, and other pertinent information. When you create a process, it inherits most of this information from its *parent process*.

1. Enter the following command to explore how a process obtains data:

   ps -l

2. Using the new subset of fields displayed by the **ps -l** command, fill in the following chart:

PID	PPID	TTY	COM[MAN]D

Essentially, each process is created, or spawned, by a previously existing process—its parent process. Specifically, in the table you just created, the PPID (**P**arent **P**rocess **ID**entifier) associated with the **ps** process is identical to the PID associated with **ps**'s parent, the shell process (**csh**, **sh**, or **ksh**). The shell process executed the **ps** and is the parent of the **ps** process. When the PID of a process matches the PPID of another process, the former process is the parent of the latter.

Processes inherit data from their parent process. When you log on to the system, your first process, usually the shell process, is started up by the login program. From then on, every utility or executable filename that you type in is executed by a process that is a child (or *n*th grandchild) of your shell process. Certain shell built-in commands are exceptions to this principle; they are commands internal to the shell process itself, so the current shell runs them rather than creating a new process. Because each new process that is created is a child process, it inherits data (such as *tty*, user id, current directory) from the parent process. Variables that are exported are passed to the child shell.

Telling Parents About Exit Status

An exit status allows you to figure out whether a program exited smoothly. There are basically two exit statuses that are important:

- Zero
- Greater than zero

When a utility exits, it tells its parent the status of its exit. If it says *0*, everything is well. But when a utility exits with anything other than *0*, there was a problem.

1. Enter the following successful program:

   grep *root /etc/passwd*

   You see lines containing the pattern *root* on your screen.

2. Check the exit status of **grep** by entering one of the following:
   On BSD:

   echo $*status*

   On System V:

   echo $*?*

   The shell variable *status* or *?* has the value of whatever the last executed process declared.

   The output shows that **grep** returned an exit status of *0* because everything went smoothly, and it found the pattern *root*.

3. Now try a pattern that does not exist, such as *I_love_UNIX*. Enter

   grep *I_love_UNIX /etc/passwd*

   You see nothing but a new prompt. The pattern *I_love_UNIX* does not exist in */etc/passwd*.

4. Check the exit status by entering one of the following:
   On BSD:

   echo $*status*

   On System V:

   echo $*?*

   The value of the exit status is now *1* because **grep** did not find the pattern *I_love_UNIX*. To **grep**, not finding a matching pattern means a "bad" exit. It tells the shell, "We're out of here—*1*."

5. Now try to get **grep** to search a nonexisting file, by entering

   grep *root filexyabmm*

You see an error message such as

```
grep: file xyabmm:  No such file or directory
```

Check the exit status with the **echo** command again. The exit status is a **2**, which is returned by **grep** when it has to exit halfway into the program due to syntax errors or inaccessible files (in this case, an inaccessible file caused the exit status of **2**).

Obtaining Detailed Information on All Processes

To this point, you have been using **ps** to display information concerning processes that are owned only by you. The output of **ps** can be expanded to include all processes, regardless of owner.

1. Enter one of the following commands:

    On BSD:

    ps -aux | more

    On System V:

    ps -ef | pg

    The output you see is a list of essentially all the processes on the system. Many of them belong to *root*, because *root* is the owner of many system processes.

■ Review 1

1. Describe the life cycle of the process that would execute the command **who**, located in */bin*.

2. Consider the following scenario: You log on to your system on *tty23*. The system starts a **csh** for you, which has a PID of *1056*. Then you start a shell script (the script is executed by a **sh** with a PID of *1080*) that in turn executes **who** (a PID of *2020*).

    ■ What is the PPID of the **who** process?

- What is the PPID of the shell executing the script?
- With information provided, can you determine with what *tty* the **who** process is associated?

8.3

Running a Process in the Background

When a process runs in the background, the shell does not wait for it to complete before asking for the next command to interpret or start another child process. The major difference between processes in the background and processes in the foreground is how the shell proceeds after it starts them.

Waiting for da Go

For the next few steps you will use a utility called **sleep**. The **sleep** utility interprets its one argument as the number of seconds to wait before exiting.

1. Type the command

   sleep *10*

   In about ten seconds you will again get the shell prompt. (The length of the pause could be more than ten seconds because of process scheduling delays, but it will be at least ten seconds.)

In these **sleep** exercises, the **sleep** utility is used here to illustrate the function of the *system call* **wait**. A system call is a special kind of subroutine call made by a utility, to get computing attention from the kernel. All requests for kernel services are made using system calls.

When you enter the **sleep** command, your shell starts a new process to run the **sleep** utility. As the **sleep** process executes (by pausing for the specified number of seconds), your shell process is **wait**ing for the child to finish before proceeding. In a distortion of *Sleeping Beauty*, the kiss that awakens your shell process is the death of the **sleep** process.

8.4

Killing Processes That Are Under Way

Generally, once a process is under way, it runs until it is finished, or you issue a keyboard interrupt by typing a Ctrl-c, or else you log out. You can also instruct the process to die by issuing a specific **kill** command from the shell.

1. Type the command

   sleep *200* **&**

2. Examine the list of current processes, with

   ps

3. Identify the PID of the **sleep** process, and kill the process with

   kill *PID*

   The shell responds with

   ```
   [1]   Terminated     sleep 200
   ```

   to show you the final disposition of the process.

The **kill** command sends one of several types of *signals*, which are like bad-news telegrams. Upon receipt of a signal, a process may be programmed to forestall its demise by *catching* the signal or it may follow the signal's instruction and die. Not all utilities can catch signals.

Many utilities can be killed from the keyboard by typing the keyboard interrupt character, usually Ctrl-c. The very same effect can be achieved by sending *signal 2* (**kill -2** *PID*) to the process. In fact, the keyboard interrupt character just causes the terminal driver to send *signal 2* to the foreground process attached to your terminal. The shell process, as well, gets *signal 2* when you type the keyboard interrupt character; but it wisely has been programmed to catch the signal and does nothing special about it.

When you used the **kill** *PID* command above, you relied on the default signal that **kill** uses when you do not indicate a preference. The default signal is *signal 15*, known as the *Software Termination* signal. The response you got from the shell indicated that the process was terminated by the signal. This is what happens when a process receives the Software Termination signal and is programmed not to catch it.

Sometimes killing a process with the default Software Termination signal has no effect because the process catches that signal, or because of the peculiarities in the way signals get delivered by the system. In these situations, the process continues to appear in the output of **ps**. Often by just sending a different signal, you can eliminate the process.

1. Once more, type the command

   sleep *200* **&**

2. Identify the PID of the **sleep** process and kill the process, with this command:

   kill -1 *PID*

   If you get a shell prompt without a message, type ⌜Return⌝ again. This time you will see this shell response:

   ```
   [2] Hangup     sleep 200
   ```

   indicating that the process was terminated with *signal 1*, the *Hangup* signal.

3. Start a child shell. Determine its PID by entering

   echo $$

4. Attempt to kill the shell by entering

   kill *PID*
   echo $$

5. If the shell catches the terminal signal, try the following until the child shell is terminated.

kill -1 *PID*
echo $$
kill -2 *PID*
echo $$
kill -3 *PID*
echo $$
kill -9 *PID*

Other signal numbers you can try to kill a process are 2, 3, and— when nothing else works—9. *Signal 9* is special; it cannot be caught by the process, so it signals certain death. However, you should always try one or more of the other signals first, because processes need to go through some cleanup procedure before they die. They may catch most signals, perform the necessary cleanup, and then put themselves to death. Sending them *signal 9* would prevent them from performing the cleanup operations.

■ Review 2

1. Let's say you start a process that appears to be taking too much time. You decide to terminate the process, but find that typing [Ctrl]-[c] doesn't do anything. How do you determine the **P**rocess **ID**entifier of the wayward process? Hint: **ps -t** *nn* lists processes attached to *tty nn*.

2. Once you determine the PID of the process in question 1, how do you kill it?

3. What would happen if you entered the following sequence of commands to your shell:

who > */dev/null* **&**
sleep *100* **&**
mail *margaret* < */etc/motd* **&**
wait

■ Conclusion

In this chapter you have used the **ps** command in some new variations that are valuable tools for system management and troubleshooting. You have also examined the composition of processes and how they come into being. This knowledge is essential for managing processes that you launch from the shell. UNIX is processes.

■ Answers to Review 1

1. The file *lbinlwho* exists on the disk. You type in the **who** command. The system loads the utility from the disk into main memory. The CPU executes the instructions in main memory, resulting in a list of users currently logged on to be printed on your terminal. When the last name is printed (the instructions are finished), the process dies, and the space in main memory taken up by the process is freed for use by other processes.

2. 1080; 1056; yes: *tty 23*

■ Answers to Review 2

1. Log on to another screen or workstation. From the second terminal run *tty* to identify the port for the second session. Then run **who** to find your original session, being careful to avoid the entry containing the port you just started. Next, run **ps** **-t** *nn*, where *nn* is the port of your original session. Look for the name of the process causing the problem, in the COMMAND column.

2. You can **kill** the wayward process with **kill** *PID*, where *PID* is the Process IDentifier you found from **ps**. If this doesn't work, try **kill** **-1** *PID*. Failing even that, use **kill** **-9** *PID*. Finally, log out of your second session.

3. The **who** command would execute, but its output would disappear; *margaret* would receive a copy of the message of the day in the mail; and your prompt would be returned in roughly 100 seconds, after all the above are complete.

COMMAND SUMMARY

ps	Lists all processes that you own.
ps -l	Generates a long listing of processes that you own.
ps -f	Outputs a full listing of processes that you own.
ps -u *login*	Lists processes that are owned by the user whose login id is *login*.
ps -t *nn*	Lists processes that are associated with the workstation *tty*.
ps -e	Prints information about all processes.
ps -a	Prints information about all processes with workstations.
kill *PID*	Terminates a process.
kill -1 *PID*	Hangs up a process. Does not work on background processes.
kill -9 *PID*	Kills a process. Usually the last form of **kill** to try. Cannot be ignored, but may not allow the utility to clean up.

Chapter Nine

Printing Files

An essential function of a UNIX system is printing files. The printing software is organized so that files can be sent to several different printers attached to one computer or another on the network. In this chapter you will print files, check the status of a printing job request, choose print options, and cancel print jobs.

There are significant differences between the commands to print files on machines running a version of System V and those running software derived from BSD UNIX. Both sets of commands are included in the following exercises and are listed in the command summary at the end of the chapter.

SKILLS CHECK: *Before beginning this chapter you should be able to*

- *Access and leave the system*
- *Execute basic commands*
- *Create, display, and print files*
- *Create and modify files using the* **vi** *editor*
- *Use the* **mail** *command to send and receive messages*

OBJECTIVES: *After completing this chapter, you will be able to*

- *Start print jobs*
- *Use command options to alter default print settings*
- *Get information on the status of your print jobs*
- *Cancel print jobs*

9.1

Sending Files to Be Printed

In earlier exercises, you sent files to be printed by either using the default command or specifying a printer by name. If your account was set up with a default printer, a variable *PRINTER* is set. To see if that is the case, enter

    echo $*PRINTER*

If a printer name is displayed, you can enter commands such as

    lpr *file*

or

    lp *file*

without specifying a printer name. If no value for *PRINTER* is displayed, ask another user or your system administrator for the name of a printer designation that you can use. The commands in this chapter contain the printer name *printer*. You'll need to substitute your printer name for *printer* when you enter each command.

    If a second printer is available on your system, get its printer designation as well, because part of this chapter involves switching a print job from one printer to another.

1. Type one of the following commands (substituting the name of your printer for *printer*).

   On System V:

   lp -d*printer* *practice*

   On BSD:

   lpr -P*printer* *practice*

   The **-d***printer* and **-P***printer* portions of these commands request a specific printer. The entire command line instructs the line printer program to send a copy of *filename* to the specified printer. Your print job waits in line in a printer queue until its turn to be printed.

2. Create a new small file called *junk1*, including some text, such as

This is a test file, and I am going to use
it to try out different print commands.

Sending More Than One File to the Queue

In one command line, you can specify several files to be printed, by listing them all as arguments to the print command.

1. Print the two files, *junk1* and *practice*, by typing the appropriate command line.

On System V:

lp -d*printer junk1 practice*

On BSD:

lpr -P*printer junk1 practice*

Printing the Output of a Pipeline

As with most other UNIX utilities, you can connect the output of another utility to the input of the print utility, using a pipe. Here are two examples.

1. You can instruct the system to print the contents of the current directory without first creating a file. Have the shell connect the output of **ls** directly to the input of **lp** or **lpr**. Type one of the following commands:

On System V:

ls | lp -d*printer*

On BSD:

ls | lpr -P*printer*

The output of the **ls** utility is sent directly to the **lp** or **lpr** utility, which sends the data to the printer exactly as if that output had been stored in a file. This piping feature allows you to make hard copy of on-line information.

2. If your system has the on-line UNIX manual, get a hard copy of the manual pages describing the **sort** utility. Type one of the following commands:

On System V:

man *sort* | **col -bx** | **lp -d***printer*

On BSD:

man *sort* | **colcrt** | **lpr -P***printer*

The **col -bx** and **colcrt** utilities remove control characters that are of value to terminals but make reading a printed version difficult.

3. Modify the previous **man** command, to print a copy of the manual pages for the **lp** or **lpr** utility.

Sending Your Job to a Different Printer

If you have more than one printer available, you can explicitly select a specific printer when you issue the print command. If you do not have an alternative printer, skip ahead to the next section.

1. Print the file *junk1* on the printer *printer2*, where *printer2* is the name of the second printer on your system. Type one of the following commands:

On System V:

lp -d*printer2 junk1*

On BSD:

lpr -P*printer2 junk1*

These commands allow you to choose your printer. That way, when one printer is down or occupied, you can send your print requests to another. Installations often use different queues for different printing styles, such as landscape, portrait, letterhead, and so on.

9.2

Using Print Command Options

The printer programs **lp** and **lpr** are UNIX utilities. You can modify the operation of each program by specifying options, identified with the usual minus sign.

Printing Multiple Copies

Suppose you need a copy of your *junk1* file for several of your colleagues. You can send the file to the printer once for each copy you need, but a more efficient way is to issue a single command line asking for multiple copies.

1. For example, request five copies of the file *junk1* by typing one of the following command lines:

   On System V:

   lp -d*printer2* **-n**5 *junk1*

   The option **-n**5 tells **lp** to print five copies of the file.

   On BSD:

   lpr -P*printer2* **- #**5 *junk1*

   The option **- #**5 instructs **lpr** to print five copies of the file.

Adding a Title Line to the Banner Page

Each of the jobs you just printed probably was preceded by a *banner page*, also called a burst page, containing information about the printer and about the user issuing the print request. If you want, you can add a title line to this banner page.

1. Add your own title and print the *junk1* file again. Type one of the following commands:

   On System V:

   lp -d*printer* **-t**"*Escaped Leopard Spotted*" *junk1*

On BSD:

lpr -P*printer* **-J***"Escaped Leopard Spotted"* *junk1*

The formats of the two print commands are as follows:
On System V:

lp -d*printer* **-t***title* *filename*

On BSD:

lpr -P*printer* **-J***title* *filename*

Notice there is no space between the **-t** or the **-J** and the *title*.

When you use either the **-t** option in System V or the **-J** option in BSD, the title you provide is printed on the banner page preceding your print job. If your title contains blank spaces, follow these guidelines.

- In System V, enclose the entire title in double or single quotation marks, or precede each space by a backslash character, as in the following examples:

    lp -d*printer* **-t***"A Title Containing Blanks"* *filename*

    lp -d*printer* **-t***'A Title Containing Blanks'* *filename*

    lp -d*printer* **-t***A\ Title\ Containing\ Blanks* *filename*

- In BSD, use quotation marks to include spaces.

TIP: *Title lines are particularly useful for identifying different versions of the same file; for instance:*

lp -dprinter -t"23june-7:31 Proposal" proposal

Suppressing Messages to the Workstation

On System V, when you use **lp** to request a print job, the system replies with a message that it has processed your request and assigned a serial number to the job:

```
request  id  is  printer-#
```

You can suppress this message by entering the following command:

lp **-s** **-d***printer junk1*

The shell prompt is then returned to you without the message.

The **-s** option suppresses the "request id…" message that is routinely sent to your workstation.

Because the BSD **lpr** command does not send a message to your screen upon receipt of your print request, there is no option to suppress the message.

Determining When a Job Is Printed

The "request id…" message tells you when the program that controls the printer has queued your print job.

1. With System V (but not BSD), you can also ask the print utility to notify you when the printer has completed your job, by typing

   lp **-w** **-d***printer junk1*

   You will first see this message:

   ```
   request  id  is  printer-#
   ```

   on your workstation. This message tells you only that the file *junk1* has been placed in the queue; it does not tell you that the file has been printed. After a few seconds (or a few minutes if your system is busy), you'll see the following message:

   ```
   lp: printer  request  printer-#  has  been  printed
   on  printer  name
   ```

The **-w** option instructs **lp** to write information to your workstation telling you when your job has finished printing.

Getting Mail Concerning Print Status

You can instruct the program to send mail to you rather than display a terminal message when the printer has finished your job.

1. On System V, type this command:

   lp -m -d*printer junk1*

   You will first see the message:

   ```
   request id is printer-#
   ```

   The shell prompt returns, and you can continue with other activities. After a few minutes, you receive the following message:

   ```
   You have new mail
   ```

2. When you read this mail, the content of the message is as follows:

   ```
   printer request printer-# has been printed on
   printer name
   ```

1. On BSD, type this command:

   lpr -m -P*printer junk1*

2. After a few minutes, you receive the following message:

   ```
   You have new mail
   ```

   When you read this mail, the content of the message is as follows:

   ```
   printer request printer-# has been printed on
   printer name
   ```

The **-m** option instructs the spooler to send you mail when a print job is complete.

9.3

Checking the Status of Print Jobs

On some systems, print jobs are sent faster than the printer can produce the output. A list or queue of jobs to run is kept. Each new job is added to the list of jobs to be done. UNIX lets you check your specific print job, or all jobs from all users in the printer queues.

Collecting the Output from a Printer

The printer programs (**lp** and **lpr**) can handle the queues for several printers. When you enter your print command, you can specify which printer is employed for each job.

1. From the shell, type the appropriate print command.

   On System V:

   lp -d*printer junk1*

   On BSD:

   lpr -P*printer junk1*

   On System V, after a few seconds, a message similar to this one will appear:

   ```
   request  id  is  printer-#  (1 file)
   ```

This message indicates that the **lp** program ran successfully. In other words, your job is in the queue and **lp** has assigned a request id to your print job (*printer-#*). The *printer* in this id is the same destination printer name you specified in the command line. The # is a sequential number assigned to your print request by the program.

Whether you are on a System V or a BSD system, if you now go to the printer expecting to see your file printed or in the process of printing, you may be disappointed. It's entirely possible your print job will be waiting in line to be printed. Each print job is queued and printed as soon as its turn arrives.

The *spooler* is the program that administers print requests. The spooler receives print requests from multiple users and sends jobs one at a time to the printer. It is the spooler that makes it possible for the system to process simultaneous print job requests from several users.

When you type a print command followed by a printer designation and filename, the spooler processes your request, assigns a request number to the job submitted, and queues the job for printing at the specified destination. If the printer you specify is free, the print request is passed to the printer, and the file starts printing. Otherwise, the job must wait for the printer to be available.

Finding the Status of Your Print Jobs

You can search the printer queue for the status of any job you send (printed, printing, or waiting).

1. Send the file *junk1* to the printer, using the print command appropriate for your system. Your file *junk1* is now queued for printing, waiting for its turn to be printed.

2. Examine the queue by typing one of the following commands.

   On System V:

   lpstat

   which provides information concerning the **line printer status**.
   On BSD:

   lpq -P*printer username*

   where *username* is the login name of your current account, and *printer* is the selected printer.

If few people are using the printer, your print job is printed immediately upon request. There would be no trace of it in the output of **lpstat** or **lpq**. If your job is queued, what you see on screen depends on whether you are using System V or BSD, as described below.

System V Printer Queue

The **lpstat** command produces the following output on System V:

```
gutenberg-2232        adrian        234        Jan 12 13:02
```

This response tells you the request id (*gutenberg-2232*), the user who initiated the request (*adrian*), the number of characters to be printed (*234*), and the date and time of the print request (*Jan 12 13:02*).

If your job is currently printing, the output is similar to the following on System V:

```
gutenberg-2232      adrian          234         Jan 12 13:02
on gutenberg
```

The final phrase, *on gutenberg*, says this request is currently printing at the printer destination *gutenberg*.

BSD Printer Queue

On BSD, the **lpq** command output is as follows:

```
Rank        Owner       Job       Files           Total Size
1st         beeching    237       /etc/motd       545 bytes
```

If your job is currently printing, the output is

```
Rank        Owner       Job       Files
active      beeching    237       /etc/motd
```

The rank of "active" means the job is currently being printed by the printer.

Listing All Print Requests on System V

The commands in System V that you have used so far report only the print requests you have made. You can also get a complete picture of all requests. This allows you to identify the printer that has the shortest queue, so you can send your print job to that printer.

1. List all print requests on your System V system by typing the following:

   lpstat -t

The **-t** option on System V gives you a total listing of current events in the spooler. The output of **lpstat -t** looks something like this:

```
scheduler  is  running
system  default  destination:  gutenberg
```

```
device   for   gutenberg:   /dev/lp
device   for   prnt2:   /dev/tty08
gutenberg   accepting   requests   since   Oct 16 16:39:05 1995
prnt2   accepting   requests   since   Jan 6 13:24:10 1996
printer   gutenberg   now   printing   gutenberg-2228.
enabled   since   Sep 5 15:29
printer   prnt2   is   idle.   enabled   since   Jan 6 13:25
gutenberg-2228   wendy   9300   Jan 6 10:57   on   gutenberg
gutenberg-2232   dave   21 Jan 6 11:00
```

This display provides you with the following information about the print requests for all printers and all users.

SCHEDULER   The first line indicates that the spooler is currently active and accepting print requests:

```
scheduler   is   running
```

DEFAULT PRINTER   The second line tells you that the default printer for this system is *gutenberg*:

```
system   default   destination:   gutenberg
```

If a user has not specified a destination printer with the **-d** option, the spooler automatically sends the job to printer *gutenberg*.

NOTE: Your system may not have a default printer. If not, you will have to specify the destination for your request or set the PRINTER variable equal to the local printer.

PORTS FOR PRINTERS   The "device" lines tell you what physical device, or port, is associated with each of the printer names:

```
device   for   gutenberg:   /dev/lp
device   for   prnt2:   /dev/tty08
```

ACTIVITY STATUS   The next lines tell you whether or not each printer is accepting requests and, if so, for how long:

```
gutenberg   accepting   requests   since   April   23
14:30:05   1991
prnt2   accepting   requests   since   Jan   6   13:24:10   1996
```

PRINTER STATUS   The "printer" lines indicate the specific status of each printer, such as whether it is idle or printing, and what it is printing:

```
printer   gutenberg   now   printing   gutenberg-2228.
enabled   since   Sep   5   15:29
printer   prnt2   is   idle.   enabled   since   Jan   6   13:25
```

JOBS ON QUEUE   Finally, a list of *all* current print requests is displayed:

```
gutenberg-2228        beeching      9300        Jan   6   10:57
on   gutenberg
gutenberg-2232        adrian          21        Jan   6   14:00
```

In this display, the user *beeching* has a request currently printing on *gutenberg*, and the request placed by user *adrian* will be printed next. The job size of *21* probably represents only a short wait. Other longer files may contain hundreds or thousands of characters, resulting in a long delay.

Listing All Print Requests on BSD

On a BSD system you can get a list of all print jobs in the queue of each specific printer. By checking a printer's queue you can see how busy it is before deciding whether to send your print job there.

1. Check the queue of *printer* by typing the following:

   lpq **-P***printer*

This command without a specified *username* option outputs printer requests for all users. The **lpq** **-P** output is similar to the following:

Rank	Owner	Job	Files	Total Size
active	norman	237	/src/sc.h	11545 bytes
1st	beeching	238	/tmp/foo	22000 bytes
2nd	adrian	238	/etc/motd	545 bytes

9.4

Canceling a Print Request

The System V and BSD commands offered in the previous sections let you observe which other files are listed in the print queue before yours. If the list represents a wait longer than you can allow, you may want to cancel your print job and process it again later or send it to a different printer.

Just as you can send a request to a printer, you can also cancel that request.

1. From the command line, type one of the following commands.

   On System V:

   lpstat -t

   On BSD:

   lpq -P*printer*

2. Edit the file *practice* using **vi,** and add enough text so that you have about 500 to 600 lines. (You can quickly accomplish this by reading into *practice* a system file such as */etc/passwd.*) Send the long file to the printer with one of the following commands.

   On System V:

   lp -d*printer practice*

   and your workstation displays a response message similar to the following:

   ```
   request  id  is  printer-1293
   ```

   On BSD:

   lpr -P*printer practice*

3. Request the file to be printed again.

On System V:

lp -d*printer practice*

On BSD:

lpr -P*printer practice*

4. Enter one of the following commands to check the status of your jobs. In both cases, this report tells you that your requests have been sent to your printer.

On System V, type

lpstat

and you'll see output similar to this:

```
gutenberg-1293 beeching 2251 Jan 12 13:32 on gutenberg
gutenberg-1294 beeching 2251 Jan 12 13:35
```

On BSD, type

lpq -P*printer*

and you'll see output resembling the following:

```
gutenberg  is  ready  and  printing

Rank        Owner        Job       Files         Total Size
1st         adrian       237       practice      12323 bytes
2nd         adrian       238       practice      12323 bytes
```

5. Because your first print job is printing, you can remove the second job from the queue. In the following command lines, substitute your printer name for *gutenberg* and your job number for *1294*.

On System V, enter

cancel *gutenberg-1294*

to instruct the spooler to cancel the request *gutenberg-1294*. Even if the job is printing, it will be stopped.

On BSD:

lprm **-P***gutenberg 238*

to instruct the spooler to cancel the request number *238*. If the job is already printing, it will not be canceled.

 SUMMARY: *The format for the command to cancel a request under System V is*

cancel *printer-jobnumber*

In BSD, the format of the command is

lprm **-P***printer jobnumber*

Sometimes you may want to remove *all* your printing jobs from the queue. In this case, use the following in System V:

cancel

and in BSD:

lprm

▪ **Review**

1. What command would you use to send more than one file to the printer for printing?

2. What command would you use to request three copies of the file *junk1* from the printer?

3. How would you add a title line to the banner page for the file *junk1* when sending it to the printer?

4. What command allows you to see if your file is queued for printing?

5. How would you cancel a print request that is not yet being printed?

6. How would you instruct the print program to print the file *mail* on the destination *gutenberg*, when you do *not* want to know immediately the request number for the job, but you *do* want to see on the workstation and through the mail that the job has finished printing?

Conclusion

In this chapter you produced hardcopy output of your files using a variety of print commands. Because printer devices are slow when compared with the speed of the computer itself, and because each print job monopolizes the printer, it is necessary to use a job queue to handle printing.

The programs that manage print queues are the *print spooler*, **lp**, and **lpr**. Its command interface allows you to add print jobs to queues, display status information about queues, and remove print jobs from queues.

Answers

1. On System V: **lp** **-d***printer* *file1 file2 file3*

   On BSD: **lpr** **-P***printer* *file1 file2 file3*

2. On System V: **lp** **-d***printer* **-n**3 *junk1*

   On BSD: **lpr** **-P***printer* **-#**3 *junk1*

3. On System V: **lp** **-d***printer* **-t***title* *junk1*

   On BSD: **lpr** **-P***printer* **-J***title* *junk1*

4. On System V: **lpstat**

   On BSD: **lpq** **-P***printer*

5. On System V: **cancel** *printer-jobnumber*

   On BSD: **lprm** **-P***printer* *jobnumber*

6. On System V: **lp** **-d***gutenberg* **-s** **-w** **-m** *mail*

   On BSD: **lpr** **-P***gutenberg* **-m** *mail*

   The **-w** option to write notifying you the print job is complete is not available on BSD.

COMMAND SUMMARY

System V Printing Commands

lp -**d***printer* *filename*	Requests that the file *filename* be printed on the destination printer *printer*.
utility | **lp** -**d***printer*	Sends the standard output of **utility** to the destination printer *printer*.
lp -**d***printer* -**n***number* *filename*	Specifies number of copies to be printed, where *number* is the number of copies desired.
lp -**d***printer* -**t***title* *filename*	Specifies that *title* be printed on the banner page.
lp -**d***printer* -**s** *filename*	Suppresses printing of request number information on the screen.
lp -**d***printer* -**w** *filename*	Specifies that **lp w**rite to the user when the request is finished printing.
lp -**d***printer* -**m** *filename*	Specifies that **lp m**ail a message to the user when the job is finished printing.
lpstat	Produces a report on the status of all your print requests.
cancel *printer* -*jobnumber*	Cancels the specified print request (whether printing or not), where *printer-jobnumber* is the request id of the requested job.
cancel	Removes all jobs of user being printed on *printer* (System V).
lprm	Removes all jobs of user being printed on printer (BSD).

BSD Printing Command Summary

lpr -**P**printer filename	Requests that the file *filename* be printed on the destination printer *printer*.
utility | **lpr** -**P**printer	The output of **utility** is piped to the destination printer *printer*.
lpr -**P**printer -#number filename	Specifies the number of copies to be printed, where *number* is the number of copies desired.
lpr -**P**printer -**J**title filename	Specifies the banner to be printed on the banner page.
lpr -**d**printer -**m** filename	Specifies that **lpr** send the user mail when the requested print job is completed.
lpq -**d**printer	Obtains the status information on all print requests (not just yours) for a destination *printer*.
lprm -**P**printer jobnumber	Cancels print request if it is not printing.

Chapter Ten

Managing UNIX Jobs

Regardless of what shell you are using, when you enter a command you are instructing the shell to perform a task. All shell command interpreters allow you to execute commands in the background, by using the ampersand at the end of a command line. In addition, the UNIX C and Korn shells provide you with the ability to manage background processes and to suspend running programs. This coordination of multiple commands by a shell is called *job control*.

The multitasking ability of UNIX allows you to manipulate as well as manage several jobs at a time. This chapter examines the particular job control features of the C and Korn shells that help you manage concurrently operating tasks.

SKILLS CHECK: *Before beginning this chapter, you should be able to*

- *Access and leave the system*
- *Rename, copy, and remove files*
- *Create and display files*
- *Access and edit files using an editor*
- *Redirect output and error messages to a file*
- *Issue complete commands to the shell*

OBJECTIVES: *After completing this chapter, you will be able to*

- *Run programs in the background*
- *Suspend and restart programs in both the foreground and the background*
- *Kill programs running in the background*

10.1

Running Jobs in the Foreground and Background

Consider a small business, whose president has one administrative assistant and places the following constraints on that assistant:

- The assistant takes requests for jobs to be done from the president, and translates them into specific instructions that are executed by temporary employees.

- The assistant assigns the tasks and then waits, doing no work, until the temporary employees have completed their assigned tasks and have reported the results directly to the president.

- The assistant is notified only that the tasks have been completed and then asks the president for the next job.

When you work on jobs in the foreground on UNIX, you are having the shell work as the administrative assistant. You type a command-line request; the shell interprets the request and starts the utilities involved. The utilities do their work while the shell sleeps. When the utilities are finished and report the results directly to you or to specified files, the shell wakes up and asks you for the next job.

More work can be accomplished if, when you assign a job, you can have the shell interpret it and start the appropriate utilities to actually do the work, and then return immediately to get instructions for additional jobs. Also of significant impact on productivity is the ability to request information about jobs in progress, move a job to the foreground so information can be added to it, and so forth.

Running Commands in the Foreground

Normally, when you give the shell a command, it starts a job in the foreground. The utilities that were specified in the command line constitute a job. The job runs while the shell sleeps.

1. Run the following UNIX job in the usual way, in the foreground. Type

   ls -R / | more

   This command line instructs the shell to connect the output from the foreground process **ls** to the foreground process **more**, which in turn writes to your screen.

   When you request a new screenful of text by pressing the (Spacebar), the space character you type is read and interpreted by the process that is *running in the foreground*, **more**, which displays the next screenful of text.

2. End the current job by entering

q

When you entered the **ls** command in step 1, you requested processes to run both the **ls** and **more** utilities by issuing a single command
line. On C and Korn shells, starting several processes with a single command line is called starting a *job*.

Preparation for Upcoming Exercises

For the tasks in subsequent sections of this chapter, you will need two
shell scripts that take a long time to execute.

1. Create a directory named *Testing* and change from your current
   directory into it by entering

   mkdir *Testing*
   cd *Testing*

2. Create a file named *sleepscript* containing the following lines:

```
echo "Sleepscript started" > file.$$
sleep 20
echo "First sleep passed" >> file.$$
sleep 30
echo "Second sleep passed" >> file.$$
sleep 50
echo "Third sleep passed" >> file.$$
sleep 2000
echo "Fourth Sleep Passed" >> file.$$
```

3. Create a second script named *longscript,* containing the following
   single line:

```
sleep  2000 ; echo  longscript  done
```

4. Make both files executable by entering this command:

   chmod *700 sleepscript longscript*

Killing the Current Foreground Job

The shell provides a convenient method for killing a current job running in the foreground.

1. Start executing *sleepscript* by entering

   sleepscript

   This command takes about 2100 seconds to execute, giving you ample opportunity to kill the current job while it is running.

2. To kill the *sleepscript* job, press

   ⌨Ctrl⌨-⌨c⌨

   Shortly after you press ⌨Ctrl⌨-⌨c⌨, the shell prompt appears. The current job has been killed and the shell is awake and asking for the next job.

3. List the contents of the current directory.

   ls

   The file named something like *file.12345*, created by *sleepscript*, is listed.

When you press ⌨Ctrl⌨-⌨c⌨, you issue a special character, called the *interrupt* signal, that kills or interrupts the current job. On your system, ⌨Ctrl⌨-⌨c⌨ may not be the interrupt character and does not kill the current job; in this case, try using the ⌨Delete⌨ key. A detailed discussion on displaying and setting the interrupt is in Chapter 23, "Modifying the User Environment."

NOTE: *Pressing the interrupt* ⌨Ctrl⌨-⌨c⌨ *will not kill all jobs. Some utilities are not affected by the interrupt signal.*

Identifying Jobs That Are Running

When you have a job that will take a long time to execute, you can run the job and wait for it to finish; or run the job and log on to another terminal and continue working; or run the job in the background while you are working on another task.

1. Again, start up *sleepscript*. Type

   sleepscript &

   The & appended to the command line tells the shell that the command should not be run as the current job, but rather should be executed *in the background* while the shell attends to other tasks that you may request.

   After you type this *sleepscript* command, a message similar to the following is displayed:

   ```
   [1] 11407
   ```

   and the shell prompt reappears. The bracketed number [1] is the *job number*, and in this case shows that you are running a single job in the background. The second number is the unique five-digit *process identification number* (PID).

2. Now confirm that the **sleep** command in *sleepscript* is running, by entering this command:

   ps

   The **ps** utility lists processes currently being executed. The screen displays the following output:

   ```
   PID      TT     STAT   TIME    COMMAND
   11407    h6     S      0:00    sleepscript
   11408    h6     S      0:00    sleep 30
   17353    h6     R      0:00    ps
   ```

The process identification number displayed by the shell after you entered the *sleepscript* command is identical to the *sleepscript* PID number displayed by **ps**.

Having the Shell Notify You When Jobs Are Complete

By using the shell variable *notify*, you can be notified when a background job finishes.

1. Enter

   set *notify*

2. Run another job in the background by typing

   wc */etc/passwd* **&**

   The shell responds with the job number and the process identification number, the prompt, and (after a few moments) the result of the word count:

   ```
   [3] 13909
        133 244 4937 /etc/passwd
   ```

3. You'll next see the following message, and a prompt:

   ```
   [3]    Done wc /etc/passwd
   ```

   The shell is notifying you that the background job has finished.

4. Unset the *notify* variable by typing

   unset *notify*

5. Run another job in the background by typing

   wc */etc/passwd* **&**

   The shell responds with the job number and the process identification number, the prompt, and (after a few moments) the result of the word count:

   ```
   133 244 4937 /etc/passwd
   ```

   but no "done" message and no prompt are displayed.

6. To redisplay the prompt, press the ⌐Return⌐ key. You'll see the prompt, plus the following message:

```
[3] Done wc /etc/passwd
```

The shell is notifying you that the background job has finished. The shell does not interrupt you; instead, it takes the opportunity of passing you the message while it is displaying a prompt.

7. Reset *notify* with

   set *notify*

Listing Multiple Jobs Running in the Background

With the C and Korn shells, you can run more than one job in the background.

1. Type

   longscript **&**
   longscript **&**

   Once again, the shell responds with the job numbers and PIDs:

   ```
   [1]   12312
   [2]   12414
   ```

2. The two *longscript* jobs are running. Check their status by typing

   jobs

   A list of jobs appears, similar to the following:

   ```
   Job number    Order    Status     Command executed
   [1]             +       Running    longscript
   [2]             -       Running    longscript
   ```

The **jobs** command is a C shell and Korn shell built-in command; it lists, among other things, all jobs that are running in the background. The **jobs** output is divided into four columns—the job number, the order (the + marks the lead job and the – marks the second job), the status (in this case, both are running in the background), and the command being executed.

Moving a Job from the Background to the Foreground

At this point in your work through this chapter, there are two jobs running in the background.

1. Verify that jobs are still running, by typing

   jobs

   You should see two *longscript* commands running. As explained above, the **+** sign marks the lead job.

2. Move the lead job into the foreground, by entering

   fg

   You'll see this message:

   ```
   longscript
   ```

   In this way, the shell informs you that a *longscript* command is now running in the foreground and is the current job. The *longscript* job does not start over, but continues as the foreground job. No prompt is displayed. No input is accepted.

3. Kill the current job by pressing

   Ctrl-c

4. Verify the current background jobs by entering

   jobs

5. Kill the remaining job by bringing it into the foreground with **fg** and then pressing

   Ctrl-c

10.2

Managing Jobs

Part of effective management is the ability to switch from one task to another. Suppose you need to print a file, but you're in the middle of writing a long letter in the **mail** utility. When you're running one program, you cannot start a new program without terminating the first program. You could either kill the **mail** letter, or you could finish the letter before printing the file—but both of those alternatives are undesirable. To move from one program to another without killing the current program, you must first *suspend* the current job.

Suspending a Job

1. Begin by starting to send a mail message to yourself. Enter

   mail *your_login*

   Or, if **mailx** is the mail program in use on your system, use that command.

2. Type a line such as the following:

   This is a test.

   and press (Return) so the cursor is on a new line.

3. Now suspend the **mail** job. Press

   (Ctrl)-(z)

   The shell responds with the message

   ```
   Stopped
   ```

   or

   ```
   Suspended
   ```

   The shell then displays a new prompt showing it is ready for new instructions. The process that is running **mail** is now *suspended*. A suspended (or stopped) job is not running, but it is not killed, either. *The system keeps track of where the program stopped its execution and can restart it at the same point later. But no computer time is consumed by the process while it is suspended.*

4. Check that the **mail** process is still there, by typing

   jobs

   The **mail** job is listed as "Stopped" or "Suspended."

Putting a Suspended Job in the Foreground

While your job is suspended, you can give any instructions to the shell that you wish. You can edit files, run other utilities, or even send other mail messages.

1. Check the date and time by typing

   date

2. Request some other tasks.

3. Restart your **mail** job again by typing

   fg

   The system responds with

   ```
   mail your_login
   (continue)
   ```

   You are back at the same place in your mail message. The **mail** program does not redisplay your previous input, but you can continue entering text.

4. To see the letter you have written so far, redisplay it by typing

   ~p

   being careful to use a lowercase **p**.

5. Add another line to the mail message, such as

   This is a second line in my test letter.

6. Suspend **mail** by pressing `Return` and then entering

`Ctrl`-`z`

The terminal now displays the "Stopped" message.

Putting a Suspended Job into the Background

At this point you have the **mail** job suspended.

1. To run the **mail** utility in the background, type

   bg

   The shell should respond with the following:

   ```
   [1]   mail your_login &
   ```

   or

   ```
   [1]   mail &
   ```

   where the bracketed number is the job number. You have now requested the shell to run the **mail** utility in the background. After the bracketed number, the response to your **bg** command is the name of the command that you just moved into the background. The ampersand (**&**) denotes that the command line is being run in the background.

2. The workstation may display this message:

   ```
   [1]   +   Stopped   (tty input)   mail your_login
   ```

   If you do not see this message, enter

   jobs

   The *tty input* part of the line tells you that this particular job needs to access your workstation's keyboard or screen but cannot do so unless the **mail** job becomes the current job. Normally, **mail** works interactively with you at your workstation. If the operating system allowed a background process such as your **mail** job to control the workstation's keyboard and screen, you would be unable to run or receive output from any other program (which defeats the purpose of backgrounding a process). So, the operating system stops or suspends a process such as **mail** if you put it in the background.

Jobs that require the user's interaction become stopped jobs if you attempt to run them in the background.

3. Verify that the **mail** process is still present by typing

ps

Stopping More Jobs

Currently, your **mail** job is probably the only suspended job. Start some more jobs so you can see how to manage several jobs at once.

1. Create a few more jobs by typing the following commands:

vi *testfile*

2. Add some text, return to command mode, then suspend the **vi** process by entering

Ctrl-z

3. Enter

vi *alsotest* **&**

4. Enter

longscript

Suspend the *longscript* job by entering Ctrl-z.

5. Check the status of the jobs by typing

jobs

Once again, the lead job is marked with a plus sign.

6. You can either move the lead job into the foreground (with the **fg** command) or into the background (with the **bg** command). In this case, the most recent job is the *suspended longscript* command. Run it in the background now, by entering

bg

7. Check the job status again. Type

jobs

Now a different job is the lead job. Usually the lead job is the most recently suspended job. The *longscript* job was started in the foreground, suspended, and then moved into the background where it resumed running.

Recalling the Most Recent Jobs Specifically

So far, you have manipulated only the lead job. You might think that to access any other job, you must either kill the lead jobs in succession, or let them run to completion.

1. Make sure you have more than two jobs pending by typing

jobs

If your *longscript* job has not finished, the output is as follows:

```
[1]         Stopped     (tty input)     mail your_login
[2]    -    Stopped                     vi testfile
[3]    +    Stopped     (tty output)    vi alsotest
[4]         Running                     longscript
```

The **vi** *alsotest* job is the most recently suspended job and it is marked with a plus sign. The **vi** *testfile* job is the next most recently suspended and is marked with a minus sign.

2. Previously, you brought the lead job into the foreground by typing **fg**. This time bring the lead job specifically into the foreground by typing

fg %+

The %+ argument to **fg** in the command line specifies the lead job. Because the **vi** *alsotest* job is the lead job, it is brought to the foreground and is now the current job.

3. Add a few lines of text.

4. Escape to command mode and suspend it again by entering

Ctrl - z

5. Check the job status by typing

jobs

The lead job **vi** *alsotest* is again marked with the plus, and the second lead job is marked with the minus.

6. Foreground the second lead job by entering

fg %-

The %- is the symbol for the job following the lead job. In the example, the suspended **vi** *testfile* job follows the lead job. This command tells the shell to bring it into the foreground.

7. Re-suspend the current **vi** job by pressing

Ctrl-z

8. Enter

jobs

Note that **vi** *testfile,* which was the second lead job, is now the lead job (marked with a +). This is because it was the last job suspended.

Recalling Jobs from the Jobs List

In the foregoing section you recalled the lead and its subsequent job. You can also bring any other job into the foreground.

1. Have the shell display a list of the current jobs. Type

jobs

and you'll see a listing of all of your stopped or background jobs.

```
[1]        Stopped    mail your_login
[2]    +   Stopped    vi testfile
[3]    -   Stopped    vi alsotest
[4]        Running    longscript
```

2. If *longscript* is not listed, enter

longscript **&**

3. Place the job listed as having job number [1] in the foreground by entering

fg %1

The **%1** is the symbol for the job with the job number **1** (in this case, probably the stopped **mail** job), which is brought to the foreground.

4. Re-suspend the job, with Ctrl - z.

5. Similarly, bring the fourth job to the foreground. Type

fg %4

Job number **4** is brought to the foreground. In the example, the *longscript* job, which was running in the background, is brought into the foreground.

SUMMARY: *In general, to recall a particular job into the foreground, you type the* **fg** *command in this format:*

fg *%job_number*

where job_number is the number of the job for the chosen command line from the **jobs** *command listing. Note that this number is not the PID for the process.*

Moving a Specific Suspended Job to the Background

You can also move a job into the background. The procedure is similar to the way you just moved a suspended job into the foreground.

1. Move the *longscript* job, which is currently in the foreground, into the background by first suspending it with

Ctrl - z

2. List the current jobs.

jobs

3. Now enter

   bg %4

4. Use the **jobs** command to verify that the *longscript* job is now running in the background.

   SUMMARY: *In general, to move a foreground job into the background, you must first suspend it, then type the **bg** command in the following format:*

bg *%job_number*

*where job_number is the number of the chosen job listed in the **jobs** command output.*

Killing a Particular Job

Earlier, you killed the current job using Ctrl-c (the interrupt signal). In this section you examine how to terminate or kill stopped jobs and jobs running in the background.

1. Find out what jobs you have pending by typing

   jobs

2. If *longscript* is running, bring it to the foreground and suspend it by entering:

   fg %4
   Ctrl-z

3. If *longscript* is not listed, enter

   longscript
   Ctrl-z

4. To complete this section, you will need five jobs in your job list. Enter

   sleepscript
   Ctrl-z

5. Enter

jobs

The display is similar to the following

```
[1]         Stopped    mail your_login
[2]         Stopped    vi testfile
[3]         Stopped    vi alsotest
[4]    -    Stopped    longscript
[5]    +    Stopped    sleepscript
```

6. Kill the most recent job in the example by entering

kill %+

7. Examine the list of jobs again, using the **jobs** command.

```
[1]         Stopped    mail your_login
[2]         Stopped    vi testfile
[3]    -    Stopped    vi alsotest
[4]    +    Stopped    longscript
```

8. Another way to kill a job is by using the job number. To kill job number *4*, type this command:

kill %4

9. The message

```
[3]    Terminated longscript
```

is displayed, which indicates that the job has been killed.

10. To avoid killing the wrong jobs, first check the currently running jobs, using the **jobs** command before using **kill**. Try this now. Type

jobs

11. Kill the second job, with

kill %2

On some systems, you may see the message

```
[2]  Suspended  (tty  output)  vi  testfile
```

It is necessary to enter **kill %2** again to kill the job.

12. Now attempt to examine the contents of the file you have been editing. Type

cat *testfile*

The shell responds with

```
testfile: No such file or directory
```

Because you never wrote the file you were editing, the file was never saved. Consequently, when the editor was killed, all of the data you typed in **vi** may be lost. On most systems, you can recover the buffer by entering

vi -r *testfile*

CAUTION: *As a precaution, avoid indiscriminate use of the **kill** command on jobs involving text editors, database programs, mail programs, or any other program that has a large amount of user interaction. The **kill** command may terminate the job without saving any of the user input or program results.*

SUMMARY: *The **kill** command takes the same arguments as the **fg** and **bg** commands. To kill the most recent job, use **kill %+**. To kill the second most recent job, use **kill %-**. In general, to kill a particular job, you use the command **kill %job_number**. You may kill the wrong job if you are not particularly careful. If you run **jobs** to determine the rank or job number of the job you want to kill and the **+** job is running in the background, that job could finish before you enter the **kill** command. If this happens, you may kill the wrong job.*

10.4

Exiting When Jobs Have Been Stopped

Job control is a very useful method for managing processes. Because background jobs and stopped jobs remain invisible to you until the jobs either write to the terminal or are finished, you might forget that processes other than the current one are running. UNIX job control provides a method of warning you of stopped or running background jobs, when you attempt a **logout** or **exit** of the process.

1. Type the **jobs** command, to make sure there are jobs running in the background or stopped.

2. If you do not have any stopped jobs, add

   vi *testfile* **&**

3. Issue the command to exit your shell:

   exit

   The shell responds with an error message:

   ```
   There are suspended jobs.
   ```

   or

   ```
   There are stopped jobs.
   ```

   In addition to the issue of stopped jobs remaining in the queue, you have not exited the shell. The assumption is that you have forgotten about your stopped jobs, so you are informed that there are stopped jobs and the current shell remains active.

CAUTION: This gives you a chance to decide whether to kill any of the unresolved jobs. Text editors and database programs are good examples of programs you do not want to kill. However, if you were to log off without resolving these programs, the process might continue. When you log on again, you would not be able to access the process from your new shell. You would then have to kill the process and lose any work done.

4. Check your jobs now by typing

   jobs

5. If you don't care whether the jobs continue running, you can ignore them and exit anyway by typing **exit** again.

   exit

   When you make this second request, the shell exits even though there are stopped jobs.

Logging Out with Jobs Running

Running a job in the background that will continue running after you log out is called running a job *independent of your controlling workstation.*

1. Log back on to your account.

2. Start a process in the background and then log off by typing

   longscript **&**
   exit

   The *longscript* will probably continue to run, even after you log off.

3. Log back on to your account.

4. Enter

   jobs

   Note that *longscript* is no longer listed as a job. You cannot use the job **kill** command to get rid of it.

5. Check the process status of the *longscript*.

   On System V, type

   ps

   The *longscript* command is not listed among the processes currently running. On System V, processes that are running at log-off time are terminated.

On BSD, type

ps -aux | grep $USER

On BSD, the *longscript* command is probably still running.

6. If the *longscript* command is still running, use the **kill** command to terminate it.

CAUTION: *Running jobs independent of your login provokes certain unresolved problems. The main issue is that once you log out, there is no way to resume control over backgrounded processes within the shell. Individual shells only manage jobs that they start, forcing independent jobs to be ignored by all other shells. Although more advanced ways exist for managing independent jobs, they don't involve features provided by the shell. To manage independent jobs, you have to resort to process control, involving the use of more complex features of the UNIX operating system, which are examined in Chapter 8.*

Review

1. What command would you use to start up a **ps** in the background?

For the next three questions, refer to the following listing:

```
[2]         Stopped     sort /etc/passwd
[3]    -    Stopped     vi .cshrc
[4]    +    Stopped     more .login
[5]         Running     find / -name foo
```

2. What command would you use to bring the **vi** editor to the foreground?

3. What is the command you would use to kill the **more**?

4. What is the command you would use to get this listing?

■ Conclusion

The UNIX C shell job-control facilities can be used to greatly increase your productivity by allowing the computer to adapt to the way you work. An informed user can switch among the **vi** text editor, the **mail** e-mail program, and the **talk** communications program on a UNIX system, as easily as switching from the telephone to correspondence or project memos in an office.

■ Answers to Review

1. **ps &**
2. **fg %3** or **fg %-**
3. **kill %4** or **kill %+**
4. **jobs**

COMMAND SUMMARY

Ctrl-c	Kills the current job.
Ctrl-z	Suspends the current job.
Ctrl-y	Allows the current job to run until input is needed, then suspends the job.
command_name **&**	Runs the command *command_name* in the background.
fg %*job_number*	Brings the job with number *job_number* into the foreground. Without an argument, **fg** brings the most recently *stopped* job into the foreground.
bg %*job_number*	Puts the job with number *job_number* into the background. Without an argument, **bg** moves the most recently *stopped* job to the background.
jobs	Prints a listing of all of the *stopped* and *background* jobs under control of the current shell.
kill %*job_number*	Kills the job with job number *job_number*. Without an argument, **kill** kills the most recent *stopped* job.
set *notify*	Forces the shell to notify the user of any change in the status of background jobs.
unset *notify*	Tells the shell *not* to notify the user of changes in the status of background jobs

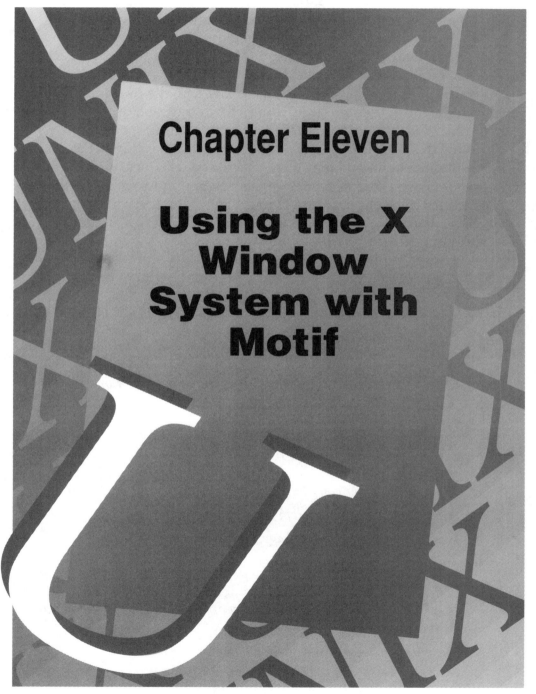

Chapter Eleven

Using the X Window System with Motif

NIX is a multitasking operating system that allows the user to do more than one job at the same time by running programs simultaneously in the background. Programs that require access to the workstation display or keyboard, however, cannot be run in the background. While such programs are being run, the user must wait, remaining idle, until the process is complete. In the past, users often kept two or more workstations on their desks to run multiple jobs.

To solve this problem, *windowing systems* were developed. By enabling a single screen to display several windows at once, with each window operating as a discrete workstation, a windowing system lets you execute a different program in every window. You can issue commands, create files, and examine output in each window without interrupting processes in other windows.

This chapter introduces the windowing system supported by UNIX, called the *X Window System*, with the Motif window manager.

SKILLS CHECK: Before beginning this chapter, you should be able to

- *Access and leave the UNIX system*
- *Create and display files*
- *Execute basic shell commands singly and in combination*
- *Access and modify files using an editor*
- *Use job control to run processes in the background*
- *Kill processes using their PIDs*

OBJECTIVES: After completing this chapter, you will be able to

- *Start the X Window System on your workstation*
- *Use the Motif window manager to modify windows*
- *Start applications using menus*
- *End an X session*
- *Issue shell commands that will start applications in specified locations on the screen*
- *Specify colors and font choices when creating a window*
- *Customize the Root window*

- *Examine the window manager's setup by looking at its run-control file*
- *Modify the window manager's setup*
- *Add menus to the window manager*

Exercises in this chapter include starting the X environment, running the Motif window manager, selecting and manipulating windows, making menu selections, cutting and pasting elements among windows, exiting properly from windows, determining window size and location, selecting window fonts and colors, and customizing the user environment.

11.1

Starting the X Window System Environment from the Command Line

This section examines the standard method of starting the X Window System. Your work environment may use a different method if your machine is configured in a special way.

 NOTE: *The X Window System (more simply, X) and the Motif window applications can be accessed in two ways. X could be the standard startup environment on your system; or you might have to start the needed programs manually. If you log on through a display that is running Motif and X, you should read through this first section on starting the environment, but do not enter the commands.*

Starting the X Window System Manually

If your system does not present you with windows when you log on, but the X and Motif programs are available, you must start the programs manually.

1. Log on to your account.
2. At the shell prompt, start X by typing

   xinit

The normal screen clears and is replaced with a gray stipple background pattern. The whole display screen is called the *Root window* in X terminology. All subsequent windows are placed on this Root window. An X-shaped *pointer* also appears on the screen, followed by a single, smaller window in the upper-left corner of the Root window.

The X Window System is now running. Once a cursor appears in the small window, the window is ready for input. This window functions as an independent terminal and is called the *console window*.

Keep this window in the upper-left corner to distinguish it from any other windows you might create. The console window functions like any other X terminal emulating window except for one thing: when you exit from the console, you terminate X as well as all other X processes currently running, and you return to the UNIX shell.

Starting the Motif Window Manager

Most windowing systems, despite their overt differences, share certain capabilities. They let you move windows, change their size, change the order in which they are stacked in the Root window, and "iconize" them (that is, minimize them to icons on the desktop). Under X, the program that handles these changes is called the *window manager*. Several window managers are available. This chapter is structured around **mwm**, the **M**otif **w**indow **m**anager (the Motif program).

1. Start **mwm** in the background by placing the pointer anywhere in the console window and typing

   mwm &

This is a request that the shell run the **M**otif **w**indow **m**anager program in the background. The pointer briefly becomes an hourglass. After a few seconds, the border of the console window changes, a title bar appears, and the window's cursor becomes a nonfilled rectangle box outline. The "hollowed out" cursor indicates that **mwm** is running. Motif will now manage all X applications and utilities in the current session until you exit, or until **mwm** is replaced by another window manager.

11.2

Getting Started When the X Window and Motif Are Running

Use the following steps if you log on to a system on which X is already running.

1. If your desktop screen has one or more windows already displayed, and one of the windows is a terminal, proceed to the next section, "Interacting with X and Motif." If a desktop is presented that does not include a terminal window, proceed to step 2 of this exercise.

2. To start a terminal window, first move the mouse pointer to a portion of the screen display that is *not* a window. You are in the Root window.

3. Click the left mouse button.

4. On the Root menu that appears (shown here), move the pointer to New Window and click on it.

A new terminal window is displayed.

11.3

Interacting with X and Motif

At this point you have at least one terminal window, called an *xterm*, open on the screen. The advantage of this system is that you can have several windows open, working on several tasks at the same time.

Moving the Pointer

When you move the mouse, the large X or I-beam pointer moves over the screen. Move the pointer in and out of the terminal window a few times, and notice the changes that take place.

When the pointer is within the bounds of the terminal emulator window (the xterm) the following activities occur:

- The mouse pointer changes shape from an X to an I-beam.
- The window's cursor changes from a box outline to a filled box.
- The window's border is highlighted.

The pointer can take other special shapes depending on what action you are performing. We will discuss these pointer shapes as you encounter them in the exercises.

Using a Terminal Emulator Window

1. Move the mouse pointer into the xterm window.

   This window is a terminal and is connected to a functioning shell, just like any full-screen display. When you move the pointer into an xterm window, the characters you type on the keyboard are sent to the shell connected to the window.

2. Type a UNIX command, such as

   date

   If the characters do not appear on the screen as you type them, that means the window manager (**mwm**) has not been told which window is the focus of your attention. To fix this, proceed to step 3.

3. Move the mouse pointer into the window and try again.

   If the characters are not entered on the screen as you type, click the left mouse button in the window. The manager is told that this window is the focus. What you type is read and the output of **date** is displayed.

4. Enter some additional shell commands, such as

who
ls -l

The output of the utility is displayed on the screen.

5. Request a report on the processes currently running. Type

ps

The **xterm** and **mwm** programs are running.

The window you are using allows you to interact with the shell in the same way as with a full-screen workstation. Hence, it is called an xterm or **X term**inal emulator window. Figure 11-1 shows an xterm window.

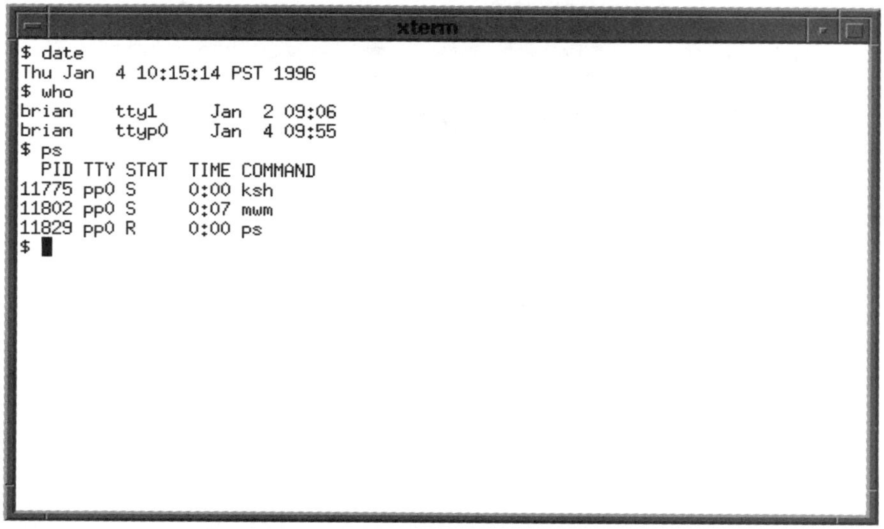

```
$ date
Thu Jan  4 10:15:14 PST 1996
$ who
brian      tty1      Jan  2 09:06
brian      ttyp0     Jan  4 09:55
$ ps
  PID TTY STAT  TIME COMMAND
11775 pp0 S     0:00 ksh
11802 pp0 S     0:07 mwm
11829 pp0 R     0:00 ps
$ ▮
```

Figure 11-1.   *xterm window displaying output of various commands*

Starting a Terminal Window Without Using a Root Menu

1. Start another xterm window by typing

   xterm &

   After a few seconds, the window appears on the screen and its icon appears in the icon box. This is shown in Figure 11-2.

*NOTE: The **xterm** utility should usually be run in the background with an ampersand, as you have done here. Otherwise, an **xterm** process runs in the foreground and blocks the use of the window from which it is invoked.*

Notice that the new window is highlighted, and the console window is no longer highlighted. Newly created windows usually receive focus automatically.

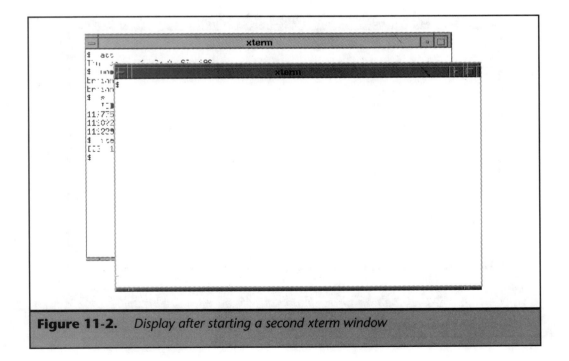

Figure 11-2.   *Display after starting a second xterm window*

The new window is 24 lines high and 80 characters wide. For now, all xterm windows created under **mwm** will be of this size. Changing the size of a window will be examined later in the chapter.

Exiting a Workstation Window

Individual windows can be exited one at a time.

1. To exit the new window, move the cursor into the window and enter the following command:

   exit

   The window and its icon disappear, and the console window becomes highlighted again.

2. Before continuing, start another workstation window by typing

   xterm &

 CAUTION: When creating and working with windows, always leave some of the Root window exposed. Certain functions of X windows, including some discussed in this chapter, require pointer access to the background or Root window.

Running an X Application

The X Window System provides a standard window interface for numerous application programs. A properly written and installed X application can be used on any machine running the X Window System. Such an application is called an *X application* or *X client*.

The **xclock** program is an X application that is provided on most systems.

1. Start a clock application window by typing the command

   xclock &

   The window containing the clock appears on the screen. The **xclock** program is now running in the background and its output is displayed (shown here). You cannot enter commands or interact with the clock. It is just an application that displays its output in a window on your screen.

11.4

Manipulating Windows

Once windows are placed on the Root window, **mwm** is used to move and resize them according to your needs.

Minimizing, Restoring, and Maximizing Windows and Their Icons

When many windows are running at the same time or, if a few very large windows are open, some windows may be obscured . Under X, you can shrink, or minimize, a window into an icon. Because icons require very little space, they help to keep the overall display orderly and uncluttered, and to maintain an adequate amount of Root window exposure.

Minimizing a Window (Iconifying)

1. Examine the title bar on top of each of the windows showing on your screen.

   As shown in the following illustration, at the right end of the title bar are two boxes, or *buttons*. The rightmost button with the larger square is called the Maximize button; we'll discuss it shortly. We'll first examine the button next to it, the one with the smaller square. This is the Minimize button.

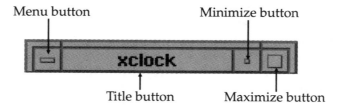

Menu button   Minimize button

Title button   Maximize button

2. Move the pointer to the Minimize button and click the left mouse button. The window disappears and the icon (the small clock in the *icon box*) is highlighted.

When the window disappears, this does not affect any processes associated with that window. They will continue to operate. The act of changing a window to an icon is called *iconifying* or *minimizing* it.

Restoring a Window (De-iconifying)

An icon is easily maximized to reveal the full window it represents.

1. Move the pointer to the icon you just created.
2. Click the left mouse button twice, quickly (called a *double-click*). The window reappears and its icon is no longer highlighted. Changing an icon to a window is *de-iconifying* or *restoring* it.

Enlarging a Window Temporarily

A window can be enlarged to the size of the entire screen, if need be. Examine the title bar again. In the title bar, to the right of the Minimize button, is the square Maximize button.

1. Move the pointer into the Maximize button, and click the left mouse button. The window fills your display.

Restoring a Window to Normal Size

A large window can be useful, but the true power of X is its ability to support access to many windows at once.

1. Move the pointer into the same Maximize button in the title bar and again click the mouse. The window is restored to its normal size.

Moving a Window

You can also move a window to a different position on the display.

1. Move the pointer into the button in the center of the title bar that contains the actual title of the xclock window. Hold down the left mouse button. Notice that the Title button appears to be pressed down.

2. Keep the left mouse button held down, and move the mouse across the screen.

   An outline of the window appears on the screen, as well as a box in the center of the display, containing two numbers separated by a comma. As you move the mouse, the window outline follows the motion of the pointer and the numbers in the box change. The numbers show the location, in pixels, of the top-left corner of the window you are moving. (The numbers measure the number of pixels to the right and down from the top-left corner of the display.)

3. Move the window's outline to a convenient location on the display and release the left mouse button. The window follows the outline and moves to its new location.

Resizing a Window

In addition to the predetermined minimized and maximized sizes, you can resize a window manually to a specific size.

1. Examine the frame surrounding any window within the Root window. Notice that it is divided into four corners and four sides (see Figure 11-3).

2. Move the pointer along the frame. Notice that the pointer changes shape as it moves from one section of the frame to another.

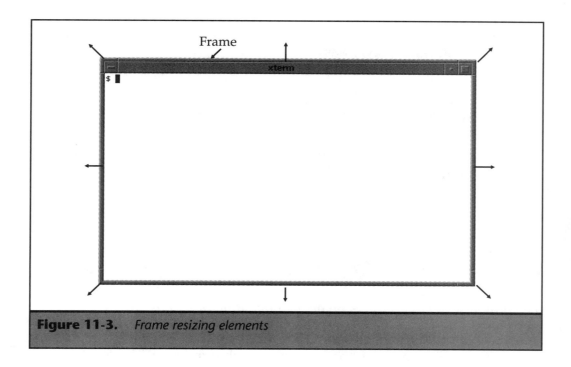

Frame

Figure 11-3. *Frame resizing elements*

3. Move the pointer to the lower-right corner of the frame.
   The pointer becomes an arrow pointing into the lower-
   right corner.

4. Hold down the left mouse button and move the mouse away
   from the window.

   An outline of the window appears, with the pointer in the
   lower-right corner. A box appears in the center of the display,
   containing two numbers separated by an *x*. The first number is
   the width of the window in columns; the second number is the
   height of the window in lines.

5. Continue holding down the button while moving the mouse in
   various directions.

   As you move the mouse, the numbers in the box change to
   indicate the changing the width and height of the window.

6. Move the mouse until the box reads "95x33." With these
   dimensions, the window is wider and taller than normal.

7. Release the left mouse button. The window has now been resized to 95 columns by 33 lines.

   You can resize the window in any direction by using the appropriate section of the frame.

8. Experiment further on your own, resizing the windows in different directions.

9. When you are finished experimenting, resize the window so that it is again 80 columns by 24 lines, using the numbers in the size box as a guide.

11.5

Manipulating the Display Using Menus

Each Motif window, including the Root window, is served by a menu listing the available *window manipulation functions.*

1. Move the pointer into the Root window and hold down the left mouse button to see the Root menu (shown here). The Root menu allows you to control your display, and **mwm** itself.

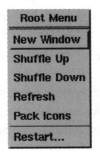

2. Keep the left mouse button held down, and move the pointer down the menu.

   As you do so, each item in the menu is highlighted. Each item on the menu functions as a button for the indicated item. When a button is selected, **mwm** is instructed to perform the associated action.

3. Move the mouse to the top of the menu and release it. The menu disappears.

4. Use the Root menu to start a new xterm by selecting New Window.

Refreshing the Screen

When you have numerous objects on display, or when your workstation is especially busy, the CPU that is running the X server sometimes gets the hiccups. When this happens, the server may draw application program windows improperly, leaving out parts of them or drawing them as blank rectangles. Under such conditions, it is best to *refresh*, or redraw, the entire display.

1. Display the Root menu by moving the pointer to the Root window and holding down the left mouse button.

2. Keep the mouse button held down while moving the pointer down the menu until the Refresh item is highlighted.

3. Release the button, and the entire display is redrawn.

Changing the Stack Order of Windows

When several windows are running, they may be arranged on screen in a tight stack that obscures all but the topmost window. Rather than laboriously dragging individual windows around the screen, you can use a handy menu command to easily adjust the stacking order.

1. Create two or three new xterms using the **xterm &** command or the New Window item in the Root menu.

2. All these xterms will have the common title *xterm*, so run a simple shell command in each window to make it somewhat unique; for instance, enter **date** in one, **who** in another, and so forth.

3. Using the mouse, move the windows into a stack so that the topmost window obscures most of the windows beneath it.

4. Call the Root menu and select Shuffle Up. The window at the bottom of the stack is raised to the topmost position.

5. You can also rotate windows in the reverse direction; that is, you can move the top window to the bottom of the stack. Bring up the Root menu again, and select Shuffle Down.

11.6

Using the Window and Icon Menus

Just as the Root window has a Root menu, the xterm and application windows have their own control menus.

1. Examine the title bar. Notice the box containing a thin rectangle or dash, at the left of the window title rectangle. This is the Menu button.

2. Move the pointer to the Menu button, and hold down the left mouse button. You see a menu similar to the one shown here.

Restore	Alt+F5
Move	Alt+F7
Size	Alt+F8
Minimize	Alt+F9
Maximize	Alt+F10
Lower	Alt+F3
Close	Alt+F4

3. While holding down the left mouse button, move the pointer through the items in the Window menu.

   Each available item is highlighted when it is touched by the pointer. Notice that the Restore item is grayed out, indicating that it is not available because the window is currently at its normal size.

4. Select the Minimize item on the Window menu. The window in which you are working becomes an icon.

5. Restore the window by double-clicking on the icon.

Moving Icons

You can move open windows around the display by "grabbing" their title bars with the mouse pointer. Although icons do not display title bars, they can be moved in a similar manner.

1. If you do not currently have an icon showing on screen, iconify (minimize) one of your full-size windows.

2. Move the pointer into an icon and click the left mouse button. An outline of the icon appears, with a pointer at its center.

3. While continuing to hold down the button, move the mouse. The outline follows the movements of the pointer.

4. To place the icon in its new position, release the left mouse button.

Changing Window Size with the Menu

In addition to the methods you've already learned, you can control the size of windows from the Window menu, as well.

1. Pull down the Window menu for one of your windows (top-left "dash" button) and click the Size item on the menu. The pointer changes shape.

2. Move the pointer to the center of an open window. The size box appears, displaying the current dimensions of the window in columns and lines.

3. Move the pointer out the bottom of the window into the Root window area. As you do this, an outline of the edge you crossed appears and follows along.

4. Move the mouse past the right edge of the window. An outline of the entire window appears.

5. When you have outlined a size you like, set the size of the window by clicking any of the mouse buttons.

Changing the Stack Order Using the Menu

Stacked windows can be manipulated individually through the Window menu. The process is similar to the Shuffle function under the Root menu.

1. If necessary, create several windows and place unique output in each one.

2. Stack the windows.

3. Call the Window menu for the topmost window in the stack, and select Lower. The topmost window is sent to the bottom of the stack.

4. Raise a window to the top of a stack. Move the pointer to the window and click the left mouse button.

Killing a Window and Its Associated Application

When you no longer need a specific window for any further work, you can completely eradicate it, or "kill" it.

1. Move the pointer into any open xterm window—*except* the console window—and type

   exit

   You are exited from the chosen window, which subsequently disappears from the screen.

   Some applications, including **xclock**, can only be killed using the UNIX **kill** command or the Window menu. Using the menu is easiest in this case.

2. Move the pointer to the xclock window. (If the xclock window is iconified, you'll need to restore it.)

3. Call up the Window menu and select Close. The window disappears and its application is terminated.

11.7

Working with the xterm Menus

Each kind of window (xclock, xterm, and others you will meet) can be manipulated individually through its own menu.

The xterm X11 Menu

1. Start a new xterm window.

   xterm &

2. Place the new xterm where you want it. Move the pointer into the window.

3. Hold down the Ctrl key and click the left mouse button.

4. When the xterm X11 menu appears (shown here) release the Ctrl key.

Main Options
Secure Keyboard
Allow SendEvents
Redraw Window
Send STOP Signal
Send CONT Signal
Send INT Signal
Send HUP Signal
Send TERM Signal
Send KILL Signal
Quit

The xterm X11 menu contains items that control the window.

Menu Item	Description
Secure Keyboard	Prevents other users from reading your input to the xterm window.
Allow SendEvents	Permits X Window SendEvents.
Redraw Window	Redraws the xterm window items.
Send Signals	The various UNIX process signals can be sent to foreground processes.
Quit	Closes the xterm window.

The items in the middle part of the menu send signals to the **xterm** process associated with the window.

Selecting xterm Options

1. Display the xterm VT Options menu (Figure 11-4) by pressing the [Ctrl] key and holding down the middle mouse button. Once the menu is displayed, you may release the [Ctrl] key.

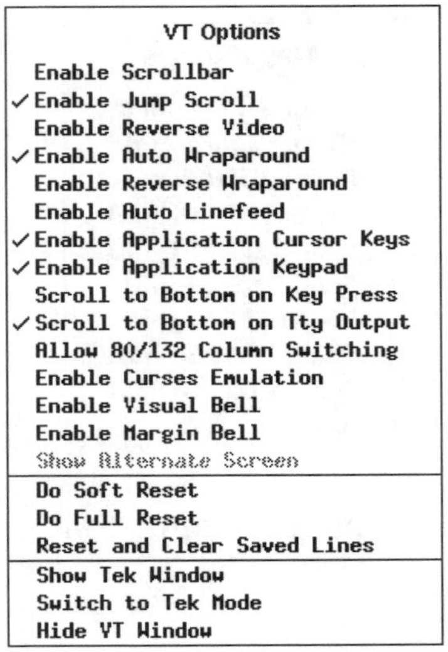

Figure 11-4. *xterm VT Options menu*

In the Options menu you can modify aspects of the xterm window. The items on the menu that have check marks beside them are currently in force in the window. Options that are not accessible from a window appear grayed out—in a lighter-colored type than the modes that are operational modes.

2. Select Enable Reverse Video on the menu. The window's background and foreground colors are reversed.

3. Display the Options menu again by pressing the (Ctrl) key and holding down the middle mouse button.

    Because you have just selected the Reverse Video option, that item on the menu now has a check mark beside it.

4. Turn off Reverse Video by again selecting the Reverse Video item.

Numerous mode settings are available through this menu. The most commonly used are summarized in the command summary section at the end of this chapter.

The VT Fonts Menu

1. Hold down the (Ctrl) key and press the right mouse button. When the xterm menu appears, release the (Ctrl) key but keep the right button depressed.

    The xterm VT Fonts menu (shown here) contains items that control the size of the fonts available in the selected window.

```
             VT Fonts
        ✓ Default
          Unreadable
          Tiny
          Small
          Medium
          Large
          Huge
          Escape Sequence
          Selection
```

2. Move the pointer to the Huge option on the menu, and release the right button.

On The VT Fonts menu, the Huge option causes the xterm window to enlarge; its text is larger.

3. Bring up the VT Fonts menu again and select Large.

This font choice is good for editing text, but keep in mind that the overall window size is quite large.

11.8

Cutting and Pasting

Moving text around the window using the mouse and pointer is one of the most useful functions in the X interface. Lines or entire blocks of text can be easily relocated inside a given window, or moved from one window to another.

1. In one of the xterms, display a file with the **cat** utility.

2. In another window, begin editing a file with **vi**.

3. Press **o** to open a new line and enter append mode.

4. Move the pointer back to the window where **cat** displayed the file.

5. Move the mouse pointer to the beginning of a line of text.

6. Press and hold down the left mouse button.

7. Move the mouse to the right until several words of the line are highlighted.

8. Release the left mouse button.

By performing these actions, you have placed the highlighted text in a portion of memory called the *stuff buffer*.

9. Move the mouse back to the window where you have **vi** in the append mode.

10. Enter the text from the stuff buffer by clicking the middle mouse button.

The buffer text appears at the current location of the cursor, as if you had typed it from the keyboard.

Thus, by copying text to and from the stuff buffer, you can quickly move text around between windows.

11. Write the file and quit the editor with

   :wq

12. In one window, enter

   ls | wc -l

13. Use the left mouse button to put **ls | wc -l** into the cut buffer.

14. Move the mouse to another xterm and press the middle mouse button. The command is placed at the cursor.

15. Press (Return) to run the command.

11.9

Clean-Up and Exiting

When an entire X session is terminated by exiting the console window, all unfinished jobs are killed and their information may be lost. To protect yourself, quit and save all open files before exiting.

> **TIP:** *Before you terminate your X session, get the status of all current processes first, by typing* **ps** *in your console window. Then do any necessary clean-up before going any further.*

1. When you are sure you want to terminate your X session, move the pointer to the console window and type

   exit

   The console and any other X applications—including **mwm**—are terminated. The entire X environment is exited, and you are returned to the full-screen display of your terminal or are logged out. Often customized menus or the Root menu include a logout option.

■ Review 1

1. Which program usually starts the X Window System?

2. What kind of program manages the look, layout, and functioning of windows in the X Window System?

3. What shell command calls up a terminal emulator (xterm) window?

4. How do you select a command from the Root menu?

5. How do you kill an application in a specific window?

6. How do you change the font size in a specific window?

7. Which window should you be most careful about closing?

11.10

■ Running X Client Applications

In the terminology of the X Window System, the process that creates the basic display format of X by drawing windows is called the *X server*. It is the program that runs the Root window. Menus, windows, fonts, size, and movement are all controlled by the X server. Applications displayed by the server—including xclock and the xterm windows—are called *X clients*, or just *clients*. The X Window System supports numerous clients. Some of them are small but useful, and similar to the desktop applications that run on other systems.

Performing Simple Calculations with xcalc

The **xcalc** client creates an operational scientific calculator in window form.

1. Start the calculator by typing

   xcalc &

   The **xcalc** application (Figure 11-5) simulates a working Texas Instruments TI-30 calculator or an HP calculator, depending on your version.

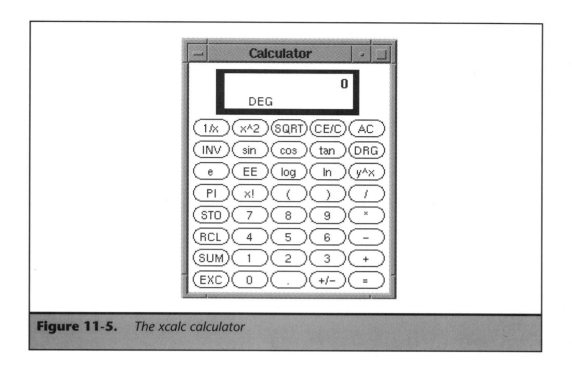

Figure 11-5. *The xcalc calculator*

The xcalc calculator can be operated with your mouse. Simply move the pointer to the appropriate button on the xcalc display and click the left mouse button. The calculator responds as though you have pressed a button on a hand-held calculator.

You can also instruct xcalc to simulate a Reverse Polish Notation (RPN) calculator.

2. Start up the RPN version of **xcalc**. Type

   xcalc -rpn &

3. On some systems, an analog calculator is available, too. Enter

   xcalc -a &

   A semifunctioning slide rule is displayed.

Finding Out When E-Mail Arrives

X has a way to alert you when e-mail arrives.

1. Start the **xbiff** application by typing

   xbiff &

   A miniaturized mailbox appears.

The mailbox tells you that the **xbiff** (the x version of **biff**) application is working. When new mail arrives, the flag on the mailbox pops up, and the system bell rings.

 NOTE: The **biff** *utility is named after a dog at UC Berkeley, and dogs do bark when mail is delivered. And no, the electronic mailbox is not used as is its counterpart in the postal system. With* **biff** *the flag is raised to signify* incoming *mail from the information highway, not outgoing mail as it is used in the rural byway.*

11.11

Customizing Windows in the X Interface

When you start up a window, it has a title bar, specific background and foreground colors, and a specific location on the screen. You can change these defaults from the command line when you start a client.

Specifying the Title of an xterm Window

1. Start another xterm by entering the following command

   xterm -title *"Test Window"* **&**

   This command line instructs the shell to run the xterm utility and pass it through arguments **-title**, *Test Windows*, and **&**. See the following illustration, which shows an xterm window with a customized title bar.

Specifying Window Colors

If you have a color workstation, you can specify the colors used in the xterm windows.

1. Type

   xterm -bg *lightblue* **-fg** *magenta* **-bd** *green* **&**

   A window is created with a light blue **b**ackground, a magenta **f**oreground, and with a green **b**order.

Most X applications understand the **-bg**, **-fg**, and **-bd** options, which are generally standard fare under X. Each option name is followed by a space to separate the option from its argument.

Specifying Color Names

The list of colors available for use can usually be found in the file */usr/lib/X11/rgb.txt*. This file contains the list of colors available for use on your system and their valid names. If the color file cannot be found in */usr/lib/X11*, you can locate it using the following command:

   find / -name *rgb.txt* **-print**

> *CAUTION:* *When colors are called from the /usr/lib/X11/rgb.txt file in a command, their names must be spelled exactly as they appear in the file. Color names may be listed twice in the file. If so, use the spelling containing no spaces between words.*

Specifying Fonts

X supports numerous fonts (*typefaces*) for use in xterm windows. These, like other window attributes, can be called from the command line.

1. The font library may be quite large. To get an idea of the fonts available on your system, type

   xlsfonts | wc -l
   xlsfonts | more

2. The names of fonts do not convey what they look like to most people. An application is available that displays the font style itself. Display a particular font in your font library by typing the following command, substituting the name of the font for *fontname*:

   xfd -fn *fontname* **&**

   A window appears, displaying each character available in the font you specified.

3. Choose a font that looks interesting. Type the following command, replacing *font* with the name of the font you want to use in your xterm window:

   xterm -fn *font* **&**

   For example, if you want to use *Serif12*, the following command line will create an xterm window using that font:

   xterm -fn *serif12* **&**

Customizing the Root Window

On color workstations, you can modify the color of the Root window.

1. From any xterm window, you can change the background of the Root window to solid black by typing

   xsetroot -solid *black*

   The Root window changes to a black background.

   The **xsetroot** utility is used to change aspects of the Root window. You can change the Root window to any color defined in the current color *rgb.txt* file.

2. Pictures, as well as solid colors and the default gray mesh, can be placed on the Root window. Examine the directory */usr/include/X11/bitmaps* by typing

   ls */usr/include/X11/bitmaps*

3. Choose one of the listed bitmap filenames to use as your Root window background. Set it by typing the following command, replacing *file* with the name of the bitmap:

xsetroot -bitmap */usr/include/X11/bitmaps/file*

After a brief processing time lag, the chosen picture will be displayed as the new background.

Resetting the Display to Default Values

Modifications made by the user to the Root window X display can be returned to default values from the command line. To reset the display, type

xsetroot -def

The background reverts to its original gray stipple texture.

Using the Screensaver

The screensaver is a specialized display that randomly energizes screen pixels to prevent image "burn-in" when a display sits unchanged on screen for long periods of time. Under X, you can turn the screensaver on and off, and you can set the period of idle time prior to its activation.

1. Set the screensaver to activate after ten seconds of idle time. Type

xset s *blank*
xset s *10*

NOTE: *Screensaver time is always expressed in seconds.*

2. Confirm that the screensaver works as specified, by waiting for ten seconds and allowing the screen to blank out. Then move your mouse to turn off the screensaver and redisplay your windows.

3. You can turn off the screensaver altogether by entering

   xset s *off*

4. Wait ten seconds. If the screensaver does not activate, turn the screensaver back on and set it for ten seconds, by typing

   xset s *10*

5. You can change the screensaver to be a display of an X logo that moves periodically around the screen. To do this, type

   xset s *noblank*

   After ten seconds, the screensaver activates, and you see the X logo instead of a blank screen. After five minutes more idle time, the X logo moves to a different location on the screen to prevent image burn.

6. Specify that the X logo should move every 10 seconds by typing

   xset s *10 10*

   The first *10* is the number of idle seconds before the screensaver is activated. The second *10* is the number of seconds before the X logo is moved.

7. Change the screensaver's idle time value to 5 minutes by typing

   xset s *300*

■ Review 2

1. How do you create a new xterm window with the name *Notes*?
2. Which command resets an X display to its default values?
3. What command do you enter to create a window with a blue background and red foreground, that uses *serif12* font and allows you to continue using the window from which you have created the new window?

11.13

Customizing the Window Manager

When the Motif window manager is invoked, the **mwm** program reads the *.mwmrc* file for instructions on how to handle everything from clients to menus. The information in *.mwmrc* is loaded into a database that affects X clients.

This section of the chapter is designed to help advanced users customize how the Motif window manager functions.

The Sample .mwmrc File

A *working copy* of the *.mwmrc* file should be in the directory */usr/lib/X11/sample.mwmrc*. The actual *.mwmrc* file on your system may vary in some ways from the example.

Examine the *.mwmrc* file either in your home directory or in */usr/lib/XII*. Notice that it is divided into two sections: the *menus* and a description of how the keys and buttons work—called *bindings*. Refer to this sample file as needed as you work through the following paragraphs. The first section examines menus.

The Bindings Section of .mwmrc

The bindings in the *.mwmrc* file determine which function is called when you press keys, click mouse buttons, and position the mouse pointer. Two types of bindings are used under X: *button* and *key*. Button bindings include the clicking of a mouse button; key bindings do not require the mouse.

Examine the following set of button bindings from the *.mwmrc* file:

```
Buttons DefaultButtonBindings
{
<Btn1Down>    frame|icon   f.raise
<Btn2Down>    frame|icon   f.post_wmenu
<Btn1Down>    root   f.menu   RootMenu
Meta<Btn1Down>   icon|window   f.lower
Meta<Btn2Down>   window|icon   f.resize
Meta<Btn3Down>   window   f.move
}
```

The first line identifies this information as a collection of button bindings named DefaultButtonBindings. The actual bindings are the lines listed within the curly braces. Each binding entry is expressed in the following format:

key<button event> cursor-location function

The parts of the entry format are defined in the following paragraphs.

Key Definition

This is the *modifier key* to be pressed to initialize the event attached to the button. Modifier key names refer to the keys on your keyboard.

Your system has either a Meta or an Alt key. They mean the same thing to X.

A specific combination of keys can be defined by listing the keys in sequence. For example, the modifier key name

```
Meta Shift
```

indicates that both the Meta and Shift keys will be pressed to initiate an event.

Button Event Definition

This is the *mouse button event*. A mouse button event occurs when a button is pressed (clicked). The standard mouse is equipped with three buttons, but allowable combinations of buttons result in a total of five buttons. They are named as follows:

Button	Mouse Button
Btn1	Left mouse button
Btn2	Middle mouse button
Btn3	Right mouse button
Btn4	A combination of the left and middle mouse buttons
Btn5	A combination of the middle and right mouse buttons

The *event element* in each line defines the actual button action that will execute the function. Four types of events are defined under X.

Event	Action
Down	Pressing the mouse button
Up	Releasing the mouse button
Click	Clicking (pressing and releasing quickly) the mouse button
Click2	Double-clicking the mouse button

Cursor Location Definition

This is the location required of the pointer for a specific event; it is also known as the *context*. The possible locations include

Context Name	Screen Location
Root	Root window
Icon	An icon
Window	A window
Title	Title area of a window
Frame	Frame of a window (including the title bar)
Border	Border of a window (not including the title bar)
App	Application portion of the window (inside the window frame)

Events can take place in more than one location. Multiple locations can be specified by separating location names with a pipe symbol.

Function Selections

The function is the program to be executed. All function calls are in the format

f. *name*

where *name* is the name of the function. A list of function names and their associated functions appears later in this section.

Interpreting a Binding Statement

1. For practice, try interpreting the following binding statement:

```
Meta<Btn1Down> icon|window f.lower
```

In the code shown here, the *lower* function will be called when the (Meta) key is pressed while the left mouse button (*Btn1*) is held *Down*, and the pointer is in an *icon* or a *window*.

2. Confirm this binding by moving the pointer into a window located at the top of a stack of windows, and holding down the (Meta) key while pressing the left mouse button.

    The window is lowered within the stack.

Keypress Bindings

In addition to bindings for mouse events, bindings exist for keypress events. Examine the following set of sample key bindings. In this listing, lines that begin with a hash sign (**#**) have been "commented out" and thus disabled; they are ignored by **mwm**.

```
Keys DefaultKeyBindings
{
Shift<Key>Escape icon|window f.post_wmenu
Meta<Key>space icon|window f.post_wmenu
Meta<Key>Tab root|icon|window f.next_key
Meta Shift<Key>Tab root|icon|window f.prev_key
Meta<Key>Escape root|icon|window f.next_key
Meta Shift<Key>Escape root|icon|window f.prev_key
Meta Ctrl Shift<Key>exclam root|icon|window f.set_behavior
# Meta<Key>Down root|icon|window f.circle_down
# Meta<Key>Up root|icon|window f.circle_up
Meta<Key>F6 window f.next_key transient
}
```

The bindings themselves are the lines within the curly braces.

A key binding statement is quite similar to a button binding statement, except that a keyboard event or events, rather than a mouse-related action, initiates the specific function. For example:

```
Shift<Key>Escape icon|window f.post_wmenu
```

In this example, the *post_wmenu* function (the Window menu) is called if the [Shift] and [Esc] keys are both pressed while the pointer is in an *icon* or *window*.

1. Try this binding by moving the pointer into the current window and then simultaneously pressing [Shift] and [Esc].
   The Window menu appears.
2. Make the Window menu disappear by pressing [Esc].
3. Examine the other key binding entries in the *.mwmrc* file. Interpret the statement, and then try out each binding.

The Function Names

A considerable number of standard functions can be called through binding events. Table 11-1 lists definitions of **mwm** functions in the sample *.mwmrc* file.

Using Menu Specifications in .mwmrc

The menus section of the *.mwmrc* file lists the menus that can be displayed by **mwm**, the window manager, and the action performed when a specific menu item is selected. The sample *.mwmrc* file has two menus: the Root menu and the default Window menu.

The Root Menu

The Root menu section of *.mwmrc* describes the options available when you activate the Root menu:

```
Menu RootMenu
{
"Root Menu" f.title
```

```
no-label f.separator
"New Window" f.exec "xterm &"
"Shuffle Up" f.circle_up
"Shuffle Down" f.circle_down
"Refresh" f.refresh
no-label f.separator
"Restart..." f.restart
}
```

1. Move the mouse to the Root window and press the left mouse button. Compare the menu with the code printed above.

The first line of the menu entry gives the name of the menu—in this case, the line

```
menu RootMenu
```

defines a menu named RootMenu. The menu contents are the lines enclosed by curly braces.

Each line in the menu specifies the name of the menu item (or *label*) and the associated function. For example, the line

```
"Refresh" f.refresh
```

stipulates that the menu includes an option Refresh and that if a user chooses the Refresh item, then **mwm** will execute the *refresh* function. The *f.* prefix identifies a function name to the process.

Some of the menu items call shell functions. For example, this line

```
"New Window" f.exec "xterm &"
```

specifies that the shell command **"xterm &** will be executed if a user chooses the New Window item on the menu. All shell commands called by a menu item are enclosed in quotes, and preceded either by the *exec* function call or a bang (exclamation mark). The *exec* function call or bang tells **mwm** to create a shell to execute the command enclosed in quotes.

Function	Action Taken
raise	Raises a window in the stack
lower	Lowers a window in the stack
resize	Resizes a window
minimize	Changes a window into an icon
maximize	Displays a window at its maximum size
normalize	Displays a window at its normal size
move	Moves a window or icon around the root display
circle_down	Moves the top window in a stack to the bottom of the stack
circle_up	Brings the bottom window in a stack to the top
menu	Invokes a specified menu
refresh	Reprints each window on the display
title	Centers a menu entry string and outlines it with a border, making it a title for a menu or section of a menu
restart	Causes **mwm** to restart
beep	Causes the keyboard to beep
kill	Kills a window and its client
quit_mwm	Exits **mwm**
nop	Does nothing
separator	Inserts a separator into the menu at the specified location; no label is printed in the menu
post_wmenu	Calls up the Window menu
next_key	Sets the keyboard focus to the next window in a stack

Table 11-1. *Motif Window Manager (***mwm***) Functions*

Function	Action Taken
prev_key	Sets the keyboard focus to the previous window in a stack
exec	Executes the given shell command
set_behavior	Causes **mwm** to restart with the default behavior or a custom behavior, depending on which behavior is the opposite of the currently configured behavior

Table 11-1. *Motif Window Manager (***mwm***) Functions (continued)*

11.14

Customizing the .mwmrc File

Now that you have examined a sample *.mwmrc* file, you can start to modify your own *.mwmrc* file.

CAUTION: Always make a copy of the original .mwmrc file before making any changes to the file.

1. If you do not have an *.mwmrc* file in your home directory, copy one to your home directory by typing

   cp /usr/lib/X11/sample.mwmrc .mwmrc

   If the file does not copy in, ask your system administrator where to find an *.mwmrc* file that you can use.

2. Create a copy of your *.mwmrc* called *.mwmrc.orig*.

Having a copy of the *.mwmrc* file ensures that a working version of that file will be available in case the other is somehow disabled during modification.

Binding Functions to Keyboard/Mouse Combinations

To create a new menu, or to add new functions to **mwm**, you must assign a keyboard/mouse combination to the functions you wish to enable. You do this in the bindings section of the *.mwmrc* file.

1. Edit your *.mwmrc* file, and locate the last binding statement in the button bindings set named DefaultButtonBindings. Right after that statement, add the following line:

```
Meta<Btn3Up> root f.refresh
```

This line tells **mwm** to *refresh* the display after you press the (Meta) or (Alt) key and release mouse button number 3 (*Btn3*), which is the right button, while the mouse is in the Root window.

2. Write and quit the editor.

3. To see this function work with the assigned keyboard/mouse combination, you must restart **mwm** to allow the new function to be enabled. Call up the Root menu and select Restart.

4. Now test your newly designed function. Move the pointer to the Root window, hold down the (Meta) or (Alt) key, click the right mouse button one time, and then release the key.

The display is refreshed. Your new function works. You can bind other functions to keyboard/mouse combinations by adding similar lines to the DefaultButtonBindings section of *.mwmrc*.

Creating Your Own Menus

One of the most common additions to the *.mwmrc* files is a user-created menu. To create one, you must define the menu and give it selectable items.

1. Edit your *.mwmrc* file, and append the following text at the end of the file:

```
menu SampleMenu
{
"Sample Menu" f.title
```

```
no-label f.separator
"Quit mwm" f.quit_mwm
"Clock" f.exec "xclock &"
"List Files" f.exec "ls"
}
```

Each line in a menu calls either a shell command or an
mwm function.

2. Edit the *.mwmrc* file, and locate the end of the button bindings
section named DefaultButtonBindings. Add the following line:

```
<Btn3Down> root f.menu SampleMenu
```

3. Restart **mwm** by selecting the Restart option from the Root menu.

4. Call up your new menu. Move the pointer to the Root window,
and hold down mouse button number 3 (*Btn3*), which is the
right button.

5. On the new Sample menu, select the List Files option. You'll
see the names of files in your current directory listed in an
xterm window.

6. Call up your menu again and select the Clock item.

7. Quit **mwm**. A box appears in the center of the screen asking if
you wish to exit **mwm**.

8. Move the pointer to the OK box and click the left mouse button.
The Motif window manager is terminated.

9. Restart **mwm** by moving the pointer into a workstation window
and typing

mwm &

■ Review 3

1. What are the different modifier keys?

2. Write a binding statement that will cause the machine to **beep** when the middle mouse button is pressed in a window's title area.

3. What steps must be performed to create a new menu?

■ Conclusion

This chapter examined the X Window System with the Motif window management package. The X Window System provides a standard and extensible graphical interface for today's large-screen displays. *A standard interface* ensures that applications written under X will function in the same manner on any machine running X. *An extensible interface* means X will be able to incorporate technological improvements as they occur. The system is complex, requires substantial computing power, and provides the user with tools to customize the interface's functionality. Because the Motif look and feel is becoming standard in the UNIX environment, mastery of its features enables a user to access a wide variety of applications.

■ Answers to Review 1

1. **xinit**

2. The window manager

3. **xterm &**

4. Move the pointer into the Root window. Press and hold the left mouse button to bring up the Root menu. Drag the pointer down the menu until your choice is highlighted. Release the mouse button.

5. Move the pointer into the specific window. Call up the Window menu and select Close.

6. Move the pointer into the selected window. Press the [Ctrl] key and the right mouse button simultaneously to get the Fonts menu. Select the font size you want.

7. The console window. Closing this window will end your X session, killing all other running windows.

■ Answers to Review 2

1. **xterm -title** *Notes*
2. **xsetroot -def**
3. **xterm -bg** *blue* **-fg** *red* **-fn** *serif12* **&**

■ Answers to Review 3

1. [Meta] or [Alt], [Shift], [Ctrl], and [Caps Lock].
2. *<Btn2Down> title f.beep*
3. Define the menu; then bind a key/button event to a *menu* function that calls that menu.

COMMAND SUMMARY

General X Window System Commands

exit   Exits the X Window System when typed in the console window; otherwise, exits the individual application window.

xterm &   Opens a new **X term**inal emulator (xterm) window.

xclock &   Starts the **xclock** application program.

mwm &   Starts the **M**otif **w**indow **m**anager.

xinit   Starts an X session and creates the console window.

Commands on the Window and Icon Menus

Restore   Restores an iconized (minimized) window to normal size.

Move   Moves the window or icon to another location in the Root window.

Size   Changes the size of the window.

Minimize   Changes the window to icon (iconizes).

Maximize   Expands the window to fill the entire display.

Lower   Moves the window or icon to the bottom of the window stack.

Close   Kills the window or icon and its associated application.

Commands on the Root Menu

New Window Starts a new xterm window.

Shuffle Up Moves the window at the bottom of the window stack to the top.

Shuffle Down Moves the window at the top of the window stack to the bottom.

Refresh Redraws the entire display.

Restart Restarts **mwm**.

Commands on the xterm VT Options Menu

Enable Scrollbar Toggles the scroll bar on and off.

Enable Jump Scroll Allows several lines to be scrolled at once when displaying long output, improving the speed of output.

Enable Reverse Video Swaps background and foreground colors.

Enable Auto Wraparound Allows long lines to wrap around to the next line.

Enable Reverse Wraparound Allows backspacing on a wrapped line.

Scroll to Bottom on Key Press Causes scroll bar to jump to the bottom of the display when a key is pressed.

Scroll to Bottom on tty Output Causes scroll bar to jump to the bottom of the display when output appears in the window.

Enable Margin Bell Rings a bell when the cursor nears a margin (like a typewriter).

Client Commands

xclock -analog	Starts an analog-style clock.
xclock -digital	Starts a digital-style clock.
xcalc	Starts a standard calculator.
xcalc -rpn	Starts a Reverse Polish Notation (RPN) calculator.
xcalc -analog	Starts a slide rule.
xbiff	Starts the e-mail notification utility.
xload	Displays a graph showing the system load.
xload -update *seconds*	Displays a graph showing the system load, with the graph updated every *seconds* number of seconds.
xterm -sb	Starts up an **xterm** with a scroll bar.

xterm Window Options

-title *WindowTitle*	Sets the title of the window to the title in *WindowTitle*
-geometry =*widthxheight*	Creates a window that is *width* characters or pixels wide by *height* lines or pixels high.
-geometry =*size+hdist+vdist*	Creates a window of the specified *size* (see above entry to specify size), *hdist* pixels from the left side of the display and *vdist* pixels from the top of the display.
-geometry =*size-hdist-vdist*	Creates a window of the specified *size* (see above entry to specify size), *hdist* pixels from the right side of the display and *vdist* pixels from the bottom of the display.

-bg *background-color*	Sets the window's background color to *backgroundcolor*.
-fg *foregroundcolor*	Sets the window's foreground color to *foregroundcolor*.
-bd *bordercolor*	Sets the window's border color to *bordercolor*.
-fn *fontname*	Sets the text in the window to use the font *fontname*.
-rv	Creates the window in reverse video (background and foreground colors reversed).
+rv	Creates the window in normal video (background and foreground colors not reversed).

Options for the xsetroot Command

The following options are available for use with the **xsetroot** command, in the following general format:

xsetroot *option*	where *option* specifies a setting for the Root window background.
-solid *color*	Sets the Root window to the color *color*.
-grey	Sets the Root window to the default gray mesh.
-bitmap *file*	Sets the Root window to contain a bitmap *file*.
-cursor *cursorfile maskfile*	Sets the pointer to the cursor bitmap defined by *cursorfile* with the mask as *maskfile*.
-def	Sets the Root window and pointer to the default values.

Options for the xset Command

The options in this section are available for use with the **xset** command, in the following general format:

xset *item option*

where *option* specifies a setting for an *item* that is not part of the display.

m	Sets the mouse velocity to be the default.
m *acceleration threshold*	Sets the mouse to accelerate by the *acceleration* factor each time the pointer moves *threshold* pixels.
b *100*	Sets the bell at maximum volume.
b *off*	Turns the bell off.
b *on*	Turns the bell on.
b *volume pitch duration*	Sets the bell's *volume* (as a percentage of maximum volume), *pitch* (in Hertz), and *duration* (in milliseconds).
c *100*	Sets the key click to maximum volume.
c *off*	Turns off the key click.
c *on*	Turns on the key click.
s *idle change*	Sets the screensaver to start after *idle* number of seconds of no screen events and to change the screen every *change* number of seconds.
s *blank*	Sets the screensaver to blank the screen.
s *noblank*	Sets the screensaver to print the X logo.
s *off*	Turns off the screensaver.
s *on*	Turns on the screensaver.

Chapter Twelve

Aliasing Command Names

When you're issuing commands in the shell, you'll often use a small set of commands repeatedly. These commands may be lengthy and tedious to type. With both the C and Korn shells, you can save yourself time and mental energy by assigning abbreviations for these repetitive commands. These abbreviations, called *aliases*, can be nicknames for very complex commands.

In our daily lives, we create aliases. When nine-year-old John Frank calls home and asks for Mom, "Mom" is an agreed-upon alias for Ms. Lillian Frank at that phone number and address. Once an alias is assigned for the name of a command or a series of commands, you can use that alias instead of, or as well as, the command or command line.

SKILLS CHECK: *Before beginning this chapter, you should be able to*

- *Utilize the UNIX directory hierarchy system*
- *Access and modify files using the **vi** editor*

OBJECTIVES: *After completing this chapter, you will be able to*

- *Create and use aliases that abbreviate or rename commands*
- *Create and use aliases that contain multiple commands*
- *Create permanent aliases*
- *Use the original command after it had been aliased*
- *Remove previously aliased commands*

12.1

Using Temporary Aliases

The simplest use of the **alias** command is to assign a new name to a utility that already exists. Often the new name is an abbreviation for the sake of convenience. The utility can then be called by its shorter alternative name as well as its original name.

Giving a Command an Alternative Name

In the C and Korn shells, you can obtain a list of commands that you have entered, with the **history** command. Using an alias for the **history** command eliminates some keystrokes.

1. If you are not currently logged on to your machine, do so now. Make sure you are in a C or Korn shell and then enter this command:

   history

2. The **history** command is a relatively long command to enter. It can be abbreviated by using an alias. Depending on the shell you are using, enter one of the following shell command lines.

   In the C shell:

   alias *h* **history**

   With the C shell, two arguments are passed to **alias**. These arguments are the new name or nickname for the command, and the original name.

   In the Korn shell:

   alias *h*=**history**

   In the Korn shell **alias** command, there cannot be spaces on either side of the equal sign. The format is the same as assigning variable values.

   You have assigned a new name, or alias, **h**, to mean the **history** command.

3. Compare the two commands now available. Type

   history

4. Now verify that **h** is interpreted the same way, by typing

   h

The two commands, **history** and **h,** can now be used interchangeably.

5. Suppose you previously worked on a different system where there was a command called **list** that gave you the same information the UNIX **ls** utility provides. Enter the command

list

The output indicates the **list** command cannot be found on your UNIX system.

6. You can create an alias for **ls** called **list** by typing the following.

In the C shell:

alias *list* **ls**

In the Korn shell:

alias *list*=**ls**

7. From the shell, type

list

The output is the same as if you had typed the **ls** command. In fact, the **ls** utility was executed by the shell. With this alias you can continue to use the command name **list** that you previously used on a different system.

SUMMARY: *The basic command lines (C and Korn) for creating a new name (an alias) for a command are as follows:*

In the C shell:

alias *nickname command*

In the Korn shell:

alias *nickname=command*

The nickname becomes a new way to execute the command.

Creating an Alias for a Command and Its Options

When a command has options, the alias you create for that command can include those options. To use more than a single word as an alias, you must enclose the whole string in single quotes so that the shell does not interpret the spaces.

1. Type one of the following command lines.

   In the C shell:

   alias *ls* **'ls -l'**

   In the Korn shell:

   alias *ls=***'ls -l'**

2. Try out the new alias. Type

   ls

   The alias **ls** displays a long listing of your current directory. When you type the command **ls**, the long listing of the current directory appears on the screen, just as if you had typed the **ls -l** command. The shell replaces **ls** with the command **ls -l**.

How Do Aliases Work?

Each time you type a command containing an alias, the shell replaces the alias with its definition before execution. For example, let's examine what happens with the **list** alias you just created.

1. A few steps back, you aliased **list** to **ls**. Try it now:

   list

   The output is not that of **ls** but of **ls -l**.

When the shell interprets your command line, it checks the command you enter with the current alias list. In this example, the shell finds that **list** is aliased to **ls,** and it then checks the alias list again. It finds that **ls** is an alias for **ls -l** and then runs the command.

Passing Arguments to an Alias

After the shell replaces an alias with its definition, the shell processes the modified command line normally, passing the original argument to the substitute command.

1. Use the **ls** alias to display a long listing of the contents of the **/** directory. Type

   ls /

   The shell replaces the **ls** with **ls -l** and interprets the command line as

   ls -l /

   The display is a long listing of the contents of the **/** directory.

2. You can also use aliases with options. For example, use the **list** alias to display all of the dot files in your home directory, by typing

   list -a

   The shell interprets the command line as

   ls -l -a

   and displays a long listing of your home directory, including the dot files (such as *.login*, *.cshrc*, *.kshrc*, and *.profile*).

Using the Original Command, Not Its Alias

On your system, **ls** is presently an alias for the **ls** command with the **-l** option. Perhaps you want to run the **ls** command with no option, but don't want to remove the alias. There are a couple of ways to do this.

1. One way to sidestep the effects of an alias is to use the complete pathname of the original command. Enter

   */bin/*ls

   The output of */bin/*ls is a plain **ls**, not the aliased **ls -l**.

2. Another way to override an alias is to specifically instruct the shell to escape the alias temporarily, by using the \ character. Enter

   \ls

   The shell runs the **ls** utility, not the alias **ls -l**.

Listing Defined Aliases

You can instruct either shell to display all aliases and their meanings.

1. To examine the aliases that have been established, enter

   alias

   The command **alias** with no arguments displays all of the assigned aliases and their definitions. The list you see should look something like the following. Notice that the aliases you defined are on the list. There may be others.

   In the C shell:

   ```
   h history
   list ls
   ls 'ls -l'
   rm 'rm -I'
   ```

   In the Korn shell:

   ```
   h='history'
   list='ls'
   ls='ls -l'
   ```

   You can also request the definition of a single alias. By checking an alias before you use it, you can determine if a command you use is actually an alias. Likewise, you can determine if a name you want to use as an alias already exists as an alias for another command.

1. Find the definition of the **list** alias by typing

   alias list

   The definition of the **list** alias is displayed on the screen:

   ```
   ls
   ```

Removing a Temporary Alias

Once you create an alias, you can remove it.

1. Remove the alias **list** by typing

   unalias list

2. Verify that the **list** alias is gone by typing

   alias

   The alias **list** no longer appears in the list of aliases.

Abandoning Temporary Aliases by Logging Off

1. You have an alias, **ls**, that is defined as **ls -l**, which prints a long listing of files. Confirm it still works by typing

   ls

2. Now log out and log back on.

3. Once you are logged on, type

   ls

   You get the usual output of **ls**, not the alias.

4. Obtain a listing of defined aliases by typing

   alias

None of the aliases that you defined before logging out and logging on again still exist.

When you define an alias from the command line, that alias remains in memory of the shell until you do one of the following:

- Kill the shell
- Log out
- Delete the alias from memory
- Overwrite the alias with a new one

When you log out, the shell you are using dies and with it all temporary information; hence the alias disappears.

12.2

Using Permanent Aliases

Each alias you have made so far has been temporary and is eliminated when you log out, kill the shell, or explicitly delete the alias. You can also save aliases, so that when you start a shell it is informed of your aliases.

Saving Aliases in a File

1. You can save each alias you create in a file. Create a file now called *.aliases* in your home directory. Depending on what shell you are using, enter the following lines:

   In the C shell:

   alias *h* **history**
   alias *lsl* **'ls -F'**
   alias *t* **date**
   alias *a* **alias**

   In the Korn shell:

```
alias   h=history
alias   lsl='ls -F'
alias   t=date
alias   a=alias'
```

2. Save the new *.aliases* file and return to the shell. By saving your aliases in a file, you can have the shell reset each alias every time you log on or explicitly at your command.

3. Log out and log on again.

4. Confirm that the aliases you created earlier are not operational. Type

   alias

   The output of **alias** shows you only the aliases that are predefined in your system files. Depending on your system administrator, you may not have any predefined aliases or you may have many—but none of the aliases you created are listed. The aliases you created are now listed in the file *.aliases,* but they have not been read by your current shell.

5. Instruct the shell to execute the commands in your *.aliases* file. Type one of the following commands.

   In the C shell:

   source ~*/.aliases*

   In the Korn shell:

   . ~*/.aliases*

   The **source** command instructs the C shell to read each line in the file as though it were the command line you entered from the shell. The **.** command is the same for the Korn shell. In this case, each line of the *.aliases* file is an **alias** command so, by reading the file, you tell the shell to create each of the aliases in the *.aliases* file.

6. Confirm that the aliases in the *.aliases* file now exist, by typing

   alias

The display now contains each of the aliases you defined in the *.aliases* file. Each time you log on, you can instruct the shell to read the file and make your aliases operational.

Making Aliases Permanent

Instead of explicitly telling the shell to read the file by typing either of these commands.
In the Korn shell:

> . ~/.aliases

In the C shell:

> **source** ~/.aliases

You can modify one of your startup files so that the *.aliases* file is automatically read each time the shell is started. The startup files are *.cshrc* (in the C shell) and *.kshrc* or *.profile* (in the Korn shell).

1. Using **vi**, edit the appropriate startup file in your home directory. Depending on what shell you are using, add one of the following lines:

   In C shell's *.cshrc*:

   > **source** ~/.aliases

   In Korn shell's *.kshrc*:

   > . ~/.aliases

2. Save the file and return to the shell.
3. Confirm that the *.aliases* file is executed automatically. Log out, then log back on and type

   > **alias**

   Each of your saved aliases and their definitions is included in the list. If you wish, you can add more permanent aliases to your *.aliases* file.

NOTE: *If the Korn shell does not read the **.kshrc** file, include the following lines in the **.profile**:*

```
ENV=.kshrc
export  ENV
```

Removing a Permanent Alias Temporarily

At this point, you have a permanent alias called **h** that is defined as the command **history**. Even though it is a permanent alias, you can remove it temporarily.

1. In either shell, to remove the **h** alias you enter

   unalias h

2. Verify that the **h** alias does not exist anymore, by typing

   alias *h*

   The **h** alias is no longer defined.

Reinstating a Permanent Alias

You can reinstate the **h** alias when you need it again. You can do this in three ways: by issuing an alias command on the command line; by logging out and logging back on, since the commands in the *.aliases* file are automatically executed each time you log on; or by instructing the shell to read the *.aliases* file without logging out.

1. Reinstate the **h** alias using the third method by typing the command that created it.

   In the C shell, type

   source *~/.aliases*

   In the Korn shell, type

   . *~/.aliases*

Removing an Alias Permanently

You may want to permanently remove an alias defined in your *.aliases* file, either because you want to redefine it or because you don't need it any more.

1. With **vi**, edit the *.aliases* file in your home directory. Locate the line where the alias **t** is defined, and then remove it. Save the file, and return to the shell.

2. Log out and log back on.

3. You removed the **t** alias from the *.aliases* file, and then you logged out. Therefore, the new login shell does not have a **t** alias. Confirm that the **t** alias is not available by typing

   alias *t*

■ Review 1

1. What is the simplest use for the **alias** command?

2. When the command **alias** is used without any arguments, what happens?

3. How would you alias **ls** to get a list of all files, including dot files, listed in a directory when you type **ls**?

4. What command removes the existing alias, **list**?

5. To create a permanent alias, where should it be entered?

6. Why don't aliases take effect immediately after you have entered them in your *.aliases* file?

7. After you have temporarily removed a permanent alias, what command would you type to reinstate it?

12.3

Working with Complex Aliases

You have defined some simple aliases for single commands. You can also create and use aliases that contain a series of commands and accept one or more arguments.

Creating an Alias for a Sequence of Commands

An alias is a handy shortcut for a series of sequential commands.

1. Define an alias called **status**. Type the following commands.

   In the C shell:

   alias *status* **'history; pwd; ls -l; date'**

   In the Korn shell:

   alias *status*=**'history; pwd; ls -l; date'**

   The command in step 1 defines **status** to perform four tasks:

   - Execute the shell command history
   - Print the working directory
   - Display a long listing of the directory
   - Display the date and time

   Notice that the semicolon is used to separate commands on the single line. Any number of commands may be used to define an alias. The single quotes tell the shell to not interpret any character as special, hence the commands listed inside are all part of the alias definition.

2. Use the new **status** alias. Type the following command and observe the results.

   status

Passing One Argument to a Multicommand Alias in the C Shell

You may want to create an alias in which the argument is needed in the middle of the definition.

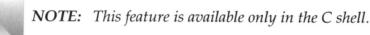

NOTE: *This feature is available only in the C shell.*

Suppose you want to create an alias called **where** that would find a specified file if it is located in a subdirectory of your home directory. You want the result of typing **where** *file* to be a display of the location of *file*. The usual way to get this result is to use the **find** command in the following way:

find ~ **-name** *file* **-print**

This instructs **find** to start looking in your home directory (~) and all its subdirectories for the name *file*, and to print the paths when files are found.

But notice that the argument (**-name** *file*) is used in the middle of the command line, not at the end of the alias definition. You can overcome this obstacle by using the characters \!^ to indicate where an argument is being used in an alias.

1. Define the **where** alias for locating files. Type

   alias *where* '**find** ~ **-name** \!^ **-print**'

   The \!^ tells the shell to expect an argument (only one) when it is used as a shell command.

2. Test the **where** alias by typing

   where *practice*

   In this command, *practice* is the name of the "misplaced" file. The **where** alias effectively expands into this complete command:

   find ~ **-name** *practice* **-print**

Passing Multiple Arguments

In many situations you will want to pass multiple arguments to a C shell. To accomplish this, the \!* notation is used much like the \!^ form.

Suppose, for example, that instead of removing files with the **rm** command, you want to move the files to a special directory called *TRASH*. By doing this, you can still have the files on hand, but they will be clearly designated as *TRASH*. You could then throw out the trash occasionally.

> *NOTE: All uppercase letters are used for this directory name in order to clearly indicate that TRASH is not a file and nor is it your ordinary run-of-the-mill directory.*

1. First create the *TRASH* directory in your home directory by entering

   mkdir *TRASH*

2. Define a **trash** alias that accepts multiple arguments, by typing

   alias *trash* **'mv** \!* ~/*TRASH***'**

   Here the \!* construct indicates that one or more arguments are to be passed to **mv**.

3. Create two files, *temp1* and *temp2*:

   cp *.aliases temp1*
   cp *.aliases temp2*

4. You now have two temporary files, *temp1* and *temp2*. Use the new **trash** alias to remove the two files.

   trash *temp1 temp2*

   The shell accepts two arguments, *temp1* and *temp2*. Both files are moved into the *TRASH* directory.

5. Confirm that the two files are no longer listed in your current directory, with

   ls

6. Confirm that the files are listed in the *TRASH* directory, with

ls *~/TRASH*

12.4

Avoiding an Alias Loop

A common error when using the C shell is *alias looping*. An alias loop occurs when an alias is defined to a name that in turn is an alias for the initial alias. Before you can practice avoiding an alias loop, you must create an alias loop.

1. Make sure that **ls** is not an alias by typing

unalias *ls*

Defining an Alias Loop

1. Create an alias **ls** so that it first prints the name of the current directory and then lists its contents. In the C shell, type

alias *ls* **'pwd; ls'**

2. Test the **ls** alias. You might (depending on your system) get an error message, such as

```
Alias loop.
```

When you enter **ls**, the shell first determines that **ls** is the nickname **pwd; ls**.

After the shell replaces an alias with its definition, the shell again examines the command line for aliases to be replaced. The command **pwd** has no alias but **ls** is the alias **pwd; ls**. After another cycle, the command becomes **pwd; pwd; pwd; ls**. The shell could continue looping, replacing one self-referencing command with another.

In earlier steps you created an alias for **ls** that was **ls -l** when you entered

alias *ls* **'ls -l'**

This is also a self-referencing alias loop and clearly should not work. However, to allow for just such aliases, the C shell does not reexamine the alias list for commands that are equal to the alias nickname and placed first in the alias definition.

Fixing an Alias Loop Quickly

There are two ways to fix an alias loop. One way is to place the command that causes the loop first in the alias definition.

1. Remove the **ls** alias by entering

   unalias ls

2. Change the **ls** command to an alias that lists the contents of a directory first and then prints the name of the directory by typing

   alias *ls* **'ls; pwd'**

3. Test this **ls** alias. Type

   ls

   The contents of the current directory are displayed followed by the name of the directory.
   Because the first word in the **ls** definition matches the alias, the shell does not "re-alias" the newly inserted **ls** command. The modified command, **ls; pwd** is not modified further, but instead is executed as it is.
   Putting the **ls** command first works, but if you want to preserve the order of the command execution (first **pwd** then **ls**), it doesn't. The solution is to *escape* the alias.

4. Define the **ls** alias in the original order by typing

   alias *ls* **'pwd; \ls'**

5. Verify the alias, with

   ls

   The **** instructs the shell to not look up a command in the alias list, but rather use the system version.

Handling Alias Looping in the Korn Shell

You do not encounter alias looping with a Korn shell because the Korn shell handles aliases differently than the C shell.

1. In the Korn shell, type

   alias *ls*=**'pwd; ls'**

2. Now enter

   ls

   The **ls** alias does not cause an "alias loop" error message to be displayed, as it did in the C shell. Rather, it functions as expected, displaying your full current directory name, and a listing of all the files there.

   Though the Korn shell, like the C shell, reexamines the command line after the **ls** alias expansion, the shell does not look in the alias list for *any* instance of the **ls** command within the expansion itself. Because the alias list is not re-referenced, there is no alias loop. The shell does find the system **pwd** and **ls** utilities and runs them.

3. In the Korn shell, enter

   alias *h*=**'history'**
   alias *multi*=**'h; hh; hh;'**

4. Now enter

   multi

   The output is a single listing of the *history* file, followed by two error messages:

   ```
   ksh:  hh:  not found
   ksh:  hh:  not found
   ```

   Though the **multi** command is self-referencing, there is no alias loop. Instead, the shell tries unsuccessfully to find a system command named **hh**.

12.5

The Disadvantages of Aliases

There are some minor problems associated with the use of aliases. Alternative names use memory space when their definitions expand, and this expansion process can be time consuming. Aliases also increase the length of the login process, too, because the shell spends time reading them each time you log on. Generally, however, these drawbacks become unimportant when an alias is used frequently enough to save you time.

Occasionally, you might define an alias to have the same name as an already existing shell command such as the **ls** alias used throughout this chapter. You may go about your business, forgetting that the shell command is aliased. Then, when you want to issue the command, you realize that it has been redefined. In order to use the original command definition you must either

- **unalias** the command
- Use the command's entire path
- Escape the alias

CAUTION: The above example of counterproductivity supports the suggestion that it's best to define aliases only for frequently used commands. Do not overdo your use of aliases.

■ Review 2

1. Suppose the output of the **who** command on your system is almost always more than a screenful, and you want to pipe the output of **who** through the **more** command. What command would you type to make the alias?

2. Let's say you wish to create an alias called **seerm**, in the C shell, which first executes **more** on files(s) that you supply as an argument and then executes **rm** on the file(s). What would that

command be? (Note: Keep in mind that you will be supplying at least one argument when using the alias.)

▇ Conclusion

The **alias** command is useful in nicknaming commands or assigning special names to a series of commands. This renaming ability allows for the creation of abbreviations or names that are more easily remembered. Arguments may be passed into aliases through the use of the special \!^ and \!* notations in the C shell only.

▇ Answers to Review 1

1. Assigning new names to commands that already exist.

2. A list of all **alias** names and their definitions is displayed.

3. **alias** *ls* '**ls -a**'

   or

   alias ls='ls -a'

4. **unalias list**

5. In your *.aliases* file if sourced; or *.profile* or *.cshrc*

6. Shell hasn't read the file.

7. Use **source** *~/.aliases,* or **.** *~/.aliases,* or re-create the alias using the **alias** command.

▇ Answers to Review 2

1. In the C shell:

   alias *who* '**who | more**'

   In the Korn shell:

   alias *who*='**who | more**'

2. **alias** *seerm* '**more \!* ; rm \!* '**

COMMAND SUMMARY

alias *name command*	(C shell) The *name* is aliased to the *command*.
alias *name=command*	(Bourne and Korn shells) The *name* is aliased to the *command*.
alias *name*	Displays the alias for *name* if there is one.
alias	Displays all aliases.
alias *name* 'cmd; cmd'*	(C shell) The *name* is aliased to a sequence of *cmd*s (commands).
alias *name='cmd; cmd'*	(Bourne and Korn shells) The *name* is aliased to a sequence of *cmd*s (commands).
alias *name* 'command \!^'*	(C shell) The *name* is aliased to a one-argument *command*.
alias *name* 'command \!*'*	(C shell) The *name* is aliased to a multiple-argument *command*.
unalias *name*	Removes an alias.

Chapter Thirteen

Accessing and Changing Previous Commands

The most fundamental way to accomplish tasks with UNIX is to type commands from the keyboard. The shell interprets and executes each command after you enter it. While interacting with the shell, you often need to cycle through a series of commands, repeat a command, or reenter mistyped commands. Sometimes you need to enter a series of commands that differ only slightly from one another. In each of these cases, having to retype the necessary command lines may take significant energy and time. The C and Korn shells' **history** mechanisms are designed to increase efficiency by making it possible for you to repeat and/or modify previously executed command lines.

SKILLS CHECK: Before beginning this chapter, you should be able to

- *Name, copy, and remove files*
- *Use several shell commands in combination*
- *Change directories throughout the file system*
- *Access and modify files using the* **vi** *editor*

OBJECTIVES: After completing this chapter, you will be able to

- *Repeat commands already executed*
- *Correct errors in previous commands*
- *Add additional elements to commands and reexecute them*
- *Print commands without having them executed*

3.1

Using the history Command

Both the C and Korn shells can maintain a listing of commands that you have entered at the command line during a login session. This *history list* is available to you for examination, and you can use it to repeat commands or to modify and reuse previous commands.

The exercises in this chapter utilize three files created in previous chapters: *practice*, *practice2*, and *journal*. If you do not currently have files by those names, create them now. The contents of the files are not important; just enter several lines of text in each file.

 NOTE: *During the course of this chapter, you should use either a C shell or a Korn shell. If both shells are available to you, we recommend you go through the chapter twice, first using one shell and then using the other.*

Starting a C or Korn Shell

The **history** feature is described for both the C and Korn shells in these exercises. The Bourne shell does not maintain a history list.

1. If you are working with a Bourne shell, you'll need to start a C or Korn child shell by typing one of the following commands.

   To start a C shell:

   csh

   To start a Korn shell:

   ksh

These commands tell your current shell to start up a C or Korn shell as a subshell. You will use either this new shell or your login C or Korn shell to run the exercises in this chapter. If you get this message:

```
Command not found
```

you probably do not have access to the requested shell on your system. If so, you will not be able to do the exercises in this chapter for that shell.

Regardless of which shell you have chosen, when you want to leave the subshell and return to your original login shell, just type the **exit** command.

Instructing the Shell to Keep a History List

The shell allows you to set the number of commands that its history list will contain.

1. Type one of the following commands.

   In the C shell:

   set *history=40*

   In the Korn shell:

   HISTSIZE=40

The C shell command not only instructs the shell about the size of the history file, but also to start maintaining a record of each command line that you enter. You must explicitly instruct the C shell, via this **set** *history=number* command, to maintain a history list.

The Korn shell's history mechanism is preset to record 128 commands. In addition, the Korn shell automatically starts updating the history file; you do not need to issue an initializing command. Setting the value of *HISTSIZE* to *40* merely resets the number of commands maintained on the history list.

Inspecting a List of Past Commands Used

The history feature keeps a record of the exact command lines that you enter, in the order that you enter them.

1. Type each of the following shell commands:

   date
   who
   cd
   ls
   cat *practice*

2. Because you have initiated the history mechanism, these five command lines are recorded in the history list maintained by your shell. Examine the list by typing

   history

   The output of **history** is similar to the following (of course, the numbers on the left of your output may be quite different).

For the C shell:

```
1   set history=40
2   date
3   who
4   cd
5   ls
6   cat   practice
7   history
```

For the Korn shell:

```
1   HISTSIZE=40
2   date
3   who
4   cd
5   ls
6   cat practice
7   history
```

The last command line on the history list is the last command that you entered. All of the commands that you typed appear on your screen as output from the **history** command. If C shell **history** was already functioning when you entered the command to initiate it (as you did just above), or if you are in the Korn shell, you will see previous commands listed in the output, as well. Each command on the list has an associated *event number* on the left.

Adding the History Event Number to the Prompt

It is useful to know what event number the shell is giving to each command as you enter it. You can change the shell prompt to include this information.

1. From the shell, type one of the following commands.

   In the C shell:

   set *prompt*="\! % "

   In the Korn shell:

   PS1="! $ "

   Notice that there is a space on both sides of the percent and dollar sign in these two commands. The *bang* (which is what many UNIX users call the exclamation mark) tells the system to read the last event number from the history list, add one to this number, and display it. The prompt will then display each event number as you work; this arrangement for the prompt remains until you change the prompt again or log out.

 NOTE: *Your prompt specifications can be made to take effect each time you log on. To do this, you'll need to modify the .cshrc file (for a C shell) or the .kshrc file (for a Korn shell). You'll find the details about modifying these files in Chapter 23, "Modifying the User Environment."*

13.2

Reissuing Previously Entered Command Lines

There are several ways to access the history list and reissue a command. You can request the shell to

- Repeat the most recently entered command
- Reissue a command identified by its event number
- Reexecute a command by specifying part of the command name

Repeating the Most Recent Command

1. Review the *practice* file by typing the following display command.

   cat *practice*

2. This utility—**cat**—moves *downward* through a file. To return to text that you passed by, it is often necessary to repeat the command. When your shell prompt reappears, tell the shell to repeat the previous command by typing the following.

   In the C shell:

   !!

   In the Korn shell:

   r

The file *practice* is displayed on your terminal screen again, because the **cat** command is repeated.

In the C shell, to repeat the last command you entered, type double exclamation points, or bang bang. In the Korn shell, the **r** command is instruction to repeat your last command.

Executing Commands by Event Number

Several of the remaining exercises use the history event numbers. The numbers that appear on your workstation are determined by the specific commands that you enter. In the following exercises, consult your history list and use the correct event numbers.

1. Examine the history list. Type

   history

2. Select one of the commands to repeat. Place its event number in the following command instead of *event_number*.

   In the C shell:

   !event_number

   In the Korn shell:

   r *event_number*

   For instance, to repeat the command associated with event number 4 at the command line, enter

   r 4

   or

   !4

   The shell examines the history list and executes the command with the specified number.

3. Call up your history list again by typing

   history

Notice that C shell commands such as **!!** or **!***event_number,* or Korn shell commands such as **r** or **r** *event_number,* are not listed. The shell instead lists the actual command that was repeated.

4. To see if someone new has logged on, repeat the **who** command by using its event number from the history list.

SUMMARY: To instruct the shell to reexecute the previous command, enter !! in the C shell, or r in the Korn shell. To reexecute a specific command identified by its history list event number, such as 6, enter !6 in the C shell, or r 6 in the Korn shell.

Executing Commands by Their Beginning Letters

Often you'll need to repeat a command but cannot recall the event number. One way to handle this is by typing **history**, locating the correct event number, and then typing the appropriate **!** command or **r** command. As is usually the case with UNIX, there is an alternative and more efficient way.

1. To repeat the last **who** command, type one of the following commands.

   In the C shell:

   !*w*

   In the Korn shell:

   r *w*

   These commands tell the shell to repeat the last command entered that begins with the letter *w*.

NOTE: Sometimes it may be necessary to type more than one letter to correctly specify the command you want repeated.

2. Type the following commands:

wc *practice*
who

3. Now count the words in the file *practice* again, by repeating the command line **wc** *practice*. Typing **!***w* in the C shell or **r** *w* in the Korn shell would instruct the shell to go back to the last command that started with a *w*, which is **who**. So, to repeat the last **wc** command, type one of the following commands.

In the C shell:

!*wc*

In the Korn shell:

r *wc*

SUMMARY: *To reissue a selected shell command from the shell, you enter* **!***letter(s) in the C shell, or* **r** *letters(s) in the Korn shell, where the argument letter(s) is one or more letters sufficient to identify the desired command.*

13.3
Modifying Previously Entered C Shell Commands

NOTE: *If you are working in the Korn shell, skip to Section 13.5. If you also have access to a C shell, return to this section later and do the exercises.*

In addition to repeating commands, C shell's **history** feature can be used to modify and reissue previous commands.

Adding to the Previous Command Line

The **history** feature allows you to add additional instructions to a previously executed command line, and then reexecute it.

1. Make sure there are some misspelled words in the file *practice* by typing

   who | **head** >> *practice*

   This adds some of the output of **who**, with its many non-English words, to the end of the *practice* file.

2. Have **spell** identify the misspelled words by typing

   spell *practice*

   The output appears on the screen.

3. Save the located spelling errors in a new file *sp.practice*, by typing the following command line:

   !! > *sp.practice*

The shell starts by reading the last command, and then appends to that line whatever you include after the **!!**. In this case, the **!!** was **spell** *practice*, so the command line actually executed is

   spell *practice* > *sp.practice*

The **spell** utility examines the content of *practice* and identifies misspelled words. The shell redirects the output of the utility **spell** to the file *sp.practice*. Because the misspelled words from the file *practice* are put in the file *sp.practice*, you must examine the file *sp.practice* to see the misspelled words.

Adding to Any Previous Command Line

1. To count the number of words in *practice*, type this command:

   wc **-w** *practice*

2. To count the words in both *practice* and *journal*, type this command:

   !w journal

   This command is instruction to access the history list, locate the most recently executed command that begins with *w*, append the word *journal* to the command line, and execute the newly constituted line. The command that is executed is

   wc -w *practice journal*

3. Another way to perform this task is to look at the history list and type a command line that includes the event number of the earlier command line. Type

   history

4. Find the event number that matches the command **spell** *practice* and use it for the next command. The command line you need to type is in this format:

   !event_number journal

   where *event_number* is the event number you located in the history file.

   You just checked the spelling of the files *practice* and *journal*. The output of misspelled words is sent to the screen.

5. The **history** command can be used to create a command line that outputs the misspelled words to the file *sp.journal*. Type

   !! > sp.journal

SUMMARY: *To recall and append to a previous command line in the C shell, type the appropriate recall command followed by the string to be appended.*

Correcting Spelling Errors in C Shell Command Lines

Command lines can be complex and we often make mistakes. The **history** mechanism can be used to make corrections.

1. Type the following command, spelled exactly as written:

   spelz *practice*

2. Type the following line. (The caret character (^) is usually Shift-6 on the keyboard.)

   ^z^l^

   This command line tells the shell to locate the first occurrence of the letter *z* on the previous command line, substitute the letter *l* for the *z*, and execute the modified command line. The altered command line appears on your screen before being executed:

   ```
   spell   practice
   ```

 NOTE: *This option also works with more than one letter or word and with spaces.*

Changing the Utility and Options Within a Command

1. The utility to be executed can also be modified. Type the following command line, which tells the shell to substitute the word count utility for **spell**:

   ^spell^wc -l^

   Thus a new utility and its option are executed instead of the original utility.

   Often, long command lines need only slight modification before they are reexecuted. Let's see how this works with the command **sort**, which has a variety of options.

2. A commonly used **sort** option, **-d**, requests the utility to **sort** in dictionary order. Type

   sort -d *practice*

3. Another option is **-r**, for a **sort** in reverse order. To change your **sort** and do it again without having to retype the whole command line, type

   ^*d*^*r*^

4. A third **sort** option is **-f** , for a **sort** in which the lines beginning with upper- and lowercase letters are folded together. Change your command line to utilize this option by typing

   ^*-r*^*-f*^

   The command line **sort -r** *practice* contains three instances of the letter *r*. The substitution changes the first one on the line. (An *r* to *f* substitution would have changed the spelling of *sort* to *soft*.) To avoid the problem, the **-r** was specified in the substitution request to indicate the minus sign and letter *r* are to be replaced with a minus sign and the letter *f*.

Printing the Command Line Without Executing It in the C Shell

Often it is useful to look at a previously entered command without having it reexecuted. You can have a command line printed to the screen and added to the history list without executing it.

1. Tell the C shell to display a previous command without executing it. Type

   !*c*:p

   The **!*c*** portion of this command instructs the shell to locate the last command beginning with a *c*. The **:p** at the end of the line prints the command on the terminal screen and adds it to the history list without executing it.

2. Make a change in this command line using the **history** syntax for the last command by entering

   *^cat^sort^*:**p**

   This printing allows you to confirm that the command formatted properly.

3. Execute the command line that you just corrected and printed, by typing

   !!

   The double bang tells the C shell to execute the last command, even if it previously was only printed on the screen and never executed.

4. Look at the history list. Type

   history

   The last four lines of the output on the terminal screen are as follows:

   ```
   28   cat practice
   29   sort practice
   30   sort practice
   31   history
   ```

   The correct **sort** command appears twice because the first time you asked for it to print and not execute; and the second time you executed the command using the **!!**.

 SUMMARY: The **:p** *command can be appended to any command line. The* **:p** *instructs the C shell to print the command line to the screen without executing it. The command is also added to the history list even though it isn't executed.*

Making More Than One Modification With the C Shell

The **:p** command is useful when multiple corrections need to be made to a single command line. This is especially helpful for long command lines.

In previous exercises, you determined the number of times a user is logged on, using the lines option of **word count**.

1. Type the following including the "**grzp**" and capital **WC**.

   who ǀ grzp *login* **ǀ WC -l**

   where *login* is your login name.

2. Correct the typing error in the word **grep** and print it to the screen by typing

   *^zp^ep^***:p**

3. Correct the case error in the **wc** command and again print it to the screen, to check that the whole command line is correct:

   *^WC^wc^***:p**

4. Once the command line is correct, tell the shell to execute it.

   !!

SUMMARY: *The caret (^) is used in the C shell history mechanism to make corrections to a previous line. The format for this usage is*

*^targetstring^replacementstring^*

Using this somewhat complex procedure to make multiple corrections is only worthwhile when the command line is long.

13.4

C Shell Procedure for Selecting Arguments from Previous Commands

Another way to reduce typing of command lines is to reuse arguments from previous commands. The C shell allows you to do this.

Selecting All Arguments

1. Look at the contents of *practice* and *journal.* Type

   cat *practice journal*

2. Run the spelling checker on these two files, by typing

   spell !*

   The !* means "Put the arguments of the previous command right here." In this case, !* is expanded into *practice journal*, the arguments in the previous (**cat**) command.

3. To verify that the shell expanded the !* sequence of characters list from the previous command into the arguments, enter **history**.

Selecting the Last Argument

1. If you have not already done so, create the directory *Desk.*

   mkdir *Desk*

2. Copy the file *journal* to the directory *Desk.*

   cp *journal Desk*

3. To move to the *Desk* directory, type the following command:

   cd !$

   The !$ means "Take the last argument in the previous command line and substitute it here."

4. View the history list to verify that this is, in fact, what happened.

5. Use the **pwd** command to verify that you are actually in the *Desk* directory.

To select the last argument in the previous command, use the **!$** in the current command.

13.5

Modifying Previously Entered Commands with the Korn Shell

If you do not have access to a Korn shell, skip to the review questions after this section.

Adding to Any Previous Command Line

Some recent versions of the Korn shell permit adding arguments to a previously issued command, using the **r** command.

 NOTE: If the following commands do not work on your system, skip to the next section.

1. Enter

    cat *practice*
    ls
    who

2. Now enter

    r | wc

    The Korn shell adds the | and **wc** arguments to the previously issued **who** command line. The output is a count of the words, characters, and lines in the output of **who**.

3. Now instruct the Korn shell to replay the last command that began with an **l**, and add a slash. The goal is to issue the **ls /** command.

r 1 /

Notice that the Korn shell issues an error statement and does not list the contents of the **/** directory. That's because you can add arguments to previous commands using the **r** command *only* if the first new addition is one of the redirection symbols **|**, **>**, **>>**, or **<**.

Adding to Any Previous Command Line with vi Mode

The Korn shell allows you to use many **vi** commands with your history list to easily make modifications to previous commands.

1. In the Korn shell, make sure that the *VISUAL* variable is set appropriately by entering

   VISUAL=**vi**

   As you may recall, assigning **vi** as the value of the variable *VISUAL* enables you to use the **vi** command to modify previously issued commands.

2. Press Esc. You can now move up and down a list of commands in your history file.

3. Enter

4. Once you have selected the command line you wish to rerun, press Return. You will be able to use most of the **vi** commands that modify text.

5. Access the previously issued **cat** command by pressing

and then

⌑k⌑

as many times as is necessary to bring up the **cat** *practice* command line.

6. Add **|** **more** to the **cat** command by entering the following commands:

A
| more

and press ⌑Return⌑ to execute the commands.

The **A** command allows you to add text to the end of the line. You added the additional shell instructions **|** and **more** to the original command line. When you press ⌑Return⌑, you instruct the shell to leave the **vi**-like command mode and run the newly modified shell command.

Searching the History List for Keywords

Rather than trying to find a previously issued command by moving through the history list a line at a time, you can find it with a keyword search.

1. Earlier, you set the *HISTSIZE* variable to *40*. Locate that command line by entering

⌑Esc⌑

/40

The command line you entered to set the *HISTSIZE* variable is displayed.

2. Now move the cursor to the *4* by pressing **w** or **l** and change the text to *30* by entering

cw*30*

You used the **/** (slash) **vi** command to first find the command that set the *HISTSIZE* variable, then the **w** to move a word to the right within the line, and finally the **cw** command to alter the original command line. In the Korn shell, the / command only locates the line containing the target string, not the target string itself.

3. Press

[Return]

The *HISTSIZE* variable is now set to *30*.

Using the History List in the Korn Shell

As you've seen, you can use most **vi** features to manipulate command lines in the Korn shell. However, you cannot use the colon commands. Editing command lines is much easier in the Korn shell because you can directly edit the text rather than use the caret substitution format.

■ Review

1. What command will reexecute the last command you entered?

2. What command would you execute to increase your history list to *100*?

3. What command would you use to instruct the shell to print out the last command you entered but not actually execute it?

4. What command could you use if you wanted to reedit the last file you edited with **vi**?

5. If you have just run the **spell** command on your file *journal* and want to place all misspelled words in a separate file called *journal.errors*, what command would you use?

6. Suppose you have entered the command

cat *food nip litter*

What would you type if you wanted to use **pg** instead of **cat** and execute it as your next command?

■ Conclusion

The history mechanisms of the C and Korn shells are used to establish how many commands should be *recorded*, to make substitutions in the command line, to recall commands and arguments, and to edit previous commands without retyping them. All this saves you time and effort.

This chapter introduced some of the more useful features of the history mechanism. For additional information, refer to the *csh* and *ksh* **man** pages or consult Chapter 23, "Modifying the User Environment."

■ Answers

1. In the C shell: **!!**
   In the Korn shell: **r**

2. In the C shell: **set** *history=100*
   In the Korn shell: *HISTSIZE=100*

3. In the C shell: **!!:p**
   In the Korn shell: [Esc] and then press [k] once

4. In the C shell: **!***v*
   In the Korn shell: **r** *v*

5. In the C shell: **!!** > *journal.errors*
   In the Korn shell: [Esc]
   [k]
   [A] > *journal.errors*

6. In the C shell: **^***cat***^***pg***^**
   In the Korn shell: [Esc]
   k
   cw
   pg
   [Return]

COMMAND SUMMARY

C Shell

set *history*=#	Sets the length of the history list to be # number of previous commands.
!!	Executes previous command.
!!*string*	Reexecutes the last command that started with *string*.
!!:p	Prints last command on the screen, but does not execute it.
!#	Repeats command that was assigned to the # event number.
!# *string*	Reexecutes the command with event number # (from the history list), but with *string* appended to the end of the command.
!*letter*	Repeats last command that began with the specified *letter*.
^*string1*^*string2*^	Looks for the first occurrence of *string1* in the last command, substitutes *string2* for it, and reexecutes the command.
^*string1*^*string2*^ **:p**	Looks for the first occurrence of *string1* in the last command, substitutes *string2* for it, prints out the command line, and places the revised command line in the history list *without* executing it.
set *prompt*=*string*	Sets the shell prompt to *string*. If there is a ! (preceded by a backslash) embedded within *string*, the command number of the command about to be entered will be included in the prompt.

Korn Shell

HISTSIZE=#   Sets the value of the history list variable to be # number of previous commands.

[Esc]   Puts you into **vi** control (command) mode for retrieving and modifying previously entered commands.

r   Repeats previous command.

r | *command*   Adds pipe and *command* to previous command.

r #   Repeats # command.

r *aa*   Repeats last command beginning with *aa*.

PART III

Working with Power Utilities

Chapter Fourteen

Locating Information with grep and Regular Expressions

The ability to search for words or character patterns with UNIX editors is an essential editing skill. However, when you use an editor to search for a word, you have to open the file and read it into the editor's memory space or buffer. Fortunately, there are powerful searching capabilities that can be used to search a file or an entire directory of files *without* reading the whole file into memory. These capabilities are offered by the utility **grep**, short for **g**lobal **r**egular **e**xpression **p**rinting.

This chapter examines the major features of **grep**, including the use of special characters to extend the search capabilities. Two additional related utilities are also explored: a faster search utility called **fgrep**, and a utility that uses an extended set of search characters, called **egrep**. These three utilities solve different problems, helping you select and extract appropriate records and data from input or files.

SKILLS CHECK: *Before beginning this chapter, you should be able to*

- *Edit files with the* **vi***sual editor*
- *Create basic shell scripts*
- *Use utilities to manage data and files*
- *Use the introductory features of* **grep** *(explored in Chapter 3, "Using Basic UNIX Utilities")*

OBJECTIVES: *After completing this module, you will be able to*

- *Select lines that match a pattern*
- *Select lines that do not match a pattern*
- *Search for a pattern using regular expressions*
- *Use command files to specify targets for searches*
- *Employ extended search metacharacters*
- *Make faster searches for target strings*

In Chapter 3, you used **grep** to search a file and select lines that contained a target string of characters. The **grep** utility also accepts specific instructions to select lines based on criteria other than an exact match to a pattern. The expressions used by **grep** for such complex searches are also employed by other utilities, including **awk** and **sed**. This chapter examines the search criteria used by **grep** and then compares **grep**'s functionality with that of its cousins, **fgrep** and **egrep**.

14.1

Creating an Example File

The exercises in this chapter use **grep** to search for specific targets in a file. To keep things orderly as you work through the chapter, we suggest that you first create a directory to hold data and programs associated with the advanced utilities.

1. Create a new directory named *Power-utilities*.

   mkdir *Power-utilities*

   This directory, used to store **grep** data and command files in this chapter, will later be used in conjunction with **sed**, **awk**, and **join**.

2. Make *Power-utilities* your current directory.

   cd *Power-utilities*

3. Create an example file called *regexp* that contains the following fairly ridiculous lines.

 NOTE: *For the exercises in this chapter to work properly, the lines of the regexp file must be entered exactly as they are presented here, including all errors.*

```
the
^the
he not formal diferent
hereby that forma is
other she different is formal
The bother that is formaldehyde
mother Thereby6a.
Bother 222
```

```
^ formally -2
\<
1A Mother.
333 this is
Brother 222A .
-2
22A 4A that$
She diffferent format sister that
themselves brother5A
222 dierent ]
```

14.2

Searching for Lines Containing Target Strings

Two tasks you will often need to accomplish are

- Identify the lines in a file that contain a word or string of characters
- Determine which of several files contains a particular word or string of characters

Finding Patterns Rather Than Words

In earlier chapters, you used **grep** to search a file and select lines that contained a target string of characters.

1. For instance, have **grep** search through the *regexp* file you just created and look for the target characters *ot*. Enter this command:

   grep *ot regexp*

2. Compare the results with the file's contents. Enter

   cat *regexp*

   The output from **grep** that is displayed on the screen shows all of the lines in the file *regexp* that contain the pattern *ot* somewhere in the line. The lines containing the words *other, mother, brother,* and *not* all contain the target pattern *ot* and so are valid matches for **grep**. The lines containing the match are selected and output by **grep**.

3. Search through several files by entering the following. (If you are using the Bourne shell, enter *$HOME* instead of the tilde.)

grep *ot regexp ~/practice ~/names.tmp*

The search target is the character string *ot* because *ot* is the first argument in the **grep** command line. The **grep** utility is programmed to interpret the first argument it receives as the search, or target, string, and all other arguments as the names of files to be opened and searched.

Searching Through All Files in a Directory

The **grep** utility searches through all files whose names are listed as arguments.

1. Enter

grep *the ~/**

The shell replaces the * with all filenames in your home directory. As a result, **grep** gets the string *the* as the first argument, followed by all the filenames in your home directory as remaining arguments. All files are then searched for the target *the*.

The **grep** utility searches all lines it reads as input, and outputs every line that contains a match to the target string and the name of the file that contains the line. The strings found do not always match whole "words" but rather a sequence or string of characters.

Listing Names of Files That Contain Matches

The **grep** utility is programmed to work in several optional ways. For instance, instead of displaying the contents of all matched lines, you can have **grep** list just the names of the files that contain a match.

1. Enter the following request to examine all files in your home directory.

grep -l *the ~/**

The names of all files in your home directory that contain the target string *the* are listed as output. The **-l** option to **grep** tells it to not display matched lines, but just list the names of all files that contain at least one match.

Counting the Number of Matches

In addition to the **-l** option's information on the names of files that have matches to the target, it is sometimes important to determine the number of matches in each file.

1. Enter

   grep -c *the ~/**

   With the **-c** option, the output of **grep** consists of two fields: the name of *all* files in your home directory, and a count of the number of matches in that file, even if there are zero matches.

Identifying the Line Number for Each Match

1. To request that **grep** inform you of the location(s) in the file for each match of the target string, enter this command:

   grep -n *he regexp*

   With the **-n** option, the output of **grep** consists of the line number and the line content for each match.

Searching for Exact Strings

Because UNIX utilities use the convention *-flag* to identify arguments, it is difficult to search for a target string that begins with a minus sign. An option makes it possible.

1. Tell **grep** to locate the lines containing a -2, by entering

   grep -2 *regexp*

   The resulting error message indicates that **grep** does not recognize the option -2, and no data is processed.

2. Now instruct **grep** to treat the -2 as a *literal expression* rather than an option, by entering

grep -e *-2 regexp*

The **-e** option to **grep** is instruction to consider the next argument as a literal character string or **e**xpression. Lines containing a literal -2 are output.

14.3

Searching for Lines Using Basic Metacharacters

In string searches like the previous examples, **grep** interprets each character in the target string as a character to match as it examines each line of input. Several utilities, including **grep**, interpret certain characters as having special meaning rather than as literal characters to be matched. These special characters are called *metacharacters*. A metacharacter symbolizes a rule that is applied in the search for a specified string.

Selecting Lines Having a Pattern at the Beginning of the Line

You can specify not only a target string, but where on the line the string is located.

1. Enter the following:

grep *'^the' regexp*

The target string *^the* is enclosed in single quotes. The quotes instruct the shell to pass the enclosed characters to **grep** as they are, rather than interpret any of them as a special shell character.

2. Compare the results of the **grep** command in step 1 with the contents of the file by entering

cat *regexp*

The line beginning with the string *the* is output; the lines with *the* elsewhere in the line are not selected.

In particular, the line containing the literal characters ^*the* is *not selected*. The fact that an exact match with the string ^*the* in the line did not result in the selection of that line indicates that the ^ (caret) does not match a caret; it has special meaning. It is a metacharacter.

Used in a search, the caret is interpreted by **grep** to mean *the beginning of a line*. The regular expression ^*the* means "look for beginning of line, then the first three characters after the beginning of line must be *t h e*." The caret can be used in front of any string to locate lines with that string placed at the beginning of the line.

Locating Lines Having a Pattern at the End of the Line

A different character is used to specify *end of line*.

   1. To locate lines in the file that end with the string *that*, enter

    grep '*that$*' *regexp*

When used in a search pattern, the dollar sign $ is not a pattern-matching character. Thus the string *that$* is in the file, but not selected. The $ in the search pattern is interpreted by **grep** to mean "end of line" locations. For the regular expression *that$* to match a target, the string *that* must be located at the end of a line.

A *regular expression* is a string of characters. Regular expressions used in searches usually include characters that are searched for literally. A regular expression may also include special characters that are not searched for literally, but instead are interpreted as specific instructions regarding the search.

Following are examples of strings that include special characters, called *special patterns*:

■ ^*the*   Search for the string *the* only at the beginning of a line

| At start of the line | t | h | e |

- *that$*   Search for the word *that* located only at the end of a line

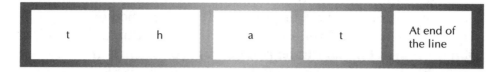

| t | h | a | t | At end of the line |

These kinds of regular expressions include the metacharacters ^ and $.

Instructing the Shell Not to Interpret Metacharacters

You have used several commands that included variables, such as *$PATH, $HOME,* and *$LOGNAME* or *$USER*. The $ next to the variable names in these commands instructs the shell to evaluate the specified variable.

1. For instance, enter one of the following commands:

   who | **grep** *$USER*

   or

   who | **grep** *$LOGNAME*

   The line from the output of **who** contains information about your login session. The shell interprets the $ as an instruction to replace *$USER* or *$LOGNAME* on the command line with the value of the shell variable *USER* or *LOGNAME*. After the value of the variable is determined, that value is passed as the first argument to **grep**.

2. Now enter

   who | **grep** '*$USER*'

   or

   who | **grep** '*$LOGNAME*'

This time, when the shell encounters the first single quote (apostrophe), the shell turns off the interpretation of special characters such as the $ until the shell reaches the next single quotation mark. Therefore, the shell treats the dollar sign as just an ordinary character to be passed to **grep**. Because the output of **who** has no line containing the literal target string $*USER,* no lines are matched, so nothing is returned.

The $ is instruction to evaluate a variable to the shell. In addition, the $ also has special meaning to **grep**. In the earlier **grep** examples, you used the $ to mean "end of line." To instruct the shell to pass the $ character to **grep** without interpreting it as a shell instruction, the string is placed inside single quotes. Whenever a character has special meaning to the shell—such as ^ * $! & and so forth—you need to place single quotation marks around the search string. The shell then passes the enclosed string to the utility without interpreting any shell special characters.

Ignoring the Case of a Letter When Searching

Metacharacters such as the beginning of line ^ are used to limit or narrow the scope of pattern searches. The caret says to "begin the definition of the target only at the beginning of the line." Metacharacters can also be used to expand searches rather than narrow them. A common application of metacharacters that expands the search using a regular expression is to find targets regardless of letter case.

1. Instruct **grep** to search for the string *he* preceded by either a capital or lowercase *t.* Enter

   grep '[Tt]*he*' *regexp*

   In this case, **grep** selects all lines containing either the string *The* or the string *the* in the file *regexp.*

The [ ] instructs **grep** to match any *one* of the characters enclosed in the brackets. The brackets contain an expanded list of characters that are acceptable for that single position in the target string.

Searching for Alternative Characters

The brackets in **grep** commands are instructions about what possible values *one* character may have at that location in the target string and be a match.

1. Enter

   grep *'b[ro]ther' regexp*

   The line returned by this command contains the word *bother* but not *brother*. It searched for a string that had a *b* followed by an *r* or an *o*, followed by the string *ther.*

2. You can use brackets to specify other elements besides differences in case or two possible values. You can also use brackets to list various acceptable targets. Enter

   grep *'[bmBM]other' regexp*

   This time the search pattern matches *Bother*, *bother*, *Mother*, and *mother*. Lines with any of the strings are selected.

Any character listed between the [and the] is acceptable for a match of one character at the specified location.

Locating a Range of Characters

1. To locate lines that contain at least one number followed by the character *A*, enter the following command:

   grep *'[0123456789]A' regexp*

   The lines containing *1A* and *222A* are selected. The line containing *333* is not selected, because there is no *A* following the number.

2. The rather laborious format of listing every number from *0* through *9* in the brackets can be replaced by a bracketed *range of numbers*. Enter

   grep *'[0-9]A' regexp*

The dash between the *0* and the *9* is a metacharacter that tells **grep** to create a range, any one member of which is a match. It is not an explicit list, instructing **grep** to look for a string containing every number from *0* through *9*. If the dash were not a metacharacter, **grep** would match a single character consisting of any one of the three characters: *0, –,* or *9*.

The presence of the dash in a range is essential. Without the dash, the results of a search using *[09]* will include only lines that have a *0* or a *9* in the position. The expression *[0-9]*, on the other hand, matches any single number from *0* to *9* inclusive, resulting in the selection of any line containing a number.

Searching for Lines Using a Range and an Explicit List

The use of brackets to enclose search parameters provides considerable flexibility. For example, both a range *and* an explicit list can be passed to **grep** in a single set of brackets as acceptable match characters.

1. Enter

    grep '[25A-Z]' *regexp*

    The above regular expression is instruction to select lines that have at least one of the specified characters—namely, a *2* or a *5* or any uppercase alphabetic character. The **grep** utility finds all lines with any one of the specified characters.

Searching for Specific Targets

Using the brackets carefully, very specific targets can be matched, letting you select particular lines from a very large file.

1. To match lines that have a lowercase letter followed by one number, followed by one uppercase letter, all at the end of the line, enter

    grep '[a-z][0-9][A-Z]$' *regexp*

With this target argument, **grep** looks for lines on which the last three characters meet the criteria specified. Each set of brackets is an instruction telling what characters are appropriate matches for one character in the target line.

2. Try the following command:

grep '[a-zA-Z]' *regexp*

The display includes all lines that have at least one lower- *or* uppercase letter somewhere in the line. Lines containing only nonalphabetic characters—such as all numbers—are not displayed.

Excluding Characters from a Search

Exclusive as well as inclusive ranges can be searched for using **grep**.

1. Enter the following command:

grep '[^a-z]' *regexp*

The output is all lines containing at least one character that is *not* a lowercase letter. When the ^ is the first character inside brackets, it instructs **grep** to locate any lines containing characters *other* than those enclosed by the brackets, rather than lines that contain at least one of the listed characters. In this position it is known as the *negation carat*.

2. Given this, you can enter the following command:

grep '[^0-9]' *regexp*

to locate lines that contain at least one character that is not a number.

The negation caret immediately following the opening bracket might be confused with a caret outside brackets that signifies "beginning of line."

3. Enter the following command:

grep '^t' *regexp*

The output is all lines that have a *t* at the beginning of the line in *regexp*.

The caret has several regular expression meanings depending on its location.

Instructing grep to Treat a Metacharacter as Ordinary

Sometimes you need to instruct **grep** to match a literal character that **grep** would normally interpret as a metacharacter. To accomplish that goal, you need to do two things:

- If the shell also attaches special meaning to the character, you must get the shell to pass it uninterpreted.

- You must instruct **grep** to treat the character as an ordinary character, not a metacharacter.

Suppose you needed to locate all lines that contained a literal caret.

1. Enter the following:

   grep '^' *regexp*

   Because the caret is placed inside single quotation marks, the shell does not interpret it, but instead passes it as a literal caret to **grep**. However, **grep** interprets the caret as a metacharacter that means "search for beginning of line." Since all lines have a beginning of line, all lines are returned.

2. To locate all caret characters, rather than the beginnings of all lines, you must instruct **grep** to interpret the caret literally—as an ordinary character, not as a metacharacter. Enter

   grep '\^' *regexp*

This time, because the backslash and caret are inside the single quotes, they are passed to **grep** uninterpreted by the shell. Hence, the first argument that **grep** receives is \^, which to **grep** is the target search pattern. The **grep** utility reads the backslash as instruction to interpret the very next single character as an ordinary character, not a metacharacter. In this example, the next character is the caret, so lines containing a literal ^ are selected and output.

3. To locate a line that *begins* with a caret, enter

   grep '^\^' *regexp*

   Here the string ^\^ is inside single quotes, so the shell passes it uninterpreted to the **grep** utility. The backslash is instruction to **grep** to not interpret the special meaning of the next character (the caret) and to interpret it literally. All lines starting with a literal caret are selected.

Preceding any character with the backslash forces **grep** to accept that character literally, ignoring any metacharacter traits the character might have.

Using Brackets to Search for Literal Metacharacters

Brackets are used to define a "list of acceptable characters." Matching a single character from the bracketed list results in selection. Metacharacters, as well as ordinary characters, can be included in a bracketed list.

1. Enter

   grep '[\2^]' *regexp*

Lines containing the characters \, 2, or ^ are returned. All the characters enclosed by brackets in this example are treated as ordinary characters in the search by **grep**. When the caret is the first character in brackets, it is the negation metacharacter. In any other position it is just a caret.

2. To search for a right bracket], enter this command:

grep '[]]' *regexp*

When the right bracket,], is the first character enclosed by brackets, it is treated as an ordinary character for searching.

3. You can take **grep** searches to the extreme and impress all your friends by locating all lines that do *not* begin with a caret. Just feed your terminal lots of carat-ene by entering this command:

grep '^[^^]' *regexp*

All lines that do not start with a caret are returned.

Each caret in the above command performs a unique function. The first signifies the beginning of a line. The second—the one immediately following the left bracket—is the negation caret. The final caret is the search-target; it says to select all lines that start with a caret. Figure 14-1 shows the multiple meanings the caret may have.

Excluded ranges are not commonly used because, to make them truly effective, it is necessary to exclude everything but the specified target.

4. In general, simply searching for an explicit target is easier. You can also use the reverse option of **grep**. Enter

grep -v '\^' *regexp*

The output is all lines that do not have a caret anywhere on the line.

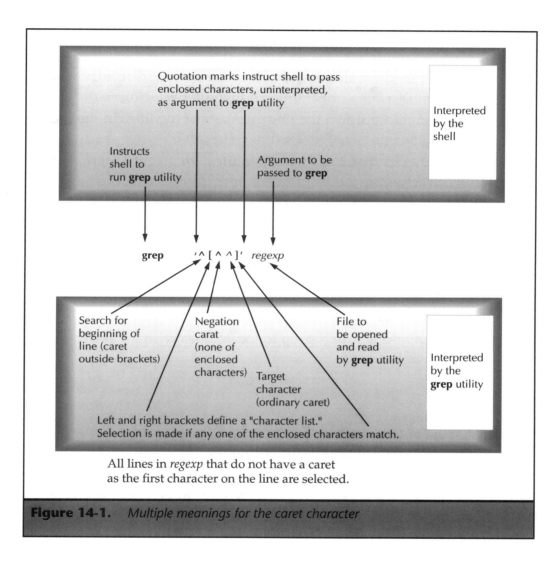

Figure 14-1. *Multiple meanings for the caret character*

Review 1

1. What command would list the files in the current directory with the number of lines in each file that include the string *security*?

2. What command outputs the line numbers of the lines in the file *project* that have a space as the first character?

3. What command searches for lines in file *outline* that contain any of the following:

   chapter1 chapter2 chapter3 chapter4

   but no other chapters?

4. What command has **grep** search for any of the following characters:

   ^ [\ ? M t

   anywhere on the line?

5. What command instructs **grep** to locate lines with a *$* at the beginning of the line?

14.4

Making Advanced Search Requests

In the previous exercises, you searched for target characters based on matches to characters, ranges, literal metacharacters, and characters symbolizing the beginning or end of a line. Additional, more complex search possibilities are available, including locating explicit words and multiple instances of specific or undefined characters.

Locating an Explicit Word

Along with its "escape" function, the backslash is also associated with certain characters to give them special meaning. In searching for a specific word, for instance, you can use the symbols for *beginning of word* and *end of word* to limit the selection to literal words only, not strings contained in words.

1. To search for the specific word *he,* enter the command

   grep '\<*he*\>' *regexp*

   When a string is enclosed by \< and \>, **grep** recognizes the string not as instruction to search for a \ followed by a < character, but as instruction to match only exact, literal occurrences of the enclosed string. The string must be self-contained (not part of a larger word), but it may be located next to punctuation or at the beginning or end of a line.

2. The **grep** utility also provides an alternative method for selecting words. Enter

   grep -w *he regexp*

   The **-w** option instructs **grep** to select lines that contain the target as a word itself, not as part of another word. With the **-w** option, word boundaries are determined by spaces, punctuation, and beginning or ending of lines.

2. Enter

   grep '\<*the*' *regexp*

   This time, lines that contain the string *the* at the beginning of a word are selected.

Matching Any Character

One of the most important metacharacters—the dot—expands to match any single character.

1. Enter the command

   grep '.' *regexp*

   As you can see by the resulting output, the command did not locate only the lines with dots.

   The dot metacharacter is interpreted by **grep** to mean "match any single character." This metacharacter, when used by itself, causes **grep** to find a match in every line containing any character.

2. Use the **vi** editor to enter two blank lines in the file *regexp*.

3. A useful application for the dot metacharacter is to select all lines that have characters, leaving out blank lines. Enter the same command:

grep *'.'* *regexp*

The new blank lines that contain no characters are ignored and not returned.

4. Now try the reverse:

grep **-v** *'.'* *regexp*

The blank lines are returned. Lines that do not have a character in them are selected.

Searching for Any Single Character

The dot is designed to work in combination with other characters.

1. To find the lines that contain a three-letter word ending in *he*, enter the following command:

grep *'\<.he\>'* *regexp*

Lines with words like *The, the, She,* or *she* are matched. The line containing *he* alone, however, is not matched.

The dot requires that one character, any character, be located in its specified position for a match. Three-letter words are matched. The first character in the word can be any character.

Searching for Zero or More Consecutive Repetitions of a Particular Character

Searching for multiple instances of target characters is an important **grep** feature.

1. Enter the following command:

grep *'if*'* *regexp*

and examine the results. All lines that contain an *i* are selected, not just lines that contain *if*.

The asterisk is interpreted by **grep** to mean *any* number, including none, of the previous character. The *, a powerful expanding metacharacter, can match zero, one, two, or fifty occurrences of the character that precedes it. This interpretation is quite different from how the shell interprets the asterisk (called a "splat") in filename expressions.

2. Examine the file *regexp* looking at the various spellings of *different*.

3. Locate the lines containing the word *different,* regardless of how many times the letter *f* is used after the *i* and before the *e* characters.

   grep *'diff*erent' regexp*

   This instruction to **grep** is as follows:

dif	Locate lines that contain the string *dif*
*f**	...followed by 0 or more additional *f*'s
erent	...followed by the string *erent*

4. When using the *, keep in mind its rather open-ended expandability (zero or more of the preceding character). For example, enter the following command:

   grep *'formal*' regexp*

   The words *formal* and *formally* are matched, as are *format* and *formaldehyde,* because these words contain the pattern *forma* followed by zero or more occurrences of the letter *l.*

5. To designate the string *formal* as the search base, preserving the single letter *l* in any match, enter this command:

   grep *'formall*' regexp*

This time no variant of the word *format* is located, but *formaldehyde* is matched because *formal* is matched with zero or more additional *l*'s.

Matching Any Number of Any Characters

The . and the * metacharacters can be combined to match any sequence of characters.

1. Enter

   grep *'s. * s'* *regexp*

   This command locates all lines that contain an *s* followed by zero or more characters, followed in turn by an *s*. Matches generated by this command include lines that have a single word, as well as lines that have an *s* in one word, followed by words and spaces, then another word containing an *s*. Spaces are also characters, so both *This is* and *sister* are matched by this regular expression.

2. Locating only single words beginning and ending in *s* requires a more precise target. Enter

   grep *'\<s[a-z]*s\>'* *regexp*

   Recall that the *[a-z]* matches any *single* letter, while the * matches any number of occurrences of the *preceding* character. When used together, they match *any* number of *any* letter.

14.5

A Comparison of grep, egrep, and fgrep

The **grep** utility has limitations. It accepts arguments, is reasonably fast, and interprets metacharacters. But it looks only for a single target and does not read a file for instructions or search patterns.

- A faster, more compact version of **grep** is called **fgrep** or fast **grep**. The **fgrep** utility accepts multiple targets, but it does not process metacharacters.

- A third version—extended **grep** or **egrep**—accepts multiple targets and also processes an expanded list of metacharacters, but is somewhat slower than **grep**.

- Both **fgrep** and **egrep** can open a specified file containing a list of targets, and then apply those targets to a search-file.

14.6

Searching for Targets Listed in a Command File

Unlike **grep**, both the **fgrep** and **egrep** utilities can read a file containing several targets to search for, then search other files for those targets.

Creating a Target File

With **grep** you must list the search target as the first argument on the command line. But with both **fgrep** and **egrep**, targets can be read from a file.

1. Create a file named *relatives* containing the following four lines:

```
father
mother
brother
sister
```

CAUTION: *Be sure to remove any blank lines accidentally entered. If an* **egrep** *target file contains a blank line, an error results.*

Reading a Target File

1. Once your *relatives* file is created, enter the following command:

fgrep -f *relatives regexp*

The following lines are displayed

```
mother Thereby6a.
She diffferent format sister THAT
themselves brother5A
```

The **-f** option informs **fgrep** that the next argument is a target (pattern) file to be read. In this example, the target file is *relatives*, which is opened and the list of targets read. All targets in the target file are then processed individually, as though you had entered a series of individual **grep** commands. The normal line-matching process then takes place, with resulting matches going to standard output.

2. Now attempt the same command with **egrep**:

egrep -f *relatives regexp*

The **egrep** utility returns the same lines as did **fgrep**. Both **egrep** and **fgrep** accept command files for instructions.

3. Try to have **grep** read the command file:

grep -f *relatives regexp*

Most versions of **grep** display the error message that tells you that **grep** does not recognize the **-f** option. It does not read from a target file. Some recent versions of **grep** do read command files.

14.7

Employing Metacharacters with grep, egrep, and fgrep

Each of the **grep** utilities uses metacharacters in markedly different ways.

Using Standard Metacharacters with fgrep and egrep

The basic **grep** utility searches for targets using metacharacters such as [ ], $, ^, and the dot character. **fgrep** and **egrep** interpret the metacharacters differently.

1. Modify the *relatives* instruction file so that it includes only the following two lines:

   ```
   [Mm]other
   [Bb]rother
   ```

2. Test how **fgrep** (fast) interprets these metacharacters by entering

   fgrep -f *relatives regexp*

   No lines are displayed, because **fgrep** interprets all target characters literally, including metacharacters. In this example, the utility searches for the lines containing the literal strings *[Mm]other*, and *[Bb]rother,*—targets that do not exist in the file *regexp*. Therefore, no lines are output.

3. Enter the same command using **egrep** (extended).

   egrep -f *relatives regexp*

   Output resembles the following:

   ```
   mother Thereby.
   1A Mother. 333 this is
   Brother 222A .
   themselves brother
   ```

   Because **egrep** does process metacharacters, the brackets have meaning. Every line from *regexp* that contains *Mother, mother, Brother,* or *brother* is displayed.

Using Extended Expressions with egrep

In addition to the standard metacharacters interpreted by **grep**, the **egrep** utility is programmed to interpret four additional or extended metacharacters.

1. So you can experiment with **egrep**'s extended metacharacters, create a new file called *test-extend* that contains the following text:

```
x
Y
4
04
x4
xY
xxY
xYY
xY
Yx
Yx444
xY4
xYY
xYY4
xYa4
0xYxY4a
0xYYYY4
0xYxYxYxYxY4
```

Specifying One or More of a Previous Character

The **grep** utility interprets the metacharacter * as an instruction to "match zero or more of the previous character." With **egrep**, you can use the "*one* or more" operator to make a match only if there is at least one of the previous character.

1. Enter

   egrep *xY+ test-extend*

   Lines that contain *xY, xYY,* or *xYYYY* are displayed. The **+** metacharacter tells **egrep** to match if the line contains an *x* followed by one or more *Y* characters.

Note that substituting a * for the + in the above command would additionally produce the lines containing just an *x*, with no *Y*—an *x* followed by zero or more *Y* characters.

Grouping Characters for Searches

With **egrep**, parentheses are used to define a substring that can then be manipulated by other metacharacters.

1. Search for the pattern *0* followed by multiple occurrences of the string *xY* followed by a *4*. Enter the following command:

   egrep *'0(xY)+4' test-extend*

   The search pattern is expanded by defining the substring *xY* with parentheses, and then operating on the substring with the "one or more" operator, **+**. The resulting display includes lines that contain a 0 followed by at least one or more instances of the string *xY* followed by a 4.

Selecting Lines with One of Several Targets

Lines that contain one or more patterns can be selected by using the | metacharacter. The pipe is the logical OR operator.

1. Enter

   egrep **"**[*Mm*]*other* | [*Bb*]*rother* **"** *regexp*

   The pipe in this command is instructed to match lines containing either *mother* or *brother*, capitalized or not.

The pipe | used with **egrep** denotes an OR operation, and is generally used on the command line. It can be used to individually define two targets in a single command.

A Summary of the grep Family of Utilities

The following table summarizes the various capabilities of the **grep** family.

Capability	grep	egrep	fgrep
Finding command-line patterns	Yes	Yes	Yes
Finding patterns in files	No	Yes	Yes
Finding multiple patterns	No	Yes	Yes
Operates especially fast	No	No	Yes
Interprets regular expressions	Yes	Yes	No
Interprets extended regular expressions	No	Yes	No

▌Review 2

1. What command instructs **grep** to select all lines from the file *receivable* that have the word *balance* in them?

2. What command instructs **grep** to locate lines in file that have *1996* followed by any number of any characters followed by *1998* at the end of the line?

3. What command instructs **grep** to select all lines from *file* that have two or more adjacent spaces anywhere on the line?

4. What command instructs **fgrep** to search through */etc/passwd* for all targets located in *targ-file*?

5. What command instructs **egrep** to locate all lines that have two or more adjacent characters in file *prog6*?

6. What is the command line if you want to search the file named *sizes* for lines containing the words *large, Large, medium, Medium, small,* or *Small*?

■ Conclusion

Using **grep** to search through input for lines that contain a specified string of characters is an essential UNIX activity. The **grep** utility facilitates selecting lines based on criteria that you specify and outputs the matched lines, line numbers, line counts, or only filenames where matches occur. Regular expressions are search strings composed of ordinary characters and metacharacters, which **grep** interprets as instructions to locate specific words, select targets by location on the line, match a range of characters, accept any number of added characters, and so forth. A faster version of the utility, **fgrep**, does not interpret metacharacters, but does read a file for a list of targets to search for. The extended version, **egrep** reads a file of targets like **fgrep**, interprets metacharacters like **grep**, and also interprets additional metacharacters allowing for more explicit searches.

■ Answers to Review 1

1. **grep** **-c** *securit* *
2. **grep** **-n** '^ ' *project*
3. **grep** '*chapter*[1-4]' *outline*
4. **grep** '[[^\?Mt]' *file*
5. **grep** '^\$' *file*

■ Answers to Review 2

1. **grep** '\<*balance*\>' *receivable*
2. **grep** '*1996*.**1998$*' *file*
3. **grep** ' *' *file* (There are three spaces before the *.)
4. **fgrep** **-f** *targ-file* */etc/passwd*
5. **egrep** ' +' *prog6* (There are two spaces before the +.)

   or

   egrep ' *' *prog6* (There are three spaces before the *.)
6. **egrep** "[*Ll*] *arge* | [*Mm*] *edium* | [*Ss*] *mall*" *sizes*

COMMAND SUMMARY

-f The file option alerts **egrep** and **fgrep** to the presence of a reference file, the name of which immediately follows the option on the command line. This file contains the target(s) that will be searched for in the input. Regular **grep** does not recognize this option.

-v The reverse option instructs **grep** to print all lines that do *not* match the pattern. This option is not recognized by **egrep** and **fgrep**.

-c The count option requests a count of the number of lines in the searched file(s) that contain a match. This option is not recognized by **egrep** and **fgrep**.

-l The list option displays a list of filenames that contain a match; matched lines themselves are not displayed. This option is not recognized by **egrep** and **fgrep**.

-n The number option displays the total number of lines in searched file(s) that contain a match. This option is not recognized by **egrep** and **fgrep**.

^ Match beginning of line.

$ Match end of line.

. Match any single character.

* Match any number of occurrences (including 0) of previous character.

[ ] Match any one character (or one from a range of characters) enclosed within brackets.

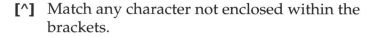

[^] Match any character not enclosed within the brackets.

\< Match beginning of a word or phrase.

\> Match end of a word or phrase.

**** Remove "magic" of special characters.

Chapter Fifteen

Editing the Data Stream with sed

Most editing sessions are conducted interactively. A file is read into an editor's memory buffer and displayed. The user enters a command to make a change, the results are observed, and the next command is issued. After all changes are completed, the editor's buffer copy is written back to disk and the editor exits. This interactivity is essential in many editing situations, but it takes up both time and resources. The modification of every instance of a date, for example, or the deletion of all blank lines in a file both entail reading the whole file into memory, making the needed changes individually or globally, then writing the file. If the file is large, it consumes even more memory and time.

With **sed**, the stream **ed**itor, the whole file is *not* read into memory for editing. Rather, one line is read into a buffer, edits are made to that line, the line is written to output, the next line is read and edited, and so on until the last line is edited. The **sed** utility interprets an expanded set of routine editing commands using a minimum number of steps. Thus **sed** can be used to effectively edit large file(s) from the shell command line or a command file.

SKILLS CHECK: *Before beginning this chapter, you should be able to*

- *Create, edit, move, copy, view, and remove files*
- *Make and change directories*
- *Use basic UNIX utilities*
- *Issue complex shell command-line requests*
- *Use regular expressions*
- *Employ the **vi**sual editor's line address commands*

OBJECTIVES: *After completing this chapter, you will be able to*

- *Use **sed** commands to edit input from a file or a utility*
- *Use files containing **sed** commands to execute several editing changes at one time*
- *Control the output of **sed***
- *Employ regular expressions with **sed***

This chapter guides you through basic **sed** editing of an example file. You will make global substitutions, specific line changes, and deletions; address lines by context and by number; and use metacharacters for matching. The last section examines how **sed** edits input and writes output.

15.1

Creating Example Files for sed Exercises

In this chapter you use **sed** to make editing changes to an example file. For ease of access in your account, we suggest you place the example file in a *Power-utilities* directory.

1. If you do not have a directory named *Power-utilities,* create it now with

   mkdir *Power-utilities*

   This directory will be used to store **sed** data and command files that you work with in this chapter.

2. Make *Power-utilities* your current directory. Enter

   cd *Power-utilities*

3. Create a file called *gdbase* containing the following lines.

NOTE: For the exercises in this chapter to work properly, the lines of the example file must be entered exactly *as they are presented here. For instance, the "v" in line 1 is lowercase. When typing the lines of this file, you need only use one space or tab between fields.*

```
Carrots    veg      .39   1   n
Milk       Dairy    .89   2   n
Magazine   Sundry  1.50   1   y
Cheese     Dairy   1.39   1   n
Sandwich   Deli    1.89   2   y
Onions     Veg      .29   6   n
```

```
Chicken    Meat      2.89   2   n
Fish       Meat      1.79   3   n
Floorwax   Hshld     2.65   1   y
Melon      Fruit      .98   3   n
Celery     Veg        .79   1   n
Napkins    Hshld      .49   6   y
```

15.2

Editing by Line Number

Lines in a file have line numbers (*addresses*) that can be used as editing reference points. The file *gdbase* that you just created contains 12 lines of text.

Deleting a Line by Number

1. Instruct **sed** to **d**elete the second line of *gdbase*, and output the remaining lines of the file, by entering

   sed '2 d' *gdbase*

   The number 2 in this command instructs **sed** to execute the specified command on line 2 of its input. The **d** is the **sed** instruction to **d**elete the specified line. Hence, line 2 is deleted in the output.

Because many of the commands used to give instruction to **sed** also have special meaning to the shell, **sed** command instructions are enclosed in single quotes, to ensure that the enclosed characters are passed to **sed** without being interpreted by the shell. In the above command, the input file *gdbase* is read by **sed**. The utility performs the specified operation, and the resulting output goes, by default, to the workstation. The original file, *gdbase*, is not affected in any way.

Deleting a Range of Lines by Number

In addition to acting on specific lines, you can also use **sed** to delete a range of lines.

1. Enter the command

   sed '2,10 d' *gdbase*

   Output consists of a copy of the *gdbase* file, with lines 2 through 10, inclusive, deleted. In this command, the range of lines is defined by the comma separating the two line numbers 2 and 10.

Substituting for the First Instance of a Pattern on All Lines

You can replace a specified pattern with another.

1. Enter the following command:

   sed 's/*Dairy***/***DAIRY***/'** *gdbase*

   Output from this command is all lines from *gdbase*, with instances of the word *Dairy* replaced with *DAIRY* in all uppercase.

   Notice that no address (line number) is specified in this command. When **sed** receives no explicit addresses, all lines of input are the target lines. In this case, because the command is to substitute one pattern for another pattern, only the lines that contain the specified pattern are changed, even though all lines are examined and output.

 NOTE: *When you use UNIX utilities, the input file (gdbase in this example) is not changed. The file is read by* **sed** *as input, but output goes directly to the workstation or is redirected to another utility or file. No changes are written back to the input file.*

The components of the command in step 1 above are as follows:

Command	Interpretation
sed	Instruction to the shell to run the **sed** utility.
' '	Shell protection; single quotes tell the shell to pass literally all enclosed characters to **sed**.
s/*Dairy*/*DAIRY*/	Editing command; tells **sed** to make a substitution. Search for the first instance on a line of the pattern *Dairy* and replace it with the string *DAIRY*.

2. Since patterns are composed of characters, you can also substitute new patterns for numbers. Enter the following:

   sed '**s**/*1*/*2*/' *gdbase*

   By instructing **sed** to search for the pattern *1* and substitute *2*, you are able to change the prices for Magazine, Cheese, Sandwich, and Fish from **$1** and change, to **$2** and change.

   Take another look at the output from the command in step 2. Notice that not all of the *1*s in the file have been changed to *2*s. The **sed** utility interprets **s**/*target*/*replacement*/ as instruction to replace only the *first* instance of the target pattern on a line.

Substituting for Multiple Instances of a Pattern on Any Line

To substitute for *all* matches of a pattern on a line, you must include the global flag in the **sed** command.

1. Enter the following:

   sed '**s**/*1*/*2*/**g**' *gdbase*

   Notice in the output that if a line includes more than one instance of the character *1*, all those instances are replaced with the character *2*. The global flag in the command is instruction to target all matched patterns on the line.

Quitting sed After a Specified Line

In the previous example, **sed** examined *all* lines in the file and made the requested changes. You can also instruct **sed** to process a specified number of lines and then quit.

1. Enter

   sed '5 q' *gdbase*

   The first five lines of the input file *gdbase* are displayed. This command instructs **sed** to begin its default process of read input, edit, write to output on the *gdbase* file. No action is called for as **sed** reads and writes lines 1 through 4. After **sed** processes line 5, the internal command **q** is followed and the editor quits.

 NOTE: The **q***uit command accepts only one address, because it is impossible to quit on more than one line.*

Creating a Script to Read
First Lines of Files

You can construct a simple script that has **sed** display the first ten lines of a file. This is especially useful if your system does not have the **head** utility.

1. In your home directory, create a file named *topp* containing this one line:

   sed '10 q' $1

2. Make the file executable by entering the following command:

   chmod 700 *topp*

3. Examine the first ten lines of a file by entering this command:

   topp *letc/passwd*

   The shell replaces the **$1** in the **sed** command in the script, with the first argument from the command line, *letc/passwd*. Hence

sed reads the file named as the first argument, */etc/passwd*, as input. When it reaches the tenth line, **sed** quits.

15.3

Structuring sed Commands

So far in this chapter you used the following **sed** command lines:

sed '2 d' *gdbase*
sed '2,10 d' *gdbase*
sed 's/Dairy/DAIRY/' *gdbase*
sed '5 q' *gdbase*

The general form of the **sed** command in these examples is as follows:

sed '*address1,address2 internal command*' *file(s)*

Single quotes protect the characters in the editing instructions from being interpreted by the shell.

Most **sed** instructions consist of two functional sections: an address and an internal **sed** command. The address, which specifies the line(s) on which the internal command should be executed, may be a single line number or a range, consisting of two line numbers separated by commas. If the address is omitted completely, all lines are examined. The internal command specifies the action **sed** is to take on the lines that were addressed. The space between the last address and the command is optional and is used to improve readability.

The following table lists the components of each of the **sed** commands used so far.

Utility	Address1	Address2	Command	Flag	File(s)
sed	2		d		*gdbase*
sed	2,	10	d		*gdbase*
sed			s/*Dairy*/DAIRY/		*gdbase*
sed	5		q		*gdbase*

Utility	Address1	Address2	Command	Flag	File(s)
sed			s/1/2/		*gdbase*
sed			s/1/2/	g	

In summary, so far you have learned that

- All **sed** command lines begin with instruction to the shell to execute the **sed** utility. The editing commands intended for **sed** are enclosed in single quotes so the shell passes the instructions without interpreting any of the characters.

- All **sed** command lines include an internal command that is executed by **sed**.

- Instructions (scripts) by **sed** work on selected lines indicated by one of the following address schemes: two addresses separated by a comma for a range, a single line address, or no address (which defaults to all lines).

15.4

Using Contextual Addresses

When a **sed** command refers to a location in the input, lines can be specified by the line number or by the contents of a line, called a *contextual address*.

Quitting After a Specified Pattern

A contextual address can initiate a **sed** editing action.

1. Enter the following command:

   sed '*/Onions/* **q**' *gdbase*

   The output consists of lines of the *gdbase* file starting with the first line through the line that contains the contextual address, *Onions*. Each line of the input file is read until the line containing *Onions* is encountered. Lines after the line containing *Onions* are not displayed because **sed** is instructed to quit after processing the first *onion* line.

A **sed** contextual address is placed within slashes.

Using Contextual Addresses in Substitutions

Contextual addresses can be used to specify a line for any action.

1. Enter the following:

sed '*/Cheese/***s***/Dairy/Deli/***g**' *gdbase*

Because no **q**uit is included in this command, the entire file, *gdbase*, is read and displayed. Each line is scanned for the contextual address, *Cheese*. When that address is matched, any instance of *Dairy* in the line is replaced with *Deli*. Here, only one contextual address is specified. The command instructs **sed** to locate lines containing the search pattern, *Cheese*, and then make the specified substitution on the selected lines.

Notice that no substitution is executed on the line containing *Milk*, even though the word *Dairy* also appears in that line. This line is not matched by the contextual address and therefore no substitution takes place.

Here are the components of the above command line.

Command	Interpretation
sed	Instruction to the shell to execute the **sed** utility.
/Cheese/	The contextual address, enclosed within slashes. Used by **sed** to select lines for editing.
s*/Dairy/Deli/*	The internal command (**substitute**) and its arguments *Dairy* and *Deli*. Both the target, *Dairy*, and the replacement, *Deli*, are identified by enclosure in slashes.

Command	Interpretation
' '	Shell protection for the script of this command. Single quotes delimit the script's instructions so it is passed intact to **sed**.
g	The **g**lobal flag instructs **sed** to execute the specified command on all instances of the contextual address *Dairy* if multiple instances occur on the same line in the input.
gdbase	The input file read and processed by **sed**.

SUMMARY: *This command line uses the contextual address /Cheese/ to instruct* **sed** *to execute the specified substitution command only on lines containing the pattern Cheese. A line number address always matches only the specified line(s), but a contextual address examines the whole file and matches from zero to all lines of input, depending on the number of matches.*

Using a Combined Numerical/Contextual Address

An address range can consist of two line numbers, two contextuals, or a combination thereof.

1. Enter this command:

   sed '7, /Fish/s/Meat/Animal/' *gdbase*

   Here two address types are combined to form the address range for this command. *Meat* is replaced with the pattern *Animal* on lines starting at line 7 and ending, inclusively, with the first line containing the pattern *Fish*. Notice that *Fish*, although separated by a comma from 7, is still enclosed by slashes.

   The following table explains the elements of the preceding command line.

Utility	Address1	Address2	Command	File(s)
sed	7	/Fish/	s/Meat/Animal/	gdbase

*NOTE: When a range is passed as the address, the elements of the range, contextual or otherwise, must be separated by a comma (e.g., **7,30** or **10,**/Fish/ or /Milk/, /Fish/).*

Using a Regular Expression to Delete Blank Lines

In addition to literal patterns, regular expressions can be used to address **sed** commands. For example, the regular expression **^$** can be used as a contextual address with the delete command, to delete all blank lines in the input.

1. Edit the file *gdbase* with **vi**. Place a blank line somewhere in the file. Save the file and quit the editor.

2. Enter this command:

   sed '/^$/ d' *gdbase*

   The output consists of a copy of the entire file *gdbase*, but with the blank line deleted.

The regular expression **^$** combines the beginning-of-line symbol (**^**) with the end-of-line symbol (**$**) to logically define a line that begins and ends but contains nothing—a blank line.

Remember that the file *gdbase* was only used as input by **sed**. The blank line that you inserted in the file remains until you explicitly remove it.

Using Regular Expression to Specify Lines

When using **sed** you often must identify explicitly which lines you want to select for editing. The regular expressions explored with **grep** are available with **sed**.

1. At the end of this chapter is a command summary of regular expressions and their meanings. Try several using as input either the *regexp* file, the output of **who**, or */etc/passwd*.

15.5

Passing Multiple Instructions to sed

More than one action can be performed by **sed** on each line it reads as input. Multiple instructions can be passed from the command line, or from a command file similar to those used with **awk**. Examples of both methods are examined in this section.

Entering Multiple Instructions on the Command Line

1. Enter the command

   sed -e 's/*Veg*/*VEG*/**' -e '**s/*Meat*/*MEAT*/**'** *gdbase*

   The file *gdbase* is displayed, with both specified strings shifted to uppercase.

   The **-e** option preceding each instruction set on the command line informs **sed** that more than one set of **e**diting instructions is included. This option is generally used when two or more sets of instructions are passed to **sed** in the same command line. It is not needed, of course, when only one instruction is specified.

Putting Multiple Instructions in a Command File

The **-e** option is convenient for passing multiple edit instructions to **sed** from the command line, but it's not the best choice for more complex **sed** scripts. Some scripts may contain 10 or 15 or more separate instructions. When this is the case, it's more reasonable to use a file containing the commands.

1. Create a command file called *modify.rec* that contains the following lines:

   s/*Magazine*/*Sunpaper*/**g**
   /*Sandwich*/ **d**

2. Have **sed** read the command file *modify.rec* for instructions and read the input file *gdbase* by entering

   sed -f *modify.rec gdbase*

   In the output resulting from this command, all instances of the word *Magazine* are changed to *Sunpaper*, and all lines containing *Sandwich* are deleted. The **-f** option instructs **sed** to open the file that follows the **-f** flag and take its instructions from that file.

Appending Text with sed

1. Create another command file named *add_item* that contains the following lines:

   /*Fish*/**a**\
   Waxpaper Tab *Hshld* Tab *1.48* Tab *1* Tab *y*
   /*Napkins*/**a**\
   Rice Tab Tab *Veg* Tab *.79* Tab *1* Tab *n*

2. Enter the following command:

   sed -f *add_item gdbase* > *gdbase_rev2*

   The components of the command line in step 2 are listed in the following table.

Command	Interpretation
sed	Execute the **sed** utility.
-f	Option passed to **sed** informing **sed** that a file, listed as the next option, is to be read for instructions.
add_item	The filename containing **sed** commands.

Command	Interpretation
gdbase	The input filename.
>	Redirect output from **sed** to the filename that follows.
gdbase_rev2	The name of the file that receives the redirected output of **sed**.

3. Examine the file *gdbase_rev2*. Its contents reflect the edits specified by the script in *add_item*. At the two contextual addresses, *Fish* and *Napkins*, **sed** is instructed to append new text as new lines to follow. The backslash *is* included after the *a* to instruct the shell to not interpret the (Return). The new *Waxpaper* entry is placed after the line containing *Fish*. The *Rice* entry is placed after the line containing *Napkins*.

■ Review 1

What do the following commands accomplish?

1. **sed** *'s/fries/chips/g' file1*
2. **sed** *'/start/,$ d' file2*
3. **sed** -**e** *'s/food/drink/g'* -**e** *'/^$/ d' file3*
4. **sed** -**f** *changes projectA*

15.6

■ Reading the Contents of a File into Input

In addition to adding text at specified addresses, you can instruct **sed** to read in the contents of external files.

Reading In a File at a Specified Address

1. Create a read-in file named *comment.file* containing the following three lines:

   ```
   * * * * * * * * * * * * * * * * * * * * * * * * * * * * * * * * * * * * * * * * * * * * * * * * * * * * * *
   J + J is our new Fish supplier, as of 12/19/97
   * * * * * * * * * * * * * * * * * * * * * * * * * * * * * * * * * * * * * * * * * * * * * * * * * * * * * *
   ```

2. Enter the following commands, substituting your actual login name for *yourlogin*.

   sed *'/Fish/* **r** *comment.file'* *gdbase*
   who | **sed** *'/yourlogin/* **r** *comment.file'*

   The entire contents of *comment.file* are added

   - After every line containing the contextual address *Fish* in *gdbase*
   - After the entry with your login in the output of **who**.

   SUMMARY: *The* **r***ead command is most useful when you need to add a large amount of text to a file. As is true for most other* **sed** *commands,* **r***ead can be used with either line numbers or contextual addresses, and requires an argument specifying the name of the file to be read.*

Replacing a File with an Edited Version

The **sed** utility always writes to standard output. Unless redirected, the output is displayed on the workstation. To capture changes made by **sed**—for checking the operation of a script, or to ultimately replace an old version of an input file with a newly edited version—the output of **sed** must be redirected from the command line to a new filename.

1. Enter the following command line:

   sed -f *add_item gdbase* > *gdbase_rev*

2. Examine the resulting new file, *gdbase_rev*. It reflects changes made by the instructions in the command file *add_item*.

Redirection of this type is used to create new files based on **sed** modifications. After the new file is created, you can check the contents to confirm that the resulting output is correct. The original input file is then either discarded or appropriately relocated.

15.7

Examining the Workings of the sed Utility

The **sed** utility is a complex stream editor that often produces unexpected results. This section is an examination of how **sed** works. With knowledge of **sed**'s operation, writing proper commands is easier.

Communicating Basic Requests to sed

Utilities that read input, then operate in some specified way on that input, and then write the result to output are often collectively termed *filters*.

1. Create a file named *explorer* containing the following line:

   s/*Veg*/*Vgtbl*/**g**

2. Enter this command:

   sed -f *explorer gdbase*

   Here, **sed** receives three arguments: **-f** and the two file names (the command file *explorer* and the input file *gdbase*). The **-f** option alerts **sed** to the presence of a command file designated, from syntax, as *explorer* (the filename immediately following the option flag). The files are opened by **sed**, and then the command file, which contains a simple substitution, is applied to every line of *gdbase* and executed at each match of the string *Veg*.

Input Buffering

Buffers are temporary storage areas for data. Buffered data may be held for simple transfer to another location, or may be processed in the buffer and then transferred. When **sed** processes input, it reads lines into buffers and there performs specified matching and other actions.

1. Modify the file *explorer,* removing its current contents and replacing them with the following:

   2,4 d

2. Enter this command:

   sed -f *explorer gdbase*

   The resulting output is all lines of *gdbase* except lines 2 through 4.

To accomplish this apparently simple task, **sed** moves through a process consisting of several steps:

- Line 1 of input is read into **sed**'s main buffer, also called the *pattern space.*

- Next, **sed** determines if the buffered line contains an address that is specified in its instructions. Because line 1 is not specified in this case (**2,4 d**), no action is taken.

- The contents of the buffer (pattern space) are simply written to standard output, clearing the buffer.

- Line 2 of input is buffered.

- Line 2 is then scanned by **sed** for a match. Because line 2 is referenced in the script, the specified command (**d**elete) is executed, and line 2 is deleted from the buffer.

- The buffer is written to output; but because the contents are already deleted, nothing reaches the workstation.

- Because lines 3 and 4 are also matched, they are processed the same as line 2—deleted.

■ Because the remaining lines of input are not matched in the instructions, they are processed the same as line 1—read in and written out.

In summary, here's what **sed** does:

■ Copies a line of input to the pattern space (buffer).

■ If the buffered line is addressed in the command, **sed** executes the specified command.

■ Writes the contents of the pattern space to standard output and empties the contents of the pattern space.

Writing Out to Files

1. Enter the following command:

   sed '1,6 w *wfile*' *gdbase*

   As the utility runs, it outputs all lines to your screen. At the same time, as a result of the **write** command, lines 1 through 6 are written to the file *wfile*.

2. Examine the contents of the file *wfile*. The command in step 1 instructed **sed** to apply the **write** command to lines 1 through 6 of the file *gdbase*. Like the **read** command, the **write** command takes a single argument—the filename to which output should be written. In this case, as lines 1 through 6 are in the buffer, the contents are written to the new file because of the edit action specified (*1,6* **w**). In each case, the buffer is then also written to output in the usual way.

Multiple Command Execution

The preceding example examined the operation of **sed** when only a single command was specified in the script. A simple test reveals how **sed** operates on multiple commands—either applied line by line to each line of input, or one command at a time to all lines.

1. Modify the file *explorer* to contain only the following lines:

   s/*Veg*/*Vgtbl*/**g**
   s/*Milk*/*Got Milk*/**g**
   q

   Let's consider what will happen with this script.

   - If the first instruction in the script is applied to all input lines before the second instruction is applied, then all input lines will be displayed with *Veg* replaced by *Vgtbl*. Likewise, *Milk* will be replaced throughout the input with *Got Milk* before **sed** quits.

   - Conversely, if the entire script is applied to one input line at a time, then **sed** will quit after processing the first line of input.

2. Enter this command:

   sed -f *explorer gdbase*

   Output consists of only the first line of *gdbase*.

The **sed** utility applies all commands in a multiple-command script to each line as it is in the buffer (pattern space). The first line of *gdbase* is buffered, read, and the substitution commands executed if there is a match. The *Veg* and *Milk* substitution lines are executed, and then the quit command is executed, terminating **sed**. The result is only a single line of output to the workstation because only a single line is read into the buffer and acted upon. If **sed** had applied the substitution commands to *all* lines of input and then processed the quit command, all lines of *gdbase* would have been edited and output before **sed** reached the **q** command and quit.

The **sed** utility is called a **stream editor** because it edits input, line by line, in a stream. It executes all edits (commands) on each line of input before reading the next line. When **sed** operates on input, it

- Reads a single line from the input stream into its buffer (pattern space)

- Executes all specified commands on that line

- Writes out the pattern space
- Reads the next line

The Interaction of sed with print

1. To see how **sed** works in conjunction with the print function, enter this command:

   sed '1,2 p' *gdbase*

   The two addressed lines are each printed twice, and the remaining lines are each printed once.

The way in which **sed** interacts with its print command produced the duplicated lines in this example, as follows:

- Line 1 of input is read and placed in the buffer.
- Line 1 matches the address, so the specified command, print, is executed on that line, printing it to standard output. It appears on the screen.
- Then **sed** performed its default "write the buffer contents to output," resulting in a second printing of line 1.
- Line 2 is placed in the buffer.
- An address match for line 2 forces a repeat of the processes that were applied to line 1, so line 2 is displayed twice.
- The remaining lines of input are read in. There is no match for the address, so they are merely written out with no further commands applied. They are written once.

A Summary of sed's Basic Operating Procedure

In summary, **sed**

- Copies a line of input to the pattern space
- Determines if the command's contextual or line address matches the contents of the pattern space

- Sequentially executes all commands if the address matches
- Writes the contents of the pattern space to the standard output (regardless of whether or not a match occurred and the command has been executed)
- Empties the contents of the pattern space

15.8

A Second Look at the substitute Command

The substitute command is one of the most powerful commands available to the **sed** user. This single, relatively simple command can quickly affect a large array of data. In this section, the substitute command is revisited to examine in detail how it works.

Substituting for a Target

1. Enter the following:

   sed ' **s**/*Dairy*/*DAIRY*/**g**' *gdbase*

   Output consists of all lines of *gdbase*, with all instances of *Dairy* changed to *DAIRY*.

Because no initial address restrictions are specified in this example, all lines of input are buffered and read, but only those lines matched by the contextual address *Dairy* are modified with the substitute command.

The global flag, the final element in the script, instructs **sed** to make the specified substitution on all occurrences of the match pattern in each line. When global is not specified, only the first occurrence of the pattern in each line is processed.

Utility	Address	Command	Flag	File(s)
sed		s/*Dairy*/*DAIRY*/	g	*gdbase*

Substituting the print Flag

1. Enter

   sed '**s**/*Dairy*/*DAIRY*/ **p**' *gdbase*

   The above command instructs **sed** to stream the lines of *gdbase* through its buffer, scanning each line for a match with the contextual address *Dairy*. When the match is made, the specified substitution is performed, and the resulting line is **printed**. However, this explicit **print** command is a separate function from the default write-the-buffer-to-output that **sed** performs on all the lines in the buffer. The line on which the substitution is performed is written to output *twice*—once by **print**, and again by **sed** 's default output of the buffer. Other lines in *gdbase* are not printed from the buffer by **p** because no address match is made. But they are written to the workstation, by **sed**'s default write to the buffer.

   NOTE: Some System V versions of **sed** *do not show duplicate lines as a result of the command in step 1.*

2. Enter

   sed '**s**/*Dairy*/*DAIRY*/' *gdbase*

   Here, no explicit call to **print** is made in the edit script. The specified substitution is performed, and the modified line is written to standard output, along with all other lines of *gdbase* that remained unmodified. No duplication takes place as it did in step 1, because of the absence of the **print** flag.

Suppressing sed's Default Output

The **print** command under **sed** is most useful for writing out specific lines from multiline files, but its side-effect of producing duplicated lines can be annoying. The **-n** option to **sed** can rectify this problem.

1. Enter

   sed -n *'1,5 s/veg/Tuber/* **p'** *gdbase*

   This time, output consists only of the one line of *gdbase* that is modified by the substitution. All other lines are **n**ot printed.

The **-n** option instructs **sed** to not perform its default write-to-output of every line. Only lines of input that are address matched and operated on by **print** are written. The **print** command copies the buffer contents to standard output and because the usual writing of the buffer at the end is suppressed, only the modified lines are output.

Figure 15-1 illustrates the steps taken by **sed**. Examine this diagram, review the previous discussion, and trace the steps on the diagram.

■ Review 2

1. What command instructs **sed** to read in the file *comment* after the line containing the word *TOTAL* in the file *accounts*?

2. What **sed** command instructs **sed** to change all instances of *1997* to *1999* in the file *projects* and then to output only the changed lines?

■ Answers to Review 1

1. Substitutes every instance of *fries* with *chips* using the file *file1* as input.

2. Deletes all lines from the first occurrence of *start* to the end of *file2*.

3. Substitutes every instance of *food* with *drink* and deletes blank lines from the file *file3*.

4. Instructs **sed** to read instructions from the file *changes* and to apply edits to file *projectA*.

■ Answers to Review 2

1. **sed** *'/TOTAL/* **r** *comment'* *accounts*

2. **sed -n** *'s/1997/1999/***g** **p'** *projects*

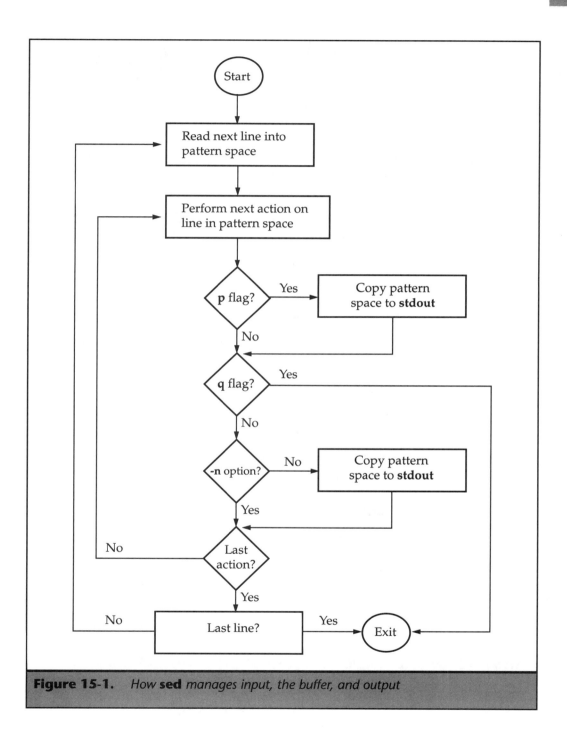

Figure 15-1.   *How* **sed** *manages input, the buffer, and output*

COMMAND SUMMARY

Summary of sed Commands

s   Instruction to substitute in pattern space; must be followed by a target regular expression and a replacement pattern separated by slashes.

g   If used as a flag for the substitute command, executes substitutions on all occurrences of the pattern in the target address, not just first instance.

p   Instruction to print pattern space.

d   Instruction to delete pattern space.

i   Instruction to insert a line before the pattern space.

a   Instruction to add a line after the pattern space.

{ } Instruction to group the commands included in the curly braces.

w *filename* Instruction to write the pattern space to the following *filename*.

r *filename* Instruction to read into the pattern space from the following *filename*.

Summary of sed Options

-n Do not print pattern space.

-e Indicates that more than one instruction per command line is passed; must precede each instruction.

-f *filename* Alerts **sed** to the presence of a command *filename*.

Summary of Metacharacters for sed Commands

^   Denotes the beginning of a line.

$ Denotes the end of a line, except when used in a comma-separated range, where it denotes the last line of a file.

. Matches any single character.

* Matches any number of occurrences of previous character (including 0).

[ ] Matches any character (or range of characters) enclosed by brackets.

[^] Matches any character not enclosed by brackets.

! Matches all lines not covered in the address.

\(Marks beginning of a pattern.

\) Marks end of a pattern.

Chapter Sixteen

Data
Manipulation
with awk

The UNIX environment supports several utilities that were created to perform specific types of data manipulation. The most powerful of these utilities is **awk** (which is an acronym of the last names of its three developers, Aho, Weinberger, and Kernighan). The **awk** utility, like **grep**, is a pattern-matching tool, but with the added ability to perform specified, often complex operations on fields in records after a pattern is matched. In addition, **awk** is fully programmable—capable of supporting the loops, conditional statements, and variables expected in a programming language.

SKILLS CHECK: *Before beginning this chapter, you should be able to*

- *Manipulate data with basic utilities*
- *Edit files with the **vi** editor*
- *Issue complex shell commands*
- *Use regular expressions*
- *Globally search and print using regular expressions with **grep***

OBJECTIVES: *After completing this chapter, you will be able to use* **awk** *to*

- *Display and manipulate lines of input that match a pattern*
- *Access, display, and manipulate specified parts of input lines*
- *Perform arithmetic and Boolean operations on input lines*
- *Operate with both command-line and command-file instructions*
- *Print reports*

This chapter introduces the powerful and comprehensive **awk** utility. You will examine command files, enhance **awk** program readability, perform arithmetic operations, format output, and explore other related advanced topics.

16.1

Selecting Records with awk

The **awk** utility can read input that is structured data either from files or from the output of another utility. In this section, several introductory forms of the **awk** command are used to manipulate the data in the file *gdbase*.

Running an Elementary awk Command

In the chapter on **sed**, you created the file *gdbase* in the *Power-utilities* directory. This file is used throughout the exercises of this chapter.

1. Change directories to *Power-utilities* and confirm that the contents of *gdbase* match the following lines:

```
Carrots    veg       .39    1   n
Milk       Dairy     .89    2   n
Magazine   Sundry   1.50    1   y
Cheese     Dairy    1.39    1   n
Sandwich   Deli     1.89    2   y
Onions     Veg       .29    6   n
Chicken    Meat     2.89    2   n
Fish       Meat     1.79    3   n
Floorwax   Hshld    2.65    1   y
Melon      Fruit     .98    3   n
Celery     Veg       .79    1   n
Napkins    Hshld     .49    6   y
```

If the file is missing or contains different information, create it or modify it to be as shown. For the exercises in this chapter to work properly, the lines must be entered as they are presented here. When creating this file, you need only use one space or tab between fields.

2. Note the placement of all special characters in the following command. Then enter the command.

awk '/*Fish*/ **{print}**' *gdbase*

All lines in *gdbase* containing the pattern *Fish* are found and displayed. The output from **awk** is displayed on the workstation. The input file is not altered.

Following are the elements of the preceding **awk** command:

Command	Interpretation
awk	Instructs the shell to execute the **awk** utility.
' '	Single quotes protect the pattern-action statement from unwanted shell interpretation, ensuring that **awk** receives this information intact.
/*Fish*/	The *target string*, or *pattern*, delimited by slashes, is the object of the search in the records of the specified database.
{print}	The action statement of the command, enclosed in braces, instructs **awk** to output selected records. The **print** statement is one of many actions supported by **awk**. Unless otherwise instructed, **print** outputs each entire record containing the target.
gdbase	The input filename; **awk** reads this file and applies the specified pattern-action statements to its lines.

The search-and-print action you just demonstrated is an example of **awk**'s basic function. After extracting records from the specified input, **awk** outputs (prints) the selected lines. The output of **awk** is routed either to the workstation or to another specified destination.

This basic command closely emulates the process of **grep**, which could have accomplished the same task, with less input from the keyboard. But when **grep** finds and prints, it is working essentially at its limit; **awk**, on the other hand, is performing only an elementary part of its functionality.

The awk Command Syntax

The basic syntax for an **awk** command is as follows:

Command	Option	Pattern	Action	Filename
awk		/Fish/	{print}	gdbase

The **awk** utility examines each line in the input file for a match with the specified pattern. If a match is found, the designated action is performed on that line. After processing a line, each succeeding line is examined until the file has been completely traversed.

Not Specifying an Action

In the preceding example, both the target and the action were specified in the command line. You need not, however, explicitly state the action in **awk**, as long as a pattern is specified.

1. Enter

   awk '/Meat/' gdbase

   All lines in gdbase that contained the target Meat are displayed.

   ```
   Chicken  Meat  2.89  2  n
   Fish     Meat  1.79  3  n
   ```

   The default action of **awk** is print (display).

Not Specifying a Pattern

1. Enter the command line

   awk '{print}' gdbase

   Here the entire file gdbase is printed.

When no pattern (target) is specified, all records contained in the input file are considered as matching the selection specification. Whatever action is specified in the **awk** statement is performed upon every record (line) in the input.

16.2

Using a Database with awk

As you have seen in previous examples, both **awk** and **grep** can be used to select records containing specified patterns. One of the principle differences between **awk** and **grep** is **awk**'s ability to select records on the basis of the *location* of values within a record. In addition, **awk** can select pieces of a record for processing. This can only be accomplished when the data are organized in a structured manner, as in a database.

Organizing the Components of the Database

A database is essentially a file that contains data. The raw content of a database tends to be in a rather elementary form that is not usually meant to be read directly. Every database is built around a central, unifying concept or definition. For example, items in the file *gdbase* pertain to the inventory of a typical grocery; that is its unifying data concept.

In database jargon, information that describes a single item or object is called a *record*. Database records are usually arranged in horizontal lines, or *rows*. The first line, or row, of *gdbase*, shown below, is its first record.

```
Carrots   veg   .39   1   n
```

The above record is divided into five interrelated segments called *fields*. Each field contributes its own piece of the overall data picture.

The following chart lists the name of each field in *gdbase*, and relates these field names to the first record in the database:

Name	Type	Unit Price	Quantity	Tax Status
Carrots	veg	.39	1	n

Printing a Field Element from a Database

Displaying a particular field contained in a record is one of **awk**'s most useful roles.

1. Note the placement of all special characters in the following command. Then enter the command.

   awk '{print $1}' *gdbase*

   The first field of each record in *gdbase* is displayed.

   ```
   Carrots
   Milk
   Magazine
   Cheese
   Sandwich
   Onions
   Chicken
   Fish
   Floorwax
   Melon
   Celery
   Napkins
   ```

Since no pattern is specified, **awk** examines all records in the file. The **print** action statement, which includes the predefined variable **$1**, instructs **awk** to print the first field of each record.

Command	Pattern	Action	Filename
awk		{print $1}	*gdbase*

Using Predefined awk Variables

In the preceding example, you used **awk** to display the first fields of all the records in *gdbase*, by specifying *$1*, a variable representing the value of a record's first field.

A *variable* is an expression that can be assigned a value other than its own literal name. These values can be defined by the user or programmer or, as is the case with certain variables in **awk**, they can be predefined.

The **awk** field variable consists of a dollar sign followed by a number and is often seen in **awk** commands. The **$** is the *field operator*, and the *1* is the literal number component. In this case, *$1* is assigned to the value of a record's first field. Likewise, *$2* represents the value in the second field, *$3* the third field, and so on, with *$0* representing the entire record.

The actual content (value) of the first field of a record may change from record to record and from database to database, but to **awk** the first field is recognized as *$1*, because this variable relationship has been predefined to **awk**.

Selecting All Fields

The **awk** utility provides a variable that explicitly denotes all fields of a record.

1. Enter

   awk *'/veg/* **{print $1}**' *gdbase*

   The pattern *veg* is matched, and the first field of its record, *Carrots*, is displayed.

2. Now enter

   awk *'/veg/* **{print $0}**' *gdbase*

   This command again matches *veg*, but displays the entire record.

The field variable *$0* denotes all fields of a record—that is, the entire line. The **{print $0}** and **{print}** statements are functionally identical, the latter being a shorthand version of the former. The all-fields variable is usually not seen in basic **awk** commands, but is sometimes used in more advanced applications to define or match the attributes of an entire record.

Displaying Multiple Fields

In addition to displaying just one field or all fields, **awk** can be used to display multiple fields. The fields can be displayed in a rearranged order, as well.

1. Enter the command

   awk '{print $3 $1}' *gdbase*

   The third field, followed by the first field of all records in *gdbase*, is displayed.

   ```
   .39Carrots
   .89Milk
   1.50Magazine
   1.39Cheese
   1.89Sandwich
   .29Onions
   2.89Chicken
   1.79Fish
   2.65Floorwax
   .98Melon
   .79Celery
   49Napkins
   ```

Formatting awk Output

Output from the command in the previous exercise was jammed together because no spaces were included between the selected fields at output. For more readable output, you can separate the fields.

1. Enter

   awk '{print $3, $1}' *gdbase*

The comma separating the two specified fields in the action statement instructs **awk** to insert a space to separate the fields in the output.

```
.39 Carrots
.89 Milk
1.50 Magazine
1.39 Cheese
1.89 Sandwich
.29 Onions
2.89 Chicken
1.79 Fish
2.65 Floorwax
.98 Melon
.79 Celery
.49 Napkins
```

Field and Record Delimiters

For database information to be organized and accessible, it must be structured in a logical manner. Fields and records provide the basic structural elements for a database.

1. Enter

   cat -tv *gdbase*

   The options **-tv** instruct **cat** to display each tab character as **^I**. If you used tab characters between fields of the database, they will be displayed.

Fields are characters separated, or *delimited,* from other fields in a record. This delimiting is accomplished by inserting a special character between the fields. The character—called the *field separator*—is chosen by the database creator. The advantage of this approach is that the number of characters contained in a specific field can vary. With a field separator in use, it is not necessary to specify a given field's length. The field separator tells **awk** where one field ends and another begins.

Fields are typically delimited by spaces or tabs, adding to the database a certain degree of readability for the user. The default field delimiter for **awk** is one or more spaces or tabs. The current example (the *gdbase* file) uses multiple spaces to align fields for clarity, but a single space or tab is sufficient.

Records, which are groups of fields, are usually delimited with a newline character. Using a newline character is advantageous because each line in the file is a record.

Changing the Field Separator

Some files have fields that are separated by delimiters other than spaces or tabs. For example, the fields of the file */etc/passwd* are delimited by colons. When alternative delimiters are used, **awk** must be informed.

1. Attempt to print the first field of *root*'s */etc/passwd* record by entering

   awk '/root/ {print $1}' /etc/passwd

   Note that if you are on a network system, you should enter

   ypcat *passwd* **|** **awk '/root/ {print $1}'**

   The entire record for *root* is displayed. (If your *root* record includes a space somewhere, your output will be only the portion of the record, up to the space.)

   In the command in step 1, the colon field delimiter in */etc/passwd* is not recognized by **awk** because it is not one of the default delimiters. There is no field-separating *white space* (spaces or tabs) between the fields in the file, and consequently **awk** is not able to find any white space-defined fields in the record. The entire record is printed because **awk** found the target pattern, and because the beginning-of-line and end-of-line characters were recognized as default record definition characters.

2. Examine some fields from your own password file record. Enter the following, which specifies the new field separator.

   awk -F: '/yourloginid/ {print $1,$4,$7}' /etc/passwd

Note that if you are on a network system, you should enter

ypcat *passwd* **| awk -F**: *'/yourloginid/* **{print $1,$4,$7}'**

This command's output is your login id, any special information (such as your name), and the name of the program that starts when you log on.

3. As another example, enter

awk -F: *'/root/* **{print $1}'** */etc/passwd*

The **-F** option informs **awk** that an alternative field separator must be processed. The colon immediately following the **-F** option defines the new separator, resulting in the first field of *root*'s */etc/passwd* record being displayed.

16.3

Selecting Records with Regular Expressions

Regular expression syntax, like that used in the **grep** family and **sed**, is understood by **awk**.

Making Selections Ignoring Letter Case

In this first example of using regular expressions in **awk** commands, you tell **awk** to select one of two possible letters in the pattern-matching process.

1. Enter

awk *'/[Vv]eg/* **{print $0}'** *gdbase*

The following output is displayed:

```
Carrots   veg   .39   1   n
Onions    Veg   .29   6   n
Celery    Veg   .79   1   n
```

The pattern /[*Vv*]*eg*/ matches either *V* or *v* followed by *eg*, allowing lines containing either *Veg* or *veg* to be matched.

Selecting Multiple Patterns

Records can be selected if they contain any one of a number of patterns by using the metacharacter for OR.

1. Enter

   awk *'/Dairy/ | |/Meat/* {**print**}' *gdbase*

   The following is displayed:

   ```
   Milk      Dairy    .89   2   n
   Cheese    Dairy   1.39   1   n
   Chicken   Meat    2.89   2   n
   Fish      Meat    1.79   3   n
   ```

The pattern */Dairy/ | |/ Meat/* is considered matched if a line contains either string—*Dairy* or *Meat*. Lines containing either string are displayed. Try it with more than two patterns in this format, separating each with two pipes. If a match fails on one or more patterns, any successful match will still be processed and the action performed on the selected records.

16.4

Selecting Records by Specific Database Components

The advantage of **awk** over the basic pattern-matching process of **grep** becomes evident when **awk** is applied to very specific components of a database.

Selecting Lines by Field Value

A database may have many records, with each record containing a "first field," a "second field," and so forth. You can select one or more records based upon the contents of one or more specified fields with **awk**.

1. Enter the following

   awk '$3 == *2.65' gdbase*

   This command instructs **awk** to print all records for which the numeric value of the third field is *2.65*. The == is the relational operator EQUAL TO, and enforces absolute equality between value of the specified field on the left, field *3*, and the number on the right, *2.65*.

2. Relative values can also be specified as an **awk** parameter. Enter the following

   awk '$3 < *2.65' gdbase*

   The output is a display of all records having a third field numeric value less than *2.65*. The < is the relational LESS THAN operator.

Matching If Two Conditions Are Met

Relational operators such as EQUAL TO and LESS THAN define a relationship between two quantities. The logical operator AND, also supported by **awk**, can connect relationships, thereby extending the scope of pattern searches.

1. Enter

   awk '$3 < *2.00* **&&** **$3** > *1.00' gdbase*

   The output from this command displays all lines in *gdbase* having third field values greater than *1.00* and less than *2.00*. Here, two relationships are connected by the logical AND operator **&&**. In this case, *both* relationships have to match before **awk** will select a line.

Matching If One of Two Conditions Is Met

The logical operator OR is supported by **awk**. It selects lines if one of two specified conditions match.

1. Enter

   awk '$2 == "*Meat*" || $5 == "*y*" ' *gdbase*

   The relationships in this command are connected by the || logical OR operator: ||. Any input line is selected if the second field is *Meat* or the fifth field is the letter *y*. Logical OR selects the record provided that *one or the other* of two stated relationships matches.

Interpreting Double Quotes

In the prior examples, items to be compared have been presented without double quotes, as in *2.00*, and with double quotes, as in "*Meat*". If you enclose an item in double quotes, **awk** regards the item as a string of characters and performs a string comparison. For example, with a string comparison, *1.0* does not equal *1*. If the item is a number and not doubled-quoted, **awk** performs a numeric comparison, if possible.

Finding Records by Searching Fields Using Real Expressions

Real expressions can be employed to specify fields for matching strings.

1. Enter

   awk '$3 == "*.89*" ' *gdbase*

   All records having a third field string value of *.89* are displayed.

2. Now enter

   awk '$3 ~ /\.89/' *gdbase*

   The use of the ~ operator tells **awk** to search the third field of the records and select the record if the string *.89* is anywhere in the field. Notice that pattern matching is not confined to the explicit, three-character *.89* string. Records with *1.89* or *2.89* (and so on) are selected. The backslash is included to indicate that the period is just a period—not a metacharacter.

3. Enter

   awk '$3 ~ /^\.89$/' *gdbase*

The ^ is the metacharacter for "beginning of a line or field."
The $ means the "end of a line or field." The string is now limited
to a field containing only the characters *.89* and no other. The
command in step 3 produces the same output as the following
awk command:

awk '$3 == ".89"' *gdbase*

Using Logical Negation

In **awk** commands, relationships can be logically excluded as well
as included.

1. Enter

   awk '! ($2 == "*Meat***")'** *gdbase*

   The output from this command is all lines having a second field
   value that is *not* the word *Meat*. The negation operator (!) forces
   this result.

2. You can use the negation operator to identify any records in a
   database file that have too few or too many fields. For example,
   confirm that each entry of *gdbase* contains exactly five fields by
   entering the following command:

   awk '! (*NF*** == 5)'** *gdbase*

   No lines from *gdbase* are displayed. The variable *NF* in this
   command line is predefined to **awk** as Number of Fields, and is
   set to the number of fields in the current line.

3. Enter

   awk '$2 !~ /*Meat***/ {print}'** *gdbase*

   In this case, the negation operator is used to search for records
   that have a specified field that does not contain a particular
   character string.

16.5

Creating and Using awk Command Files

Many **awk** commands can be entered quite effectively from the command line, but when commands grow into more complex scripts that take full advantage of this utility's power, the command line alone becomes a less-efficient means of putting **awk** to work. Entering complex **awk** commands is tedious, time consuming, and a perfect environment for input errors—especially when the command must be used more than once. When you place these complex **awk** statements in their own files, and then associate these files to **awk** on the command line, you reduce both complexity and the potential for errors.

The following examples show you how to create a command file and then instruct **awk** to read the file for instructions. The examples are basic, yet still apply to more-complicated commands.

Creating a Basic Command File

1. Create a file called *print.dairy* that contains the following line:

   /Dairy/ {print **$1**, **$3**}

The command line in *print.dairy* breaks down as follows:

Command	Pattern	Action	Filename
None	/Dairy/	{print $1, $3}	None

Command files such as *print.dairy* are not true executable files, but merely text files that are specifically written for and read by **awk**.

Passing a Command File to awk

1. Enter

   awk -f *print.dairy gdbase*

The resulting output is the first and third fields of all records in *gdbase* that contain the string *Dairy*. This is the same result that would be obtained if the following had been entered:

awk '*/Dairy/* **{print $1, $3}**' *gdbase*

The components of the complete command that is ultimately executed are as follows:

Command	Interpretation
awk -f	This **awk** command instructs the shell to run the **awk** utility and pass the **-f** option. To **awk**, the **-f** is instruction to open the file named as the next argument for instructions.
print.dairy	This argument, the command filename, immediately follows the **-f** option; it specifies the name of the command file to read.
gdbase	The input file **awk** reads as input and applies that pattern-action statement located in the command file.

The file *print.dairy* contains an **awk** pattern-action statement. Neither an actual command (**awk**) nor an input file is present. Special character protection in the form of single quotes is absent, as well. This is permissible because the shell never sees the contents of the command file, so there's no need to protect its special characters from unwanted shell interpretation. The shell merely passes the unopened reference filename to **awk**, which then opens the file and reads its contents for instructions.

Selecting Lines by Record Number

Records can be selected based on field value or content. They can also be selected based on the record number.

1. Create a new command file named *findNR* containing the following **awk** statement:

   NR == 6 **{print}**

2. Enter

awk -f *findNR gdbase*

The following output is displayed:

```
Onions   Veg   .29   6   n
```

Examine the file *gdbase*. This output is the sixth record (line) of that file. The output is determined by the contents of the command file *findNR* that you just created; specifically, by the statement **NR == 6**. The element **NR** is another predefined **awk** variable, denoting **N**umber of the **R**ecord. Here, if the value of **NR** is 6, the line is selected.

After **awk** reads in the contents of *findNR*, the overall command to the utility becomes, "If the current record is the sixth record, then perform the specified action (in this case, print)."

■ Review 1

1. What command do you enter to print the third field of *file1*?

2. What command will print the third field, followed by a space, followed by the second field of *file2*?

3. Using **awk**, write a command line that functions like the following **grep** command:

   grep *pattern file3*

4. What would you enter to print out any lines of *file4* that do not contain four fields?

5. Which option of **awk** allows **awk** to read from a command file?

16.6

■ Making awk Programs Easier to Read

To some degree, the syntax of **awk** itself enforces the formatting of its command files. For example, action statements must always be enclosed by braces. As long as its basic syntax is not violated, **awk** permits a reasonable freedom in formatting to enhance readability for users and programmers.

Formatting awk Command Files

Following is an example of **awk** code written in a linear, command-line style:

/*Dairy*/{**print $1,$3**}

It is possible to write the identical code in an expanded style that is much easier to interpret visually, without violating the command syntax—like this:

```
/Dairy/ {
    print $1, $3
    }
```

1. Reformat the *print.dairy* file. Its lines should read exactly as shown above.

   This new version of *print.dairy* provides identical results. In this second version, however, the intent of the command file is more immediately apparent. The **awk** utility can use a command file in which multiple spaces and tabs are equivalent to one space, and newline characters are often ignored, thus allowing the second format to work. Each action associated with a given pattern is placed on a line by itself, with action statements indented with multiple spaces for clarity. You can see that, in a more complex command file, this simplification is a valuable aid.

   Notice that the pattern /*Dairy*/ is followed by an opening brace on the same line. This is done to connect the indicated action(s) on the next line with the line containing the pattern /*Dairy*/.

2. Verify that the reformatted file performs identically to the original version. Enter

   awk -f *print.dairy gdbase*

   and examine the output.

Improving Readability with Variables

Several predefined **awk** variables have been used in this chapter so far. *User-defined variables* are also supported by **awk**, and they work well when you are trying to improve code readability.

1. Copy the file *print.dairy* to a new file named *print.dairy2*.

2. Modify the new file by deleting the old action and inserting three new lines, as follows:

```
/Dairy/ {
    name  = $1        ⟵
    price = $3        ⟵
    print name, price ⟵
    }
```

3. Enter the following command:

   awk -f *print.dairy2 gdbase*

   and examine the output.

   Some new syntax has been included in this example of **awk** command file formatting. You've seen how the == provides a test for equality. In this case, the single = symbol is the *assignment* operator.

   Here, the variable *name* is assigned the value of the first field, **$1**. The variable *price* is assigned the value of the third field, **$3**. Assignment is, essentially, the process of storing the value of an expression in a variable; the value is *assigned*. Assignment proceeds from right to left. With the assignments in the command above, the **print** statement displays the variable's values, not the literals *name* and *price*.

   Assignments can be made from predefined expressions, such as the field specifiers in this example, as well as from constants, user-defined expressions, and arithmetic statements.

4. Compare the new code:

```
/Dairy/ {
  name = $1
  price = $3
  print name, price
  }
```

with the original version:

```
/Dairy/ {print $1, $3}
```

Both versions of the code produce the same output. Although the original version is more compact, it is somewhat harder to understand. Using variable names that imply the role of the variable in the code, as *name* and *price* do, is always good practice and is permitted by **awk**. In this example, storing the values of predefined expressions such as *$1* in word-based variables makes the intent of the code more understandable. Assigning the value of *$1* to a variable called *x* would also be permitted, but would hardly improve readability.

Including Literal Words in awk Print Statements

To this point in the chapter, the **print** statements you have used displayed very simple output—numbers, the values of variables, and so on. More complex output, such as phrases or sentences, can also be passed to **print** in combination with variables and code-generated values. Doing this can greatly clarify the operation of an **awk** program, as well as make its output more friendly.

1. Create a file called *quoting* that contains the following lines:

```
{
  price = $3
  print cost is price
}
```

2. Enter

awk -f *quoting gdbase*

Output from this command is limited to the third field value of *gdbase*.

The words *cost is* did not display because of the way **awk** interprets its code. Unless otherwise specified, any string passed to **print** in **awk** code is taken as a *variable* to be evaluated. Thus **awk** attempted to find the current value of the variables *cost is price* and to display their values. Because *price* was the only variable with an assigned value, that value was the only output for each record of *gdbase*.

3. Quotation marks are the key to defining a string of characters as literals. To display the phrase *cost is,* you'll need to modify the file *quoting* as follows.

```
{
  price = $3
  print "cost is " price
}
```

For readability, a space is inserted within the quoted section, at the end of the phrase *cost is.* The output is

```
cost is  3.49
```

instead of

```
cost  is3.49
```

4. Rather than entering a space after the word *is,* you could use a comma:

print *"cost is",* *price*

5. Enter

awk -f *quoting gdbase*

Now for each selected line, **print** displays *cost is* and the value of the variable *price.*

Using Variable Names as Words

In **awk**, literals are always enclosed in quotation marks, as demonstrated in the preceding exercise. Variables, on the other hand, are not quoted. To illustrate this fact, a string can be passed both literally and as a variable in the same command.

1. Enter

   awk '{*item* = **$1**; **print** *item*, *item*}' *gdbase*

2. Notice the output of this command. After the variable *item* is assigned the first field value of *gdbase* for each record, the resulting value in each record is printed twice per line.

3. Now enter the following:

   awk '{*item* = **$1**; **print** "*item*", *item*}' *gdbase*

   Here, the first argument to **print** is enclosed in quotes, forcing a literal interpretation. Accordingly, each line of output contains one literal instance of the word *item* followed by a space and then the value of *item* as a variable.

■ Review 2

1. What is an **awk** command file?
2. When is an **awk** command file useful?
3. What is the advantage of using variable names over field names?
4. Why would you want to avoid naming a variable something like *x* or *int*?
5. Why is it important to properly format an **awk** command file?
6. What does the following command line accomplish?

   awk '{**print** "*Name*", **$3**, "*Phone*", **$1**}' *fowl.db*

16.7

Performing Arithmetic Operations in awk

In addition to manipulating character strings, the **awk** utility can apply arithmetic operations to variables and data.

Subtracting a Constant from a Numeric Field

1. Create a new command file called *change* containing the following program:

```
{
    print $1, $2, $3 - .10, $4, $5
}
```

Notice that the number *.10* is not enclosed in quotes. Numerical arguments are considered by **awk** to be variables having values equal to their inherent numeric values.

2. Have **awk** read the new command file by entering

awk -f *change gdbase*

The **-** used in the *change* command file is **awk**'s *subtraction operator.* Here, this operator instructs **awk** to subtract a constant from the value of a field in each record output by the **print** statement. Output is all of *gdbase,* but with its original third field values reduced by *.10,* as follows:

```
Carrots   veg   0.29   1   n
Milk   Dairy   0.79   2   n
Magazine   Sundry   1.4   1   y
Cheese   Dairy   1.29   1   n
Sandwich   Deli   1.79   2   y
Onions   Veg   0.19   6   n
Chicken   Meat   2.79   2   n
```

3. Create another **awk** command file to reduce prices by thirty-five cents.

4. Apply the file to *gdbase* and examine the output.

Adding a Constant to a Variable

Employing user-defined variables can make the command file *change* easier to read. Once defined, they can be used in arithmetic operations.

1. Modify *change* to read as follows:

```
{
name = $1
type = $2
price = $3
quantity = $4
taxable = $5
print name, type, price + .10, quantity, taxable
}
```

2. Enter the following command to instruct **awk** to read commands from *change,* and data from *gdbase*:

awk -f *change gdbase*

You have assigned the values of all five fields of *gdbase* to variables, which are ultimately passed to **print**. Focus here is on the third field variable, *price,* which has its value increased by the constant *.10* before printing. Although it seems that **awk** has added a number to a word, remember that the word *price* is the name of a variable (a character string storing the value of the third field of *gdbase,* which is a number).

Multiplying One Variable by Another

Assigning code elements to user-defined variables is good general practice. The intent and operation of code is almost always clarified by the presence of variables. Although constants tend to be concise and compact by nature, their functions can be clarified by assignment to a variable. Once this is done, for example in the *change* file, variables can be used in an arithmetic operation.

1. Modify the *change* file as follows:

```
{
name = $1
type = $2
price = $3
quantity = $4
taxable = $5
change = .50
print name, type, price * change, quantity, taxable
}
```

2. Enter

awk -f *change gdbase*

The third field of the output is a new price of one half the old price. In this version of the commands in the *change* file, a new user-defined variable, *change*, is defined and assigned the value *.50*. The value of the variable *price* is multiplied by the value of the variable *change* and the result becomes the third output field for all records of *gdbase*.

Using Variable Division Outside the print Statement

The clarity already afforded the program by variables can be further enhanced by performing arithmetic operations on their own lines, assigning the results to a third variable, and then passing it to **print**.

1. Modify *change* as follows:

```
{
name = $1
type = $2
price = $3
```

```
        quantity  =  $4
        taxable  =  $5
        change  =  3
        saleprice  =  price / change
        print name, type, price, saleprice, quantity, taxable
        }
```

2. Apply the newly modified file to *gdbase,* with the following command:

   awk -f *change gdbase*

   In this example, each record's *price* is divided by the value of the *change* variable 3 and the result assigned to the variable *saleprice.* The **print** line outputs the value of the new variable *saleprice* as the fourth field.

Maintaining a Running Total

The way in which **awk** creates and initializes (that is, assigns initial value to) variables can be used to maintain an updated or "running" total on items in a database.

1. Create a new command file called *running* that contains the following lines:

```
        {
        name  =  $1
        price  =  $3
        quantity  =  $4
        total  =  price * quantity
        running  =  running + total
        print name, total, running
        }
```

2. Have **awk** read the commands from the *running* file and use *gdbase* as the input.

   awk -f *running gdbase*

The output includes one line for each item, showing the item's name, total cost (price multiplied by quantity purchased), and the current running total.

```
Carrots  0.39  0.39
Milk  1.78  2.17
Magazine  1.50  3.67
Cheese  1.39  5.06
Sandwich  3.78  8.84
Onions  1.74  10.58
Chicken  5.78  16.36
Fish  5.37  21.73
Floorwax  2.65  24.38
Melon  2.94  27.32
Celery  0.79  28.11
Napkins  2.94  31.05
```

Calculating the Running Total

The mechanism of accumulating a running total is the following line

running = running + total ,

This line generates the running total, which seems to appear "out of nowhere," without the definitions and assignments that usually accompany a new variable.

The variable *running* is actually created when **awk** processes the first record of *gdbase*. In **awk**, a new variable has a value of zero *at the time of its creation,* and this line of code tells **awk** to literally "Create a new variable, and assign to it the sum of zero plus the current value of *total*."

By the time the next record is processed, the variable *running* has a nonzero value, and the statement translates as follows: "Assign to the variable *running* the sum of its present value plus the value of *total*." This process continues until all records in the file are processed. The value of *running* increases as each *total* is added.

Combining the Addition Operation and Variable Assignment

An addition operation and the assignment of its result can be combined with a single operator.

1. Open the file *running* and locate this line:

   running = running + total

2. Change this line to read as follows:

   running += total

3. Apply the modified *running* file to *gdbase*:

   awk -f *running gdbase*

   The code has been condensed by the combining operator **+=** which instructs **awk** to set the value of *running* to its current value plus the value of *total*. The result is the same as before.

The operator **+=** takes the value held by the variable to the left of the operator, adds to it the value specified on the right of the operator, and assigns the result of the sum back to the variable on the left of the operator. For example, *a += 1* is equivalent to *a = a + 1*.

> **SUMMARY:** *The arithmetic operations addition, subtraction, multiplication, and division are supported in* **awk**. *These operations can be performed with either constants or variables. They can be performed in a* **print** *statement or in conjunction with variable assignment. They are floating-point operations. The operate-and-assign operators (+=,– =, *=, and /=) are also supported. A variable to the left is operated on (+, –, *, /) by an element to the right. The result is then assigned back to the variable to the left.*

16.8

Using the printf Function to Format Output

The **awk** utility borrows some of its notation and functions from the C programming language, in which the utility is written. Maybe Kernighan, who was an author of both, had something to do with it. The C function, **printf**, is commonly used in **awk** code to provide additional formatting capabilities over basic **print**.

Printing Strings

1. Create a new command file called *taxes* that contains the following lines:

   $5 == "*y*" {*price* = $3;
     taxedprice = *price* + *price* * .065;
     printf "%*s* %*s**n*", $1, *taxedprice*
        }

2. Apply this tax-calculating file to *gdbase* by entering

   awk -f *taxes gdbase*

   This application selects all records having *y* in the fifth field, indicating that the associated item is taxable. The *taxes* program then calculates a *taxedprice* equal to *price* plus 6.5% of *price*. The output is as follows:

   ```
   Magazine   1.5975
   Sandwich   2.01285
   Floorwax   2.82225
   Napkins    0.52185
   ```

The **printf** statement introduced in this example contains the following elements:

   printf "%*s* %*s**n*", $1, *taxedprice*

Command	Interpretation
printf	The formatting statement begins with the **printf** function itself.
"%s %s\n",	The *control string,* also called the *format string,* has symbols enclosed in double quotes that specify how **printf** will ultimately format its output. The % is a placeholder for variables that are named later in the **printf** call. The % tells **printf** that a variable will be supplied and to replace the % with the value of the variable. The *s* specifies the type of variable to be inserted; here a **string** of characters. The \n at the end of the control string tells **printf** to print a new line at that position. Unlike **print**, **printf** must be explicitly instructed to print new lines.
$1, *taxedprice*	The arguments to the **printf** call; the values of these two variables will be the formatted output.

Left- and Right-Justifying the Output

The arguments **$1** and *taxedprice* in the previous example could also have been displayed by regular **print**. When more complex demands are made on the format, however, **printf** is the stronger function.

1. Reopen the file *taxes*. Modify the **printf** statement as follows:

   printf "%-20s %-10s\n", $1, *taxedprice*

2. Run the *taxes* application again. The output resembles the following:

```
Magazine   1.5975
Sandwich   2.01285
Floorwax   2.82225
Napkins    0.52185
```

The newly added format specifies *-20* and *10* have altered the appearance of the output. They also provide insight into how **printf** handles format and variable arguments. Formatting specifiers and the variables to which they refer must appear in the same order in their respective locations in the overall **printf** line. Here, the specifier **%-20s** refers to the variable **$1**, and *%10s* applies to *taxedprice*. These numerical specifiers create minimum field widths of 20 and 10 characters. Their respective variables are left- and right-justified against the boundaries of each field width.

Aligning the Decimal and Truncating Numbers

Although the output produced by the command in the preceding section shows some improvement in formatting over the **print** command used in the "Printing Strings" exercise earlier in this section, it could still be made better. For instance, all decimal points in the output should be aligned, and the monetary values held to two decimal places.

1. Reopen the command file *taxes*. In the **printf** statement, change the *s* in *%10s* to *.2f*, as shown here:

   printf "%-20s %10.2f\n", $1, *taxedprice*

2. Enter

   awk -f *taxes gdbase*

   and you'll get the following output:

   ```
   Magazine    1.60
   Sandwich    2.01
   Floorwax    2.82
   Napkins     0.52
   ```

This modification instructed **printf** to express the variable *taxedprice* as a floating-point number held to a precision of two decimal places rather than a string. This results in an improved alignment.

> **NOTE:** *For a quick reference to the* **printf** *commands used in this chapter, refer to the command summary at the end of this chapter, under the heading "Summary of* **awk** *Printing Commands."*

16.9

Using the BEGIN and END Patterns

The basic **awk** process consists of receiving input, operating on that input in some specified manner until it has been completely processed, and then terminating. This entire sequence of **awk** operation is also called the *main loop*. When it becomes necessary for **awk** to perform other tasks before or after its main loop is executed, the **BEGIN** and **END** statements can be used to embed these additional routines in the code.

Using BEGIN in a Command File

1. Reopen the file *running*. Modify it as follows:

```
BEGIN {
  print "The running totals are: "
  }
{
  name = $1
  price = $3
  quantity = $4
  total = price * quantity
  running += total
  print name, total, running
}
```

NOTE: *Correct syntax requires that the word* **BEGIN** *be followed by an opening brace* { *on the same line.*

2. Run **awk** with the new command by entering

   awk -f *running gdbase*

   The **BEGIN** statement instructs **awk** to execute the associated instructions before any processing whatsoever of the input file *gdbase.* Here, only after printing the quoted phrase "The running totals are: " does **awk** enter its main loop.

Using END in a Command File

1. Reopen the file *running.* Modify it as follows:

BEGIN {
   print "*The name and price for each of your items is:* "
   }
{
   name = **$1**
   price = **$3**
   quantity = **$4**
   total = *price* * *quantity*
   sum += *total*
   print *name*, *total*
}
END {
   print "*the total cost of all items is:* " *sum*

      }

NOTE: *As is the case with* **BEGIN***, the word* **END** *must be followed by an opening brace* { *in the same line.*

2. Enter

   awk -f *running gdbase*

Here, the **END** statement is used to clarify the final output of this application. This application of *running* is identical to the preceding version except that the running total is not printed as each line is processed. Instead, it is printed after *all* records are processed. Because no pattern is initially specified with the action that accumulates the running total *sum* += *total*, this action is performed as every line is processed. After all lines have been processed, the **END** statement is executed and its associated action—printing the running total—is performed.

■ Review 3

1. How would you create a variable named *animals* and assign it the value of the second field of a record multiplied by the fourth field?

2. What will be the result of the following lines?

```
fowl     = $0
duck     =    $1
geese    =    $2
swans    =    $3
subtotal    =    duck    +    geese    +    swans
print    fowl    subtotal
```

3. What advantages do the **BEGIN** and **END** statements give you?

4. The statement **duck += *1*** is equivalent to what?

5. What **awk print** statement will multiply the contents of the third field times the fifth field and then print the results after first printing all the original fields?

6. What effect on an **awk** command file does the **BEGIN** statement have when it's placed at the beginning of a file?

■ Conclusion

This chapter examined the pattern-matching and data-processing utility **awk**, including database structure, basic **awk** syntax, and a variety of advanced features. You extracted specific fields from a database, employed command files to pass pattern-action statements, improved the readability of **awk** code, used arithmetic operators in **awk** commands, and used the **printf** function to create formatted output. Using the **BEGIN** and **END** statements, you employed arithmetic operators in the context of a database application.

Answers to Review 1

1. **awk** '{**print** $3}' *file1*

2. **awk** '{**print** $3, $2}' *file2*

3. **awk** '/*pattern*/ {**print**}' *file3*
   or
   awk '/*pattern*/ {**print** $0}' *file3*

4. **awk** '! (*NF* == 4)' *file4*

5. **-f**

Answers to Review 2

1. A file containing **awk** instructions.

2. When you have lots of long, complicated **awk** instructions; or when you are going to use the same instructions over and over; or when you wish to keep a record of what you are doing.

3. Using variables names makes their contents easier to identify and therefore easier to work with.

4. Variable names such as *x* or *int* have little specific meaning and thus are no better than field names for helping a programmer read code and identify variables.

5. A poorly formatted program is also difficult to read and understand. This can cause problems when you are debugging or modifying the program at a later date.

6. For all records the word *Name*, a space, third field, a space, the word *Phone*, a space, and the first field are output.

Answers to Review 3

1. *animals* = $2 * $4

2. Add the fields $1, $2, and $3 together and print the result after printing the entire record.

3. The **BEGIN** and **END** statements allow you to have actions performed either before the database file is processed or after all records have been processed.

4. *duck = duck + 1*

5. {**print** $0, $3 * $5}

6. The **BEGIN** statement tells **awk** to execute the instructions that immediately follow it, before even looking at the contents of the database file. Only after completing the instructions found in **BEGIN** does **awk** do the normal processing of records.

COMMAND SUMMARY

Summary of the awk Command

-F_character_ The field separator flag. When used on the command line, the **-F** flag informs **awk** to use the specified _character_ (which follows without a space) as the field separator.

-f _filename_ The command file flag. When used on the **awk** command line, the **-f** flag instructs **awk** to reference a _filename_ containing commands.

' ' Shell quotation marks used on the command line to protect **awk** pattern-action statements from unwanted interpretation by the shell.

/_pattern_/ The _pattern_ to be matched and then operated on by **awk**. Practically any pattern recognized by **sed** or **grep** can be matched by **awk**.

/_pattern_ | _pattern_/ The syntax for passing two patterns to **awk**. The separating pipe symbol, logical OR, permits both of the specified _patterns_ to be matched and processed.

{ Begins a block of actions.

} Ends a block of actions.

; Separates actions in a block.

BEGIN Instructs **awk** to perform the following block of actions before processing the database.

END Instructs **awk** to perform the following block of actions after processing the database.

Summary of awk Operators

Type of Operator	Operators	Function
Logical	*a* || *b*	Evaluates to true if either *a* or *b* is true.
	a && *b*	Evaluates to true if both *a* and *b* are true.
	!*a*	Evaluates to true if *a* is not true.
Assignment	*a* = *b*	Assigns the value of *b* to *a*.
	a += *b*	Assigns to *a* the value that results from adding the value of *b* to the value of *a*.
Arithmetic	+	Addition operator.
	-	Subtraction operator.
	*	Multiplication operator.
	/	Division operator.
Relations	*a* == *b*	Evaluates to true if *a* matches *b*.
	a < *b*	Evaluates to true if *a* is less than *b*.
	a > *b*	Evaluates to true if *a* is larger than *b*.
	a ~ *b*	Evaluates to true if field *a* contains the string *b*.

Summary of awk Predefined Variables

**$#** The value of *$#* is the content of the #th field in the current record.

$0 The value of *$0* is the content of all the fields in the current record.

NF The value of *NF* is the Number of Fields in the current record.

NR The value of *NR* is the Record Number of the current record.

FS The value of *FS* is the value of the Field Separator. Default separators (delimiters) are one or more spaces, or a tab.

RS The value of *RS* is the value of the Record Separator; the default separator is a newline character.

Summary of awk Printing Commands

print *variable*	Prints the value held by *variable* (for example, *cost*) followed by a new line.
print *"string"*	Prints, literally, the characters enclosed by the double quotes, followed by a new line.
print *variable1, variable2*	Prints *variable1* and *variable2*, separated by a blank space (for example, *price quantity*) and followed by a new line.
printf *"string"*	Prints the *string* enclosed by the double quotes
printf *" \tstring\n"*	Prints the *string* enclosed by the double quotes, preceded by a tab and followed by a new line.
printf *"string %s\n", variable*	Prints the *string* enclosed by the double quotes; replacing % with the value held by *variable,* and starting a new line.
printf *"%ns", variable*	Prints the value held by *variable,* right-justified to *n* number of spaces.
printf *"%-ns", variable*	Prints the value held by *variable,* left-justified to *n* number of spaces.

printf "%*nf*",   Prints the value of *variable* as a floating-point
    variable   number, right-justified against the end space of a
                field *n* characters wide.

printf "%*n.nf*",   Prints the value of *variable* as a floating-point
    variable   number, rounded to the *n*th decimal point,
                right-justified to the *n*th space.

Chapter Seventeen

Accessing Relational Data with join

Much of the data stored in modern computers consists of detailed, organized information about individuals, agencies, companies, vehicles, art work, inventory, taxes, and other components of our civilization.

Usually data concerning something as complex as an individual is stored as records in different files and identified by a unique number, such as the social security number.

The ability to match or join appropriate records from separate files that relate to one individual is critical to using the wealth of information. Creating a view of data from different files relating to one automobile, building, or person is the central task in the design and maintenance of a relational database application.

A primary role for modern UNIX systems is to provide the computing power needed to manage the data in complex database applications.

The **join** utility performs appropriate matches of records from files and is employed by users to create small database applications that manage local or limited data.

SKILLS CHECK: *Before beginning this chapter, you should be able to*

- *Create, edit, move, copy, view, and remove files*
- *Create directories and move around the file system*
- *Employ the basic utilities*
- *Use the shell to issue complex commands*
- *Issue basic commands using the* **awk**, **sed**, **sort**, **grep**, *and* **join** *utilities*

OBJECTIVE: *Upon completion of this chapter, you will be able to*

- *Create a simple relational database application*
- *Locate records from multiple files that include the same value in a specified field*
- *Output selected fields*
- *Manipulate the locations of fields in the output of* **join**

In this chapter you create three files containing various records about individuals, **join** the files, manipulate the output, and then create a series of scripts to obtain various reports from the data. The features of **join** required for effective use of the utility are examined and then applied to an example relational database.

17.1

Creating Example Database Files

In the directory *Power-utilities*, create the following three files. Enter the data as shown without changing the order of the lines.

1. Create the file *employee* by entering

    101 [Tab] *Bob* [Tab] *Place*
    102 [Tab] *Bob* [Tab] *Koettel*
    104 [Tab] *Kenny* [Tab] *Joyce*
    106 [Tab] *Mary* [Tab] *Lloyd*
    107 [Tab] *Catherine* [Tab] *Cavette*

2. Create the file *title-dept* by entering

    101 [Tab] *manager* [Tab] *30*
    102 [Tab] *programmer* [Tab] *30*
    103 [Tab] *president* [Tab] *20*
    106 [Tab] *manager* [Tab] *20*
    107 [Tab] *vice-president* [Tab] *20*

3. Finally, create a file called *salary*.

    101 [Tab] *48000* [Tab] *96*
    101 [Tab] *36000* [Tab] *95*
    102 [Tab] *30000* [Tab] *95*
    102 [Tab] *29000* [Tab] *94*
    106 [Tab] *48000* [Tab] *96*
    107 [Tab] *68000* [Tab] *96*
    107 [Tab] *63000* [Tab] *94*

17.2

Identifying Relationships in Database Files

The file *employee* has a record for each employee containing one employee's number and corresponding name. In the *title-dept* file, each line or record consists of the employee's employee number, title, and department number. The file *salary* contains at least one record for each employee listing the employee's number, a salary, and the year in which the employee's salary was established.

Mentally Examining Relationships Between Files

1. Carefully examine the files *employee*, *title-dept*, and *salary*, either as printed above, or by displaying both files contiguously by entering

   more *employee title-dept salary*

   In the *employee* file, the name *Mary Lloyd* is assigned the employee number *106*. In *title-dept*, employee number *106* is related to the title *manager*, and the department number *20*. In *salary*, employee number *106* is related to the salary *48000*, and the date of the salary assignment, *96*. The common element relating the records from the three files is employee number *106*. We conclude that Mary Lloyd is the manager and that her salary is $48,000.

   The employee number *106* is in the field called a *join field* (or match field): the field held in common in all records in all the data files.

   It is this sort of elementary relationship, projected and replicated, that lies at the heart of relational database applications.

   What you did mentally to identify the connections among the records of the files using the join field to select the appropriate data concerning Mary Lloyd is depicted in Figure 17-1.

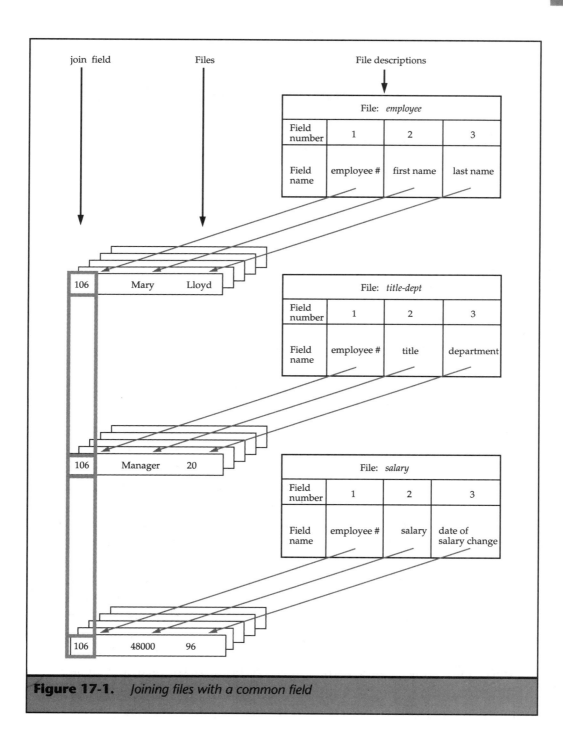

Figure 17-1. *Joining files with a common field*

17.3
Combining Selected Records with join

The **join** utility provides output that matches data from two files if the value of the join field is the same.

1. Display two of the files by entering

   more *employee title-dept*

   A basic **join** command instructs **join** to output a composite of the matched records.

2. Enter

   join *employee title-dept*

   The output is

   ```
   101  Bob Place manager 30
   102  Bob Koettel programmer 30
   106  Mary Lloyd manager 20
   107  Catherine Cavette vice-president 20
   ```

The first line of example output consists of *101*, the value that is common in the first field of the first record in both files. The values of the remaining fields of the first line of output come from the two files: *Bob Place*, from the 101 line in *employee*, and manager 30, from the *title-dept* file.

The output, termed a *joined composite*, consists of all fields from the pair of records located in the two files that have the same value in the join field. All possible joins of the input data are included. The output demonstrates the complete relationship of "person to employee number to title and department." Unless otherwise instructed, **join** attempts to join records from the files based on the value in the first field of each input line.

The output from **join** includes only those lines that have the same value in the first field—the join, or match, field. Although the *employee* file contains a record for *Kenny Joyce*, there is no matching record in *title-dept*, and *Kenny Joyce* is not in the output from **join**. If a line does not have a match in the other file, the default operation is to not include it in the output.

Combining Three Relational Files

In the previous example, records from two files were combined to produce a composite showing the names, titles, and departments of the employees. Data from the third file, *salary*, was not included. The complete relationship description of the employees can be examined only if all three files are joined. The **join** utility does not accept three arguments. However, **join** can create composite data using two of the files that can then be joined with the data from the third file.

1. Enter

    join *employee title-dept* **>** *emp-title-dept*
    join *emp-title-dept salary*

    The first command line instructs the shell to execute **join** and gives it two arguments, the first two files. The **join** utility then creates a composite join of the records from the first two files. The output of **join** is written to a new file *emp-title-dept*. The second command line results in a joining of the file containing the output of the first **join** (*emp-title-dept*) with the data in the third, *salary* file.
        The output is

    ```
    101  Bob Place manager 30 48000 96
    101  Bob Place manager 30 36000 95
    102  Bob Koettel programmer 30 36000 95
    102  Bob Koettel programmer 30 29000 94
    106  Mary Lloyd manager 20 48000 96
    107  Catherine Cavette vice-president 20 68000 96
    107  Catherine Cavette vice-president 20 63000 94
    ```

    Because there are two entries in the *salary* file for some of the employees (two *101*s, etc.), there are two composite records in the output.
        The joining of three files can also be accomplished using one command line.

2. Enter the following:

join *employee title-dept* | **join** - *salary*

This command, which results in joining records from all three files, uses two processes running **join**. Both are executed from the same command line, connected with a pipe. The first **join** process opens two files and creates a composite join of the data it reads from the two files. Its output is piped to a second **join** process. The second **join** is also given two arguments, the - and the third data file, *salary*. The **join** utility interprets the - as "read from standard input instead of a file." As a result, **join** reads the output of the first **join** (standard input) and creates a composite join with the data it reads from the file *salary*. The output is displayed on the screen.

17.4

Examining the Operation of the join Utility

In the example database files you entered at the beginning of the chapter and have been using since, all records are in ascii order. The **join** utility properly operates on input lines only if they are in ascii sorted order.

Unsorting the Datafiles

To examine how **join** works and why the input must be sorted, this exercise instructs you to modify an input file to have records out of order.

1. Change the *employee* file as follows: Move record *102* to after record *106*, and move record *104* to the end of the file.
   The *employee* file now is

   ```
   101 [Tab] Bob [Tab] Place
   106 [Tab] Mary [Tab] Lloyd
   102 [Tab] Bob [Tab] Koettel
   107 [Tab] Catherine [Tab] Cavette
   104 [Tab] Kenny [Tab] Joyce
   ```

Processing a File That Is Not Sorted

With the modifications you just entered in the first input data file, *employee*, it is no longer in sorted order.

1. Have **join** create a join composite of two files. Enter

   join *employee title-dept*

   The output displayed is

   ```
   101 Bob Place manager 30
   106 Mary Lloyd manager 30
   107 Catherine Cavette vice-president 20
   ```

   Comparing the input files with the output of **join** indicates that something is lost in translation—specifically, the record of *Bob Koettel*. The join field value of *102* is present in both input files, *employee* and *title-dept*; but a composite join record is not output by **join**. The missing line is not the result of an error, but is the expected output when **join** is provided input files that are not in sorted ascii order. The "missing" join results from the comparison process used by **join**. The following abbreviated discussion of how **join** works is tied to the steps in Figure 17-2.

   - Step 1: The first line of the file *employee* and the first line from *title-dept* are read and found to contain a match in the join field, the first field of each line. The records are joined and the composite record is output.

   - Step 2: The second line from the *title-dept* file is read. It is *102*, which does not match *101*, so the second line from the *employee* file is read; it is 106.

   - Step 3: The two new records, *106* from *employee* and *102* from *title-dept*, are compared. They do not match each other.
     The line from the file *title-dept* with number *102* in the join field is discarded because the join field value of the current line from the other file, *employee*, is already at *106*, a higher number. Because **join** makes decisions based on the assumption that the files are sorted, there can be no line with

a value less than *106* in the *employee* file; so a match for *102* (Bob Koettel) in *employee* is impossible.

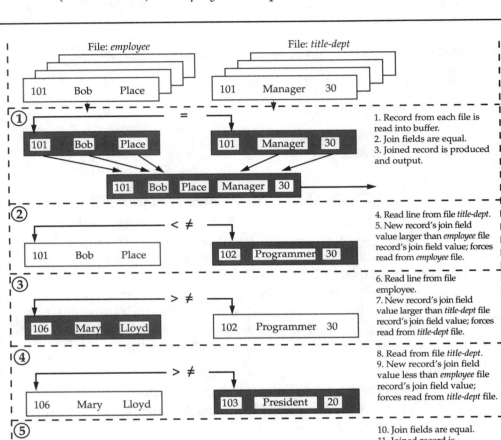

Figure 17-2. *Joining unsorted lines*

- Step 4: The record with *106* is retained, and **join** reads in the next line from *title-dept*. This line contains *103* in the join field. Again, with *106* as the value in the current line from the *employee* file, there can be no *103*, so the *103* is discarded and a new line read from *title-dept* file.

- Step 5: The next line is *106*; finally a match. A join is made and the composite line is output.

  When a value in one of **join**'s input buffers has a greater ascii value than that contained in the second buffer, the lesser value is discarded and the greater value retained against a possible future match. The *102* records are not matched because *102* follows *106* in the file. This seesaw operation continues until all records are processed. The resulting joins when input files are not sorted are merely a result of circumstance; reasonable joins can be missed.

Sorting a File Directly

To continue with the exercises in this chapter, re-sort the *employee* file.

1. Enter

   sort -o *employee employee*

   In this command line, the **sort** utility is given three arguments: **-o**, *employee*, and *employee*.

Argument	Description
-o	Instruction to **sort** that when it is finished sorting, it should write its output to the file listed as the next argument, *employee*. Without this **-o** argument, **sort** writes output to standard output often connected to the display.
employee	This argument directly follows the **-o** option and is interpreted by **sort** as the filename for writing output.

Argument	Description
employee	Any remaining arguments, such as this one, are interpreted by **sort** as files to be opened for input. Hence, **sort** reads from the file *employee*, and when finished writes its results back to the same file. If you used shell redirection to accomplish this task, either the file would be emptied by the shell or an error message presented depending on whether you have **noclobber** set. This option to **sort** allows users to sort a file without resorting to writing to intermediary files.

Sending the data files to **sort** before using them with **join** satisfies **join**'s need for ascii order.

2. Confirm the files are in proper order by entering

join *employee titles-dept*

Joining Files with Missing Information

In its basic form, **join** does not output a record unless the join fields of the records match. Through the use of a specific option, **join** can be instructed to include the input records in its output that do not contain a matching value in the join field of the other file.

1. Enter

join -a1 *employee title-dept*

Output is

```
101 Bob Place manager 30
102 Bob Koettel programmer 20
104 Kenny Joyce
106 Mary Lloyd manager 30
107 Catherine Cavette vice-president 20
```

This command instructs **join** to make all valid composites in the usual way and to also include in the output all unjoinable lines from the first file. The **-a1** option is instruction to include **all** records from file **1**. Although both input files contain unjoinable lines, the only line that is output is the sole unjoinable line from the first file, *104 Kenny Joyce.*

2. The same process can be applied to request a listing of all lines in the second file and from both files. Enter

   join -a1 *employee title-dept*
   join -a2 *employee title-dept*
   join -a1 -a2 *employee title-dept*

   By including the **-a** option, **join** lists records from either or both files that are not joinable.

17.5

Determining the Order of Output

By default, **join** outputs fields in the order they are found in the input files. You can explicitly choose the output order, as well as the exact fields you want displayed.

1. Enter

   join -o *1.3 2.1 2.3 employee title-dept*

   The resulting output is only a few of the joined fields, and in a different order.

   ```
   Place 101 30
   Koettel 102 30
   Lloyd 106 20
   Cavette 107 20
   ```

   The **-o** argument instructs **join** to rearrange the order of its output as specified by the arguments that follow the option. Each dot-separated number in the argument list denotes a file and field number in the format *file.field*

In this example, the specified order of the output is

File one's third field
File two's first field
File two's third field

Examining the Code

The following table summarizes the components and functions of the command line

join -o *1.3 2.1 2.3* *employee title-dept*

Command	Option	Argument to the Option	Input
join	-o	1.3 2.1 2.3	*employee title-dept*

The **-o** option and its arguments determine the fields chosen and their order:

Argument	Description
-o	Instruction to **join** that the output of fields is to be explicitly requested rather than the default output consisting of all fields in input order.
1.3	Instruction that the first output field is to be taken from the first file, *1*. The *3* specifies the third field from the file.
2.1	The second output field is to be the second file's first field.
2.3	The third output field is to be the second file's third field.

17.6

Specifying the Delimiter Character

In the examples used thus far, all fields are separated from each other in the input files by a tab character. By default, the **join** utility recognizes the tab and/or space characters as field separators, but will also accept other characters, if instructed.

1. Create a file, called *friends*, containing the login ids of several of your friends with accounts on your system, using the colon as the field delimiter, and using the following format:

   loginid:real name:phone number

   For example, enter

   cassy:catherine thamzin:ext222

2. Sort your *friends* file by entering

   sort -o *friends friends*

3. Now obtain a join of your *friends* file with the */etc/passwd* file:

   sort */etc/passwd* | **join -t***: - friends*

   The output displayed consists of records containing your friends' login ids, their names, phone numbers, and the remaining information located in the */etc/passwd* file.

   Both the */etc/passwd* and *friends* files employ the colon to separate fields within the records.

   The **-t***:* flag instructs **join** to interpret the colon character, instead of a tab character, as the field delimiter. Essentially, any character can be specified as the delimiter if entered with the **-t** option. If the character you choose has special meaning to the shell, place it in quotes. For example: **-t** ";" would make the semicolon the field separator.

Limiting the Number of Output Fields

In the last exercise, the output included all fields from both the *friends* file and */etc/passwd*.

1. Instruct **join** to limit the output by entering

   sort */etc/passwd* | **join -t**: **-o 2.1 2.6 -** *friends*

   The output consists of only the login name from the *friends* file and the home directory from */etc/passwd* for users who are also listed in the *friends* file.

Changing the Delimiter of the Input

At times input is available with one field separator character in one source, and another character in the second source. The input character can be changed using UNIX utilities. Output of the **who** utility consists of fields separated by one or more spaces.

1. Run **who** on your system and examine the format of the output.

   ```
   anna    ttyh5   Nov   23   10:05
   marty   ttyi1   Nov   23   09:47
   kyle    ttyi7   Nov   23   08:43
   cassy   ttyie   Nov   21   08:53
   ```

In files that use white space (tabs and/or spaces) to delimit fields, such as this example, the number of spaces between two fields varies with field length. If, for example, the login name is short, more spaces are included before the *tty*.

The **sed** utility can be used to replace delimiting spaces with specific character delimiters. Enter

   who | **sed** '**s/   */:/g**'

Two spaces precede the asterisk. They define the search target to **sed** as a single space, followed by zero or more spaces. The **sed** utility can be used to change delimiters from variable white space to a specific character, such as : in this case.

Determining If Friends Are Logged On

Using a multi-pipe command, **join** can create a composite of the output of the **who** command and the file *friends*, resulting in a list of your friends who are currently logged on.

1. Create a file named *friends-on* and enter the following text:

   who | **sort** | **sed** 's/ */: /g' \
   | **join** -t: -o *1.1 1.2* - *friends*

2. Make the script executable and run the script:

   chmod *755 friends-on*
   friends-on

   Output is a composite of names from *friends* and matched current logins. Only currently logged-in friends are displayed.

Examining the Code

The preceding command consists of the following components:

Arguments	Description
who	Instructs the shell to execute the **who** utility.
|	Instructs the shell to connect the output of **who** to the input of **sort**.
sort	Instructs the shell to execute the **sort** utility.
|	Instructs the shell to connect the output of **sort** to the input of **sed**.
sed	Instructs the shell to execute the **sed** utility.
' '	Instructs the shell to not interpret enclosed command but pass as is to **sed**.
s/ */:/g	Instructs **sed** to replace all strings of one or more spaces with a : character.

Arguments	Description
\	Instruction to the shell to not interpret the (Return) that follows as having special meaning. Without the return key interpreted, the command line continues to the next line of text.
|	Connects the output of **sed** to the input of **join**.
join	Instructs the shell to execute the **join** utility.
-t:	Specifies an alternative field delimiter, here the : symbol, to **join**.
-o *1.1 1.2*	Instructs **join** to output only the first file's first field and the first file's second field. (In this case, the first file is the data read from standard input.)
-	Instructs **join** to read from standard input instead of a file. Here the input of **join** is the standard output from **sed**.
friends	The second input filename.

■ Review 1

1. Which option of **join** allows unpairable/unjoinable lines to be included with normal output?

2. What does the **-o** option of **join** do?

3. What option do you use to tell **join** that field separators are colons (:) and not (Tab)?

17.7

■ Changing the Field to Be Joined

By default, **join** uses the first field of each input file as the join field, but also permits other join fields to be specified.

The file */etc/passwd*, containing user-related data, is maintained on all UNIX systems. The fields of */etc/passwd* are delimited by colons. An example *letc/passwd* file is shown below. The fourth field contains each user's group id number:

```
tammy:7HRtmKLyY:631:800::/lurnix/tammy:/bin/csh
mike:4DffTWMgh:462:800::/lurnix/mike:/bin/csh
lela:F2kkURvTp:136:900::/lurnix/lela:/bin/csh
caitlin:8FRthKLyS:540:800::/lurnix/caitlin:/bin/csh
mary:9QPSrGDIO:73:850::/lurnix/mary:/bin/csh
stephanie:8RgGvVSSL:246:850::/lurnix/stephanie:/bin/csh
```

1. Examine the first two lines of the example *letc/passwd*. Both contain the value *800* in the fourth fields, designating users *tammy* and *mike* as members of group *800*. Group memberships are used by system administrators to permit common file access to selected users. *Data Entry*, *Management*, *System Administrators*, *Operators*, and *Specific Application Users* are common group designations.

2. Examine the password file on your system using **pg** or **more** with a command such as

   more *letc/passwd*

   or

   pg *letc/passwd*

   Locate the fourth field and write down several of the group id numbers used on your system.

3. Create a new file called *groups* containing the group ids from the preceding step, and their possible name designations. Separate the numbers and designations with a colon. Precise group designations are not mandatory here. Make them up if necessary. Following is an example *groups* file shown as a general guideline (not to be copied, because the group id values on your system are probably different).

   800:Administrators
   850:Data Entry
   900:Programmers

The example above is shown as though it had been run through an ascii sort, but your *groups* file may still need to be sorted to ensure that **join** can properly operate on it.

4. Sort your *groups* file at this time by entering

sort -o *groups groups*

With the *groups* file now sorted, **join** can be called to create a composite of all users on your system in each group. But, because the group ids are contained in the fourth field of */etc/passwd*, both **sort** and **join** must be instructed to reference that field in their respective operations.

5. Enter

sort +3 -4 -t: */etc/passwd* | **join -t: -j1 4 -** *groups*

Output consists of a composite of your *groups* file and the */etc/passwd* file sorted by group affiliation (group id). It should resemble, in format, the following:

```
800:caitlin:8FRthKLyS:540::/lurnix/caitlin:/bin/csh:Administrators
800:mike:4DffTWMgh5po:462::/lurnix/mike:/bin/csh:Administrators
800:tammy:7HRtmKLYiCv:631::/lurnix/tammy:/bin/csh:Administrators
850:mary:9QPSrGDIOYqY:73::/lurnix/mary:/bin/csh:Data Entry
850:stephanie:8RgGvVSSL:246::/lurnix/stephanie:/bin/csh:Data Entry
900:lela:F2kkURvTp:136::/lurnix/lela:/bin/csh:Programmers
```

Examining the Code

The command

sort +3 -4 -t: */etc/passwd* | **join -t: -j1 4 -** *groups*

is noteworthy in the way it focuses the activity of both **sort** and **join**:

Arguments	Description
sort +3 -4	Arguments to **sort** instructing **sort** to restrict its sorting to only the fourth field of its input, the group id.
-t:	Argument to **sort** changing field separator to colon.
-j1 4	Instruction to **join** to join lines from the first file using its fourth field as the join field with the colon as field separator. The *1* indicates the first file; the *4* specifies the field to be used for joining.
- groups	Instruction to **join** to read from standard input for the first file and *groups* for the second. In this example, **join** is instructed to read the output of **sort** as one input file and read the file *groups* as the other input file.

Selecting Only Group and User

The following table summarizes the fields and field numbers for *groups* and the first part of */etc/passwd*.

Field Number	File 1: */etc/passwd* Field Name	File 2: *group* Field Name
1	login	*group number*
2	*password*	group name
3	*user id*	
4	*group number*	

The next command line instructs **join** to restrict its output to three fields: *group number*, *group name*, and *login*. The length of this command forces it to the next screen line, requiring a backslash before the [Return] to instruct the shell to not interpret the newline character as having special meaning.

1. Enter

   sort +3 -4 -t*:* **/etc/passwd **
   | join -t*:* **-o 2.1 2.2 1.1 -j1 4 -** *groups*

   Exact output depends on the contents of your *groups* file and your system's **/etc/passwd** file, but resembles the following in format:

   ```
   800:Administrators:caitlin
   800:Administrators:mike
   800:Administrators:tammy
   850:Data Entry:mary
   850:Data Entry:stephanie
   900:Programmers:lela
   ```

Examining the Code

The addition of the output option (**-o 2.1 2.2 1.1**) instructs **join** to output fields in this order:

File	Field	Field Name
2	1	group number
2	2	group name
1	1	login

Entering Long Command Lines

Command lines involving **join**, as well as other powerful utilities and their options, can become quite long. Following are some hints for successfully entering long commands:

- Enter the command on two or more lines, with a backslash (\ ) before pressing each Return.

- Enter the command as one line, allowing the terminal to wrap the display.

- Place the command in a file, make the script file executable, and then run the script. The script approach can be very useful when working through chapter activities, and is recommended. When naming scripts, avoid using command names such as **join** for script names to avoid confusion with utilities.

17.8

Examining Basic Database Design

Two approaches to database application design currently exist: *single file* and multiple file, or *relational*, application. Organizing the same example database, using each approach, can illustrate their similarities and differences.

Designing a Single-File Application

If a database for company records used a single-file approach, it would have all records for each current employee in one file. Its fields would include all required information, such as

```
first name
last name
title
department
salary
date
salary
date
```

Using a Single-File Application

Administrative users of such a database would add a record to the general file for each employee hired. As salaries are changed, dates are added in the respective fields. If an employee continues to receive the same salary, only two of the fields allocated are used, and the remainder left blank. If an employee is promoted or changes departments, relevant new data is written over the old.

Adding a different type of information about employees requires the addition of new fields to all records.

Examining the Advantages and Limitations of the Single File

Data-access efficiency is probably the foremost advantage of the single-file method. When all data resides in one file, the system can quickly access it. Only one file must be opened, precluding the need to match records in several files.

But despite potential savings in CPU time, the single-file approach contains some inherent disadvantages.

Data Loss

When replacement data, such as a new address, are added, old data is probably lost or becomes very difficult to locate in backups of the general file. For example, a listing of all past positions held by an employee is not possible using the single-file approach, because every time the person changed positions, the new position would be entered, overwriting the old. There is no continuing record.

Inefficient Use of Disk Memory

A single large database will probably reserve many unused memory addresses, locking these addresses out of other uses while the database is being used. For example, a company database will necessarily contain multiple fields for salaries. However, not all employees will have the same number of salary changes. Some salary fields and their associated date fields will remain empty. Empty fields in a given employee's record necessarily become reserved, unusable memory. Addition of fields in the middle of each record can be cumbersome. If disk space is not a problem, and if employees rarely have salary changes or if the company has few employees, the single-file approach may still work adequately.

The "All Things to All People" Problem

A single database must contain all conceivable entry fields, thereby adding to its overall size and the associated memory-use inefficiencies. For example, if an employee's salary may change often, each employee record must contain fields to accommodate these multiple changes, even if some employees may never need them.

17.9

Examining a Relational Database Design

Single-file design problems can be solved using the multiple-file, relational database approach. Although relational databases may have some impact on the CPU, they seldom overtax modern processors. A relational database uses multiple files that can be linked with join fields. Each file must be joinable to at least one other file through a common field, even though records may differ from file to file. For example,

File: *title-dept*

```
1 employee identification number [join to employee, salary]
2 employee title
3 department name
```

File: *salary*

```
1 employee identification number [join to title-dept, employee]
2 new salary
3 date of salary change
```

File: *employee*

```
1 employee identification number [join to title-dept, salary]
2 first name
3 last name
```

The three files outlined above describe all needed information about the employee. The files are related through the employee information number.

17.10

Implementing a Relational Database

An example database using the relational structure can organize and track simplified employee records. The files in this example are processed by **join** and other utilities to extract appropriate data for reports. The *employee*, *salary*, and *title-dept* files you created will sufficiently serve to demonstrate a relational database. You may add additional records, following the example formats, to the files if you wish.

Examining the Relational Application

When each new employee is hired, a new entry is created in the file *employee*. New job titles and/or department changes are made by adding relevant information to the *title-dept* file. The changing of salaries is supported by the file *salary*, which includes the salary amount, date of salary change, and employee id number. No modification of preexisting records is needed.

In the relational model, management, expansion, and alteration of data becomes primarily file based, not field based as in the single-file approach. If a new data type such as "requested vacations" must be incorporated into the overall database, a new, joinable file can be added, instead of forcing one or more new fields to be wedged into an existing structure.

Creating a Simple Report with join

The files *employee* and *salary* can be joined on the employee id number, the common field in both, to produce a composite report.

1. Create a file named *salary-rpt* and add the following line:

   join -o *1.3 1.2 2.2 2.3 employee salary*

2. Make the script executable and run it by entering

chmod 755 *salary-rpt*
salary-rpt

The resulting output is

```
Place Bob 48000 96
Place Bob 36000 95
Koettel Bob 30000 95
Koettel Bob 29000 94
Place Mary 98000 96
Lloyd Mary 48000 96
Cavette Catherine 68000 96
Cavette Catherine 63000 94
```

Although **join** used its default first field (employee id) as the join reference, that field was not written to output. Output, as specified by the **-o** option and its arguments, displayed only employee names, salaries, and the dates of the salary changes.

The **join** utility took input from the two files, recognized the tab as the field delimiter, created a join field based on the value in the *employee identification number* field, then output four fields: *1.3*, *1.2*, *2.2*, and *2.3* using the standard numbering scheme. The results are depicted in Figure 17-3.

Modifying Data

The report script you just created can remain constant even though the data it reads changes.

1. Modify the *salary* file to include a new salary entry:

102 [Tab] 34000 [Tab] 96

2. Make sure the input file *salary* is sorted and run the script again.

sort -o *salary salary*
salary-rpt

Without modifying the report script, the output reflects the change made in the data file.

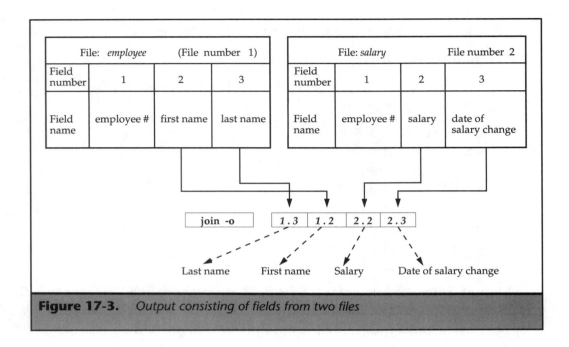

Figure 17-3. *Output consisting of fields from two files*

17.11

Creating Complex Reports from Relational Data

A database application consists of files that store data and programs that retrieve the data for use. The **join** utility is used to formulate a view or report of data that is stored in multiple files. The files used in this chapter to maintain information concerning salaries, employees, departments, etc., can be used to create a variety of reports such as the previous example.

A report that lists all employees by department and includes the most recent salary for each is an essential report. To accomplish such a report requires several steps.

Sorting the salary File

The data in the *salary* file is listed in sorted order by the first field. The last field, the year the salary was established, can be in any order.

1. Create a new file named *dept-sal-rpt* and include the following line:

   sort +0 -1 +2 -3 -r *salary*

2. Make the file executable and run the script.

   chmod **755** *dept-sal-rpt*
   dept-sal-rpt

   The output is a sorted version of the file *salary* using the first field as the primary sort field and the third field as secondary sort.

   ```
   107   68000     96
   107   63000     94
   106   48000     96
   102   34000     96
   102   30000     95
   102   29000     94
   101   48000     96
   101   36000     95
   ```

Examining the Code

The command line consists of the following:

Argument	Description
sort	Instruction to the shell to run the **sort** utility.
+0 -1	Instruction to **sort** to perform a normal sort using field 1 (employee number) as the sort field. (Skip 0, stop after the first field.)
+2 -3 -r	The secondary sort field is the third field. (Skip 2, stop after 3.) When multiple records share the same employee number, those records are sorted on the basis of the value in the third field, date of salary change, in reverse order (latest year first).

The data flow is depicted in Figure 17-4.

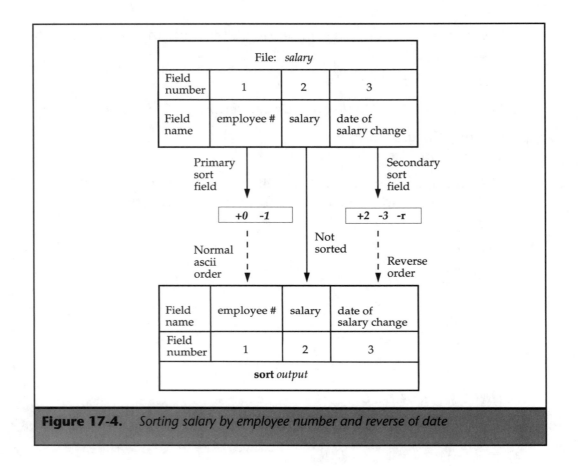

Figure 17-4. *Sorting salary by employee number and reverse of date*

Retaining Only Most Recent Salary

The output from the previous exercise includes every historical instance of the salary for each employee. To provide a report of current salaries, only the most recent should be retained.

1. Modify the script *dept-sal-rpt* to include a \ at the end of the first line and add a second **sort** line.

   sort *+0* **-1** *+2* **-3** **-r** *salary* \
   | sort *+0* **-1** **-um**

2. Run the script *dept-sal-rpt* with its modifications. The output is

```
107   68000      96
106   48000      96
102   34000      96
101   48000      96
```

Only the most recent salary for each employee is output. This second **sort** command line has **sort** read its input from the previous **sort** line, and because of the options **-um** selects only the first record among a group of records containing identical values in the first field (employee number). The **-u** option is **sort**'s unique option and results in discarding records that have multiple values in the specified field. (See Figure 17-5.) Because

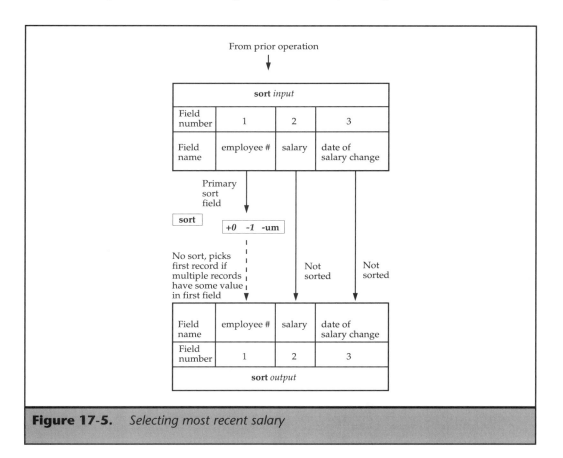

Figure 17-5.   *Selecting most recent salary*

the file is already sorted according to the first field, the **-m** option is included, which **sort** interprets to mean "Accept the present order; don't do another sorting."

Including Employee Names in Report

The output of the script now includes the most recent salaries attached to the employee number. To make the report useful, names should be added.

1. Modify the script *dept-sal-rpt* to be as follows:

   sort +0 -1 +2 -3 -r *salary* ****
   **| sort +0 -1 -um **
   | sort | join -o *1.1 1.2 2.2 2.3* **-** *employee*

2. Run the script, which produces the following:

```
101  48000  Bob Place
102  34000  Bob Koettel
106  48000  Mary Lloyd
107  68000  Catherine Cavette
```

The additional line in the script is instruction to pass the output from the second **sort** to the **join** utility. Figure 17-6 describes the data flow. The instructions to **join** are to read from standard input and the file *employee*, creating a composite join, then to output only the first and second fields from the first file, and the second and third fields from the second file.

Organizing Output by Department

A salary report is produced, but it lacks information concerning departments.

1. Modify *dept-sal-rpt* to be as follows:

   sort +0 -1 +2 -3 -r *salary* ****
   **| sort +0 -1 -um **
   | join -o *1.1 1.2 2.2 2.3* **-** *employee* ****
   | join -o *2.3 1.2 1.3 1.4* **-** *title-dept* **| sort**

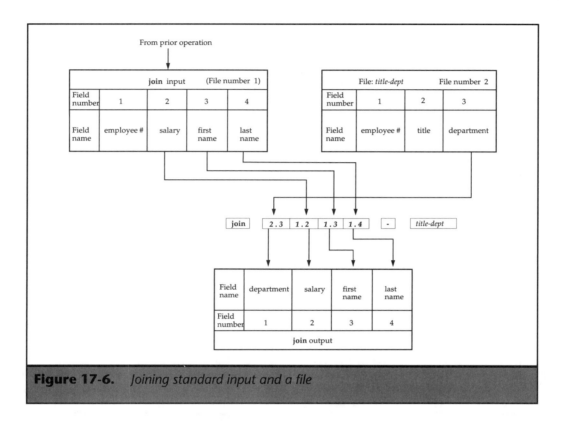

Figure 17-6. *Joining standard input and a file*

2. Run the script. The output is

```
20  48000  Mary Lloyd
20  68000  Catherine Cavette
30  34000  Bob Koettel
30  48000  Bob Place
```

Department number, most recent salary, and employee name are displayed.

In the last line of the script, the output from **join** is passed to another process running **join** with instruction to form a composite join with the data in the file *title-dept*, output the department number followed by the other fields, and then to sort on the department number.

The data can change; this script will produce the report using the most recent data. If you want employee number or any other field in

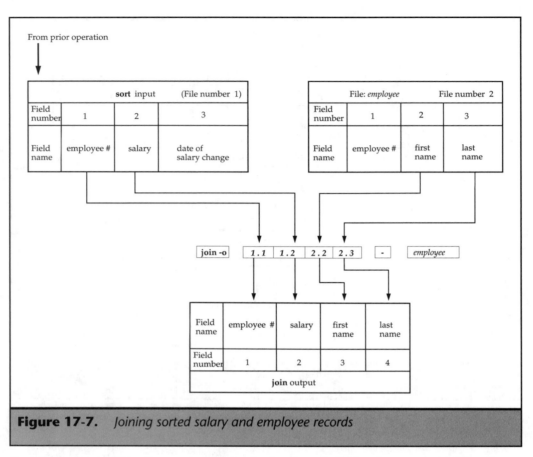

Figure 17-7. *Joining sorted salary and employee records*

the report, modify the script to include that field in the output. The data flow is described in Figure 17-7.

■ Review 2

1. What is the minus (-) between **4** and *file2* in the following command line for?

   sort +3 */tmp/file1* | **join** -j1 **4** - *file2*

2. Explain what each option of **join** in the following command line does:

   join -t: -j1 **2** -o **2.3** **2.1** **.1.1** **1.4** **2.6** *fileA* *fileB*

■ Conclusion

Material in this chapter demonstrated the use of **join** to locate records in files that have a common value in a specified field. The ability to join files in this manner permits the development and manipulation of relational database applications. An example relational database was incrementally built, and operated on by **join** and other utilities commonly used with **join**.

■ Answers to Review 1

1. **-a**

2. It allows the output order of **join**ed files to be modified.

3. **-t***:*

■ Answers to Review 2

1. The minus (**-**) is a placeholder for standard input from the **sort** utility.

2. **t***:*   Tells **join** that the delimiters are colons (*:*).
   -j1 2   Instructs **join** to join lines from *fileA* (listed as first file on command line) using the second field as the join field.
   -o 2.3 2.1 1.1 1.4 2.6   Outputs all joined fields in the following filename and field order: field 3 of *fileB*, field 1 of *fileB*, field 1 of *fileA*, field 4 of *fileA*, and field 6 of *fileB*.

COMMAND SUMMARY

-a1 *filename1 filename2*	Outputs *all* records in *filename1* and only those that are matchable from *filename2*.
-a1 -a2	Outputs all records of each corresponding file, joining the matchable files.
-o *1.2 2.3 1.1*	Outputs all joined records in the following filename and field order: field 2 of *filename1*, field 3 of *filename2*, and field 1 of *filename1*.
-t:	Use the colon instead of the [Tab] for the field separator.
-	Instructs **join** to read from standard input.
-j1 4	Instructs **join** to join lines from the first file using its fourth field as the join field. The *1* indicates the first file. The *4* specifies the fourth field of the first file as the join field.

Chapter Eighteen

Using
Advanced
Visual Editor
Features

The visual editor is used to create and edit files. In the previous **vi** chapter, you entered many of the editor's basic commands for operations such as adding and deleting text, manipulating blocks of text, and moving to specific locations in the file.

In this chapter you will explore other available **vi** features. You'll use commands that invoke **vi** from the shell and pre-position the cursor in the file you are going to edit. You'll examine how to make text changes globally predicated upon finding specific target strings, and how to use marked lines for editing. You'll also customize your editing environment with specific editing features, such as keystroke "aliases," word wrapping, and auto-indenting.

SKILLS CHECK: Before beginning this chapter, you should be able to

- *Access and leave the system*
- *Execute basic shell commands*
- *Create, display, and print files*
- *Access and modify files using the **vi** editor*

OBJECTIVES: After completing this chapter, you will be able to

- *Use the command-line features of **vi** to set the editing environment*
- *Use buffers for cutting and pasting lines*
- *Create maps and aliases*
- *Run shell utilities without exiting **vi***
- *Make global search and replace changes*
- *Edit multiple files in succession*
- *Mark text for editing*

18.1

Accessing Specific Locations in a File

There are several ways to use **vi** to access a file. Thus far in this book you have been instructed to enter **vi** with a *filename* argument, and your editing began with the cursor at the first line of the file. You can also instruct the editor to begin editing at other locations in the file or to open the file for examination but prohibit writing of changes.

Starting at a Specific Line

The editor facilitates beginning at a specified line in the file.

1. To place the cursor on the eighth line of the *practice* file, enter this command line:

   vi +8 *practice*

   Notice that a single space separates the **vi** command and the *+8*, and another space separates the *+8* from the filename, *practice*. The shell sends two arguments to **vi**: *+8* and *practice*. The editor interprets these arguments to mean open the file *practice* and place the cursor at the beginning of the eighth line.

2. Make some changes in the file, such as adding a new line of text.

3. Return to the shell by pressing Esc and entering **:wq**.

The general format of the **vi** command to access a file at a specific line is

   vi +*n filename*

where *n* is a line number in *filename*.

Starting at a Specific Word

You can also instruct the editor to begin editing a file on the first line that includes a specific word or string of characters.

1. Enter the following command:

   vi +/*the practice*

   If the file *practice* contains the string *the* as a word or within some other word, the file is displayed with the cursor positioned on the first line containing that pattern.

The general format of the **vi** command to access a file at a specific word is

vi +/*string filename*

where *string* is any set of contiguous characters in the file.

Accessing a File for Reading Only

On some occasions, you will want to examine a file using the power of **vi** search commands, yet protect the file from being modified. To prevent accidental changes while examining the file, you can use the **visual** editor to only **view** the file.

1. Examine the file *practice*, by entering

   view *practice*

2. Move through the file, using this series of commands:

   /*word*
   Ctrl-d
   ?*word*

   where *word* is any string in your file.

3. Even though you intended to just read the file, make a change or two to the text.

4. Attempt to save and exit the file. Enter

   :wq

   You are informed with an error message that the file is read only.

5. Exit **view** by quitting the editor without writing. Enter

   :q!

   With **view**, you can also insist that you really do want to make changes, and write the file.

6. Call up the *practice* file again with **view**, and make some changes to the text of the file.

7. Write the changes to the file by entering

   :w!

The **view** command functions like **vi**, except that changes cannot be written to disk unless you force a write with the **!** character. The **view** command is very useful for preventing accidental changes to important files that you want to examine.

18.2

Modifying the Editing Environment

You can tailor how the editor works for you, using a series of commands that customize the visual editor environment. In this section, you see how to use line numbers, automatic line indenting, special character listings, margin wrap, and other **vi** features.

1. First, bring up the file *practice* by entering

   vi *practice*

   and make certain you are in **vi** command mode.

Employing Line Numbers

Editing blocks of text, moving to a specific line, and identifying your location in a file are all easier tasks if lines in the display are numbered.

1. If you do not have line numbers displayed next to the lines of your *practice* file, request them by entering

   :set *number*

2. To remove the numbers, enter

   :set *nonumber*

   NOTE: *In* **vi**, *you may abbreviate the* **number** *command as* **nu** *and the* **nonumber** *command as* **nonu**.

3. Instruct the editor to include the line numbers again using the abbreviations.

4. To determine which editor options are currently in, enter

:set

The display is a list of the options, which at this moment are set in the editor.

SUMMARY: *The **number** command option is a typical **set** option in the **vi**sual editor. To make a **set** option take effect, you enter*

:set *option*

and press (Return). *To turn off the feature (that is, to return to the state before the option was set), you enter*

:set *nooption*

and press (Return). *To determine what options are currently on, enter*

:set

and press (Return).

Setting Automatic Indenting

There are times when you'll want every line you type to be indented one or several tabs. When you don't want to have to remember to press (Tab) every time you start a new line, you can set the editor to automatically indent.

1. Open a new line in your file, and at the left margin insert one or more tab characters (press (Tab) or insert several blank spaces by pressing (Spacebar)).
2. Add a word of text.
3. Press (Return), and add another line. The new line is at the left margin. No automatic indenting takes place.
4. Leave append mode by pressing (Esc).
5. From command mode, enter

:set *autoindent*

*NOTE: The abbreviation for **autoindent** is **ai**, which can be used as well.*

6. After you have set automatic indent, open up a new line, indent spaces with tabs, and enter a few characters of text.

7. Press Return and add more text. The added line is indented to match the previous one.

Escaping autoindent
Occasionally, automatic indenting becomes a nuisance.

1. Add another line of text that is auto-indented, and press Return.

2. To cancel **autoindent** for one line, you can move the cursor back to the left. While still in append mode, press

Ctrl-d

This moves the cursor one shift-indent to the left. If this doesn't move you back far enough, press Ctrl-d again.

3. To shut off **autoindent** altogether, enter command mode by pressing Esc, and then enter

:set *noai*

which sets *no autoindent*.

Ignoring Upper- and Lowercase in Searches
To the editor, *Father* and *father* are different strings of letters, because the uppercase *F* is not the same as lowercase *f*. When you need to, you can instruct the editor to ignore case during searches. As you did to turn auto-indent on and off, you use a **:set** command option to turn case consideration on and off.

1. From the command mode, enter

:set *ignorecase*

With *ignorecase* in effect, the editor will find words whether they are capitalized or lowercase, even when you have specified a search for lowercase.

NOTE: *You can abbreviate **ignorecase** as **ic**.*

2. Search for all instances of the word *the* by entering

/tHe

Even though the letter *H* is capitalized in the search command, all instances of the word *the* are found when you move through the matches by pressing ⓝ.

Listing Special Characters

The editor can be instructed to display special characters, such as tabs, in a readable format.

1. From the command mode, enter

:set *list*

In your display, a **$** appears at the end of each line in the text and tabs are displayed as **^I** throughout the text.

2. Turn listing off by entering

:set *nolist*

Matching Programming Language Special Characters

A common programming error involves improper matching of parenthesis and braces. The editor can help.

1. From command mode, enter

:set *showmatch*

2. Enter the following text. The first line has four open or left characters. As you *close off* each pair of parentheses and curly brackets in the last three lines, the cursor flashes on the matching open left parenthesis or curly bracket that is being closed.

(xx(xx[xx{yy zz
end
}}
]]
))

The editor shows you which opening parenthesis or brace is matched when you enter the closing character.

3. Add additional right parenthesis. The workstation beeps, flashes, or in some way notifies you that there isn't a matching open left parenthesis.

4. The square bracket [is not matched.

Being able to match programming characters is useful when you are writing in a variety of programming languages.

Setting the Size of a Window

Thus far you have used the basic toggle mechanism for on/off **set** options in the **vi**sual editor. Some types of features require that you set a value rather than a toggle.

1. Determine the current value for the editor variable *window* by entering

   :set *window*

2. To change the workstation window size variable, enter this command:

   :set *window=12*

   Make sure there are no spaces around the equal sign.

3. Now enter

z.

Be sure to enter the dot; it's essential to redraw your screen.

Because the *window* option is now *12* instead of the usual value, there are only 12 lines displayed on the screen. As your screen scrolls, the upper portion will fill, but every time you invoke a command that causes the screen to be redrawn, only 12 lines will be used.

The following commands change the display on your screen and are affected by the *window* value: **z.** for redraw; Ctrl - f to move forward a screen; and Ctrl - b to move backward a screen.

4. Before continuing, reset your window to the original number of lines by entering

:set *window=original-num*

Setting the Number of Spaces for Tabs

The *tabstop* option allows you to set the number of spaces used when **vi** displays the tab character.

1. In command mode, enter

:set *tabstop=4*

2. Open a new line and press the Tab key. Notice that the editor now puts a tab stop at every four spaces, all the way to the right margin, whenever you press the Tab key.

*NOTE: The **tabstop** abbreviation is **ts**.*

3. From the command mode, change the *tabstop* setting to *10* and try pressing Tab again.

Setting the *tabstop* option only affects the visual display of the text while you're in **vi**. When the file is printed, the printer will use its own settings for tabs, and the file output may be spaced differently from the display you see in **vi**.

Using shiftwidth

The *shiftwidth* value determines the number of spaces you can shift the cursor line and the line immediately below it. This is how it works.

1. First enter

   :set *shiftwidth=4*

   and press [Return].

NOTE: *The* **shiftwidth** *option may be abbreviated as* **sw**.

   Now, while still in **vi** command mode, simultaneously press [Shift] and the [>] key, followed by [Return]. Two lines of text are shifted to the right four spaces.

2. Move the two lines back flush with the left margin, by simultaneously pressing [Shift] and the [<] key, followed by [Return].

3. Try shifting only one line. Place the cursor on the line you want to shift and press the [>] key twice. (Do not press the [Return] key in this case.) The moment you press the [>] the second time, the line shifts to the right.

4. If you have not done some other text changing commands in the meantime, you can shift the same line to the left by simply typing **u** to undo your last command.
   Notice that the cursor doesn't have to be on the line to accomplish the reversal. If you cannot undo the command because you have entered some other text-changing command in the meantime, and you want to shift the line to the left, position the cursor on the line and press [<] twice.

5. You can also augment the effect of the shiftwidth command. For instance, to shift lines 11 through 15 (that's five lines: 11, 12, 13,

14, and 15) to the right, position the cursor at line 11 and enter this command:

5 > >

6. You can also shift lines without the cursor being positioned at the first line to be shifted. For instance, if you want to shift lines 16 through 21 to the right, and you are elsewhere, such as at line 5, you can simply enter this command from the command mode:

:16,21 >

and press (Return).

The advantage of the method demonstrated in step 6 is that it also permits you to shift a line or a range of lines more than a single shiftwidth.

7. For instance, to shift lines 3 through 8 *three* shiftwidths to the right, enter

:3,8 >>>

and press (Return).

8. Experiment with various *shiftwidth* values until you can shift lines easily using any of the methods described in this section.

SUMMARY: The three **set** *commands examined just above—for setting shiftwidth, tabstop, and window—all follow the same formula:*

:set *option=value*

In all of these commands, value is the number that is given to the option by the **set** *command.*

Automatically Returning to a New Line

The visual editor processes very long lines, usually 512 characters. The workstation display is only 80 characters wide.

1. To demonstrate how **vi** handles display of long lines, enter the following:

:set *wrapmargin=0*
:set *number*

2. Now open a new line and start typing real words separated by spaces. Type past the screen's right margin.

   The editor continues displaying the long line on the screen. The remainder of the line does not get a new line number because it is not a new line, just a continuation.

3. Press (Return) and add another short line.

4. Press (Esc) and move the cursor up one line. The cursor "skips" the extended portion of the long line. The editor forces new lines when a line gets long, if you wish.

5. In command mode of the **vis**ual editor, enter

   :set *wrapmargin=50*

NOTE: *You can abbreviate **wrapmargin** as **wm**.*

Open a new line and start typing another long line of text. You cannot type lines longer than about 30 characters, at which point the editor automatically returns the cursor to the beginning of a new line, and a new line number is added.

The *wrapmargin* option allows you to set the position of the screen's right margin, which determines the maximum number of characters the editor can display on a line. Once that limit is reached, each line automatically continues on, or *wraps,* to a new line. The smaller the *wrapmargin* value, the closer to the right side of the screen you can type.

6. A more reasonable *wrapmargin* value uses more of the screen. Enter

   :set *wrapmargin=10*

When you use the *wrapmargin* option, the editor determines the line length by subtracting the value of *wrapmargin* from the standard line length of 80 characters.

To shut off *wrapmargin*, give it a value of *0*.

Determining the Current Value of an Option

1. From the command mode, enter

   :set *window*

   At the bottom of your screen, the editor displays

   ```
   window=23
   ```

   Note that the window size may vary depending on your display.

When you want to see the current value for an option that has been set, you can enter

:set *option*

where *option* is the name of the option whose value you are interested in. The option name and its value are displayed.

Determining the Current Value of All Options

1. To find out the value or state of all options, enter

   :set *all*

   The report indicates what options are on or off, and the current values for options that accept values.

If you forget the name of one of the **set** options, you can use the **:set** *all* command to obtain a listing.

■ Review 1

1. How can you call up the file *practice*, with the cursor placed at line 50 when the file is opened?

2. What command line would you use to begin editing the file *practice* at the first occurrence of the string *help*?

3. What command calls up the full screen editor in read-only mode?

4. What command do you enter to instruct **vi** to add a (Return) creating a new line whenever your current line comes within 15 characters of the right margin?

5. What command instructs the editor to list the current values for all editor options?

18.3

■ Using Numbered Buffers for Manipulating Text

Whenever you delete one or more whole lines of text, the editor automatically saves the lines in a *buffer*—a temporary holding area for your text. These buffers are numbered from 1 through 9. Individual words and characters that are deleted are not saved in a buffer. Numbered buffers are essential for retrieving deleted lines if you have made editing changes since you made the deletions.

Placing Text in a Buffer

1. From the command mode of the **vi**sual editor, delete one line of text, using this command:

   dd

2. Reposition the cursor on a new line, and delete two lines of text, with

   2dd

3. Reposition the cursor on a new line, and delete three lines of text, using

   3dd

   You have now deleted three text blocks that are one, two, and three lines long, respectively. When a text block is deleted, the deleted block is placed in buffer 1. Any old, deleted text that was in buffer 1 is shifted into buffer 2; old, deleted text in buffer 2 is shifted to buffer 3; and so forth. This process of shifting deleted blocks of text from buffer to buffer continues up to buffer 9, thus saving your last nine text blocks. The most recent text block deletion always resides in buffer 1. Figure 18-1 illustrates how the buffers are utilized for holding the text.

Retrieving Text from Buffers

Retrieve the block of text residing in buffer 2 consisting of 2 lines of text, which you deleted in the previous procedure.

1. Position the cursor on the line above where you want the lines from buffer 2 to appear, and enter the following command. The first character in the command is a quotation mark, or double quote:

   "2p

In this command, the **"** instructs the editor to access a buffer; the **2** indicates which buffer; and the **p** says to put the text in a line *below* the cursor. If no text existed in buffer 2, you would receive a message saying

```
Nothing in register 2
```

You may use either the lowercase **p** or uppercase **P** command, depending upon your needs. **P** places a copy of the buffer text *above* the current line, and **p** places a copy of the buffer *below* the current line. For

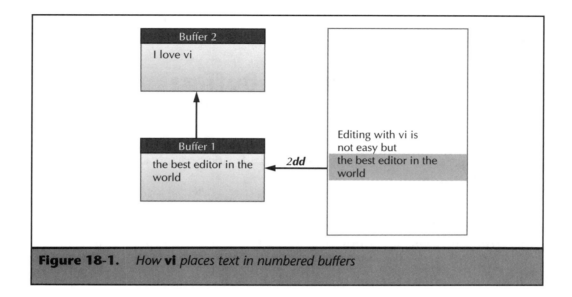

Figure 18-1. *How **vi** places text in numbered buffers*

example, the command **"2P** would copy the deleted text in buffer 2 to the line above the current cursor position.

Figure 18-2 illustrates how text is retrieved from the numbered buffers.

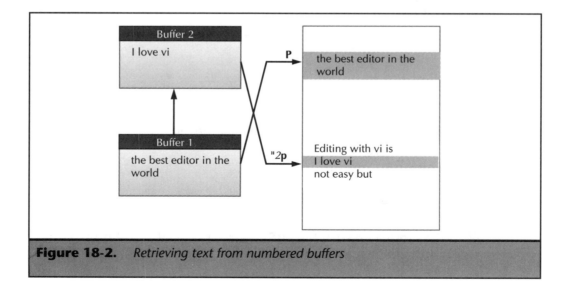

Figure 18-2. *Retrieving text from numbered buffers*

18.4

Working with Lettered Buffers

In addition to the numbered buffers, the **vi** editor maintains a set of lettered (*a* to *z*) buffers where you can store yanked or deleted blocks of text. Text blocks placed in these buffers remain there during the entire editing session and can be accessed at any time through the use of the appropriate command.

Placing Lines in Lettered Buffers

Unlike the numbered buffers just described—in which deleted text is automatically deposited for *safekeeping*—you must direct the editor to save text in a lettered buffer.

1. Move the cursor to a line of text. Use the **yank** command to copy this line into the lettered buffer a:

   "ayy

   In this command, **"** is the quotation mark, or double-quotes (*not* two single quotes); the *a* is the lettered buffer a; and **yy** is the yank command, which copies a line of text into the lettered buffer.

2. In the following command, five lines of text are yanked and saved in lettered buffer q. Try it:

   "q5yy

 CAUTION: *If you yank lines to a buffer that already contains text, you overwrite the old entry.*

Accessing a Lettered Buffer

1. Move the cursor to a different line in the file. Enter the following to access the text stored in buffer a:

   "ap

In this command, the **"** is the quotation mark to signal using a buffer; *a* is the lettered buffer *a; and* **p** is the put command. Text in the lettered buffer *a* is thus copied to the line just *below* the current cursor location.

Saving Deleted Text in a Lettered Buffer

You can also use lettered buffers to save text blocks that you have deleted.

1. To delete a line of text and place it in lettered buffer b, enter

   "*b*dd

2. To delete five lines of text and place them in the lettered buffer m, enter

   "*m*5dd

3. Move your cursor to the end of the file, using the **G** command.

4. Recover the text you stored in lettered buffer m, by entering

   "*m*p

Deleting and Putting Words or Characters

The **P** and **p** commands can also be used to put deleted characters or words in a different location in your file, even though single characters and words are not saved in a buffer.

1. Move the cursor to the beginning of a word, and delete the word:

   dw

2. Now move the cursor to the space between two other words, and enter the lowercase **p** command:

   p

   The lowercase **p**ut command combined with the **x** command can be used to quickly transpose characters in your text.

3. Move the cursor to the first letter of any word in your text and type

x

4. Now type

p

and notice that the two characters are transposed.

Table 18-1 describes text-changing commands. Read the table and try all the commands several times. The table summarizes commands introduced in this and earlier chapters.

18.5

Searching and Substituting for a Word

So far you have used the colon commands to copy, move, and remove blocks of text. You can also use the colon commands to search for a word and substitute a different word.

Substituting for the First Occurrence of a Word

The substitute, a colon command, is used to substitute one regular expression for another in a file.

1. Move the cursor to a line containing the word *creating*. (If the word *creating* does not appear in the file, add it to the end of a line and keep the cursor on that line.)

2. Change the word *creating* to *producing*, by entering

   :s/*creating*/*producing*/

   The first instance of the word, *creating* is changed to *producing*.

The substitute command requires two words separated by slashes. The action performed by the **s** command is to check the addressed line(s) for the pattern on the left (the *target* pattern) and, if it is found, substitute the expression on the right (the *replacement* pattern) for the target pattern. Thus, this command told **vi** to find the word *creating* on the current line and substitute the word *producing*.

If **vi** cannot find the target pattern you specify, the following error message appears:

```
Substitute pattern match failed
```

Command	Function
x	Erases (x's out) only the letter under the cursor.
dw	Deletes only the word under the cursor.
dd	Deletes the entire line.
D	Deletes the rest of the line (from the cursor position on).
r*x*	Replaces the letter under the cursor with *x*, where *x* is the letter to be substituted. For instance, **rb** replaces the character under the cursor with the letter *b*.
J	Joins cursor line with the next line in your text by appending the next line onto the end of the cursor line.
yy	Yanks the cursor line.
*n*yy	Yanks the specified number (*n*) of lines. For instance, **6yy** tells **vi** to "make a copy of 6 lines (starting with the current line), remember them, and put them where I tell you to." (See **put** commands, just below.)
P	(uppercase P) Puts the **y**anked or **d**eleted line(s) just above the cursor line.
p	(lowercase p) Puts the **y**anked or **d**eleted text just below the cursor line.

Table 18-1. *Text-Changing Commands*

Substituting for the First Occurrence of a Word on All Lines

An extension of the **s** colon command instructs the editor to act on *all* lines in the file.

1. Add the following lines to your file:

betty	*1994*	*1995*	*1996*
alan	*1995*	*1996*	
betty	*1995*	*1995*	*1995*
bob	*1995*	*1996*	
margot	*1995*	*1995*	*1995*

2. To implement a change, enter the command

   :1,$ s/*1995/1996Y/*

   This command instructs the editor to check all of the addressed lines through the last, looking for the pattern *1995* and, on lines where this pattern is found, substitute the pattern *1996Y*.

3. Undo the changes by entering the **U** command.

Selecting All Lines Containing a Particular Word and Changing a Different Word

It is possible to select lines containing a specified word or string of characters and replace the occurrence of some other pattern on the line.

Substituting on All Selected Lines

Previously, you substituted a new pattern for an old one on all lines using this command:

:1,$ s/*pattern1/pattern2/*

1. To select lines based on the presence of a target, and make a substitution using another target, enter

   :g */betty/***s***/1995/1996Z/*

   This instruction asks **vi** to select all lines containing the word *betty*, then locate instances of the string *1995*, and then substitute *1996Z* for all occurrences of that pattern, as outlined in the following table:

Command	Interpretation
:	Use line command mode.
g	Search on all lines (globally).
betty	Identify the line containing the word *betty*.
s	Make the following **substitution**.
1995	Target string to be substituted for.
1996Z	Substituted string.

2. Undo the changes by entering the **U** command.

18.6

Substituting for the Line Target

In the previous exercises you provided a line target, then for selected lines, a search target was specified.

1. You can also make changes to the target you specify for selecting lines.

   :g */1995/***s***//1776/*

The target *1995* is used to select lines and then is used as the target for substitution because no substitution target is specified between the first two slashes after the **s**.

Here the **//** in the substitute command receives the last word matched—in this case, *friend*. This instruction has the same result as the following:

:1,$ s/*1995/1776/*

If no substitution target is specified, the *line* target is assumed.

The main difference between the two commands is execution time. The command using a **g** and default target takes longer to execute on larger files than the shortcut and is only presented here because it is often used.

2. Undo the changes.

Substituting for Multiple Occurrences on All Lines

You may have noticed that the substitute command only works on the first occurrence of a pattern on an addressed line. If a line has more than one instance of the target pattern, only the first is affected. You can also have this command work on all occurrences of a pattern within a line.

1. Enter the command

:1,$ s/*1995/2000/***g**

This command instructs the editor as shown in the following table:

Command	Interpretation
1,$	Go from line 1 to the last line in the file…
s	and make substitutions…
1995	replacing the string *1995*…
2000	with the string *2000*…
/g	globally in the file.

The **g** at the end of the **s**ubstitute command is called a *flag*. It works differently from the **g** at the beginning of the command line, which is the default address for all lines in the file (*1,$*). The **g** flag, **g**lobal, instructs the substitute command to perform the replacement on *all* occurrences of the target pattern within the addressed line(s).

18.7

Using Text Marking in a File

It is possible with the **vi**sual editor to mark a place in a file and then later return to it or act on it. You can use marks to specify text to be deleted, moved, written, or copied.

Marking Your Place in a File

In a file, the line number assigned to a particular line of code or text will change if lines are added or removed between that line and the beginning of the file. During editing, you often need to return to a particular line of text; but if the number has been changed, it can be difficult to find the line you want.

With the visual editor's **m**ark command, several positions in a file may be marked. Once a line of text is marked, you can return to that line, even if its line number has changed during the editing session. Your markings last only for the current editing session.

1. Make certain line numbers are displayed for the *practice* file. (If they are not, enter **:set** *nu* and press ⎡Return⎦.)

2. Go to a line in the middle of your file, and note its line number. With the cursor on that line, enter the following command:

   m*b*

   This command **m**arks the line and assigns it the label *b*. You can replace the *b* with any letter from a through z.

3. Move the cursor to another location near the beginning of the file. Remove or add a few lines of text at this new location.

4. Return to command mode.

4. To return to the line of text that you marked in step 2, type a single quote mark, followed by the letter you used in the **m**ark command. In this case, enter

'b

The cursor moves to your original marked location, even though its line number is clearly different.

Deleting Lines from the Current Position to a Marked Spot

Sometimes you need to delete all text from the current line to a marked line.

1. Place the cursor on any line of text, and mark the line:

m*a*

where *a* is any letter from a through z.

2. Now move the cursor a few lines above or below the line just marked, and enter the following:

d'*a*

All the text between your present location to and including the marked line is deleted.

3. To replace the text, enter

u

Deleting, Moving, or Copying Marked Blocks

You can use the **m**ark command to simplify the tasks of deleting, moving, and copying large blocks of text.

1. Move the cursor to the first line of some text you want deleted. Mark that line by entering

m*a*

2. Next, move the cursor to the last line of text to be deleted. Mark that line by entering

   m*b*

3. Now delete the marked text from *a* to *b*, with this command:

   :'*a*,'*b* d

   All text between and including lines marked *a* and *b* is deleted. The command you just entered did the same thing as a delete line number command such as **:16,32 d**. Both commands identify lines and call for action.

4. Undo the previous command, so that the deleted text reappears.
   Marked lines can be used to specify lines for all colon commands: **c**opy, **m**ove, **d**elete, and **w**rite. Lines in a file can be identified by either line numbers or by marks, and all colon or line commands can be used with lines identified by either element.

5. Before continuing to the next section, practice using marks to move, delete, and write blocks of text.

18.8

Having a Single Key Accomplish a Complex Task

Like many editors, the UNIX visual editor allows you to connect one or more commands to a single key. This lets you perform a complex editing task with a single keystroke. In the command mode of **vi**, this is called *mapping*.

1. A *map* is a set of keystrokes called by a single key. For instance, enter

   :map # Go*This is new text*

   and press ⟨Return⟩.

2. Nothing appears to happen. Press

   ⟨#⟩

The editor follows the instruction as mapped:

Command	Interpretation
G	Go to last line in file.
o	Open a line below cursor and enter append mode.
This . . .	Text that is added.

3. To get out of append mode, press

   Esc

Entering Control Characters in Text

In this section you will be using commands that include *control characters*, such as **^M** for Return or **^[** for Esc. It is possible to include them in text files. Here's how to enter them:

1. In **vi** append mode, press

   Ctrl-v

   On the screen, you see only the **^** symbol displayed.

2. Next, press

   Return

   Displayed now on the screen is the control character for the Return key:

   ^M

3. Add more text, and while still in append mode, press

   Ctrl-h

4. As expected, the cursor moves back one space. You can also insert the control character for Ctrl-h in your text. Try the following sequence:

   Ctrl-v
   Ctrl-h

A **^H** has been added to your screen.

Whenever you wish to insert special characters in your text, precede that character with a `Ctrl`-`v`.

Mapping Keys in the Command Mode

There are many different uses for mapping in **vi**. Many programming languages include a basic *if-then-else* statement, similar to the following:

```
if X
  then a
  else b
```

When you are writing a program, instead of typing these lines again and again, you can simply map them to a keystroke.

For this example we will use the @ key as the key to be mapped.

1. From the command mode of **vi**, enter the following **map** command, all on one line. (Recall that in the previous section you learned how to enter control characters by using `Ctrl`-`v`.)

   :map @ o*if X* `Ctrl`-`v` `Return` `Tab` *then a* `Ctrl`-`v` `Return` `Tab` *else b* `Ctrl`-`v` `Esc`

   and then press `Return`.

2. Move the cursor to a line where you would like to add an *if-then-else* statement, and press @.

The map Command Syntax

The **map** command takes two arguments: the first argument is the key you would like to map, and the second argument is what you want the mapped key to symbolize.

We started the previous map with an **o**, which is the **vi**sual editor command to **o**pen a new line below and move into the append mode. Everything from **o** until the `Esc` character (^[) is entered in the append mode.

The text that is appended is interpreted by the append mode. The words *if X*, *then a*, and *else b* are interpreted as text. The `Ctrl`-`v` allows you to enter the (Return) and (Esc) keys into the command sequence. The resulting ^M and ^[produce a carriage return and escape command, respectively.

The key mapping is illustrated in Figure 18-3.

Using Abbreviations in the Append Mode

In the command mode, you can use mapping to cut down on the amount of time spent on repetitive editing. In the append mode, you can use **ab**breviations to accomplish the same goal.

1. From the command mode of **vi**, enter the following all on one line, using (Ctrl)-(v) to request special characters.

   :ab ift *if* X (Ctrl)-(v) (Return) (Tab) *then a* (Ctrl)-(v) (Return) (Tab) *else b*

   and then press (Return).

2. Move into the append mode with the **o** command.

3. Type a few words, including the abbreviation **ift**. As soon as you type the abbreviation **ift**, it is expanded to

   ```
   if X
      then a
      else b
   ```

   Figure 18-4 illustrates the use of **ab**breviation.

18.9

Editing Multiple Files

There are times when you need to edit two or more files at once. But every time you enter **vi** and a filename, you start a new process running the **vi** program. You can avoid this by instructing the editor that you want to edit several files; hence, the **vi** program is started only once.

1. Enter the following shell command line, substituting *file1*, *file2*, and so forth, with names of files from your directory:

   vi *file1 file2 file3*

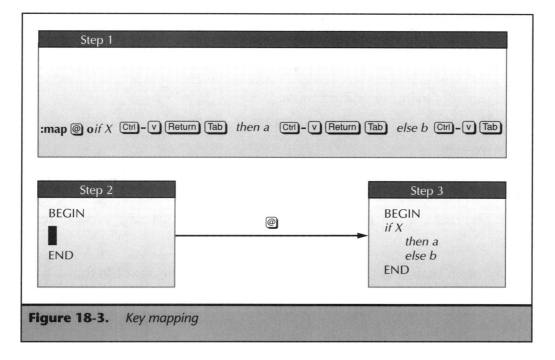

Figure 18-3. *Key mapping*

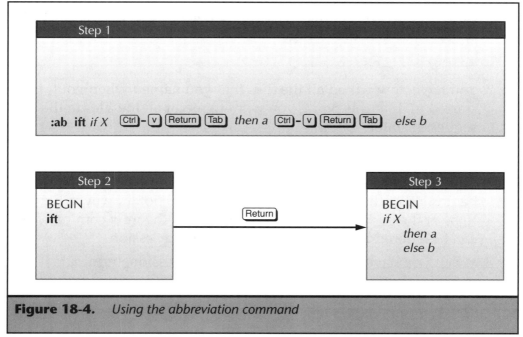

Figure 18-4. *Using the abbreviation command*

You will see this message:

```
3 files to edit
```

2. The first file accessed is *file1*. Make some changes and add text to this file, using **vi** editing tools.

3. When you have finished editing *file1*, enter

   :w

   which writes all your changes that you made in the buffer copy of *file1*. Notice that this command does *not* include the **q** for **q**uit.

4. The first file has been written; the editor is still active. Now enter

   :n

   The **:n** instructs the editor to open or access the next file for editing. It follows the series of filenames that you listed when you entered the initial **vi** command.

5. Make changes and write this second file.

6. Continue using the **:w** and **:n** commands as you edit your way through the series of files. When you reach the last file and enter **:n**, you will see the message

```
No more files to edit
```

7. You have now edited all the files that you named when you started **vi**. If at this point, you want to reedit all the files in the sequence, enter

   :rew

   This **rew**inds all the files originally listed and places you at the beginning of the series of files again. You do not, however, have to be at the end of the series of files to enter the **:rew** command. It can be entered at any time during an editing session.

8. When you have finished with this editing session, terminate it by entering

   :q |

18.10

Changing the Order in Which Files Are Edited

As you are editing a series of files, you can get a list of the files you chose for editing.

1. Pick four files from your home directory and call them up for editing, using

   vi *file1 file2 file3 file4*

2. To check the names and order of files to be edited, get into the command mode and enter

   :args

   In a line at the bottom of the screen, the editor displays the names of the files you requested to edit. These are the arguments to the **vi** command you entered.

3. Add to or reorder the entire editing series, with this command:

   :n *newfile1 newfile2 newfile3*

   where the three *newfiles* are filenames you want to edit, whether or not they were among the initial **vi** command arguments. These new filenames replace the previously entered ones.

Ending an Editing Session Early

You can instruct the editor to quit, even when there are more files remaining to be edited.

1. Write the current file (if it's open) with the **:w** command.

2. Then enter

   :q

You will see a message:

```
n more files to edit
```

where *n* is the number of files (arguments) left in your editing sequence.

3. Enter **:q** again to end the editing process.

Storing Text for Use in Editing Other Files

You have just seen one advantage of editing several files at once—the editing program is initiated only once, saving time and resources. In addition, an editing environment spans several files. For instance, editing environment settings and text saved in lettered buffers all remain in memory as you move to another file.

1. Call up a series of *practice* files with the following command, using actual filenames:

   vi *file1 file2 file3*

2. Use the following command to save any four lines of text from the first file into the buffer a:

   "a4yy

3. Put that file away, and call up the next file with these two colon commands:

   :w
   :n

4. Move the cursor to any line on the screen and enter

   "ap

   The text stored in the lettered buffer a from the first file is now placed in the second file.

18.11

Accessing Shell Commands from Within the Editor

Often while you are editing a file, you need to access the shell to get information from a utility such as **who**, **date**, or **ls**. You need not leave the editor to access the shell.

Performing a Single Shell Command

1. Select and open a *practice* file with **vi**.
2. From the command mode, enter

   :!*date*

   The shell command **date** is executed. Once the command is completed, the following message appears at the bottom of your screen:

   ```
   [Hit return to continue]
   ```

3. When you press Return, you are returned to the editor. You can execute any single shell command from within **vi** by entering

   :!*command*

   where *command* is the desired shell command. The **!** is the shell escape character in the **vi**sual editor.

Creating a New Shell

You can also instruct the visual editor to call up a new shell for you to use.

1. From **vi** command mode, enter

   :!ksh

   or

   :!csh

   You are greeted by a shell prompt indicating that you have created a temporary shell. You can now invoke any number of shell commands.

2. Enter some shell commands, such as **date** to check the current date, or **who** to find out who is logged on.

3. To terminate this shell and return to the editor, press

   Ctrl -d

   The screen clears, and your *practice* file reappears. (If Ctrl -d doesn't work, enter **exit**.)

18.12

Incorporating the Output of a Shell Command

You can incorporate the output from any shell command into a file that you are editing.

1. To get the results of a **spell** command to appear at the top of the file, enter the following command from the **vi** command mode:

   :0r !spell *filename*

   where *0* is a zero, and *filename* is the file you are editing.

2. To have the output of spell added to the end of your file, enter

   :$r !spell *filename*

   Any time you want the output of a shell command line to be read into your file, you can use this command:

   :r !*command_line*

where *command_line* includes a shell command and the command arguments (options, filenames, and so forth).

Review 2

1. What command line would you use to call up the files *practice1*, *reminders*, and *practice2* for editing?

2. While in **vi**, with four files queued up for editing, what command moves you to the next file?

3. What is the command to place three lines of text into the lettered buffer a, starting at the current cursor position?

4. What is the command to obtain a listing of your current directory without leaving **vi**?

5. How would you start a new Korn shell while still in **vi**?

6. What command would you use to read the result of the **date** command into a file you are editing?

7. You have a number of files queued up for editing. You have just entered the **:q** command, and the message

   ```
   3. more files to edit
   ```

   is displayed. What do you enter to terminate the session?

8. If, after entering the command **vi** *first second*, you decide you want to move to the file *other*, what would you enter?

9. How would you map the ⌗ key to tell the editor to go to line 1, to open a line above, enter your name, and then exit append mode?

Conclusion

In this chapter, you examined powerful features of **vi**. With the **vi** editor, you can access a file with the cursor positioned at any desired line or word. You can use many different methods of deleting, moving, copying, and changing blocks of text; and you can move blocks of text between files. Furthermore, you can customize your editing environment to suit your specific application. The editor allows editing of multiple files in succession, maping of single keys, and in-line abbreviations. Although command rather than mouse driven, it is a full-featured editor.

■ Answers to Review 1

1. **vi** *+50 practice*
2. **vi** *+/help practice*
3. **view** *filename*
4. **:set** *wrapmargin=15*
5. **:set** *all*

■ Answers to Review 2

1. **vi** *practice1 reminders practice2*
2. **:n**
3. **"a3yy**
4. **:!ls**
5. **:!ksh**
6. **:r** *!date*
7. **:q**
8. **:n** *other*
9. **:map** # *1Goyourname* [Ctrl]-[v] [Esc]

COMMAND SUMMARY

Alternative vi Entry Methods

vi +*n filename* — Start editing a file on line *n*.

vi +/*the filename* — Start editing a file on the line where the string first occurs.

view — Allow user to view a file, but not write to it, except by using **w!**.

Setting the Editor

:set *option* — Basic format of the **:set** *option* command to use the options described in this section.

:set *nooption* — Basic format to turn off the editor *options*.

:set *number* — Tells editor to include line numbers on your display. Can be abbreviated as **:set** *nu*.

:set *nonumber* — Removes line numbers from your display. Can be abbreviated as **:set** *nonu*.

:set *window=value* — Defines the number of lines drawn on your display.

:set *autoindent* — Automatically indents each new line. Can be abbreviated as **:set** *ai*.

:set *noai* — Turns off automatic indenting.

:set *tabstop=value* — Sets the number of spaces used to display a tab character. Can be abbreviated as **:set** *ts=value*.

:set *ignorecase* — Tells the editor to ignore upper- and lowercase. Can be abbreviated as **:set** *ic*.

:set *shiftwidth=value* — Sets the distance for left and right text shifting. Use the > to shift the text left and use the < to shift the text right.

:set wrapmargin= *value*	Defines the distance between the right margin and the right edge of the display.
:set	Shows you all the *options* you have set.
:set all	Shows you all the set *options* available.
:set list	Tells the editor to display tab characters as **^I** and end-of-line characters as **$**.
:set showmatch	Right (closing) parentheses and brackets are matched with their left (opening) parentheses and brackets.

Text-Changing Commands

x	Deletes the one character under the cursor and retains it in memory, not in buffer.
dw	Deletes one word from text and retains it in memory, not in buffer.
dd	Deletes cursor line of text and places it in the buffer.
D	Deletes the rest of the line (from the cursor position on) and places it in the buffer.
r*x*	Replaces the letter under the cursor with the letter *x*. For instance, **rw** replaces character under cursor with letter *w*.
J	Joins cursor line with the next line in your text by appending the next line onto the end of the cursor line.
yy	Yanks the cursor line to the buffer.

*n***yy** Yanks the specified number (*n*) of lines. For instance, **6yy** tells **vi** to "make a copy of the next 6 lines, remember them, and put them where I tell you to." (See **p**ut commands just below.)

P (uppercase P) Puts the yanked or deleted line(s) just above the cursor line.

p (lowercase p) Puts the yanked or deleted text just below the cursor line.

Using Buffers

"*n***p** or "*n***P** Puts line from buffer numbered *n* below or above where cursor is located.

"*x***dd** or "*x***yy** Places designated line into a lettered buffer *x* (a–z).

"*x***p** or "*x***P** Puts line from lettered buffer *x* below or above cursor's line.

Marking Lines

m*x* Marks a line with any letter *x* (a–z). Line stays marked even if line is moved.

'*x* Positions the cursor on a line previously marked *x* (a–z).

Line Command Summary

:*n,nn* **mo** *nn* Moves lines *n* through *nn* after line *nn;* for example, lines 1 through 26 after line 82. (You select the line numbers.)

:*n,nn* **co** *nn* Copies lines *n* through *nn* and places them after line *nn;* for instance, lines 1 through 26 after line 82. (You select the line numbers.)

:*n,nn* **d** Deletes lines *n* through *nn,* for instance 1 through 26. (You select the line numbers.)

:*n,n***w** *newfile* Creates a new file named *newfile* and copies text lines *n* to *n* from the present file into *newfile*. (You select the line numbers.)

:*n,n***w** >> *oldfile* Appends copy of lines *n* to *n* to end of an existing file named *oldfile*. (You select the line numbers.)

:*n,n***w!** *oldfile* Overwrites (replaces) *oldfile* with contents of lines *n* to *n*. (You select the line numbers.)

:*n***r** *report.old* Reads in the file named *report.old* after text line *n* in the present file. (You select the line numbers.)

:*'a,'b* **d** Deletes text between and including lines previously marked in lettered buffers a and b. See information about letter buffers.

Text Editing with Line Commands

:s /*string*/*other-string*/ Finds first occurrence of *string* and substitutes *otherstring*.

:1,$ s/*string*/*other-string*/ Finds first occurrence of *string* on each and every line and substitutes *otherstring*.

:g /*string*/**s**/*other-string*/ Same as command just above.

:1,$ /*string*/**s**/ *string2*/*string3*/ Finds first occurrence of *string* on each and every line and substitutes *string3* for *string2*.

:g /*string*/**s**/ *string2*/*string3*/   Finds first occurrence of *string* on each and every line and substitutes *string3* for *string2*.

:1,$ s /*string*/*other string*/**g**   Finds all occurrences of *string* in a file and substitutes *otherstring*.

Maps and Abbreviations

:map # **a**string   When in command mode, adds to a line *string* and
[Ctrl]-[v] [Esc]   returns to command mode. The # character may be any key, **a** may be any append mode (**a,i,o**, etc.), and string can include other control characters if each is masked by a [Ctrl]-[v].

:ab *string other-string*   When in append mode, *otherstring* is substituted for *string*. Control characters may be included in *otherstring* if each is masked by a [Ctrl]-[v].

Append Mode Special Characters

[Ctrl]-[h]   Backspaces one character.

[Backspace]   Backspaces one character.

[Ctrl]-[w]   Backspaces one word.

[Ctrl]-[v]   Allows input of control characters.

[Esc]   Escapes to command mode.

Editing Multiple Files

vi *file1 file2 file3*   Creates **vi** session with multiple files.

:n	Moves to next file in session.
:rew	Rewinds to *file1*. You can **rew** while editing any *filename* for this **vi** session.
:args	Displays names in order specified at the beginning of the **vi** session.
:n *newfile1 newfile2*	Replaces files previously specified for this **vi** session.
"*an***yy** **:w** **:n** **"ap**	Sequence to move text from file currently being edited to the next file to be edited. See information on letter buffers, **yy** commands, and **p** commands.

Shell Commands from vi

:!*command*	Allows the invoking of shell *command*.
:csh or **:ksh**	Creates a new shell. Use [Ctrl]-[d] or **exit** to return to **vi**.
:r !*command_line*	Reads into *filename* the output of *command_line*.
:0r !spell *filename*	Runs **spell** command on *filename* and places output at beginning of *filename*.

Saving the Editing Environment

setenv exinit 'set *option1 option2***'**	In *.login* file, sets the **vi** editing environment for C shell.
exinit 'set *option1* *option2***'** **export exinit**	In profile file, sets the **vi** editing environment for Bourne shell.

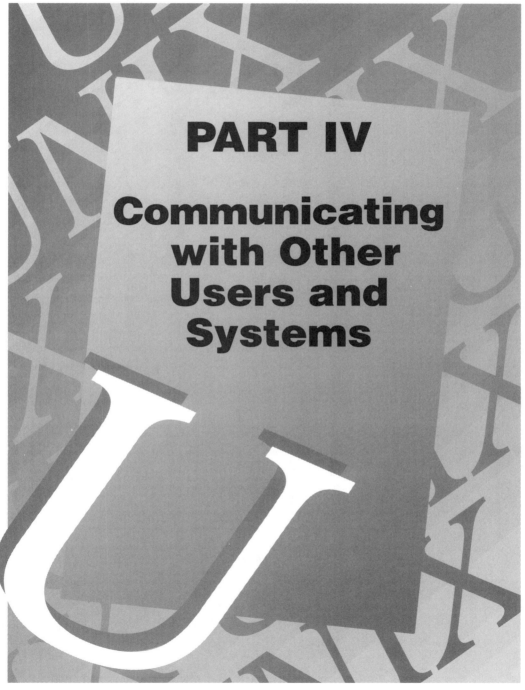

PART IV

Communicating with Other Users and Systems

Chapter Nineteen

Sending and Receiving Mail Messages

Maintaining the flow of information among all the users of a system is an essential component of a successful computing environment. Critical information such as changes in the system, updated project schedules, and other corporate information must be given to system users quickly. The **mail** utility is a popular tool that can be employed by all users to communicate throughout a UNIX system, between systems, and often across the network. With **mail**, you can send specific messages or files to one person or to a group. Recipients are automatically notified that they have mail, and they can then read their mail, send a reply, and save or discard the message, as needed.

SKILLS CHECK: *Before beginning this chapter, you should be able to*

- *Log on and issue basic UNIX commands*
- *Copy, rename, and remove files*
- *Access and modify files using the* **vi** *editor*

OBJECTIVES: *After completing this chapter, you will be able to*

- *Send a mail message to one recipient or to several recipients*
- *Receive mail*
- *Save messages*
- *Delete messages from your mailbox*
- *Respond to mail messages you receive*
- *Send files to other users*

In this chapter you send a series of mail messages, read your mail, and use advanced features for other tasks when you're using the **mail** utility.

19.1

Sending Messages Using the mail Utility

UNIX electronic mail allows each user to send messages, including files, to other UNIX users. You can send mail to other users whether or not they are currently logged on to the system.

Determining Which mail to Use

Throughout this chapter, reference is made to the **mail** utility. On many machines there are two versions of mail: **mail** and **mailx**.

1. To find out which **mail** utility you have, enter

   man *mail*
   man *mailx*

   If you have both versions on your computer, use **mailx** for this section. If not, use **mail**.

Initiating the Command to Send Mail to Yourself

To learn how to use **mail**, you will first practice by sending yourself messages.

1. Because the objective of this exercise is to send mail to yourself, substitute your own login id for *login* in the following command line. Type

   mail *login*

Using the Subject Line

A user receiving mail is informed of both the sender and the subject of the message. When you are sending a message, the **mail** utility may ask you to enter the title (subject) of your message, depending on how your account is set up. If it doesn't ask, the feature is not turned on at the moment. If the subject line feature is enabled in your **mail** utility, you receive a prompt:

Subject:

If you receive this prompt, you can type a short title (half a line or so) for your message, and press Return. Or you can just press Return without entering a subject.

When you make an entry in the subject line, you give the recipient of your message the opportunity to easily choose which **mail** messages to read first. If you leave your subject line blank, some versions of the **mail** program will repeat the first few words of your message in the subject field of the message header.

Entering the Append Mode of mail

Locate the **mail** *login* command on the abbreviated conceptual map shown in Figure 19-1. It leads from the shell to the **mail** append mode. Once you type **mail** *login* (and possibly a subject line), you are in the **mail** append mode. Notice that the **mail** *login* command has a one-way single-headed arrow in the conceptual map, indicating that you are not automatically returned to the shell.

With the **vi**sual editor, you are first placed in command mode. In contrast, when you use **mail**, you are *automatically* placed in the append

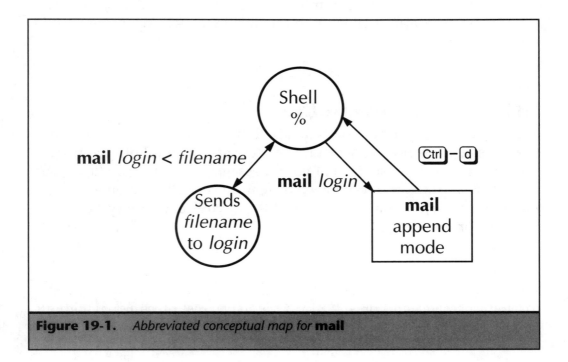

Figure 19-1. *Abbreviated conceptual map for* **mail**

mode. You do not have to type a command (such as **vi**'s **a** or **i** commands) to go from command mode to append mode. Whatever you type is sent as mail.

Entering Your Message

The cursor is now at the beginning of a line. The **mail** program is waiting for input from the keyboard.

1. Type a short message, such as

   ```
   This is message number 1.
   ```

   and press (Return).

2. Add another line or two, ending each line by pressing (Return).

3. If you make a mistake on a line, enter

   (Backspace)

   or

   (Ctrl)-(h)

   to return to the point where you made the mistake. You can then correct it, as long as the cursor is still in the same line as the mistake.

Ending Your Message

When you have completed typing your message, you must inform **mail** that you have finished and want to send the message.

1. Press (Return) to move the cursor to the beginning of the next line.

2. With the cursor on a new line, press

   (Ctrl)-(d)

   The shell prompt returns. Whatever you typed is sent as a message to the user *login*, the **mail** program dies, and you are returned to the shell.

Again examine the abbreviated conceptual map in Figure 19-1. To exit the append mode of **mail**, you press Ctrl-d.

Receiving Your Message

The message you just sent will be delivered to your personal *mailbox* within a few minutes. Your mailbox is actually a file, stored in a different place on the system from most of your files.

1. You are at the shell. Check for the existence of mail, and start the process of reading it by typing

   mail

2. If the mail you sent has not yet arrived, you will see this message:

   ```
   No mail for login
   ```

   and your shell prompt reappears. It may take several minutes for the message to be delivered to your mailbox. Try checking again after a minute or so.

3. If you do have mail, your workstation displays something like the following:

   ```
   mail version 3.0 Type & for help.
   "/usr/mail/yourname": 1 message 1 new
   >N 1 sender Wed Jun 24 08:13 13/315 Subject
   ?
   ```

4. If the actual contents of the first message appear on your screen instead of a header, you are using an old version of **mail**. To use a new version of **mail**, exit **mail** by entering

   x

   Start over by entering

   mailx

Interpreting the Header

The mail display includes a summary line or header describing the message you just sent yourself, followed by the **mail** prompt, which is either a **?** or a **&**. The summary line, which starts with the > symbol, indicates that a **new** (**N**) mail message, numbered *1*, is in your mailbox. (New mail means unread mail.) The header then tells you the new message has been received from *sender* on the indicated date. Finally, the subject of the message appears at the end of the line.

If other users have sent you mail, you will see additional summary lines, one for each additional message.

1. Find the message number for your message (it is *1* unless you have other messages).

2. To read the message, type

   1

   and press Return. The message you sent earlier is displayed on the screen.

3. If the message is more than a page long, press Spacebar or Return to see the next screenful. After you complete your examination of the message, a new **mail** prompt is automatically displayed.

To see a particular message, you must type its message number at the **mail** prompt and press Return.

Deleting a Message from the Mailbox

Your mail file (mailbox) will become unmanageably large if you do not delete unneeded messages from time to time.

1. After reading the message you just sent yourself, delete it by typing

   d

2. End your session with **mail** and return to the shell by typing

   q

Later in this chapter you will use other commands that read and save your mail.

Since you have just deleted the message you sent to yourself, send another one now so that you can explore more of the **mail** command.

3. Type the following command, replacing *login* with your own login id:

mail *login*

4. If you receive the subject prompt, type the following for your subject:

Here is my subject.

5. Type the text of your message:

Here is the body of my message.
This is message number 2.

6. End the message by moving to a new line and entering

Ctrl - d

19.2

Sending Files Through mail to a User

In the preceding section you typed text for a **mail** message to be sent. You can also send an existing file with **mail**. In this section you create and edit a message (file), and when it is ready, send it.

1. Use **vi** to create a file called *letter*. Write a few lines in it, including one mentioning that this is your third message.

2. Save the file and quit **vi**, so that you're back at the shell prompt.

3. To send the letter, type the following command, again substituting your login id for *login*:

mail *login* < *letter*

The shell prompt returns. This time, you don't have to type the message. This command line instructs **mail** to send mail to *login* just like before, but now the file *letter* is opened, read, and sent as the message. The *input* to **mail** is redirected from the keyboard to the file *letter*.

The less-than symbol < is used to tell the shell to open the file *letter* and connect it to the input of **mail**. If you don't specify the input with a < *filename* on the command line, input will be read from your keyboard just like the earlier two messages. When input is read from the keyboard, a Ctrl-d is used to end the input. That is why Ctrl-d is called "end-of-file" or "EOF." When you specify a file for input, the end of input is the end of the actual file.

In summary, you have thus far examined two types of mail messages:

- If you send mail by typing **mail** *login*, input is from the workstation, and you conclude the message by pressing the end-of-file command Ctrl-d.

- If you type **mail** *login* < *filename*, the file is the input that is sent to *login*. The end of the file concludes the message.

19.3

Sending Mail to Multiple Recipients

The **mail** utility can be used to send messages or files to several accounts at the same time. This function allows you to quickly send a memo or letter to a select group, or to every user on your system.

Sending a Message to More Than One Recipient

For the fourth practice message that follows, select a person you know and substitute his or her login id for *neighbor.login*.

1. Type the following command line, substituting your friend's login id for *neighbor.login* and your login id for *login*:

mail *login   neighbor.login*

2. At the subject prompt, type

   Multiple mailings

3. After pressing (Return), type the following text:

   This is message number 4.
   I am sending it to more than one login.

4. End the message by pressing (Ctrl)-(d) on a new line.
   Now the message you typed in step 3 is sent to both you and
   your neighbor, because you specified both your login id and your
   neighbor's as arguments on the command line. You can send a
   message to as many people as you want with this command line:

   mail *login1   login2   login3 ...*

   where *login1*, *login2*, *login3*, and so on are the login ids of each
   recipient.

Sending a File to More Than One Recipient

You can also send a file to multiple recipients, using the standard input
redirection symbol, <, like this:

   mail *login1   login2   login3 ... loginx   <   file*

Review 1

1. What is the command to mail a file called *letter1* to a user whose
   login id is *user1*?

2. What do you type to indicate that you have finished typing a
   mail message?

3. What is the effect of the following command?

   mail *andy   fred   joe   <   form.letter*

19.4

Receiving Mail

When someone sends a **mail** message to you, it is put in your system mailbox and saved for you to read at your convenience. When you log on, your mailbox file is examined. If there are any new messages there, the notification

```
You have mail.
```

appears automatically on your screen.

Depending on how your account is set up, the system looks at your mailbox every one to ten minutes. If someone sends you mail while you are logged on, you don't have to wait until the next time you log on to be aware of it. If there is mail for you, you will be told at the next shell prompt:

```
You have new mail.
```

Accessing Your Mail

Earlier, you read the first message you sent to yourself. You later deleted it. To support the exercises in this section, you need to send yourself some more mail.

1. Create and send yourself five more messages. Be sure to put a message number in the text of each message, so you will be able to see later the order in which they are displayed.

2. Once you've sent the messages, type the following command from the shell prompt:

   mail

   A message header list similar to this one appears on your screen:

   ```
   mail version 3.0 Type ? for help.
   "/usr/mail/yourname": 8 messages 8 new
   >N 1 sender Wed Jun 24 08:33 13/315 Subject
   ```

```
N 2 sender  Wed Jun 24 08:55 13/315 Subject
N 3 sender  Wed Jun 24 08:59 13/315 Subject
. . . .
?
```

You have sent yourself five new messages. You do not have to wait for the message telling you that you have new mail in order to read your mail. When you type **mail** with no arguments, you access your mailbox.

Interpreting mail Output

The message header display is rich with information. The header was introduced in an earlier exercise. What follows is a closer look at the header's contents. For each message, the header tells you the following:

- The first field indicates whether the message has been read. The **N** means that a message is new and has not been read. In this display, all of your message headers are preceded by **N**. If the **N** is missing, you already looked at the message.

- The next field is the message number. This number reflects the order in which your messages were received. The times of receipt correspond to the order of the message numbers. You can use these numbers to refer to your messages.

- The third field is the sender field. It is the login of the user who sent the message.

- The fourth field is the date and time the message was received, followed by the length of the message. The length is in number of lines and characters, separated by a slash.

- Finally, each header has a subject field. If the sender typed in a subject at the prompt, it appears here.

- The > that marks message *1* indicates that message *1* is your current message. Whenever you are reading your mail, one of the messages is the current message, and it is always marked with a > .

Working in the mail Command Mode

Whenever you type **mail** without an argument, you read rather than send mail. You enter the **mail** command mode. The **?** or **&** prompt at the end of the message list is your **mail** command mode prompt.

Examine Figure 19-2, and locate the box that says "Mail command mode." Once you're in **mail**'s command mode, the commands you enter are two-way commands, which return you to the command mode prompt once they finish executing. You can see this represented on your conceptual map by the double-headed arrows that connect commands to the "Mail command mode" box.

Getting a Listing of Commands in mail

1. Get the command line for **mail**. Request help by typing either

   help

   or

   ?

   The resulting screen output displays a list of commands and what they do.

2. Read through the help screen. The list you see when you type **?** is not exhaustive. Check **man** *mail* for more details.

Using the header Command

After looking at the **help** screen of commands, you'll find that the message header list you had displayed when you first entered the command mode has disappeared. You can call up this header list at any time.

1. Type the command

   h

   Once again, you see the list of message headers and the **mail** prompt.

   The **h** stands for **header**. To produce the header list, you can type **h**, **he**, **hea**, **head**, and so forth, up to and including the entire word, **header**.

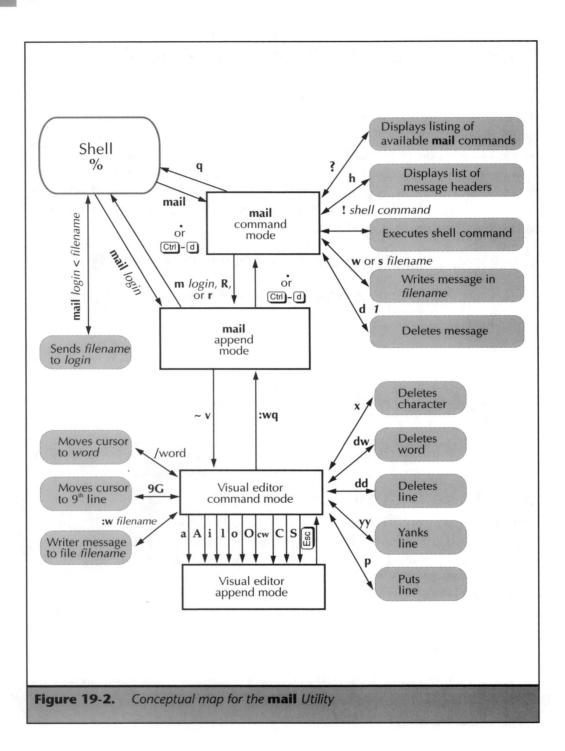

Figure 19-2. *Conceptual map for the* **mail** *Utility*

TIP: *Whenever you can abbreviate a command in such a way that it does not conflict with the abbreviation of another command,* **mail** *will understand the abbreviation.*

Selecting Messages by Number for Viewing

One way of viewing your messages is to type just the message number, and press [Return].

1. To view message 3, type

   3

   Message 3 is displayed.

19.5

Deleting Messages from Your Mailbox

Messages from other users can really pile up in your mailbox. An essential skill is deleting messages you've already read and don't want to save. UNIX lets you delete the current message, a specific message, or a range of messages.

Deleting the Current Message

One way to delete a message is to read it first, and then delete it before reading another message.

1. Look at message 3 again. Type

   3

2. When the message appears on the screen and you get your **mail** prompt (**?**), read the message and then type

   d

   This instructs **mail** to **d**elete message 3, which is the current message, from the list of messages.

3. To verify that the header for message *3* is gone from the header list, type

h

Deleting a Message That Is Not Current

In addition to deleting a message you have just read, you can delete specific messages.

1. Delete message *6* by typing the following:

d *6*

By specifying which message to delete, you avoid having to access it to make it current. The **mail** program deletes the specified message.

2. Verify that message *6* was deleted, by typing

h

3. Review the list of message headers. Messages *2*, *3*, and *6* are gone.

Deleting a Range of Messages

Besides deleting messages one at a time, you can also delete groups of messages.

1. With the list of messages displayed, delete messages *2*, *3*, and *4* by typing

d *2-4*

The hyphen is used to specify a *range* of messages.

2. Look at the list of messages again, with the **h**eader command:

h

Messages *2* through *4* have been deleted from the list of message headers.

Exiting mail Without Affecting the Mailbox

You have been reading and deleting mail. When you have finished, you need to get back to the shell.

1. One way to exit **mail** is to type a lowercase

   x

   This command is equivalent to **exit**, **xit**, and so forth.

2. Now that you have used **x** to get out of **mail**, return to the **mail** command mode again by typing

   mail

   Look carefully at the messages that are listed. The messages that you deleted in your last exercise have returned. The command **x** tells **mail** to exit your mailbox without writing changes to it. Your mailbox is left exactly as it was before you brought up **mail** the previous time.

19.6

Quitting the mail Program and Processing Your Changes

You use another command for leaving the **mail** program when you want to also write your changes to the mailbox.

1. Delete messages *2* through *4* again by entering

   d *2-4*

2. Type one of these commands:

   q

   or

   quit

A message similar to the following appears on your screen:

```
Held 5 messages in /usr/mail/login
Held 5 messages in /usr/spool/mail/login
```

This message indicates that the **mail** program is retaining (or holding) five messages that you have not yet read.

The **q**uit command records all changes made to the mailbox through the **d**elete command, and returns you to the shell.

3. At the shell prompt, call up **mail** again and inspect the list of messages. This time messages **2** through **4** have indeed been deleted. If you started with eight messages, you are now left with five in your mailbox.

4. Notice that several messages have a **U** (for **u**nread) at the left of the message number, whereas they were previously marked **N** (for **n**ew). This is because when you quit **mail** with a **q**, the messages are marked according to what you did during the preceding session. They are no longer new—just unread.

5. Examine the header list. The messages have been renumbered. At this point, what used to be message **5** has moved up to the number 2 position. The numbers now correspond to the current **mail** list.

▌ **Review 2**

1. If you receive mail while you are logged on, do you have to wait until the next time you log on to find out you have mail?

2. If a user named *topaz* has sent you mail, what is the command to read it?

3. How do you read the fifth message?

4. How do you display the list of messages held for you in your mailbox?

19.7

Using the undelete Command

It may happen that you accidentally delete a message. Fortunately, there is a **mail** command that will bring back any deleted messages, until you exit **mail** with the **quit** command.

1. Remove message 2 by typing

   d 2

   The commands **d2** *and* **d 2** *are equivalent.*

2. To bring back message 2, type

   u

   The **u** command **u**ndeletes the last deleted message. All deleted messages are held until you type **quit**.

3. To verify that the last message has been undeleted, type

   2

4. You can also **u**ndelete a range of messages. Delete messages 2 through 4 and check the results by typing

   d 2-4
   h

5. To undelete this range of messages, type the following:

   u 2-4

6. Even if you have deleted a range of messages, you can **u**ndelete a specific one. For example, delete messages 2 through 4 again with

   d 2-4

7. Bring back message *3* by typing

   u *3*

8. Now check the results by typing

   h

   Message *3* is there, but messages *2* and *4* are still deleted.

   With **mail**'s **u**ndelete command, there is no need to panic. It provides you with an escape in case you have made a mistake or changed your mind about deleting a message. When you use the **u**ndelete command before you **q**uit **mail**, the message you have undeleted remains in your mailbox. When you **q**uit **mail** and leave messages deleted, you will *not* be able to undelete them in a later session.

19.8

Creating and Adding to mbox

As you have seen, when you use the **x** command to exit **mail** after reading your messages, they remain in your mailbox, and any new messages that arrive are added to the existing ones. The size of your mailbox can thus reach enormous proportions if left unattended. On the other hand, if you use the **q**uit command to leave **mail** after reading your messages, all messages that you have read but not deleted are transferred to another file, called *mbox*, located in your home directory.

Some systems are set up so that messages that have been read are retained with unread messages. If your system works that way, you may wish to skip the following exercise related to *mbox*.

Creating the mbox File

1. You should still be in the command mode of **mail**. If you are not, call up **mail**.

2. Read a message and then **quit**. The status message that appears will be similar to one of the following:

```
Saved 1 message in mbox
Held 4 messages in /usr/mail/login_id
Held 4 messages in /usr/spool/mail/f6
```

In the last two examples, the *4* indicates how many messages are left in your mailbox. When you **quit** in step 2 after reading one message, that message was added to the file *mbox*. Because *mbox* did not exist earlier, the file was automatically created for this purpose. The other five messages were treated as unread mail. They were left in your mailbox, marked **U** for **u**nread.

In the first example, where **mail** has responded with

```
Saved 1 message in mbox
```

it is telling you that the one message you read but did not save or delete was *added* to your *mbox* file.

19.9

Saving mail Messages as Files

If someone sends you an important file or program, you may want to save the information in a specific file for editing, printing, or archiving.

1. Return to the command mode of **mail**. Inspect the list of message headers, and notice which message is marked as your current one (>).

2. At the prompt, type the following:

   s *friend-mail*

   This command puts your current message in the file called *friend-mail* in the current directory.

3. If you want to save a message other than the current one, you must specify also the message number. Save message **2** in *friend-saved* by typing the following command:

s 2 *friend-saved*

You receive a message saying that the message is *appended* to the *friend-saved* file.

4. Quit mail by typing

q

5. Examine the file named *friend-saved* to confirm that the mail messages are saved.

19.10

Replying to Mail

Often when you receive mail, you will want to reply to certain messages, to pose questions, write answers, or make comments.

1. Mail yourself another message, by typing

mail *login*

2. At the subject prompt, type
RSVP

3. Type in the following message:

I'm planning a party to celebrate
my mastery of mail.
Will you attend?
Ctrl-d

4. Let some minutes pass, to make sure the message has time to arrive in your mailbox. Then call up **mail**.

Using Reply and reply

Rather than going through the mail-sending process, you can use a received message as the basis of a reply directly to the sender of the message.

1. Read the message you just sent yourself, and then type an uppercase

   R

   The following information appears:

   ```
   To: login
   Subject: Re: RSVP
   ```

   There is no prompt—you are already in the append mode of **mail**. The program is waiting for your input, just as if you had entered the **mail** *login* command.

2. Type in a reply message accepting your party invitation, and on a new line press [Ctrl]-[d].

3. Return to the command mode by pressing

   [Ctrl]-[d]

4. Look back at Figure 19-2. Notice that the two reply commands, **r** and **R**, bring you into the append mode, and the append mode command [Ctrl]-[d] brings you back to the command mode.

5. At the **mail** prompt, type

   x

   to return to the shell without writing changes.

6. From the shell, call up **mail** again. Your header list now includes a line that looks something like this:

   ```
   N n login  Wed Jun 24 08:13 13/315 Re: RSVP
   ```

This is the header for a completely new message—your **Reply** to the RSVP message. Notice that the subject was retained, but that it was altered to indicate the message is a reply.

NOTE: *On most systems, when a message goes to more than one login name, and you are included among the recipients of the message, using* **R** *to* **R***eply allows you to reply privately to the author of the message. The other recipients of the original message do not receive copies of your answer.*

Using reply to Send Copies of a Reply

You have seen how to use **R** to send a private reply to the author of a message that was sent to more than one user. If you wish to reply to the author of the message, as well as send a copy of your reply to all of the recipients of the original message, use the lowercase **r** command.

SUMMARY: *You use* **R***eply and* **r***eply in the same way. The difference is that on most systems* **R** *directs your answer to the sender, but not to the other recipients of the original message;* **r** *directs it to the sender* and *all of the recipients.*

NOTE: *On some Sun systems, the function of* **R** *and* **r** *is reversed. To be certain of what happens on your system, consult the manual entry for* **mail***.*

■ Review 3

1. What is the command in **mail**'s command mode to save the current message as the file *letter*?

2. Which of the following commands to exit **mail** command mode will *not* remove deleted messages from your mailbox?

   q
   x

3. What command will allow you to send a mail message reply to the author of a message as well as to all of its original recipients?

19.11

Editing Your Messages

Making corrections to what you type when you're using **mail** is a bit difficult, since you cannot return to a previous line.

1. From the shell, enter

   mail *login*

   where *login* is your own login name.

2. If there is a subject prompt, press Return.

3. At this point, mail is waiting for your input. Enter the following lines:

   This is a test
   of the editing capabilities of mail.

4. Now suppose you want to change this line:

   This is a test

   to read as follows:

   This will be *a test.*

   You can always use the Backspace key or Ctrl-h to go backward in a line and correct your mistakes *within the line,* but how do you move the cursor around the various lines in the message?

Changing the Content of a Message

1. After the last word in the message, press Return.

2. On a line by itself, enter the following:

   ~v

   Your screen clears. You see your two lines of text at the top, and the message

   ```
   "/tmp/Re00727"  2  lines,  52 characters
   ```

at the bottom. You are now in **vi**, and you can edit your message exactly as if you had written it with **vi**.

3. Use **vi** commands to change the text so that the first line now says

This will be a test

4. Add some more text. When you have finished, press ⎡Esc⎤.

5. Save and quit the file by entering

:wq

The following message appears:

```
"/tmp/Re00727"  2 lines,  57 characters
(continue)
```

You have quit editing with **vi**, but you are *not* back in the shell.

Instead of bringing you to the shell, as **:wq** usually does, it brings you back to **mail**—the place where your **vi** session started. Now you are back in **mail** with the cursor on a blank line just after your edited message. With **mail**, the ~ **vi** command calls **vi** as a child process. When **vi** ends it lets its parent—your **mail** process—know. Examine Figure 19-2 to review how **mail** and **vi** interact.

Notice that the modified message does not appear on the screen. Whatever you add now will be a continuation of the message since you are still in the append mode of **mail**. Continue entering text, the **vi** information that you still see on your workstation will scroll up and disappear.

Displaying the Content of a Message

Tilde ~ commands must be on lines by themselves.

1. On the next line, enter the following:

~p ⎡Return⎤

This is the **print** command of **mail**'s append mode. It instructs **mail** to display the message you are writing. The following appears on your screen:

```
-------
Message contains:
To:  login
This will be a test
of the editing capabilities of mail.
More text
More text
(continue)
```

Notice that the ~ **v**, the **vi** line count information, and the ~ **p** do not appear. The ~ entries were actual commands, and the **vi** information appeared only on the screen for you. It was not actually added to the message.

Getting Help for the Tilde Commands

What else can you do with a tilde?

1. On a line by itself, enter

   ~?

   A list of tilde commands is displayed. Read the list to discover which tilde commands are available on your system.

Reading In a File

1. Still in the append mode of **mail**, enter the following on a line by itself:

   ~**r** *practice*

   and press (Return). The display is a single line like

   ```
   "practice"  15/224
   ```

   The number 15 represents the number of lines, and 224 represents the number of characters in the file *practice*. You have just read the text of the file *practice* into your message. You will not see the text of the file *practice* itself, but the message tells you that it read the file.

2. To see the whole message as it stands now, enter

~p

Executing Shell Commands

You just read the file *practice* into your **mail** message. Could you determine which files are in your current directory without leaving **mail**?

1. Enter the following:

~! ls

You see a listing of the contents of your current directory, including the filename *practice*. The tilde command, followed by an exclamation mark (!), followed by a shell command, permits you to execute the shell command.

2. Determine if **vi** displayed the correct information about *practice*, by entering the following:

~! wc -lc *practice*

■ Review 4

1. When sending a mail message, how can you obtain a listing of files in your current directory?

2. How can you read the file *picnic* into the **mail** message?

3. How can you invoke the **visual** editor from within **mail**?

■ Conclusion

In this chapter, you sent electronic mail to other users on your system, and read mail that you received from other users. You learned that messages can be saved as files, deleted, or stored in *mbox*. The **mail** program is augmented by a series of tilde commands that allow you to read a file, invoke the **vi**sual editor, and escape to the shell. With electronic mail, you and other users can efficiently exchange ideas, files, and information.

▇ Answers to Review 1

1. **mail** *user1* < *letter1*
2. Ctrl-d on a new line
3. Mail the contents of a file called *form.letter* to colleagues who have login ids *andy*, *fred*, and *joe*.

▇ Answers to Review 2

1. No. Your mailbox is checked periodically by the shell while you are logged on, and you are informed of any new mail at the next shell prompt.
2. **mail**
3. Enter 5.
4. Type **h** from the command mode of **mail**.

▇ Answers to Review 3

1. **s** *letter*
2. **x**
3. **r** (usually)

▇ Answers to Review 4

1. ~! **ls**
2. ~**r** *picnic*
3. ~**vi** or ~**v**

COMMAND SUMMARY

?   Prints a help screen of selected **mail** commands.

p *message-list*   Prints messages on screen.

d *message-list*   Deletes current message, or message list if specified.

u *message-list*   Undeletes deleted messages.

R   Sends **R**eply to author of message.

r   Sends **r**eply to author of message, as well as all original recipients of the message.

x   Exits **mail**, preserving all messages.

q   Quits, registering all changes (read, delete, and so on) made to the messages in the mailbox file.

h   Prints active message header.

s *message-list*
filename   Saves, including header, the current message (or message list if specified) into *filename* (if specified) or into *mbox*.

w *message-list*
filename   Writes, without header, the current message (or message list if specified) into *filename*, which must be specified.

-f *file*   Command line option to read *file* for mail messages.

Chapter Twenty

Connecting to Local Network Machines

omputers are often connected in a *network* so that users on individual machines, called hosts or systems, can communicate and exchange information with other users and hosts in the network. Some UNIX workstations, like those in an office, are connected in a small *local network* and communicate with one another almost constantly. In other environments, host machines are connected to large nationwide (and sometimes worldwide) networks but communicate much less often. There are specific UNIX utilities that allow users to set up communication links via these networks, large or small.

In this chapter, the exercises call for you to access other hosts connected to your local host through a local network. Check with your system administrator to see if your host is connected to a network, if you have access to the network, if the network is working, and if your network system is derived from the Berkeley network programs. If you don't have access to a network, you will not be able to do the exercises in this chapter.

SKILLS CHECK: *Before beginning this chapter, you should be able to*

- *Access and leave the system*
- *Execute basic commands*
- *Create, display, and print files*
- *Rename, copy, and remove files*
- *Access and modify files using the* **vi** *editor*
- *Send and read e-mail using the* **mail** *program*

OBJECTIVE: *After completing this chapter, you will be able to*

- *Determine what hosts are on your local network*
- *Get information about users on other hosts*
- *Communicate with users on other hosts*
- *Access accounts on other hosts*
- *Transfer files between accounts on different hosts*

20.1

Getting Information About Local Hosts

In this chapter, you collect information about other host machines and users on your local network, log on to remote hosts, send e-mail to other users on the network, and transfer files between accounts.

Hosts (machines) are connected on a local network so that users on individual hosts can access shared files, use the same programs, and otherwise work together. UNIX utilities will report the names and other information about the hosts on your local network.

1. Every host on a network has a name. Request the name of your host by entering the command

   hostname

   The output is the unique name of your system on your network.

2. Find out the status of every host machine on your network by typing

   ruptime

   If the computer responds with one of the following messages:

   ```
   No hosts!?!
   ruptime: not found
   ```

   it means either your host is not part of a network or there is some problem with the network and you should ask your system administrator for help.

Normally, if you're on a network and the network is up, the computer responds with a list of computers on your network and the status of each. The output is similar to the following:

```
Host        Status  Time       Users     Load
vanilla     down    4+02:34
chocolate   up      13+18:28,  1 user,   load 0.25, 0.24, 0.00
strawberry  up      2+08:33,   0 users,  load 0.33, 0.26, 0.01
rocky-road  up      2:44,      0 users,  load 0.24, 0.24, 0.00
pistachio   up      5+22:10,   15 users, load 8.13, 6.17, 4.19
```

The components of the **ruptime** output are as follows:

Component	Description
Host	The names of the various computers—the hosts. These computers are given names so that users can identify them.
Status	Whether the host is up or down (operational or not).
Time	Time host has been in the current state, in the format *days + hours*: *minutes*.
Users	Number of users on this host.
Load	Three numbers indicate how busy the host machine is. The load is the average number of processes runable and in the queue waiting for CPU attention. Numbers represent, from left to right, average load over 1 minute, over 5 minutes, and over 10 minutes—the larger the number, the busier the host.

To be able to report this list, **ruptime** maintains a data file. Every minute, each host on the network sends out a message to all of the other hosts; this message describes the host's status. If any host is not heard from for 5 minutes, it is listed as being down.

By knowing the status of the hosts on your network, you can use the network more efficiently. For example, if you have a task that requires substantial system resources, a host with a small load number, or one that is not very busy is best. You can use **ruptime** to find out which host is least busy.

Another way to see what hosts your local host has information about is to examine the */etc/hosts* file. Enter

   more */etc/hosts*

The host names and numerical addresses are displayed.

20.2

Obtaining Information About Users on the Network

You have determined what hosts are on your network. On each of those host machines are users. UNIX utilities provide information about these users, as well as their host machines.

Determining Who Is Logged On to Local Hosts

The **who** command tells you which users are logged on to your local host. It is also useful to find out which users are on other hosts on your network. If certain network programs are running, you can obtain user information from other network systems, as well.

1. Find out what users are on your local network by typing

   rwho

2. If the listing is long, you might want to pipe the output through the **pg** or **more** command. To do this with **pg**, type

   rwho | pg

   If your installation is running **rwho**, the output is a list similar to the following:

   ```
   smith      chocolate:ttyp0     Jun 27 10:22
   root       pistachio:console   Jun 27 10:14
   roberts    pistachio:ttyh2     Jun 27 10:20
   salinger   pistachio:ttyh3     Jun 21 18:11
   bronte     pistachio:ttyh5     Jun 27 09:41
   naipaul    pistachio:ttyi3     Jun 27 09:06 :01
   guest      pistachio:ttyi5     Jun 27 09:10 :0
   mitchell   pistachio:ttyi7     Jun 27 08:25
   ```

```
maugham    pistachio:ttyie    Jun 23 16:00
guest-4    pistachio:ttyj1    Jun 27 08:51
guest-1    pistachio:ttyp0    Jun 27 09:40
guest-3    pistachio:ttyp1    Jun 27 09:07 :24
```

Each line of the **rwho** output is in the following form:

user host_name:tty_port login_date login_time

The first column lists the users on hosts connected to the network. The middle column names the host machine and terminal where the user is logged on. The last column shows when the user logged on and, if the user has been idle for more than a minute, the amount of idle time. Users who are idle for more than an hour are not listed at all.

The **rwho** command can be helpful when you need to communicate with another user. The output will tell you whether a user is logged on, where they are logged on, and how long they have been idle.

Checking Who's Logged On to a Specific Host

The **rwho** command displays the logins of users who are on all of your local systems. This might be too much information to sift through if you want to find a specific host on the network. Fortunately, there is also a UNIX utility that will tell you who is on a specific network host machine.

1. Type the following command:

   finger

   The output is a display similar to this:

```
Login      Name            TTY   Idle  When         Office
root       Super User      co    11    Tue 10:14    767-2676
matt       Matthew Adams   h2          Tue 10:20
smith      Jean Smith      h3    19    Wed 18:11
sam        Sam Silver      h5          Tue 09:41
guest-4    ???             j1          Tue 08:51
guest-1    ???             j2          Tue 09:40
guest-3    ???             j4    1     Tue 09:07
```

The **finger** command displays all users logged on to your host, their "real" names (if known), terminals, idle times, and login times.

2. You can also check a network host by specifying the name of the host machine. Pick a host machine (*host_name*) on your network and find out who is logged on it by typing

finger *@host_name*

You get an output similar to the earlier output for **finger**. The *@host_name* address tells **finger** to check for users on the host machine named *host_name* instead of on your host.

Finding Out How Recently a Specific User Logged On

Besides using **finger** to check who is logged on, you can use it to find information about a specific user.

1. To find out when the user *root* (which has an account on every system) last logged on your system, type

finger *root*

The output should be similar to this:

```
Login name: root                   In real life: Super User
Directory: /                       Shell: /bin/csh
Last login Mon Jun 26 18:41 on console
No Plan.
```

There are four lines in the display. The first line tells you the login id and real name of the account user if that information is in the fifth field of the *passwd* file. The second line tells you the account's home directory and default shell. The third line says when *root* last logged on and which *tty* port was used. (If *root* is currently logged on, this line tells you when *root* logged on and which *tty* port *root* is using.) The last line says that *root* doesn't have an optional file called *.plan*. The *.plan* file, located in the user's home directory, usually contains a short description of the account's purpose as conceived by the owner.

2. If you know the login ids of friends on your system, use **finger** to determine when they last logged on.

3. You can also check this same information for a user on another system by specifying the user and the host. Pick a host machine, and find out when the user *root* last logged on there by typing

   finger *root@host_name*

   where *host_name* is the name of the host. This output tells you when *root* last logged on at that host machine. As before, the *@host_name* address tells **finger** to check the specified network host named *host_name*, instead of your local machine. In this way, @ is a special character that separates the login id from the host name.

The general form for **finger** is as follows:

finger *user@host_name*

This tells you either that *user* is logged on, or when *user* last logged on.

Determining a User's Account

Not only can you find the name of a user of a given login id and when that user last logged on, but you can often determine the login id for a user, given the user's real name.

1. If you have a friend with an account on another host, type

   finger *friend_name@host_name*

   where *friend_name* is either the first or last name of your friend. The output either tells you your friend's login id and **finger** information, or it displays the following:

   ```
   Login Name: friend's_name        In real life: ???
   ```

This line means that finger couldn't find the login id matched with *friend_name*.

The **finger** command checks both the login id list and the real name list in the fifth field of the *passwd* file. If **finger** finds a name in the real name list, it will display the information for the login id matching the name.

20.3

Communicating Over a Network

For users on individual hosts to work together effectively, they have to be able to send messages and data back and forth.

Sending E-mail to Users on Other Hosts

Electronic mail provides fundamental communication among users on a network. You have already sent mail to users on your local host by using the **mail** *login_id* command. You can also send mail to users on other hosts, as long as you know their login ids and host names.

1. Try sending mail to a friend with an account on another system. If you don't know the login id, use **finger** to find it out.

2. If you do not have the login of a friend on another host, send mail to the user */dev/null* on another host. Type this command:

   mail */dev/null@host*

   where *host* is the name of a host other than your own.

3. Type the following lines in your outgoing e-mail:

   ```
   Hi,
   I'm trying mail.
   Could you please answer this.
   Thank You.
   ```

   and then press

   Ctrl - d

   to end the message.

(Don't expect an answer. On some host machines, this mail will be thrown away. On other host machines, you will get a reply saying that the user */dev/null* doesn't exist.)

In general, to send a message to a user on another host, you have to type a **mail** command in the following format:

mail *loginid@host_name*

where *loginid* is the user's loginid, and *host_name* is the name of the host machine where the user's account is located.

Talking to Users Logged On to Other Hosts

Using **mail** is not the fastest way to communicate over a network. With e-mail, you have to type the message or letter, send it, and wait for a reply. It is often necessary to communicate in real time with another user (like using a telephone). On most systems, you can use a UNIX utility to establish a communication link, by typing, to another user.

1. Try **talk**ing to a friend on another host. Type the following command:

talk *friend@host*

where *friend* is your friend's login id, and *host* is your friend's host name.

NOTE: *Some versions of UNIX don't have the* **talk** *command installed or may run a version of the program that is incompatible with yours. If your version of* **talk** *doesn't work to communicate with another system, ask your system administrator for more information about it.*

2. If your friend is not logged on, try another user, or try this command at another time. If your friend is logged on, the **talk**

command clears your screen and divides it into two parts. Meanwhile, your friend's terminal gets beeping messages like this:

```
Message from Talk_Daemon@host at 12:23 ...
talk: connection requested by login_id@host
talk: respond with: talk login_id@host
```

Once the connection is established, whatever you type will appear on the top half of your screen and the bottom half of your friend's screen, and vice-versa. It's just like talking on the telephone, except that you are typing instead of talking.

3. Either you or your friend can end the **talk** by pressing
   Ctrl - c

The general form of the **talk** command line is

talk *user@host*

Notice that the *user@host* address argument for **talk** is exactly the same as for **mail** and **finger**. This address tells the network software where the person is logged on. When you want to **talk**, it does the same as when you want to use **finger** or **mail**.

■ Review 1

1. What command displays the names of the hosts on your local network?
2. What is the main difference between the **rwho** and **finger** commands?
3. How would you send mail to the user *strawberry* whose account is on the host *red*?
4. What do you do to leave **talk**?

20.4

Accessing an Account on Another System

Before continuing with this chapter, ask your system administrator if you have access to an account on any other hosts besides the one you normally use. If the answer is no, find out if you can get one. Be sure you know the host name, the login id, and the password of the new account that you are allowed to access.

By having access to more than one account, you have access to another system that may not be as busy as your normal system. This can improve your productivity during high-usage periods.

Logging On to a Remote System

You can log on to an account on another system (the *remote host*) from your account (the *local account*), by using the **rlogin** utility.

1. Request a logon to a remote host by typing

   rlogin *host_name*

   If the remote host machine is up and running, after a short wait the host replies with the following prompt:

   ```
   Password:
   ```

   Notice that the system doesn't ask you for the login id, because **rlogin** assumes that the account you are logging on to has the same login id as your local account.

2. If the account you are attempting to use does have the same login id as your local account, enter the password. At this point you can proceed with your task.

3. If the account you are logging on to has a different login id, press

   [Return]

The system now prompts you with

```
Login:
```

4. Enter the correct login id and then the password, just as you would if you were logging on to the host directly.

Note that you can also log on to another account by using the **-l** option of **rlogin**, using the syntax

rlogin *host_name* **-l** *login_id*

where *login_id* is the login id of the account you are accessing.

Executing Commands on a Remote System

Now that you are logged on to an account on a remote host, you can execute commands just as if you were on your own local host.

1. Create or modify a file called *kilroy_was_here* in your home directory with the **vi** editor. Add some text to the file.

2. Now **write** and **quit** the file.

3. Determine the name of your remote host, by entering

   hostname

4. List the files in the directory */tmp*.

   ls */tmp*

   You are connected to a different host that has its own name and its own */tmp* directory, which is different from your local system.

5. Use an editor to create a file in the remote host's */tmp* containing the following lines:

   ```
   This file was created on _____
   machine while rlogged in from _____ machine
   ```

6. Write the file and quit the editor.

Logging Out at the Remote System

Now that you have finished using this other account, you need to log out.
To log out from an account on a remote host, go through the same process
that you would use if you were logging out from your local account.

1. Log out from the other account.

   logout

2. Press **pwd** to confirm that you are back at your local host.

3. Request the name of your host by entering

   hostname

4. Check the */tmp* directory to see that the file *kilroy-was-here* is not
   on this host. It is on the one you remotely logged into.

Connecting to a Remote System
Using telnet

Many systems do not allow **rlogin** connections. You can also log on to a
remote system by using the **telnet** utility. This command uses a slightly
different method of connecting to the remote host. For now, use **telnet**
to connect the same remote system that you accessed in the preceding
section.

1. Type the following command:

   telnet *host_name*

   where *host_name* is the name of the remote system.

2. The output that appears will be something similar to the
   following. Notice the message is similar to a "normal" login
   prompt, as opposed to the one used for **rlogin**.

   ```
   Trying...
   Connected to machine_name.
   Escape character is '^]'.
   ```

```
Machine-OS Release X.X (machine_name)

login:
```

3. Enter the account login and password when prompted for it. You'll be connected to the remote machine just as you are when using the **rlogin** command.

4. Request the host's name by entering

   hostname

5. Run several other standard commands on the remote system.

6. Exit from the remote system by typing one of the following:

   exit
   Ctrl-d
   logout

20.5

Copying Files from a Remote Host

The **ftp** interactive copying program enables you to copy files between accounts over a network.

1. Start up **ftp** by typing

   ftp

   You get a prompt that looks like this:

   ```
   ftp>
   ```

   which tells you that you are in the **ftp** program and can execute **ftp** commands.

2. Find out what **ftp** commands are available by typing

   help

3. There are many **ftp** commands, but you will only need to know a few of them to copy normal files. If you want to get a short synopsis of an **ftp** command, type

help *command_name*

where *command_name* is the name of one of the **ftp** commands listed.

Logging On

Before you can use **ftp** to copy files between your account and a remote account, you need to log on or connect to the remote host.

1. Log on to the remote host that you have been using so far in these exercises.

open *hostname*

where *hostname* is the name of the remote host. The **open** command tells **ftp** to open a connection between your host and the specified remote host.

2. Enter the account name and password. These tell **ftp** what account you want to access.

*NOTE: Logging on with **ftp** is not the same as using **rlogin**. Although you are connected to the remote host, you cannot execute shell commands on the remote host. You can only execute **ftp** commands.*

Finding Out What Files You Can Copy

Before you can copy a file using **ftp**, you need to know what files you can copy.

1. Get a list of files by typing

ls

The screen displays a single-column listing of all files in the home directory of the remote account.

Within the **ftp** utility, the command **ls** is exactly the same as the **ls** UNIX shell command, except that the **ftp** version doesn't have any options.

Copying a File from a Remote Host

Files that exist on a remote host can be copied to the local host using **ftp**.

1. Pick a file on the remote account. Copy the file by typing this command:

   get *filename*

   where *filename* is the name of the file you are **get**ting from the remote host. The **get** command copies files *from* the remote account *into* your account.

   If **ftp** does not copy the file, you may have to tell **ftp** you want to transfer in ascii format. At the **ftp** prompt, enter

   ascii

   and enter the **get** *filename* command again.

2. To make sure that the file has been copied, type

   !ls

   You get a listing of all the files in your current directory on your local host account.

   The **!** command tells **ftp** that you want to run a shell command (**ls**) on your local host.

3. You can also specify the filename you want to give the copy after it is transferred. Choose another file stored on the remote account. Then copy it and give it a new name, by typing

   get *filename filename.copy*

   where *filename* is the name of the file you are copying from the remote host, and *filename.copy* is the name you want to give the copy on your local host.

4. Now check what files are listed in your account.

!ls

The file *filename.copy* is in the listing on the local host.

In general, to copy a remote file with **ftp,** you type a **get** command in the following format:

get *remote_original local_copy*

where *remote_original* is the name of the file you want to copy, and *local_copy* is the name you want to call the copy.

Putting Copies into an Account on a Remote Host

You have just used the **get** command to copy files from a remote host into your local host account. You can also use **ftp** to copy files from your local account into a remote account.

1. Choose a file on your local account to copy over to the remote account. Copy it by typing

   put *filename filename.copy*

   where *filename* is the name of the file on your local host that you want to copy, and *filename.copy* is the name you want to give the copy on the remote host. The **put** command copies files *from* your account *into* the remote account.

2. Check that the copy was made. Type

   ls

   This time you get a list of all the files in the home directory of the remote host; notice that the copy has been added.

In general, to use **ftp** to copy a file from your local host account to a remote host account, you type a **put** command in the following format:

put *local_original remote_copy*

where *local_original* is the name of the original file in your account, and *remote_copy* is the name you want to call the copy in the remote host account.

Changing Directories in a Remote Account

Other users have their own directory scheme for managing their files. When you're looking for files to copy, you'll often need to change directories to find the file.

1. Move to the parent directory of the remote account by typing

   cd ..

   The **ftp** command **cd** *directory_name* allows you to change directories on the remote host.

2. Just as on your account, you sometimes need to know the path to the current directory. Type

   pwd

   The output of the **ftp** command, **pwd** is the path to the remote account. In **ftp**, the **pwd** command works exactly as it does with the shell.

Now that you know how to move around remote directories and find out what directory you are in, you can explore the directories on the remote account and copy files into your account.

Logging Out of ftp

Eventually, you will want to leave **ftp**.

1. Type the following command to leave **ftp**:

   bye

   You are now back in the shell on your local host. The **bye** command tells **ftp** to close the connection to the remote host and return to your regular shell.

There are many other **ftp** commands that you will find helpful. You can use the **help** command in **ftp** to investigate these further.

Review 2

1. How would you log on from your account to the account *vanilla* on the host *shake*?

2. What command would you enter to copy the file *television* from your account to the remote account *green* on the host *grass*, naming the copy *radio*?

Conclusion

In this chapter you established connections on the local network to send e-mail, obtain information about users on remote hosts, and transfer files. By using the network, you can boost your resources and your productivity.

Answers to Review 1

1. **ruptime**

2. **rwho** displays all users on every host connected to the network, and **finger** displays users according to host or for a specific host.

3. **mail** *strawberry@red*

4. Press Ctrl-c.

Answers to Review 2

1. **rlogin** *shake* **-l** *vanilla*

2. **ftp** to host *grass*; log on as *green*; enter **put** *television radio*

COMMAND SUMMARY

Commands for Communicating on a Network

ruptime	Displays the status of all hosts on the local network.
rwho	Displays a list of users logged on to hosts on the local network.
finger @ *host_name*	Displays all users logged on to the host named *host_name*.
finger *user@* *host_name*	Displays when *user* last logged on to the host named *host_name*.
mail *login_id@* *host_name*	Sends e-mail to the user with login id *login_id* whose account is on the host named *host_name*.
talk *login_id@* *host_name*	Sends a **talk** request, which might or might not be answered, to the user with login id *login_id* whose account is on the host named *host_name*.
rlogin *host* **-l** *login_id*	Logs on to account with login id *login_id*, on the host named *host*.

ftp Commands

open *host*	Opens a connection between your account and the host named *host*.
help	Displays the list of available **ftp** commands.
help *command*	Displays a brief synopsis of the **ftp** command named *command*.

get *original* *copy* Copies the file *original* from the remote account into a file named *copy* on the local account.

put *original* *copy* Copies the file *original* from your local account into a file named *copy* on the remote account.

Chapter Twenty-One

Accessing Resources on the Internet

The Internet gets described in a variety of ways. Some observations are

- "Somewhat organized anarchy."

- "Possibly the greatest human achievement, it employs more human effort, connects more people, and breaks more barriers than anything else in our history."

- "It is the thing more people know nothing about than anything else."

- "It is the biggest waste of time ever inflicted on people."

- "My window to the world."

The Internet is a series of connections among computers that allow individual users to access other computers or other users essentially anywhere in the world. On the Internet, daily reports and personal mail from a conference in China can be read by colleagues in California, Italy, Russia, Malaysia, and India within minutes; or a student can request a copy of a report and have the first page ready to read within minutes.

This chapter explores making basic connections to other hosts on the Internet, communicating through e-mail to other users, using tools to locate information, accessing the Web, navigating through the net, and transferring information back to your system.

SKILLS CHECK: *Before beginning this chapter, you should be able to*

- *Log on and issue basic UNIX commands*

- *Use the X Windows graphical interface*

- *Issue basic commands to the shell*

- *Navigate around the file system*

OBJECTIVES: *After completing this chapter, you will be able to*

- *Describe the Internet and its origins*

- *Transfer files from a remote host on the Internet to your local host*

- *Identify hosts on the Internet by their full names*

- *Locate files available from anonymous servers*
- *Use electronic mail to subscribe to electronic mailing lists*
- *Access files and directories on remote Gopher servers*
- *Search many servers for files and directories that match a simple search string*
- *Access the World Wide Web using Lynx, Mosaic, and Netscape Navigator*

This chapter begins with a brief introduction to the development and structure of the Internet, followed by exercises in accessing a remote server and transferring files. You will then use the Internet to send mail. Fundamentally, the Internet is an access door to an unimaginable number of pages of information and comments about essentially any topic. Much of the programming and effort spent on the Internet is aimed at facilitating searches for appropriate information. Several search engines are examined and used in the next set of exercises. You can perform these activities without the X graphical interface. However, the last section examines interface programs that facilitate rapid searches and movement to sites, and seamless accessing of Internet facilities. These programs, called *browsers*, require a Windows interface.

21.1

Developing the Internet

Although the Internet is a relatively new communication phenomenon, much of the basic technology (used in computers, phone systems, data links, and even a limited Internet) has existed for many years. Improvements in hardware and software, and an astonishing increase in the number of connected computers, have pushed the Internet from research labs into the front office and front page.

The Internet's Origin

The Internet began as a network connecting computers located at United States Department of Defense facilities, laboratories of military contractors, and several large universities. The network was called the

ARPAnet, an acronym for **A**dvanced **R**esearch **P**rojects **A**dministration **net**work. The goal of the designers of the ARPAnet was to develop a robust, fault-tolerant network that would continue to function even if some sites were destroyed. The ARPAnet was considered successful because it allowed for two-way communication across the continent and would automatically reroute traffic around disabled sites or congested bottlenecks. Since most universities participated in defense research projects, the ARPAnet grew to connect virtually all colleges and universities in the United States.

The ARPAnet soon became an essential communications tool for thousands of people not really associated with the Department of Defense. The military users who were paying for the telephone lines and computers to conduct their communications consumed only a fraction of the computing power and network capacity of the ARPAnet. It was quiet much of the time. Students and faculty members' communications began to consume the idle time and network space. The web of campus networks connected by the ARPAnet became indispensable as a tool for collaboration of researchers, professors, and students. The technology that was developed for ARPAnet was used to build other, smaller independent networks, which were then connected to the ARPAnet. Local networks in private corporations that held defense contracts were connected to ARPAnet, allowing their employees to communicate to other hosts.

Organizations were formed to provide long-distance network services. These networks, with names like SURAnet (serving the southeastern U.S.), BARRnet (serving California), and UUNET (providing national, long-distance service) were connected to one another and to ARPAnet. This interconnection of networks, or *inter-net*works, is what we call the Internet.

The Department of Defense decided that the ARPAnet no longer met its research goals and decided to terminate funding of the project. Universities and laboratories protested, prompting the National Science Foundation to seek funding from Congress and assume responsibility for maintaining the ARPAnet, renaming it the NSFnet. Recently, a consortium of corporations called the Commercial Internet Xchange (CIX) assumed responsibility for what little administration is a part of

NSFnet. The U.S. government has ceased almost all direct funding of Internet services.

UNIX and the Internet

It is no accident that UNIX and the Internet are closely related. At the time that the ARPAnet project was started, most major universities across the U.S. had installed UNIX. Due to the ease of programming, relatively low cost, and widespread use, UNIX was the preferred research platform. ARPA researchers selected UNIX as the operating system for development of the ARPAnet and underlying software. Development of the networking software took place on UNIX systems. The Internet is largely a series of connections between UNIX machines and programs running on those systems.

Management of the Internet

There is no one agency, corporation, or group that controls the Internet. Because all industrialized countries of the world are now connected, central management of the Internet could be a political nightmare. The Internet grew in a spirit of community (or cooperative anarchy), and that approach is what keeps it running more or less smoothly.

A few organizations have evolved as clearinghouses to keep things as orderly as they are. When the National Science Foundation assumed the mantle of responsibility from ARPA, it created InterNIC, the **In-ter**net **N**etwork **I**nformation **C**enter. The InterNIC coordinates the assignment of unique network addresses so no two machines in the world have the same address. It also organizes top-level group or domain names (such as *.com* for commercial enterprises), which you will examine shortly. Network Information Centers from other countries cooperate with InterNIC in the management of network addresses and domain names.

The *Internet Society* is an international organization created to promote standardization of Internet technology and policies. It sponsors the Internet Architecture Board, the Internet Engineering Task Forces, and liaisons with international standards organizations to assist in the evolution, growth, and operation of the Internet infrastructure.

The Internet is a cooperative, self-policing network of networks of computers—ultimately, of users on those computers. The remainder of this chapter is a guided tour of the features and resources of the Internet.

21.2

Transferring Files from Remote Hosts

In a previous chapter, you used the **ftp** utility on a local area network (LAN) to transfer files from one host to another. In this section, you will transfer files from hosts outside of your LAN to your home directory using the same program. Many machines or hosts on the Internet allow any user who wishes to log on using **ftp** to copy files from their FTP archives back to their local systems.

Selecting an FTP Server

One Internet FTP site is often so popular that it cannot accommodate all of the requests from around the world. To accommodate more requests, other FTP site administrators volunteer some of their resources to share the burden, creating a "mirror" of the overburdened FTP archive on their own host. These mirror FTP sites are important, not just because they allow more simultaneous access to the same files, but because a mirror site is often closer to your physical location, and hence faster to access, than the original FTP site.

One popular FTP site is *rtfm.mit.edu*, long an authoritative repository for files called Frequently Asked Questions (FAQs) on various topics. In the following series of steps, you may be unable to connect to *rtfm.mit.edu* because it is sometimes overloaded. If so, select one of the mirror sites listed in the following table.

Continent	FTP Mirror Site	Directory
North America	*ftp.uu.net*	*Iusenet/news.answers*
	mirrors.aol.com	*Ipublrtfm/usenet*
	ftp.seas.gwu.edu	*Ipublrtfm*

Continent	FTP Mirror Site	Directory
Europe	*ftp.uni-paderborn.de*	*/pub/FAQ*
	ftp.Germany.EU.net	*/pub/newsarchive/news.answers*
	ftp.sunet.se	*/pub/usenet*
Asia	*znctuccca.edu.tw*	*/USENET/FAQ*
	hwarang.postech.ac.kr	*/pub/usenet/news.answers*
	ftp.hk.super.net	*/mirror/faqs*

Connecting to a Server

In the steps that follow, you may use one of the FTP sites listed above in place of the name *rtfm.mit.edu*.

1. Initiate an FTP session to the FTP server.

   ftp *rtfm.mit.edu*

   A connection message similar to the following is displayed.

   ```
   Connected to BLOOM-PICAYUNE.MIT.EDU.
   220 rtfm ftpd (wu-2.4(34) with built-in ls);
   bugs to ftp-bugs @rtfm.mit.edu
   Name (rtfm.mit.edu:brian):
   ```

   Notice that the first line says "BLOOM-PICAYUNE.MIT.EDU." This is just a second name by which *rtfm.mit.edu* is known.

2. The last line is a prompt to identify yourself. Instead of your user name, log in by entering

   ftp

   or

   anonymous

   If anonymous access to the server is permitted, you will get another prompt:

```
331 Guest login ok,
send your complete e-mail address as password.
Password:
```

3. At this prompt, enter your e-mail address consisting of your *login* followed by the @ and then your *hostname*. For example,

brian@cybernaut.com

Type carefully. It is easy to make errors, because the characters are not echoed back to you as you type.

A message confirming that you are granted access is displayed:

```
230 Guest login ok, access restrictions apply.
ftp>
```

The last line is the standard FTP command prompt.

Navigating Around the Remote Host

Just as you can change directories on your local host, you can ask **ftp** to issue the proper commands to change directories at the FTP host.

1. Change directories by entering the following. (On mirror sites, you have to substitute a slightly different path. See the table in the preceding section, "Selecting an FTP Server.")

cd */pub/usenet/news.answers/mail*

After the remote host has completed the change of directories, it will send you the following message and prompt you for your next command:

```
250 CWD command successful.
ftp>
```

2. Get a listing of the current directory on the remote host by entering

ls

Your results should resemble

```
200 PORT command successful.
150 Opening ascii mode data connection for /bin/ls.
total 239
drwxrwxr-x  2  8726  3    512  Jan 2 01:03   archive-servers
drwxrwxr-x  2  root  3    512  Dec 19 01:11  college-email
-rw-rw-r—  16  root  3  31795  Dec 30 00:42  country-codes
-rw-rw-r—   4  root  3  49952  Apr 29 1995   filtering-faq
-rw-rw-r—  14  root  3  34266  Dec 22 00:47  inter-net-guide
drwxrwxr-x  2  root  3    512  Dec 26 00:52  list-admin
-rw-rw-r—   6  root  3  11934  Dec 6 06:15   mailclient-faq
drwxrwxr-x  2  root  3    512  Dec 8 07:55   mailing-lists
226 Transfer complete.
ftp>
```

3. Change to the *mailing-lists* directory.

   cd *mailing-lists*

   If all is well, the following is displayed:

   ```
   250 CWD command successful.
   ftp>
   ```

4. List the directory contents.

   ls

   The directory listing is a long listing of the files in the current directory on the remote host. The files in this directory are a mailing list broken into 17 parts. On some mirror sites, the files are compressed and have a *Z* or *.gz* extension.

5. Set the file transfer mode to binary. (This is optional if the files are not compressed.) At the ftp> prompt, enter

   binary

   FTP replies with

   ```
   200 Type set to I.
   ```

6. Transfer the first part of the list by entering

   get *part01*

   If using a mirror site that compresses the files, substitute the corresponding filename. Depending on the speed of the network connections between you and the FTP site, the transfer may take several seconds or minutes.

7. After the transfer is complete, exit from FTP by entering

   bye

   You may receive a farewell message:

   ```
   221 WU ftpd exiting.
   Good night and have a pleasant tomorrow.
   ```

8. List the files in your current directory:

   ls

   You should have one file that you just transferred from the FTP site.
       If the filename has an extension such as *.Z* or *.gz*, it is compressed. Use the **uncompress** utility to decompress those files with the *.Z* extension. The GNU **gunzip** utility can decompress either the *Z* or *.gz* files.

9. If it is compressed, decompress it with the **uncompress** or **gunzip** utilities.

   uncompress *part01.Z*

   or

   gunzip *part01.gz*

10. Examine the file contents:

    more *part01*

The file has contents like the following:

```
Newsgroups: news.lists,news.answers

Path:

senator-bedfellow.mit.edu!bloom-beacon.mit.edu!newsxfer.itd.umich.edu!news

ucla.edu!newsfeed.internetmci.com!swrinde!news.uh.edu!bonkers.taronga.com!arielle

From: arielle@taronga.com (Stephanie da Silva)

Subject: Publicly Accessible Mailing Lists, Part 01/21

Approved: arielle@taronga.com

Archive-name: mail/mailing-lists/part01

Previous-maintainer: spaf@purdue.edu (Gene Spafford)

Last-change: 25 November 1995 by arielle@taronga.com (Stephanie da Silva)


[This is the first of twenty-one articles on mailing lists.]


Quick Summary of Changes

-----------------------


Added since last list:

    ALZHEIMER          Art Comics Daily          Border Collie

    Boston             CE                        The City Discussion

    The City Updates                             CLASS-ADS

                       DMC-News                  Easton, Sheena

    EMF-L              Excel Telecommunication

    Gargoyles          Guiding Light Discussion  Guiding Light Updates

    Hawaii NewsList    HOUDINI                   INKLINGS
```

The first 20 or so lines are a header used by the USENET news service on the Internet, where this file was first posted. The remainder is the first part of the mailing list.

11. Quit **more** with the command

    q

    You have logged on to a remote host, changed directories, located a file, and transferred the file back to your account. This file is used later in the discussion on mailing lists.

21.3

Naming Internet Hosts

In the preceding section, you saw names of FTP sites, such as *rtfm.mit.edu* and *ftp.uu.net*. Each aspect of the name has meaning, which makes it possible to locate the machine on the Internet.

One of the challenges of connecting a world of computers together is being able to identify each host uniquely from all other hosts. In the United States, each person is uniquely identified by his or her social security number. On the Internet, each host is identified by a unique address, called an IP address. InterNIC assigns unique IP addresses. IP addresses are often represented as four numbers, separated by periods, such as *204.75.208.10*. Every machine on the Internet has an address like this. Your host machine keeps a file of the addresses of other machines it contacts directly.

1. Examine the *hosts* file on your system by entering

   more */etc/hosts*

   The file contains information about the hosts that your system contacts. The file contains a name and the IP address for each host.

When you want to access another machine, both the IP address and the name are acceptable ways to identify the host. It is easier to remember names than IP addresses, so most humans specify target hosts by employing the name. When you refer to a host by its name, computer software translates the name into a corresponding IP address by checking the host's file or other network services that provide translations.

Grouping Hosts into Domains

Each host has a name that must be guaranteed to be unique. In a small, isolated network, this is simple—just keep a list somewhere. In a world of millions of connected computers, the short-list solution won't work. The list would become impossible to maintain and share among all computers in the world, and it would become virtually impossible to distinguish a host named *snoopy* at Otterbein College in Ohio from another host named *snoopy* at the University of California at Berkeley.

To solve both of these problems, *domain names* were developed. The InterNIC grants a site a unique domain name such as *berkeley.edu* or *muster.com* or *nasa.gov*. At each site, the network administrators are permitted to name hosts anything they want, providing the host name includes the domain name the site was granted by the InterNIC. As an example, a host named *snoopy* at UC Berkeley has a full name of *snoopy.berkeley.edu*. The domain name *berkeley.edu* is assigned to UC Berkeley by the InterNIC, and it is in the top-level domain *edu*, which is used for *edu*cational institutions. Similarly, *snoopy* at Otterbein College has a full name of *snoopy.otterbein.edu* which makes it unique. On the Internet, there are hundreds of hosts named *snoopy*, but each is guaranteed to be unique worldwide because each domain is uniquely assigned.

Locating One Host Among the Host of Hosts

The issue of uniqueness for machines is solved by using IP addresses and domain names. Given the name of a host you want to reach, how do you find it? To solve this problem, a set of programs called the *Domain Name Service* was developed.

Each domain, such as *berkeley.edu*, is required by the InterNIC to maintain at least two servers, called *name servers*, that each keep a list of the host names and IP addresses for the hosts within its domain. For example, NASA, the National Aeronautics and Space Administration, has a name server called *ns.nasa.gov*, which maintains a list of many of the hosts throughout the NASA offices, laboratories, and research centers around the world.

However, even NASA is too large to keep one list of all of its Internet hosts. The domain *nasa.gov* is further divided into subdomains, each of which has its own name servers. For instance, the NASA Ames Research Center in California has its own name server, *ns.arc.nasa.gov*, which maintains the IP addresses and names for all the hosts associated with the Ames Research Center.

Contacting a Name Server

Your machine is on the Internet. It knows about many hosts. It cannot possibly have access to the addresses of all the systems in the world.

1. A utility is available that asks name servers for information about its hosts. Look up the address of the Ames FTP server by entering

   nslookup *ftp.arc.nasa.gov*

   After a few seconds, you should get a reply like

   ```
   Server:    odin.community.net
   Address:   140.174.119.10
   Name:      sage.arc.nasa.gov
   Address:   128.102.194.144
   Aliases:   ftp.arc.nasa.gov
   ```

   This reply indicates that the host *ftp.arc.nasa.gov* is an alias for the *sage.arc.nasa.gov* machine.

The events that happen following your entering the **nslookup** command depend on what server you are attempting to locate. In this case, the events are as follows:

- The request for the address is passed to the name server of your local domain.

- The local name server on your network probably didn't have the answer, so it gave **nslookup** the address of one of the several name servers maintained by the InterNIC (called *root name server*).

- The root name server probably pleaded ignorance about *ftp.arc.nasa.gov*, but referred your **nslookup** process to the name server *ns.nasa.gov*, which maintains information about all *nasa.gov* hosts that are name servers.

- The name server *ns.nasa.gov* probably didn't have the answer either, but referred **nslookup** to the Ames Research Center (*arc*), name server, called *ns.arc.nasa.gov*.

- Finally, *ns.arc.nasa.gov* replies to **nslookup** with the answer, which is displayed.

As long as things function well, users are not told that name servers are doing all the search and identify work. Without host names, IP addresses, and name servers, your network would just be the hosts in your local network. With those facilities you have a way to access the whole net.

Sending Mail Across the Internet

The way e-mail is sent to the correct host illustrates how domain names are used. To send mail to a friend with a login of *friend-login* on your local host, you enter

mail *friend-login*

Your friend has a login id that is unique on the local host, so only your friend receives mail addressed to *friend-login*. Your local mail program can handle that level of complexity.

On a small local network, you may have to enter the name of the machine as well (though some e-mail configurations may do this automatically):

mail *friend@remote-host*

Across the Internet, you could specify the domain name with the host name through which your friend receives e-mail.

mail *friend@very-remote-host.subdomain.top-domain*

In practice, however, most mail is sent to a domain name, such as

*john@muster.***com**

or

*cassy@arc.nasa.***gov**

The name server at the remote domain gives the address of the host that accepts mail for the domain. This way the details of an organization's internal network are hidden from view, not so much because outsiders shouldn't know about it, but so they need not remember it.

Overview of Top-Level Domains

There are many domains in the top level in addition to the *.edu, .com,* and *.gov* seen so far.

Top-Level Domain	Description
com	Commercial enterprises
edu	Educational institutions
gov	Governmental agencies
mil	U.S. military
net	Internet infrastructure organizations
org	Noncommercial, nongovernmental organizations

These organizational domains were developed before the Internet went global, so are traditionally limited to U.S. organizations. With the explosive growth of the Internet worldwide, another set of domain names was developed based on geography.

Top-Level Domain	Description
au	Australia
us	United States
ca	Canada
uk	United Kingdom
de	Germany (Deutschland)
tw	Taiwan
jp	Japan

Within each country, the local Network Information Center (NIC) abides by its own domain name scheme. In the U.S., a domain called "The Well" is *well.sf.ca.us*, indicating that it is in (or near) San Francisco,

California, in the United States. In Taiwan, domain names are modeled after the original U.S. domain names, such as *moevax.edu.tw,* which is the Ministry of Education DEC/VAX computer in Taipei, Taiwan.

With this domain name scheme, it is possible to represent all Internet host names in a hierarchical map very much like files and directories, where domains are directories (and can have subdomains just as directories can have subdirectories) and hosts (files) reside within those domains (directories). Figure 21-1 depicts such an organization of hosts.

21.4

Locating FTP Resources with Archie

It is one thing to be able to transfer a file like one of the mailing-list files on *rtfm.mit.edu* to your home directory, but with the thousands of FTP servers available, how can you locate FTP servers that have files of interest to you? One tool designed to help is *Archie,* which maintains a list of

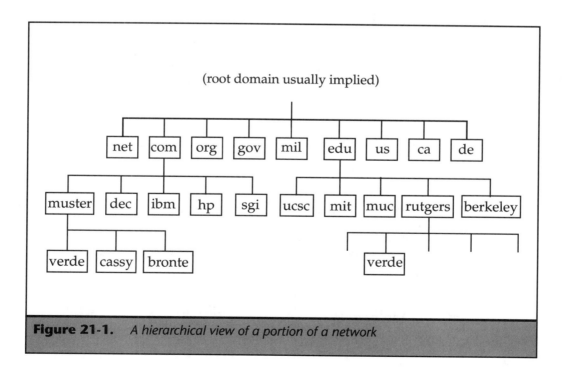

Figure 21-1. *A hierarchical view of a portion of a network*

FTP sites and files that they provide. The name probably is related to *archive,* but it is not clear where the name originates.

The Archie servers are able to provide information about the files available on FTP sites because the Archie servers run processes that skulk about the Internet in the wee hours of the morning (when network traffic is low) and automatically log on to anonymous FTP servers around the world. They issue one **ls -lR** command to get a recursive, long listing of the files available from that server. The retrieved information is placed in a database on the Archie server that can be searched. Archie client programs search the database of filenames when users make a search request.

Archie can be used in one of two ways: through an Archie client installed on your local host, or by using **telnet** to log on to a public access Archie host and issuing a search.

1. Ask Archie to launch a simple search through its database looking for the string *mailing-list* by entering the following:

   archie *mailing-list*

   If Archie is not available, you are told. If you made an error, an error message is displayed. If all went well, after a few seconds or minutes results should appear in the following format:

```
Host brolga.cc.uq.oz.au
   Location: /pub/reve
   DIRECTORY drwxr-xr-x 512 Jun 28 1991 mailing-list

Host software.watson.ibm.com
   Location: /pub/mobile-ip
   FILE -rw-r-r- 187 Jul 5 1994 mailing-list
```

   The list continues, but you get the idea.

   Each entry identifies the Internet host name that is an anonymous FTP server, the path to the filename that matched your search string, and the long listing of the name that was found. For example, the host *software.watson.ibm.com* has a file *mailing-list* in the directory */pub/mobile-ip*. The file is 187 bytes long and was last updated July 5, 1994, at least according to this Archie's latest information.

Listing Archie Servers

In the above example, the Archie client has a built-in list of Archie servers to use for the search.

1. To list the servers your client knows about, enter

   archie -L

   The results should resemble

   ```
   Known archie servers:
           archie.ans.net (USA [NY])
           archie.rutgers.edu (USA [NJ])
           archie.sura.net (USA [MD])
           archie.unl.edu (USA [NE])
           archie.mcgill.ca (Canada)
           archie.funet.fi (Finland/Mainland Europe)
           archie.au (Australia)
           archie.doc.ic.ac.uk (Great Britain/Ireland)
           archie.wide.ad.jp (Japan)
           archie.ncu.edu.tw (Taiwan)
         * archie.sura.net is the default Archie server.
         * For the most up-to-date list, write to an Archie
           server and give it the command 'servers'.
   ```

2. You can specify an alternative server to search. Tell Archie to use a specific server for the same search string. Enter

   archie -h *archie.rutgers.edu mailing-list*

   In the next section, you will get a list of alternative Archie servers from a known server.

Employing Regular Expressions in a Search

You can also use search arguments that are more powerful than simple strings.

1. Have Archie search for names that match a regular expression pattern by entering the command

   archie -r *"mail.*list"*

   This regular expression pattern also matches *mail-list*, *mailing_list*, and any other string that starts with *mail* and ends with *list*.

Using Public Access Archie Servers

It is not always possible to use a local Archie client to access an Archie server. In such cases, an alternative is to use Telnet to log on to an Internet host that allows public access to Archie. A list of such servers is found appended to this chapter. In the steps below, substitute an Archie server geographically near you in place of *archie.sura.net*.

1. At the shell prompt, enter the command

   telnet *archie.sura.net*

   You should receive the reply

   ```
   Trying 192.239.16.130...
   Connected to kadath.sura.net.
   Escape character is '^]'.

   SunOS UNIX (kadath.sura.net)

   login:
   ```

2. You do not have an account on this machine, but it accepts anyone who logs on as *archie*. At the login prompt, enter

   archie

   You receive a welcome message followed by an archie> prompt indicating that you are in an interactive Archie session.

3. At the Archie prompt, enter the command

   find *mailing-list*

   Archie responds with a confirmation that the search is underway and provides an estimated time to completion. This is followed eventually by a list of servers and files. Several pages of output scroll by, ending with the archie> command prompt.

For each host in the listing, the time of last update is reported, indicating the time the FTP server was last checked by this Archie server. Servers that have not been visited in awhile may no longer have the indicated file. The server may not even exist anymore.

Permitting Regular Expressions in Searches

Archie also reported that your search type was *sub*, meaning *substring*. While the *sub* is **set**, you can only search using character strings.

1. At the Archie prompt, set the search type to regular expressions with the command

   set *search regex*

2. Launch a more general search using a regular expression pattern:

   find *mail.*list*

   Archie responds with a summary of several pages in response to the search request, probably slightly more than the substring search found.

Identifying Related Servers

The Archie server you contacted maintains a list of other Archie servers.

1. Get a list of other servers known to this one with the command

   servers

The results should resemble the list at the end of this chapter. Interactive Archie also supports many other commands to fine-tune your search.

2. A list of the commands supported by Archie can be requested. At the Archie prompt, enter

   help

3. Finally, exit the Archie server with the command

   exit

21.5

Subscribing to Mailing Lists

As simple and arcane as it is, text-based e-mail is still extensively used on the Internet to promote collaboration, cooperation, and commiseration among people with similar interests. People interested in a topic subscribe to a mailing list on that topic. Users post questions or opinions. Other users answer—and the whole interaction is sent to all subscribers. Literally thousands of mailing lists operate on the Internet.

Obtaining a List of Mailing Lists

In the first exercise in this section, you used **ftp** to transfer one part of an ever-growing list of mailing lists. In this section, you will subscribe to one or more mailing lists.

> *CAUTION: A word of warning, however: when you no longer need to receive information sent to all members of the mailing list, be sure to unsubscribe from it. Mailing list administrators are forever cursed with mail bouncing back from addresses that are no longer valid or are otherwise inaccessible.*

1. View the file *part01* that you transferred from *rtfm.mit.edu* (or a mirror site) earlier.

Each list is described by its title, a synopsis of its purpose, the name and e-mail address of the list administrator, and instructions to subscribe. Most of these lists allow anyone to subscribe automatically by sending the correct magic words to a program on the server that maintains the subscription list, called the list service *robot*. Some lists are private; subscribers are screened based on one or more criteria.

2. Select a mailing list that appeals to you and is open to all comers. If none appeal to you from *part01*, use **ftp** to retrieve more parts of the list of mailing lists.

Subscribing to a Mailing List

Two common methods for subscribing can be used, corresponding to the two mailing list robot software packages that are used to administer the lists. One rule is critical: Save the first few e-mail messages you receive from the mailing list and print them out on paper. Save them. They are important. They contain instructions for *unsubscribing* from the list, which proper "Netiquette" demands you do when you no longer want the list. If you ever change e-mail addresses, be sure to unsubscribe your old address and subscribe your new one.

1. Send an e-mail message to the list robot. ListServ robots typically use commands in the body of your e-mail message like

   subscribe *listname Harry Reed*

   where *listname* is the published name for the list you want to join. After the name of the mailing list is the subscriber's full, real name. Do not put any other information in the body of the message and do *not* use the subject line because the robot does not read the subject line. The mailing-list robot will extract your Internet e-mail address from the mail header information that arrives with your message. For this reason, you can only issue the subscription request when logged on to the host you want to receive the messages (though mail aliases and *~/.forward* files can redirect all incoming mail to other places).

2. Another type of list is maintained by a program named *Majordomo*. To subscribe to a Majordomo-operated list, send e-mail to the Majordomo robot with the following command in the body of the message:

   subscribe *listname*

   If you enter any information after the list name, you will likely confuse the robot. Again, Majordomo typically ignores the subject line of the message.

Soon you should receive one or more welcome messages from the robot or an explanation of why your request was denied. Again, the welcome messages are important. Don't lose them.

Interacting with Others on the Mailing List

Those welcome messages will also include the e-mail address to which you may send a message to have it broadcast to the subscribers on the list. However, you should spend some time in read-only mode, just browsing the incoming mail for awhile before you post a message to the list. It is not only the polite thing for "newbies" to do, but some group members take great offense at a newcomer violating implied or stated rules of conduct. Observe how postings are phrased, what kind of information and language is appropriate, and how others on the list respond. In a limited medium like ascii text, even the way a message is capitalized and punctuated has connotations.

Beware of subscribing to too many lists too fast. It is easy to subscribe to several lists in one day then return from a long weekend to find several hundred messages in your in box. Also, be sure to keep up with your incoming mail. If you congest the mail spool because you went on a sabbatical, you will not be popular with your local e-mail administrator.

1. After you have satisfied yourself with the wealth of information in your e-mail in box, unsubscribe from the list. You should

receive confirmation from the list robot when you have been successfully removed.

■ Review 1

1. In **ftp**, what is the command to get a listing of the current directory?

2. How do you change your transfer mode from ascii to binary to **ftp**?

3. How do you exit from the **ftp** program?

4. What is the command to search for the file *gzip.tar.Z* on the server *ftp.mla.com*?

5. How do you get a list of available commands at the archie> prompt?

21.6

■ Mining the Internet with Gopher

Archie is a useful tool, but it is limited. It only catalogs files and directories by their names. Hopefully, the names of the files and the directories in which they reside say something about the content. This cannot always be relied on, however, especially with the various ways that FTP site administrators abbreviate names.

Enter Gopher, a method of publishing search information on the Internet that is organized and searchable based on content. Developed at the University of Minnesota, the "Home of the Golden Gophers," Gopher was designed to present simplified access to files and indexed databases using easy-to-follow text menus. The computer science researchers at the University of Minnesota sought to create a user-friendly, uniform interface to the various department servers across campus. What worked across campus now works around the world. Gopher can deliver text and binary files, launch Telnet sessions, and access virtually any text-based information, including searchable databases such as library catalogs.

Calling the Default Gopher

Several Gopher client programs exist for both text-mode terminals and X graphical workstations. The features of Gopher clients are basically the same; however, they differ in details. For the following steps, the Gopher client developed by Camosun College is used, which may not be the one your system uses. Generally, it should work the same.

1. To launch Gopher and access whatever default Gopher server your system calls, enter the command

   gopher

   You may also specify a different Gopher server by including an argument on the command line. A brief list of other Gopher servers is found in the next section. Select a Gopher site and launch Gopher with the command

   gopher *gopher-server-name*

   where *gopher-server-name* is a Gopher server such as *panda.uiowa.edu*.

Using Public Access Gophers

If **gopher** is not available on your local host, you may **telnet** to one of the publicly available Gopher hosts from the following list:

Hostname	IP Address	Login	Area
consultant.micro.umn.edu	134.84.132.4	gopher	North America
ux1.cso.uiuc.edu	128.174.5.59	gopher	North America
sailor.lib.md.us	192.188.199	gopher	North America
panda.uiowa.edu	128.255.40.201	panda	North America
gopher.msu.edu	35.8.2.61	gopher	North America
gopher.ebone.net	192.36.125	gopher	Europe
gopher.sunet.se	192.36.125.10	gopher	Sweden

Hostname	IP Address	Login	Area
info.anu.edu.au	150.203.84.20	info	Australia
tolten.puc.cl	146.155.1.16	gopher	South America
ecnet.ec	157.100.45	gopher	Ecuador
gan.ncc.go.jp	160.190.10.1	gopher	Japan
gopher.th-darmstadt.de	130.83.55.75	gopher	Germany
hugin.ub2.lu.se	130.235.162.12	gopher	Sweden
gopher.uv.es	147.156.1.12	gopher	Spain
hugin.ub2.lu.se	130.235.162.12	gopher	Sweden
info.brad.ac.uk	143.53.2	gopher	United Kingdom

Select a host that is in your geographic region.

1. After you make a **telnet** connection to a Gopher host, you are asked to log on. Use the login name listed in the Login column in the table.

   One authoritative list of Gopher sites is maintained by the InterNIC.

Burrowing with Gopher

Once you have established either a default or Telnet Gopher connection, a display similar to the following appears.

```
Camosun College Gopher System
Default Gopher Server (gopher.camosun.bc.ca)

  1 <DIR> Camosun College
  2 <DIR> Camosun Wide Information Service (CWIS) Gopher
 12 <DIR> Weather/Travel/Accomodation Information
 13 <TEL> Victoria Freenet


[1-18], Help, Quit, =, Bookmarks, Save, List, Previous, Up, or Down:
```

The actual menu varies, depending on the default server your Gopher client accessed and the current resources available on that server.

The list consists of items that are mostly directories (lists) of yet other items, as indicated by the <DIR> label after the number. Items preceded with a <TEL> label launch Telnet sessions to a host. Other labels include <TXT> for text documents, <BIN> for binary files, and <IDX> for searchable indices.

1. Select an item of your choice by its number. For example, entering *12* (for the Weather/Travel/Accomodation Information item) leads to another menu:

```
Camosun College Gopher System
Weather/Travel/Accomodation Information (gopher.uvic.ca)


   1 <TXT> BC Weather: Coast (Environment Canada)

   2 <TXT> BC Weather: Marine Forecast

   3 <IDX> BC Accommodations (Victoria Freenet)

   4 <DIR> Canadian Weather Forecasts (Environment Canada)


[1-6], Help, Quit, =, Bookmarks, Save, List, Previous, Up, or Down:
```

Note that this page was provided by the Internet host *gopher.uvic.ca*, which is maintained by the University of Victoria. By selecting this item you obtain information from a different server.

2. From this menu, select item *3*.

This option produces a searchable index of accommodations in British Columbia (maintained by a group called Victoria Freenet).

```
Please enter your search criteria
   (you may use 'and' and 'or'):
```

3. Enter

bed and breakfast

The following results are displayed:

```
Searching...

Camosun College Gopher System

Index Search Results (freenet.victoria.bc.ca)

  1 <TXT> A B & C BED & BREAKFAST OF VANCOUVER

  2 <TXT> COPES' CHOICE BED & BREAKFAST ACCOMMODATIONS

  3 <TXT> TOWN AND COUNTRY BED & BREAKFAST IN BC

  .

  .

 14 <TXT> HIBERNIA BED AND BREAKFAST


[1-40], Help, Quit, =, Bookmarks, Save, List, Previous, Up, or Down:
```

4. Enter a *14* for Hibernia Bed and Breakfast. A description of the selected Bed and Breakfast is displayed.

    At this point, the text can be saved to a local file with the **S** command, mailed to an Internet e-mail address with the **M** command, or discarded by simply pressing ⎡Return⎤.

5. To return to the previous list, press ⎡Return⎤. The prompt at the bottom of the menu should resemble this:

```
[1-40], Help, Quit, =, Bookmarks, Save, List, Previous, Up, or Down:
```

6. To return to the previous list, enter

    P

7. To see a description of the item you are presently viewing, enter

    =

    In the above example, the list is described as follows:

```
Type:     DIR
Title:    Weather/Travel/Accomodation Information
Host:     gopher.uvic.ca
Port:     70
Selector: 1/weather
```

This text describes the type of information you are viewing, its title, the Internet host name of the server, and some information of interest to administrators who maintain Gopher services.

8. Exit from Gopher with the command

q

You are returned to your shell prompt.

Once you have successfully reached a Gopher server, you may navigate with simple text commands in response to the menus.

9. Select another Gopher site and examine its contents.

Searching Gopherspace with Veronica

While Gopher servers allow Internet sites to present information in a structured, navigable format, there is still so much information to wade through that finding the exact file item you want could require an enormous amount of patience and perseverance. To aid in the task of searching Gopher servers, Veronica was invented. Veronica is to Gopher as Archie is to FTP. Veronica skulks about Gopher servers at weird hours of the night, building a database of all of the Gopher directories that it finds.

Veronica servers are accessed from Gopher menus. With Veronica, you can search Gopher directories or all of "Gopherspace" for keywords, identifying Gopher sites of interest. Search criteria can include Boolean operators AND and OR to focus the search. Veronica servers can usually be found by connecting your Gopher client to *gopher.tc.umn.edu* and browsing from there.

1. User **gopher** to connect to a Veronica server and explore.

There is also a Gopher-based database called *Jughead*. The *Jughead* version searches only a well-defined subset of Gopherspace, such as "All Gopher servers at the University of Minnesota." Jughead indices look just like the output from Veronica, but the scope of the search is intentionally limited by the site administrator.

21.7

Browsing the World Wide Web Using a Character-Based Interface

The notion of presenting a variety of information resources using a common, uniform interface struck other people outside of the University of Minnesota. Researchers at the CERN European Laboratory for Particle Physics sought a user-friendly interface for exchanging files, reading and posting news, publishing research in progress, and viewing pages of documents. With these goals, they developed what became the World Wide Web.

Defining the Web

The idea was to create a user interface program called a *browser* that could access servers of various types, including FTP, Gopher, USENET newsgroups, and Telnet. In addition, they developed a way to present documents using *hypertext*, a structure facilitating in-context links to other resources. More types of information, including audio, video, still graphics, and "executable content," are still being incorporated into the Web.

The World Wide Web, or simply "The Web," is made up of all of Gopher, FTP, News, Telnet, and Hypertext servers on the Internet because Web user browsers can access all those kinds of servers. The servers you can access are limited only by the capabilities of your access program—your browser. Many browsers have been developed. Some are text based, others require a graphical interface. In the following section, you will examine a character-based browser: Lynx. Two graphical browsers are explored in the next two sections: NCSA Mosaic and Netscape Navigator.

Accessing a Remote Server with Lynx

Lynx is a text-based Web browser. Even though most Web browsers are graphical and can incorporate fine pictures in their presentation, graphic data is large and takes a long time to transfer across congested network links or slow serial connections to the Internet. Many users call on the text-based program Lynx when speed is more important than pictures.

In an earlier exercise, you transferred a file of mailing lists from *rtfm.mit.edu* or one of its mirror sites to your account.

Use the same site or another mirror site in the example that follows. Remember, it is usually faster to use a site that is in your geographic region, if possible.

1. Start up a Lynx session by entering

   lynx *ftp://rtfm.mit.edu/pub/usenet/news.answers*

   This command line passes an argument to Lynx that is a *Uniform Resource Locator*, or *URL*. URLs were developed early in the history of the Web to make names for information hosts or resources, well, uniform. This URL has three parts:

Command	Interpretation
ftp:	Because there are now several protocols in use on the Internet, you must specify to your browser which one you want. This calls for anonymous FTP. Others could be **gopher**, **http**, **archie**, etc.
//	The double slash indicates that the name that follows is an Internet host name. The browser will establish a connection to the host.
rtfm.mit.edu	The specified host name.
/pub/usenet/news.answers	This instruction resembles a directory path, which was the way URLs were originally defined. This is the absolute pathname to an object, as understood by the *rtfm.mit.edu* FTP *server*. In this case, the path is to a directory.

If you are using a mirror site, the absolute path may well be different. Refer to the table of mirror sites for *rtfm.mit.edu* in the section "Selecting an FTP Server," earlier in this chapter.

After Lynx has negotiated a connection with the FTP server at *rtfm.mit.edu*, it displays a listing of the directory as shown in Figure 21-2.

2. Browse down the list one page at a time by pressing the [Spacebar]. Stop when you find the directory *mail*, as shown here:

Examining Hypertext Links

The output from Lynx includes phrases and words displayed in reverse video or highlighted text. As you will soon see, when you select one of the highlighted objects you are connected to other parts of the FTP

```
                                              news.answers directory (p1 of 27)
                                  NEWS.ANSWERS

      Up to usenet

Jan  2 06:55    text/plain      .#index    255Kb
Jul 17 16:50    text/plain      .message    639 bytes
Dec 21 01:52    text/plain      1996-olympics-faq    20Kb
Apr 30  1995    Directory       386bsd-faq
Nov 29 01:23    Directory       3b1-faq
Nov 21  1994    Directory       3b2-faq
Dec  7 07:47    text/plain      3d-programmer-info    2Kb
Dec 14 16:53    text/plain      abdominal-training    25Kb
Dec  2 02:29    text/plain      acedb-faq    46Kb
Dec 21 05:43    Directory       acorn
Sep 26 06:45    Directory       active-newsgroups
Dec 10 03:26    text/plain      active-noise-control-faq    49Kb
Nov 15 07:43    text/plain      advertisers-blacklist    42Kb
Nov  4 01:34    Directory       african-faq
Dec  3 02:21    text/plain      afs-faq    111Kb
-- press space for next page --
  Arrow keys: Up and Down to move. Right to follow a link; Left to go back.
  H)elp O)ptions P)rint G)o M)ain screen Q)uit /=search [delete]=history list
```

Figure 21-2. *Output from Lynx*

archive or some other specific action is taken. It may be hard to find on your screen, but there is a cursor that you can move from one link to the next.

1. Use only the ⬆ or ⬇ keys or the Ⓚ and Ⓙ keys to move the cursor from link to link.

   Do not use the ⬅ or ➡ keys or the Ⓗ or Ⓛ keys; they will move you to different directories.

2. Place the cursor on the text *mail* on the screen and press ⟨Return⟩ or Ⓛ or the ➡ key. This is interpreted as instruction to take you to the *mail* directory, which looks like the output in Figure 21-3.

   If at times Lynx gives a message like

   ```
   Alert! Unable to access document
   ```

   it usually means that the FTP server is heavily loaded with many people accessing it. Repeat the attempt to access the directory. If

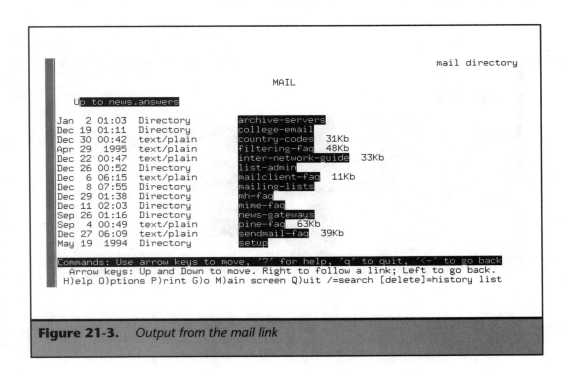

Figure 21-3. *Output from the mail link*

the problem persists, you may do well to quit from Lynx with the **q** command and either try again later or try another mirror site.

3. Place the cursor on the *mailing-lists* link and press Return again. Lynx displays the *mailing-lists* directory. See Figure 21-4.

Transferring a File with Lynx

In the first FTP section, at the beginning of this chapter, you transferred *part01* of this list of mailing lists. You will now use Lynx to transfer *part02*.

1. Use the ↑ or ↓ keys to place the cursor on the link *part02* and press Return. Lynx begins the file transfer.

   If you accessed a site that doesn't compress the files, Lynx transfers the file and displays it. Your screen resembles Figure 21-5.

2. This file is not saved to your directory, yet. To save it, enter

   P

   Lynx displays the Printing Options menu. See Figure 21-6.

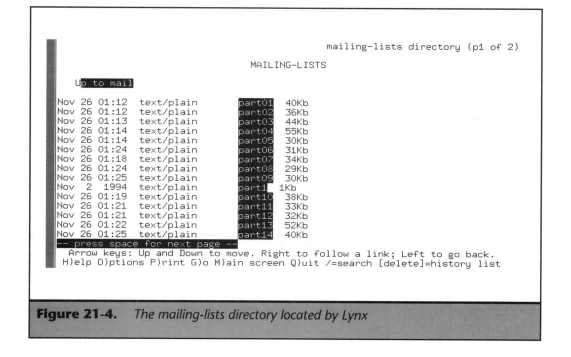

```
                                          mailing-lists directory (p1 of 2)
                                MAILING-LISTS

      Up to mail
Nov 26 01:12    text/plain       part01    40Kb
Nov 26 01:12    text/plain       part02    36Kb
Nov 26 01:13    text/plain       part03    44Kb
Nov 26 01:14    text/plain       part04    55Kb
Nov 26 01:14    text/plain       part05    30Kb
Nov 26 01:24    text/plain       part06    31Kb
Nov 26 01:18    text/plain       part07    34Kb
Nov 26 01:24    text/plain       part08    29Kb
Nov 26 01:25    text/plain       part09    30Kb
Nov  2  1994    text/plain       part1     1Kb
Nov 26 01:19    text/plain       part10    38Kb
Nov 26 01:21    text/plain       part11    33Kb
Nov 26 01:21    text/plain       part12    32Kb
Nov 26 01:22    text/plain       part13    52Kb
Nov 26 01:25    text/plain       part14    40Kb
-- press space for next page --
  Arrow keys: Up and Down to move. Right to follow a link; Left to go back.
  H)elp O)ptions P)rint G)o M)ain screen Q)uit /=search [delete]=history list
```

Figure 21-4. *The mailing-lists directory located by Lynx*

```
                                                                  (p1 of 57)
Newsgroups: news.lists,news.answers
Path: senator-bedfellow.mit.edu!bloom-beacon.mit.edu!newsxfer.itd.umich.edu!new
s.kreonet.re.kr!usenet.kornet.nm.kr!agate!news.ucdavis.edu!library.ucla.edu!inf
o.ucla.edu!newsfeed.internetmci.com!swrinde!news.uh.edu!bonkers.taronga.com!ari
elle
From: arielle@taronga.com (Stephanie da Silva)
Subject: Publicly Accessible Mailing Lists, Part 02/21
Approved: arielle@taronga.com
Followup-To: poster
Supersedes: <1995OctPt02@taronga.com>
Reply-To: arielle@taronga.com
Keywords: An-Az
Sender: arielle@bonkers.taronga.com (Stephanie da Silva)
Expires: Fri, 19 Jan 1996 00:00:01 GMT
Organization: Taronga Park BBS
Message-ID: <1995NovPt02@taronga.com>
References: <1995NovPt01@taronga.com>
Date: Sat, 25 Nov 1995 18:01:32 GMT
Summary: 1516 mailing lists in twenty-one postings
-- press space for next page --
  Arrow keys: Up and Down to move. Right to follow a link; Left to go back.
 H)elp O)ptions P)rint G)o M)ain screen Q)uit /=search [delete]=history list
```

Figure 21-5.   *File transfer output from Lynx*

```
                                                          Lynx Printing Options
                              PRINTING OPTIONS
   There are 1122 lines, or approximately 18 pages, to print.
   You have the following print choices
   please select one:

   Save to a local file

   Mail the file to yourself

   Print to the screen




 Commands: Use arrow keys to move, '?' for help, 'q' to quit, '<-' to go back
  Arrow keys: Up and Down to move. Right to follow a link; Left to go back.
 H)elp O)ptions P)rint G)o M)ain screen Q)uit /=search [delete]=history list
```

Figure 21-6.   *Printing options menu in Lynx*

3. The first item allows you to save the current document to a file. Press ⟨Return⟩ to select option one.

4. Lynx prompts you for a filename to use in your local directory. You may accept the default or assign your own.

5. To save the file press ⟨Return⟩.

Running a Command on the Local Host

You can tell your local Lynx program that you want to have access to a subshell to issue UNIX utilities.

1. Escape to a shell by entering

   !

   A shell prompt is displayed.

2. At the prompt verify that the file was saved by entering

   ls

3. To leave the shell and return to Lynx, enter

   exit

Changing Internet Sites Using Lynx

Lynx allow you to jump to another Internet site. At this moment you are at an FTP site, and have transferred a file with **ftp**. You can not only change sites, but you can change the type of site.

1. To go to another site, press

   g

   Lynx will prompt you for a new URL, Uniform Resource Locator.

2. To change to a different site, this time a Gopher site, enter

   gopher://*gopher.tc.umn.edu*

   or another site of your choice from the list of Gopher servers. This URL specifies the following:

Address Element	Interpretation
gopher:	Use the Gopher protocol.
//gopher.tc.umn.edu	Connect to the site shown after the double slash.

Lynx soon displays a list like Figure 21-7. This is the same list accessed by Gopher earlier in this chapter.

Exiting from Lynx

1. Practice navigating around cyberspace with Lynx and when you are ready to exit, enter

   q

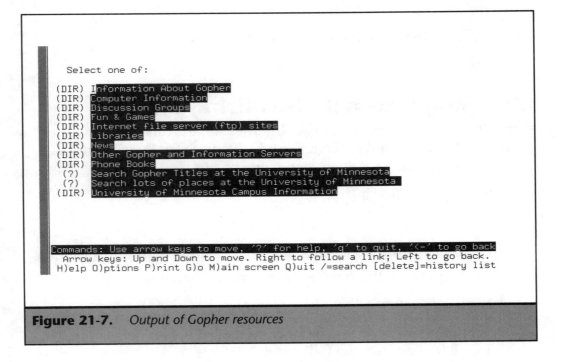

Figure 21-7. *Output of Gopher resources*

In the history of the Internet, simplified access tools like Gopher and Lynx were phenomenal improvements over groping in the dark with Telnet and FTP. Today, both Gopher and Lynx are used extensively from ascii terminals, and from graphical workstations when speed of data transmission is more important than the graphical interface or pictures.

21.8

Surfing on a Graphical Ocean of Information

With the growth of graphical user interfaces, point-and-click navigation became possible—and therefore necessary.

Getting Hyper About Text

The first major advance in ease of navigating was refinement of contextual links, or *hypertext*. When you read a book, you are often limited to starting at the front and reading the material one page after another, linearly, until you reach the back.

Along the way, the author may insert footnotes, endnotes, margin notes, and references to other works in the Bibliography. Readers often look at the footnotes, occasionally read some endnotes, but seldom go to the bibliography unless they are doing research.

With hypertext, information is organized into pages that allow for linear reading, but embedded in the pages are highlighted references to other resources available to the user. Rather than including a mere mention of the University of Illinois, an author can create a button or link in the text. If the reader chooses to activate the button, the program immediately jumps the reader to another page, located anywhere, that introduced various facets of the university. A reader can satisfy a curiosity, then jump back and continue with the original topic.

This ability breaks the mold of the linear book and allows authors to create collections of documents that could be linear, hierarchical, circular, or chaotic. More important, the author's ideas of the proper linear order can be countermanded by a reader who chooses an independent path. See Figure 21-8.

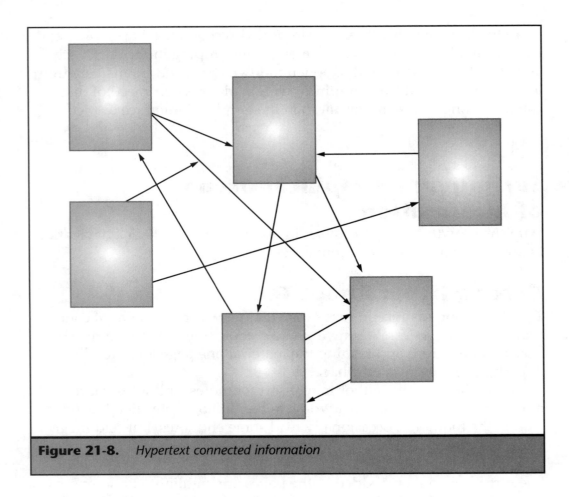

Figure 21-8. *Hypertext connected information*

Putting the Mosaic of Pieces Together

Once hypertext ideas were well developed and the graphical interface tools available, all it took was student energy to develop a graphical browser. For that, students at the University of Illinois, Urbana-Champaign, developed an improved Web browser, and named it Mosaic. To run Mosaic on UNIX, you must be using an X11 graphical workstation.

1. Start the Mosaic browser by entering the command

   mosaic &

Depending on how Mosaic is installed on your system, the command to start it may be **mosaic**, **Mosaic**, or **xmosaic**. If Mosaic is not found, try the other commands. The Mosaic client displays in a new window. See Figure 21-9.

The document, or Web page of Mosaic, that is first displayed is called the *home page* for your browser. You will have a chance to customize your browser to start with a home page of your choice.

Jumping to Another Server by Selecting Text

On a gray-scale screen, some text is underlined. On a color monitor the text is also displayed in a different color. Each of these underlined phrases is a link to another document. Often it is another Web page, but it could easily be a file on an FTP server, a Gopher resource, or even a

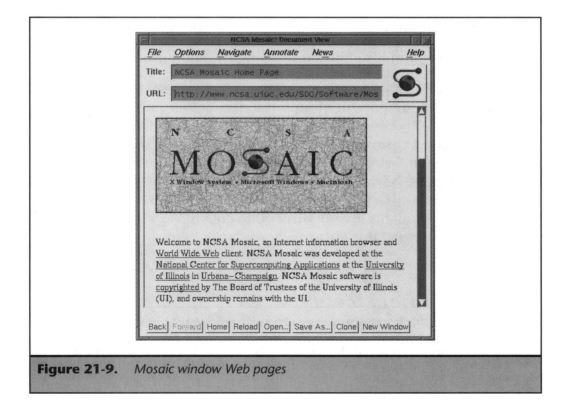

Figure 21-9.   *Mosaic window Web pages*

link to a database or other application. The links can be on any server, anywhere on the Internet.

1. Move your mouse pointer to the link *University of Illinois,* but do not click any buttons. Note what appears just between the Web page and the bottom row of buttons. It is the uniform resource locator information.

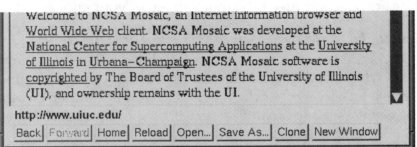

The URL **http://*www.uiuc.edu*/** is the Web server for the data that would be used concerning the University of Illinois.

2. Click on *University of Illinois* to see what happens.

Clicking on the underlined text instructs the browser to jump to the specified Web server, which transfers a default Web page to your browser since no other resources are specified. Mosaic contacts the server *www.uiuc.edu* using **http**, the **HyperText Transfer Protocol**. Mosaic requests the default Web page, which is transferred to your local host. Once the Web page is transferred, Mosaic displays it. See Figure 21-10.

The Web page is in a format called HTML (HyperText Markup Language). Such documents are not difficult to create. More information on HTML can be found at this URL:

http://*www.ncsa.uiuc.edu/General/Internet/WWW/HTMLPrimer.html*

Getting Help from Mosaic

This Web page can also be accessed from the Mosaic Help menu.

1. Open the Help menu by clicking on the word *Help* above the NCSA revolving earth logo. See Figure 21-11.

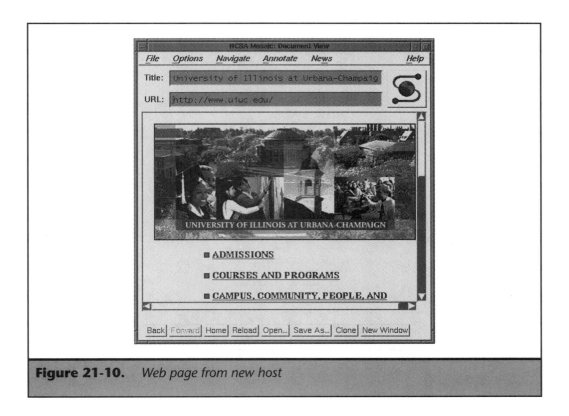

Figure 21-10. *Web page from new host*

A page of helpful information is displayed.

2. Select On HTML... from the menu. The *HTML Beginners Guide* is displayed. The text is in Hypertext format, permitting you to explore topics of interest.

3. Browse through *HTML Beginner's Guide.*

Navigating in Hypertext

After you have made several hypertext selections, you are deep into hyperspace...but where?

1. Navigation buttons are in the bottom row of the Mosaic window, on the left. To return to the previous location, click on the button labeled Back. This moves you back to the Web page preceding the page that is currently displayed.

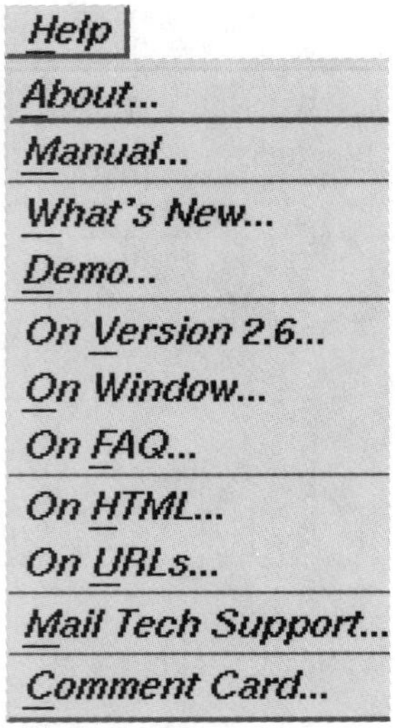

Figure 21-11. *Mosaic Help button*

Maintaining a List of Interesting Sites

The Mosaic browser maintains a list of sites you find interesting, called a *hotlist*.

1. To add the URL for this page to your Mosaic hotlist:

   a. Pull down the Navigate menu.

   b. Select the Add Current to Hotlist option

   The following illustration shows the menu for adding to the hotlist.

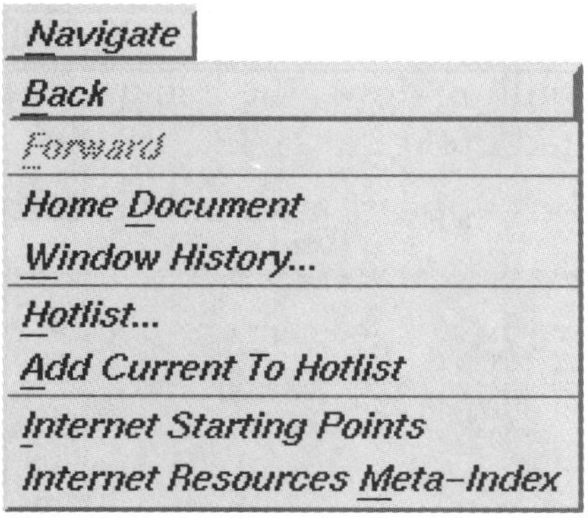

Navigate
Back
Forward
Home Document
Window History...
Hotlist...
Add Current To Hotlist
Internet Starting Points
Internet Resources Meta–Index

2. To access the hotlist, pull down the Navigate menu again and select Hotlist.

   A dialog box appears. See Figure 21-12.

3. At the Hotlist dialog box,

   a. Click once on the title of the Web page you just saved.

   b. Click the Go To button.

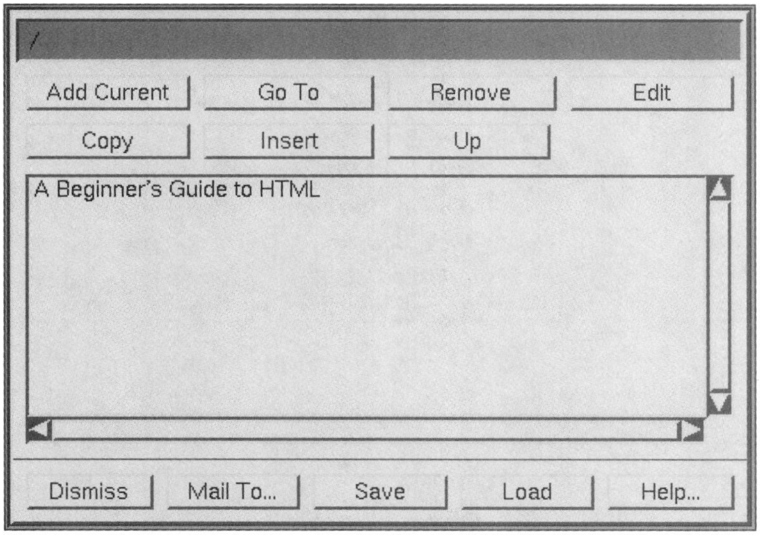

Add Current	Go To	Remove	Edit
Copy	Insert	Up	

A Beginner's Guide to HTML

| Dismiss | Mail To... | Save | Load | Help... |

Figure 21-12.   *Dialog box for accessing Hotlist*

Mosaic loads the selected Web page and displays it.

4. Exit Mosaic by pulling down the File menu and select Exit Program, depicted in Figure 21-13.

5. When a dialog box appears asking for confirmation, select Yes.

> Are you sure you want to exit NCSA Mosaic?
>
> Yes   No

Browsing with Netscape Navigator

Lynx and Mosaic were once the favored Web browsers for UNIX environments. Although used extensively, many sites now include Netscape

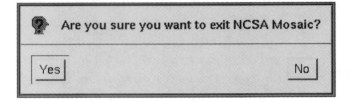

Figure 21-13. *File menu in Mosaic*

Navigator, designed by the same students who designed Mosaic, after they graduated from the University of Illinois.

Accessing Netscape

The Netscape user software is essentially free. If it is on your system, when you start Netscape, a window is launched.

1. Start the Netscape Navigator by entering

   netscape

   Surprise. The Netscape Navigator window that appears resembles that of Mosaic. See Figure 21-14.

   The appearance and use of hypertext links is very similar to Mosaic. However, the Back button is located just under the menu bar near the top of the window instead of at the bottom. The Hotlist of Mosaic is replaced by Bookmarks.

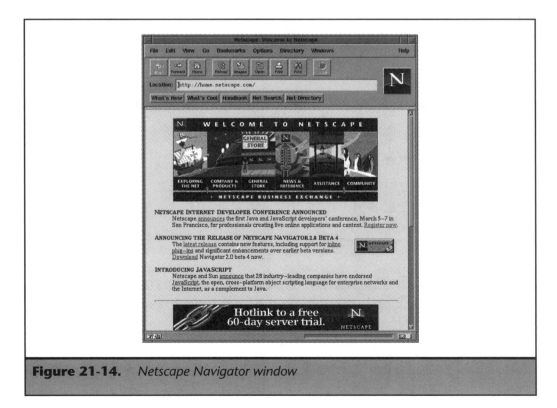

Figure 21-14. *Netscape Navigator window*

2. Experiment with some hypertext links in the text to confirm that Netscape Navigator is similar to Mosaic, but is a lot faster.

Quitting Netscape

If it was difficult getting Netscape up and running, skip this step until you are ready to exit.

1. When time or energy runs out, to quit from Netscape Navigator pull down the File menu and select Exit.

Changing Remote Hosts

When you start Netscape, you are jumped to a Netscape welcome or home page.

1. Start Netscape again. You can easily change sites.

2. To open a new URL, click on the Open tool button:

A dialog box appears.

3. In the Open Location dialog box, enter the following URL.

   http://www.yahoo.com

4. Click the Open button.

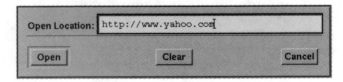

Searching Web Pages for Specific Information

The Web page that appears can be a starting point for searching the Web with purpose instead of aimlessly wandering from island to island in the sea of hypertext. The search engine for Web pages is called *Yahoo*. See Figure 21-15.

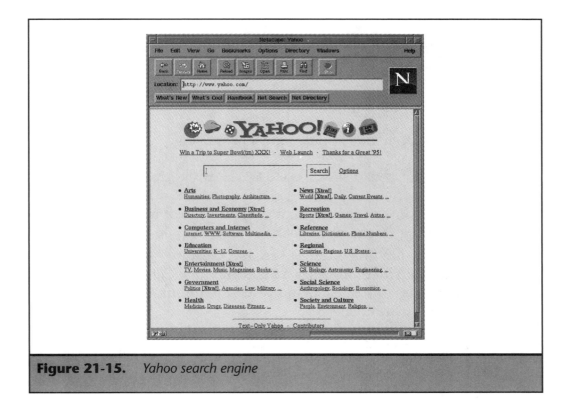

Figure 21-15.   *Yahoo search engine*

Yahoo provides a Web page indexing and search service for the Web community. The indexes are built not just from the title of the documents, as with Archie and Veronica, but from the content as well. Yahoo derives funding by selling advertising space in their Web pages, very much like the Yellow Pages. The remaining steps in this section use the Yahoo search service. The first task is to search for recipes for brewing beer.

1. In the text entry field next to the Search button, enter the search criteria

   brew

2. Click the Search button.

Your browser displays several links that contain references to brewing.

In this search, one appears most promising.

Entertainment:Drinks and Drinking: Alcoholic Drinks: Beer: Home**brewing**

3. Click on the link to see where it goes. A page of references to homebrewing resources appears.

4. Near the top is a link entitled *Recipes*. Select it.

    In the page that follows is a link called the *Cat's Meow 3*. Yahoo rates that as a "cool site," as indicated by the sunglasses in the following illustration.

- Bee's Lees, The – a collection of mead recipes
- Cats Meow 3 👓 – Largest and most diverse collection of beer recipes on the net
- Cock's Fine Brews – Recipes

5. Select the *Cat's Meow 3*.

6. From here, see if you can find a recipe for *oatmeal stout* or your favorite beer.

7. When you have explored as much as you want, return to the Yahoo main page.

8. Pull down the Go menu, which lists the titles to several sites you've visited during this session.

9. Select Yahoo. If you cannot find Yahoo under the Go menu, you can open the URL with the Open tool button. The URL is

    http://*www.yahoo.com*

The browser changes your connection to a new site. Examine the Yahoo title graphic. It changes from time to time. The example shown in this illustration is a picture of an *image map*. By clicking on certain parts of the picture, you activate specific URLs.

10. Click on the New part of the picture. Your browser goes to the newest Web pages listed in Yahoo's index.

11. Be sure to create a bookmark for each Web page you find interesting.

12. Click on the sunglasses to visit the really cool sites.

13. Gamble by clicking on the die. Clicking the die asks Yahoo to select a URL at random and connect your browser there.

14. Click on the Extra! newspaper. A page of news headlines from the Reuters news service is displayed.

15. Click on the information icon. The display is information about Yahoo.

    The Add URL picture allows you to contribute an entry to Yahoo's index.

Examining Other Search Engines

The Yahoo search mechanism is only one of several available with Netscape.

1. In the Netscape browser, click on the button labeled Searches. Several search engines are listed here and can be explored.

   The following search programs are available by accessing the site listed on the right.

Service Name	URL
Alta Vista	**http://*www.altavista.digital.com***
Inktomi	**http://*inktomi.berkeley.edu***
Lycos	**http://*www.lycos.com***
Open Text	**http://*www.opentext.com***
Webcrawler	**http://*webcrawler.com***
Yahoo	**http://*www.yahoo.com***

■ Review 2

1. What does the equal sign (=) do in **gopher**?

2. How do you escape to the shell in Lynx?

3. How do you exit Lynx?

4. In the following URL, state the protocol, server name, and filename:

http://*webcrawler.com/spider-surfer.gif*

Protocol: _____

Server name: _____

Filename: _____

■ Conclusion

The Internet is a collection of computers and communication links that provide you with information, mail connections, and computing resources. Two kinds of programs have been created to make accessing the Internet more productive—search engines and interface browsers. The most advanced browsers allow you to jump from site to site by clicking on hyperlinks, transfer files with point and click, search using a menu, and access information easily. Because this aspect of UNIX is changing rapidly, new resources programs and sites are added daily.

■ Answers to Review 1

1. **ls**
2. **binary**
3. **bye**
4. **archie -h** *ftp.mla.com.gzip*
5. **help**

■ Answers to Review 2

1. Gives description for current item

2. !

3. **exit**

   http
   webcrawler.com
   spider.surfer.gif

COMMAND SUMMARY

Commands

ftp *server*   Connects to *server* to begin file-transferring process.

uncompress *file*.**Z**   Decompress *file*.**Z**, which was compressed by the **compress** utility.

gunzip *file*.**gz**   Decompress *file*.**gz**, which was compressed by the **gzip** utility.

nslookup *server*   Looks up information about *server*. Output contains IP address and alias of *server*.

archie *pattern*   Searches for *pattern* on anonymous FTP servers and returns with matching data.

gopher *server*   Connects to a **gopher** *server* to search the Internet. If the *server* argument is omitted, a default server is selected by **gopher**.

veronica   Contains a database of **gopher** directories for searching purposes, accessed via **gopher**.

jughead   Contains a more well-defined database of **gopher** directories, accessed via **gopher**.

lynx *protocol*   Starts up the Lynx text-based Web browser with the specified *protocol* (e.g., **ftp**, **gopher**, or **http**).

Mosaic   Starts up the graphical Mosaic Web browser.

netscape   Starts up the graphical Netscape Navigator Web browser.

List of Active Archie Servers

Hostname	IP Address	Country
	Last Update	
archie.au	139.130.23	Australia
archie.univie.ac.at	131.130.1.23	Austria
archie.belnet.be	193.190.248.18	Belgium
archie.bunyip.com	192.77.55	Canada
archie.cs.mcgill.ca	132.206.51.250	Canada
archie.uqam.ca	132.208.250.10	Canada
archie.funet.fi	128.214.6.102	Finland
archie.univ-rennes1.fr	129.20.254	France
archie.th-darmstadt.de	130.83.22.1	German
archie.ac.il	132.65.16	Israel
archie.unipi.it	131.114.21.10	Italy
archie.wide.ad.jp	133.4.3	Japan
archie.hana.nm.kr	128.134.1.1	Korea
archie.kornet.nm.kr	168.126.63.10	Korea
archie.sogang.ac.kr	163.239.1.11	Korea
archie.uninett.no	128.39.2.20	Norway
archie.icm.edu.pl	148.81.209	Poland
archie.rediris.es	130.206.1	Spain
archie.luth.se	130.240.12.23	Sweden
archie.switch.ch	130.59.1.40	Switzerland

Hostname	IP Address	Country
archie.switch.ch	130.59.10.40	Switzerland
archie.ncu.edu.tw	192.83.166.12	Taiwan
archie.doc.ic.ac.uk	146.169.16.11	UK
archie.doc.ic.ac.uk	146.169.17	UK
archie.doc.ic.ac.uk	146.169.2.10	UK
archie.doc.ic.ac.uk	146.169.32	UK
archie.doc.ic.ac.uk	146.169.33	UK
archie.doc.ic.ac.uk	146.169.43.1	UK
archie.doc.ic.ac.uk	155.198.1.40	UK
archie.doc.ic.ac.uk	155.198.191.4	UK
archie.hensa.ac.uk	129.12.43.17	UK
archie.sura.net	192.239.16.130	USA (MD)
archie.unl.edu	129.93.1.14	USA (NE)
archie.internic.net	192.20.225.200	USA (NJ)
archie.internic.net	192.20.239.132	USA (NJ)
archie.internic.net	198.49.45.10	USA (NJ)
archie.rutgers.edu	128.6.18.15	USA (NJ)
archie.ans.net	147.225.1.10	USA (NY)

PART V

Shell Programming and Customizing the Environment

Chapter Twenty-Two

Programming with the Shell

I n previous chapters, you employed UNIX utilities in complex command lines that you entered from the shell prompt, as well as in shell scripts. In this chapter, you create Bourne and/or Korn shell scripts containing programming statements that control operation of the shell and UNIX utilities. These scripts can be used to perform repetitive, complex, and routine tasks. New shell commands are introduced here—both interactively at the prompt and within scripts.

In this chapter you will explore the **sh** and **ksh** programming languages. Most shell scripts on UNIX systems are written in the Bourne shell, which is available on all versions of UNIX. The Korn shell, which is an extension of the Bourne shell in its programming features, is gaining in popularity. The C shell programming language is very similar to Bourne and Korn shell programming, but has important differences. The C and Korn shells are not available on all UNIX systems.

SKILLS CHECK: *Before beginning this chapter, you should be able to*

- *Issue complex command lines to the shell*
- *Employ UNIX utilities*
- *Create and run basic shell scripts*
- *Create, access, and change shell variables*
- *Correctly employ single and double quotation marks in command lines for communicating with the shell*
- *Have the shell make substitutions as specified with back quotes*
- *Effectively use input, output, and error redirection in command lines*

OBJECTIVES: *After completing this chapter, you will be able to*

- *Access variables from within a script*
- *Write a shell script that will get input from and write output to the user*
- *Utilize looping and branching control structures within a script*
- *Provide error checking in a script*
- *Manage error messages*
- *Properly lay out code in a script*

- *Provide for branching as a result of user input*
- *Exiting with status messages*

This chapter guides you through development of several typical shell scripts: an interactive script that determines how many times any selected user is logged on; an interactive menu program that allows the user to select programs to be run; a program for accessing a phone list; and a complex utility that determines which members of the user's group are currently logged on.

22.1

Determining How Many Times You Are Logged On

Three steps are generally involved in implementing a shell script: creating the shell script with an editor; making the script file an executable file; and then executing the shell script itself.

Working in the Korn or Bourne Shell

This chapter examines the Korn and Bourne shell programming language. As you work through the exercises in this chapter, you need to be in one of those shells.

1. If you are using another shell, start a Korn shell if it is available; otherwise, start a Bourne shell. Enter one of the following commands:

   ksh

   or

   sh

2. Two variables used with shells have the value of your login id, namely *LOGNAME* and *USER*. Depending on the operating system you are using, one or both of these variables is available. Examine the list of your shell's variables by entering

   set

If *LOGNAME* is listed as having the value of your login id, use that variable in the following exercises. If *LOGNAME* is not listed, the variable *USER* will be, and you should use it.

Creating a Simple Script

When writing shell scripts, it is most efficient to start with a simple portion of the script, make it work, and then include additional features. As each new feature is added, if the script fails, you know approximately where the error is located.

1. Create a new file named *checkuser* containing the following line:

   who | grep $*LOGNAME* | wc -l

2. Make *checkuser* executable, by entering

   chmod *755* *checkuser*

3. Run the script by entering

   checkuser

4. If you receive the error message

   ```
   checkuser: not found
   ```

   then the current directory is not in the *PATH* variable that the shell uses to locate utilities. Add the current directory to your shell's search path by entering the following commands:

   PATH=$PATH::
   export *PATH*

5. After you've added your current directory to the search path, you can run the script by entering

   checkuser

   The output from the script **checkuser** is the number of times that the user running the script (in this case, you) is logged on. This output is identical to what you would see if you enter the script's command line at the shell prompt.

Examining the Code

When you run the *checkuser* script, the various components of the command line are interpreted as follows:

Command	Interpretation
who	Instruction to the shell to execute the **who** utility.
|	Instruction to the shell to connect the output of **who** to the input of the next utility, **grep**.
grep	Instruction to the shell to execute the **grep** utility.
$LOGNAME	Instruction to the shell to evaluate the variable *LOGNAME* and place its value on the command line, replacing the string **$LOGNAME**. The shell then passes the value of the variable (your login id) to **grep** as an argument. To **grep**, the first argument, your login id, is interpreted as the target string to look for in the input. Only lines that contain your login id are output by **grep**.
|	Instruction to the shell to connect the output of **grep** to the input of the next utility, **wc**.
wc	Instruction to the shell to execute the **wc** utility.
-l	Instruction to the shell to pass the argument **-l** to **wc**. The **wc** utility interprets **-l** as instruction to output only the count of *lines* it receives as input, not characters or words.

22.2

Obtaining Information from the User of a Script

The shell provides the programmer (through the script) with a mechanism to communicate with the user interactively—both getting and giving information.

Echoing Fixed Strings in a Shell Script

The **echo** utility reads all its arguments and writes what it reads to standard output, usually connected to the workstation display. Programmers often use **echo** commands in shell scripts to send information to the user.

1. Edit the executable file *checkuser* to match the following:

   echo *The number of times you are currently logged on is:*
   who | **grep** *$LOGNAME* | **wc** **-l**

2. Run the script again.

   checkuser

Including the **echo** command line makes the script's output a bit more friendly, but as you will see, the real power of using **echo** in a script lies in displaying more essential information.

Passing User Input into a Script

Keyboard input from the user of a script can be read by the shell and used in a script.

1. At the command-line prompt, enter the following command:

   read *name*

   The cursor moves to a new line.

2. Complete the process by entering your name, and press (Return).

Accessing the Value of a read Variable

Whatever you typed in step 2 just above was read by the shell and became the value of the variable *name*, which was created because *name* was the argument to **read** on the command line.

1. Confirm that the variable *name* was set to whatever you typed by entering

   echo *$name*

The syntax of the **read** command is **read** followed by one argument, which is used as the name for a new variable created by the shell. The new variable takes the value of whatever is entered as input by the user, terminated by pressing the (Return) key.

Modifying and Running the Script

1. Modify all lines in the *checkuser* script as follows, so that it includes reading input from the user:

   echo *Please enter the login name of the user you want to check*
   read *name*
   echo *The number of times $name is currently logged on is:*
   who | **grep** *$name* | **wc** -l

2. Run the modified script.

   checkuser

3. When prompted, enter the login id of a user who is currently logged on and then press (Return).

Originally, *checkuser* produced a count of current logins for the user who ran the script. Now, it will do the same for any login name entered by the user when asked by the script.

Examining the Code

The *checkuser* script now contains the minimum components needed for an interactive shell script.

Command	Interpretation
read *name*	Instruction to create a new variable called *name* and assign it the value of whatever is read from the keyboard.
echo *The...$name...is:*	Information line written to the screen, including the value of the variable *$name*.

Command	Interpretation
who | grep $name	Instruction to the shell to run **who**, pass its output to **grep**, and give **grep** the evaluated variable *name* as an argument. Hence, **grep** searches its input for the specified user and outputs only lines that include the user string.
| wc -l	The output of grep is passed to **wc**, which counts the number of lines.

22.3

Communicating with Scripts Using Command-Line Arguments

Scripts can receive input interactively, as in the preceding section, or by incorporating an argument from the command line.

Passing Command Arguments into a Script

Specific user-supplied information can be passed to utilities inside scripts by employing arguments on the command line.

1. Create another script named *scriptarg* and include the following lines:

   date
   echo $1
   sleep 2
   echo $2
   sleep 2
   echo $*

2. Make the script executable.

3. Run the script, by entering the following command lines:

scriptarg *A B C D*
scriptarg *Red Blue Green Yellow*

The shell assigns to the variable named *1*, the value of the first argument entered at the command line. The variable *2* is the second argument. When the shell interprets the command **echo $1**, it replaces the string **$1** with the value of the variable *1*, the first argument from the command line. Likewise, **$2** is the value of the second argument and **$*** is the value of all arguments.

Modifying the Script to Process Command-Line Arguments

Command-line arguments can be used to pass information as needed in scripts.

1. Reduce the script *checkuser* to the following lines:

    echo *The number of times* **$1** *is currently logged on is:*
    who | grep $1 | wc -l

    The **read** statement and the **echo** command line requesting input are removed, and a new element—the variable statement **$1**—is added as an argument to **grep** and to **echo**.

2. Run the modified script by entering the following command, replacing the argument *loginname* with your login name or the login of a user currently logged on:

    checkuser *loginname*

    Output should resemble the following:

    ```
    The number of times loginname is currently logged on
    is: 1
    ```

    In this version of the script, the shell is asked to evaluate the variable **$1**, a *positional parameter,* which has the value of the first argument on the command line, the *loginname* you entered. In the script, **$1** always has the value of the first command-line argument, regardless of where in the script it is used.

3. Run *checkuser* again using the login name of a user currently logged on.

22.4

Making Decisions in Shell Scripts

Logic control structures such as "if this is true, then do this" are commonly used, because they effectively add power and flexibility to a script.

Creating a Decision-Making Script

The script in this next example makes a simple decision: to run, or to prompt the user for necessary input and then run.

1. Modify *checkuser* to match the following. (New or modified lines are identified with an arrow.)

```
if [ "$1" ]        ←
then               ←
    name=$1        ←
else
    echo Please enter the login name you want to check on   ←
    read name ←
fi                 ←
echo The number of times $name is logged on is:   ←
who | grep $name | wc -l   ←
```

2. Run the modified script by entering the following command line, replacing *loginname* with the login name of a user currently logged on.

   checkuser loginname

   The output from *checkuser* is information about the number of times the user you specified as an argument to the command is logged on.

3. Now run the script without an argument.

checkuser

4. When prompted by the script, enter a login name.

In this version of *checkuser*, the output is information concerning the login id you enter when prompted.

Making Decisions Using if-then-else

Four lines in the current script are the decision-making logic.

```
if [ "$1" ]
then
    ...
else
    ...
fi
```

The essence of this script is how the value of the variable *name* gets assigned. The variable is given whatever is entered as an argument at the command line, or if there is no argument, the variable is assigned whatever value is entered after the script prompts the user. The decision pivots on whether or not an argument is included by the user on the command line.

The following table analyzes the elements of the decision-making structure in the final version of *checkuser*. The **echo** line has been truncated to fit the table.

Command	Interpretation
if ["$1"]	If there is a value for the **$1** variable…
then	Then do the following…
name=$1	Set a new variable, *name*, equal to the value of the variable **$1**, the first argument from the command line…
else	Otherwise do the following.
echo *Please*…	Display the message "Please…".

Command	Interpretation
read *name*	Set value of the variable *name* to be the user's input from the keyboard.
fi	End of the **if** structure.

The overall **if-then-else** structure translates as follows: "**if** the first argument exists, **then** set the value of *name* to it, **else** prompt for it and set the value of *name* to whatever is entered." All **if** structures are terminated with **fi** (yes—that's **if** spelled backward). If an argument is passed on the command line, then **$1** exists and control passes to the **then** portion of the structure. The shell then creates a new variable *name* and assigns it to be the value of the variable **$1** (which is the login name included as the first argument on the command line). If the argument is *not* included on the command line, the variable **$1** does not exist and control moves to the **else** statement. The action specified in the **else** is the **echo** prompt and the **read** command, which gets the needed information for the variable *name* from the user.

Either by supplying a command-line argument or by answering the scripts inquiry, the variable *name* is created and assigned a value. The shell then replaces $*name* with its value in the argument to **echo** and as an argument to **grep** in the remaining lines of code.

■ Review 1

1. What does the following accomplish?

   echo *Choose 1 or 2*
   read *choice*

2. What code would determine if a second command-line argument existed and, if so, would **echo** its value to the screen? If the second argument does not exist, it displays the message "There is no second argument."

22.5

Interactively Choosing Options from a Menu

A common use of interactive scripts is to present menu-like interfaces for users so that they need not directly face the hazards of communicating with the shell. Menus work much like the above *checkuser* script: a menu prompts the user for input, sets the value of a variable equal to the user's input, and then performs some action based on the value of that variable. In this exercise you create a script that presents a short menu interface.

1. Create a new script named *menu* containing the following lines. Use either **USER** or **LOGNAME** as appropriate.

> **NOTE:** *The first line is a request that the script be evaluated by a Korn shell. If you do not have access to the Korn shell and are using the Bourne shell, change the line to read **#!/bin/sh** instead.*

#!/bin/ksh

cat **<<++**
            MAIN MENU
        1**)** *Print current working directory*
        2**)** *List all files in current directory*
        3**)** *Print today's date and time*
*Please enter your selection **$LOGNAME**:*
++
read *selection*
echo *Your selection was **$selection***

2. Make the file executable and then run it by entering

chmod **755** *menu*
menu

3. When you are prompted for input, type either a *1*, *2*, or *3*, followed by a Return.

4. After the program confirms the selection you typed, it exits, and the shell prompts you for your next command.

Examining the Code

The *menu* script includes two new constructs. Following are the elements of the script.

Command	Interpretation
#!/*bin/ksh*	Specifically requests that the script be interpreted by the Korn shell (or **sh** if you changed it). This serves two purposes: reminding the programmer what shell is used, and ensuring that the required shell is the one actually doing the interpreting. When you tell your interactive shell to run this script, your shell reads the first line and then executes the appropriate shell to interpret the script.
cat <<++	Instruction to read the lines following this command line in the script as input to **cat**. The file is read as input to **cat** until a line is reached that has ++ characters located at the beginning of the line.
++	The ++ is the *tag* indicating the end of the text to be read as input to **cat**.

The way to indicate that you want to have standard input come from the lines that follow in the file is to use a double input redirect << followed by a *here document*, as this kind of redirection is called. After the text lines, the closing tag is included on a line by itself. The ++ that serves as the tag in this example is discretionary; you can use any string of characters. The two occurrences of the tags must match exactly, and the closing tag must appear alone at the beginning of a line, with no spaces or tabs before it. Often programmers use the string *EOF* as a tag, signifying **End Of File**.

Using **cat** in a *here document* such as this, instead of using multiple **echo** statements, is more efficient and permits greater flexibility (you can arrange the display text as desired).

22.6
Debugging a Script

When you're creating scripts, there is little room for error. The shell expects exact syntax to be followed. Fortunately, you can have the shell run in *debugging mode* to see what is happening. (Use **sh** if appropriate.)

1. Enter the following command:

   ksh -x *menu*

This command explicitly calls the Korn shell with the **-x** option and the script name as an argument. Because the *menu* file is included as an argument, the commands in *menu* are executed. This is just a variation on one of the many ways to run a shell script. It is starting a child shell and giving it two arguments, the **-x** option and the script file, to execute.

Deciphering the -x Output

The output of the command you've just entered is initially confusing. The menu is displayed twice, commands are listed—output is, in general, a jumble.

Normally when the shell interprets a script, the shell reads each line, processes the line (performs variable substitution, expands filenames, and so forth), and then executes the specified commands. When you run a script with the **-x** option, however, the shell

- Reads each line and processes the line
- Displays the results of its processing of the command line
- And then actually executes the specified commands.

Each interpreted command line is displayed on the screen preceded by a plus sign. The first line now on your screen should be

```
+ cat
```

This tells you that a **cat** command is being processed. What follows on your screen is the remainder of the **cat** *here document*: the menu text to be displayed. Next comes the *result* of the **cat** command: the menu being displayed on your screen a second time.

The next command is an **echo** statement, again preceded by a plus sign. What follows is the result of that command: the variable *name* replaced with your login name.

Finally, you see another plus sign followed by a **read** statement. The shell is waiting for you to enter input from the keyboard.

1. Enter a response and conclude the script.

Debugging an Error

One of the most instructive exercises you can do to learn how the shell works is to return to a working script and intentionally include an error to see how the shell identifies it.

1. Make a copy of the *menu* script, and name it *menu-err*.

2. Call up the *menu-err* file, and remove the closing **++** tag after the menu display.

3. Run the script in debug mode by entering

   ksh -x *menu-err*

   (use **sh** if you do not have **ksh**) and examine what happens.
   The **cat** utility reads the remainder of the file, code and all, and the script quits. There is no *tag* indicating when to stop reading input.

4. Fix the problem, and run the script again to make sure it works.

5. Make another error in *menu-err*, such as deleting the variable *name* after the **read**. Practice bugging and debugging until you are comfortable with the process.

As you complete the exercises in this chapter, you should use the **-x** debug option to locate errors you may make accidentally, and also use **-x** on working scripts to see how they function.

> **TIP:** *It's a good idea, once a script is working, to make intentional errors and observe how the shell communicates its findings to you. Reading the shell's error messages is most instructive when you already know the error you introduced. By running through that exercise several times, the shell's error messages become familiar, and even possibly reasonable.*

22.7

Using Control Structures

The parts of a programming language used to control what a program does based on some condition, such as the **if-then-else** construct you have already seen in action, are called *control structures*. This section presents several more control structures, which you incorporate into the *menu* script to refine its operation.

Handling Multiple Choices with the case Statement

To accomplish tasks using the menu you have been developing, you need to be able to control which of several possible courses the menu will take, based on the value of a new variable *selection*.

1. Use **vi** to edit your *menu* script and replace the line

   echo *Your selection was $selection*

   with the following lines:

   case *$selection* **in**
   1)
    pwd
    ;;
   2)
    ls -l
    ;;
   3)
    date

> *;;*
> **esac**

2. When you have added these lines, run the script again.

   menu

3. When prompted, enter one of the three choices: *1, 2,* or *3.*
   What happens next depends on your entry. The action specified in the code after the script's **case** segment that matches your selection is performed for you.

4. Rerun the *menu* script and select each of the other two choices, observing the results.

5. Run the script in debug mode by entering

   ksh -x *menu*

The Components of the case Statement

You have just used the control structure called **case**. The **case** control structure determines which one of several actions is taken based on the value of a variable. The **case** control structure and others like it are often referred to as *branching* structures.

The following table contains a somewhat stilted English-language translation of the **case** structure you just used in your *menu* script. In the lines of code preceding the **case** structure, the value of the variable *selection* was determined by the number entered by the user at the **read** command. The **case** structure takes action based on the value of *selection*.

Command	Interpretation
case $*selection* **in**	Based on the value of the variable *selection*, do one of the following:

1)
    pwd
    ;;
	In the case where *selection* has the value *1*:
	    Run **pwd** to print working directory
	    End of this course of action

Command	Interpretation
2) **ls -l** **;;**	In the case where *selection* is 2: Run **ls -l** to list the files in this directory End of this course of action
3) **date** **;;**	In the case where *selection* is 3: Run **date** to print the date and time End of this course of action
esac	End of this **case** control structure

A complete **case** control structure should always include at least three major components:

- The **case** statement itself is used to indicate the beginning of the control structure and to specify the *variable* to be evaluated.

- The *condition segment* begins with a character followed by a right (closing) parenthesis. This specifies a string of letters and/or numbers to be compared to the value of the variable specified in the **case** segment. If the **case** value matches the string preceding the **)**, the *actions* specified following the **)** are performed.

- The **esac** segment indicates the end of the **case** structure. (And yes, **esac** is **case** spelled backwards.)

In addition to the above required components, conditions are terminated with two semicolons (**;;**). This part of the **case** structure indicates the end of a branch or course of action.

Identifying Errors in Case Code

1. Call up the *menu* script, remove the **esac**, write the file, and debug with **ksh -x** *menu*.

2. Correct the previous error, remove the **;;** after option *1*, write the file, and run the script in debug **ksh -x** *menu*, choosing option *1*.

Making a Script Loop Continually Using while

As it stands now, the *menu* script quits after you make one choice. Usually, a menu script should perform the desired action and then present the menu display again to continue. The process of repeating actions within a program is called *looping*.

If you are going to make the menu loop, you will also need to provide a choice for users to select when they wish to exit.

1. Use **vi** to edit your script file so it looks like the following. Arrows indicate lines to modify. Add three lines before **cat** and a new *x* option in the menu and the *x)* option in the **case**.

NOTE: Be sure to enter all five spaces in the **while** *statement; they are critical.*

```
#!/bin/ksh
leave=no                     ←
while [ $leave = no ]        ←
do                           ←
cat <<++
                MAIN MENU
          1) Print current working directory
          2) List all files in current directory
          3) Print today's date and time
          x) Exit      ←
Please enter your selection $LOGNAME:
++
read selection
case $selection in
   1)
     pwd
     ;;
   2)
```

```
        ls -l
        ;;
    3)
        date
        ;;
    x)                      ←
        leave=yes           ←
        ;;                  ←
    esac
    done                    ←
    exit 0                  ←
```

2. Once your modifications to *menu* are complete, run the script again. Make a few selections and observe the results.

3. When you are ready, indicate your wish to exit by typing **x** when prompted.

4. Once the script works, introduce an error into the code, run the script in debug mode, examine error messages, and repair the code.

Interpreting the while Loop Code

The **while** loop is a major control structure. Call up your *menu* script again, to examine the code.

In general, the form of the **while** loop looks like this:

while [*expression*]
do
    statement 1
    statement 2
    .
    .
    .
done

The **while** statement causes the shell to continue executing the code between the **do** and its closing line **done**, as long as the expression on the **while** line evaluates as true. (And no, **done** is not **do** spelled backward.)

The expression used in this example is

while [$*leave* = *no*]

In other words, "**while** the variable *leave* has the value *no*, keep repeating the actions called for in the code following the **do** statement to the **done** statement."

The new condition section in the ***menu*** script, for the *x* option on the menu, changes the value of the variable *leave* from *no* to *yes*. Once this has happened, the shell completes the **while** loop and because *leave* does not equal *no*, proceeds on to the statements following the **done** statement. In this example, the only command following the **done** statement is **exit**. So, choosing selection *x* ends the whole loop and exits the program.

> **NOTE:** *The* **exit** *statement in this menu does not accomplish much, because every program has an automatic, implicit* **exit** *at the end of the file, anyway. If your code lets the interpreting shell reach the bottom of the file, it exits automatically. It's better programming practice, however, to call* **exit** *explicitly, with an argument of* **0**. *This is a way to indicate specifically how the shell script ended. The UNIX convention for exiting is that* **0** *means "everything was okay." Any other number usually means something went wrong.*

Clearing the Screen

You may have noticed that the screen would be easier to read and work with if it were cleared before each display of the menu.

1. Call up your *menu* script and add a **clear** statement, like this:

```
#!/bin/ksh
leave=no
while [ $leave = no ]
do
clear          ←
cat <<++
```

2. Save your file.

3. Run the menu again, make a few selections, and then exit. The screen clears before the menu is redisplayed.

Pausing the Script

With the clearing of the screen, the displays in the *menu* program are easier to read. However, the results of each choice you make on the menu go by very quickly—sometimes too quickly to see. You can fix that, too.

1. Change your file to add a **sleep** statement, as follows:

    esac
    sleep 2   ←
    done
    exit *0*

2. Run the script again, and make a few selections. Notice how the **sleep** command helps.

The **sleep** utility causes the shell that is reading this script to stop and take a breather after the results of the **case** choice and before the menu is displayed again. The argument in the **sleep** statement is the number of seconds you want this little coffee break to last.

Waiting for User Response

The **sleep** statement forces a prescribed wait, but the wait may not be long enough when there's a lot of output. A better solution is to wait until the user indicates a readiness to continue.

1. Modify your *menu* file, replacing the **sleep** statement with two new statements. If you're using System V, modify the file as follows:

    esac
    echo "*Press Return to continue* \c"   ←
    read *hold*   ←
    done
    exit *0*

If you're using BSD, modify the file as follows:

esac
echo -n *"Press Return to continue"* ←
read *hold*   ←
done
exit *0*

2. Run the script again to check your modifications. Make two or three selections. After each selection, you must press (Return) to get back to the menu.

The **\c** (in System V) or the **-n** (in BSD) portion of the **echo** statement instructs the shell to eliminate the newline at the end of the line and allow the cursor to park at the end of the line until a selection is made. Having the cursor remain on the prompt line makes the menu more user friendly, and its presentation somewhat more elegant. The **read** statement causes the shell to wait for input to assign to the variable *hold*. The new variable *hold* is created but its value is never accessed. You don't need the variable, you just need the shell to pause and the **read** statement is a good way to do it.

This version of the menu is a little easier to work with, because the user can move as quickly or slowly as desired.

Handling the Selection of an Invalid Option

So far, the menu performs actions based on four possible entries. What happens if the user enters some other value? Try it and see.

1. Run your script and, in response to the prompt, type *8*.

    You are prompted to press (Return) to continue, and the menu is simply redrawn, with no action taken. The shell cannot locate an option *8* after the **case** before it reaches **esac**. It would be better if some more explicit action occurred, such as an error message.

Declaring a Default Condition

When the user enters an invalid option, you can display an appropriate error message.

1. Exit from the *menu* script.

2. Use the editor to add a new condition after the *x*) condition, as follows:

```
x)
    leave=yes
    ;;
*)                          ←
    echo "Invalid choice. Try again."      ←
    ;;                      ←
esac
```

3. Run the script again, this time entering some value other than *1*, *2*, *3*, or *x*. The script alerts you about incorrect input.

The **)* condition contains statements that are performed if the shell encounters any value *other* than those already designated in previous condition statements. If an unexpected value is entered, an appropriate error message is displayed.

Including Multiple Values in a case Segment

As it stands now, your script terminates when a lowercase *x* is entered by the user.

1. Run your *menu* script again, and see what happens when you type X instead of *x* as your selection. You are told that you made an invalid choice.

2. Exit the script by typing *x* and pressing [Return].

There are two ways to modify the script so that the user can exit by typing either an uppercase *X* or lowercase *x*. One way is to have two separate **case** segments that perform the same thing; one matches *X*, the other *x*. There is an easier way.

3. Using **vi**, modify the exit segment of *menu* so that it looks like this:

x I *X*)
    leave=yes

4. Run the script, and exit by typing an uppercase *X*.

5. Run the script again, and exit with a lowercase *x*.

When you wish to have the same set of instructions followed in a **case** statement when the user enters any of several values, use the pipe symbol I between the accepted values. This symbol is interpreted in **case** code as the OR statement. It indicates that the **case** statements following it should be executed if the variable being tested contains one of the listed values. You are not limited to two possibilities, but instead may include many values, each separated from the others with a pipe character.

The **case** statement has the following format. Note the indentation for readability.

case *$variable* **in**
    string I string2)
        statement(s)

        ;;
    string3)
        other statement(s)

  ;;
  *)

        default statement(s)

  ;;
esac

Taking Actions When the if Statement Evaluates to False

You can further modify the script so that it alerts the user that a nonexistent filename has been entered.

1. Modify your *menu* file so that condition 4 looks like this:

   4)
       echo "*Enter a filename*"
       read *fname*
       if [-f $*fname* **]**
       then
         echo *The contents of* $*fname:*   ←
         more $*fname*
       else   ←
         echo $*fname does not exist*   ←
       fi
       ;;

2. Run this version of the script, again selecting the new option 4, and typing a fictitious filename.

   This time you are told that the file does not exist.

   The **else** statement made this screen response possible. The **else** statement is used to specify a list of one or more commands to run when the condition specified in the **if** statement is evaluated as False.

   A form of the **if** control structure is

   if [*expression* **]**
   then
      statement(s)
   else
      other statement(s)
   fi

This form makes a provision for what should be done whether the **if** statement is evaluated as True or False. If True, then.... If not True (else).... All possibilities are covered.

Repeating an Action on Multiple Objects

So far you have used one looping control structure, **while**. The **while** structure is used to repeat a sequence of actions as long as some condition remains true. Another type of Bourne and Korn looping repeats a sequence of actions on all of a specified list of objects, such as filenames or variables.

1. Make backup copies of two of the files in your current directory by typing the following Bourne or Korn shell command, replacing *file1* and *file2* with the names of two files in the current directory:

   for *fn* **in** *file1 file2*

   When you press (Return), you are greeted by a > prompt. Because you entered the **for** *command* from the command line, the shell prints a secondary prompt > to let you know that it is expecting more instructions.

2. Give the shell what it is waiting for. Type the following lines in response to the prompts you receive:

   do
   cp *$fn $fn.bak*
   done

   The **for** command you entered in step 1 instructs the shell to create a new variable *fn* and to give it all values listed after the **in**. It also specifies that the statements between **do** and **done** are to be repeated **for** each value of the variable *fn*. The statements here tell the shell to create a copy of each named file, giving it the same name as the original with the added extension *.bak*.

3. Use **ls** to take a look at the files in your current directory. Included in the list should be two new files with the *.bak* extension, created with the **for** command.

Examining the Code

Command	Interpretation
for *fn* **in** *file1 file2*	The **for** command takes as its first argument a *variable* name followed by **in** and a *list* of words that are used as different values for the variable. It performs the same set of *statement(s)* for each variable value in the list. The value of the named variable (in this case, *fn*) is set to the first word in the word list. Then the statements between the **do** and **done** are executed. Next, the value of the variable is set to the second word in the list, and the statements are executed again. This process is repeated until the end of the word list is reached.
do	The word **do** alone on a line starts the body of the loop, which is ended with **done**, which is also alone on a line. Within the body of the loop, you may specify as many statements as you wish. They should all be indented when used in a script for clarity.
cp $*fn* $*fn.bak*	This command instructs the shell to evaluate the current value of the variable *fn*, making a copy of the file named *file.bak*.

The general syntax of the **for** command is as follows:

```
for variable in list
do
   statement(s)
done
```

The command must begin with the word **for** followed by a variable name, then the word **in**, and then a word list.

Remove the files now (unless you find them useful), by typing

rm **.bak*

Using a for Loop in the Menu Script

You just used a **for** loop at the command line. You can use the same structure in a script.

1. Use **vi** to edit your script *menu* once again, modifying the menu, adding a fifth option:

   1) Print current working directory
   2) List all files in current directory
   3) Print today's date and time
   4) Display contents of a file
   5) Create backup file copies   ←
   x) Exit

2. Add the following new condition statement after condition 4 and before *x*:

   5)

   > **echo** *Enter filenames*
   > **read** *fnames*
   > **for** *fn* **in** *$fnames*
   > **do**
   >   **cp** *$fn* *$fn.bak*
   > **done**
   > *;;*

3. Run a test of this version of the script, creating two or three backup file copies.

Examining the Code

The code included in the *menu* is described as follows:

Command	Interpretation
echo *Enter filenames*	Once the user has chosen option *5* the message requesting filenames is displayed.
read *fnames*	A new variable is created containing the name(s) of file(s) entered by the user in response to the previous **echo** request.
for *fn* **in** $*fnames*	The value of a new variable *fn* is to cycle through all names listed in the variable *fnames* and for each value complete the following **do** loop.
do **cp** $*fn* $*fn.bak* **done**	This **do** loop is to be completed for each value of *fn*. The file is copied into a new file with a name consisting of the old filenames with a *.bak* extension.

■ Review 2

1. What are the three major components of the shell's **case** structure?

2. To write a shell script that performs a series of actions as long as some condition is true, what control structure would you use?

3. What is the best way to have a script pause so that a user has time to read what is on the screen?

4. What is the * (splat) used for within **case** structures?

5. How can you get **case** to accept several alternatives as acceptable conditions for the same set of actions?

6. What is the closing part of an **if** structure in the shell?

7. What closes a **do** loop?

8. What is wrong with the following code segment?

   3)

   ```
   echo "Enter a filename"
   read $fname
   if [ -f fname]
      echo The contents of fname:
      more fname
   else
      echo < No such file
   ;
   ```

22.8

Finishing Up Your Menu Script

Your script is now a fully functional menu. In this section you will
make a small modification to your code that will make your menu a
little friendlier. You will also be introduced to an alternative method for
exiting a **while** loop.

Eliminating Returns from the echo Statements

When you used an **echo** command in this menu, the cursor was placed
on the line that followed (with one exception). In menus it is helpful
to have the cursor remain on the prompt line until the user enters a
response and presses Return.

1. Use **vi** to edit the *menu* script. Modify all lines that have the form:

   echo *prompt string*

   to look like one of the following.

   On System V:

   echo "*prompt string*: \c"

On BSD:

echo -n *"prompt string:* "

The **-n** (on BSD systems) and **\c** (on System V) are instruction to the shell to eliminate the return at the end of the line. The quotes allow you to use a blank space between the end of the prompt and the cursor.

2. The first prompt for input at the end of the menu display is inside the *here document.* To make it remain on the line, you must use **vi** to remove the line from the input to **cat** and include it in a separate **echo** statement. Your code should look like the following. (If you are using a BSD system, use **echo -n** instead of the **\c** in the last line.)

4) Display contents of a file
   5) Create backup file copies
   x) Exit
++
echo *"Please enter your selection $LOGNAME: \c"*

3. Make a few selections.
4. Exit the menu.

Using an Alternative Exit

Up to now, the method of exiting a **while** loop within the menu includes an explicit exit condition within the **while** structure itself. There is another method of exiting, which uses a loop with no exit condition (an *infinite loop*) and then uses an explicit call to the shell **exit** code to end the program.

1. Use **vi** to edit *menu*.
2. Replace the third line, which is

while [*$leave* = *no*]

with the line

while :

3. Replace the code in the last **case** selection.

x | X)
  leave=yes
  ;;

with the line

x | X)
  exit 0
  ;;

4. Delete the last line, **exit 0**.

The **while** loop continues to recycle the **do**...**done** code as long as **while** evaluates its argument as true. In the previous version, a variable value was evaluated. As long as the variable value was evaluated as true, the **while** loop continued. In the shell, two arguments to **while** are *always* evaluated as true (the word "true" and the colon). Once the **while** loop is started with one of those two arguments, it continues indefinitely. Some other mechanism has to be used to end the program.

The **exit 0** in the **case** statement causes the current shell that is running the script to terminate when that option is selected.

22.9

Making the Finished Product Easier to Read

Now that you have a user-friendly menu that works, it's important for the script that runs your menu to be easily readable, as well. No program is ever really complete, and someday, someone (quite possibly you) will need to change the program. Modifying a program is considerably easier when you can read what is already there and decipher what each line of code does and what each variable contains. To ensure that your program is readable, now and in the future, you should always complete the following finishing touches. Each of these practices is discussed further in the paragraphs that follow.

- Verify that each variable has a name that describes its content.
- Check your line indentation and use of blank lines between sections.
- Add comment lines where they will be helpful to another reader, including a header comment at the beginning of the program.

The listing of the code for this program at the end of the chapter includes comments for your inspection.

Selecting Names for Variables

Notice that the variable names we have employed so far are words or derivatives of words. They describe the data contained in the variable. This is good programming practice. For example, when you're thinking of a name for a variable that will contain a filename, call it *filename* or *fname* or *filnme*, but not *x*.

Some Notes on Line Indentation

Review the indentation of lines in the scripts examined thus far. Consistent indentation is very important for maintaining the readability of code. Here are some guidelines to follow:

- In general, the components of a control structure should be located in the same column. The body of the structure should be indented one level. For example, the associated **if**, **then**, **else**, and **fi** statements should all start in the same column. So should a **while** with its associated **do** and **done**.
- Do not indent unnecessarily; only indent within statements that suggest a need for it.
- Use the same indentation distance for all levels. Use one, two, and three tabs, for instance; or four, eight, and twelve spaces. Be consistent.

Providing Comments for Future Users

A professional programmer includes comments attached to and inside programs; these comments explain how the code works. When the shell finds a pound sign (#) on a line, the shell does not interpret the remainder of the line. Thus, helpful comments can be added to a script without affecting how the script works—provided that a # precedes the comments on the line.

Comments should be used to explain the parts of the code that will likely be less understandable to other people (or even to you, after some time has passed). In addition, a comment header at the beginning of the program should specify the name of the program, its author, date of creation, and its function.

Explicitly Calling the Shell to Interpret a Script

There is one exception to the rule about comment lines beginning with the # character. Notice that the first line of the scripts in this section begins with a # followed by an exclamation mark (!), or "bang." The bang indicates that the script should be interpreted by whatever command interpreter is named following the bang—in this case, */bin/ksh*, the Korn shell. A line that begins with #! is *not* a comment line. This line is instruction to your interactive shell to have a particular kind of child shell interpret the script. This explicit call avoids the possibility of having the wrong shell interpret the script.

If a user's interactive shell is a C shell, and the first character in a script is a # but is *not* followed by the bang and the absolute path to a command interpreter, a *child C shell* will interpret the script. Many a programmer has created a Bourne or Korn shell script that worked perfectly at first but then failed after comments were added, because they had placed a comment as the first line. A C shell was thus handed the script, found the Bourne or Korn syntax unintelligible, and failed to execute the program. To avoid this error, many programmers explicitly call the shell they want with a beginning line such as

#!/bin/ksh

22.10

Creating a Phone Search Script

You can create shell scripts to perform various tasks. One useful task is to search a phone list file for a desired number.

The Korn shell script that follows can be used to search a phone list file by name or phone number. The script is invoked from the command line by typing the name of the script, followed by an argument that specifies the pattern to use in the search.

1. Create a new file called *phone.list* with the **vi**sual editor, which contains the following lines of names and phone numbers:

```
Phil Barnhart 123-4567
Walter Mitchell 234-1029
Walter Mitchell 543-9681
Lillian Frank 567-4823
Mabel Joyce 123-4567
```

2. With **vi**, create a script called *phon* that has the following lines:

#!/*bin/ksh*
grep *$1* *phone.list*

3. Make your script executable and run the script, by entering

chmod **755** *phon*
phon *Mabel*

The output consists of the line from the *phone.list* file that contains the string *Mabel*, which is the first argument from the command line.

```
Mabel Joyce 123-4567
```

4. Try another phone request. Type

phon *123*

The output is

```
Phil Barnhart 123-4567
Mabel Joyce 123-4567
```

Two lines were printed because **grep** displays all lines from the file *phone.list* that contain the target string *123*.

Examining the Code

Command	Interpretation
#!/*bin*/*ksh*	Instruction to the shell to have the script interpreted by the Korn shell.
grep *$1 phone.list*	Instruction to the shell to run the **grep** utility and to pass **grep** two arguments: the value of the variable *$1*, and *phone.list*. The shell evaluates *$1* as whatever string the user entered as the first argument on the command line. For instance, *Mabel*. You don't type *phone.list* on the command line that runs the *phon* script. The *phone.list* argument is hard coded within the shell script. As a result of the two arguments, **grep** looks for lines containing the string *Mabel* in the file *phone.list*.

Quoting Multiple-Word Arguments

As it stands now, the *phon* script is mildly useful. It saves you from having to type the name of the file to be searched with **grep**. However, it has more than one flaw that you might not notice for a while. If your *phone.list* file grew, however, and eventually included six people with the first name of *Walter*, you might want to enter the whole name, first and last, as the first argument to the *phon* script.

1. Type the following:

   phon "Walter Mitchell"

   Instead of getting the expected output,

```
Walter Mitchell 234-1029
```

you get something like this:

```
grep: can't open Mitchell
phone.list:Walter Mitchell 234-1029
phone.list:Walter Mitchell 543-9681
```

When you typed the command line *phon "Walter Mitchell"* to your login shell, it started a child shell to interpret the *phon* script and passed to it the first argument, consisting of two words: *Walter Mitchell*. Within the *phon* script, the shell read the command line

```
grep $1 phone.list
```

and then processed the commands in the script according to the shell's evaluation rules. The variable **$1** was evaluated and replaced on the command line with its value, *Walter Mitchell*. Once this was done, the **grep** command line in effect looked like this:

```
grep Walter Mitchell phone.list
```

Where there were two arguments before, the shell now sees three. So the shell starts the **grep** utility and passes it the three arguments.

To the **grep** utility, the three arguments mean

Walter	The pattern to search for
Mitchell	The first file to search
phone.list	The second file to search

When **grep** searches through more than one file for a pattern, **grep** prefaces each line of its output with the name of the file where the match was found. Hence, the output contains the name of the *phone.list* file. The first file, *Mitchell*, does not exist, so **grep** reports the error message.

The *phon* script would be a more useful utility if it did not have this behavior for arguments that contain embedded blanks, such as *Walter Mitchell*. The script should treat the value of **$1** as a single word. You can use quoting *within* the script to accomplish this.

2. Change the **grep** line of the *phon* script to read

   grep "$1" *phone.list*

3. Try the script again, using the same argument from the last example. Enter

   phon "Walter Mitchell"

   This time, you don't receive an error message that the file *Mitchell* cannot be located.

Putting the variable **$1** within double quotes fixes the problem. Now when the shell that is interpreting the script expands the variable **$1**, it produces (internally) the intermediate command line

   grep *"Walter Mitchell" phone.list*

The double quotes within the script instruct the shell to pass *Walter Mitchell* as a single argument. The double quotes do not prevent the shell from interpreting the dollar sign as a variable identifier, they just prevent interpretation of the space.

Performing Multiple Searches

You can use looping to make your script search for several patterns.

1. Modify the *phon* script to include the following **for** statement. Make sure that the first argument to **grep** is **$i** and not **$1** as it was before.

   #!/bin/ksh
   for *i* **do**
   grep "$i" *phone.list*
   done

2. Try the modified *phon* script by entering

   phon Walter Mabel

You get the following output, consisting of lines that match either target.

```
Walter Mitchell 234-1029
Walter Mitchell 543-9681
Mabel Joyce 123-4567
```

The **for** statement in the script loops over all the command-line arguments, setting the variable *i* to each one in turn. For each value of the variable *i*, the shell runs the **grep** utility, evaluating the current value of the variable *i* for **grep**'s first argument. The outputs of both of the **grep** runs appear together in the output.

Removing Duplicate Output Lines

The *phon* script is more useful now because it accepts multiple search patterns. These patterns do not have to be names; any characters will do. In this section you examine how to handle patterns that produce duplicate output.

1. For example, type

   phon Walter 234

   You get the following output

   ```
   Walter Mitchell 234-1029
   Walter Mitchell 543-9681
   Walter Mitchell 234-1029
   ```

   Notice that the first line of the output appears twice—first because the argument pattern *Walter Mitchell* matched it, and again because of the match with the pattern *234*. Although this output is entirely consistent, it seems unnecessary to show lines from the phone list more than once. The output can also appear cluttered if several entries are repeated. And since **grep** runs multiple times, the output may be haphazard and unsorted.

2. Enter the following:

   phon Walter Mabel

You get the output

```
Walter Mitchell 234-1029
Walter Mitchell 543-9681
Mabel Joyce 123-4567
```

The output is not in alphabetical order, even though the source file, *phone.list*, is sorted. The output results from two runs of the **grep** utility: the first, using the argument *Walter*, selects the first two lines of output and the second run, using the argument *Mabel*, selects the remaining line. The pattern arguments *Walter* and *Mabel* were not in alphabetical order, so the output is not alphabetized, either.

3. You can fix both problems—duplicate output and unsorted output—with a minor addition to the *phon* script. Change the **done** line of the script to the following:

done | sort -u

4. Try the new version of *phon* on the two earlier examples. Type the following commands and observe the output:

phon *Walter Mitchell 102*
phon *Mabel Joyce Walter Mitchell*

Both commands now produce sorted output with no duplicates.

This illustrates an important property of the Bourne shell and Korn shell control constructs: they can be treated just like commands. In this case you can think of the **for** construct—that is, everything from the keyword **for** through the keyword **done**—as a single command. Its output is the output that prints on your screen. The modified line now takes the output of the **for** command and pipes that output to the **sort** utility, which alphabetizes it. The **-u** option to the **sort** utility causes **sort** to produce unique output lines—duplicates are eliminated.

Ignoring Case in Searches

The *phon* utility you just created is case sensitive. To successfully find Phil Barnhart, for instance, you must capitalize his names.

1. Modify the script to include the **-i** option for **grep,** instructing **grep** to ignore case during a search.

   #!/bin/ksh
   for *i* **do**
      grep -i *"$i"* *phone.list*   ←
      done | *sort* **-u**

2. Run the script by entering

   phon *walt phil mabel*

   The output is appropriate, even though you entered search strings in lowercase.

This version of the *phon* script is considerably more useful than the first one you created, yet it remains simple. It uses a few features of the Korn shell programming language to significantly increase its capabilities.

22.11

Creating a Complex Group Member Script

The remaining sections of this chapter guide you through development of a complex script that determines which members of your UNIX group are currently logged on.

The file */etc/passwd* contains a single-line record for each user account on the system. All users can quickly access the record in the password file associated with their account. Each record consists of fields separated by colons, like this:

```
cassy:CsTg7.KnyE/xhG:376: 200:Catherine Thamzin:/mla/cassy:csh
```

The fields represented are as follows:

```
loginid:password:userid:groupid:info:home-directory:start program
```

Searching for the Login Character String Anywhere in the File

The **grep** utility searches each line in a file looking for a match to a string of characters. When it finds a match anywhere on a line, **grep** selects the line.

1. To search for your own record in *letc/passwd*, enter the following command. (Use *$USER* if appropriate.)

   grep $LOGNAME /etc/passwd

   or if you are on an NIS network, try

   ypcat *passwd* | **grep $LOGNAME**

When the shell interprets a command line, the $ indicates a variable. For *$LOGNAME*, the shell locates the value of *LOGNAME* (the user's login id) and substitutes that value for the variable in the command line. When the shell executes **grep**, the user's login id is passed as the first argument.

In this case, **grep** is given two arguments: the user's login id and *letc/passwd*. The **grep** utility then opens *letc/passwd* and searches through all lines of the file, selecting those lines that have the user's login character string *anywhere* in the line. If a person's login were *student1*, then **grep** would locate *student1*, as well as *student10*, *student11*, and so on. Likewise, if the string *student1* is included in any other field of a record in the password file, the record would be selected.

Searching for Matches in a Specific Field

To make searching the password file more useful, it should be limited to the first field of the record, and should respond only to exact matches.

1. Create a script file called *mylogin*.

2. Enter the following commands in the script file, substituting your own login id for the string *yourlogin*:

   echo *Your entry in the password file is:*
   awk -F*: '*$1* == "*yourlogin*" {**print $0**}' *letc/passwd*

or on a network

ypcat *passwd* | **awk** -F: '*$1* == "*yourlogin*" {**print** *$0*}'

3. Make the script *mylogin* executable.

4. Run the script. The output is the arguments to **echo** and the */etc/passwd* entry for your login.

Examining the Code

The **awk** command line instructs the **awk** utility to locate all lines in */etc/passwd* that have a first field that matches your login id exactly, and then to output all fields of each selected line. The elements of the **awk** command line are as follows:

Command	Interpretation
awk	Instructs the shell to execute the **awk** utility.
-F:	This argument is passed by the shell to **awk** and instructs **awk** to use the colon as the Field separator.
' '	Instruction to the shell to pass enclosed characters to **awk** without interpreting any characters.
**$1** == "*yourlogin*" {**print** *$0*}	This entire string of characters, enclosed by single quotes, is passed, uninterpreted by the shell, to **awk**. The **awk** utility receives and then interprets this code, as described below.
/etc/passwd	This argument, passed to **awk**, is interpreted by **awk** as the file to open and read for input.

The code between the single quotes, which is received and interpreted by **awk,** instructs **awk** to examine the first field of each record and select all records where the first field is a character string exactly matching the value of *yourlogin*. The **awk** utility *requires* that any character match string must be enclosed by double quotes. This allows spaces between characters to be passed uninterpreted as part of a target string. Within this code, the command elements are as follows:

Command	Interpretation
$1	Instructs **awk** to examine the first field of each record, looking for matches.
== "*student1*"	The double equals is an absolute equality operator telling **awk** that an *exact* match to field *1* is needed. Given the ==, if the *yourlogin* string is *student1*, **awk** selects the line that includes *student1* in field one for whatever action follows. The character string must be inside double quotes. Only the record from *letc/passwd* with *student1* in the first field is matched. Other records with entries such as *student10*, *student11*, and so forth are *not* selected, even though the target string is part of *student10*, because they are not *exact* matches.
{print $0}	The code {**print** *$0*} is the action to be taken on selected lines. It instructs **awk** to print *all* fields of each selected record.

Therefore, all fields in the *letc/passwd* entry for *yourlogin* become the output of this instance of **awk**.

22.12

▌ Locating Group Ids

Each user on the system has a group identification number (group id) that permits the sharing of files and programs among group members. The group id is the fourth field in the *letc/passwd* file.

Obtaining a Specific User's Group Id

With **awk**, records can be selected according to a specific criterion. From these records, specific fields can then be output.

1. Modify both lines of the script *mylogin* to be as follows:

   echo *Your login and groupid are:*
   awk -F*: '$1 == "yourlogin"* {**print** *$1, $4*}' */etc/passwd*

2. Run the script. The output is the login id and group id of the specific login that is hard-coded into the script as *yourlogin*.

3. Modify the *mylogin* script to process information about another user, such as ***root***.

4. Run the script again.

In this version of the *mylogin* script, the **echo** statement is modified to reflect the script's new task, and the **awk** line is modified to output two specific fields rather than all fields of each selected record. Instead of the action **print** *$0*, the new action to be taken for selected lines is {**print** *$1, $4*}.

Examining the Code

This action code of the command instructs **awk** to do the following for each selected record:

Command	Interpretation
{	Start action.
print *$1*	Print the first field.
,	Print a single space, and then…
$4	Print the fourth field.
}	End action.

Quoting Special Characters

When the shell encounters a command line, it scans the elements of the line for any special characters that might be present. The shell then expands special characters or makes necessary substitutions where indicated. Then the shell executes the utilities called in the command and passes the remaining arguments to the utilities. This section reviews special characters and how the shell interprets them.

Evaluating Variables and File Expansion Characters

The **echo** utility has a simple task: it reads whatever arguments it receives and writes them to standard output. The output is connected to the workstation display unless it is redirected to a file or another utility.

1. For instance, enter the following:

   echo *Preparing the shell is quite fun*

   Six arguments, separated by spaces, are passed to **echo** and subsequently written by **echo** to standard output. In this case, standard output is not redirected, and the output of **echo** is displayed on the screen.

2. The shell completes interpretation of all special characters on the command line before the arguments are passed to **echo**. For example, enter the following:

   echo *$LOGNAME has a home directory of* **$HOME**

   In the above line, the variables *LOGNAME* and *HOME* are evaluated by the shell before the seven resulting arguments are passed to **echo**.

3. Enter the following:

   touch *my myfiles lye2 llye2*
   echo [*mls*]*y**

   Files are listed that have names beginning with *m*, *l*, or *s* followed by a *y* and then zero or more other characters. The brackets have special filename expansion meaning to the shell.

4. Double quotes instruct the shell not to interpret certain characters, such as braces and the asterisk. Enter the following:

echo "[*mls*]*y**"

The brackets and asterisk are not interpreted.

echo "[*My login is* $*LOGNAME*]"

In this case, the double quotes instruct the shell to pass the brackets without interpretation. On the other hand, the $*LOGNAME* variable *is* evaluated although it is enclosed by double quotes. The shell evaluates variables even when enclosed in double quotes.

5. Contrast the effect of single quotes. Enter the following:

echo '[*My login is* $*LOGNAME*]'

In this case, the variable $*LOGNAME* is not evaluated but is displayed as a literal string.

Examining the Code

When the shell reads a command line and encounters a single quote, it turns off interpretation of essentially all special characters such as [and $ until it encounters the next matching quote.

1. You can demonstrate the "on-off" nature of shell interpretation by entering this somewhat unlikely command line:

echo ' $*LOGNAME* ' $*LOGNAME* ' $*LOGNAME* '

The first and last instance of $*LOGNAME* in this command are echoed literally, because both instances are enclosed by single quotes. Only the middle instance is not quoted and, therefore, is evaluated by the shell.

Envision the arguments to **echo** in this command as shown in Figure 22-1.

The shell always begins command-line processing at the left with interpretation switched on. The process moves from left to right. When the first single quote is encountered, interpretation is

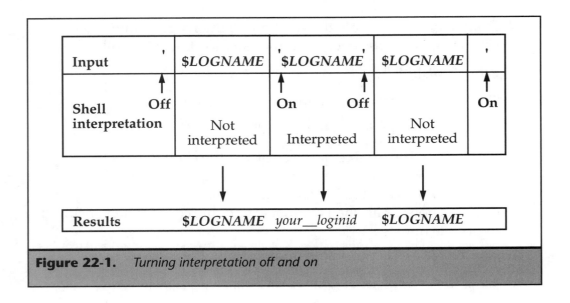

Figure 22-1. *Turning interpretation off and on*

switched off. In the previous command, the first instance of
$LOGNAME is not interpreted and is passed literally to **echo**.
When the second single quote is encountered, shell interpretation
is reactivated. The second instance of **$LOGNAME** is then read.
Because interpretation is back on, the string is evaluated as a
variable. The *value* of the variable is then passed. The third
instance of **$LOGNAME** is enclosed in quotes like the first and
passed literally to **echo**.

2. Single quotes instructs the shell to not interpret double quotes.
   Enter the following

   echo '"$LOGNAME"'

   When the shell encounters the first single quote, it turns
   interpretation off until it reaches the next matching quote, at the
   far end of the command line. Because the double quotes in this
   command are encountered by the shell when interpretation is
   switched off, they are passed literally to **echo**.

3. For a more complex example of turning interpretation on and off, enter the following:

echo *'My login is '"$LOGNAME'" on this machine'*

This command is depicted in Figure 22-2.

At first glance, **$LOGNAME** appears to be well protected by single and double quotes, but appearances can be deceiving. The first single quote does its work; interpretation is switched off until the shell reads the next matching quote. The string *My login is "* is inside the section surrounded by single quotes, hence safe from shell interpretation. Included in this uninterpreted section is a double quote. The **$LOGNAME** is not inside single quotes. The first single quote on the command line turned off interpretation. The second single quote, just to the left of **$LOGNAME**, reactivates shell interpretation. Hence, **$LOGNAME** is not quoted and therefore is evaluated as a variable. The single quote immediately following **$LOGNAME** switches off shell interpretation again, allowing the string *" on this machine* to be passed literally to **echo**.

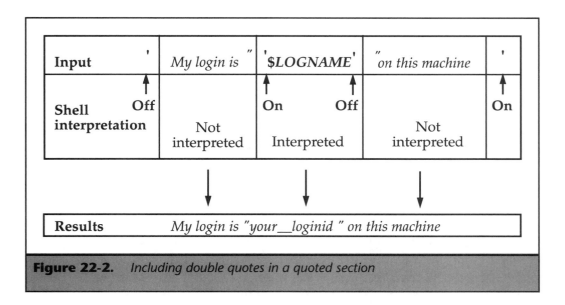

Figure 22-2. *Including double quotes in a quoted section*

The final output of **echo** in this case is

```
My login is "yourlogin" on this machine
```

The double quotes in this command are passed *uninterpreted* because the shell encountered both with interpretation off. The evaluation of *$LOGNAME* is therefore displayed in the output of **echo** with double quotes on each side.

Locating the Group Id of the User Executing the Script

The use of quotes in command lines has an especially practical implementation in shell scripts. In the current version of the script *mylogin*, the output of the login id and group id from the password file is determined by the login that is hard-coded in the **awk** line of the script. To obtain information about a different user, you must explicitly change *login* in the script.

You might be tempted to modify the script to replace the hard-coded *yourlogin* with the variable *$LOGNAME*. If you did, the variable would be inside the single quotes that surround the line, and so would not be interpreted.

1. To make the script determine information about the user who runs the script, modify the script as follows, taking care as you enter the single and double quotes:

   echo *The user login and group id for* **$LOGNAME** *are:*
   awk -F*: '$1 == "'$LOGNAME'"* {print $1, $4}' */etc/passwd*

2. Run the script. The **echo** line is displayed, as are the login id and group id of the user.

The single quotes in this version of the **awk** line are essential to its correct function, because certain elements of this line must be passed uninterpreted to **awk**, while other portions must be interpreted by the shell. The **awk** line components are depicted in Figure 22-3.

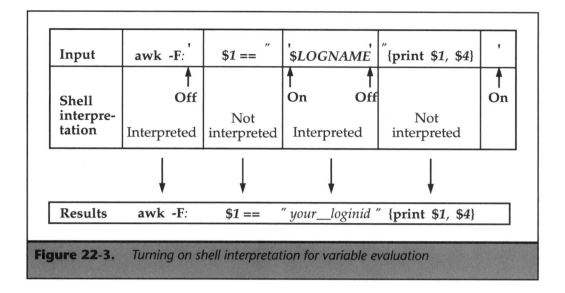

Figure 22-3. *Turning on shell interpretation for variable evaluation*

Examining the Code

Command	Interpretation
'$1 == "'	The string $1 == " is enclosed by single quotes and is not interpreted by the shell. The unevaluated $, all alphanumeric characters, special characters (double quotes), and white space are passed to **awk** as is, not interpreted by the shell.
$LOGNAME	When the shell encounters the $ in front of *LOGNAME*, it is *after* the second single quote. Interpretation is back on and the shell evaluates this variable as the login of the user who executes the script. Hard-coding a user name reference in the script is no longer necessary. The *LOGNAME* or login id of the user who is running the program is substituted here.

Command	Interpretation
'" {print $1, $4}'	Shell interpretation is switched off again by the first of another pair of single quotes, and the characters " {print $1, $4} are passed to **awk** uninterpreted. Again, the double quote is not interpreted because it is inside single quotes.

Interpretation by awk

After shell interpretation has finished, the three arguments shown below are finally passed to **awk**. Now **awk**, and not the shell, handles the remaining processing of the command.

-**F**:

$1 == "*yourlogin*" {print $1, $4}

/etc/passwd

The following table describes how **awk** interprets the elements of this code.

Command	Interpretation
-**F**:	This option to **awk** tells it to consider the colon as the field separator as it reads the input.
$1 == "*yourlogin*"	Specifies the selection criteria. All records where the value of the first field is an exact match to the string that is *yourlogin* are selected for action. Because *yourlogin* is a character string, not a numeric value, **awk** requires it to be enclosed by double quotes. You had the needed double quotes passed by the shell to **awk** as part of the quoted section above.
{print $1, $4}	This string directs **awk** to take action on all selected lines. The first and fourth fields of the selected record(s) are printed (output).

Command	Interpretation
letc/passwd	This argument is interpreted by **awk** as a file to open and read for input.

Passing User-Defined Data into a Script

The ability of the shell to transfer command-line arguments into scripts can be used to make scripts adaptive to user input. Even with the presence of the variable *$LOGNAME*, which lets the script automatically conform to the current user, the script is still unnecessarily restrictive. With the following modifications, the user can specify any login id as an argument on the command line, and the script will locate information pertaining to that user.

1. Create a new script file called *groupon,* containing the following lines:

   #!/bin/ksh
   echo *The user group id for the login* **$1** *is:*
   awk -F: *'$1* **==** *'''$1''' {print $1, $4}' /etc/passwd*

2. Make the script executable.

3. Run the ***groupon*** script by entering the following command, substituting your own login id for the string *yourlogin*:

   groupon *yourlogin*

   The output is your login id and your group id.

4. Make a note of your group id. My group id is _____ .

5. Try the script again, using as argument a login id other than your own (such as ***root***).

Examining the Code

The critical element of the script ***groupon*** is the variable *$1*, which replaces *$LOGNAME*. This variable is evaluated by the shell as the first command-line argument entered by the user when ***groupon*** was entered. If a user named *bob* had been specified in the command, and the following command line was entered,

 groupon *bob*

the shell would have placed the string *bob* in the script replacing the **$1** variable. With *bob* in the search-pattern quotes, **awk** would have extracted and printed the specified data about this user. Figure 22-4 depicts the interpretation of this code.

The script ***groupon*** illustrates an interesting aspect of variable evaluation. (See Figure 22-4.) Two instances of **$1** reside on the **awk** line. The instance of **$1** outside the single quotes, in the middle of the command line, is interpreted by the shell as the first argument on the command line. The other instances are quoted, so the shell passes them uninter-

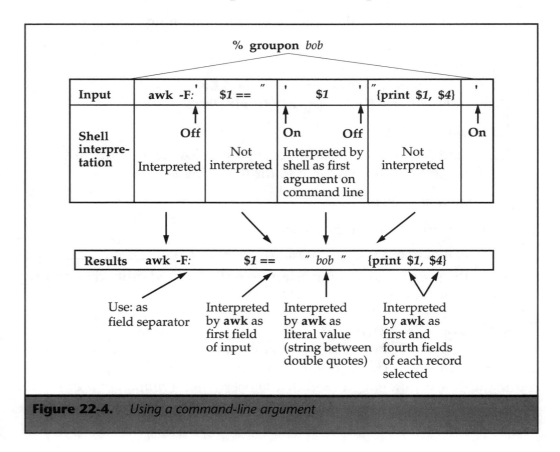

Figure 22-4.   *Using a command-line argument*

preted to **awk**, which does interpret them. To **awk**, they indicate the first field in the specified records. The same variable notation, because of command-line quoting, can be individually evaluated and passed to different command interpreters and have very different meanings.

> **SUMMARY:** *Information can be passed to a utility inside a script in three ways. You can*
>
> ■ *Hard-code the exact information in the script*
>
> ■ *Set the value of a variable that the shell can read*
>
> ■ *Pass the value as an argument to the script on the command line*

22.13
Determining Group Membership

On a normal UNIX system, many users may be members of the same group. They share the same group id, which is a number assigned by the system administrator. Like login ids, group ids can be matched and extracted from the password database.

Extracting Logins for All Members of the Group

Because the group id is a standard field of each user's record in the */etc/passwd* file and always occupies the same position in each record, it can be readily obtained.

1. Enter the following command, substituting your own group id number, which you obtained and made note of in the preceding exercise:

    grep *groupid /etc/passwd*

The output of **grep** is the records of all users with your group id, as well as all lines in */etc/passwd* that have the specified group id string of characters anywhere else in the line. For example, if your group id is **400** and another user has a user id number of **4009**, that user record is selected by **grep** and is output as well.

Selecting Group Ids Only

The **awk** utility can be used to extract records that have an exact match in a specific field.

1. From the shell, request a listing of all members of your group by entering the following command. Substitute the group id for your account, obtained in the earlier exercise.

   awk -F: *'$4 == groupid* {**print $1**}*' /etc/passwd*

Examining the Code

The login names are output for all users who have the same group id as you.

Command	Interpretation
$4 == *groupid*	Instructs **awk** to select only lines where the fourth field matches the number you supplied (*groupid*). Notice the absence of double quotes around the match string; **awk** does not require *numbers* to be enclosed by double quotes. Only *character strings* require this.

Obtaining a Group Id from /etc/passwd with Command Substitution

The **awk** utility can also be used to explicitly select the group id.

1. From the shell enter the following command:

   echo *my Gid* `**awk -F:** *'$1 ==* "'*$LOGNAME*'" {**print $4**}*' /etc/passwd`

The output is

```
my Gid ###
```

where ### is your group id number.

The back quotes (`) enclosing the entire **awk** command line tell the shell that all characters within constitute a command to be executed by a subshell, and that the output of this command is to be substituted for the back-quoted section in the command line. Here, the output of the back-quoted command is placed on the **echo** command line, where it becomes an argument to **echo**. For a user whose group id is *300,* **echo** receives and displays these arguments:

```
my Gid 300
```

22.14

Identifying Group Members Who Are Logged On

Users on larger networks often look at the output of **who** to determine if any of their colleagues are logged on. This section of the chapter continues the development of the *groupon* script to identify users who are both logged on *and* members of a particular group.

Selecting Group Id and Group Members from Login

Back-quote enclosure can be used in a script to set the value of a variable to the results of a command.

1. Modify the script *groupon* as follows:

   #!/*bin/ksh*
   grpnum=`awk -F: '$1 == "'$1'" {print $4}' /etc/passwd`
   awk -F: '$4 == '$grpnum' {print $1}' /etc/passwd | sort

2. Execute the script by entering the following command line, substituting your own login id for *yourlogin*:

   groupon yourlogin

   The output is a sorted list of all login ids who are members of the same group as the user whose login is entered as an argument to *groupon*.

3. Try the script again, using the *root* login id instead of your own, to see which accounts are in the same group as *root*.

There are two code lines in this script. The first sets the value of a new variable *grpnum* equal to the output of the back-quoted **awk** command line. This **awk** command outputs the fourth field (group number) for the user whose login was included as the first argument on the command line (*$1*). Hence, *grpnum* is set equal to the group id of the specified user.

The second **awk** command line outputs the first field (login id) for all records in the password file that have a fourth field equal to the value of the variable *grpnum*. Because *grpnum* is a variable with a numerical value, it does not have to be quoted for **awk**.

Examining the Code

The following table describes the elements of this latest version of *groupon*.

Command	Interpretation
grpnum=` `	The variable *grpnum* is assigned the value of the output of the **awk** command that is in back quotes. The back quotes around the command instruct the shell to have the command executed and to have the output replace the back-quoted portion of the command line.
awk -F: '$1 == "'$1'" {print $4}' /etc/passwd	This **awk** command is the code between the back quotes. The command line argument *$1* is placed outside the single quotes. Hence, the *$1* is interpreted by the shell. If that value is equal to the first field in a record from the password file, the fourth field, group id, is output.

The next line of code has the shell evaluate the variable *grpnum* in the middle of the **awk** line. The **awk** utility then selects all lines where the fourth field is equal to the value of *grpnum*, and prints the login, field one. The result is the logins of all users who have the same group id as the user supplied as an argument to the command.

Locating Group Members Who Are Logged On

As it now stands, the *groupon* script identifies the group id for a chosen login id, and then locates all users who have the same group id. The following changes to the script enable it to determine not only login ids who are members of the chosen group, but also those who are logged on at the time the script is run. For this section, use **rwho** if you are on a network.

1. Change *groupon* to be as follows:

```
#!/bin/ksh
grpnum=`awk -F: '$1 == "'$1'" {print $4}' /etc/passwd`
awk -F: '$4 == '$grpnum' {print $1}' /etc/passwd \      ←
| sort > /tmp/grplist$$        ←
who | awk '{print $1}' | sort > /tmp/loglist$$      ←
comm -12 /tmp/grplist$$ /tmp/loglist$$        ←
rm /tmp/grplist$$ /tmp/loglist$$        ←
```

2. Run the script, giving your login id as an argument to *groupon*.

3. Try it again, using *root* as the login id argument.

Examining the Code

Following is an analysis of this new version of *groupon*.

Command	Interpretation
\	The \ at the end of the third line tells the shell not to interpret the newline character that follows. The shell accepts this line and the next line from the script as one command line, from **awk** to *grplist$$*.

Command	Interpretation
sort > */tmp/grplist***$$**	The output of the **awk** is piped to **sort** and its output placed in a file. This output consists of all system users who are members of the same group. From **sort** the output is redirected to a new file */tmp/grplist***$$**. The **$$** variable is the process id (PID) for the current process, which when appended to the string *grplist* gives the file a unique name. Each instance of this command is run from a new shell having a unique PID. If several people are using this book at the same time, each will have a uniquely named file in */tmp*.

Next are new lines, as follows:

who | **awk** '{**print $1**}' | **sort** > */tmp/loglist***$$**

The components of these lines are

Command	Interpretation
who	**awk**	The output of **who** is passed (piped) to **awk**.
{**print $1**}	Instruction to **awk** to select only the first field (*login*).
	sort > */tmp/loglist***$$**	The output, consisting of a list of logins of users currently logged on, is sorted and placed in the temporary file, *loglist* with the process's PID appended.

Command	Interpretation
comm *-12* */tmp/grplist$$* */tmp/loglist$$*	The **comm** utility compares the two temporary files just created. Entries common to both files (*-12*) are selected, producing a list of users who are both in the selected group and currently logged on.
rm */tmp/grplist$$* */tmp/loglist$$*	Removes the temporary files.

Using Standard Input

One temporary file can be eliminated by properly reading standard input.

1. Modify *groupon* as follows:

```
#!/bin/ksh
who | awk '{print $1}' | sort > /tmp/loglist$$
grpnum=`awk -F: '$1 == "'$1'" {print $4}' /etc/passwd`
awk -F: '$4 == '$grpnum' {print $1}' /etc/passwd | sort \
| comm -12 - /tmp/loglist$$
rm /tmp/loglist$$
```

2. Run the script with your login id as the argument.

3. Run the script with a different login id argument.

Examining the Code

The change in this version is the addition of a minus sign as an argument to **comm**.

```
awk -F: '$4 == '$grpnum' {print $1}' /etc/passwd | sort \
| comm -12 - /tmp/loglist
```

The **comm** utility always compares two files. The command previously used was in this form:

comm *file1 file2*

In this **awk** command line, no second filename is listed as an argument to **comm**; instead, a minus sign is the first argument and the second argument is */tmp/loglist*. The minus sign is interpreted by **comm** to mean "Read from standard input," which in this case is the output of **sort**. The minus sign included as an argument to **comm** tells **comm** to retrieve information from standard input *as though it were the name of a file located at this place in the command line*. Given this, **comm** compares the following: (1) data supplied from standard input (the output of **sort**), and (2) the data from the filename supplied as an argument on the command line, */tmp/loglist*.

22.15

Developing a Script That Handles Errors

Some error-checking capability is beneficial to any shell script. Users will regularly make typing errors or enter the wrong type of data. A script should inform its users when this has occurred and assist them to use it properly.

Modifying the groupon Script

This final version of *groupon* contains three additional sections inserted at the beginning of the script. The new sections handle error checking and the creation of the correct value for a variable *person* (the login id to be used for searching). The new variable, *person*, is defined in the error-checking section and passed into the main script. This is the only change to this part of the script.

1. Modify the *groupon* script to include the following:

```
#!/bin/ksh
############## User enters 2 or more arguments ######
```

```
if [ "$2" ]
then
    cat <<+1
        You entered more than one argument.
        Please enter:
            groupon
        or
            groupon login id
+1
    exit 1
################## User enters 1 argument ######
elif [ "$1" ]
then
    person=$1
    grep "^$person": /etc/passwd >> /dev/null
    if [ $? != 0 ]
    then
    cat <<+2
    The login id you requested does not exist.
    Please use a valid id.
+2
        exit 2

    fi
################# User enters 0 arguments ######
else
    person=$LOGNAME
fi
################## Main Program ######
echo
echo Members of the same group as $person logged on are:
who | awk '{print $1}' | sort > /tmp/loglist$$
grpnum=`awk -F: '$1 == "'$person'" {print $4}' /etc/passwd`
awk -F: '$4 == '$grpnum' {print $1}' /etc/passwd | sort \
| comm -12 - /tmp/loglist$$
rm /tmp/loglist$$
exit 0                          ←
```

2. Run the program without any arguments.

3. Run the program, with your login id as an argument.

4. Run the program, with a different login id as an argument.

5. Run the program, giving a login id that does not exist on your system.

6. Run the program, giving two legal login ids as arguments.

Responding to Multiple Arguments

The first section you added to *groupon*:

```
################# User enters 2 or more arguments ######
if [ "$2" ]
then
    cat <<+1
      You entered more than one argument.
      Please enter
        groupon
      or
        groupon login id
+1
    exit 1
```

As the comment line indicates, this section of the script responds to an incorrect number of inputs. The script is designed to accept only one argument or no arguments, and if two or more are entered the script displays an error message, as well as examples of correct input.

Examining the Code

Command	Interpretation
if ["$2"]	If there is a second command-line argument, the variable $2 is set equal to that argument. If the variable 2 exists, the **test** statement enclosed in brackets ["$2"] evaluates as true, and indicates the existence of an illegal second argument.

Command	Interpretation
cat<<+1	Marks the beginning of the *here document* that contains the error message and correcting prompts. This message is displayed if the preceding line evaluates as true.
+1	The *+1* that follows the message text is *not* indented because it marks the end of the *here document*.
exit 1	Exits the script with the status set to the value *1*. Recall that *0* is a successful exit status. Setting the exit status to *1* specifies that the script processed an error.

Verifying the Login Id

```
############### User enters 1 argument ######
elif [ "$1" ]
then
   person=$1
   grep "^$person": /etc/passwd >> /dev/null
   if [ $? != 0 ]
   then
      cat <<+2
   The login id you requested does not exist.
   Please use a valid id.
+2
   exit 2
   fi
```

Examining the Code

When the user inputs a single argument (the correct number), but the input is not a legal login id, this code processes the error by displaying the appropriate message. The correct input for this script has a very specific attribute, and this error section looks for that attribute.

Command	Interpretation
elif ["$1"]	This part of the **if** structure checks for the presence of a single argument. If one argument is there, the following is run.
person=$1	The variable *person* is set to the first command-line argument. This assigned value is carried through the error check into the main body of the script, where it becomes the search target. But first the script checks to see if *person* is a real user.
grep "^$*person*": */etc/passwd*	Performs the type error check. The variable *person* is passed to **grep**, which will output lines containing the variable's value only when it is at the beginning of a line in */etc/passwd* and is followed immediately by a colon. In a regular expression, the caret means beginning of line. All logins in */etc/passwd* are at the beginning of a line and followed by a colon. If the string the user entered is not found at the beginning of an */etc/passwd* line, it is not a login id.
>> */dev/null*	Because **grep** is used here only to test for correct input, its output need not be displayed or stored in a readable file. Given this, the file named */dev/null* becomes the destination of **grep** output. This special file serves as a system wastebasket and incinerator. Output sent there is never seen again. The >> is instruction to add to an existing file.

Command	Interpretation
if [$? != 0]	This **if** statement checks the exit status of **grep**. The **?** is a shell variable set to the exit status of the previous command that was run. If **grep** finds matching lines, it exits with a status of **0**. Otherwise, it exits with nonzero indicating an error condition, in which case the login entered was not a valid argument and an error message is printed. If the status is zero, then the login is valid, and the related error section that follows is skipped.
cat<<+2	The *here document* is used to print the error message if **grep** exits indicating an error. The *+2* is *not* indented because it marks the end of the *here document*.
exit 2	Instructs the shell running the script to exit the script with the status of **2**. Because the script did not finish successfully, the status it reports to your interactive shell is not **0**.

Setting the Variable for Login Id to the User

The next section of code is

```
################# 0 arguments ######
else
```

> *person=$LOGNAME*
> **fi**

This section runs when the script is given no arguments on the command line. No error checking is needed in this case because the current user's login id is always available as a default argument. Accordingly, the variable *person* is set to the user's login id.

The Main Section of groupon

If the user enters two or more arguments, the error section of the code (prior to the main section) displays an error message. If the user enters one argument, the variable *person* is set to the value of the argument and tested for correct type. If the user enters no argument, the variable *person* is set to the user's login id. In the latter two cases, the main section of the program is given a value for *person*. It instructs **awk** to look for password records that have the first field matching the value of the variable *person*. The main program now completes the processing, searching for the group id number, other members of the group, users currently logged on, and ultimately the set of members of the selected group who are currently logged on.

■ Review 3

Describe the actions of the following lines in a script:

1. #!*/bin/ksh*

2. *datetime=* ` **date** `

3. **if ["$3"]**
   then
       echo *Three arguments or more*
   fi

4. **cat** * > */dev/null*

■ Conclusion

This chapter illustrates the development of several practical shell scripts. These programs might be installed on a system to allow users to identify other users of specific groups who are currently logged on; to access phone numbers; and to determine the number of times they or other users are logged on. As the scripts were developed through the exercises of the chapter, you observed the addition of features that gave the scripts added flexibility and scope. Alternative methods of accomplishing the tasks were presented. You also saw error-checking routines installed to verify the correct amount and type of user input. The major programming features of the Bourne and Korn shells were examined in this chapter. To explore shell programming further, consult both the **man** pages for **ksh** and **sh**, as well as a text in shell programming.

■ Answers to Review 1

1. Displays "Choose 1 or 2" and waits for a response. Whatever the user enters is stored as the value of variable *choice*.

2. **if ["$2"]**
   then
      echo $2
   else
      echo *There is no second argument*
   fi

■ Answers to Review 2

1. **case**, a condition statement, and **esac**

2. **while**

3. Use **echo** to prompt them to press a key to continue and **read** to wait for their input.

4. To signify the default condition.

5. Separate each alternative with a | pipe.

6. **fi**

7. **done**

8. **read** *fname*
   if [-f $fname]
   there is no **then** section.

      echo *The contents of $fname*
      more *$fname*
      else
      echo *No such file*
    fi
  ;;

■ Answers to Review 3

   1. Instruct the current shell to run the current script using a Korn shell.

   2. The variable *datetime* is assigned the value from the output of **date**.

   3. If the user enters three or more arguments for the script, the string "Three arguments or more" is **echo**ed to the screen.

   4. No output. A copy of each file in the current directory is sent to */dev/null*, never to be seen again.

■ Listing of menu Program

```
#!/bin/ksh


#  Program  name:  menu
#  Written  by:  your  name  here
#  Date:  current  date  here
#  Description:
#      This program prints a menu and executes the selected choice.
#      Then it reprints the menu for another selection.
#      This goes on until the user enters the exit option.
#      Choices are:
#          1)     Print  current  working  directory,
#          2)     List  all  files  in  current  directory
#          3)     Print  today's  date and  |time
#          4)     Display  contents  of  file
#          5)     Create  backup  copies  of  files
#          x)     Exit  back  to  the  shell.

# start infinite loop .. exit is in case x
while :
do
```

```
clear

# print menu display
cat <<++
                    MAIN MENU
        1) Print current working directory
        2) List all files in current directory
        3) Print today's date and time
        4) Display contents of a file
        5) Create backup file copies
        x) Exit
++


# prompt for user input
echo -n "Please enter your selection $LOGNAME: "
# set variable named selection to value of user input
read selection

# start case based on variable selection
case  $selection in

# selection 1 ... print working directory
    1)
       pwd
       ;;
# selection 2 ... list files
    2)
       ls -l
       ;;
# selection 3 ... display today's day and time
    3)
       date
       ;;
# selection 4 ... view a file
    4)
        echo -n "Enter a filename: "
        read fname
# or
# echo "Enter a filename: \c"
        if [ -f $fname ]
        then
            echo "The contents of $fname: "
```

```
                more $fname
         else
                echo $fname does not exist
         fi
         ;;
# selection 5 ... make backup copies of a list of
# user entered files
    5)
         echo -n "Enter filenames: "
         read fnames
         for fn in $fnames
         do
                cp $fn $fn.bak
         done
         ;;
# selection x ... exit
    x | X )
         exit 0
         ;;
# default case
    *)
         echo "Invalid choice. Try again. "
         ;;
# end the case
esac

# pause before redisplaying menu
echo -n "Press Return to continue "
read hold

# end the while
done
```

Listing for phon Program

```
#!/bin/ksh
for  i  do
    grep  -i  "$i"  phone.list
    done  |  sort
```

Listing for groupon Program

```ksh
#!/bin/ksh
############# User enters 2 or more arguments ######
if [  "$2"  ]
then
        cat  <<+1
            You entered more than one argument.
             Please enter:
                    groupon
                or
                    groupon  login id
+1
        exit  1
################ User enters 1 argument ######
elif  [  "$1"  ]
then
        person=$1
        grep  "^$person":  /etc/passwd  >>  /dev/null
        if  [  $?  !=  0  ]
        then
        cat  <<+2
        The  login  id  you  requested  does  not  exist.
        Please  use  a  valid  id.
+2
        exit  2


    fi
################ User enters 0 arguments ######
else
        person=$LOGNAME
fi
################ Main Program ######
echo
echo  Members  of  the  same  group  as  $person  logged  on  are:
who | awk  '{print  $1}'  | sort  >  /tmp/loglist$$
grpnum=`awk  -F: '$1 == "'$person'" {print  $4}'  /etc/passwd`
awk  -F: '$4 == '$grpnum' {print  $1}' /etc/passwd | sort \
| comm  -12  -  /tmp/loglist$$
rm  /tmp/loglist$$
exit  0
```

Command Summary

if-then

```
if [ expression ]
then
    command-list
fi
```

if-then-else

```
if [ expression ]
then
    command-list
else
    command-list
fi
```

case

```
case variable-list in
    string)
        command-list
        ;;
    string)
        command-list
        ;;
    *)
        command-list
        ;;
esac
```

while loop

```
while [ expression ]
do
    command-list
done
```

for loop

```
for varname in word-list
do
    command-list
done
```

Control Structures

cat << *tag*   Instructs **cat** to read from file to *tag*.

clear   Clear the screen.

echo **-n**   Do not add a new line at end of **echo** output (BSD).

echo " \c"   Do not add a new line at end of echo output (System V).

exit #   Exit the program giving the shell # exit status.

read *var*   Assign a new variable *var* whatever user enters from keyboard to next Return.

Chapter Twenty-Three

Modifying the User Environment

UNIX was created to provide an operating system of great flexibility. You, as a user, can choose from a large variety of options that affect how the system behaves. If you want the editor to include numbers on the screen when you are editing, you simply make that request. When interacting with a program, you can, on the fly, modify the way it works. Additionally, many programs read startup control files located in your home directory when they are executed. You can put instructions in the control files that request the program to function in ways that are tailored to your personal needs. Each control file is read by one or more specific programs. To further customize your account, you can also create personal housekeeping files and request that your shell read them. In addition, keyboard key mapping is often a matter of personal choice. Some keys can be defined to function as you wish. This chapter examines various ways that UNIX helps you customize the system's interaction with you.

SKILLS CHECK: *Before beginning this chapter, you should be able to*

- *Execute basic commands*

- *Create, display, and print files*

- *Use several shell commands in combination*

- *Access and modify files using the* **vi** *editor*

- *Automate commonly used procedures by invoking aliases*

- *Set local and environmental variables*

- *Evaluate local and environmental variables*

- *Have the shell read a file and execute its contents using* **source** *and the dot command*

OBJECTIVES: *After completing this chapter, you will be able to*

- *Use the shell initialization files to set up your system environment when you log on*

- *Incorporate a file of aliases that are available whenever you are using a shell*

- *Use initialization files that instruct child shells how you want your environment tailored*
- *Explore various system variables and commands that affect your environment*
- *Use the editor initialization file to tailor how the editor works*
- *Use the mail initialization file to customize how mail works*
- *Modify keyboard terminal characteristics*

The features you are able to control depend on the shell and version of UNIX you are using, as well as the changes added by the administrator of your system when your account was established. The Korn, Bourne, and C shells have different capabilities, and there are further differences between older System V shells and BSD shells. How you employ the initialization files is largely determined by what you want to happen—what features you want running.

This chapter first guides you through exercises to determine which files you are currently using to control your login shell and child shells. Next, the chapter assists you in using other control files to further customize your account. Specific commands and utilities for both the C and Korn shells are examined, with recommendations for where they could be employed. Startup files for other utilities and keyboard customizing conclude the chapter.

23.1

Having Startup Files Announce When They Are Read

Manufacturers and local system administrators employ the control files in different ways to achieve their specific goals. The control files and their content that you are using as you log on may be quite different from the files and commands employed by other users on a different system.

This first exercise is designed to assist you in identifying which files are employed in your account. You will make backups of the standard files and then add the **echo** command to each of the original files to inform you when the file is read. You will also set a variable in each original file so you can test to see if the file was read. Because shell control files are read before the shell asks you what you want to do next, an error in the control file can cause the shell to behave very badly or fail completely. On some systems you do not have ownership or write permission on one or more of your control files. If you are not able to get write permission on a file, proceed to the steps that follow.

Creating or Modifying the .login File

The startup control files are located in your home directory. Make certain that your home is your current directory and obtain a listing of the housekeeping (dot) files.

> **cd**
> **ls -a | more**

Begin by making a backup copy of your working *.login* file, if you have one.

1. Enter

   cp *.login* *.login.BAK*

   If you are told that the file does not exist, check to be sure you included the dot and spelled it correctly. If you are using the Korn or Bourne shell as your login shell, the *.login* file may not exist.

2. Use **vi** to start editing the existing *.login* file, or create a new one if one does not exist.

   vi *.login*

3. Add the following three lines to the end of the file:

   # *Following are my additions to .login file*
   setenv *LOGIN* "*login file was read*"
   echo *running of .login file completed*

   Quit and write the file.

Creating or Modifying the .profile File

As with the *.login* file, you should take precautions before you change the *.profile* file.

1. Make a backup copy of the working *.profile* file, if it exists, by typing

    cp *.profile .profile.BAK*

2. Use the editor to create a new *.profile* or modify your current version of the file. Add the following four lines to the end of the *.profile* file.

    # *Additions I have made follow:*
    PROFILE="*profile was read*"
    export *PROFILE*
    echo *The .profile has been read*

3. Quit the editor and save the file.

Creating or Modifying the .cshrc File

1. Make a backup copy of the *.cshrc* file, if you have one, by typing

    cp *.cshrc .cshrc.BAK*

2. Create or modify the *.cshrc* file placing the following three lines at the end of the file:

    # *Following are my additions to .cshrc file*
    setenv *CSHRC "cshrc was read"*
    echo *running of .cshrc file completed*

3. Quit the editor and save the file.

Creating or Modifying the .kshrc File

1. Attempt to make a backup of the *.kshrc* file, by typing

    cp *.kshrc .kshrc.BAK*

2. If you do not have a *.kshrc* file, create one. Place the following four lines at the end of the existing or new *.kshrc* file.

```
#  Following are my additions to .kshrc file
KSHRC="kshrc was read"
export  KSHRC
echo running of .kshrc file completed
```

3. Quit the editor and save the file.

Creating Aliases Files

Both the Korn and C shells allow you to make aliases for commands that you issue.

1. Create a file named *.aliases-ksh* and add the following line:

   alias *winnie*=**"echo** *the pooh —ksh*"

2. Create a second aliases file named *.aliases-csh* and add the following line:

   alias *and* **"echo** *tigger too —csh*"

23.2

Determining Which Startup Files You Are Using

At this point you have placed commands in some of your control files that will allow you to determine which files are read and when they are read.

Logging On with Modified Startup Files

With the files modified, the next step is to carefully examine the control files' effects on the processes you run when you log on.

1. Log out of your session.

   One of the ways UNIX programs are informed of your specific requests is through initialization of files. Whenever you log on, your shell reads some of the files you just modified. Because these files determine how programs run, they are often called *run-control* or *run-command* files. Hence, the *rc* at the end of *.cshrc* and *.kshrc*.

You are about to log back on. When you do, you will see some of the messages resulting from the **echo** commands you just placed in the control files. Keep a record of the order of whatever messages you receive.

2. Log back on. On the lines below, note the message you see.

_____

_____

The messages you receive depend primarily on what shell you are using. The last entry in your */etc/passwd* file record determines the startup program, usually a Bourne (**sh**), Korn (**ksh**), or C (**csh**) shell.

On some X Window or menu-driven systems, the startup shell is not attached to your terminal but is used to launch windows. If you are at such a system, the control file messages are not displayed; however, you can determine what files were read by examining the variables that were set and exported to the child shells.

Examining Login Shell Variables Messages

The **echo** messages are one way to see what files were read. You included commands to create environmental variables in the control files. If a file was read, its variable is now set.

1. Evaluate the variables by entering

    echo *$LOGIN*
    echo *$PROFILE*
    echo *$CSHRC*
    echo *$KSHRC*

If a variable has a value, the control file that set it and exported it was read.

2. Depending on the type of shell you are using, you will see the following:

- In the C shell: The variables *LOGIN* and *CSHRC* were set and have values. The messages you previously received from the C shell are from *.cshrc* and then from the *.login* control files.

- In the Bourne shell: You received only one message, from the *.profile* file. Likewise, only one variable, *PROFILE*, is set.

- In the Korn shell: The *.profile* file is read, and possibly the *.kshrc* file. If *.kshrc* was read, the variable *KSHRC* was set.
    Whether or not the *.kshrc* file is read is determined by whether or not *.profile* includes another environmental variable, *ENV*.

3. Call up *.profile* with the visual editor. If your **ksh** read the *.kshrc* file at login, the following lines are in your *.profile*.

    ENV=~/.kshrc
    export *ENV*

    or

    export *ENV=~/.kshrc*

    If you do not have the lines that create and export the variable *ENV*, add them to the file.

4. If you are using the Korn shell and just added the *ENV* lines to your *.profile*, log off and back on to see that *.kshrc* is now read at login.

Reading Files When a Child Shell Is Created

Whenever you create a child shell, some of the control files may also be read. The following exercises ask you to create child shells and determine which control files, if any, are read.

Starting a Child C Shell

1. From your login shell, start a new C shell by entering

csh

The message from *.cshrc* is displayed.

Regardless of which login shell you are using, when you tell it to start a child C shell, the new C shell reads only the *.cshrc* file, not the *.login*.

2. Exit the child C shell.

Starting a Child Bourne Shell

1. From your login shell, start a child Bourne shell with the command

sh

No messages are displayed and no control files are read.

2. Exit the Bourne shell

Starting a Child Korn Shell

1. From your login shell, start a new Korn shell

ksh

One of two things happens. Either no files are read, and therefore no **echo** messages are displayed, or else the *.kshrc* file is read and its message displayed.

If you are using a Korn shell as your login shell, and if the variable *ENV* is set as above, then child Korn shells read the *.kshrc* file. If the *ENV* variable is not set, child Korn shells do not read the *.kshrc* control file.

Starting a Korn Shell from a C Shell

If you are using a C shell as your login shell and you start up a Korn shell, no control file is read unless the environment variable *ENV* is set in *.login* or *.cshrc*.

1. Exit from the child Korn shell.

2. Edit your *.login* to create the needed environment variable by including the following line:

setenv *ENV ~/.kshrc*

This instructs the shell to create a new variable *ENV*, give it the value *~/.kshrc* and export its value to child processes—all child process, even Korn shells.

3. Instruct your C shell to read the *.cshrc* by entering

source *.cshrc*

4. Start another child Korn shell. This time the *.kshrc* control file message is displayed.

5. Test for the variables with

echo *$KSHRC*

The C shell passes environmental variables to the child Korn shell. Because the Korn gets the *ENV* variable, it reads *.kshrc*.

6. Exit the child Korn shell.

Summarizing When Control Files Were Read

The specific control files that are read at login and when child shells are created is a function of the shell employed and the value of the *ENV* variable.

Login Shells

The following table summarizes the control files that are read by the C, Bourne, or Korn shells when they are the login shell.

Shell	First File Read	Second File Read
C shell	*.cshrc*	*.login*
Bourne shell	*.profile*	
Korn shell without *ENV*	*.profile*	
Korn shell with *ENV*	*.profile*	*.kshrc*

At login, the C shell reads the *.cshrc* file first, followed by *.login*. The Bourne shell reads *.profile* only. The Korn shell reads the *.profile* file only, unless *.profile* includes the line *ENV=~/.kshrc*. If the *ENV* variable is set, the login Korn shell goes on to read the file *.kshrc* located in your home directory. The *ENV* variable could be set to some filename other than *~/.kshrc*. The filename *.kshrc* is chosen because of convention, not necessity.

Child Shells

The following table summarizes the control files that are read by the C, Bourne, and Korn shells when they are started as child shells.

Child Shell	File Read
C shell	*.cshrc*
Bourne shell	
Korn shell without *ENV*	
Korn shell with *ENV*	*.kshrc*

Child C shells automatically read *.cshrc*. Child Korn shells read no files unless the environment variable *ENV* is set and exported from the parent shell. If *ENV* is set, the child **ksh** reads the specified file (usually *.kshrc*). Child Bourne shells read no files when they are started.

23.3

Properly Using the Control Files

The control files facilitate tailoring your environment to a high degree. You must decide what to put in each file to reach your desired goals.

All the shells use shell environmental variables. In the C shell, you must use the **setenv** command. In the Korn shell, you must create the variable and then use its **export** command to make the variable environmental. Once created, the variables are then available to all child processes including subshells of any type (C, Bourne, Korn, etc.). Keep in mind, though, that some variables, like *CDPATH* in the Korn shell, can be exported to a child C shell and not work. The C shell uses the local variable *cdpath* to provide the directory finding feature.

All the shells use local variables, the value of which are not passed to a subshell. However, by including commands to create local variables in the *.cshrc* or *.kshrc* files, you can ensure that frequently used local variables contain the values you want and will be available to child shells.

Deciding When to Use Each Control File

The way files are read by the shells affects what happens. If you want all C shells to act in a specific way, put the command or set the variable in the *.cshrc* file because it is read by all C shells when they are started.

Users often want the login shell to have information that is not passed on to child shells. Sometimes variables are set to make it easy to change directories to an often-used directory. You can give instruction to a login shell by entering the information as a local variable in the *.profile* file for the Korn shell and the *.login* file for the C shell. Because child shells do not read those files, they are not given the information. If you do want the information passed to the child shells, you can put it in the *.cshrc* or *.kshrc* files, or use environmental variables in the *.login* or *.profile* files.

The order of reading of the startup files has consequences for users of the shells.

Using C Shell Control Files

With the C shell, if a variable is set to different values in the two control files, the value in the *.login* file is read second, so it overwrites whatever value was set in the *.cshrc* file.

1. If you are using a C shell as your login shell, create an environmental variable named *ABCD* in each control file. Assign a different value to each *ABCD*, as below.

   In the *.login* file add the lines

   setenv *ABCD A-login*
   echo *$ABCD*

In the *.cshrc* file add the lines

setenv *ABCD* *A-cshrc*
echo $*ABCD*

2. Log off and log back on. As the control files are read, the first variable displayed is the one set in the *.cshrc* file. It is quickly changed as the *.login* file is read.

3. Evaluate the variable's resulting value with

echo $*ABCD*

The value that was set in the *.login* file is displayed.

4. Create a child shell and evaluate the variable with

csh
echo $*ABCD*

The value set in the *.cshrc* file is now displayed. Unlike in the login shell, the variable *ABCD* is not changed to the value set in the *.login* file because the child shell never reads *.login*.

If you set your prompt to be one way in the *.login* file and another in the *.cshrc* file, the prompt for your login shell will be whatever you set it to be in the *.login* file. It is read second and overwrites whatever was read in a *.cshrc* file. All other (child) shells have the prompt as set in *.cshrc* because the child C shells do not read the *.login* file at all.

Using Korn Shell Control Files

You can have the login shell for the C shell behave differently from all child shells because *.login* is read after *.cshrc* by the login shell. In the Korn shell, the *.profile* is read first, not second.

1. Create the environmental variable *EFGH* in both of the Korn shell control files. In the *.profile* file add the line

EFGH=A-profile
export *EFGH*

In the *.kshrc* file add the line

EFGH=A-kshrc
export _EFGH_

2. Log off and log back on.

3. Evaluate the variable by entering

echo _$EFGH_

The value as set in the _.kshrc_ file is reported.

4. Create a child Korn shell and evaluate the variable with

ksh
echo _$EFGH_

The same value is reported. The Korn shell reads _.profile_ first and then _.kshrc_. Children read _.kshrc_ only. Either way, whatever is set in _.kshrc_ takes effect.

Consequently, if you set your prompt in _.kshrc_, all Korn shells will have it. If you set it only in _.profile_, only your login shell will have it and the child shells will get a system default prompt.

Reading a File of Aliases

In an earlier exercise you created two files for aliases and put an alias in each.

1. Evaluate those aliases now by entering

winnie
and

Neither alias is in effect. The shells have not read the alias files.

2. With the editor, add the following line to the _.kshrc_ file:

. _~/.aliases-ksh_

This line in the _.kshrc_ file is instruction to the shell to read the file .aliases-ksh in the home directory. When Korn shell starts, it reads _.kshrc_ and will also read the aliases in the **_aliases-ksh_** file.

3. Start a child Korn shell and try the aliases.

ksh
winnie
and

The alias *winnie* that was set in the *.aliases-ksh* file is now available, and the C shell alias *and* is not.

4. Exit the child Korn shell.

5. With the editor add the following line to the *.cshrc* file.

source ~/*.aliases-csh*

6. Start a child C shell and try the aliases.

csh
winnie
and

The alias set in the *.aliases-csh* file is read by the child C shell and is now working. The **source** command in the C shell instructs the C shell to read the file just like the dot command does with the Korn shell. When the child shell is started, it reads *.cshrc* and because of the **source** command, the child shell reads the alias in the *.aliases-csh* file. The aliases are then available to the child shell.

7. Add some more aliases to each file utilizing the proper syntax for each shell and try them out.

Identifying Other Files Read at Login

One other factor may affect how the shells behave at startup. Your administrator may have included **source** or dot commands telling the shell to read other files located on your system.

1. Use **more** or **pg** to read through the control files in your home directory and locate any **source** or dot commands.

On some systems, the C shell has been modified to read a system-wide initialization file, such as HP-UX's */etc/csh.login*. If you have such a file, examine it.

23.4

Tailoring How the Shell
Interacts with You

In the previous exercises, you examined which control files are read at startup and which are read when you create child shells. This section examines a variety of commands that you can include in one of the control files to modify how your shell functions.

Using Environmental
and Local Shell Variables

Many of the C shell variables mentioned in the following pages will be local variables (lowercase). Because the C shell program reads the *.cshrc* file each time it is started, those local variables set in *.cshrc* are read by child shells. This means that they function virtually as environmental variables. Consequently, the C shell uses these in its operation.

However, the C shell also maintains a number of environmental shell variables (uppercase) of the same name. Since they are environmental variables, they are passed to child Bourne or Korn shells. Additionally, Bourne and Korn shells must have certain variables defined explicitly as environmental variables if they are to be used.

When creating C shell environmental variables, you must use the C shell command **setenv**. However, the format of the value of the variable to be passed must be acceptable to the Bourne or Korn shells (for example, *ENV=~/.kshrc*).

Setting the Search Path for the Shell

When you request that the shell execute a utility, the shell must find the executable. Where it looks is determined by the *path* variable in the C shell and *PATH* in the Korn and Bourne shells. Your current startup files have path variables.

1. If you need to add a new directory such as a local bin for your scripts or a new application is added to the system, add the directory to the path variable in the control file.

Setting the Terminal Variable

The *TERM* variable has a value that is the name of the type terminal that you are using. The *letc/termcap* file contains this name and associated information that enables the terminal and computer to communicate correctly.

When you log on, if you are asked for a terminal type, and if you always enter the same response, you can just set the variable in the *.login* or *.profile* run-control files.

Setting Where the User's Shell Program Is Stored

The value of the *SHELL* variable is loaded at login from the entry in your *letc/passwd* record. This variable is used, for example, when you ask for a shell from within **vi**. If you wish to use some other shell, you can change the value of *SHELL*.

Avoiding Accidental Logout
or Exits from a Shell

In earlier chapters you set the C shell and Korn shell variable *ignoreeof* to instruct the shell to not exit when you enter a Ctrl-d to a shell or sub-shell. You must use the **exit** command to leave a shell if *ignoreeof* is set. If you are in your login shell, the **logout** command will also kill your shell. You can include setting this variable in your run-command files.

Preventing Overwriting of Files

The C shell and Korn shell *noclobber* variable prevents overwriting of existing files when the shell redirects the output of a utility to a file. If the file already exists, an error message is displayed.

Customizing Shell History

The C and Korn shells maintain a history list of commands you have issued. Two aspects of the history mechanism are determined by variables that you can set in the run-control files.

CUSTOMIZING C SHELL HISTORY   You must tell the C shell to record your commands. Include **set** *history=50* in the *.cshrc* file.

1. You can also request that the shell keep its history record after you log off and make it available when you log on. The command is

   set *savehist=50*

Setting the *savehist* variable to 50 instructs the shell to save the last 50 commands you used in a file named *.history* when you log off. When you next initiate a C shell, the contents of the *.history* file are included at the beginning of your history list. The *.history* file resides in your home directory. This option is not available on all systems.

CUSTOMIZING KORN SHELL HISTORY   Unlike in the C shell, you do not need to set any history variable for the Korn shell to provide the history facility. The history mechanism is preset to save 128 commands. You can change the number of saved commands by entering a command like the following, from either the command line or in your *.profile* file.

   HISTSIZE=50
   export *HISTSIZE*

Requesting Notification When C Shell Jobs Are Completed

You can request the shell to notify you immediately when a background job is completed, rather than waiting until it issues a new prompt. Include the following in a C shell run-control file:

   set *notify*

Including File Completion

If the file completion feature of the Korn and Bourne shells is useful, include the appropriate instruction in the control files.

In the C shell (*.cshrc*):

set *filec*

In the Korn shell (*.profile* or *.kshrc*):

set **-o** *vi-tabcomplete*

Including a Personalized Prompt

The C shell allows you to have different prompts for login versus all other shells. The Korn shell has a primary prompt, and a different secondary prompt for requesting additional information.

Enabling the umask Built-In Command

The value for **umask** masks the owner, group, and other permission fields for each file or directory that you create. To select a suitable **umask**, refer to the chapter on file permissions. The command is the same for both the C and Korn shells and can be included in control files.

Including Command-Line Editing with the Korn Shell

To take advantage of command-line editing in the Korn shell, you need to tell the shell which editor you prefer. You can use just the common name of the editor you wish, or you can specify a full pathname, provided that the last item in the path is **vi**, **emacs**, or **gmacs**.

The Korn shell furnishes you a command-line editor that has similar characteristics to the editor you have specified. The Korn shell checks the variable *VISUAL* first. If it has not been set, the variable *EDITOR* is used. You can also set your editor preference using the **set -o** *vi* syntax. If you use this approach, the value assigned with the **set -o** command takes precedence over other variables.

23.5

Passing Variables to Other Utilities from Control Files

This far you have modified the control files to affect how the shells function. Another powerful way to customize your account is to set environmental variables in the control files so they are passed to applications when they are executed.

Setting the EDITOR, VISUAL, and Other Editor Variables

Certain applications allow the user to edit files while still running the application. The application will start up a particular editor based on the value of the environmental variable. *EDITOR* is the most commonly referenced of the various editor shell variables. In addition, different programs may use one of the other editor shell variables, such as *VISUAL* or *ED*. Generally, you assign the pathname of the editor you want as the value of the shell variable. If you don't define *EDITOR*, the **mail** utility, for example, will select a system default editor for you to use in *mail*.

1. To set the *EDITOR* variable, enter the following:

   In the C shell:

   setenv *EDITOR* */usr/ucb/vi*

   In the Korn shell:

   VISUAL=vi
   EDITOR=vi
   set -o *vi*
   export *EDITOR VISUAL*

Setting EXINIT, the Editor Environment Variable

The *EXINIT* initialize variable allows you to preset your editor options.

1. To create the variable, enter the following:

   In the C shell:

   setenv *EXINIT* 'set **wm**=5 *ai number*'

   In the Korn shell:

   EXINIT='set **wm**=5 *ai number*'
   export *EXINIT*

With this value for *EXINT*, whenever you use your editor, with this example's settings, your wrap margin is set to 5, and the auto-indent and numbering options are enabled.

> *NOTE: The shells (C or Korn) of different systems may have different ways of handling the interaction of this variable and the .exrc file. Editor options specified in this variable may be added to or ignored depending upon options specified in the .exrc file. Conversely, options specified in the .exrc file may be added to or ignored. It all depends on the system.*

The best solution probably is to put your editor options in a *.exrc* file and not use the *EXINIT* variable unless the variable is specifically required for some application.

23.6

Creating Variables for Shortcuts

The modifications made to the run-control files thus far have changed the ways the shells and utilities work. You can also create entries that are very specific to your needs.

Creating Shell Variables to Save Work

You can create variables that contain pathnames that you frequently use and then use the variables instead of long pathnames. For instance, if an environmental variable *PSC* is set to *~/Projects/Secret/Code/* you can enter **cd** *$PSC* and you are changed to the targeted directory.

Calling Other Files To Assist

You can create a *.logout* file that is read whenever you log out of the system.

The C shell automatically looks for a *.logout* file in your home directory when you log out.

1. Create a *.logout* file in your home directory and put in some useful information that you should see at logout.

2. To get the Korn shell to access the *.logout* file, you need to **trap** the shell's exit signal. Enter

trap *'~/.logout'* **0**

3. When you log out, the *.logout* file is read.

4. To make reading the file permanent, enter the **trap** in your *.profile*.

Accessing a Reminder File at Login

You can create a file that contains reminders for the day that automatically is displayed when you log on. Have the file read by the shell when it processes either *.login* or *.profile*.

■ Customizing the Visual Editor

The initialization file for the editor **vi** is the file *.exrc*. Most users create the *.exrc* file in the home directory. You can have different *.exrc* files in different directories to create specialized editing environments in those directories.

All of the commands within **vi** can be placed in the *.exrc* file. They will be read in at the beginning of every editing session in the directory containing the *.exrc* file. Be aware, though, that the variable *EXINIT* (and the *.exrc* file in your home directory if you are not in your home directory) will affect your editing environment.

How the **vi** or editing environment is set up depends on what options you select, where you specify them, and what system you are using.

On some systems, if *EXINIT* is set, the *.exrc* file is not read. If you have such a system, you will need to decide which method you will use in the future to set your editing environment.

When the visual editor is started up, it checks for and reads the options in *EXINIT*. If *EXINIT* does not exist, the editor checks for the *.exrc* file in your *home* directory. If it does not exist, it checks for the *.exrc* file in your current directory. If your systems reads *.exrc* files when *EXINIT* is set, all options not in common that are set will remain set. Any option in common will have its value set in the last *.exrc* file read.

23.8

Using the Initialization File for Mail

The initialization file for **mail** is called *.mailrc* and it belongs in your home directory together with the *.cshrc* and the *.login* files.

Check the command summary at the end of this chapter and the **man** pages for **mail** for other useful options that you can include in your *.mailrc* file.

Review 1

1. What command lists your environmental variables and their values for the current session?

2. You set *filec* in your *.login* file. You unset it in your *.cshrc* file. Is it on in your login shell? Is it on in your child C shells?

3. What do you put in your *.profile* file so that your *.kshrc* file is read each time you start a Korn shell?

4. In the Korn and Bourne shells, what command would you use to ensure that subshells inherit the variable *deptname*?

5. In which file would you place all assignments of (a) environmental variables and (b) local variables? In the C shell? In the Korn shell?

6. In the C shell, what command would you use to have the shell re-read the *.login* file immediately? What command would you use to have the Korn shell read *.profile* immediately?

7. What do you enter to enable the file completion feature in the C shell? The Korn shell?

8. What is the name of the file for customizing your interaction with **mail**?

23.9

Using stty to Set Input and Output Options on a Terminal

You often modify the terminal display using keys such as Ctrl-h for backspace or signal a program interrupt with Ctrl-c. These and other keystroke bindings can be changed through the use of the **stty** utility. This feature of UNIX is particularly useful in situations where you are used to one keyboard configuration but must work on another. Both versions of **stty**, for BSD and System V, are examined in this section.

Setting Terminal Control Characters

You can examine the current terminal settings by typing

>   **stty all**

or

>   **stty -a**

The output of this command contains lines similar to the following:

```
erase kill werase rprnt flush lnext susp  intr quit stop  eof
^H     ^U   ^W     ^R    ^O    ^V    ^Z/^Y ^C   ^\   ^S/^Q ^D
```

or

```
speed 1200 baud; line = 1; intr=DEL; quit = ^|; erase = ^h;
kill = @; eof = ^d; eol = ^'; swtch = ^'
```

Depending on your system, you will see a number of special commands to the terminal and the characters that are bound to those commands. It is possible to remap the commands to any key that you wish. In the following exercises, you will rebind keys in some rather strange ways, but when you log out and log back on, the original bindings take effect.

One of the commands is the *erase* command. This **^h** or **^H** (case in-sensitive) command erases the character to the left of the cursor and is usually mapped to the ⌷Backspace⌷ key on your keyboard. To demonstrate that it is possible to map these commands to any key on your keyboard, the following exercises instruct you to map commands from the above list to the numerical keys 2 through 0.

1. To map *erase* to the ②key, type

   stty *erase* **2**

2. Try out your new *erase* key by typing

   ls -al 222222

   The 2 works as the backspace or erase key.

3. The next command is the line kill (*kill*) command. This command erases the entire input line that was typed in. To map line *kill* to the ③key, type

   stty *kill* **3**

4. Try out your new line kill by typing

   more */usr/dict/words* **3**

   The line is killed and a new one started.

5. The *eof* (end-of-file) command is used to end input such as letters sent with the **mail** utility, and also to log off a system. Usually, it is ⌷Ctrl⌷-⌷d⌷. To map it to the ⑨key, type

   stty *eof* **9**

6. Try out this modification by sending **mail** to yourself. Type

   mail *your_login*
   This is a test.
   9

7. When the *intr* key is typed, an interrupt signal is sent to the running process. To map it to ⓪, type

   stty *intr* **0**

8. Try to interrupt a process by typing

   more */usr/dict/words*

   0

9. So far, all of the examples presented here make one change to each terminal command at a time. It is possible to combine all of the previous commands into one long command. An example could look like this:

   stty *erase* `Ctrl`-`h` *intr* `Ctrl`-`c` *eof* `Ctrl`-`d`

   The basic syntax is

   stty *command command_key command command_key . . . options*

10. We have now modified most of the normal terminal command keys to rather unusual settings. To set them back to more normal key strokes, you can log off and log back on again, or on some systems, type

    stty *sane*

■ Review 2

1. What command would you put in which file to allow the use of the abbreviation *org* for the word *organization* in the visual editor?

2. What command would you put in which file to send a copy of a mail message to other users?

3. What command would you use to change the interrupt key to @?

■ Conclusion

In this chapter, you have been customizing many aspects of your user environment. You created or modified several initialization files (*.login*, *.profile*, *.cshrc*, *.kshrc*, *.mailrc*, *.exrc*), which makes it possible to customize aliases, the shell variables, the editor, mail, and the keyboard.

One of the strong points of UNIX is the flexibility the user has in setting up his customized environment.

Chapter 11 has further references to dot files used with the X Window and Motif programs. Additional information about shell variables can be found in the **man** pages for **sh**, **csh**, and **ksh**.

■ Answers to Review 1

1. On BSD: **printenv**

   On System V: **env**

2. Yes, it is on in your login shell because the login file is read after *.cshrc* during login.
   No, because only *.cshrc* is read when a child shell is started.

3. *ENV ~/.kshrc*
   export *ENV*

4. **export** *deptname*

5. In the C shell:
   a. *.login*
   b. *.cshrc*

   In the Korn shell:
   a. *.profile*
   b. *.kshrc* or whatever *ENV* is set to

6. **source** *.login*
   . *.profile*

7. **set** *filec*
   set -o *vi-tabcomplete*

8. *.mailrc*

■ Answers to Review 2

1. **ab** *org organization* in the file *.exrc*

2. **askcc** *.mailrc*

3. **stty** *intr* @

COMMAND SUMMARY

Shell Variables

HOME   Home directory of user.

PATH   Path searched when looking for command issued by user.

SHELL   The path and filename of the user shell.

TERM   Terminal type (e.g., vt100).

EDITOR   Used to set default editor.

EXINIT   Contains options for editing session.

VISUAL   Used to set type of command-line editor for the Korn shell.

CDPATH   Korn shell: Sets paths that the shell will search for directory names.

HISTFILE   Korn shell: Sets name for history file used for saving history list when shell exits.

HISTSIZE   Korn shell: Changes history list size.

MAIL   Bourne and Korn shells: Enables notification of mail arrival; specifies location to check.

MAILPATH   Bourne and Korn shells: Allows user to set multiple paths instead of one path, like *MAIL*.

MAILCHECK   Bourne and Korn shells: Sets time interval shell waits to check for mail.

ENV   Has the value that is the name of a file where local variables are set and tells shell to read that file each time a Korn shell is started.

PS1   Korn shell: Sets prompt variable.

Shell Modifiable Features

biff   Enables immediate notification of mail arrival.

mesg y   Enables other user's ability to write to your terminal.

umask   Sets permission mask that blocks specified file directory permissions given to files and directories when they are created.

.mailrc Options

ask   When set, mail offers subject line creation.

askcc   Allows you to send copies of your mail message to other users.

crt   Sets number of lines displayed by **mail**.

Local Shell Variables

cdpath   C shell: Sets paths for shell to search to locate directories.

filec   C shell: Turns on file completion.

ignoreeof   Instructs shell to provide error message when it receives end of file signals, rather than exiting.

mail   C shell: Enables notification of mail arrival; allows setting of checking interval and location to check for mail.

noclobber   Prevents overwriting files with redirection.

notify   Instructs shell to inform user immediately of change in background jobs.

prompt   C shell: Set prompt.

savehist	C shell: Instructs shell to store history list when shell exits.
set -o ignoreeof	Instructs shell to provide error message when it receives end of file signal, rather than exiting.
set -o noclobber	Prevents overwriting files with redirection.
set -o vi	Korn shell: Sets type of command-line editor.
set -o vi-tab complete	Korn shell: File completion.

Shell Commands and Functions

set	Display current variables with their values.
set *name=value*	Set the variable *name* to the value *value* (C shell).
name=value	Set the variable *name* to the value *value* (Korn and Bourne shells).
unset *name*	Delete the variable *name*.
env	Display current environmental variables with their values (System V).
printenv	Same as **env** (BSD).
setenv *name value*	Set the environmental variable *name* to the value *value* (C shell).
unsetenv *name*	Delete the environmental variable *name* (C shell).
source *filename*	*Current* shell reads the file *filename* (C shell).
. *filename*	*Current* shell reads the file *filename* (Korn and Bourne shells).

alias *name* *command*	When *name* is entered *command* is run (C shell).
alias *name=command*	When *name* is entered, *command* is run (Korn and some Bourne shells).
stty *all*	Displays various terminal information, such as baud rate and the characters to be used to perform actions such as deleting characters (BSD).
stty **-a**	Similar to **stty** *all* (System V).
stty *action character*	Changes the character used to perform various actions, such as deleting a character.
stty *raw*	Tells the terminal driver program to pass all characters along without interpreting them.
stty *cooked*	Tells the terminal driver program to process characters (normal mode).

Index

G

H

X

Z

Thank You

*for teaching yourself UNIX using the
Learning Guides in UNIX Made Easy. The
staff at MLA and Osborne/McGraw-Hill put
a lot of effort into creating UNIX Made Easy,
and find it rewarding that the book is so well
used. Your comments, thoughts, and
suggestions are welcome and appreciated.*
- John Muster

If you found this approach useful, a companion Video, a Computer-Based Training program,
Classroom Education, and other Learning Guides on advanced topics are also available.

Teach Yourself UNIX-the Video

This series of four half-hour programs
examines the concepts in the basic chapters of *UNIX Made Easy*.
Normally $185. Order with a copy of this page attached, $85.

Computer-Based Training

Several interactive computer-based Education programs, running on
either PCs or UNIX, and tied to *UNIX Made Easy*, are available from
Uniworx. 800/864-UNIX. 10% discount to *UNIX Made Easy* owners.

Learning Guides on Advanced Topics

Self-paced Learning Guides like the chapters in *UNIX Made Easy* are
available on advanced UNIX topics such as Shell Programming, System
Administration, C Programming, and Using X Windows with Motif.

Classroom Education

Learning Guides like the chapters of this book are the central student
handbooks for on-site and public classes in Introductory, Intermediate,
and Advanced UNIX topics.

Muster Learning Architects   P. O. Box 10164, Berkeley, CA 94709
510/ 849-4479